An Introduction to the History and Sources of Jewish Law

An Introduction to the History and Sources of Jewish Law

Edited by

N.S. Hecht, B.S. Jackson, S.M. Passamaneck,
D. Piattelli, A.M. Rabello

THE INSTITUTE OF JEWISH LAW
BOSTON UNIVERSITY SCHOOL OF LAW

Clarendon Press • Oxford
1996

The Institute of Jewish Law
Boston University School of Law
765 Commonwealth Avenue
Boston, MA 02215
Publication No. 22

Oxford University Press, Walton Street, Oxford OX2 6DP
Oxford New York
Athens Auckland Bangkok Bombay Calcutta Cape Town Dar es Salaam Delhi
Florence Hong Kong Istanbul Karachi Kuala Lumpur Madras Madrid Melbourne
Mexico City Nairobi Paris Singapore Taipei Tokyo Toronto
and associated companies in
Berlin Ibadan

Oxford is a trade mark of Oxford University Press

Published in the United States
by Oxford University Press Inc., New York

British Library Cataloguing in Publication Data
Data available

Library of Congress Cataloging in Publication Data
Data available

ISBN 0-19-826226-4
ISBN 0-19-826262-0 (Pbk)

Typeset by Deborah Charles Publications

Printed in Great Britain on acid-free paper by
Bookcraft Ltd, Midsomer Norton, Avon

We express our appreciation to Mr. David Landau

through whose generosity this volume has been published

in memory of his parents

Rabbi Irwin Landau and Mrs. Alfreda Landau

CONTENTS

In the summer of 1988, at the Fifth Biennial Conference of the Jewish Law Association, a number of the attendees met informally to discuss a serious gap in the materials then available for the teaching of Jewish Law. Professor Bernard Jackson and Professor Daniela Piattelli conducted the meeting. The discussions focused on the need for a single volume introduction to Jewish Law, designed especially to provide essential background information for those seriously encountering Jewish Law for the first time (particularly, students of Law and Jewish Studies in the Diaspora, and the intelligent laity). This book is the result of that meeting.

Soon after the Conference, Professor Jackson and Professor Piattelli enlisted the help of Professor Neil Hecht, Professor Stephen Passamaneck, and Professor Mordechai Rabello. These five became the Editorial Board and began to work toward the development of such a book under the auspices of the Association. In the latter stages of the editing work, Mr. Jonathan Cohen was recruited as an editorial assistant and rendered invaluable help; Mr. Jonathan Burnside kindly undertook final proof checking.

The Board developed a basic chapter outline, which each contributor would be expected insofar as possible to follow. This outline required each author to remark upon the political and juridical background of the particular period, the character of the sources from it, and some salient features of its substantive law and legal practice, as well as present a brief list of major authorities of the period and a basic bibliography. The search for contributors then commenced.

The Editorial Board was gratified that so many outstanding scholars agreed to contribute chapters to the volume. The Editors wish to thank all the contributors for their painstaking efforts and their attention to the basic design of the book, and also to those who have devoted considerable labour to the translation of the articles written originally in Hebrew. The task of reducing centuries of complex legal development into relatively brief and coherent essays is difficult — especially so, very often, for specialists who are writing for a non-specialist audience. What is here presented is a truly collective work, rather than a series of independent essays. Many of the articles look quite different from the drafts originally submitted: the authors have collaborated with the Editors in pruning, supplementing and clarifying the material, in the interests of the primary audience. The major responsibility for such revision and supplementation was assumed by the writers of this Introduction.

The Editors also decided early in the planning stage of the book that it would include more than the 'mainstream' approach of presenting the transformation of Biblical law into ancient rabbinic law, and that in turn into medieval rabbinic law and so on to the present. Instead, the work would take a broader view and include material from the Dead Sea Scrolls, Hellenistic Egypt, Roman law, the Samaritans and the Karaites. The book would thus endeavour to present various dimensions of Jewish Law rarely included in any general discussion of the subject. The growth of rabbinic law from ancient roots to modern applications would, of course, be given full attention, but the reader would have a much expanded sense of all the streams that historically were part of or related to Jewish Law. The sixteen scholars whose essays appear here have amply fulfilled the Editorial Board's hopes for such a comprehensive introduction to the history of Jewish Law.

Since so many individuals contributed to this book, one could not expect complete uniformity in approach or opinion from chapter to chapter. The contributors represent various positions on the philosophical or theological context of Jewish Law, but their several positions are not germane here. The focus is history. The philosophy of the law and its theological component must be studied in detail elsewhere. These components of Jewish Law are significant in their own right, but undue emphasis on them would have injected a particular point of view which could blur the emphasis on history. Nevertheless, the final chapter presents one particular viewpoint on the legal significance of the religious dimension of Jewish law, designed to stimulate further reflection, on the part of students and teachers alike.

This book is about Jewish Law, it is not a book of Jewish Law. There is no attempt to trace the development of several, or even one, specific topic, although examples of family law are more often provided than examples of other types of law. The theme remains the history and development of the whole. This general theme by its nature requires references to various major events and developments in the history of Europe and the Middle East since Jewish Law spread both eastward and westward from ancient Judaea. At various times Jewish Law grew and thrived in communities as diverse as fifth century C.E. Babylonia and eighteenth century Poland. Jewish communities from the Euphrates to the North Sea, and beyond, adapted their traditional law to meet changing times and circumstances. The reader is introduced to this sprawling and complex historical progression, filled with attractive byways which can only be noticed before one must pass to new settings in time and place. The Editors hope that the reader will find the historical journey worthwhile and that the reader will be encouraged to go more deeply into periods which he or she will find particularly fascinating.

During all stages of preparation, the Editors emphasized the needs of those who might use this book. The needs of students received special attention. The work could not be too technical (it was not designed as a *Handbuch* for researchers); nor could the pages bristle with unexplained terminology. While a knowledge of Hebrew, or of law, would be most helpful, neither is assumed. The secondary literature noted is usually in English, although much of the best work in Jewish Law is published in Hebrew, and indeed many extremely valuable studies appear in German, French, Italian, and other languages. The materials provided here form an introduction; the more serious student must necessarily be prepared to consult non-English publications. Lawyers, judges, students of Jewish history, and others with an informed interest in Jewish Law and life will also find this book a useful resource.

The Editors were aware of the fact, as the work proceeded, that Professor Menachem Elon's *magnum opus*, *Hamishpaṭ Ha'Ivri*, was being translated into English. It has recently appeared in a magnificent four-volume set. That work was written originally for the needs of students of Jewish Law in Israeli Universities. Our audience is that of students in the Diaspora, whose background knowledge, language, and needs are all different. Nevertheless, we hope that our readers will be encouraged to enhance and broaden their knowledge of this field through Elon's monumental work.

Teachers of Jewish Law will certainly augment the bibliographies here provided. This is as it should be. An introductory work cannot, and should not, articulate in detail the full range of opinion and perspective in the field. The Editors hope that they have laid a solid foundation on which others can build.

The Jewish Law Association wishes to express its sincere gratitude to The Jewish Law Publication Fund, and in particular to Mr. David Landau, whose material support for the commissioning and translation costs, kindly offered in 1990 in response to a speculative appeal made by one of the Editors in the course of a public lecture, is genuinely appreciated. Continuing, and generous, support for the publication programme of the Jewish Law Association has also been provided by the Institute of Jewish Law, Boston University; the Jewish Law Association owes much to the Institute, and particularly to its Director, Professor Neil Hecht.

The work of preparation has concluded. The work of learning begins anew. May this book serve to instruct and to enrich.

BERNARD S. JACKSON   STEPHEN M. PASSAMANECK
Liverpool   Los Angeles

1

BIBLICAL LAW

by

RAYMOND WESTBROOK
Johns Hopkins University

1. *Political and Juridical Background*

The biblical period of Jewish Law dates from the mid-second millenium to the fourth century B.C.E. Traditionally, it covers five sub-periods: patriarchal (sixteenth?), exodus (thirteenth?), judges (twelfth-eleventh), monarchy (eleventh-sixth), and post-exilic (sixth-fourth).

In the narratives of the book of Genesis, the patriarchs are characterized as autonomous legal units, whose relationship to a wider legal system resembles that of states in international law. Indeed, each patriarch is head of an independent household which often appears as the equal of local rulers (*Gen.* 14). At other times, however, a patriarch may appear as an individual in an uneasy relationship of dependence upon the host society: Abraham and Isaac in Egypt and at Gerar (*Gen.* 12:10-20; 20:1-18; 26:6-11), Abraham and the Hittites (*Gen.* 23). There is no mention of a court to whose jurisdiction they might be subject, but when Jacob is accused of theft by Laban, he proposes submission to an *ad hoc* tribunal composed of members from both sides (*Gen.* 31:36-37).

Nonetheless, the substantive law of the period does not differ significantly from that of later periods. The main difference would appear to lie in the fact that enforcement of legal rights is through self-help, e.g. the rape of Dinah in *Gen.* 34. Where individuals are intended to represent later political units, political disputes are placed in the context of family law. Thus the later decline of the tribe of Reuben is depicted in terms of the partial disinheritance of Reuben by his father for the offence of sleeping with the latter's concubine (*Gen.* 49:3-4).

The head of household would appear to have had total jurisdiction over its subordinate members (*Gen.* 42:37), but the latter could appeal to a divine tribunal (*Gen.* 16:6).

According to the account in Exodus and Deuteronomy, the 40 years spent by the Israelites in the desert on their way from Egypt to the promised land are a seminal period, during which the laws and institutions of the later polity were established. Leadership, temporal and spiritual, is in the hands of Moses, to whom Aharon as high priest is subordinate. Moses judges the people, i.e. is head of the administration of justice, but there are several accounts of the delegation of his authority (see below, p.9). The substantive law is given by God to Moses at Mount Sinai, in the form of the Ten Commandments and of 'judgments' — rules concerning everyday social and economic relations (*Ex.* 22-23). Further rules are established by God as precedents when consulted by Moses on cases that occur during the journey through the desert (e.g. *Num.* 9:6-14).

The degree of historical reality present in the biblical account of this period is a matter of dispute among scholars. The legal system is idealized, and has long been recognized as a projection back into Israel's past of institutions of later periods or even of ideological programmes that may never have been put into practice. Much of the substantive law can be shown to be part of a wider ancient Near Eastern tradition, which stretches back at least to the third millenium B.C.E.

As in the previous period, political events are presented in terms of private law: the elaborate division of the promised land among the tribes by Joshua is structured upon the division of an estate by heirs, in accordance with general ancient Near Eastern practices.

After the settlement in Canaan, there existed a loose confederation of tribes which was occasionally united by charismatic war leaders known as judges. It was regarded by later generations as a period of anarchy, 'when each man did what was right in his own eyes'. Nonetheless, there was a universally accepted code of conduct, as epitomized by the incident of the Levite's concubine (*Judg.* 19-20). When a traveller had sought hospitality in a city of the Benjaminites, the local inhabitants had seized and raped to death his concubine. The crime was regarded as so shocking that he was able to recruit all the other tribes for a war against the Benjaminites.

Government of cities was in the hands of local 'lords' (*Judg.* 9:6; 20:5). For the administration of justice, the focal point was the city gate, where the elders judged local cases and citizens transacted their affairs. The book of Ruth claims to describe events that took place 'in the days when the judges judged' (*Ruth* 1:1). It paints a picture of an agricultural community with an established customary law that is well known to its members, who apply it before the elders at the city-gate (*Ruth* 4:1-12). Again, the substantive law, in its secular aspects at least, does not differ radically from that found in other periods. On the other hand, there is no consciousness of a code of Mosaic law that has to be followed by the local courts.

The period of the 'judges' ends with the establishment of a monarchy (c.1000 B.C.E.), first by Saul but then giving way to a dynasty founded by David, and consolidated by his son Solomon (under whom the First Temple was constructed). On Solomon's death, the kingdom divided into two (922 B.C.E.): 'Israel' in the north, 'Judah' in the south, with its capital at Jerusalem.

During the monarchy, the king was the head of the legal system, but a dual system of courts appears to have existed beneath him, consisting of the local courts of the elders and courts presided over by royal officials. There was no legislature in the modern sense; the king issued decrees (*I Sam.* 28:9) and made judgments which might be regarded as precedents (cf. *I Sam.* 30:23-25). There are occasional references to the *torah* of Moses (e.g. *II Kings* 14:6 = *II Chron.* 25:4), but these may be anachronistic insertions. Even if genuine, it is not clear that they refer to the body of pentateuchal commandments later identified in rabbinic jurisprudence. The 'book of the law' (*sefer torah*) discovered in the Temple during the reign of Josiah (*II Kings* 22:8) has generally been associated with the book of Deuteronomy or a part thereof.

The Kingdom of Israel fell to the Assyrians in 722 B.C.E. and disappeared from history. The Kingdom of Judah survived until 587 B.C.E., when it was conquered by the Babylonians under Nebuchadnezer. Here begins the 'exilic' period: many of the leaders of the community were taken to Babylon, where they appear to have thrived. The Babylonian Empire itself fell to the Persian conqueror Cyrus in 538 B.C.E., and the latter permitted the exiles to return to Jerusalem, and to re-establish their political and legal institutions. The Temple, destroyed when the city had fallen to the Babylonians, was rebuilt (the 'Second Temple'), and was later to be much enlarged under Herod.

Under the Persian empire, Judah was no longer a sovereign state but a province (called *Yehud*). Nonetheless, it retained a high degree of local autonomy under the rule of indigenous governors. The seminal figure of the period was Ezra, who came from Babylonia with an imperial commission to appoint judges to administer the community's own law (*Ezra* 7:25). Described as a priest and a 'scribe skilled in the *torah* of Moses', he may be credited with laying the jurisprudential foundations of Jewish Law as we

understand it today. For he and his fellow priests read 'from the book, from
the *torah* of God, with interpretation' before the assembled people (*Neh.* 8:1-
8). Thus the legal system became based upon the idea of a written code of
law interpreted and applied by religious authorities.

2. *Sources*

The term sources has two meanings: authoritative texts applied by the
courts in determining the law in a particular case and primary data used by
historians as evidence of the law in force at a particular period. In the post-
biblical period the laws contained in the first five books of the Bible, the
Torah, constituted a source of the first type, but as we have seen they did not
achieve this status until almost the end of the biblical period. The main
sources of law were tradition, precedent (*Jer.* 26:17-19), and royal decree (*I
Sam.* 14:24; *Jer.* 34:8-10), with divine authorship frequently being attributed
to the latter two forms (e.g. *Num.* 27:1-11; *Ex.* 20:22-26).

As regards historical sources, there is only one extant contemporary legal
text: the *Metsad Ḥashavyahu* inscription, a petition by a corvée worker to the
local military commander dated to the reign of Josiah (seventh century
B.C.E.). The principal source is of course the Bible itself, but its historical
value is qualified by the fact that the version that has come down to us is the
result of hundreds of years of compilation and redaction; much of it cannot be
dated with any certainty. Within the Pentateuch, scholars in the tradition of
biblical criticism (deriving from Wellhausen and Graf) have identified several
sources from different streams of tradition that have been interwoven in the
final version. With very tentative dates, they have been labelled: J — eighth
century B.C.E.; D(euteronomy) — seventh; E —seventh; P(riestly) — fifth.
J, E and P are interwoven in the first four books of the Pentateuch, while the
Deuteronomic author is also regarded as responsible for the redaction of the
historical narrative found in *Joshua-Kings*. Traditional scholars continue to
maintain the claim to the unity of the Pentateuch. This chapter follows the
critical approach.

The events of the monarchy are recorded in two parallel accounts: the
books of *Samuel-Kings*, which are regarded as closer to the events that they
portray, and *I-II Chronicles*, which are of post-exilic authorship. Moreover,
much of the material used by biblical authors came from existing traditional
sources such as songs, proverbs, rituals and laws. Scholars have attempted
to isolate these sources on the basis of form, but the results are necessarily
speculative and rarely datable.

The Pentateuch contains two discrete collections of non-sacral laws (i.e. laws governing relations between man and man). *Ex.* 21:1-22:16 forms the core of a series of various cultic, ethical and legal rules known as the Covenant Code (*Ex.* 20:23-23:19), which is regarded by scholars as an independent source inserted into the account of the events at Sinai at some stage during the editing and combining of the J and E narratives. Its dating is uncertain, but it is generally considered to be of great antiquity, although not contemporary with Israel's sojourn in the desert. The agricultural content of many of the laws (e.g. *Ex.* 22:4-5) places it after settlement in Canaan, while the absence of any mention of a king would seem to indicate the period of the judges (twelfth-eleventh century). Many scholars claim to see signs of development within the individual laws, either by way of reforms (e.g. in the law of *talion* in *Ex.* 21:22-25) or scholastic exegesis (e.g. *Ex.* 22:8). The strong affinity between the laws of 21:1-22:16 and the cuneiform law codes (see below) points to a separate origin for this unit within the Covenant Code.

The second collection of non-sacral laws is *Deut.* 21:1-25:13. Since the cultic laws of Deuteronomy are associated with the reforms of King Josiah (7th century, Judah), the non-sacral laws too must have received their present form at the same time, although they contain earlier traditions. Several parallels to the Covenant Code suggest that the Deuteronomic author used the earlier code as a source or at least that there was a source common to both. It has also been suggested that the Deuteronomic author was responsible for redactional additions to the Covenant Code (e.g. *Ex.* 21:8b). The style of the Deuteronomic laws is more heterogeneous than those of Exodus, with motive clauses, exhortation and admonition. There are also scattered non-sacral laws found outside the main corpus, e.g. homicide (*Deut.* 19:13), evidence (*Deut.* 19:15-21), slave-release (*Deut.* 15:12-18).

A further body of laws known as the Priestly Code, and dealing mostly but not exclusively with sacral matters, is to be found scattered through the narrative of Leviticus and Numbers (P-source). Within this source, a compact unit of mostly cultic rules in *Lev.* 17-26 has been identified as a separate corpus, referred to as the Holiness Code. It is generally dated to the exilic period, due to close parallels with the writings of the prophet Ezekiel.

The Ten Commandments in themselves constitute an independent source which is found in two narratives: *Ex.* 20:1-17 and *Deut.* 5:6-21. Strictly speaking, however, they are not to be regarded as laws to be applied by the courts but as moral exhortation to the individual, since they contain no sanctions for disobedience.

An influential theory of A. Alt distinguished between two types of laws in the codes: casuistic laws, which are framed as a hypothetical case with the corresponding legal solution (e.g. 'If an ox gores a man ..., ... its owner shall be put to death...'), and apodictic laws, which are framed as concise commands (e.g. 'Thou shalt not steal', 'He who curses his father and mother shall be put to death'). The former were said to derive (via a putative Canaanite law) from the Mesopotamian law codes (see below, p.7), which share the casuistic form, while the latter were regarded as a native Israelite creation. Subsequent evidence has not confirmed this theory, but the distinction between casuistic and apodictic laws is still routinely used by scholars in discussing their origins.

The law codes are by no means the only source for law in the Bible. The P narrative contains four reports of judicial decisions which supposedly represented the original precedents for later rules of law: a case of blasphemy (*Lev.* 24:10-23), a second Passover for persons ritually impure (*Num.* 9:1-14), the gatherer of wood on the Sabbath (*Num.* 15:32-36), and the rights of daughters (here, those of Zelophehad) in intestate succession (*Num.* 27:1-11; 36). Similar reports are found in juridical parables — a realistic account of a legal case presented to a king for judgment with the aim of leading him to draw a parallel with his own conduct: the poor man's lamb (*II Sam.* 12:1-14), the woman of Tekoah (*II Sam.* 14:1-20), and the negligent guard (*I Kings* 20:35-43).

Many of the narratives in Genesis, the historical books and Ruth describe in a more incidental fashion legal institutions and procedures, such as a formal search for stolen goods (*Gen.* 31:30-35), a herding contract (*Gen.* 29:15-18; 30:31-4; 31:38-9), a treason trial (*I Kings* 21:8-14), and levirate marriage (*Ruth* 4:1-10). A further source of law is the use of metaphor by the prophets: the relationship between God and Israel is described in terms of human legal relationships such as guardianship and marriage, revealing modes of formation and penalties for breach, etc. (e.g. *Hos.* 2).

To reconstruct the legal system of ancient Israel, however, further sources are needed that can supplement the fragmentary information provided by the Bible and place it in context. One possibility is to look to the abundant material from the period immediately following: the *Mishnah* and early strata of the *Talmud*, the New Testament and the Dead Sea Scrolls, and commentaries on the biblical codes such the *Mekhilta* and that of Philo of Alexandria. While they undoubtedly preserve many earlier traditions, two difficulties arise in using these sources. First, the legal sources and commentaries do not represent academic historical inquiry, but the needs of practical jurists to produce a system suited to the conditions of their own society, which were very different from those of biblical times. Second, the intellectual background of all authors of this period is Greek philosophy, which contains concepts far more sophisticated than those employed by the drafters of the biblical codes. It is very difficult therefore to distinguish in these later sources between genuine tradition on the one hand and legal development, interpretation or rationalization on the other.

There is, however, a more closely related source that has come to light through the archaeological discoveries of the past 100 years: the legal systems of Israel's contemporary and earlier neighbours. Records from the ancient Near East, mostly in cuneiform script, begin at the end of the fourth millenium B.C.E. and continue until Hellenistic times. (Special note should be made of an archive of some sixty legal documents in Aramaic from a fifth century B.C.E. Jewish community at Elephantine in Egypt.) They include not only thousands of legal documents but records of all aspects of their societies' life and thought, providing their legal systems with a context that is mostly lacking in the biblical evidence.

These sources are of more than mere comparative value; there emerges from the cuneiform record evidence of a common legal tradition that stretched across the whole of the ancient Near East. That tradition is reflected especially in a form of jurisprudence that was developed in Mesopotamia as part of a wider intellectual system and transmitted beyond its boundaries through the medium of cuneiform scribal schools. An individual case is reformulated as a hypothetical problem (the casuistic form mentioned above) and discussed by considering variants on the facts, often according to a set pattern (e.g. varying the status of the victim). The system, however, lacks the ability to formulate abstract concepts or to define legal terms; it produces instead endless lists of examples. In the third and second millenia this technique finds expression in law codes that are remarkably similar in form and content. Six such codes have been recovered to date, in Sumerian, Babylonian, Assyrian and Hittite, the best-known being the code of King Hammurabi of Babylon. The law codes of the Bible are heirs to this tradition, in varying measure. In the earliest of them, the Covenant Code, some three quarters of its content can be traced back to standard legal problems found in the cuneiform codes.

The later codes already show the first signs of the revolution in thought that was to replace the Mesopotamian science of lists by Greek philosophy, albeit the bulk of their material still derives from the old tradition. The shift from the Mesopotamian concept of a law code as a pedagogical tool to that of an authoritative source of law is, however, achieved only in the latest stratum of the Bible. For most of the biblical period the climate of thought and practice in which the Law of Israel was created is that represented by the cuneiform sources.

3.   *Legal Practice*

A.   Courts

The *local court* sat in the open space behind the city gate. It consisted of leading citizens usually referred to as elders (*Deut.* 21:18-21; 22:13-21; 25:5-10; *I Kings* 21:8-11; *Lam.* 5:14). In the P-source, the term 'assembly' (*'edah*) seems to designate the same body (*Num.* 35:12, 24-5; cf. *Josh.* 20:1-9). The elders also have the power to extradite a fellow townsman from a city of refuge in order to stand trial for murder (*Deut.* 19:12) and they are responsible for unsolved murders (*Deut.* 21:2-3). They appear to have sat as a college.

The king is *ex officio* the supreme judge, and sits alone (e.g. *I Sam.* 8:5; *Ps.* 72:1-4; *Jer.* 22:15-16; cf. *Judg.* 4:5). Solomon judged from a throne situated in the 'courtyard of judgment' (*I Kings* 7:7). The king could judge cases at first instance (*I Kings* 3:16-28), possibly where a difficult question arose (cf. *Ex.* 18:26). A party might petition him directly, by 'shouting' to the king (*II Kings* 6:26-9), using the formula 'Save, O king!' (*II Sam.* 14:4-11). There is no evidence of a formal system of appeals from the lower courts, but the petition may have been a method of overcoming failure to obtain justice at the local level (*II Sam.* 12:1-6; cf. *II Kings* 8:3-6).

God in his capacity as divine king is also regarded as a judge (*Jer.* 11:20). He may be petitioned directly, through prayer (e.g. *Lam.* 3:59), or on behalf of others (*Gen.* 18:25). God was the ultimate guarantor of justice when the human system had failed because of abuse by its officers (*Is.* 3:14).

During the period of the monarchy a system of *royally appointed judges*, connected in some way with the military administration, was active in the capital and the provinces. Its relationship to the local courts of the elders is unclear. King Jehoshaphat (Judah, ninth century B.C.E.) is reported (*II Chron.* 19:5-11) to have appointed both (a) 'judges in all the fortified cities of Judah' and (b) a special court in Jerusalem, consisting of levites, priests and heads of households (i.e. elders). The scope of the latter's jurisdiction is not specified beyond the statement that it was presided over by a priest for 'all matters of God' and by the governor (*nagid*) for 'all matters of the king'.

The three different accounts in the Pentateuch of Moses' appointment of subordinate judges have been interpreted by scholars as attempts to legitimize reforms of the court system by Jehoshaphat and other kings. In *Ex.* 18:13-26 Jethro proposes the appointment of commanders (*sarim*) of thousands, hundreds, fifties and tens to lighten the burden of judging for Moses, who is only to take the difficult cases. The model is that of the royal military organization. The appointees are to be able men from among all the people, but in *Deut.* 1:9-17 Moses makes the same appointments from among all the 'heads of the tribes', i.e. the elders, while in *Num.* 11:16-25 seventy elders are appointed from the 'elders and officials' (*shotrim*).

In the trial of Jeremiah (*Jer.* 26) the court consists of commanders and 'all the people', but it may be an *ad hoc* court. It should be noted that in the *Metsad Hashavyahu* document a petition is presented to the local military commander.

In the post-exilic community the Persian emperor's mandate to Ezra authorized him to appoint judges (*Ezra* 7:25).

In *Ezekiel's ideal constitution* the levitical priests are to be judges (*Ezek.* 44:24). Evidence for the role of priests as judges in practice is less clear. In Chronicles the levites are mentioned as officials and judges in Solomon's reign (*I Chron.* 23:4), but this may be an anachronism from a post-exilic source. The Chronicler also gives a priest jurisdiction over 'all matters of God' in Jehoshaphat's reform, which could refer to sacral matters or simply to the priests' traditional forensic function of administering evidentiary procedures (cf. *Deut.* 17:9 and 19:17-18 and see below). Possibly priests had jurisdiction within the precincts of the Temple: cf. *Jer.* 20:1-3.

B.   Procedure

In *private disputes*, if the defendant is not present, the plaintiff must bring him to court to face charges (*Deut.* 21:18-21) or the court itself may summon him (*Deut.* 25:8; *I Sam.* 22:11). Some sources suggest a formal procedure of claim (*Is.* 5:1-7) and reply (*Mic.* 6:2-4; *I Sam.* 22:14-15) or counterclaim (*Jer.* 2:29), but it is not always strictly observed (*I Kings* 3:17-22).

Evidence is usually given in the form of oral testimony; documentary evidence is not mentioned in a forensic context (although *Job* 31:35 appears to know of a written bill of indictment), but must have been admitted, since documents were sometimes used to attest to transactions. Reliance is also placed on evidentiary presumptions (*Deut.* 22:24-7) and material evidence (*Ex.* 22:12; *Deut.* 22:16-17). An exculpatory oath procedure is applied for a bailee accused of fraud (*Ex.* 22:10) and a wife accused of adultery (*Num.* 5:21-3). It was administered by the priests (*Num.* 5:21-3; cf. *Deut.* 21:5), as were other supra-rational evidentiary procedures — the oracle (*Ex.* 22:8; *Josh.* 7:10-18; *I Sam.* 14:38) and possibly the ordeal (*Num.* 5:23-8). Perjury was punished by the talionic principle (*Deut.* 19:19-21).

The verdict in actions *in personam* was a formula directed to the winning party: 'You are in the right' (*tsadik 'atah*: *Prov.* 24:24); in actions *in rem* it was declaratory: 'She is its mother' (*I Kings* 3:27).

For *public offences* such as blasphemy, treason and sacrilege the accused was brought to trial on the basis of a denunciation (*Deut.* 17:4, 7; *I Kings* 21:9-13) and held in custody until judgment was pronounced (*Lev.* 24:12; *Num.* 15:34). The denouncer, sometimes called a *satan*, stands to the right of the accused (*Zech.* 3:1). In the trial of Jeremiah the 'priests and prophets' act as his accusers and demand the death penalty (*Jer.* 26:11). A minimum of two witnesses is required for a conviction (*Deut.* 17:6; 19:15; *I Kings* 21:10), a principle apparently extended to all capital cases (*Num.* 35:30).

Where the injured party is a hierarchical superior, he may act as both plaintiff and judge, bringing the defendant before his own court, e.g. Saul against Ahimelech (*I Sam.* 22:11-16), God against the elders and commanders of Israel (*Is.* 3:13-15).

Most *contracts* were oral (e.g. *I Kings* 20:39-41), but some could be attested by documents: when Jeremiah buys land, it is recorded in a 'double document' consisting of sealed and open parts (*Jer.* 32:11). A document might accompany divorce (*Deut.* 24:1, 3; *Is.* 50:1; *Jer.* 3:8). Some transactions were witnessed at the city gate: Boaz convenes ten elders to witness an agreement over redemption of family land (*Ruth* 4:1-11).

4.   *Principal Legal Institutions*

A.   Marriage and Divorce

Marriage in biblical Israel was not so much a personal relationship as an alliance between two families for the purpose of producing legitimate heirs (*Gen.* 34:8-10; *I Sam.* 18:22; cf. *Judg.* 11:1-2). Polygamy was permitted. On the question of prohibited degrees, the laws of *Leviticus* appear to be more restrictive than the practice attested in the narratives. The latter contemplate marriage between a half-sister and half-brother who do not share

a common mother (*Gen.* 20:12; *II Sam.* 13:13), but even this degree is forbidden by *Lev.* 18:9. Similarly, Jacob marries two sisters, but *Lev.* 18:18
forbids such a union.

There are four stages in the formation of marriage:

(i) Agreement between members of the two families that the bride will
be given in marriage to the groom. The parties are usually the father of the
bride and the groom or his father. Jacob and David act for themselves,
whereas Abraham sends his own agent to procure a bride for his son Isaac
(*Gen.* 24). Even where the son chose his own bride, it was considered proper
for his parents to open the negotiations (*Gen.* 34:4; *Judg.* 14:1-2, 5). Adult
sons might participate with their father in the negotiations over their sister
(*Gen.* 34:13-18). The bride was thus the object of the agreement rather than
a party thereto, but a widow or divorcee could contract on her own behalf (*I
Sam.* 25:39-42; *Hos.* 2:16-22; cf. *Ezek.* 16:8, an orphan bride).

A subsidiary term of the agreement was the amount of betrothal payment
(*mohar*) to be made by the groom to the bride's father. From ancient Near
Eastern evidence this would normally have been in silver, as is provided in
Ex. 22:16. The two examples given in the biblical narratives are atypical:
seven years' labour by Jacob (*Gen.* 29:15-19) and a hundred Philistine
foreskins from David (*I Sam.* 18:25).

(ii) Bringing of the *mohar* by the groom, who would customarily
provide a banquet on the occasion (*Judg.* 14:10). From this point in time
the bride is betrothed (*'oraṣah*). She is referred to as a wife (*Deut.* 22:24;
Judg. 15:1) and as far as outsiders are concerned she is a fully married
woman — rape or seduction by a third party will be treated with corresponding severity (*Deut.* 22:22-25). In the cuneiform sources breach of the
agreement by the father results in damages (see *Codex Hammurabi* §160).
On the same principle, the Philistines recognize that Samson has a just
claim when breach by his father-in-law leads him to take revenge, albeit
immensurate (*Judg.* 15:1-2, 6). Nonetheless, it does not appear that a formal
divorce was necessary to dissolve betrothal, as was the case in later law.

(iii) Claiming of the bride by the groom, on the strength of payment of
the *mohar*. On completion of his 7 years' service Jacob says to his father-in-
law Laban: 'Bring me my wife, for my days are completed' (*Gen.* 29:21).

(iv) Completion of the marriage. It is the father-in-law's turn to give a
banquet before delivering his daughter to the groom (*Gen.* 29:22). Legal
completion appears (in the absence of evidence as to special ceremonies or
rites) to be constituted by consummation, which is referred to as the groom
entering the bridal chamber, described variously as a tent (*Gen.* 24:67), room

(*Judg.* 15:1) or *ḥuppah* (*Joel* 2:16; *Ps.* 19:6), the term used in post-biblical periods for the bridal canopy under which the wedding ceremony takes place.

A man might be forced to marry under certain circumstances. According to *Ex.* 22:15-16:

> If a man seduces an unbetrothed virgin and lies with her, he shall marry her with payment of *mohar*. If her father refuses to give her to him, he shall pay 'the *mohar* of virgins' (i.e. the customary amount) in silver.

If the offence is rape, the conditions are harsher (*Deut.* 22:28-9):

> If a man finds an unbetrothed virgin and seizes her and lies with her and they are caught, the man who lay with her shall pay the girl's father fifty shekels of silver and she shall be his wife. Because he degraded her, he shall not be able to divorce her all his days.

Under the law of the levirate, a man might be obliged to marry his deceased's brother's widow. If he refused, he was subjected to a humiliating ceremony (*Deut.* 25:5-10):

> If brothers dwell together and one of them dies and has no son, the wife of the deceased shall not be married outside to a stranger; her husband's brother shall go in to her and take her as his wife and perform the duty of a husband's brother to her. The first son whom she bears shall rise up upon the name of his deceased brother, that his name be not expunged from Israel. If the man does not wish to marry his brother's wife, then his brother's wife shall go up to the gate to the elders and say: 'My husband's brother refuses to raise up a name to his brother in Israel; he will not perform the duty of a husband's brother to me.' Then the city elders shall call him and speak to him, and if he persists, saying, 'I do not wish to marry her,' then his brother's wife shall go up to him in the presence of the elders, pull his sandal off his foot, spit in his face and declare: 'So shall it be done to the man who does not build up his brother's house.' And his name shall be called in Israel: 'The house of the one whose sandal was pulled off.'

The biblical levirate, unlike the later institution, applied not only to brothers. In their absence, the duty fell upon the closest relative. In *Gen.* 38, after Tamar is twice widowed and her father-in-law refuses to allow his third son to marry her, she tricks her father-in-law into performing the levirate himself. In *Ruth* 4:1-6, a more distant relative is potentially liable. On the other hand, the circumstances under which the law applies are narrower than in the later law: see section B on 'Inheritance' below (p.15).

Although it receives scant mention in the Bible, the dowry (*shiluim*) must have played an important role in Israelite marriage. In *Josh.* 15:18-19 (= *Judg.* 1:13-15) and *I Kings* 9:16, it consists of land. More typical items are personal slaves (*Gen.* 29:24, 29; cf. 16:2-3; 24:59), jewellery and clothing (*Ezek.* 16:10-12). It is typically furnished to the bride by her father (being the functional equivalent of an inheritance share), but in *Ezek.* 16:10-12, where the girl is an orphan, it is provided by the groom and in *Gen.* 24:53 it is supplemented by gifts from the groom's father. During marriage the dowry merged into the husband's property, but the wife might maintain control of certain personal items (*Ezek.* 16:16-18), especially personal slaves (*Gen.* 16:2-3; cf. *melug* in the *Mishnah* (*Yeb.* 7.1) = Akkadian *mulugu*, Ugaritic *mlg*). From the usage of neighbouring societies, it may be presumed that a primary purpose of the dowry was to support the wife in widowhood.

A special problem that is dealt with by several of the ancient Near Eastern law codes is that of the wife whose husband fails to return from a foreign country (e.g. *Hammurabi* §§133-7). Under certain circumstances the wife is allowed to remarry, but the second marriage is subject to annulment should the first husband return. There are no legal provisions of this nature in the Bible, but the story of David and Michal seems to reflect the same principles, in contrast to the harsher attitude of later Jewish Law (*M. Yeb.* 10:1). After David has fled from Saul (*I Sam.* 19:11-17), the latter gives David's wife Michal to one Paltiel (*I Sam.* 25:44). After Saul's death David claims Michal back from his successor Ishbaal, who feels obliged to comply, in spite of the tearful objections of Paltiel and the fact that he is at war with David (*II Sam.* 3:14-16).

Divorce is a unilateral act by the husband, by means of a formal declaration such as: 'She is not my wife and I am not her husband' (*Hos.* 2:4), following the practice prevalent throughout the ancient Near East. The possibility of a wife divorcing her husband is not raised in the Bible, but the right existed at least in theory in the surrounding societies and is attested in practice among the Jewish community at Elephantine (see Porten and Yardeni, texts B2.6; B3.3; B3.8).

The husband is mentioned in sources from the period of the later monarchy as providing his wife with a 'document of separation' (*sefer keritut*: *Deut.* 24:1, 3; *Is.* 50:1; *Jer.* 3:8) upon divorce. Possibly it served to furnish the wife with documentary evidence that she was free to remarry.

The main legal provision concerning divorce is *Deut.* 24:1-4. While rabbinic jurisprudence regarded it as the basis of divorce law, the biblical text does not lay down any general principles. Rather, it deals with an exceptional case:

> If a man takes a woman and consummates the marriage and it happens that
> she displeases him because he found in her some indecency and he writes her
> a document of separation, gives it to her and sends her from his house, and
> she leaves his house and becomes the wife of another and the latter hates her,
> writes her a document of separation, gives it to her and sends her from his
> house or the second man who married her dies: her first husband who divorced
> her may not take her again as his wife, after she has been made unclean to
> him...

It presents a complicated scenario: (1) a husband finds 'some indecency'
(*'ervat dabar*) in his wife and divorces her; (2) she remarries and her second
husband either 'hates' and divorces her or dies and leaves her a widow; (3) the
first husband is then forbidden to remarry her.

The rationale for this provision becomes clear if it is placed against the
background of the wider ancient Near Eastern legal tradition. If a husband
divorces his wife without cause, the technical phrase being 'hates and
divorces', he must restore to her her dowry and pay compensation. If on the
other hand she has done something to justify her being divorced (cf.
M. Ket. 7.6: immodest conduct), he may keep her dowry and need pay her
nothing.

In the Deuteronomic law, then, the wife left the first marriage penniless,
but not the second, whether as divorcee or widow. In prohibiting remarriage,
the law imposes an estoppel on the husband to prevent him from profiting
twice from his wife: first by claiming that she was not fit to be his wife, and
subsequently by conceding that she *is*.

A husband is forbidden to divorce his wife altogether in two instances: in
Deut. 22:28-9, where he had raped a maiden and was forced to marry her, and
in *Deut.* 22:13-19, where he had falsely accused his wife of pre-marital
infidelity:

> If a man takes a wife, has intercourse with her and hates her, then makes a
> false statement about her and gives her a bad reputation, saying, 'I married
> this woman but when I slept with her I did not find in her the signs of
> virginity,' but the girl's father and mother take the girl's signs of virginity
> and bring them out to the city elders at the gate, the girl's father saying to
> the elders, 'I gave my daughter as a wife to this man and he hated her, so he
> made a false statement, namely: 'I did not find the signs of virginity in your
> daughter,' but here are the signs of my daughter's virginity' and spreading
> out the garment before the city elders: the city elders shall take that man and
> beat him, fine him one hundred of silver and give it to the girl's father,
> because he gave a virgin of Israel a bad reputation. She shall be his wife; he
> may not divorce her all his days.

B.   Inheritance

The basic family unit was the 'house of the father', a patriarchal household of three (or more) generations (*Gen.* 7:7). On the death of the head of household his sons (or grandsons inheriting *per stirpes*: *Josh.* 17:1-6) divided the estate by lot (*Num.* 26:55). The first-born was entitled to an extra share. A father could transfer that share to another son, but not to the son of a different mother, if his preference was based on favouritism towards the other wife (*Deut.* 21:15-17). The first-born could, however, lose his extra share by misconduct (*Gen.* 49:3-4). He could also trade his future right to it: Esau sold his for a bowl of soup! (*Gen.* 25:27-34).

The brothers could choose to postpone division and remain as joint owners — technically known as 'dwelling together' (*Gen.* 13:1-6; *Ps.* 133:1). If one died childless during this period, the other brothers could simply divide without him. To ensure the deceased his share, another brother was obliged to marry his widow, the product of this levirate marriage being deemed the deceased's heir who would divide on his behalf (*Deut.* 25:5-6). The levirate duty also applied if the brother predeceased his father and the estate was therefore still undivided (*Gen.* 38) or if an undivided inheritance that had been sold was restored to the family by redemption (*Ruth* 4).

If there were no heirs in the house of the father, the estate passed to the nearest agnate in the clan (*mishpaḥah*), in the order of brother, uncle, etc. (*Num.* 27:8-11). In the absence of sons, daughters counted as heirs (*Num.* 27:8), but because their share was regarded as dowry, they were obliged to marry within their clan (*Num.* 36:8).

5. *Bibliography*

5.1 General

Daube, D., *Studies in Biblical Law* (Cambridge: Cambridge University Press, 1947, reprinted New York, Arno, 1969).

Falk, Z., *Hebrew Law in Biblical Times* (Jerusalem: Wahrmann Books, 1964).

Greengus, S., 'Law', *Anchor Bible Dictionary* (New York: Doubleday, 1992), IV 242-52.

Jackson, B.S., 'Law' in *Harper's Bible Dictionary,* ed. P.J. Achtemeier (San Francisco: Harper & Row, 1985), 548-51.

Jackson, B.S., 'Ideas of Law and Legal Administration: a Semiotic

Approach', in *The World of Ancient Israel: Sociological, Anthropological and Political Perspectives,* ed. R.E. Clements (Cambridge: Cambridge University Press, 1989), 185-202.

Patrick, D., ed., *Thinking Biblical Law* (Atlanta: Scholars Press, 1989, *Semeia* 45).

Welch, J., ed., *Biblical Law Bibliography* 1989- (available from J. Reuben Clark Law School, Brigham Young University, Provo UT 84602).

Westbrook, R., *Studies in Biblical and Cuneiform Law* (Paris: Gabalda, 1988).

Yaron, R., 'The Evolution of Biblical Law', in A. Theodorides et al., *La Formazione del diritto nel vicino oriente antico* (Rome: Edizioni Scientifiche Italiane, 1988), 77-108.

5.2   *Juridical Background*

Dearman, J., *Property Rights in the Eighth Century Prophets* (Atlanta: Scholars Press, 1988).

Noth, M., *The Laws in the Pentateuch* (Edinburgh: Oliver & Boyd, 1966), 1-107.

5.3   *Sources*

Alt, A., 'The Origins of Israelite Law', in *Essays on Old Testament History and Religion* (Oxford: Clarendon Press, 1966), 81-132.

Fishbane, M., *Biblical Interpretation in Ancient Israel* (Oxford: Clarendon Press, 1985), 89-277.

Jackson, B.S., 'The Problem of Exodus 21:22-25', in *Essays in Jewish and Comparative Legal History* (Leiden: E.J. Brill, 1975), 75-107.

Patrick, D., *Old Testament Law* (London: SCM Press, 1985).

Paul, S., *Studies in the Book of the Covenant in the Light of Cuneiform and Biblical Law* (Leiden: E.J. Brill, 1970).

Porten, B. and Yardeni, A., *Textbook of Aramaic Documents from Ancient Egypt* (Winona Lake: Eisenbrauns, 1989).

Pritchard, J., ed., *Ancient Near Eastern Texts relating to the Old Testament,* (Princeton: Princeton University Press, 1969, 3rd ed.): contains translations of the cuneiform law codes and of selected private legal documents.

Roth, M., *Law Collections from Mesopotamia and Asia Minor* (Atlanta: Scholars Press, 1995).

Westbrook, R., 'Biblical and Cuneiform Law Codes,' *Revue Biblique* 92 (1985), 247-64.

Yaron, R., 'Biblical Law: Prologomena', in *Jewish Law in Legal History and the Modern World*, ed. B.S. Jackson (Leiden: E.J. Brill, 1980), 27-44.

5.5 Legal Practice

Boecker, H.J., *Law and the Administration of Justice in the Old Testament and the Ancient East* (London: SPCK, 1980).

Frymer-Kensky, T., 'The Strange Case of the Suspected Sotah', *Vetus Testamentum* 34 (1984), 11-36.

Jackson, B.S., *Theft in Early Jewish Law* (Oxford: Clarendon Press, 1972), 203-50.

McKenzie, D., 'Judicial Procedure at the Town Gate', *Vetus Testamentum* 14 (1964), 3-13.

Reviv, H., 'The Traditions Concerning the Inception of the Legal System in Israel', *Zeitschrift für die alttestamentliche Wissenschaft* 94 (1982), 566-75.

5.6 Marriage

Ben-Barak, Z., 'The Legal Background to the Restoration of Michal to David', *Supplements to Vetus Testamentum* 30 (1979), 15-29.

Levine, B., 'Mulugu/Melug: The Origins of a Talmudic Legal Institution', *Journal of the American Oriental Society* 88 (1968), 271-85.

Neufeld, E., *Ancient Hebrew Marriage Laws*, London: Longman, 1944.

Westbrook, R., 'The Prohibition on Restoration of Marriage in Deuteronomy 24:1-4', *Scripta Hierosolymitana* 31 (1986), 387-405.

Yaron, R., 'On Divorce in Old Testament Times', *Revue Internationale des Droits de l'Antiquité* 4 (1957), 117-28.

5.7 Inheritance

Daube, D., 'Consortium in Roman and Hebrew Law', *The Juridical Revue* 62 (1950), 71-91.

Mendelsohn, I., 'On the Preferential Status of the Eldest Son', *Bulletin of the American Schools of Oriental Research* 156 (1959), 38-40.

Westbrook, R., *Property and the Family in Biblical Law* (Sheffield: JSOT Press, 1991).

2

JEWISH LAW DURING THE SECOND TEMPLE PERIOD*

by

DANIELA PIATTELLI
Pontificia università Lateranense
Università di Salerno

and

BERNARD S. JACKSON
University of Liverpool

1. *Political and Juridical Background of the Period*

A. Introduction

The period of the Second Temple extends from the restoration of the institutions of the Judaean community under Ezra and Nehemia, authorized by the Persians (Ch.1, pp.3f., above) to the destruction of the Temple, and the institutions which went with it, on the failure of the first great revolt against Rome in 70 C.E. In it, we encounter a great diversity of approaches — reflecting differences between the cultural environments of Palestine and the more thoroughly Hellenised community of Egypt, and within Palestine between rival groups for Jewish political hegemony (including Sadducees and Pharisees) and those who adopted an oppositional stance to the Jerusalem establishment (Samaritans, Zealots, the Dead Sea community, followers of charismatic leaders like Jesus). It is with the wisdom of hindsight that many of these groups are characterized as 'sects', by comparison with the Pharisees, who are viewed as proto-Rabbis, forming the bridge in Jewish legal history between the late biblical period and that of the *Mishnah*. An historical approach must view this period without regard to later conceptions of what was 'authentic' in the history of Jewish law. In the period of the Second Temple, all these various groups considered themselves authentic heirs to, and developers of, the biblical tradition.

Until recently, our knowledge of Jewish law in this period was extremely scanty. There appeared to be a chasm between the world of the Bible, and that of postbiblical (rabbinic) Judaism, which emerged in a seemingly well-developed form in the tannaitic sources (Ch.5, below). Though some literature has survived from this period (including the later books of the Bible), the fourth century B.C.E. in particular forms an important gap, and until the discovery of the Dead Sea Scrolls none of the literature could be described as 'legal'. There is literature, historical and philosophical, which to greater or lesser degrees reflects the Hellenistic environment of the period from the early third century C.E. — some of it, including the 'Septuagint' (the Greek translation of the Bible) written in Egypt (see further pp.79-81, below). The books of the Apocrypha (books not included in the canon of the Bible, but regarded as having a certain sanctity), the scrolls from Qumran, the writings of the Alexandrian Jewish philosopher Philo, and much of the New Testament (such as the Pauline letters), were written within the period; much of the rest, including the histories of Josephus and the Synoptic Gospels describe events in the period and were written down shortly thereafter. The later rabbinic sources also make claims about the pre-70 *halakhah*, but their reliability in this regard has frequently been questioned.

The discovery of the Dead Sea Scrolls has provided, for the first time, substantial normative material which can be firmly dated between the codes of the Bible and the *Mishnah* and other collections of tannaitic literature. Much of the focus of this chapter, therefore, is directed towards these sources.

The period was one of considerable political turmoil. The Persian dynasty fell to Alexander III of Macedon ('Alexander the Great'), who between 334 and 330 B.C.E. conquered Phoenicia, Palestine, Egypt and Mesopotamia. In 331, the oracle of Amun Re in Egypt proclaimed Alexander divine, and in the same year he founded the city of Alexandria. On the death of Alexander, his empire split between two dynasties, the Seleucids controlling Syria and Palestine, the Ptolemies Egypt. Syrian rule in Palestine became increasingly oppressive and intolerant of Jewish religious practice. Ultimately, there was a successful revolt (led by 'the Maccabees') against 'the Greeks', leading to the establishment of an indigenous Jewish dynasty in Judaea, that of the Hasmoneans (161-37 B.C.E.). There was thus a period of over a century during the Second Commonwealth period when something approaching full autonomy was enjoyed by the Jewish political and legal institutions in

Judaea. Then the Romans appeared in the area (Ch.6, below). After the conquest of Pompey in 63 B.C.E., Judaea became a client kingdom to Rome, though still nominally headed by Hyrcanus II, a member of the Hasmonean dynasty. In 37 B.C.E. the Romans influenced the replacement of the Hasmoneans by a new ('Idumaean') dynasty founded by Herod the Great (who was half-Jewish). But this arrangement did not long survive the death of Herod, and in 6 C.E. Palestine lost its formal independence and was incorporated into the Roman empire (at first, as a sub-province under the control of the governor of Syria). But though the monarchy was lost, and with it all vestiges of secular political authority, the institutions of the Temple, particularly the High Priesthood, survived — perhaps with an enhanced status in the eyes of many, as representing the principal remaining focus of national identity. It was only with the destruction of the Temple, in 70 C.E., that the Priesthood and its institutions also disappeared.

It is clear that the existence of Jewish autonomy during the Second Temple period did not result in uniformity in the development of Jewish law. With the close of the Biblical canon — so that no new books would be accepted as divinely dictated or inspired — new forms of institutional authority were required. But as in the period of the Bible itself, tensions developed between (royal) political authority and religious authority and indeed between different religious institutions *inter se* — between King and Sanhedrin (Assembly of Elders), King and High Priesthood, Sanhedrin and High Priesthood. Nor were religious tensions restricted to the formal institutions. Groups opposed to these institutions (including both political and religious zealots) developed their own, rival claims to religious authority. The Temple Priesthood in Jerusalem, for example, emerges as a major target of opposition in some of the Dead Sea Scrolls. Frequently, disputes centred upon authority to interpret the Biblical text, and the manner in which it ought to be interpreted or supplemented.

What, then, was Jewish law in this period? At least three approaches to this question are possible. Traditional Jewish scholars, for whom Jewish law is defined by the later rabbinic tradition, tend to seek a 'Second Commonwealth *halakhah*', being those elements within this period from which rabbinic *halakhah* may be thought to have originated; anything else is then regarded as 'sectarian'. A second, 'historical' approach, is to look at the totality of trends within the period, without privileging any one, and thus to conclude that Jewish law at this time was 'pluralistic'. A third approach may be labelled 'positivistic': it would privilege Jewish law as developed and enforced by the formal institutional sources of the period (King, Sanhedrin,

High Priesthood) irrespective of (often later) views of its religious authenticity. Writing about the law of this period inevitably involves the making of choices amongst these approaches, but these choices are not always made explicit.

B. The *Halakhah* in the Postbiblical Era

We know that the great treatises of the *Mishnah* (Ch.5, pp.116-20, below) and *Talmud* (Ch.7, below) were prepared in order to perpetuate the values of a tradition which had grown up over the centuries, and which ran the risk of disappearing if it was not written down. Israel's will to survive prevailed, on that occasion, despite the inhibition against writing anything other than that which had been given in writing on Sinai. By committing the 'Oral Law' to writing, the Rabbis sought to perpetuate traditions which had grown up over time with the consent of the community of Israel. But the conception of the 'Oral Law' was not universal in Judaism in this period. Other groups, such as the Dead Sea community, displayed no inhibitions against codifying their own practices and understandings of the Biblical text. We shall consider shortly their halakhic writings. But first a word about their general organization and ideology.

The people of Qumran termed their congregation a *yahad* (meaning 'unity'), with a rigid, vertical organization under the leadership of Priests.[1] An important role was played also by the levitical priests, who were given the task of enforcing the rules according to which the community was organized, under the leadership of the Zadokite priests (derived from *Ezek.* 44). The writers of the so-called *Damascus Covenant* (*CD*) seem to have been anticipating the future coming of a 'Teacher of Righteousness' (*moreh hatsedek, CD* 1:1), who would have a profound knowledge of the Divine Word and a capacity to make it easily intelligible by the people (*doresh hatorah*). Pending his arrival, the initiates invested authority in an official called the *mehokek* as one who would teach the priests the necessary techniques to clear up the meaning of the Law.

Josephus (*Ant.*, xi.121-23) a little later records a tradition according to which Ezra was regarded, in popular consciousness, as 'the priest, the reader of the Law, the just man who enjoys the consent of the multitude'. The just man whom the Qumran initiates were awaiting appears to have been a personage with features not unlike those of Ezra, who had brought back the people to Jerusalem, freeing them from an exile which had been not only material, but also spiritual, since then too people had strayed from the strict observance of the Law.[2]

Without entering into the discussion about the identification of the *moreh hatsedek*, or his relationship, in the view of the Qumran community, to the *mehokek*, it is still fundamental to realize that they felt themselves to be awaiting a future event. They appear to have viewed themselves as depositaries of readings of the Law that would ultimately find full acceptance by the whole of Israel; they were conscious, however, that a necessary condition for extending to the whole of Israel 'their' reading of the Law was for the moment lacking.

General consent was regarded as necessary in order to establish the compulsory value of any given reading of the Law. We may recall the detailed description of the solemn reading of the Law preserved in the *Book of Nehemia* (*Neh.* 8:1-18). The narration begins with the rebuilt Temple in the background. The principal actors are Ezra (the scribe-priest), Nehemia (the 'excellent man'), the levitical priests, and the people (comprising men, women, and all those who can understand). Ezra, assisted by the levitical priests, who have the task of teaching the people, begins the reading of the law, translating it and providing its meaning in a way that is understandable to all. The reading lasts the whole day, and at the end the people are urged to go and celebrate joyfully the solemn event.

Similarly, to prove the acceptance of the compulsory value for the Jewish communities living in Egypt of the Greek translation of the Hebrew Bible, the *Letter of Aristeas* was written, according to which, after the Seventy translators had completed the required version (the Septuagint) it was read before Israel's congregation in Egypt (see further pp.79-81 below).

Parallel disputes are attested amongst other groups regarding the character of the binding law. Josephus (*Ant.*, xiii.297-8) says that the Pharisees[3] had given the people some rules of behaviour worked out by the past generations but not included in the law of Moses, but that these rules were, therefore, rejected by the Sadducees, who considered compulsory only the traditions that had been set down in the written *Torah*. Nevertheless, the Sadducees are said (in *Megillat Ta'anit*, perhaps of the second century B.C.E., and accepted as authentic by the rabbinic sources: *M. Ta'anit*, 2:8) to have had their own Book of Decrees (*Sefer Gezerot*) which provided rulings on the different forms of capital punishment, and the cases in which these various forms — stoning, burning at the stake, beheading, strangulation — were to be applied. This source is of undoubted importance also from the point of view of the capacity of the Jewish community to impose capital punishment. It does not follow, however, that these decrees enjoyed general efficacy.

Megillat Ta'anit (probably of second century B.C.E.) attributes the ban on writing down the 'Oral Law' to opposition to this Sadducean *Book of Decrees* (see further Ch.5, section 3A). Clearly, the Sadducees did not think they were transgressing any principle by committing their extra-biblical traditions to writing, and this too is relevant to the problem of the origins of the Oral Torah.

In what spirit did the initiates of Qumran set about their editing activity? To be more precise: what was the value they ascribed to writing and what purpose did they seek to fulfil by preserving in writing the results of their speculative activity? How did they regard the material whose memory they wished to preserve?

Specialists who have investigated the editing techniques of Qumran have shown that their halakhic material seems to have been constructed through the use of close textual exegesis (*Midrash Halakhah*, cf. pp.121-24 below). The community seems not to have felt any inhibition against writing down the results of their speculative activity — unlike the later Rabbis who decided to commit to writing their great mass of decisions (elevating them to the status of Oral Torah) only under the threat of total dispersion following the fall of the Second Temple in 70 C.E. Indeed, Neusner claims that the very conception of Oral Torah was elaborated only in the period following the destruction of the Temple, which seemed to open an historical era recalling the Babylonian exile and when, moreover, the centre of activity shifted from Jerusalem to the study of the *Torah* in the Yavneh academy.[4] Schiffman agrees with Neusner on this point, but does not think that the absence of Oral Torah in Qumran is proof of its later origin.[5] However we resolve the problem of the origin of the conception of Oral Torah, the initiates of Qumran appear to have adopted a form of reading of the text (a *pesher*) that was the result of a scribal type of activity — one which stipulated the (often deeper) meaning of the words, but did not engage in formal arguments regarding verbal interpretation.

2.   *General Character of the Sources*

A.   The Pentateuch

First and foremost of the sources of Jewish law in the Second Commonwealth period is the Pentateuch (the 'Five Books of Moses'). None of the different sects within this period rejected the Pentateuch; indeed, some — such as the Samaritans (Ch.3, below) and later the Sadducees — maintained that it was the exclusive source of law. The recognition of the Pentateuch's importance was not confined to the Jews of Palestine. Already in the third century C.E., it was translated into Greek: Modrzejewski (pp.79-81 below) argues that this may have been for a legal purpose.

According to critical Biblical scholars, the Pentateuch grew in stages (Ch.1, section 2). The very (Greek) name *Deuteronomy* suggests a 'second law', and indeed Moses purports to recapitulate the story and content of the Sinaitic revelation, though with significant differences. The view is frequently taken that it was only in the exilic or early post-exilic period that the Pentateuch received its present form. It is not easy to determine what document is actually referred to when we read, in various sources, of the "Book of the Law", but by the time of Ezra (pp.3f., above) we may be confident that the "*torah* of Moses" is indeed the Pentateuch, in more or less the form in which we have it today.

The term "canonization" is sometimes used to refer to the process by which writings achieved the status of holy writ. That means not only that they are regarded as sacred, but that the text is closed against further amendment. The beginnings, at least, of that sentiment are found in the pre-exilic period itself, where *Deuteronomy* insists that nothing shall be added or taken away from the text (*Deut.* 4:2, 12:32). Previously, it had been accepted that changes could indeed be made, especially by authorised prophets. A rabbinic tradition later dates the cessation of prophetic authority to the destruction of the First Temple.

The status of the Pentateuch was confirmed through ritual means. *Deut.* 31:11 had ordained a septennial reading of the *Torah* during the feast of *sukkot*, and several Second Commonwealth sources attest to this practice.[6] Some scholars have noted that the period of the canonization of the Pentateuch was also the period of codification in Greece and Rome. Whether the Jewish development stemmed from purely internal religious considerations or from external legal influences, or from a combination of the two, cannot be determined. What is clear, however, is that canonization provided Jewish law with a text of supreme authority, to which all later development had to relate (whether by way of interpretation or supplementation).

B. The Aramaic Papyri

The 'Aramaic Papyri' are a collection of documents which have survived from a Jewish military colony established at Elephantine, near the southern border of Egypt, written during the fifth century B.C.E. Two collections have been published: A. Cowley, *Aramaic Papyri of the Fifth Century BC* (Oxford: Clarendon Press, 1923); and E.G. Kraeling, *The Brooklyn Museum Aramaic Papyri* (New Haven: Yale University Press, 1953), the latter being a set of documents from Elephantine which had been obtained by an American Egyptologist (C.E. Wilbour), but which were not available to Cowley, and only became generally known some years later. Kraeling provides further information regarding the military colony from which the documents come, including the political, social and religious background. We also have from this period some instructions written by the Persian Satrap of Egypt and other high ranking Persian officers to their subordinates: see G.R. Driver, *Aramaic Documents of the Fifth Century B.C.* (Oxford: Clarendon Press, 1954). Reuven Yaron, *Introduction to the Law of the Aramaic Papyri* (Oxford: Clarendon Press, 1961), takes account of all of these sources, insofar as they are relevant to our understanding of the private law of the community.

Yaron offers the following classification of the contents of the documents relevant to private law: some concern complaints before a court, and there are references to such judicial proceedings in others; one appears to refer to an action for the recovery of a debt; another appears to be a declaration on oath; there are three marriage contracts, and two fragments relating to marriage; there is one document of manumission and one concerning adoption. By far the largest group of documents concern property matters. There are deeds concerning barter, sale, gift, and property arrangements subsequent to litigation. There are also provisions for the reversion of property, division of inheritance, and arrangements arising from the grant of building rights. In the area of contract, there are three deeds of loan and further fragments reflecting creditor-debtor relations. There is one deed of lease, providing for a crop-sharing tenancy. Yaron's book provides a detailed analysis of these documents, with chapters on courts and procedure, law of persons, marriage and divorce, succession, law of property, and law of obligations. He also discusses the place of these documents in the history of Jewish law (their relationship both to the Bible and to later Jewish sources), as well as the contacts they manifest with the laws of the surrounding cultures. Further literature is cited by Modrzejewski, Ch.4, n.3, below.

C. The Books of The Apocrypha and Pseudepigrapha

The term 'Apocrypha' comes from the Greek word meaning 'hidden (things)'. It was sometimes used in Second Commonwealth times to refer to books regarded as so sacred that they must be hidden from the general public and reserved for an inner circle of initiates or believers. The sacred writings of some sects (such as that of the Dead Sea Scrolls) may have been regarded in this light. To others, however, such writings were regarded as secondary to those accepted by all Israel (the scriptures now found in the Hebrew Bible) and were regarded as heretical.

These different usages of the term 'Apocrypha' reflect the very processes of 'canonization' (pp.24f., above). With the exception of the Second Book of Esdras, the books of the Apocrypha were all included in the Greek version of the Old Testament made for the (Greek-speaking) Jews in Egypt (the 'Septuagint': see further pp.79-81 below). They were not, however, accepted as part of the Palestinian Canon (i.e. were not regarded as part of the Hebrew Bible[7]), though they were accorded a limited sanctity.

Jerome defined the Apocrypha as those books that were not accepted as part of the Palestinian Canon but were accepted by the early Church; similarly, the Rabbis use the term *sefarim hitsyonim*, meaning books 'external' to those included in the Biblical canon. The differences within Jewish tradition (as reflected in the acceptance of the Apocrypha by the Septuagint but not by the Palestinian circles who defined the content of the Hebrew Bible) were later to be reflected also within the Church. The books known as the Apocrypha are accepted by the Roman Catholic and some Orthodox churches (following the Septuagint), but are not included in the Bible of the Protestants and some Orthodox churches.[8]

The list of books accepted in the Hebrew Bible was not finally deter-mined until the tannaitic period, in the second century C.E., and is thus attributable ultimately to the Rabbis. The latter determined that the form of revelation determinative of the status of books as Biblical was 'prophetic' (Moses himself had been described in the Pentateuch as a prophet). In their view, prophecy has ceased at the time of Ezra. Therefore, books written after Ezra could not be included in the Hebrew Bible even if there was evidence that they had originally been written in Hebrew, as was the case for *Ben Sira* and *1 Maccabees*. Perhaps because of their adoption as part of the Christian Bible, traditional Jewish scholarship largely ignored the Apocrypha, until the development (particularly from the nineteenth century) of academic Jewish scholarship outside the world of the rabbinical academy.

The Apocrypha consists of the following books:

The First Book of Esdras
The Second Book of Esdras

Tobit
Judith
The Rest of the Chapters of the Book of Esther
The Wisdom of Solomon
Ecclesiasticus or the Wisdom of Jesus son of Sirach
Baruch
A Letter of Jeremiah
The Song of the Three
Daniel and Susanna
Daniel, Bel, and the Snake   ·
The Prayer of Menasseh
The First Book of the Maccabees
The Second Book of the Maccabees

For historical purposes, *1 and 2 Maccabees* are particularly important, since they tell the story (from the Hasmonean point of view) of the struggle of the Maccabees against the Syrians, leading to the establishment of the Hasmonean dynasty.   Some of the books elaborate Biblical stories or attribute new ones to Biblical characters: *1 Esdras* combines part of the Biblical book of *Ezra* with extracts from *Chronicles* and *Nehemiah*, retelling the story of Ezra.   There are additions to the books of *Esther* and *Daniel* (the latter including the book of *Susanna*).   There are also works of an apocalyptic character, describing events at the 'end of days' (*2 Esdras*). *Ben Sira* (= *Sirach* or *Ecclesiasticus*) is a Wisdom work, originally composed in Hebrew, and representing a genre comparable to that of the Biblical *Book of Proverbs*.   The wisdom tradition is preserved also in a book called the *Wisdom of Solomon* (discussing themes such as immortality and the nature of divine wisdom, and attributing the discussion to the Biblical King Solomon).

The Pseudepigrapha is the name given (following the Protestant tradition[9]) to a collection of books written between about 250 B.C.E. and 200 C.E. which are not included in the Apocrypha, but are associated with Biblical books or Biblical characters, and indeed are often written in the name of some Biblical character (hence 'Pseudepigrapha', meaning 'written under a false name').   They purport to convey further revelations from God.

The Pseudepigrapha includes a genre called 'apocalypse', a revelation of divine secrets regarding the cosmos and the 'end of the age' (*1 Enoch, Apocalypse of Zephaniah, Apocalypse of Abraham to Enoch*, and part of *2 Esdras*).   Others take the form of testaments, purporting to be the words of the Biblical character in whose name the book was written (the *Testaments of the Twelve Patriarchs*, the testaments of *Job, Moses, Abraham, Isaac, Jacob, Adam and Solomon*). Others represent elaborations of Biblical stories, sometimes with some affinity to rabbinic *midrash*. The most significant is the *Book of Jubilees,* which comments on *Genesis* and part of *Exodus*. Material of this kind was found also at Qumran (e.g. the *Genesis Apocryphon*, which comments on the story of Abraham in *Genesis* 12-13). Other examples of this genre are *The Letter of Aristeas* (written in the name of a Greek in the court of Ptolemy II Philadelphus (285-46 B.C.E.) to his brother Philocrates, telling the story of the translation of the Hebrew Bible into Greek); the *Martyrdom of Isaiah*; the *Life of Adam and Eve*; the *Lives of the Prophets*; and the *Ladder of Jacob*. Other works express the Wisdom tradition, with some links to contemporary philosophical speculation (e.g. *3-4 Maccabees*).

There is some, though not much, explicit halakhic material in the Apocrypha and Pseudepigrapha. Perhaps the most important is the *Book of Jubilees*, composed originally in Hebrew and then translated into Greek. It is thought that some later Jewish *midrashim* may have known the Hebrew original.[10] Views have differed as to its dating, but some twelve fragments of the manuscript of *Jubilees* were found at Qumran, and a mid-second century B.C.E. date appears likely.[11]

Since *Jubilees*' retelling of the Biblical story concludes at *Exodus* 14, it does not cover the giving of the law to Moses on Mount Sinai. However, it is written in the form of a revelation given to Moses on Mount Sinai by an angel, and thus suggests (contrary to the Pharisaic and later rabbinic view[12]), that *halakhot* not found in the Biblical text were already committed to writing on Mount Sinai, rather than being given to Moses for oral transmission. In this respect, the book seems closer to the Sadducean position, and indeed to that of the sect at Qumran. In fact, the book is explicitly quoted in one of the Qumran sectarian documents, the *Damascus Covenant* (16:3f.). Parallels have been observed between the *halakhah* in *Jubilees* and that adopted by the sect.[13] The author was particularly interested in the religious calendar (culminating in the institution of the Jubilee itself). The Biblical patriarchs are portrayed as celebrating festivals prescribed later in the Biblical text. Biblical stories are used as vehicles for halakhic commentary, on such matters as marriage to foreign spouses, circumcision, incest. Towards the end of the book there is a particularly detailed account of the norms relating to the passover sacrifice, and the sabbatical and jubilee years.

While many of the apocryphal and pseudepigraphical books cast incidental light on legal matters, the 'historical' books relating to the Maccabaean revolt (*1* and *2 Maccabees*) are particularly important insofar as the revolt itself was motivated in part by a desire to rescue Jewish law from oppression at the hands of the Syrian ruler (who had forbidden practice of much of Jewish ritual law), and the Wisdom books of *Ben Sira* and the *Wisdom of Solomon* attest to contemporary mores and values. This body of literature, however, does not represent a single genre nor a single tendency within the *halakhah*. It is defined largely by the indeterminacy of its date and provenance: it belongs to the Second Commonwealth period, but is not included in the Hebrew Bible, nor is it assignable to particular, known groups. Nevertheless, one attempt has been made to summarize what we know of law in the Apocrypha (here not including the Pseudepigrapha): Ralph Marcus, *Law in the Apocrypha* (New York: Columbia University Press, 1927, reprinted New York: Ams Press, 1966) collects and considers those passages relating, inter alia, to the Covenant, reward and punishment, chastisement, conversion of gentiles, the concept of *torah* and of command-ments, study of the law, the written law, tradition, and ceremonial obser-vances relating to the Sabbath, festivals, the Temple, sacrifice, and offerings.

D. Qumran

The discovery in 1947 of a cache of manuscripts in caves overlooking the Dead Sea at Qumran, together with the excavation of a nearby settlement, has proved to be the most dramatic development for biblical and early Jewish history in the twentieth century. The identity of the sect (or sects) which authored the 'Dead Sea Scrolls' has been a matter of considerable scholarly discussion. The most popular view remains that they were Essenes (a sect described by both Philo and Josephus), but points of both commonality and opposition can be identified with all known Second Commonwealth sects.[14] The library of Qumran includes representatives of the various genres of Second Commonwealth literature found also in the Apocrypha. A full study of its thinking about Jewish law involves recourse to all these texts — including its own versions of Biblical texts, and its biblical commentaries.

Qumran, however, is particularly important in having provided us with a number of 'halakhic' works — collections of rules often independent in substance from those of the Bible (but sometimes, as in the *Temple Scroll*, following the arrangement of the laws in the Bible) and anticipating (as a genre) the *Mishnah* and *Tosefta*, collections of rabbinic law dating from about three centuries later, at the end of the tannaitic period (see Ch.5, below). Four such documents containing major assemblages of halakhic material will be briefly reviewed.

i.   The *Damascus Covenant*

The history of the *Damascus Covenant* is rather complex. The first indication of its existence came from the discovery in the Cairo Geniza (see Ch.8, pp.212f., below) of two manuscripts, one (A) dating from the tenth century C.E., the other (B) from the eleventh or twelfth century. More recently some fragments that were recognized as an integral part of the Document were found in caves 4, 5 and 6 at Qumran. Most of these fragments date from the Herodian period. There is, however, one which appears to be datable between 100 and 75 B.C.E. If we rely on this latter, the document could therefore be earlier, but not later, than 100/75 B.C.E.

However, R.H. Charles, the editor of the Apocrypha and Pseudepigrapha of the Old Testament, observed that the document makes a reference to the *Book of Jubilees*, which dates it after 106 B.C.E. Moreover, he observed that the writer transmits the expectation of a Messiah coming from 'Aaron and from Israel'. He therefore proposed that the *Document* was written when Alexander and Aristobulus, sons of the Hasmonean Mariamme (who was of Aaronite stock), and of Herod (of an Idumean family, and therefore considered a Jewish proselyte) were still living.[15] The fact that fragments of the document, datable from the Herodian period, were found in Qumran, could confirm Charles' intuition.

The editors of the new Schürer (see p.51 below) noted that the compiler of the statutes of the Community in the form found in the *Damascus Covenant* followed the scheme of the final chapter of the *Book of Jubilees* (p.29 above), endeavouring to put the halakhic material into a systematic order according to the techniques for the composition of codes. We may ask what efficacy the writer sought to impute to his composition. Did he view it as a set of rules of behaviour which only the initiates of the sect were obliged to keep within the narrow ambit of their group, or did the Community, considering themselves as the depositary of the correct reading of the Law, see themselves also as elected to the task of propagating the code to the whole of Israel when the conditions which the Community awaited were fulfilled.

The *Damascus Covenant* begins with an account of the origins of the sect, and includes provisions regarding accusations (one who has another sentenced to death 'under the laws of the gentiles' is himself to be put to death); a law on the bearing of grudges (elaborating *Lev.* 19:18), a law against forcing people to take involuntary oaths, laws on lost property, on evidence, judges, and ritual matters. The roles of the priest and the camp overseer are stated.

ii. The *Manual of Discipline*

The *Manual of Discipline* (sometimes called the *Community Rule*) regulates the manner of initiation into the sect, and lays down a procedure of annual review. It sets out the internal discipline of the community (such as the duty of each one to obey his superior in rank, to dine together, worship together and take counsel together). Initiates are to keep awake for a third of all nights during the year, studying the *Torah* and worshipping together. A general council is described, with a hierarchy consisting of priests, elders and then the rest of the community. There are sections on impermissible forms of speech, on fraud and on misconduct in public sessions. Further rules regulate slander and accusations against the community as a whole. Others deal with indecorous conduct (such as 'raucous, inane laughter', spitting in a public session, etc.). Within the community, there are 'men of perfect holiness', who have special privileges and to whom a special discipline is applied.

iii. The *Temple Scroll*

The *Temple Scroll* is the largest preserved scroll from Qumran. It rewrites laws of the Pentateuch in accordance with the sect's interpretation. The scroll takes its name from a major section dealing with the temple building and the altar. The cycle of religious festivals and sacrifices is extensively regulated. A section on laws of purity includes dietary laws, laws relating to burial, and to various forms of bodily discharge. There is a section on the judicial system, based on *Deut.* 16:18-20 (see p.39 below) and a section on the relationship between vows and family status. A number of offences relating to idolatry and false prophecy are detailed. There is a section on positions of authority: the monarchy (including the Queen), the priesthood and prophets (including false prophecy), followed by a treatment of problems of proof in crime. The sequence of family laws in *Deut.* 21 is followed, culminating in that of the stubborn and rebellious son. Much of *Deut.* 22 is rehearsed, and *Deut.* 23:1 leads to a section summarizing incest laws taken from a number of pentateuchal sources.

The scroll now appears, from palaeographic examination, to have been the work of different editorial hands, between the middle and the end of the Herodian period. Nevertheless, the fragment in the Rockefeller Museum had induced scholars to consider the whole scroll as the expression of a current of thought active during the period of the last Hasmoneans. The scroll mentions the use of rings to bind animals for slaughter and the practice of hiring mercenaries — both of which are institutions which may be ascribed to John Hyrcanus.

iv. *Miktsat Ma'aseh Hatorah* ('MMT')

The most recently published sectarian legal collection is *miktsat ma'aseh hatorah*.[16] The six manuscripts which comprise it date from between 75 and 50 B.C.E. It commences with a calendar of sabbaths and festivals, followed by a halakhic section of eighty-two lines (shorter than the other documents), and concludes with an epilogue which reflects upon the carrying out of the blessings and curses of *Deuteronomy* in the future, and commends observance of this version of the Law to those who seek happiness 'at the end of time'. The *halakhah* is presented as a sequence of 'polemically formulated legal statements' (1994:110) — polemical in that the sect's understanding is juxtaposed against that of its opponents. Some sections commence: 'And concerning x: we are of the opinion ...', while other practices are described as what 'they are accustomed to do.' In addition to these 'we' and 'they' parties, another group is also addressed (in the second person plural): the 'you' party, to whom the author sometimes appeals for support, as being a group knowledgeable of the correct interpretation of the Torah. The editors of the MMT think that it may be the halakhic treatise which the 'Teacher of Righteousness' is said in another scroll to have sent to the 'Wicked Priest', and on account of which the latter tried to have the Teacher of Righteousness put to death (1994:119f.). The halakhic positions of the 'they'-party 'is that attested in Tannaitic literature for the Pharisees and for the later rabbinic consensus' (1994:116). The editors hypothesize that the document goes back to the early history of the sect, in the mid-second century B.C.E., and represents an attempt by this ('Zadokite') group to enlist the support of a Maccabaean political leader — the very one who, after his usurpation of the High Priesthood, came to be known to the sect as the 'Wicked Priest' (1994:121).

The polemical character of the *halakhah* in this scroll dominates the choice of material. It is a collection specifically of topics on which the sect differs from its opponents, principally in ritual and cultic matters: the cultic calendar; ritual purity (especially in connection with the Temple) and the sacrificial cult; and marital status (in connection with the priests and the Temple). Frequently, the sect's views are supported by reference to the biblical text.

E. Philo

Philo was a Greek-speaking philosopher in Alexandria, in the first half of the first century C.E. (c. 15 B.C.E-50 C.E.). According to Josephus, Philo was highly respected by his local community; indeed, he was a member of an embassy of Alexandrian Jews which went to Rome in 40 C.E. to protest to the Emperor Caligula against anti-Jewish riots. Philo himself discusses these events in two books: *In Flaccum* and *Legatio ad Gaium*. Philo's main works, however, were philosophical. He wrote an allegorical commentary on *Gen.* 1-17 and a four book treatise, *De Specialibus Legibus* ('On the Special Laws'), in which he provided a commentary on both the Ten Commandments and the specific provisions of Mosaic law. In it, he emphasized both the literal requirements of the law and their symbolic interpretation. Philo's writings — particularly, his allegorical interpretations of the Bible — became popular in early Christianity. No doubt because of this, his work was ignored in rabbinic circles, until medieval times.

Philo was concerned to show his Alexandrian audience that Jewish literature was philosophically sensitive. Moses is presented as a philosopher, and indeed the source of later philosophy. In his book *On the Creation* (*De Opificio Mundi*), Philo argues that the Pentateuch opens with the story of creation because this demonstrates harmony between the laws of nature and the laws given on Sinai. In *De Specialibus Legibus*, he arranges the specific Biblical laws under one or other of the Ten Commandments, seeking to show how they exemplify and elaborate the principles of the Decalogue itself.

Scholars have debated the extent to which his account of Jewish law is in accordance with rabbinic conceptions. S. Belkin, *Philo and the Oral Law* (Cambridge, Mass.: Harvard University Press, 1940), stresses such points of contact, while I. Heinemann, *Philons Griechische und Jüdische Bildung* (Breslau: M. & H. Marcus, 1932) sees Philo's work as reflecting primarily his Hellenistic philosophical environment. E.R. Goodenough, *The Jurisprudence of the Jewish Courts in Egypt* (New Haven: Yale University Press, 1929, repr. Amsterdam: Philo Press, 1968), argued that Philo in fact provides us with an account of the actual practice of Jewish courts in Egypt (on which see further Ch.4, p.75 below), but this view has not attracted support. G. Alon, *Jews, Judaism and the Classical World* (Jerusalem: Magnes Press, 1977), 89-137 links particular legal teachings of Philo with other Second Commonwealth sources (Apocrypha, Josephus) to argue that Philo frequently represents a pre-rabbinic *halakhah* deriving from Palestine, and not merely a local Hellenistic tradition. He discusses, in particular, the bringing of capital cases before the Great Sanhedrin in Jerusalem, rather than in local Sanhedrins.

F. Josephus

Flavius Josephus is the principal Jewish historian of the first century C.E. Born in Jerusalem around 37 C.E., he spent some time in his youth with the Essenes but later regarded himself as an adherent of the Pharisees. On the outbreak of the first Jewish revolt against Rome in 66 C.E., he was appointed the general in charge of Galilee. His forces were swiftly overrun by Vespasian, in circumstances which led to some suspicion. Josephus surrendered to the Romans, ingratiated himself with Vespasian by predicting that he would become Emperor (which he did), and later attached himself to the entourage of Titus (the conqueror of Jerusalem in 70 C.E.). Josephus spent the rest of his life in comfortable exile at Rome. There, he wrote *The Jewish War* (*Bellum Judaicum*), beginning his account in the early second century B.C.E. He also wrote a major work, *The Jewish Antiquities*, designed for a Roman intelligentsia which was showing considerable interest in Judaism. Part of it paraphrases and expands the historical writings of the Hebrew Bible.

In his account of Biblical law, he appears to have followed the then Palestinian *halakhah* (Schürer, 1973, I.49). He summarizes the Decalogue (Ant. iii.91-92), but omits the Covenant Code, remarking that he intended to reserve the major portion of the law for a special treatise — a work which unfortunately appears never to have been completed, but to which he alludes on various occasions (mentioning its 'four books': *Ant.* xx.268). Nevertheless, the *Antiquities* does contain a large number of passages relating to Biblical law. Josephus gives a full description of the tabernacle (iii.102f.) the various ritual objects inside the temple and the vestments of the priests, and discusses their symbolism. He gives an account of the sacrificial law (iii.224ff.), and the festivals. He continues with purity and dietary laws. The issue of woman's purity after childbirth leads him to the law of adultery (the ordeal of the suspected wife), and then to forbidden marriages. He describes the sabbatical year, the year of the Jubilee, followed by the levitical cities and the tithes for the support of the Levites (iv.67ff.) and the priestly dues. His account of the conquest of the land leads him to consideration of the cities of refuge for those who had committed 'manslaughter' (iv.172f.). After Moses' valedictory speech, Josephus embarks on a summary of various aspects of the law, despite still claiming to reserve much of it for the treatise noted above. Among the topics he here considers are blasphemy (iv.202), administration of justice (iv.214-18), witnesses and false witnessing (iv.219), undetected murder (iv.220), the law of the King (iv.223-4), the prohibition of the removal of landmarks (iv.225), the rights of the poor (iv.231-43), marriage laws including divorce and levirate marriage (iv.244-56), women captives (iv.257-9), the rebellious son (iv.260-65), loans, interest and securities (iv.266-70), theft (iv.271-2), slavery (iv.273), restitution of lost property (iv.274), quarrels and bodily injury including the lex talionis (iv.277-80), the goring ox (iv.281-2), deposit (iv.285-7), individual responsibility (iv.289), and the law of war (iv.292-300). Thus, despite Josephus's failure to write the treatise he had promised, and notwithstanding the somewhat disorganized account of the laws in the context of his Biblical narrative, the *Antiquities* provides a good deal of information about Jewish law as understood by an educated layman in the middle of the first century C.E.

G. The New Testament

Much of the New Testament was written by Jews, in a Jewish milieu. The life and death of Jesus is set in the first decades of the first century C.E., the crucifixion normally being dated around 33/34 C.E. Jesus and his Galilean followers clearly regarded themselves, and were regarded by others, as Jews, despite the fact that they opposed the teachings of the Jewish establishment (variously described as 'scribes', 'Pharisees', and ultimately the High Priesthood).

Our principal sources for these events are the four Gospels, of *Matthew*, *Mark*, *Luke* and *John*. The first three are called 'Synoptic'. They have a close literary inter-relationship. The precise nature of that relationship is much debated by scholars, but the most popular view is that *Mark* is the oldest, and that both *Matthew* and *Luke* used it (perhaps with another source, which has not survived: 'Q'). *John* is thought to represent an independent, somewhat later tradition, although it also contains elements which appear to be early. The Gospels represent the ultimate writing[17] of material which may have developed earlier through oral tradition. While presented as the evidence of the Apostles, there is more than a generation between the death of Jesus and the writing of the Gospels.

On the other hand, the letters of Paul in the New Testament undoubtedly pre-date the destruction. Paul (born as Saul) was a near contemporary of Jesus, and was brought up in the Jewish community of Tarsus, moving to Jerusalem for the final stages of his education (under the guidance of a leading Rabbi: Gamliel — *Acts* 22:3, 26:4). He became a prominent Pharisee, and some have suggested that he was a member of the Sanhedrin (based on *Acts* 26:5, *Phil.* 3:5). In the earliest days of the church, he persecuted the Judaeo-Christians, and it was while travelling to Damascus in pursuit of some of them that he had the vision which caused his conversion and adherence to the Church. Much of his career, and the history of the early Church, is recounted in the *Acts of the Apostles*, usually ascribed to the writer of *Luke*, but including parts which may derive from a companion of Paul. Paul's writings, including the *Letters* written to the Churches being established in various parts of the Mediterranean world, also make incidental reference to the life of Jesus, and represent a source closer in time than the Gospels to those events.

The Gospels provide accounts of the attitude of Jesus towards the *halakhah*, in a variety of forms. There are stories of conflict with the establishment over particular rules of law (for example, healing on the sabbath, plucking corn on the sabbath); there are parables which presuppose a knowledge of contemporary laws and customs; and there are specific teachings to Jesus' own disciples (for example, the famous Sermon on the Mount in *Matthew* 5). An immense amount of scholarship has been written seeking to clarify both Jesus' own attitude to Jewish law (on the assumption that his own attitudes are recoverable from the New Testament literature), and the attitudes of the various New Testament writers (including Paul). A wide variety of attitudes is discernible: on the one hand, Matthew's Jesus claims not to seek to alter a single tiny detail (at least, until the end of days), while some passages of Paul describe the written law as a source of death, redemption being available only to those who entrust their faith to Jesus. Elsewhere, Jesus is portrayed as promising a 'New Covenant', one in which revelation will take the form not of the communication of written rules, but rather direct inspiration to each individual through the Holy Spirit.

Scholars have recognised increasingly the use made by the New Testament of Jewish tradition, even where a radical critique of Jewish institutions appears to be offered. For example, the 'New Covenant' echoes the words of *Jeremiah* 31. Indeed, it has been suggested that many aspects of the life — and even the death — of Jesus are formulated in the New Testament in terms deliberately reminiscent of figures in the Hebrew Bible, notably Moses, Elijah, Jeremiah.

There is no doubt that the New Testament contains evidence of Jewish thought on halakhic matters during the first century C.E. As such, it can be used — in combination with other Second Commonwealth sources — not only to add to our knowledge of Second Commonwealth *halakhah* but also to distinguish those elements of tannaitic literature (Ch.5, below) which go back to the Second Commonwealth period from those which do not. Jewish scholars have, perhaps, been understandably reluctant to use this material.[18]

The accounts in the Gospels of the trial of Jesus represent, potentially, a very valuable source of information regarding the actual practice of Jewish law in serious criminal cases in the early first century C.E. But enormous controversy surrounds their historical reliability. Many aspects of them do not appear to make historical sense, notably, the relationship between the Jewish and Roman authorities, the charge of blasphemy, and the attitudes of Pilate (not least in releasing Barabbas, under popular pressure). The issues are complex, and neither Jewish nor Christian scholars can hope to approach the matter with full objectivity.[19] Jackson has recently argued that many of the details are modelled upon the trial of Jeremiah in *Jer.* 26, while the selection of blasphemy reflects the false accusation of Naboth in *1 Kings* 21.[20]

The issue of jurisdiction exemplifies the problems. There is internal inconsistency in the Gospels: *John* claims that the Jews deny having jurisdiction to authorize a capital sentence while *Mark* and *Matthew* appear to presuppose such a competence. Similarly, there is a conflict in the rabbinic sources: a tradition in the Jerusalem Talmud (*Y. Sanh* 1:1) says that capital cases were taken away from the Jewish court (conveniently?) 40 years before the destruction — thus, just a few years before the trial of Jesus, while another talmudic tradition dates the cessation of capital jurisdiction at the destruction of the Temple itself 70 C.E. (*B. Sanh.* 37b).[21] But whatever was the normative position at the time of the trial — whether the Jewish courts did or did not have the authority to pass a capital sentence — is not conclusive as to what happened: even if the Jews did have such authority, it does not follow that they chose to exercise it without seeking endorsement from the Roman Governor; nor, if they lacked such authority, is it excluded that they determined to have Jesus executed extra-legally.

3. *The Legal Practice of the Period*

A. The Hasmoneans and their Successors

In the absence of a secure dating of the Scrolls, the reconstruction of the practice of the courts, lacking as it does a firm place in the overall chronology of Israel's judicial traditions, remains difficult. We have seen that a fragment of the *Damascus Covenant* dates between 100 and 75 B.C.E. and that the *Temple Scroll* seems datable to the period of John Hyrcanus. Both sources, therefore, bring us to the period of the Hasmoneans. Even if the editing of the text can probably be ascribed to that period, we cannot exclude the possibility that Qumran's traditions represent the crystallization of a line of thought whose origin is earlier.

The period of the Hasmoneans, during which the texts appear to have been edited, is exceptional in the history of Israel in many, both positive and negative, respects. On the one hand, we can observe one of those rare moments when the people attained their sovereignty, as a result of the valiant deeds of the Maccabaean brothers, who succeeded in freeing the Jewish nation from the Seleucid yoke. On the other hand, their descendants, the Hasmoneans, caused a real subversion of Israel's institutions by claiming for themselves both the priestly and kingly crowns. The consequences of this may be illustrated from column 64 of the *Temple Scroll*, as we shall see presently.

In reality, it seems that the Maccabaean brothers themselves produced a period of some exceptionality in the history of the organization of justice. *I Macc.* 3:35 affirms that at the very moment when Judas Maccabaeus organized the revolt against the Seleucides, he creates chiefs of thousands, of hundreds, of fifties, and of tens — divisions which had not only an administrative, but also a judicial character. This was evidently modelled on the practice of Moses, when he, on the advice of his father-in-law, decided to delegate the decision of minor cases to minor judges (*Ex.* 18). The text, however, may express rather an aspiration on the part of the writer (to make Judas appear like Moses) rather than provide evidence of an actual reconstruction of the normal judicial organs. In the same *Book of Maccabees* (*I Macc.* 9:73) it is said that Jonathan Maccabaeus settled in Machmas and from there began to judge the people and to exterminate the impious.

It has rightly been observed[22] that Jonathan is here considered by the writer as one who exercises the role of judge of the people in arms, as one who has control, first of all, of the functions connected with military activities. From this point of view, though not explicitly described as *shofet* he is considered as entitled to prosecute the impious of Israel, and it is not difficult to apprehend who they were. The Maccabaean insurrection had begun as a rebellion against the Seleucids, who tried to profane the Jewish cultic institutions (as in the story of Ḥanukkah), but that movement certainly encompassed a desire to punish the Hellenizing Jews.

The same sources (*I Macc.* 4:44) say that, on the day following his first success, Judas chose pure, law-abiding priests to purify the Sanctuary. Together, they decided to destroy the altar of burnt-offerings, which had been profaned by the Seleucids, and deposited its stones on the Temple mountain, awaiting a faithful prophet who could decide what to do with them. This is an indication that the Maccabeans did not feel themselves fully entitled to exercise all forms of jurisdiction. Confirmation of the authenticity of this episode comes from the rabbinical sources themselves, which contain a story much to the same effect (*M. Middot* 1:6, *B. A. Zar.* 52b).

Overall, the Maccabaean sources offer a picture of the legitimation of the Maccabeans and the Hasmoneans to assume a role corresponding to that of *shofet* but not that of the recognized chief of a *Bet Din.*

We find a court of ten operating at Qumran, comprising one priest, three Levites, and six Israelites, all of whom were required to be well versed in the sectarian interpretation of the Bible. Schiffman (1983:40) notes that one of the functions of the judges was to collect a proportion of the income of each member of the sect (eight per cent) to be used for social welfare and charitable purposes.

On the other hand, the rabbinic sources themselves offer evidence of the establishment of a *Bet Din shel Ḥashmonaim*, though of imprecise date, but which may reasonably be attributed to the moment when the Maccabeans succeeded in establishing their power. Talmudic passages (*B. Sanh.* 82a and *B. A.Zar.* 35b) attribute to that court the decision to consider impure (*niddah*) a gentile woman who had had relations with a Jew, on the presumption that she had been violated. That a Hasmonean court would have interested itself in such a matter is supported by passages from the Apocrypha, from which we know that among the severest criticisms made of the Hellenizing Jews was the charge of having violated the Covenant precisely by having relations with gentile women (*I Macc.* 1:15). In particular, the *Testament of Levi* 14:5-6 represents the union with gentile women as comparable to the sin of Sodom and Gomorra; moreover, the *Book of Jubilees* (30:7-10) compares the father who gave his daughter in marriage to a non-Jew to the father who gave her to Moloch. For the writer both are liable to the same punishment, lynching.

We now pass to the reign of John Hyrcanus II (63-40 B.C.E.). Josephus preserves a story (in some respects detailed, in others, obscure) which well illustrates the complexity of the evaluation of our sources regarding jurisdictional activity, and of the forms it assumed under both Maccabeans and Hasmoneans: that of the trial of Herod when he was governor of Galilee (*Ant.* xiv.159). The historian says that Herod, having heard that Hezekias (very probably a nationalist, a new Maccabee, but described by his opponents as a brigand) was about to cross the Syrian border with a strong army, took him prisoner and put him to death. The elders of the Jews intervened with Hyrcanus to convince him to punish Herod's behaviour, not least because the mothers of those killed by him insisted on asking for justice. Hyrcanus, therefore, brought Herod before the Sanhedrin. Following the advice of his father Antipater, Herod appeared — contrary to the tradition according to which a defendant appeared poorly dressed and crying for mercy — accompanied by an escort, not too numerous to appear too powerful, but also not too small to seem unarmed and lacking the capacity to protect him. In the background there lurks the dominating presence of Rome, which, through the governor Sextus, let it be known that the defendant should be acquitted because of the help he had given Rome in suppressing a revolt in Galilee. When Herod appeared before the Sanhedrin, none of those who had denounced him dared to confirm the accusation. The only one to rise to his feet was Samea, a disciple of the Pharisee Pollion. His words of reproach for so great an act of cowardice were about to have their effect when Hyrcanus adjourned the trial to another day and secretly helped Herod to leave the city.

Josephus provides a shorter version of this episode in *The Jewish War* (i.272); here the Sanhedrin is not mentioned, but rather a 'public court'. Some authors see a close connection between this story and that concerning the trial of King Alexander Jannaeus, discussed at p.43 below.

Given the procedure described in the story, we must wonder if it is proper to use the term Sanhedrin for so peculiar a trial. Also unsolved is the problem of the relations between the Sanhedrin and the *Beth Din shel Ḥashmonaim*. Was the latter a special court, so called precisely to avoid giving the impression that the Maccabeans re-established a regular Sanhedrin? Or does it in fact coincide with the organ recognised in Jewish tradition?

B. The *Sanhedrin*

Schürer describes the Sanhedrin as an aristocratic council, with its seat in

Jerusalem and endowed with total or quasi-total power in matters of government and jurisdiction over the Jewish people (II.200). In that form, we have evidence of it from the Greek era. But a court with powers resembling those of the later Sanhedrin seems to have begun to develop from the Persian period. This is the role of the 'elders' in the book of *Ezra* (5:5, 9; 6:7, 14; 10:8). In *Ezra* 2:2 (= Neh: 7:7) twelve men are named as leaders of the exile, but *Neh.* 5:17 mentions 150 Jewish dignitaries (*seganim*). Schürer (II.201) quotes Hecataeus of Abdera, a contemporary of Alexander the Great, as asserting (II.202, in Diodorus 40, 3) that Moses appointed men as priests on the basis of ability, and appointed them judges in all major disputes. Supreme authority was vested in whichever priest was regarded as superior to his colleagues in wisdom and virtue, and he was called the High Priest. Josephus mentions a *gerousia* (Council of Elders) as operating during the period of Antiochus the Great (223-187 B.C.E.). The office of High Priesthood was hereditary but the dynasty could change — as it did after the Maccabaean uprising. Increasingly, scribes and Pharisees entered the *gerousia* but the term Sanhedrin was used for the first time in relation to the court in Jerusalem before which the young Herod had to answer for his actions in Galilee (Josephus, *Ant.* xiv, 165-79, discussed above). From that period, it is used consistently to refer to the supreme court in Jerusalem. When Herod came to the throne, he executed 'all' (*Ant.* xiv.175) the members of the Sanhedrin and reconstituted it with persons sympathetic to himself. Conflict between Pharisees and Sadducees in the Sanhedrin is reflected in Josephus *Ant.* xx.200, where the Sadducean High Priest Ananus 'convened the judges of the Sanhedrin' to condemn James, brother of Jesus, but the Pharisees sought to have him (Ananus) removed, on the grounds that he had no authority to convene the Sanhedrin without the Roman governor's consent.

The rabbinic sources speak of a 'Great Sanhedrin' and also a 'Sanhedrin of 71' (in opposition to local Sanhedrins, of 23). This has led some to suggest that there were two (or even three) bodies each called Sanhedrin, with different functions. Schürer, however, argues (II.208) that the Sanhedrin of 71 as described in the *Mishnah* has judicial, administrative and governmental functions, in the same way as the Sanhedrin described in the Greek sources. There was, they argue, a single institution under the Presidency of the High Priest (in the absence of the King).[23] The Sanhedrin, however, ceased to exist in its previous form after the destruction of Jerusalem in 70 C.E.[24]

The *Mishnah* records activities of the Sanhedrin as the court which sat in the chamber of 'hewn stone' (*Lishkat hagazit*), and records questions being sent there (*M. Eduy.* 7:4) and of Rabban Gamliel going there to receive a reply to a question which he had put (*M. Peah* 2:6). The competence of the Sanhedrin is described in *Mishnah* Sanhedrin and parallels, but there is debate over whether this account, written much later, reflects an ideal or a memory of an historical reality. In *Acts* 23:6 the Sanhedrin is described as being 'one part Sadducees and the other Pharisees', while the rabbinic sources play down the Sadducean and priestly element in it.

4. *Principal Authorities of the Period*

A. *Shimon ben Shetah*

Active during the reign of King Alexander Jannaeus and Queen Alexandra Salome (103-76 B.C.E.), he played a leading role in the Sanhedrin. A Pharisee during a period when the authority of the Sadducees was dominant, he succeeded, perhaps with the aid of the Queen, in obtain the repatriation of the Pharisees whom Alexander Jannaeus had exiled to Egypt. The rabbinic sources represent him as having restored the splendour of the Torah (*B. Kidd.* 66a).

The influence of Shimon ben Shetah on the *halakhah* is seen in a number of areas, to be considered below (pp.48, 50f.): in particular, he enacted a *takkanah* securing the wife's interest in the bride-price (*mohar*); took emergency measures to combat witchcraft; and sought the careful examination of witnesses. His status is attested also by a story told in the Jerusalem Talmud (*Y. Ber.* 7:2, 11b, and, with slight variations, in *Tanhuma shofetim*, 6) of an incident which would have taken place in the time of King Alexander Jannaeus. The King was called before the Sanhedrin to answer for a crime committed by his slave. When the King sat down, as was the custom in Israel for those who, like Moses, fulfilled judicial functions, Shimon ben Shetah admonished him to stand up and to let the witnesses give their evidence, because: 'It is not before us that thou standest, but before Him who spoke and the world came into being.' But the King refused to obey this order, encouraged by those present who, fearing him, dared not contradict him. Those who had supported the King in this way perished, punished by divine intervention. Since then, the sources tell us, the principle was established that a king not belonging to the House of David must neither judge nor be judged.

B. The Pharisaic Chain of Tradition and the 'Pairs'

The Pharisees were a 'religious and political party or sect during the second temple period which emerged as a distinct group shortly after the Hasmonean revolt, about 165-160 B.C.E.' (*Enc.Jud.* 13.363). The name appears to come from the term *parash* ('to be separated'), perhaps indicating the sectarian origin of the group. They were thought to have 'set themselves apart' from others for reasons of ritual purity. They sought to bring ritual practices, on analogies from the ritual of the Temple, into the home; they stressed teaching. Ultimately, they came into conflict with the Sadducees (the name deriving from that of the Zadokite priests). Their differences with the Sadducees became both political and theological. Unlike the Sadducees, the Pharisees believed in resurrection of the dead. They also preached divine providence (but combined with free will), while the Sadducees are said to have thought that God took little interest in human affairs. They held that God had given an oral tradition to Moses, which was handed down along with the written law; this was denied by the Sadducees.

When the tannaitic rabbis came to write the history of Jewish law in accordance with their conception of the Oral Law, they put it thus:

> Moses received the Law from Sinai and committed it to Joshua, and Joshua to the Elders, and the Elders to the Prophets; the Prophets committed it to the men of the Great Synagogue ... Simeon the Just[25] was of the remnants of the Great Synagogue ... Antigonus of Sokho received [the Law] from Simeon the Just ... (*M. Av.* 1:1-3).

From there, five 'pairs' of authorities are said each to have 'received the law' from their predecessors, thus linking the Great Synagogue (viewed as the Elders who came back from exile with Ezra, thus representing the end of the Biblical period) with the rabbinic schools whose disputes dominate tannaitic literature. The five pairs are: (1) Yose b. Yoezer and Yose b. Yohanan (who lived during the religious persecution under Antiochus Epiphanes, 174-64 B.C.E.); (2) Joshua b. Perahiah and Nitti the Arbelite; (3) Judah b. Tabbai and Shimon b. Shetah (during the period of Alexander Jannaeus and Salome Alexandra); (4) Shemaiah and Avtalyon (period of Herod the Great); and (5) Hillel and Shammai. Rabbinic tradition holds the 'pairs' to have mirrored their own organizations: the first member of the pair was the *Nasi* (head of the Sanhedrin) while the second was the *Av Bet Din* (deputy). It is difficult to gauge the historical reliability of rabbinic statements about the Pharisees. These traditions have been studied in detail by J. Neusner, *The Rabbinic Traditions about the Pharisees Before 70* (Leiden E.J. Brill, 1971, 3 vols), who concludes that the account which has survived is historically sketchy.[26]

5. *Characteristic Features of the Substantive Law of the Period*

A. Polygamy, Divorce and Attitudes to the Monarchy

In the *Damascus Covenant (CD* V:1-4) we have a rule which reveals the thought of the community on both family law (marriage, divorce and especially polygamy) and the duty of the Kings of Israel to observe the Law. It lays down the rules of behaviour to which the 'prince' must conform:

> As regards the prince, it is written: He will not multiply wives for himself; but David did not read the sealed Book of the Law which was in the Ark (of the Covenant) because it was not opened in Israel after the deaths of Eleazar, Joshua and the Elder's death; so it [this rule] was concealed and was not revealed until the rising of Zadok. Hence the deeds of David were overlooked.

As regards polygamy, what is the relationship between this rule, which seems to bind the king only, and that which immediately precedes it in the *Damascus Covenant* (CD IV:20f.), according to which it is prohibited to 'take two wives during their lifetimes'?

As regards *CD* IV:20f., Davies (1982, p.116) agrees with the earlier view of Murphy-O'Connor[27] in adopting a literal interpretation, according to which the writer rejects *any* new conjugal union whatever (apparently even after divorce or death of the first wife), perhaps because marriage is justified only because of procreation. Davies notes also the parallel view attributed by Josephus (*War* 2, 8, 13) to the Essenes, who discouraged relations even with their own wives when they had had a child, to show that the proper purpose of intercourse was not pleasure, but only the creation of posterity.[28]

The *Temple Scroll* has a section called 'The Law of the King', in which we find the following passage (col. 57, lines 15-19, tr. Yadin):

> And he shall not take a wife from all (16) the daughters of the nations, but from his father's house he shall take unto himself a wife, (17) from the family of his father. And he shall not take upon her another wife, for (18) she alone shall be with him all the days of her life. But should she die, he may take (19) unto himself another (wife) from the house of his father, from his family.

The *Temple Scroll*, though it contains a detailed account of the rules of behaviour to which the king must conform, does not include any comments on their actual behaviour. The writer of the *Damascus Covenant*, by contrast, claims by way of justification of David's polygamy that he did not know the sealed text of the Torah. In this context, we may recall the story told in the Bible of the finding of the *ṣefer torah* in the time of King Josiah (King of Judah, 640-609 B.C.E.)

II Kings 22:8ff. records that the priest Hilkiyahu gave to Shaphan, the King's secretary, a Book of the Law which he had found in the Temple. When the Book was read to the King, he rent his clothes, observing that his fathers had not complied with the words of the Law. The prophetess Huldah, whom the King consulted, confirmed that the wrath of the Eternal God would be great for having been abandoned by the people, who had sacrificed to other divinities. Still, having seen the King's pain at the violation of the Law, He promised to save him from His vengeance. Josiah then assembled the people, and had the Law solemnly read out, to confirm their promise to respect the Covenant. Substantially similar is the version found in *II Chron.* 34. Here too the king's responsibility is mitigated by the fact that he did not know that the Law had been violated.

The writer of the *Damascus Covenant* similarly utilizes King David's ignorance in order to show his innocence: he practised polygamy because the sealed Scroll of the Law had had to be kept concealed (because of the commitment of the people at that time to the cult of Ashtoreth). It thus appears that the attitude of the sect reflected in the *Damascus Covenant* is not negative towards monarchy.

As regards the rules regarding monogamy and remarriage, expressed in lines 17-19, Yigael Yadin, editor of the text of the *Temple Scroll* and author of a detailed commentary, published first in Hebrew and then in English, connected this passage with that already quoted from *CD* (IV:20f.) and concluded that the prohibition of polygamy and divorce should be understood as referring to the length of the lives of *both* the man and the woman, and thus that the sect opposed both polygamy and divorce.[29]

As regards the same passage, Murphy-O'Connor, on the other hand, objects to this approach of Yadin. To conflate the passages from *CD* and the *Temple Scroll* is to presuppose that there existed in the sect(s) no differences of view or historical development between positions found in the different texts. Taken alone, for example, the *Temple Scroll* appears to provide no opposition to divorce, either by the King or ordinary citizens.

The New Testament reflects similar tensions within the early Christian community regarding the permissibility of divorce.[30] According to *Luke* 16:18, 'Every one who divorces his wife and marries another commits adultery' (cf. *Mk.* 10:11), while *Matt.* 5:32, 19:9, admits an exception ('on the ground of unchastity', *porneia*).

As for the prohibition against the King's contracting a marriage with a gentile woman (*TS* 57:15-17), Yadin compares *Deut.* 7:13 and the reform of Ezra (9:12; cf. *Neh.* 10:31; 13:25) and, in particular, *Neh.* 13:26, which criticizes King Solomon's marriages with such women, saying that it was they who had led him into sin.

It was not only the Qumran community for whom the strictures of Ezra and Nehemia proved influential. Yadin quotes also the *Book of Jubilees* 30:11 which imposes the prohibition 'not to give their daughters to the Gentiles and not to take for their sons any of the daughters of the gentiles, for this is abominable before the Lord'. Yadin refers also to *M. Sanh.* 9:6: 'If a man ... made an Aramaean woman his paramour, the zealots may fall upon him.'

Yadin sees the rule which requires the King to choose a wife from the family of his own father as based on *Gen.* 24:37ff. and *Num.* 36:6-8. It contrasts markedly with the later attitude of the Rabbis, as reflected in *Tosefta, Sanh.* 4:2: 'He chooses for himself wives from wherever he wishes: the daughters of priests, Levites, or Israelites.' By this time, of course, the Jewish monarchy was but a distant memory; nevertheless, it is significant to find the Rabbis expressing opposition to an inherently aristocratic principle.

B.   Securing the Wife's Position on Divorce

When the biblical Book of Deuteronomy was compiled, a written document (called *sefer keritut*) was required only on repudiation (divorce) of a legitimate wife (*Deut.* 24:1). This deed gave back to the wife her freedom to contract a new marriage without the risk of being accused of adultery. Probably, it also regulated repayment of the bride-price (*mohar*). At any rate, a promise in a written document (called *ketubah*, after its written form) was one of two forms of financial protection for the divorced wife which emerged in the Second Temple period. The Aramaic Papyri of Elephantine include documents which arguably may be considered *ketubot*, but the first clear indication of such a marriage contract occurs in the Apocrypha, in relation to the union between Sarah and Tobias (*Tobias* 7:13). There, immediately after the oral declaration of marriage (according to a formula similar to that in the traditional text of the *ketubah*), we are told that the father wrote a document. But the form of that document does not seem to be the closed and sealed form peculiar to the *ketubah*.

The Rabbis themselves appear unsure of the origins of the institution. Indeed, there is conflict even in respect of the views of one particular Sage: Rabban Shimon ben Gamliel. According to some, he claimed that the wife's *ketubah* was Biblical (*midivre torah*): according to others, that it was rabbinic (*midivre ṣoferim*) (*Ket.* 10a); elsewhere, the former view is attributed to R. Meir, the latter to R. Judah (*Ket.* 56a). Rabban Shimon ben Gamliel was a contemporary of Josephus, and a leading figure of the last decades of the Second Temple period. The dispute thus provides further evidence that the *ketubah*, whether regarded as biblical or rabbinic, was already in use by this time.

A second form of protection was the mortgaging of the husband's property to ensure repayment of the bride-price. This radical solution is attributed in the *Talmud* to Shimon ben Shetaḥ:[31]

> So it was also taught elsewhere: At first they used to give merely a written undertaking in respect of (the *kethubah* of) a virgin for two hundred *zuz* and in respect of that of a widow for a *maneh*, and consequently they grew old and could not take any wives. It was then ordained that the amount of the *kethubah* was to be deposited in the wife's father's house. At any time, however, when the husband was angry with her he used to tell her: 'Go to your *kethubah*'. It was ordained, therefore, that the amount of the *kethubah* was to be deposited in the house of the father-in-law. Wealthy women converted it into silver, or gold baskets, while the poor women converted it into brass tubs. Still, whenever the husband had occasion to be angry with his wife, he would say to her: 'Take your *kethubah* and go'. It was then that Simeon ben Shetaḥ ordained that the husband must insert the pledging clause: 'all my property is mortgaged to your *kethubah*'. (*B. Ket.* 82b (Soncino transl.), cf. *Y. Ket.* 8, 32b-c).

The documents of the Judaean desert also show that the promise to repay the *mohar* was considered equivalent to any other debt and that the same types of guarantee were applied to it.[32] But whether the guarantee was already incorporated in a written *ketubah* in the time of Shimon ben Shetaḥ — indeed, whether such a written marriage contract had yet come into existence — cannot be certain. Though the *Talmud* certainly claims that Shimon ben Shetaḥ knew of such an institution, this passage dates from centuries after the event, and may well not reflect the *ipsissima verba* of Shimon. We may ask therefore whether it provides evidence that the document was indeed already in use. This need not, however, cast doubt on Shimon's role on protecting the wife's position through the mortgage: the creation of a legal mortgage over all the property of the husband in order to secure the obligation to make a real payment of the *mohar* is not necessarily dependent on incorporation within a written document.

C. Hanging as a Form of Capital Punishment

According to the reading proposed by Yadin, col. LXIV of the *Temple Scroll* considers the following hypotheses:
  (a) one who gives the enemy information against his people and delivers them to a foreign nation;
  (b) one who commits a crime liable to capital punishment and flees to the Gentiles, where he curses his people and the children of Israel.

For both, the prescribed punishment is one which some scholars identify with crucifixion, others with hanging.[33]

Neither offence appears to correspond with biblical sources. It is possible to find a distant echo as regards (b) with *I Kings* 21:10, where Naboth was stoned for having uttered blasphemous words against the Eternal God and King Ahab. But the form of execution is stoning and not 'hanging from a tree'.

Hanging, according to *Deut.* 21:22, is supplementary to the form by which capital punishment is executed; it is not the form of execution itself, and this view is followed in *M. Sanh.* 6:4.[34] The Biblical text reads: 'When a man committed a capital crime and was executed, you shall hang him from a tree.' Hanging, in fact, is clearly seen in the biblical sources as a form of execution peculiar to peoples other than Israel: *Gen.* 40:22; *II Sam.* 21:6-12; *Ezra* 6:11. Cf. also Josephus, *Ant.*, 12, 256. That view is echoed in rabbinic sources. *Sifre* to *Deuteronomy* 21:12 comments:

> It could be supposed that he must be hanged live according to the fashion of those who reign; for that the Scripture says: 'let him be put to death (and *then*) you will hang him from a tree'.

This tradition of *Sifre* is adopted in the Babylonian Talmud (*B. Sanh.* 46b):

> Our Teachers taught: 'If he sinned, you must hang him.' I could have said that he is hanged and then put to death, like those who reign do. Therefore the Scripture says: 'and he is put to death, and you must hang him'. First he is put to death and then hanged.

Yet the *Temple Scroll* is not alone amongst Second Commonwealth sources in attesting a practice of execution by hanging. According to Josephus (*Ant.* xiii.380) King Alexander Jannaeus had 800 Jewish opponents crucified, while banqueting with his concubines.[35] It is thought that the Qumran commentary on Nahum (*4 Q.p. Nah.* I.6-8)[36] may refer to some such incident when it speaks of the 'furious young lion who ... hangs men alive'.[37]

Recollections of such events are preserved in rabbinic literature. The

Talmud (*Kidd.* 66a) also attributes to Alexander Jannaeus an episode which Josephus (*Ant.* 13, 288) ascribes, with slight variations, to John Hyrcanus. The Pharisees opposed the wearing by the king of the priestly as well as the royal crown, because it was claimed that his mother had been a prisoner at Modi'in and would therefore be presumed to have been raped and thereby have become impure. Angry at the request of the Pharisees to give the priestly crown to Aaron's descendants, the king had them massacred and 'the world was desolate until Shimon ben Shetah came and restored the Torah to its ancient splendour'.

Another incident is ascribed to Shimon ben Shetah. The *Mishnah* (*Sanh.* 6:4, cf. *Y. Sanh.* 6:9, 23c) tells that when Shimon perceived the necessity to uproot witchcraft from Israel, he took the exceptional measure of ordering the hanging of 80 women accused of witchcraft on a single day.

These various sources appear to have a common element: they make reference to particular incidents, each characterized by exceptional circumstances, and to a form of execution perhaps not inflicted by a regular court. Such practices were clearly condemned by both the author of the *Pesher Nahum* and the Rabbis.

Is it possible to infer the view of the author of the *Temple Scroll*? While in general his attitude towards the authority of the King is restrictive,[38] it is difficult to infer whether the law on hanging was constructed with a view to condemning such royal practices or, on the contrary, to justify their departure from the rules of behaviour sanctioned in the biblical text on the grounds of the exceptionality of the offences to which they are here applied. It may, however, be noted that both the offences so treated in the *Temple Scroll* are forms of treason against the state,[39] and that the 800 whom Alexander Jannaeus executed were leaders of a revolt against the King, in which the aid of Demetrius, ruler of Syria, had been sought.[40]

D. Testimony

Deut. 17:6 requires 'two witnesses or three witnesses' for capital punishment.[41] While rabbinic tradition regards two witnesses as sufficient, *CD* IX:16-23 adopts the higher number as a minimum for execution: there, *three* witnesses are required. Schiffmann (1983:75) has noted that Josephus appears to be in agreement with the Qumran tradition: in *Ant.* 4:219 he opines that three witnesses are preferable to two, and in his version of the trial against Naboth for blasphemy (*I Kings* 21:10-13), he has increased the number of witnesses from two (as found in both the Hebrew Bible and the

Septuagint (Greek) translation) to three.

Concern in the Second Temple period over the *quality* of evidence emerges from a dictum ascribed to Shimon ben Shetah in *Mishnah Avot*:

> Shimon ben Shetah said: Examine the witnesses diligently and be cautious in thy words lest from them they learn to swear falsely. (*M. Avot* 1:9)

This may possibly reflect Shimon's reaction to the controversy prompted by his execution of the witches (p.50, above). According to the talmudic sources (*Sanh.* 6:4, cf. *Y. Sanh.* 6:9, 23c), a group of 'liars', relatives of the executed women, decided to seek revenge and gave false testimony against Shimon's own son, so bringing about his condemnation to death. Moved, however, by the cries of innocence of the accused as he was led to the place of execution, the false witnesses tried to retract their evidence. Shimon ben Shetah was about to change the sentence when his son himself admonished him to let justice proceed on its course, if he really wanted Israel to be strengthened.

6. *Bibliography*

Two major handbooks provide much detailed information on the history and literature of this period:

E. Schürer, *The History of the Jewish People in the Age of Jesus Christ* (175 B.C.- A.D. 135), ed. G. Vermes & F. Millar (Edinburgh, T. & T. Clark, 1973-87), 3 Vols. (Vol. III in 2 parts)

M. E. Stone, ed., *Jewish Writings of the Second Temple Period*, in *Compendia Rerum Iudaicarum ad Novum Testamentum*, Sect. II (Assen: Van Gorcum, and Philadelphia: Fortress Press, 1984). See especially I. Gafni, 1-31 (for the historical background); D. Dimant, 483-550 (Qumran); P. Borgen, 233- 282 (Philo); H.W. Attridge, 185-232 (Josephus), all with bibliographies.

The development of scholarship relating to the Qumran Community may be followed in the specialist journal: *Revue de Qumran.*

On biblical interpretation at Qumran, see M. Fishbane, 'Use, Authority and Interpretation of Mikra at Qumran', in *Mikra, Text, Translation, Reading and Interpretation of the Hebrew Bible in Ancient Judaism and Early Christianity*, ed. M.J. Mulder (Assen/Maastricht: van Gorcum, 1988), 339-75, with bibliography.

For the principal Qumran documents relevant to law, see P.R. Davies, *The Damascus Covenant. An Interpretation of the 'Damascus Document'* (Sheffield: JSOT Press, 1982); P. Wernberg-Møller, *The Manual of*

Discipline (Leiden: E.J. Brill, 1957); Y. Yadin, *The Temple Scroll* (Jerusalem: Ḥevrah leḥakirat Erets Yisrael ve'atiḳotehah, 1977, Heb.; Engl. ed., Jerusalem: Magnes Press, 1984); J. Maier, *The Temple Scroll, An Introduction, Translation and Commentary* (Sheffield: JSOT Press, 1985).

On *Halakhah* at Qumran, see L.H. Schiffman, *The Law of Testimony*, in *Sectarian Law in the Dead Sea Scrolls. Courts, Testimony and the Penal Code* (Chico, CA: Scholars Press, 1983), reviewed by Milikowsky, 'Law at Qumran. A critical Reaction to Schiffman, Sectarian Law ...' *Revue de Qumran* 12 (1986), 237-49. See also J. Pouilly, 'L'évolution de la législation pénale dans la Communauté de Qumran', *Revue Biblique* 82 (1975), 522-51; J. Baumgarten, 'The Duodecimal Courts of Qumran. Revelation and the Sanhedrin', *Journal of Biblical Literature* 95 (1976), 59-78.

Notes

[a]   Sections 1B, 2Di and iii, 3A, 4A, 5 and 6 were drafted by Piattelli; the other sections by Jackson.

1   Sons of Zadok, High Priest in the time of King David, assisted by *rashe avot edah*, the same council of notables that, according to *Num.* 31:26, Moses ordered to assist the High Priest Eleazar in the fulfilment of the most important religious functions in the life of the community.

2   There is also some evidence that the model of the 'prophet like Moses' of *Deut.* 18 was important in the sect's eschatological thinking. See *1QS* 9:11, *4QTest.*, and B.S. Jackson, 'The Prophet and the Law in Early Judaism and the New Testament', in *The Paris Conference Volume*, ed. S.M. Passamaneck and M. Finley (Atlanta: Scholars Press, 1994), 67-112 (Jewish Law Association Studies, VII), at 74.

3   A proto-rabbinic group to whom the origins of the Oral Law are traditionally ascribed, often found in the sources in opposition to the Sadducees (who opposed the Oral Law), and also in the New Testament sometimes disputing with Jesus. The tannaitic Rabbis saw the Pharisees as their immediate predecessors. See J. Neusner, *The Rabbinic Traditions about the Pharisees before A.D. 70* (Leiden: E.J. Brill, 1971, 3 vols).

4   Neusner, *supra* n.3, at Vol.III, 164ff.; 'The Problem of Oral Transmission', *Journal of Jewish Studies* 22 (1971), 3ff.; 'Oral Tradition and Oral Torah. Defining the Problematic', in *Studies in Jewish Folklore*, ed. F. Talmage (Cambridge, MA: Association for Jewish Studies, 1980), 25-71.

5   L. Schiffman, *The Halakhah at Qumran* (Leiden: E.J. Brill, 1975), 20.

6   D.Piattelli, "Riflessi giuridici sulla celebrazione delle feste d'Israele: Sukkot et la lettura della legge", *Appollinaris* 59 (1986), 701-719.

7   The original language of some was Hebrew, though for the most part the works have survived only in the Greek versions of the Septuagint.

8   On the history of the Apocrypha in the church, and divergent approaches even amongst Protestants after the Reformation, see R.C. Dentan, in *The Oxford Companion to the Bible*, ed B.M. Metzger and M.D. Coogan (New York and Oxford: Oxford University Press 1993), 37-39.

9   The Roman Catholic and Eastern Orthodox churches accept the Apocrypha as part of the Bible, sometimes calling them 'Deuterocanonical'; they apply the term 'Apocrypha' to the books here (and conventionally) termed Pseudepigrapha.

10 G.W.E. Nickelsburg, 'The Bible Rewritten and Expanded', in M.E. Stone, ed., *Jewish Writings of the Second Temple Period*, 104 (see bibliography), citing R.H. Charles, *The Book of Jubilees* (Oxford: Clarendon Press, 1902), lxxv-lxxvii; see further 152f. for a bibliography on the Book of Jubilees.

11 See Nickelsburg, *supra* n.10, at 101-103, concluding that it was written around 168 B.C.E.

12 On the oral law, see E.P. Sanders, *Jewish Law from Jesus to the Mishnah, Five Studies* (London and Philadelphia: SCM Press and Trinity Press International, 1990), ch.2 ('Did the Pharisees have Oral Law?'), at 27-130.

13 See further J. Vanderkan, *Textual and Historical Studies in the Book of Jubilees* (Scholars Press: Missoula, 1977), 253-83.

14 For a brief overview, see E. Tov, in *The Oxford Companion to the Bible*, *supra* n.8, at 159-161; in greater detail, G. Vermes, *The Dead Sea Scrolls. Qumran in Perspective* (London: Collins, 1977).

15 'Fragments of a Zadokite Document', in *The Apocrypha and Pseudepigrapha of the Old Testament*, ed. R.H. Charles (Oxford: Oxford University Press, 1963-4), vol. II, p.788.

16 E. Qimron and J. Strugnell, *Qumran Cave 4 V: Miqsat Ma'ase Ha-Torah* (Oxford: Oxford University Press, 1994). Qimron contributes the chapter on the halakhic content of the scroll (123-177), including a bibliography on *halakhah* at Qumran (124-130); there is also an Appendix by Y. Sussman, 'The History of the Halakha and the Dead Sea Scrolls', at 179-200.

17 Whether this process commenced before the destruction of the Temple in 70 C.E., or a few years earlier, is a matter of scholarly controversy.

18 A Christian scholar who has written on it extensively, and who argues that many of the teachings of Jesus reflect a midrashic style of argument, using sophisticated allusions to Biblical sources, is J.D.M. Derrett, *Law in the New Testament* (London: Darton, Longman & Todd, 1970), who studies, amongst many others, the parables of the unmerciful servant, the unjust steward, the prodigal son, and the Good Samaritan, together with the teachings of Jesus on marriage and divorce, his decision in the case of the woman taken in adultery, and the principle of 'Render Unto Caesar ...'. A classic collection of shorter studies is provided by David Daube, *The New Testament and*

Rabbinic Judaism (London: Athlone Press, 1956: reprinted New York: Arno Press, 1973). Part I considers the 'messianic types' which may be reflected in the New Testament: Joseph, Moses, Samuel, Saul, Elijah, Ruth and Boaz; Part II discusses Legislative and Narrative Forms; Part III treats Concepts and Conventions (including rabbinic authority, semikhah, talion, terms for divorce). E.P. Sanders, *Jewish Law from Jesus to the Mishnah, Five Studies* (London and Philadelphia: SCM Press and Trinity Press International, 1990) considers various aspects of the relationship between the law and Jesus in the synoptic Gospels, including the sabbath, temple tax, oaths and vows, blasphemy, and the place of Jesus within contemporary conflicts over the law (especially the Essenes and Pharisees), concluding that Jesus did not seriously challenge the law as it was practised in his day.

19 Amongst the most important recent books on the issue are P. Winter, *On the Trial of Jesus* (Berlin: Walter de Gruyter, 1961; 2nd revd. ed. by T.A. Burkill and G. Vermes, 1974); S.G.F. Brandon, *The Trial of Jesus of Nazareth* (London: Batsford, 1968; Paladin, 1971); H.H. Cohn, *The Trial and Death of Jesus* (New York: Harper & Row, 1971); J.D.M. Derrett, *Law in the New Testament* (London: Darton, Longman & Todd, 1970), ch.17; J. Blinzler, *The Trial of Jesus* (Westminster MD: Newman Press, 1959; E. Bammel, ed., *The Trial of Jesus* (London: SCM Press, 1970).

20 Jackson, *supra* n.2, at 108f.

21 See further B.S. Jackson, 'On the Problem of Roman Influence on the Halakhah and Normative Self-Definition in Judaism', in *Jewish and Christian Self-Definition,* ed. E.P. Sanders (London: SCM Press, 1981), vol.II, 157-203 (text), 352-379 (notes), at 353f. n.11.

22 Cf. F.M. Abel, *Les Livres des Maccabées* (Paris: Editions du Cerf, 1949), 184ff.

23 For a summary of views on whether there was one Sanhedrin or more, see *Encyclopedia Judaica* 14.838f.

24 See further E. Schürer, *The History of the Jewish People in the Age of Jesus Christ* (175 B.C.- A.D. 135), ed. G. Vermes & F. Millar (Edinburgh, T. & T. Clark, 1973-87), II.210-218, on the composition of the Sanhedrin, and II.218-226 on its competence, the time and place of sessions, and its judicial procedure. See also H. Mantel, *Studies in the History of the Sanhedrin*, (Cambridge: Harvard University Press, 1961); S. Hoenig, *The Great Sanhedrin* (Philadelphia: Dropsie College, 1953). Mantel contributes the article on Sanhedrin to the *Encyclopedia Judaica* (14.836-839), noting that the first historical notice is in the statement of Josephus (*Ant.* xiv.91) that Gabinius divided the country into five *synedria*.

25 Ca. 280 B.C.E., Josephus *Ant.* xii.2.5, or Simeon II, High Priest around 200 B.C.E., *Eccles.* 50:1.

26 On Hillel, see pp.130f. below.

27 J. Murphy-O'Connor, 'Remarques sur l'exposé du Prof Yadin', *Revue Biblique* 89 (1972), 99-100.

28 J.R. Müller, 'The Temple Scroll and the Gospel Divorce Texts', *Revue de Qumran* 10 (1980-81), 247-56, finds in Temple Scroll Col. LXVI:12-17 confirmation of the view of J. Fitzmyer, 'The Matthean Divorce Texts and some Palestinian Evidence', *Journal of Theological Studies* 37 (1976), 221, regarding the concept of *zenut* at Qumran, as reflected in *CD* 4:20.

29 Y. Yadin, 'L'attitude essénienne envers la polygamie et le divorce', *Revue Biblique* 79 (1972), 98-99; *idem*, *The Temple Scroll* (Jerusalem: Ḥevrah leḥakirat Erets Yisrael ve'atikoteḥah, 1977), 353-57. But serial polygamy is permitted, perhaps even recommended, for the King in the *Temple Scoll*, 57:18-19.

30 Mueller and Fitzmyer, articles cited *supra* n.28. See also J.D.M. Derrett, *Law in the New Testament* (London: Darton, Logman & Todd, 1970), ch.16. There was dispute also amongst the rabbinic schools, though here those requiring adultery represented the more restrictive view: 'The School of Shammai say: A man may not divorce his wife unless he has found unchastity (*devar ervah*) in her, for it is written, *because he has found some indecency* (*ervat davar*) *in her*. And the School of Hillel say: [He may divorce her] even if she spoiled a dish for him, for it is written, *because he has found some indecency in her*. R. Akiba says: Even if he found another fairer than she, for it is written, *if then she finds no favor in his eyes*.' (*M. Gitt.* 9:10).

31 M. Geller, 'New Sources for the Rabbinic Ketubah', *Hebrew Union College Annual* 49 (1978), 227-45, thinks that the institution of such a mortgage over all the property of the husband, as guarantee for the payment of the *ketubah* (in the Bible, the *mohar*, 'brideprice') originated from Egyptian practice. He reminds us that Shimon ben Shetaḥ was a Pharisee and that many members of his wing were forced to find shelter in Egypt at the time of Alexander Jannaeus' persecutions. Specialists in the Egyptian sources have shown, however, that in Egypt marriage contracts, not infrequently written after children had already been born, fulfilled the function of establishing community of property between husband and wife. On the other hand, the rabbinic text shows Shimon ben Shetaḥ's provision as concerned exclusively with the desire to provide a certain guarantee for the repayment of the *mohar*. See most recently M. Satlow, 'Reconsidering the rabbinic *ketubba* payment', in S.J.D. Cohen, ed., *The Jewish Family in Antiquity* (Atlanta: Scholars Press, 1993, Brown Judaic Studies), 133-151; H. Cotton, 'A Cancelled Marriage Contract from the Judaean Desert (*XHev/Se Gr.2*)', *Journal of Roman Studies* 84 (1994), 65-86, reviewing evidence from eight marriage contracts from various sites in the Judaean desert.

32 See the document published by P. Benoit, 'Une reconnaissance de dette du IIème siècle en Palestine', in *Studi Calderini Paribeni* (Milano: Ceschina, 1956-57), II.258, dated 161 C.E.; see also *P.Mur.* 18, in P. Benoit, J.T. Milik and R. de Vaux, *Discoveries in the Judaean Desert, II. Les Grottes de Murabba'at* (Oxford: Clarendon Press, 1961), 100-104, and ch.4 n.61, below.

33 See J. Baumgarten, 'Does TLH in the Temple Scroll refer to Crucifixion?', in *Studies in Qumran Law* (Leiden: E.J. Brill, 1977), 172-83.

34 Though with differences of view as to the scope of the rule's application: 'All that have been stoned must be hanged. So R. Eliezer. But the Sages say: None is hanged save the blasphemer and the idolator.'

35 On 'hanging live on a tree' as meaning crucifixion, see the discussion in Schürer, *supra* n.24, at I, 224f. note, commenting on this incident and other sources referring to Alexander Jannaeus.

36 Scholars discuss the meaning to be assigned to the term *pesher*: whether it is nearer to *targum* or to *midrash*. The problem is complicated by the fact that the term *pesher* designates not only exegetical techniques and literary form, but also the work itself. The Qumran fragments of the *Pesher Nahum* were found in a manuscript which dates from between the end of the Hasmonean period and Herod. Two Greek kings are named in it, Antiochos, identified with Antiochos IV Epiphanes (175-164 B.C.E.) and Demetrios III Eukairos (95-88 B.C.E.). See further Y. Yadin, 'Pesher Nachum (4Q pNach.) Reconsidered', *Israel Exploration Journal* 21 (1971), 1-12.

37 Schürer, *supra* n.24. See also D.J. Halperin, 'Crucifixion. The Nahum Pesher and the Rabbinic Penalty of Strangulation', *Journal of Jewish Studies* 32 (1981), 32-46.

38 From the section on the law of the King in the *Temple Scroll* (cols. 57-58) it appears that the writer considered the king chiefly as a military chief; but, even in this capacity, his authority was strongly limited: even the prerogative to decide to make war requires also the authority of the High Priest (58:18-21).

39 See Yadin, *supra* n.28; Schürer, *supra* n.24, at I.225 note.

40 Schürer, *supra* n.24, at I.224.

41 On this expression in the Bible, see B.S. Jackson, *Essays in Jewish and Comparative Legal History* (Leiden: E.J. Brill, 1975), ch. 6; on its interpretation in CD 9:16-23, Jackson, *ibid.*, ch.7, at 172-83; J. Neusner, 'By the Testimony of two Witnesses in the Damascus Document IX, 17-22 and in Pharisaic-Rabbinic Law', *Revue de Qumran* 8 (1972-75), 197-217; B.S. Jackson, 'Damascus Document IX, 16-23 and Parallels', *Revue de Qumran* 9 (1977-78), 446-450.

3

SAMARITAN HALAKHAH

by

MICHAEL CORINALDI
University of Haifa

[The Samaritan *halakhah* is not traditionally treated in books on Jewish law. Here we seek to present more fully the diversity of historical strands, and not to exclude those which came to be regarded by the dominant (rabbinic) tradition as sectarian. The period reviewed in Chapter Two was one characterized by such diversity. This chapter considers the history of a tradition which commenced even earlier, in the period of the First Temple, and which has survived to the present day. Apart from its intrinsic interest, it therefore provides a valuable comparative perspective for the rabbinic tradition — the history of a form of Jewish law based on the Bible but rejecting the Oral Law of the Rabbis. — Eds.]

1. *The Name*

Originally the name *Shomronim* ('Samaritans'), mentioned in *2 Kings* 17:29 meant the ancient inhabitants of the Assyrian province of Samaria. The city of that name, built by Omri in the ninth century B.C.E. (*1 Kings* 16:24) was at first the capital of the tribe of Ephraim, and upon its capture by the Assyrians at the end of the eighth century became the local Assyrian provincial centre. Hence its name is applied to the inhabitants of the region. The root of the sect's name, *Shomronim*, refers to a separate group from that of the Samarian inhabitants, and is said to be *shomer* (guardian) — the Samaritans referring to themselves as the authentic guardians of the Scripture and of the original tradition of the Jewish people, *al ha'emet* (truth of the *Torah*).

2. *Origins*

There are, in fact, three different theories of the sect's origin. According to *2 Kings* 17, in the ninth year of the rule of Hoshea, the son of Elah, in Samaria (722 B.C.E.), Shalmanezer V, King of Assyria, conquered Samaria and exiled the Israelites to various places in Assyria replacing them with a number of disparate peoples from different areas (Babylon, Cuth, Ava, Hamath, Sepharaim) who knew nothing of the God of Israel. These were attacked by wild animals (lions) and almost annihilated. In their distress they appealed to the King of Assyria, who restored one of the exiled priests to Bet El and under whose guidance they were converted to the worship of the Lord. But the conversion was neither genuine nor complete, and alongside worship of Jehovah they continued their previous idolatrous practices and usages. This account explains their being called Cutheans and in some traditions in tannaitic times 'the proselytes for fear of lions' (*B. Kidd.* 75b).

Traditionally, the Samaritans regard themselves as descendants of the tribes of Ephraim and Menasseh which had constantly occupied their ancestral lands in Samaria and guarded the authentic original Israelite traditions. In the days of the priest Eli (c. 1050 B.C.E.) they split away from the Jews as a result of a quarrel over the 'chosen place', which some identified as Mount Gerizim, whilst others set up a separate shrine (*mishkan)* in Shilo. The majority of the people followed Eli to the latter place. Until then a time of 'Divine Favour' (*rahutah*) had prevailed but when the larger part of the people forsook Shiloh for Gerizim, a period of 'Divine Disfavour' (*fanutah —* literally, the concealment of the Presence) began.

Modern research is critical of both the Biblical and the Samaritans' traditional approach. The story of the exile of the Israelites in the Book of Kings presents difficulties. Under Josiah (639-609) Jews survived in Samaria (*2 Chron.* 34:6-9). Josiah destroyed the 'high places' at Bet El and the cities of Samaria (*2 Chron.* 23:15-20), but the attachment of what remained of the Kingdom of Israel to Jerusalem and the *mishkan* may be found in the account of the pilgrimage (*Jeremiah* 41:5). The upper classes alone went into exile; according to the Annals of Sargon II, some 27,290 were sent into captivity. Thus there are strong grounds for rejecting the accepted biblical and talmudic account and accepting the view that the vast majority of the people of Ephraim and Menasseh were not exiled and the Samaritans today stem from them.[1] Assyrian sources also indicate that the local population was augmented by several small migrations from Babylonia.[2]

The Samaritan assertion of an early religious schism is also rejected, as demonstrated by the affinity of Samaritan *halakhah* to pre-tannaitic Jewish *halakhah*. The schism was in fact a process stretching over a lengthy period.

3. *History*

Samaritan history consist of three main periods. In the Persian period friction between Jews and Samaritans accompanied by mutual estrangement began to manifest itself. When the Jews returned from Babylon (from 538 B.C.E. onwards) the Samaritans offered to cooperate in the rebuilding of the Temple but the returnees rejected the offer (*Ezra* 4:1-6), thus contributing to the isolation of the Samaritans. Apparently social and political considerations lay behind the opposition to them, in particular the alien extraction of the Samaritans and their polytheistic religious rites. Under Ezra and Nehemiah mutual hostility increased; Nehemiah expressly forbade inter-marriage and a son of the High Priest who married a daughter of Sanballat I, the ruler of Samaria, was expelled by Nehemiah (*Neh.* 13:28). Sanballat I was avowedly hostile to Nehemiah (*Neh.* 6 *et pass.*).

According to Josephus (*Ant.*, xi.21) the division grew wider in the second half of the fourth century, on the removal of a brother of the High Priest in Jerusalem from his priestly functions as a result of the marriage of his daughter to Sanballat III, the Governor of Samaria. This marriage aroused the hostility of the Jerusalem priesthood, and its annulment was only avoided by a promise of Sanballat to erect a temple on Gerizim and instal his son-in-law to serve there. The opportunity to build this temple came in 312 with the conquest of Palestine by Alexander the Great.

Alexander the Great was assisted by the Samaritans and in return he permitted the building of the temple on Gerizim. Subsequently, relations between Jews and Samaritans became strained. *Megilat Ta'anit* records an attempt by the Samaritans to attack the Temple in Jerusalem. Later the Samaritans and the forces of Alexander the Great fell out. The Samaritans revolted against Alexander the Great; Samaria was destroyed and settled by soldiers. This event may account for the Samaritans finding refuge in Shechem, which became their capital city and their religious centre in rivalry with Jerusalem. When Alexander the Great moved into Egypt he took with him Samaritan auxiliaries who eventually constituted the nucleus of the Samaritan community in Egypt.

The anti-Jewish decrees of Antiochus Epiphanes (second century B.C.E.) applied equally to the Samaritans. It is not, however, clear what attitude the Samaritans adopted to the Hasmonean revolt. In 128 B.C.E. John Hyrcanus sacked the Temple on Gerizim and imposed upon the Samaritans the Jerusalem version of Judaism. Later Hyrcanus destroyed Shechem, and this event may have led finally to the complete separation of the two communities.

The Roman conquest under Pompey (63 B.C.E.) did not change the situation. Although the Samaritans did not enjoy the status of a recognized religious group, they remained loyal to the authorities and lived unmolested for most of the Roman period as a small body that presented little threat. During the time of Pontius Pilatus (c. 26 C.E.), when messianic fervour moved the Samaritans and aroused suspicions, suppressive measures were taken against them and many were killed. Throughout this period relations between Jews and Samaritans were further strained. The latter did not join the Jews in their revolt against Rome and at the beginning of the Bar Kochba uprising even acted against them. The fatal consequences of that uprising to the Jewish community made the Samaritans an important element in the local population and also strengthened their diaspora. The Samaritan tradition was not, however, an officially recognized religion, and at the end of the third century C.E. increasing persecution led, among other things, to the prohibition of circumcision.

A considerable part of the administrative organization of the Samaritans was introduced by Baba Rabbah in the fourth century; he also created a judicial system of seven judges and set up a council of twelve 'leaders' (nesi'im), parallel to the institutions found in the Jewish community.

During the Byzantine period, the Samaritans were regarded as heretics to be converted to Christianity, and indeed many of them were converted. Persecution by the Christians prompted a revolt, which was cruelly put down. Many of the Samaritans' synagogues were destroyed; they suffered from economic and other restrictions; and many were even sold into slavery. This repression is one of the main reasons for their decline in the Middle Ages. Whilst as a consequence of repression many foreign elements penetrated Samaria, the Samaritans remained the majority of the local population.

The Arab period (638-1517) was critical for Samaritan history. As a result of persecution and exile, their numbers declined from 350,000 to some few thousands by the time of the Crusades. It may be assumed that the Arabs treated them as a client group like the Jews and Christians: although they enjoyed a certain degree of autonomy, they were not regarded as a distinct people but rather as a religious sect.

During the Crusades the Samaritans were controlled like the other non-Christians in Palestine on a traditional community basis. Their condition did not worsen, although the major sites under their rule in Shechem were seized by the Crusaders and turned into churches. An important literary source for their position in this period is provided by Benjamin of Tudela, who informs us that they numbered about 2000 families. The struggle, however, between the Crusaders and Moslems at the end of the twelfth century seriously harmed the Samaritans.

Under the Mamelukes the pressure to convert to Islam continued, but a counter movement sprang up to reinforce their religious belief, which manifested itself in renewed cultural creativity and revival of ritual traditions and a new poetical flowering. An educational centre was established in Shechem, their law texts were rewritten and chronicles and prayer books were compiled.

Under the Ottomans the Samaritan communities outside Shechem ceased to exist. The remaining individuals turned to Shechem, which now became the only Samaritan centre. A clear indication of decline is the disappearance of the family of high priests claiming direct descent from Aaron. The last of this line died in 1624 and the priesthood passed to a family of Levites related to Uzziel ben Kehat. Their numbers dropped to some 200, all living in Shechem. In 1842 even this remnant was almost annihilated by the local Arab population on the pretext that they were neither Jews nor Christians recognized by Islam. It was only after obtaining confirmation from the then Chief Rabbi, Abraham Hayyim Gaguine, that 'the Samaritan people is a branch of the Jewish people that acknowledge the truth of the *Torah*',[3] that their persecution ceased. The community, however, remained in a parlous social and economic state.

After the British conquest of Palestine in 1917, conditions began to improve and upon the establishment of the State of Israel in 1948 (which recognized them as Jews for the purpose of the Law of Return), the community began to revive. A new centre was set up in Holon. Numbers rose to the present population of over 560, half of them living in Shechem and Kiryat Luza on Mount Gerizim and half in Holon. The latter participate fully in the life of the State, serve in the army and find employment in all areas of the economy. The community continues to adhere to its religious tradition. It is headed by a high priest from the Avta family, who is also the supreme authority in matters of family status.

4. *Literature*

The basic religious text is the Samaritan Pentateuch. No special status attaches to the rest of Scripture or to postbiblical Samaritan literature.

According to most scholars, the Samaritan version of the Pentateuch is later than the traditional version.[4] The earliest and most prized of the copies is the *Ṣefer Avisha*, thought to be of great antiquity and zealously preserved. It dates back to medieval times — some of its early parts from the tenth and eleventh centuries, and additions were made later, as early as the fourteenth century. It has been found that the Samaritan version differs from the traditional Jewish version of the Pentateuch in 6000 particulars, a third of which agree with the Septuagint. Most of the differences are verbal in nature but some, as in the tenth command of the Decalogue, also reflect differences of substance: the Samaritan version requires the erection of stones engraved with 'all the words of this *Torah*' on Mount Gerizim, and the raising there of an altar.[5] The fundamental textual differences involve the Samaritan belief that Mount Gerizim is the place 'which God has chosen' instead of (as traditionally) 'the place which God will choose', in order as it were to emphasize the choice of Mount Gerizim as the site of the Temple. Again in *Deut.* 27:4 instead of the traditional

> When you have crossed the Jordan you shall set up these stones on Mount Ebal, as I command you this day, and cover them with plaster

the Samaritan version is:

> When you have crossed the Jordan you shall set up ... on Mount Gerizim ...

The oldest prayer book, the *Defter,* in Aramaic, goes back to the fourth century with later additions in Aramaic and Hebrew. Over the ages important religious poets (*paytanim*) wrote in Aramaic and Hebrew, incorporating halakhic matters into their compositions. Highly esteemed is the midrashic *Memar Markah*, by the great poet Markah of the fourth century,[6] which recounts the events mentioned in the Pentateuch, such as the miracles that happened to Moses (the crossing of the Red Sea). Another important midrashic composition dating to the sixteenth century, is *Molad Mosheh*, in Arabic, by Ismail Arumeyhi: it indicates the special regard the Samaritans have for Moses, unlike the other prophets mentioned in the Bible.

The historical compositions of Samaritan scholars are an important source for their history, but only few have been preserved. These also contain midrashic and aggadic material and occasionally halakhic observations. Of these, the most important are the following:

1.   *The Asatir*, in Aramaic (tenth and eleventh centuries), the oldest preserved of the chronicles.
2.   *The Al Tolidah*, a genealogical work compiled by Jacob b. Ishmael (fourteenth century, in Hebrew and Aramaic). It is based on a

book by the High Priest Elazar b. Amram of the twelfth century, containing genealogical tables from Adam down to the conquest of Palestine together with a history of the high priests.

3. The Samaritan *Book of Joshua*, in Arabic, written by an anonymous author, describes Samaritan history from the time of Joshua down to Baba Rabbah, the great Samaritan leader of the fourth century.

4. *Kitab al Ta'arih,* a chronicle by Abu'l Fath (mid-fourteenth century, in Arabic) — the most detailed chronicle that has survived from the Middle Ages.

5. *Shalshalah* (The Chain, or The Annals), a genealogy of the High Priests attributed to Pinhas b. Elazar in the fourteenth century and now containing supplements down to the present century.

The basic Samaritan halakhic texts still extant are all in medieval Arabic.[7] These date from the medieval period:

— *Kitab al-Kafi* (The Fully Sufficient Book) by Yusuf b. Salamah, written in 1042 and dealing with the 613 biblical precepts;

— *Kitab al-Tabakh* (The Book of Insight), composed in the first half of the eleventh century by Abu al Hasan of Tyre, part of it dealing with the laws of ritual slaughter of animals (*shehitah*) and prohibited foods;

— *Kitab al-Khilaf* (The Book of Differences) by Munajja b. Sadaqah in the twelfth century, concerned with the differences between the Samaritans, the Rabbis and Karaites;

— *Kitab al-Fara'id* (The Book of Precepts) by Abu'l Faraj ibn Kathar in the fourteenth century, of which only part has survived and which lists the 613 precepts.

Post-medieval texts include:

— *Kitab Kasif al-Ghayahib* (The Uncovering of Obscurities), a comprehensive commentary on the Pentateuch other than Deuteronomy, written at the end of the seventeenth and the beginning of the eighteenth centuries by various authors;

— *Kitab al-Tukusaat* (The Book of Religious Practices), dealing with principles and religious practices, including *responsa* on questions of faith and *halakhah*, extant in two versions, one by Khidr b. Ishaq and one by Ya'qub b. Harun (late nineteenth century);

— *Kitab al-Irshad w'al Ishaad* (The Book of Differences in Teaching), dates back to the nineteenth century and attributed to Pinhas b. Joseph HaCohen or Jacob b. Aaron, the High Priest, dealing in ten chapters with the halakhic differences between Samaritans and Jews due to variations in the text of the *Torah*. The first chapter of this work recounts the history of various communities that have disappeared, which seems to show that the book is made up of extracts from ancient writings that have been lost. The last part of the book deals with the problem of death, divine retribution and resurrection.

— Finally there is the *Kitab al-Madaris* (The Book of Students), a student's text written by the priest Pinḥas b. Yitsḥak in the second half of the nineteenth century.

None of the above has achieved a complete and systematic redaction of Samaritan *halakhah*; the nearest to that is *Kitab al-Fara'id*.

Samaritan halakhic compilations generally derive from and supplement each other. They include polemics against the Rabbis and Karaites, as well as Islam and Christianity. Large parts include commentary on biblical chapters. Noteworthy are also the *responsa* of the Community's priests on halakhic matters given at the beginning of the twentieth century in answer to two questionnaires from Moses Gaster. These *responsa* are intended for 'external' consumption, so that non-Samaritans might understand the foundations of Samaritan *halakhah*.

The paucity of Samaritan halakhic texts is to be explained by the fact that, as already indicated, only the Pentateuch is hallowed by the Samaritans, in contrast to the Jewish *halakhah* where the Oral Law is vitally important. Further, pressure from alien rulers, persecution and pogroms, as well as poverty and dwindling numbers, have led the Samaritans to concentrate on those few halakhic texts sufficient to provide them with the information they require to pursue a minimal religious life. Three books — *al-Tabakh*, *al-Kafi* and *al-Khilaf* — cover the ordinary daily religious life of the community and these books have been copied much more frequently than the other halakhic books.

5. *The Legal Sources of the Samaritan Halakhah*

The sources of the law are the *Torah*, as the basic norm and the springhead of the entire Samaritan *halakhah*; tradition (*nakl*) possessing divine authority, based on *midrash* (homiletic interpretation); and reasoning by analogy of the biblical text (*qiyas*) delivered to Moses and the Seventy Elders: 'they will teach the precepts to Jacob, the law to Israel' (*Deut.* 33:10).

Samaritan *halakhah* differs largely from rabbinic *halakhah* by its strictness both in interpretation of the written word and observation of the biblical commandments (*haḥmarot*). Its logical reasoning (*akl*) is similar to the *ṣevarah* of rabbinic *halakhah*. A passage from *Sharh Surat al-Irbot*[8] may conveniently be quoted here:

> The use of the verb 'to speak' [*d-b-r*] ('Speak to the Children of Israel', *Lev.* 18:2) refers to addressing the people with the actual words spoken and recorded in the text of Scripture. The use of the verb 'to say' [*a-m-r*] refers to what is obscure to ordinary people and involves deductive interpretation (*qias*), inversion [by inference] (*wa-aks*) and consistency of theme (*wa-illah*) of the verses revealed in a particular passage. Moses was told by God to explain the verses to the people. Thus 'to speak' may be taken to refer to what is written in the text and 'to say' to what is not so written. The latter is recondite but can be derived from the text and it has been transmitted from the time of Moses in the writings of his ancient successors. Moses was so instructed by divine authority equally with that which is plainly and clearly set down. This is what is called 'judgment' (*mishpaṭ*) as in the familiar phrase 'one *Torah* and one judgment' (*Numbers* 15:16). '*Torah*' refers to whatever is found clearly stated in the *Torah* and '*mishpaṭ*' (judgment) to whatever can be perceived from interpretation of the text and has been transmitted down the ages from Moses, to the extent that it is accessible to reason (*aql*).'

This interrelationship of the text, tradition and logic can be regarded as the essential theoretical principle of Samaritan *halakhah*. The Samaritans recognize that although the text of the *Torah* is perfect and needs no supplementing, it is not possible to derive *halakhah* from the text of Scripture because of the limited capacity of all mortals except Moses. Hence traditional knowledge is required and exegesis cannot take the place of tradition. The *halakhah* is known by means of traditionally transmitted exegesis going back to the Seventy Elders of the time of Divine Favour, who received it from Moses. Some of the *halakhah* can also be perceived by the priests with the help of tradition believed to be transmitted by Moses and the Seventy Elders.

The Samaritans do not possess a hallowed (authoritative) book of law besides the Pentateuch, and there is almost no record of halakhic judgments. The priest judges a case on reasoning supported by the *Torah* as the binding source as well as by such halakhic books and interpretations of the *Torah* that were written down in medieval times. Nevertheless, real attempts are made to contend with contemporary problems and their profound effect on the community.

Most of the sources of Samaritan religion go back to the Middle Ages and do not reflect the religious reality of earlier periods, although the basic principles were already known. Four major dogmas exist :

(a) belief in the singularity and unity of the God of Israel;
(b) the existence of a single prophet Moses, no subsequent prophet being recognized;
(c) exclusiveness of the *Torah* of Moses, no other book of scripture being acknowledged;
(d) the exclusiveness of Mount Gerizim as the holy site.

In addition there is a messianic belief in Messiah (*Taheb*) ben Joseph who will be a prophet like Moses and will appear at the millennium to effect final judgment.

The highest religious authority rests in the high priest. Up to the seventeenth century the Samaritans were led by a dynasty of high priests traditionally related to Pinhas b. Elazar ben Aaron the Priest. The priesthood descended by inheritance to the oldest succeeding priest by age ('one among his brethren', *Lev.* 21:10).

6. *Traditional Customs and Usages of the Samaritans*

We may note some examples of traditional customs and usages of a distinctive character. Sacrifices are still today offered on Mount Gerizim. Samaritan synagogues are oriented towards Mount Gerizim. Footware is removed before entering the synagogue (*Ex.* 3:5). During prayers conducted mainly on Sabbath and Festivals the congregants sit on carpets.

The prohibition of kindling on Sabbath includes the lighting of candles on the eve of Sabbath and leaving them lit. They do not leave their houses to walk beyond their immediate districts for purposes other than to go to synagogue to pray and sing psalms. The calendar is a lunar one of 354 days and the Festivals vary in date from the rabbinic festivals. The Samaritans have seven festivals, four called *mo'adim* (Passover, the New Year, the Day of Atonement and *Shemini Atseret*) and three called *haggim* (the Feast of Unleavened Bread as distinct from Passover, Tabernacles and Pentecost), when pilgrimage is made to Mount Gerizim. The Samaritans are very careful to observe the law relating to pure and impure things. The menstruating woman is separated from society as is also the man who experiences nocturnal discharges. Boys enter into the observance of the prescriptions after reaching maturity and study of the *Torah*, usually between the ages of 6 and 10.

7. Marriage and Divorce Laws

Samaritan *halakhah* understands strictly the biblical injunctions regarding incest and forbidden marriages (with the daughter of a brother or sister, contrary to Jewish *halakhah*). It also prohibits the marriage of a priest and a divorcee.

There are three main grounds for divorce

(a) where differences between the spouses lead to mutual dislike or hatred after a period of one year for conciliation has been to no avail;

(b) where one spouse is guilty of practices contrary to the spirit of the *Torah* or does not observe his or her conjugal duties although living with the other spouse (after a hearing to determine who is to blame for the situation and the imposition of penalties);

(c) where a spouse engages in extra-marital relations, the guilty party suffers excommunication, because the halakhic alternative is stoning — which cannot be applied under modern circumstances.

On the other hand a woman cannot be divorced for sterility. In such a case the woman may permit the husband to marry another woman. (Today, bigamy is prohibited under Israeli state law.) In the event of the man's disappearing, the high priest may dissolve the marriage even against the wish of the woman.

Cases of divorce are very infrequent in the community. Because of the intense family orientation of Samaritan marriage, divorce may well lead to bitter dispute. The seriousness of divorce has meant strict examination of witnesses who must have observed the grounds to support divorce. Divorce judgments including the depositions of the witnesses are published, although they do not constitute precedents. Whilst there are no means for enforcing a divorce judgment and any penalties it may involve, the social sanction of ostracism is common, particularly where the woman is the guilty party and refuses to pay the penalty that may have been imposed. No priest will remarry her until she has complied. The divorce ceremony is carried out in the presence of the parties' relatives, along with the priests and tribal elders and three or four of the witnesses. The high priest reads the divorce aloud and then appends his signature; the witnesses also sign the document which is then delivered by the man to the woman and subsequently destroyed.

8. The Halakhah and the Samaritans

The Samaritans, called *Cuthim* in Rabbinic literature, are frequently mentioned in various ways; a separate tractate, *Cuthim*, composed after the completion of the *Talmud*, is devoted to them.[9] Apparently the Rabbis were aware of the Samaritan claim of descent from the tribe of Joseph, but they did not acknowledge it.[10]

Two main periods may be distinguished within rabbinic literature dealing with relations with the Samaritans. The first was during the period of the Second Temple and soon after its destruction. Then, the Samaritans were trusted to observe most of the biblical prescriptions, the majority concerning matters of prohibition and permission. The *halakhah* was largely influenced by R. Shimon b. Gamliel's dictum that 'every commandment observed by the Samaritans was kept more scrupulously by them than by the Jews' (*T. Pes.* 1:15, *B. Kidd.* 76a, *Gitt.* 10a). Thus animals slaughtered according to their rules and their produce were not prohibited. Socially, of course, the Samaritans were not treated as a part of the Jewish people; hence restrictions developed on the use of wine produced by them and limitations on the sale of land and houses to them.

In the second period their status came into dispute: R. Ishmael took the view that they had became Jews under compulsion, 'through fear of lions', and were therefore not truly Jewish, while R. Akiba maintained that they were 'true' converts (*B. Kidd.* 75b). The reasons for excluding them lay in the problems arising from their deficient observance of the *halakhah* regarding marriage. Despite an earlier 'liberal' attitude towards them (as in the view of R. Akiba), a period of 'deterioration' set in later, as a result of which they were treated more stringently and gradually subjected to a number of restrictive rulings with the purpose of keeping them separate from the Jews. Thus R. Meir prohibited the use of their wine and later R. Gamliel prohibited the consumption of animals slaughtered by them. Then, by the end of the talmudic period, the Rabbis enacted that they be treated as Gentiles, and thus the rift became complete.

The change in view reflects historical differences between these two periods: in the first, the Samaritans were more exacting in the commandments they actually observed; in the second, they wandered from the life of the *Torah* because of their assimilation into the idolatrous environment in which they lived in the coastal cities of Palestine, to which they gradually moved after the Bar Kochba uprising. The Rabbis even claimed that the image of 'a dove' was to be found on Mount Gerizim, imitating their idolatrous practices. Modern scholars, however, take the view that the dove is the 'magic' dove which the Romans set up to snare the Samaritans and not a native practice.[11] In any event, mutual distancing led to the second period in which they were treated as Gentiles.

The worsening of the situation between Jews and Samaritans is attributed not only to pure halakhic considerations, but also to the tension between the two communities that manifested itself after the Bar Kochba uprising as a result of the hostility to the Jewish cause shown by the Samaritans in the course of that uprising and their settling in those areas which the Jews had left in the wake of anti-Jewish Roman decrees. The deterioration of the situation is indeed expressed in the observations of R. Akiba and his disciples who lived at the time of the uprising.

Prohibition of intermarriage had already been mentioned in Nehemiah, and the Rabbis were particular in its observance. Originally the status of the Samaritans was a matter of dispute. Some held that the ban on marriage with them was merely rabbinic and that in truth they were genuine converts so that their marriages were valid (in the sense that a Jewish woman married to a Samaritan would require a *get*). Others took the view that although they were considered genuine converts, they were disqualified as regards their *shehitah* and the laws of evidence because they had become idol worshippers. In this respect their status was different from that of the Gentiles, since they were bound to observe the commandments which they denied.

Maimonides, however, abrogated the rule that they were genuine converts, holding that they should be treated completely as Gentiles from the viewpoint of Jewish law. The Rabbis treated the Samaritans as the offspring of the Cutheans mentioned in talmudic literature. The *Shulhan Arukh, Yoreh De'ah* 2:8 holds that 'the Cutheans of today are like idol worshippers', i.e. 'after they were interdicted in talmudic times' (*Taz, ibid*). Nevertheless their marriages are effective, since the *Shulhan Arukh* decides that a woman marrying one of them would require a *get* (*Shulhan Arukh, Even ha'ezer* 44:10), a ruling which involves serious problems of bastardy. Some later authorities tend to adopt the more stringent attitude, in accordance with Maimonides, and decide that they are Gentiles in every respect, and even their marriage does not take effect at all (e.g. *Shakh* on *Shulhan Arukh, Yoreh Deah* 159:5). Thus today the marriage of Samaritans with Jews is permitted only provided that they convert completely.[12]

9. *The Legal and Personal Status of the Samaritans in Israel*

With regard to the personal status of Samaritans in the State of Israel, matters of marriage and divorce are administered by the Samaritans' High Priest, the community's sole religious authority. Under State law (going back to the Mandate) he is empowered to act as their Registrar of marriages.[13] The High Priest's authority has been enhanced in practice by the fact that the State enrols in the Population Register not only the marriage certificates issued by the High Priest but also his divorce certificates.

The community today comprises five major families, each as a separate unit from the others. These families are rivals for influence and hegemony within the community. They are ranged in a hierarchy depending on historical prestige. Socially the most esteemed are the family of priests (ha-Cohen), the religious leaders of the community. The other families are that of Tsedakah, the Danfi (Altif and Sasoni) and Marchiv. Under these conditions inter-family marriage is unusual; each family considers it an obligation to remain intact to the extent that sometimes they will refrain from marrying off their girls altogether. All this creates difficulties, especially because the number of unmarried males is almost double that of unmarried women. In the past the High Priests also did not permit marriage with a non-Samaritan but the situation has now somewhat changed: whilst male Samaritans alone may marry Jewesses, that permission is on condition that the woman accepts the principles of the Samaritan religion. Even so, intermarriage is not always received with pleasure, particularly in Shechem. Whilst the Samaritan High Priest carries out marriages which are recognized by the State, up to the present the question of the validity of mixed marriages celebrated in Israel has not been authoritatively considered in the civil courts. The jurisdiction of the High Priest extends neither to non-consensual divorces nor to divorces involving an inter-married spouse; and such cases must be brought to the civil courts.

The Government of Israel decided in 1949, in answer to a question by the then future president, Itzhak ben Zvi, that Samaritans who had immigrated since the establishment of the State were to be treated like any Jewish immigrant coming from an Arab state.[14] Since then the Samaritans have received all the rights available to immigrants under the Law of Return and each of them is registered as a Samaritan or a Samaritan Jew in the Population Registry. Support for this procedure is also provided by the holding of Chief Rabbi Gaguine that they are a branch of the children of Israel (see p.61, above).

On the other hand, the Chief Rabbinate and the Rabbinical Courts decided in 1989 that the Samaritans are to be treated as Gentiles; this holding was in connection with an application by two Samaritan sisters to be converted in order to marry Jewish men. The Tel Aviv Rabbinical Court held that they required full conversion.[15] The problems surrounding the halakhic status of the Samaritans mainly concern intermarriage.

In 1992 the Government, decided that in view of the 1970 amendment of the Law of Return,[16] which defines a Jew ('a Jew means a person born to a Jewish mother or converted to Judaism and who is not a member of another religion') the Samaritans cannot be included in its provisions, because they are of 'another religion'. The Samaritans objected to this change of government policy and claimed that Samaritan tradition regarding their relations with the tribes of Israel (as distinct from those of Judah) did not exclude them from the definition of Jew in the Law of Return. Indeed no one would today dream of inquiring into the tribal affiliation of a Jew, the tribes having intermingled so extensively. Moreover, Ethiopian Jewry (Beta Israel) is considered in Rabbinic tradition as of the tribe of Dan and no one uses this fact to question their Jewishness.[17] It is also noteworthy that the Jewishness of the Karaites and other groups that do not follow Rabbinic tradition is not questioned.[18]

The changed attitude of the Government was consistent with the halakhic test of who is a Jew. However, this test governs the Rabbinical Courts Jurisdiction (Marriage and Divorce) Law[19] whereas interpretation of the definition of 'Jew' in the Law of Return is subject to a secular-national test, including a series of positive and negative components, both objective and subjective, such as Jewish descent, affiliation with a Jewish community and not belonging to another religion in everyday life.[20] These criteria, the policy of granting the Samaritans the right of return until 1992, and the arguments above, put into doubt the legality of the Government's 1992 decision.

In 1994, as a result of a petition by the Samaritans to the High Court of Justice, the Israeli Government reversed its position and signed an agreement — which was approved and became the judgment of the court — to the effect that:

> A Samaritan who comes to settle in the State of Israel is entitled to get an *oleh* visa [immigrant visa given to Jews] according to the Law of Return 5710-1950,[21] and will be treated in the same way as those Samaritan community members who settled in Israel from the establishment of the State until 1992.

Bibliography

Ben Ḥayyim, Z., *Ivrit ve-Aramit Nosaḥ Shomron* (Jerusalem: Mosad Bialik and Academy of the Hebrew Language, 1957-77, Hebrew, 5 vols).

Ben Zvi, I., *Sefer Hashomronim* (Jerusalem: Yad Itshak Ben Zvi, 1970, 2nd ed., Hebrew).

Boid, I.R.M., *Principles of Samaritan Halakhah* (Leiden: E.J. Brill, 1989).

Coggins, R.J., *Samaritans and Jews* (Oxford: Blackwell, 1975).

Crown, A.D., ed., *The Samaritans* (Tübingen: J.C.B. Mohr, 1989).

Gaster, M., *The Samaritans, Their History, Doctrines and Literature* (Oxford: Oxford University Press, 1925).

Montgomery, J.A., *The Samaritans, the Earliest Jewish Sect* (Philadelphia: J.C. Winston, 1907).

Rabello, A.M., *Giustiniano, Ebrei e Samaritani alla luce delle fonti storico-letterarie, ecclesiastiche e giuridiche* (Milan: Giuffrè, 1987-88, 2 vols.).

Shur, N., *History of the Samaritans* (Frankfurt am Main: Verlag Peter Lang, 1989).

Notes

1   S. Talmon, "Biblical Tradition of the Early History of the Samaritans", in *Eretz Shomron* (Jerusalem: Hahevrah lahakirot Erets Yisrael va'atikoteha, 1974), 19-37.

2   See H. Tadmor, "Introductory Remarks to a New Edition of the Annals of Tiglath-Pileser III", *Proceedings of the Israel Academy of Sciences and Humanities* 2/9 (1967), 168-87.

3   See I. Ben Zvi, *Sefer hashomronim* (Jerusalem: Yad Yizhak Ben Zvi, 1970, 2nd ed.), 57, 367 (in Hebrew).

4   The Samaritan script developed over the centuries before the Christian era as a branch of ancient Hebrew script which was abandoned by the Jews in favour of the Assyrian script. The original script is to be found on ancient Jewish documents and in archaeological remains. It is still retained by the Samaritans in their writings. Their pronunciation differs from Hebrew. Hebrew writings as such among the Samaritans have been preserved since the 14th century. In early times Greek was widespread among them but little of this remains. The Samaritan translation of the Bible into Greek is called *Samareitikon* and was composed apparently in Palestine between the 1st and 4th centuries. There exists another translation, in Arabic, by Abu Sayid (13th century). Most of the Samaritan literature extant today is written in Samaritan Aramaic and Arabic.

5   See M. Greenberg, "The Decalogue Tradition Critically Examined", in *The Ten Commandments in History and Tradition*, ed. B.Z. Segal (Jerusalem: Magnes Press, 1990), 91, 94.

6   See Z. Ben Hayyim, *Tevat Markha* (Jerusalem: Israeli National Academy for Sciences, 1988).

7 See in particular the survey by I.R.M. Boid, "The Samaritan Halakha", in A.D. Crown, ed., *The Samaritans* (Tübingen: J.C.B. Mohr, 1989) 625-51; *idem, Principles of Samaritan Halakhah* (Leiden: E.J. Brill, 1989).

8 Written by Naji b. Khidr, ms. Sulzberger 18 of the Jewish Theological Seminary. The passage is cited as translated by Boid, "The Samaritan Halakha", *supra* n.7, at 638.

9 See H. Higger, ed., in *Sheva Maṣekhtot Ḳetanot* (New York: Bloch, 1930), and his introduction therein.

10 See *Bereshit Rabbah*, ed. Albeck, 1178.

11 Ben Zvi, *supra* n.3, at 367.

12 Cf. n.15 below and references therein.

13 In accordance with the Marriage and Divorce (Registration) Ordinance of 1919 (Drayton, *Laws of Palestine*, vol. II, p. 903).

14 See the statement of the Minister of Foreign Affairs, M. Sharet, in the Knesset (Ben Zvi, *supra* n.3, at 365).

15 See the decision of the Tel Aviv Regional Rabbinical Court headed by Rabbi Shlomo Dikhovsky (1985). This decision was adopted by the former Chief Rabbi of Israel, Abraham Kahane Shapira (File no. 100/86 of the Supreme Rabbinical Court of Israel). The full text of the decision was published in *Torah Shebe'al peh* 29 (1988), 59-67.

16 Law of Return (Amendment no. 2) 1970, s.4B, *Laws of the State of Israel* 24 (1969/70) 28.

17 See M. Corinaldi, *Ethiopian Jewry — Identity and Tradition* (Jerusalem: Rubin Mass, 1988), 179-229 (in Hebrew).

18 See M. Corinaldi, *The Personal Status of the Karaites* (Jerusalem: Rubin Mass, 1984), 101-75 (in Hebrew). On the Karaites, see Ch.9, below.

19 *Laws of the State of Israel* 7 (5713/1952-53), 139.

20 See H.C. 265/87 *Beresford* v. *Minister of Interior* (1989) 43 P.D.(4) 793, *per* Justice Barak; Justice Elon, on the other hand (in *Beresford, ibid.*), put the emphasis on the *halakhah*, but extended the test's substance and scope in accordance with "the universe of Judaism with all its spiritual and historical components". If this test had been applied, the problem of the Samaritans' rights, according to the Law of Return, would probably have remained unsolved.

21 H.C 4200/93 *The Samaritan Community in Israel* v. *The Prime Minister of Israel* (unpublished).

4

JEWISH LAW AND HELLENISTIC LEGAL PRACTICE IN THE LIGHT OF GREEK PAPYRI FROM EGYPT

by

JOSEPH MÉLÈZE MODRZEJEWSKI
Université de Paris I - Sorbonne

1. *Sources and Literature*

Papyrus is an Egyptian plant of the family of sedges, or Cyperaceae (*Cyperus Papyrus*), with a tall triangular stem and a feathery crown. Formed into scrolls or sheets, it was the principal substance conveying the written word during Antiquity. Consequently, 'papyrology' is the science devoted to the study of these texts. By scholarly consensus, however, the term 'papyrology' is restricted to texts written in Greek and (more rarely) Latin, while the study of papyri written in Egyptian remains a branch of 'Egyptology'.[1] Documents in Aramaic and Hebrew must be left to specialists in Semitic languages.[2]

The story of papyrology begins on Egyptian soil just over 100 years ago. Towards the end of the nineteenth century, a great harvest of documents written on papyrus was reaped on the desert borders of the Nile valley and in the oasis of the Faiyum, heralding the emergence of a new scientific discipline. Subsequent excavations and purchases have incessantly augmented the impressive inventory of ancient texts written on papyrus and discovered in Egypt. When it brought to light long-lost works of Greek literature, such as Aristotle's *Constitution of Athens*, papyrology made the headlines. But its principal focus has been the discovery of the tens of thousands of documentary texts, documents in the literal sense: legal rules and regulations, contracts, wills, fiscal receipts, accounts, correspondence both administrative and private, etc.

This documentation is of capital importance for Jewish legal and social history. Aramaic documents discovered on the island of Elephantine, near Aswan (ancient Syene), afford us a glimpse into the life of a Judaean military colony in the fifth century B.C.E., when Egypt was a province of the Persian empire.[3] Since the conquest of the country by Alexander the Great (332/331 B.C.E.), numerous Greek papyri dealing with the Jews and Jewish affairs have afforded us fresh insights into the world of the Diaspora in Egypt under the Ptolemies, and later under Roman domination.[4] They furnish unparalleled material for the study of Jewish legal practice during the Graeco-Roman period.[5]

Greek papyri and ostraca from Egypt concerning Jews and Judaism have been collected in the *Corpus Papyrorum Judaicarum* (= *CPJud.*).[6] We do not possess a comprehensive study of Jewish legal practice in Ptolemaic and Roman Egypt based on the now-available papyrological evidence, but we do have general manuals on that body of law.[7] They pay but little attention to the Jews and their legal problems. The present chapter appears as a first attempt in this field.

2. *Personal Status*

The author of the *Letter of Aristeas* (§§12-14), followed by Josephus,[8] informs us that Ptolemy I deported 100,000 Jews from Judaea to Egypt, between 320 and 301 B.C.E. Our knowledge of the first Jewish settlements in Egypt favors the opposing tradition attributed to Hecataeus of Abdera, according to which the Jews followed the king voluntarily.[9] Whichever is correct, Jewish slaves doubtless existed in Ptolemaic and Roman Egypt. A document dating from Diocletian's reign relates how a Jewish maid and her two (or three) children were redeemed from slavery by the Jewish community of Oxyrhynchus, in conformity with the principles of talmudic law.[10]

The causes of enslavement varied; however, slavery for debts must be excluded. Victor Tcherikover supposed that he had found an example of such enslavement for debt in a Ptolemaic testament dated 238/237 B.C.E., in which a Jewish debtor, Apollonios *alias* Jonathas, was mentioned alongside the slaves of the testator.[11] But since enslavement for private debts was illegal in Ptolemaic Egypt, this may be doubted.[12] In any case, voluntary immigration and not captivity was by far the principal source of the Jewish settlement in the Ptolemaic kingdom, as it was for other Greek-speaking immigrants.

The Greeks who came to Egypt after the Macedonian conquest retained their original mainland citizenship. Some of them acquired new citizenship in the cities founded by Alexander and Ptolemy I, Alexandria and Ptolemais. An Athenian who had settled in Krokodilopolis remained 'Athenian' (*Athenaios*), as did his descendants, since citizenship was hereditary. His great-grandson would certainly have serious difficulties in being recognized as a fellow-citizen of the 'true' Athenians in Athens. But in Egypt, this reference to a civic homeland was a vital matter for the immigrants' descendants: it guaranteed their belonging to the community of Hellenes.

The status of 'Hellene' was recognized as extending to a mass of individuals stemming from the North and Northwest regions, as well as those from lands such as Macedonia or Thrace, once considered as barbaric but which were now included in the expanding cultural sphere of the Greek universe. By extension, Asiatics and Semites from the countries Alexander had conquered were also considered 'Hellenes', provided they spoke Greek and served the royal dynasty. The community of 'Hellenes' guaranteed to each of its members a status reconciling the maintenance of his own national identity with his incorporation into the dominant group. This state of affairs suited the Jews perfectly.

Some scholars have imagined that the Jews in Egypt were divided into distinct autonomous bodies called *politeumata*.[13] But the term *politeuma* (πολίτευμα), as applied to the Jewish diaspora in Egypt, is attested only in a literary text dealing with Alexandrian Jews, the *Letter of Aristeas,* where it does not have a precise technical meaning. No mention of a Jewish *politeuma* in the *chora* (the countryside, in opposition to Alexandria) occurs in Ptolemaic documents published so far. There is, indeed, reference to *politikoi nomoi* ('civic laws') in a royal regulation quoted by a Jewish litigant at Krokodilopolis,[14] but this is not sufficient evidence for the existence of a Jewish *politeuma* in that town: the regulation was issued for all Greek-speaking immigrants, not for the Jews alone. The same applies to the poetical use of the terms *politai*, 'fellow-citizens', *polis*, 'city', and *politarches,* 'ruler of a city', in the epigraphical material from the necropolis of Tell el-Yehoudieh; these texts hardly support the supposition that the Jewish settlement in Leontopolis was 'organized as a politeuma'.[15] The concept of Jewish *politeumata* as independent political units must be regarded as a 'historiographical legend'.[16]

If the Jews in Ptolemaic Egypt enjoyed a kind of 'civic status', it was not because they were organized in 'civic communities'; the deciding factor was their inclusion in the community of Hellenes, a 'civic body', as opposed to the native population. From the Greek viewpoint, the ethnic designation *Ioudaios* opened the portals of this community to the Jews, as other 'foreign' ethnic designations did for all those who adhered to Greek culture by adopting its tongue and its social customs, and who could give proof of a respectable origin outside Egypt, regarded as 'Greek'. In the third century B.C.E., in Trikomia (Faiyum), a village having a considerable Jewish population, a number of persons — most of whom, if not all, are Jewish — are listed as 'Hellenes living in the house of Maron'.[17] We can draw a parallel between this document and the complaint of the Macedonian Ptolemaios, son of Glaukias, concerning an outrage which has been committed on him 'although he was a Hellene' (παρὰ τὸ ῞Ελληνά με εἶναι).[18] To be a *Ioudaios* in Ptolemaic Egypt was not very different from being a *Makedon*. As distinguished from the native Egyptians, both were 'Hellenes'.

A considerable part of the Jewish population lived in Alexandria. Traditionally, this settlement is supposed to have begun during Alexander's lifetime;[19] by the beginning of the Roman period the Jews are thought to have represented roughly a third of the inhabitants of Alexandria: 180,000 Jews for a population of 500,000–600,000.[20] According to the author of the *Letter of Aristeas* (§ 310) they had their 'elders', *presbyteroi* (πρεσβύτεροι), and their 'leaders' (ἡγούμενοι τοῦ πλήθους); at the end of the Ptolemaic period and at the beginning of the Roman domination an ethnarch administered Jewish affairs in Alexandria.[21] However, like so many other inhabitants of that great cosmopolitan city, the Jews were not Alexandrian citizens, barring a few exceptional cases, as rare as those of Alexandrian Jews who were granted the Roman citizenship (such as that of the alabarch Alexander, brother of the philosopher Philo, and his sons, Marcus Julius Alexander and Tiberius Julius Alexander, who became procurator of Judaea and prefect of Egypt[22]). Since they were not 'Alexandrians' (Ἀλεξανδρεῖς), citizens *stricto sensu,* they were 'Jews of Alexandria' (Ἰουδαῖοι οἱ ἀπὸ Ἀλεξανδρείας).[23]

In this respect, the Jewish settlement in Alexandria did not differ from those we encounter in the *chora*: Jews *of* this or that town (ἀπό) or residing *in* such and such a place (ἐν).[24] They had their representatives, called *presbyteroi* (πρεσβύτεροι), the 'elders', or even *archontes* (ἄρχοντες), the 'rulers'.[25] The first mention of a Jewish community as such, termed *synagoge* (συναγωγή), 'assembly', dates from the reign of Diocletian, in the late third century C.E.[26]

The heightened self-awareness of the Jews in Ptolemaic Egypt under the influence of the Septuagint did not change the legal situation.[27] Neither 'citizens' nor 'autonomous aliens', the Jews were just one of the various elements composing the society of Greek-speaking conquerors. Nothing but his religion distinguished a Jew from his Graeco-Macedonian neighbours. He was a fully-fledged member of the dominant group of 'Hellenes', the equal of any other Greek-speaking immigrant. His personal status determined his legal behaviour in everyday matters: adhering to Greek culture, the Jew adopted Hellenistic legal customs.

The community of 'Hellenes' did not survive the Roman conquest of Egypt (30 B.C.E.). The new organization of Egyptian society under Roman rule was unfavourable to the Jews: they were not included in the orders of provincial notables created by the Imperial Government with the aim of 'saving' the Greek elements, on whom it depended to staff the local administration.[28] However, this detorioration of their status did not change the behaviour of the Jews as far as private law was concerned. In this respect, the papyrological evidence of early Roman Egypt supplements that of the Ptolemaic period.

3. *The Torah*

At the end of the fourth century B.C.E., the Jews who returned to Egypt in the wake of the Macedonian conquest took with them their most treasured possession: the *Torah* of Moses in the form that Ezra had established a century earlier. We can lend credence to the words of Hecataeus of Abdera, when, in a 'revised version' elaborated in Judaeo-Egyptian circles and quoted by Josephus, he relates the arrival in Egypt, towards 300 B.C.E., of a Jewish 'high priest' (*archiereus,* a member of the sacerdotal aristocracy) Ezekias, bringing a scroll of the *Torah* for public reading.[29] It was customary at the time to read the *Torah* aloud on Sabbath days or on one of the Jewish festivals. Ezekias read from the Hebrew text, but the problem of a Greek translation was soon to arise.

Who decided to translate the *Torah* into Greek, and why? Two opposing doctrines are currently professed. A Jewish legend (later adopted by the Christians) first recorded in the *Letter of Aristeas to Philocrates*[30] attributed the initiative for the translation to King Ptolemy II Philadelphus, who commissioned the translation for the Library of Alexandria.[31] This thesis coincides with rabbinical tradition, which considered the translation to have been intended for the King Ptolemy ('Talmai').[32] In modern times, Elias Bickerman was among the scholars accepting this thesis of a royal initiative.[33]

A second opinion, defended by Paul Kahle and more recently by Arnaldo Momigliano,[34] places the translation of the *Torah* within the perspective of synagogal practice. The Jewish immigrants adopted the Greek language so rapidly and so completely that they no longer understood Hebrew, and were in dire need of a version of the Scriptures they could understand. Just as an Aramaic translation, the *targum*, was to accompany the reading of the *Torah* in Jerusalem and in Judaea, a Greek translation was used in Alexandria and throughout Egypt. The future Septuagint was, at first, a kind of Greek *targum*, which existed in different variants. Towards the end of the second century B.C.E., a decision was made to provide a unified text. According to Kahle, it was this 'revised version', later to become the official text of the Christian Church, that the *Letter of Aristeas* was supposed to promote.

To choose between the thesis of a royal commission for the Library of Alexandria, and the thesis of a Greek *targum* designed uniquely to fulfill the needs of the Jewish diaspora would amount to placing us needlessly on the horns of a dilemma. The mere fact that the Jewish subjects of King Ptolemy no longer understood the language in which their national Law was couched probably was the least of the King's worries. But the Jews accounted for a considerable percentage of the Ptolemaic kingdom's population, in Egypt as well as in Judaea (which was an integral part of the realm throughout the third century B.C.E.). Assimilated to the reigning minority with regard to their language and social status, they were set apart by their religion, which referred to a Law reputedly of divine inspiration. Guaranteeing the respect of this Law could only prove advantageous to the régime. However, for its effective application, the royal judges and officials needed a Greek translation. The practical concerns of the monarchy were convergent with the religious needs of the Jews of Egypt.

In this respect, it is highly instructive to confront the Greek *Torah* with what we know of the Ptolemaic régime's attitude toward the national traditions of the native Egyptian population. The ancient Egyptians did not find it necessary to possess a corpus of written law. The first collection of Egyptian legal rules was apparently made only during the Persian domination, on the initiative of Darius I (522-486 B.C.E.). Its substance might have survived the Macedonian conquest in the Egyptian priestly *Case-Book*.[35] The latter is known by several demotic papyri from the Ptolemaic period. The most important of these is a long text discovered in Tuna el-Gebel during the 1938-1939 season of excavations, but published only in 1975 under a misleading title: *The Demotic Legal Code of Hermopolis West*;

other fragments from the late Ptolemaic period have recently come to light among the papyri of the collections in Florence and in Copenhagen.[36]

The *Case-Book* was a collection of practical prescriptions devised to assist native judges and notaries in their daily routine, by furnishing models for the drafting of documents and legal decisions, and suggestions for the solution of difficult cases. It was kept in existence by the Egyptian priests, guardians of their national law, as a 'holy book' in local variants which might differ from one religious center to another. In the first half of the third century B.C.E., under the reign of Ptolemy II Philadelphus, it was translated from the original demotic into Greek (P. Oxy. XLVI 3285). The Greek version preserved by that document corresponds only partially to the Hermopolis text.[37] The translation was based on another variant of the compendium, its 'official version', which did not come down to us. It made the rules of Egyptian law, noted down by the priests in their 'holy books', accessible to the Greek-speaking agents of the royal administration.

The parallel between the two 'holy books' translated into Greek under the first Ptolemies — the Egyptian priestly *Case-Book* and the *Torah* of Moses — helps us to determine the conditions under which the *Torah* could continue to play its fundamental role amongst the Jewish Diaspora in Egypt. We cannot follow Tcherikover's supposition that the right 'to live according to their ancestral laws' had been granted to the Jews of Egypt by the Ptolemies in the same form as it was to the Jews of Jerusalem and Judaea by the Seleucids.[38] In Egypt, the confirmation of the Jewish Law did not take the form of a 'charter', nor could it refer to the Temple, as had been the case with the *Torah* of Ezra, confirmed as a royal law for the Jews of the realm after the return from captivity in Babylon. It was achieved by the bias of a translation guaranteed by the authority of the Ptolemaic monarchy. Its purpose was to serve the administration of justice within the framework of a system established to protect the laws and customs of the kingdom's inhabitants.

4.   Courts and Procedure

The confirmation of the *Torah* did not lead to the establishment of autonomous Jewish jurisdictions. The existence of Jewish tribunals in Alexandria is highly questionable. Philo's book *De Specialibus Legibus* reflects his own interpretation of the Biblical laws rather than the actual jurisprudence of Jewish courts.[39] The competence of the ethnarch in the judicial domain was limited to a kind of arbitration;[40] the same applies to the

Alexandrian *beth-din* mentioned in rabbinical sources.[41] Papyrological documents show the Jews in Egypt bringing their claims and business affairs before the regular instances of State justice. This fact can be easily explained in the pluralistic context of the Ptolemaic organisation of the courts.

Ptolemaic Egypt offers the legal historian a particularly interesting example of legal pluralism.[42] As we have seen, Egyptian local law, which the Greeks called *nomoi tes choras* (νόμοι τῆς χώρας), the 'law of the land', was still in force for the indigenous population. The immigrants had imported their own legal traditions: the Greek *nomoi*. In the cities — Alexandria, Naucratis, Ptolemais — these took the traditional form of written legislation, often influenced by the reigning monarch. In the *chora*, they spread as a substantially homogeneous customary law, the 'common law' of the Greeks. Over and against the Greek and Egyptian *nomoi*, the will of the Ptolemaic sovereign was expressed in royal regulations, *diagrammata* (διαγράμματα), and orders, *prostagmata* (προστάγματα).

Faced with the problems created by the existence of legal rules of unequal weight and of various provenance, the Ptolemies did not strive to unify the content of these various legal sources. Another solution was found: the kingdom was blanketed by a double network of jurisdictions, each one authorized to deal with the cases falling within its specific nationally-determined competence: the dicasteries in the cities and in the *chora* for the Greek-speaking immigrants, and the courts of *laocritae* ('people's judges'), staffed by Egyptian priests, for cases involving the indigenous population; the king reserved the right of intervention in any and all litigation, either directly or indirectly, through the *chrematistae,* royal judges.[43]

How did the Law of Moses fit into this picture? A lawsuit involving Jewish litigants, Dositheos and Herakleia daughter of Diosdotos, affords us our first glimpse of the system in action.[44] The case was to be judged in 226 B.C.E., in the dicastery of Krokodilopolis (Faiyum). All the judges were Greek. Dositheos had accused Herakleia of insulting him in public and ripping his coat, causing him 200 drachmas' worth of damages. At the last minute, however, he lost his nerve and failed to appear before the court. Herakleia did not desist but, appearing in her own defence, produced, *inter alia,* an extract from a royal regulation, a *diagramma,* concerning the rules of law to be applied by the local dicasteries to Greek-speaking litigants. According to this regulation, priority lay with royal legislation, represented by the *diagrammata.* But the king, well aware of the limits of his legislation (which was restricted to administrative and fiscal matters), had decided in the *diagramma* that, in the absence of an available disposition of the royal law, the judges should resort to 'civic laws', *politikoi nomoi* (πολιτικοὶ νόμοι); if these were insufficient to guide them to a decision, they had to follow the 'most equitable view', *gnome dikaiotate* (γνώμη δικαιοτάτη). Any Hellene could require the judges of the dicasteries to try him according to 'civic laws'. As a 'Hellene', a Jew could invoke the royal *diagramma* bearing this authorization. There was thus a close link between royal justice and the law applicable to Jews. But what exactly was this link?

To answer this question, we must be sure that we understand the exact meaning of all the terms of the regulation. The *diagrammata,* an expression *par excellence* of the king's will, create no major difficulties. Neither does the 'most equitable view', *gnome dikaiotate,* a well-known traditional Greek notion responding to the problem of gaps in the law. The term 'civic laws', *nomoi politikoi,* is more obscure. According to Hans Julius Wolff, it designated the 'national laws' of the litigants. If these latter were of common origin — citizens of the same city or their descendants or, as in the present case, members of the same ethnic group — Wolff believed that the king, in the absence of the appropriate royal legislation, had authorized the judges to apply the laws of the litigants' homeland.[45]

A curious problem arises here, since one never hears of an Athenian law, for example, being applied in Egypt to plaintiffs of Athenian origin. This is why Wolff's hypothesis should be interpreted *cum grano salis:* the regulation should be taken more as an intention than a reality. The Alexandrian law-makers may well have envisaged the possibility of applying the litigants' national law as a subsidiary law, to fill the gaps of the royal legislation. But that project was not carried out, and the term 'civic laws' came to designate the actual legal practice of the Greek-speaking immigrants; this practice was 'civic', since it was based on the traditions of Greek cities, as opposed to the village world of the native population. In other words, the term became synonymous with Greek 'common law', the legal *koine.*

The intentions of the legislator had, nonetheless, important practical consequences. Whether the 'civic laws' stemmed from the litigants' national legislation (as the legislators had intended) or from the documents actually employed in practice (everyday reality), the legal traditions of the Greek-speaking population became the official legal corpus for the dicasteries, liable to enforcement by the courts. Egyptian law (*nomoi tes choras*), for its part, became the legal corpus for the courts of the *laocritae,* applicable to native litigants. The two groups of *nomoi,* corresponding to the two groups of the population, had been raised to the status of 'laws of the court', *leges fori,* for their respective tribunals.[46] One might speak of a 'judicial legalisation' of legal rules which did not originate in the royal legislative activity.

For the Jews, this decision had still another meaning. When they immigrated to Egypt, the Greek-speaking colonists did not import their ancestral laws. The Jews did: they are the one exception of whom we surely have knowledge. In accordance with the royal *diagramma,* the *Torah* of Moses, 'the Books of the Law of the Jews' (τοῦ νόμου τῶν Ἰουδαίων βιβλία) as the *Letter of Aristeas* (§30) calls it, was a *politikos nomos,* applicable to Jewish litigants by the royal justice. In other words, the Septuagint became a 'civic law' for the Jews of Egypt.

This conclusion is supported by a Ptolemaic papyrus containing the complaint of a certain Helladote, daughter of Philonides, married to a Jew named Jonathas.[47] Helladote is referring to her marriage concluded 'in accordance with the civic law of the Jews', κατὰ τὸν νόμον πολιτικὸν τῶν Ἰουδαίων.[48] The *politikoi nomoi* could be invoked before the dicasteries as well as before royal officials who examined the complaints (*enteuxeis*), formally addressed to the king. The 'civic law of the Jews' (νόμος πολιτικὸς τῶν Ἰουδαίων) is nothing else than the *Torah* of Moses, in the Greek version established in Alexandria half a century before the date of this document.

5. *Family Law*

A. Status of Women

During the proceedings before the dicastery in Krokodilopolis, described above, the Jewess Herakleia was accompanied by her legal guardian, Aristides son of Proteas, an Athenian born in Egypt. Herakleia was following a Greek custom. So were other Jewish women whom we meet in papyrological documents from the Ptolemaic and early Roman periods assisted by their guardians (*kyrioi*) in judicial and legal activities; this evidence is corroborated by Philo, in contradiction to talmudic law, which did not require women over the age of 12 to employ guardians.[49] We can subscribe to Tcherikover's conclusion that the life of a Jewish woman in Hellenistic Egypt 'was far more like that of her Greek neighbour than that of her sister in Palestine'.[50]

Fiscal documents from Apollinopolis Magna (modern Edfu) show that Jewish fathers in Egypt exercised their rights and duties in family life in a manner which corresponded both to Jewish tradition and local custom. The father was fiscally responsible for the members of his family.[51] Another fiscal document shows that Jewish girls in Egypt were betrothed and married at a very early age, in accordance with a usage common to Jews and Greeks. A young woman aged 20 had two children, one of them being five years old: she had been married at the age of 14 years, if not earlier; this was also the case of two other young women, both aged 22, who each had children four years old.[52] The paucity of children attested by these documents might lead to the remark that the biblical exhortation of *Gen.* 1:28, 'Be fruitful and multiply', was not perfectly followed by Egyptian Jews; it does not justify the conclusion that they had adopted the Greek custom of exposing new-born children.[53]

B. Marriage

A Jewish *ketubbah* (marriage contract) in a papyrus from the Cologne University collection was published in 1986.[54] Written in Antinoopolis on 15 November 417 C.E., this is the only dated Jewish document of this period. It records the marriage of Samuel, son of Sampati (Sampathaios), and Metra, daughter of Eleazar and Esther, an Alexandrian family. The Aramaic text is strewn with Greek words in Hebrew transliteration, including items of the trousseau and the consular date: an important testimony to the continuing use of Greek by Jews in Byzantine Egypt.

Nothing similar to the Cologne *ketubbah* has been found in the papyri from the Ptolemaic and early Roman periods prior to the revolt of 115-117 C.E. The late Edoardo Volterra suggested that the wording of Helladote's complaint, against a man 'holding her as a wife (ἔχειν με γυναῖκα) according to the civic law of the Jews', might reproduce the traditional formula of the *ketubbah* declaring the marriage 'conform to the Law of Moses and Israel', *kedat Moshe veYisrael* (כדת משה וישראל). Since the Ptolemaic judge would not have been able to understand the expression 'Law of Moses', νόμος Μοϋσέως in Greek, Helladote preferred to speak of the 'civic law of the Jews', νόμος πολιτικὸς τῶν Ἰουδαίων.[55] She invoked the *Torah*, although the marriage formula is not to be found in the biblical text.

Volterra's hypothesis could be reinforced by the variant of the formula in which 'Israel' is replaced by 'Jews', *Yehudaei* (כדת משה ויהודאי) — an exact counterpart of the Greek 'of the Jews' (τῶν Ἰουδαίων) in Helladote's complaint; that variant is attested in documents found in the Dead Sea region[56] as well as in Palestinian marriage and divorce acts from the Cairo Geniza;[57] according to the Talmud, it was also employed by Alexandrian Jews.[58] This convergence does not inform us what exactly was the form of

Helladote's marriage contract; the verb συγγράφεσθαι, 'to draw up a contract' in her complaint refers to a Greek rather than to a Jewish document, although *syngraphe* would be a reasonable translation of *ketubbah*.[59] A contemporary document concerning a Jewish family in the Faiyum clearly mentions a Greek 'deed of cohabitation', *syngraphe synoikisiou* (συγγραφὴ συνοικισίου).[60] In all likelihood, the *syngraphe* was the usual form of concluding marriage among Hellenized Jews in Egypt. At the beginning of the Roman period, the *synchoresis* (συνχώρησις), 'judicial compromise', was used by Alexandrian Jews. This does not exclude recourse to traditional Jewish forms, a duality which is attested by the Babatha 'archive' for the provincial practice in *Erets Israel* under the Roman Principate.[61] Parallel recourse to both Jewish and Greek forms is not directly attested.

C. Intermarriage

A mixed marriage between a Jew and an Egyptian woman (or between an Egyptian and a Jewish woman[62]) was not totally unthinkable, but very difficult to imagine in the light of the documentary material now available. Marriages between 'Hellenes', under which heading the Jews fell, and native Egyptians were a very rare occurrence in Hellenistic Egypt. Not that they were forbidden by law, as were mixed marriages in Athens at the epoch of the orators, but because a kind of 'cultural agamy' rendered them impracticable. Exceptionally, in certain circles and at certain times, the barriers were lifted.[63]

The problem the Jews of Egypt had to solve was not the avoidance — or the acceptance — of family alliances with Egyptian notables; they had to find a way to reconcile their friendship with their Greek comrades-in-arms and their desire to preserve their proper identity, which mixed marriages could jeopardize. During the third century B.C.E., intermarriage between Jews and Greeks did not create special difficulties from the legal point of view: a pagan woman who married a Jew was integrated into her husband's group. Helladote daughter of Philonides, to judge from her name and patronymic, was Greek. She was accepted into the community of her husband at the moment when she became the spouse of the Jew Jonathas.

In the second century B.C.E., after the process of conversion to Judaism had been 'invented', the question became more serious.[64] No clear answer seems yet to have been given, either in practice or in theory: compare Philo's vigour in defending the prohibition of mixed marriages with his apology for matrimonial ecumenism, which he simultaneously recommended.[65] The novel *Joseph and Asenath* sets forth a simple and optimistic solution of the problem: conversion to Judaism of the Greek woman who wished to espouse a Jew.[66] Modern Rabbinic Judaism was to reject it. But as early as the *Pirke de-Rabbi Eliezer,* ch. 38, Asenath is not the daughter of a heathen priest, as she was in the novel: she is the child of Jacob's daughter Dinah, who had been ravished by Shechem, son of Hamor the Hivite. In that version, Joseph marries his own niece, who is Jewish because born of a Jewish mother: between Alexandria and the *Midrash*, the *Mishnah* had instituted the strict rule that the child's status followed that of the mother.[67] The Alexandrian solution became inadequate because of the high priority placed on lineage in the classical rabbinic period.

D. Divorce

The Jewish law of divorce was applied in the case of Helladote, the unhappy wife of the Jew Jonathas: Jonathas had repudiated his spouse in the traditional manner sanctioned by *Deut.* 24:1.[68] The Jewish institution was in flagrant contradiction to current Greek matrimonial custom: in the marriage contracts preserved in the papyri, the husband promised formally not to repudiate, literally not to 'throw out' (μὴ ἐκβάλλειν) his wife.[69] Now Helladote had well and truly been 'thrown out'. This discrepancy between Jewish law and Greek practice was the cause of Helladote's outrage and the prime motive for her complaint.[70] Unfortunately, we ignore its outcome. The last line of the document indicates that Helladote requested the return of her dowry; we may suppose that the case has been decided in her favour.

Two hundred years later, in 13 B.C.E., Apollonia, daughter of Sambathion and Eirene, and Hermogenes, son of Hermogenes, a Jewish couple from Alexandria, put an end to their union by mutual consent in the shape of a 'judicial compromise' (*synchoresis*), in defiance of the biblical ruling.[71] The Jewishness of the couple has been questioned, but it is proved by the names of the parties. Sambathion is one of the Greek forms of Shabtai (שבתי), a Jewish name related to the sabbatical rest. Since the first century C.E. it was borrowed by non-Jews, but this could not be the case of Apollonia's father, a man who was born about the mid-first century B.C.E. (he had a married daughter in 17 B.C.E.).[72] Eirene, 'the Peaceful', is a good semantical equivalent to Salome. Apollonia, paradoxically enough, is a quite suitable name for an Alexandrian Jewess; another Apollonia, almost certainly Jewish[73], and several Jews named Apollonios appear in papyrological and epigraphical sources from Egypt.[74]

As to Apollonia's husband, Hermogenes, scholars regarded him as a Greek, or a Jew granted Alexandrian citizenship. But the reading of the word which was supposed to indicate his deme ('Αρχηγέτης or 'Αρχηγέτειος) or his tribe ('Αρχιστράτειος) is very uncertain.[75] The restoration ἀρχηγ(οῦ) would make more sense; *archegos* (ἀρχηγός) is a term employed by the Septuagint, Josephus, Philo, and epigraphical evidence for Jewish 'leaders'.[76] Hermogenes might have exercised official functions in the Jewish community of Alexandria, e.g. as the head of a synagogue, *archegos* being in this case an equivalent to *archisynagogos* (ἀρχισυνάγωγος) or *archiprostates* (ἀρχιπροστάτης), terms attested by a contemporary Alexandrian inscription.[77]

Under these circumstances, this Alexandrian *synchoresis* remains an important witness to the 'egalitarian divorce' in use among Hellenized Jews of the diaspora in the Second Temple period, alongside the bill of divorce (*get*) provided for in biblical law and rabbinical doctrine. These two methods of divorce are attested in Jewish practice of that period: one subscribed to the unilateral repudiation of the wife by the husband, while the other recognized reciprocity in this domain. The principle according to which the wife could initiate divorce proceedings had already been adopted by the Jews in Elephantine.[78] Greek influence obviously abetted the egalitarian tendency by affording it a favourable social climate. Spurred, doubtless, by a desire to accentuate the difference between Jews and non-Jews, rabbinical Judaism was to have the last word, eventually imposing unilateral repudiation as the sole accepted procedure.[79] Egalitarian pressure persisted for a long while, however, as is attested by clauses in marriage contracts in which the wife could initiate divorce proceedings with the court's assistance.[80]

6. *Contracts*

In the province of commercial transactions the Greek environment must have exercised a stronger influence on Jewish legal practice than in family life. The prohibition of loans with interest will serve as a touchstone.

The Jews of Egypt could not yet have known of the talmudic doctrine, condemning not only interest itself, *ribbit* (רבית), but any form of enrichment resembling interest, 'the dust of interest', *avaq deribbit* (אבק דרבית); but they must have been aware of the biblical interdiction, thrice repeated in the *Torah* (*Ex.* 22:24; *Lev.* 25:35-37 and *Deut.* 23:20-21).[81] Hellenistic practice did not require them to distance themselves from the straight and narrow path: the free loan was well established in Greek tradition.

Two contracts from the second century B.C.E., involving Jews from the Faiyum, afford us some insight into the manner in which everyday practice gave concrete expression to this situation. The first specified the conditions under which Apollonios son of Protogenes lent two talents 3,000 drachmas of copper money without interest (*atoka*) for one year to Sostratos son of Neoptolemos, on the security of a house belonging to him.[82] The second contract records a transfer of credit between Jewish soldiers, Judas son of Josephos and Agathokles son of Ptolemaios; Judas is accredited with a sum of 12,500 drachmas, in the form of a one-year loan bearing a 24% interest rate, the legal norm.[83]

At first glance, it seems that Apollonios and Sostratos followed the precepts of the *Torah*: 'unto thy brother thou shalt lend without interest' (*Deut.* 23:21). Contrariwise, Judas and Agathokles, as well as their co-religionists who served as witnesses, appear to be transgressors. But can we be sure that the law of *ribbit* did apply in the Hellenistic economy? During that remote epoch when agriculture was the principal activity and source of revenue for the Jews, loans were essentially consumers' loans and interest would have been unthinkable; with the beginnings of commerce, interest could no longer be condemned out of hand. This position was defended by John Calvin and Charles Dumoulin, a distinguished French jurisconsult in the sixteenth century, and shared by some traditional Jewish commentators.[84]

The controversy may well have its roots in the Graeco-Roman period. Our document could mirror the opinion holding that necessary investment could legitimately produce interest. Since the question was still open to debate, Egyptian Jews were perhaps persuaded, in all good faith, of the legitimacy of their operations, which the *Talmud* was only to condemn some centuries hence. Evidence from the Faiyum of the second century B.C.E. would thus attest a peculiar *halakhah*, proper to the Hellenistic precursors of Calvin and Dumoulin.

How, then, are we to interpret the terms of the first contract, recording a loan without interest? In the majority of instances, a loan granted 'without interest', *atokon*, was not a truly free loan, but a loan with built-in interest: the debtor had to reimburse more than he received. Another twist was the obligation to mortgage one's property as a guarantee, the creditor knowing full well, from the outset, that the debtor would be unable to repay the loan. This sort of operation, technically 'free of interest', actually concealed an iron-bound buying-and-selling deal, enabling the creditor to acquire property or real estate at prices well below the market level.[85] We have no serious reason to insinuate that Apollonios wanted to swindle his 'brother'

Sostratos, lending him money for the sole purpose of buying his house at a bargain price one year later. But in the light of such usages, hypotheses concerning the 'disinterestedness' of the Jews and its possible influence on their pagan neighbours must be abandoned.[86] In the final analysis, Greek influence dominated Jewish practice.

7. Conclusions

From the viewpoint of legal history, there is no contradiction between the desire of the Egyptian Jews 'to follow old national and religious traditions' and their ambition 'to participate vigorously in all aspects of Hellenistic life'.[87] The influence of Greek models in social life as well as in everyday legal practice is indisputable. But it did not inevitably lead to apostasy. Renegades like Dositheos son of Drymilos or Tiberius Julius Alexander were rather exceptional.[88] Adherence to Greek culture was compatible with the maintenance of Jewish identity. To paraphrase the author of the *Third Book of Maccabees,* the great majority of Jews in Egypt 'remained faithful to the religion of their fathers'. Whatever the degree of the Jews' acculturation, including the use of Hellenistic law, there were never any signs of Judaeo-pagan syncretism.

Fidelity to Jewish law is demonstrable in family life. Occasionally, we can observe a kind of convergence between Jewish tradition and Hellenistic custom. Sometimes, an apparent deviation was in fact a manifestation of the pluralistic character of Jewish law itself during the Second Temple period. The hypothesis of a *halakhah* proper to the Jewish diaspora in Egypt could also be envisaged.

In the majority of cases, however, the choice of language and of formulae appears decisive. Language is the vehicle of law. Jews who drew up Greek contracts followed Greek law. From Alexander the Great to the revolt of 115-117 C.E., the Jews in Egypt applied, by anticipation and in a manner that modern orthodox Judaism might deem excessively liberal, the well-known principle which the Babylonian Amora Mar Samuel was to enunciate in the third century C.E.: *dina demalkhuta dina* (דינא דמלכותא דינא), 'the law of the governing State is law'.

8. *Selective Bibliography*

Papyrology:
> Pestman, P.W., *The New Papyrological Primer* (Leiden: E.J. Brill, 1990; 2nd ed., 1994).
>
> Oates J.F., Bagnall R.S., Willis W.H. and Worp K.A., *Checklist of Editions of Greek and Latin Papyri, Ostraca and Tablets* (Atlanta: Scholars Press, 1992, 4th ed.).

The Jewish Diaspora in Egypt:
> Mélèze Modrzejewski, J., *The Jews of Egypt from Rameses II to Emperor Hadrian*, trld. R. Cornman (Philadelphia and Jerusalem: The Jewish Publication Society, 1995).

Greek documents from Egypt concerning the Jews:
> Tcherikover V., Fuks A. and Stern M., *Corpus Papyrorum Judaicarum* (Jerusalem and Cambridge, MA.: Harvard University Press, 1957-1964, 3 vols.);
>
> Horbury W. and Noy, D., *Jewish Inscriptions from Graeco-Roman Egypt* (Cambridge: Cambridge University Press, 1992).

Legal history of Graeco-Roman Egypt:
> Taubenschlag, R., *The Law of Greco-Roman Egypt in the Light of the Papyri, 332 B.C.-640 A.D.* (New York: Herald Square Press, 1944; 2nd ed., Warsaw: Panstwowe Wydawnicto Naukowe, 1955; repr. Milano: Cisalpino-La Goliardica, 1972).
>
> Wolff, H.J., *Das Justizwesen der Ptolemäer* (Munich: Beck, 1962, 2nd ed. 1971).
>
> Mélèze Modrzejewski, J., *Droit imperial et traditions locales dans l'Égypte romaine* (Aldershot: Variorum, 1990).
>
> Mélèze Modrzejewski, J., *Statut personnel et liens de famille dans les droits de l'Antiquité* (Aldershot: Variorum, 1993).

Notes

1 On papyri and papyrology see E.G. Turner, *Greek Papyri. An Introduction* (Oxford: Clarendon Press, 1968, 2nd ed. 1980); P.W. Pestman, *The New Papyrological Primer* (Leiden, E.J. Brill, 1990; 2nd ed., 1994).

2   A catalogue of papyri and parchments in Hebrew script (*ktav 'ivri*) found in Egypt has been published by C. Sirat, *Les papyrus en caractères hébraïques trouvés en Égypte* (Paris: C.N.R.S., 1985); it contains about one hundred and fifty fragments of books and documents from the 2nd to the 10th cents. C.E., most of them being subsequent to the Arab conquest.

3   A. Cowley, *Aramaic Papyri of the 5th Century B.C.* (Oxford: Clarendon Press, 1923); E.G. Kraeling, *The Brooklyn Museum Aramaic Papyri* (New Haven: Yale University Press, 1953). For an overview, see ch.2, section 2A, above. See now B. Porten and A. Yardeni, *Textbook of Aramaic Documents from Ancient Egypt*, 1. *Letters*, 2. *Contracts*, 3. *Literature, Accounts, Lists* (Jerusalem: The Hebrew University, Department of the History of Jewish People, 1986-1993); vol. 4 (forthcoming) is devoted to Ostraca. See also a previous study of B. Porten, *Archives from Elephantine. The Life of an Ancient Jewish Military Colony* (Berkeley and Los Angeles: University of California Press, 1968). On the legal problems presented by these texts, see R. Yaron, *Introduction to the Law of the Aramaic Papyri* (Oxford: Clarendon Press, 1961); Y. Muffs, *Studies in the Aramaic Legal Papyri from Elephantine* (Leiden, E.J. Brill, 1969; 2nd ed. New York: Ktav, 1973).

4   For a more detailed study, see my book *Les Juifs d'Égypte de Ramsès II à Hadrien* (Paris: Armand Colin, 1991/1992). In the present chapter I refer to the updated English version of this work, *The Jews of Egypt from Rameses II to Emperor Hadrian*. transl. by R. Cornman (Philadelphia and Jerusalem: The Jewish Publication Society, 5755/1995).

5   This chapter concentrates on Jewish legal history as reflected in Greek papyri from Egypt. As for documentary papyri and parchments found in the caves of the Dead Sea region, see, e.g., N. Lewis, 'The World of P. Yadin', *Bulletin of the American Society for Papyrology* 28 (1991), 35-41; H. Cotton, 'The Guardianship of Jesus Son of Babatha. Roman and Local Law in the Province of Arabia', *Journal of Roman Studies* 83 (1993), 94-108; B. Isaac, 'The Babatha Archive. A Review Article', *Israel Exploration Journal* 42 (1992), 62-75; and ch.6 section 3Bii below.

6   V. Tcherikover, A. Fuks, M. Stern, *Corpus Papyrorum Judaicarum* (Jerusalem and Cambridge, Mass.: Harvard University Press, 1957-1964, 3 vols.) (= *CPJud.*). A new volume of the *Corpus,* containing material published since 1964 with *addenda* and *corrigenda* to volumes I-III, is now being elaborated under the responsibility of Professor I.F. Fikhman (Jerusalem). A special section of the *CPJud.* (vol. III, Appendix I), based on the 2nd vol. of J.-B. Frey's *Corpus Inscriptionum Judaicarum* (Vatican, Pontificio Istituto di Archeologia Cristiana, 1952) (= *CIJ*), is devoted to 'The Jewish Inscriptions from Egypt'; a new collection is now available in W. Horbury and D. Noy, *Jewish Inscriptions from Graeco-Roman Egypt* (Cambridge: Cambridge Univ. Press, 1992) (= Horbury and Noy). Biblical papyri are listed in J. van Haelst, *Catalogue des papyrus littéraires juifs et chrétiens* (Paris: Publications de la Sorbonne, 1976). New sources and bibliography are

reported in the present author's continuing surveys, *Revue historique de droit français et étranger*, 1961 onwards; *Archiv für Papyrusforschung und verwandte Gebiete*, 1976-1978, for the years 1962-1972, and *Archiv* 1985-1988, for 1972-1982; *Studia et Documenta Historiae et Iuris* 1975-1983, for the years 1970-1982, continued in *Journal of Juristic Papyrology*, since 1990. Greek and Latin literary texts concerning Jews and Judaism are to be found in Th. Reinach, *Textes d'auteurs grecs and romains relatifs au Judaïsme* (Paris: Ernest Leroux, 1895, repr. Hildesheim: G. Olms, 1983), and M. Stern, *Greek and Latin Authors on Jews and Judaism* (Jerusalem: Magnes Press, 1976-1984, 3 vols.) (= Stern).

7   See especially the treatise of R. Taubenschlag, *The Law of Greco-Roman Egypt in the Light of the Papyri, 332 B.C.–640 A.D.* (New York: Herald Square Press, 1944; 2nd edition, revised and enlarged, Warsaw: Panstwowe Wydawnicto Naukowe, 1955); E. Seidl, *Ptolemäische Rechtsgeschichte* (Glückstadt: J.J. Augustin, 1962, 2nd ed.). See also the unfortunately interrupted work of H.J. Wolff, *Das Recht der griechischen Papyri Aegyptens in der Zeit der Ptolemäer und des Prinzipats*. Only one volume, the second of a projected trilogy, appeared: *Organisation und Kontrolle des Privaten Rechtsverkehrs* (Munich: Beck, 1978: Handbuch der Altertumswissenschaft, Rechtsgeschichte des Altertums).

8   Josephus, *Ant.* xii.12-33. See also the tradition preserved by Agatharchides of Cnidus and reproduced by Josephus: *C. Apion.* 1, 208-211; *Ant.* xii.5-6. On its historicity, see the discussion of I. Biezunska-Malowist, *L'esclavage dans l'Égypte gréco-romaine*, I. *Période ptolémaïque* (Wroclaw: Zaklad Narodowy im. Ossolinskich (Polish Academy of Sciences), 1974), 19ff. The principal document concerning this problem is a *prostagma* of Ptolemy II Philadelphus dated 260 B.C.E., *PER* 24552 = *C.Ord.Ptol.* 21-22.

9   Josephus, *C. Apion.* 1, 183-204 (Stern no. 12).

10   *P. Oxy.* IX 1205 = *CPJud.* III 473 (291 C.E.). The duty to redeem Jewish slaves was prescribed to Jews by talmudic authorities: *M. Gittin* 4:9; *Y. Gittin* 45d-46a; *B. Gittin* 46a.

11   *P. Petrie* III 7 (*P. Petrie*[2] I 14) = *CPJud.* I 126. Tcherikover's hypothesis, *supra* n.6, at 229f., is followed by A. Kasher, *The Jews*, quoted *infra*, n.13, at 69f.

12   A better solution would be to consider that what has been bequeathed in this testament was not the debtor himself, but a claim from creditor to debtor. The notary who had drawn up the testament confused debt and debtor. The hypothesis of personal service for paying off the debt, in conformity with both Jewish law and Greek usage, could explain Jonathas' relationship to the testator; the notary made no allusion to the service contract.

13   So especially A. Kasher, *The Jews in Hellenistic and Roman Egypt* (Tübingen: J.C.B. Mohr (Paul Siebeck), 1985).

14   *CPJud.* I 19, l. 44; *infra*, n.44.

15 Kasher, *supra* n.13, at 108-109, referring to *CIJ* II no. 1489 = Horbury and Noy, no. 114 (1st cent. B.C.E.) and *CPJud.* III, Append. I, no. 1530a = Horbury and Noy, no. 39 (mid-2nd cent. B.C.E.-early 2nd cent. C.E.).

16 C. Zuckerman, 'Hellenistic *politeumata* and the Jews. A Reconsideration', *Scripta Classica Israelica* 8-9 (1985-1988), 1989, 171-185. An unedited Ptolemaic papyrus in Cologne is supposed to mention Jewish *politeumata*. It would prove that the Jews in Egypt, like other immigrants, could possess *politeumata*, but not that they were 'citizens of their *politeumata*'; the *politeuma*, a kind of military-religious club, was not in the position of producing citizens in the formal sense of the term.

17 *CPR* XIII 4, col. VII, 109. See W. Clarysse, 'Jews in Trikomia', *Proceedings of the 20th International Congress of Papyrology, Copenhagen, August 1992* (Copenhagen: Tusculanum Press, 1994), 193-203.

18 *P. Par.* 36 = *UPZ* I 7, 13-14, and *P. Lond.* I 44 (p. 33) = *UPZ* I 8, 14 (161 B.C.E.).

19 Josephus, *Bell. Iud.* 2, 487, *C. Apion.* 2, 25 and 42.

20 D. Delia, 'The Population of Roman Alexandria', *Transactions of the American Philological Association* 118, (1988), 275-292.

21 Strabo cited by Josephus, *Ant.* 14, 117. The powers of the ethnarch should not be overestimated, as they are by Tcherikover, 'Prolegomena' to *CPJud.*, *supra* n.6, at 10.

22 See further my *Jews of Egypt*, *supra* n.4, at 185ff.

23 This is the term a certain Helenos, son of Tryphon, used to identify himself, when the rank of citizen he claimed to have directly inherited from his father had been put into question: *CPJud.* II 151. See my *Jews of Egypt*, *supra* n.4, at 164f., and D. Delia, *Alexandrian Citizenship During the Roman Principate* (Atlanta: Scholars Press, 1991), 26f.

24 This applies e.g. to 'the Jews of Xenephyris' (οἱ ἀπὸ Χενεφύρεως Ἰουδαῖοι); 'the Jews living in Nitriai' (οἱ ἐν Νιτρίαις Ἰουδαῖοι); 'in Athribis' (οἱ ἐν Ἀτρίβει Ἰουδαῖοι); or 'in Krokodilopolis' (οἱ ἐν Κροκοδίλων πόλει Ἰουδαῖοι). See *CIJ* II nos. 1441, 1442 (both 140-116 B.C.E.) and 1443 (2nd or 1st cent. B.C.E.) = Horbury and Noy, nos. 24, 25 and 27.

25 A recently published papyrus from the 2nd cent. B.C.E., *P. Monac.* III 49, mentions Jewish *presbyteroi* in Tebetnoi and Jewish *archontes* in Herakleopolis. *Archontes* may here designate the heads of the local synagogue: this is the meaning of this term in the only other document in which it appears, *P. Lond.* III 1177, p.181 = *CPJud.* II 432 (113 C.E.) l. 57. On this whole question see the commentary of the editor, D. Hagedorn, at 9ff.

26 *P. Oxy.* IX 1205 = *CPJud.* III 473 (291 C.E.).

27 See S. Honigman, 'The Birth of a Diaspora: The Emergence of a Jewish Self-Definition in Ptolemaic Egypt in the Light of Onomastics', in *Diasporas in Antiquity* (Atlanta: Scholars Press, 1993), 93-127.

28 See my *Jews of Egypt*, *supra* n.4, at 163.

29 (Ps.-)Hecataeus quoted by Josephus, *C. Apion.* I, 185-189 (Stern no. 12); C.R. Holladay, *Fragments from Hellenistic Jewish Authors, I: Historians* (Chico, CA: Scholars Press, 1983), 277-335, esp. at 306f.

30 And by the philosopher Aristobulus: see R.J.H. Schutt, 'Letter of Aristeas', in J.H. Charlesworth, ed., *The Old Testament Pseudepigrapha* (Garden City: Doubleday, 1983-1985), II, 7-34; A.Y. Collins, 'Aristobulus', *ibid.*, 831-842.

31 Coupling him, rather awkwardly, with the Athenian statesman, Demetrius of Phalerum, counsellor to Ptolemy I Soter. Clement of Alexandria, *Strom.* 1, 22, 143, testifies to this ambiguity: he follows a tradition which hesitated between Ptolemy I and Ptolemy II Philadelphus. Historical context appears to favour the son, rather than the father.

32 Rabbinical sources and discussion in G. Veltri, *Eine Tora für den König Talmai. Untersuchungen zum Übersetzungsverständnis in der jüdisch-hellenistischen und rabbinischen Literatur* (Tübingen: J.C.B. Mohr (Paul Siebeck), 1994).

33 E.J. Bickerman, 'The Septuagint as a Translation' (1959), reprinted in his *Studies in Jewish and Christian History* (Leiden: E.J. Brill, 1976), I, 167-200.

34 P. Kahle, *The Cairo Geniza* (Oxford: Clarendon Press, 1947), 132-179; 2nd ed., 1959, 209ff.; A. Momigliano, *Alien Wisdom. The Limits of Hellenization* (Cambridge: Cambridge University Press, 1975), 91ff.

35 For more details see my study '«Livres sacrés» et justice lagide', in *Acta Universitatis Lodziensis, Folia Juridica* 21 (*Symbolae C. Kunderewicz*) (Lodz: Wydawictwo Uniwersytetu Lodzkiego [Lodz University Press], 1986), 11-44.

36 G. Mattha and G.R. Hughes, *The Demotic Legal Code of Hermopolis West* (Cairo: Institut Français d'Archéologie Orientale, 1975). See now K. Donker van Heel, *The Legal Manual of Hermopolis [P. Mattha]. Text and Translation* (Leiden: Leiden Papyrological Institute, 1990, Publication no.11), combining the edition of Mattha and Hughes with corrections proposed by P.W. Pestman and some unpublished interpretations of the late M. Malinine. Other fragments: E. Bresciani, 'Frammenti di un «prontuario legale» demotico da Tebtuni nell'Istituto Papirologico G. Vitelli', *Egitto e Vicino Oriente* 4 (1981), 201-215; M. Chauveau, 'P. Carlsberg 301: Le manuel juridique de Tebtunis', in *The Carlsberg Papyri 1.Demotic Texts from the Collection* (Copenhagen: Museum Tusculanum Press, 1991), 103-129.

37 See P.W. Pestman, 'Le manuel de droit égyptien de Hermoupolis: les passages transmis en démotique et en grec', *Textes et études de papyrologie grecque, démotique et copte* (Leiden: E.J. Brill, 1985), 116-143.

38 V. Tcherikover, *Hellenistic Civilization and the Jews* (Philadelphia and Jerusalem: The Jewish Publication Society of America and Magnes Press, 1959), 300-301 (and p.506, notes 11-12); 'Prolegomena', *CPJud.* I, p.7. On

the Seleucid charter (*Josephus*, Ant. xii.138-144) see E.J. Bickerman, 'La charte séleucide de Jérusalem' (1935), in *Studies*, *supra* n.33, at I, 44-85. A Jewish legend attributed the authorship of this privilege to Alexander himself: Josephus, *Ant.* xi.317-336; see my *Jews of Egypt*, *supra* n.4, at 50ff. See also ch.2, pp.20f., above.

39 As argued by E.R. Goodenough, *The Jurisprudence of the Jewish Courts in Egypt* (New Haven: Yale University Press, 1929, reprinted Amsterdam: Philo Press, 1968).

40 Διαιτᾷ κρίσεις: Strabo quoted by Josephus, *Ant.* 14, 117. On arbitration and arbitrators in Greek and Roman Egypt see my art. 'Private Arbitration in the Law of the Papyri', *Journal of Juristic Papyrology* 6 (1952), 239-256.

41 *Tosefta Ket.* 3:1 = M. *Peah* 4:8; B. *Ket.* 25a., cf. Y. *Ket.* 2, 26d. Cf. V. Tcherikover, 'Prolegomena', *CPJud.* I, *supra* n.6, at 32f. n.84, and 93 n.87. Under Roman domination, provincial justice became a monopoly of the Imperial government, excluding the action of any other autonomous jurisdiction.

42 H.J. Wolff, 'Plurality of Laws in Ptolemaic Egypt', *Revue internationale des droits de l'Antiquité*, 3d ser., 7 (1960), 20-57.

43 H.J. Wolff, *Das Justizwesen der Ptolemäer* (Munich: C.H. Beck, 1962; 2nd ed., 1971).

44 *P. Petrie* III 21g + *P. Gurob* 2 = *CPJud.* I 19.

45 'Plurality of Laws', *supra* n.42, at 213ff.

46 Wolff, 'Plurality of Laws', *supra* n.42, at 197f., 217f.

47 *P. Ent.* 23 = *CPJud.* I 128 (118 B.C.E.).

48 The reading πολιτικὸν τῶν 'Ιουδαίων is certain; κατὰ τὸν νόμον, restored by Wolff, may be accepted as quite probable.

49 Philo, *De spec. leg.* 3, 67. See Tcherikover, 'Prolegomena', *CPJud.* I, *supra* n.6, at 35.

50 *Ibid.* On the condition of the Greek woman in Egypt see S.B. Pomeroy, *Women in Hellenistic Egypt from Alexander to Cleopatra* (Detroit: Wayne State University Press, 1990, 2nd ed.).

51 See *CPJud.* II, Section IX, 108ff.

52 *W. Chr.* 61 = *CPJud.* 421 (73 C.E.).

53 See Tcherikover's introduction to the document quoted above, *CPJud.* II, p.205. On exposure of newborn children see Pomeroy, *supra* n.50, at 135f., quoting Diodorus of Sicily, who rightly observed that, in contradiction to the Greeks, the Egyptians (*Bibl. hist.* 1, 80) and the Jews (*ibid.* 15, 3) never exposed their infants.

54 *P. Colon.* inv. 5853, ed. C. Sirat, P. Cauderlier, M. Dukan, M.A. Friedman, *La ketouba de Cologne. Un contrat de mariage juif à Antinoopolis* (Opladen: Westdeutscher Verlag, 1986) (Papyr. Colon. XII). See my remarks on this document in *Revue historique de droit* 67 (1989), 381f.

55 E. Volterra, 'Intorno a P. Ent. 23', *Journal of Juristic Papyrology* 15 (1965), 21-28.

56 *P. Yadin* 10, l. 3-4 (restored); probably also *P. Mur.* 20, l. 3, one of the two surviving *ketubbot* from Murabba'at, and *P. Mur.* 19, ll. 8, 21, a divorce document.

57 On the Palestinian *ketubbot* from the Geniza see M.A. Friedman, *Jewish Marriage in Palestine. A Cairo Geniza Study* (Tel Aviv and New York: Jewish Theological Seminary of America, 1980), Vol. I, 156 n.23 and 162-167.

58 *Y. Ket.* 4:8, 29a (*Y. Yeb.* 15:3, 14d). See Z.W. Falk, *Introduction to the Jewish Law of the Second Commonwealth* (Leiden: E.J. Brill, 1972-1978), Vol. II, 280ff.

59 *P. Ent.* 23 = *CPJud.* I 128 (218 B.C.E.), line 1: συνγραψα[μένου].

60 E.g. *CPR* XVIII 9 (Samaria, August-September 232 B.C.E.), l. 179-180: ... φερνὴν τῆς θυγατρὸς αὐτῆς [κατὰ τ]ὴν συγγραφὴν συνοικισίου (cf. *Revue historique de droit* 71, 1993, p.263).

61 *P. Yadin* 10, an Aramaic *ketubbah*, and 18, a Greek contract, between members of the same two Jewish families. See N. Lewis' commentary on *P. Yadin* 18 and the first edition of this document: N. Lewis (Text, Translation and Notes), R. Katzoff (Legal Commentary) and J. C. Greenfield (The Aramaic Subscription), *Israel Exploration Journal* 37 (1987), 229-250. See further ch.2, section 5B, above.

62 This might have been the case of Psenamounis, husband of Esther and father of Ruben, in the demotic papyrus *P. Berl.* P 7057 (47/48 C.E.), ed. K.-Th. Zauzich, 'Ein Hauskauf in Soknopaiou Nesos', *Studi E. Bresciani* (Pisa: Giardini, 1985), 607-611.

63 See my article, 'Dryton le Crétois et sa famille: les mariages mixtes dans l'Égypte hellénistique' (1984), in *Statut personnel et liens de famille dans les droits de l'Antiquité* (Aldershot: Variorum, 1993), no. VIII.

64 Shaye J.D. Cohen, 'Conversion to Judaism in Historical Perspective: From Biblical Israel to Post-Biblical Judaism', *Conservative Judaism* 36/4 (1983), 31-45; *idem*, 'Religion, Ethnicity, and «Hellenism» in the Emergence of Jewish Identity in Maccabean Palestine', in P. Bilde et al., eds., *Religion and Religious Practice in the Seleucid Kingdom* (Aarhus: Aarhus University Press, 1990), 204-223, esp. 209ff.: 'The Emergence of Conversion'.

65 *De spec. leg.* 3, 29 and 3, 25. See Shaye J.D. Cohen, 'From the Bible to the Talmud: The Prohibition of Intermarriage', *Hebrew Annual Review* 7 (1983), 23-39.

66 C. Burchard, 'Joseph and Aseneth', in J.H. Charlesworth, ed., *The Old Testament Pseudepigrapha, supra* n. 30, at Vol. II, 177-247. See my *Jews of Egypt, supra* n.4, at 67ff.

67 On this 'mishanic innovation' see Shaye J.D. Cohen, 'The Origins of the Matrilineal Principle in Rabbinic Law', *Journal of the Association for Jewish Studies* 10 (1985), 19-53.

68 See section 4 above, at n.47.

69 See 'La structure juridique du mariage grec' (1981 and 1983), in my *Statut personnel et liens de famille*, *supra* n.63, at no. V.

70 A document of 232 B.C.E. concerning a Jewish family in Samaria (Faiyum), *CPR* XVIII 9 (quoted *supra*, n.60), records the restitution of the dowry (*pherne*) in simple amount, and not with the usual penalty of 50%; the Greek model seems to have been adapted to Jewish rules.

71 *BGU* IV 1102 = *CPJud.* II 144. See, *inter alia*, R. Yaron, 'CPJud. 144 et Alia', *Iura* 13 (1962), 170-175; A.M. Rabello, 'Divorce of Jews in the Roman Empire', *The Jewish Law Annual* 4 (1981), 79-102, esp. 97f.

72 V. Tcherikover, Prolegomena', *CPJud.* I, *supra* n.6, at 94f.; cf. *CPJud.* III, AII (Prosopography), p.189, and Section XIII ('The Sambathions', 43-87).

73 *P. Tebt.* III 882 = *CPJud.* I 28 (155 or 144 B.C.E.), l. 28.

74 *CIJ* II, No. 1425 = Horbury and Noy, No. 4 (3rd cent. B.C.E.): [...]אפלל = Apollo(nios), Apollo(doros) or Apoll(odotos). Another Apollonios, transcribed אפלניס (without vav), is to be found in the Aramaic accounts of 'Abihi, a Jewish merchant in Egypt towards the turn of the 4th/3rd century: B. Porten and A. Yardeni, *Textbook* 3, C 3.28 (Cowley, no. 81); one wonders however whether he was a Jew, and not one of the Greek clients of 'Abihi. A certain Apollonios son of Philippos, indubitably Jewish (*Ioudaios*), is to be found in *CPR* XVIII 7, a recently published lease contract concluded in Samaria (Faiyum) in 232 B.C.E. Apollonios son of Dositheos, in Edfu (*CPJud.* I 70-72; 114 B.C.E.), and Ap(ollonios?) son Sollaios or Salamis (*CPJud.* I 67 and 68; 139 B.C.E.), might be regarded as Jews. See also *supra*, § II, *P. Petrie* III 7 = *P. Petrie²* I 14, and *infra*, § VI, *P. Tebt.* III 817 = *CPJud.* I 23.

75 D. Delia, *Alexandrian Citizenship*, *supra* n.23, at 59-60.

76 The sources are collected by B.J. Brooten, *Women Leaders in the Ancient Synagogue* (Chico, CA: Scholars Press, 1982), 35-39. αρχηγετου (Schubart, the first editor, confirmed by G. Poethke) must be interpreted not as a demotic, but as a title, ἀρχηγέτης being a substitute for ἀρχηγός: *op.cit.*, 39.

77 Horbury and Noy, no. 18 and pl. VII (Alexandria, 3 C.E.). On *archisynagogoi* see now T. Rajak and D. Noy, 'Archisynagogoi: Office, Title and Social Status in the Greco-Jewish Synagogue', *Journal of Roman Studies* 83 (1993), 75-93.

78 Yaron, *Introduction*, *supra* n.3, at 53f.; cf. my *Jews of Egypt*, *supra* n.4, at 35f.

79 See now Irwin H. Haut, *Divorce in Jewish Law and Life* (New York: Sepher-Hermon Press, 1983).

80 Details in Falk, *Introduction*, *supra* n.58, at Vol.II, 307f.

81 For the details see A. Weingort, *Intérêt et crédit dans le droit talmudique* (Paris: L.G.D.J., 1979).

82 *P. Tebt.* III 817 = *CPJud.* I 23 (Krokodilopolis, November 182 B.C.E.).

83 *P. Tebt.* III 818 = *CPJud.* I 24 (Trikomia, April 174 B.C.E.).

84 Weingort, *supra* n.81, admits to have been initially seduced by these rationalistic arguments, which contended that Moses would not have prohibited interest 'had he known that it could be profitable'. Further investigation led him to the conviction that the Sages of the Talmud were already aware of this reasoning, and had rejected it, maintaining the interdiction under all circumstances.

85 P.W. Pestman, 'Loans Bearing no Interest?', *Journal of Juristic Papyrology* 16/17 (1971), 7-29.

86 See especially the discussion between V. Tcherikover and M. Heichelheim, 'Jewish Religious Influence in the Adler Papyri?', *Harvard Theological Review* 35 (1942), 25-45.

87 Tcherikover, 'Prolegomena', *CPJud.* I, *supra* n.6, at 36.

88 See my *Jews of Egypt, supra,* n.4, at 56ff. and 185ff.

5

JEWISH LAW DURING
THE TANNAITIC PERIOD

by

PERETZ SEGAL
Tel-Aviv University

1. *Historical Introduction: Autonomy of the Law*

The tannaitic period (a *tanna* is a reciter of the law; see p.114) was one of great political turmoil, and dramatic change and development in Jewish Law. It is conventionally understood as commencing with the destruction of the Second Temple and its institutions by the Romans in 70 C.E. This chapter, however, traces the beginnings of tannaitic literature to the early first century. The period closes in the early days of the third century.

The Jewish population did not immediately reconcile itself to the new situation: the loss of the Temple, the symbol of Jewish spiritual independence, and Roman rule. There were Jewish uprisings in Cyrenaica, Egypt, Mesopotamia and according to some sources also in Palestine in 115-117 C.E., in the last years of the reign of the Roman Emperor Trajan. Trajan's successor, Hadrian, offended the Jews by a decree against castration, which was interpreted (not necessarily correctly) as directed against circumcision, and by attempting to rebuild Jerusalem as a Roman city, *Aelia Capitolina*. Many of the causes of the first Jewish revolt — a combination of political opposition and messianic/apocalyptic expectation — remained in existence, and led to a major revolt in Palestine, led by Simon ben Kosiba ('Bar Kochba') and supported by Rabbi Akiba, in the years 132-135 C.E. By the end of the second century, the Jewish population became more resigned to Roman rule, and a more pragmatic approach was adopted by the Jewish leadership, resulting in Roman recognition and support for the position of *Nasi* ('Prince' — a position assumed by leading rabbis, but involving political as well as religious administrative responsibilities).

The legal sources, literary sources and institutions of Jewish Law reflect the nature of this particular political-legal situation and the changing needs and functions that transformed Jewish Law throughout this period. They address problems presented by the edicts of the Roman administration issued in reaction to the particular political situation of the land of Israel and provide evidence as to the extent of the autonomy granted to Jewish Law during the period. At the same time, they bear witness to the far reaching changes that Jewish Law underwent in terms of the function of its institutions, its new literary sources, and the understanding of its legal sources. The tannaitic period was, indeed, primarily the period of the crystallisation of *halakhah*. *Halakhah* is the Hebrew-Aramaic name assigned to the newly formed Jewish Law during this period. It was both a general term referring to the whole corpus of Jewish Law from that time onwards, and a specific term ascribed to a particular law regarding any specific matter (in the plural: *halakhot*). This term appears to be founded upon the metaphoric use of 'a path to walk on' taken from the Biblical verse: 'And thou shalt warn them regarding the laws and statutes; and instruct them concerning the path on which they shall walk' (*Ex.* 18:20: *halakhah* is a noun derived from the Hebrew root *h-l-kh*) 'to walk'). It may, for our purposes, be said that from this period onwards *halakhah* becomes the normative framework for the Jewish people, in matters of both religion and law.

Our discussion of *halakhah*, below, concentrates on its development and expression in the context of changes in the understanding of legal sources. We also aim to describe the compilation of different literary sources during this time. Our discussion of the literary sources emphasizes the debate regarding the need and authority to record the law in writing, which takes place while the new literary sources are formed. We attempt to describe these literary sources, introduce their different functions, and trace the traditions they represent. This chapter further introduces the legal institutions as they develop throughout this period (against the background of the destruction of the Second Temple) and the leading authorities that contribute to these transformations at the time. It concludes ends with a discussion of the law of betrothal and marriage during the tannaitic period.

To begin with, however, let us examine the quality and extent of the autonomy of Jewish Law throughout this period. In order to appreciate the nature of this autonomy we shall examine some points of contact between Jewish and Roman Law, as evidenced in the sources of Jewish Law. (For further discussion of the relationship between Roman and Jewish jurisdiction, including the evidence of the archive of Babatha, see Ch.6, pp.146f. below.)

During the main part of the tannaitic period the Land of Israel was an independent province of the Roman Empire. Its governor was initially given the title of *praefectus* (later *procurator*); in this capacity, he controlled the standing army stationed in the province, and also supervised the administration, the levying of the various taxes, and the legal system. According to Roman Law, the governor was given all necessary powers to ensure the supremacy of Roman rule, first and foremost amongst these being jurisdiction over capital matters (which had been taken away from the local courts), as well as authority to expropriate land and levy taxes.

A. Capital Crimes

As already noted, the Roman governor was authorized to impose the death penalty; more precisely, he was empowered with the 'right of the sword' or *ius gladii*. This is reflected in the statement of the *Tosefta*:

> Four death penalties were granted to the *Bet Din* (according to Jewish Law), but the Government (of the Romans) had (under Roman Law) only (the use of) the sword. (*T. Sanh.* 9:10)

This was also the background to a tannaitic dispute regarding the Jewish form of capital punishment by the sword. According to the *Mishnah*:

> The ordinance of them that are to be beheaded [is this]: they used to cut off his head with a sword in the way that the (Roman) Government does. R. Judah says: This is shameful for him; but, rather, they lay his head on a block and cut it off with an axe. They said to him: There is no death more shameful than this. (*M. Sanh.* 7:3)

In the *Tosefta*, a version of R. Judah's view is repeated, followed by his justification: 'as it is said (*Lev.* 18:3), and in their statutes thou shall not walk' (*T. Sanh.*, 9:11), thus apparently regarding beheading with a sword as the Roman form. From the language of the dispute itself, we are unable to discern whether it accurately reflects the actual practice of an autonomous Jewish jurisdiction functioning according to Jewish Law. In fact, the following passage adds credence to the view that the Jewish courts by this time lacked jurisdiction to deal with capital crimes:

> More than forty years prior to the destruction of the Temple, jurisdiction for capital crimes was taken away from Israel. (*Y. Sanh.* 1:1)

However, both the sources of Jewish Law and external evidence indicate that capital crimes did fall under the jurisdiction of the Jewish courts both before and after the destruction of the Temple. For example:

> R. Eliezer b. Zaddok said: There was a case of the daughter of a Priest who was unfaithful, and they wrapped her up in rolls of vines and burnt her. (*M. Sanh.* 7:2)

> and they did the same thing to Ben Stada in Lydda ... they stoned him. (*T. Sanh.* 10:11)

It seems therefore that despite the fact that theoretically the Jewish Court had been denied its jurisdiction over capital crimes, as a matter of practice Jewish autonomy in this field was maintained, apparently for as long as it did not interfere with the interests of the Roman Government. The claim that Jewish jurisdiction had been abrogated with respect to capital crimes must be restricted to particular occasions only. In this connection the historian Emile Schürer makes the following instructive remark, based on Origen:

> There are also secret legal proceedings in accordance with the Law, and many are condemned to death without any general authority having been obtained for the exercise of such functions, and without any attempt to conceal such doings from the governor. This was the state of matters during the third century. In the first decade after the destruction of Jerusalem, they would not have ventured to go so far. Yet this was the direction in which things were tending! (*A History of the Jewish People in the Time of Jesus Christ*, Pt.1 Vol 1 §21(1) at note 32)

B. Expropriation of Lands

The authority of the governor to expropriate lands was seen by Jewish Law as theft, and was referred to as *sykarikon*. But Jewish Law nonetheless reflected the reality that had been created by Roman Law in the region:

> The land of Judah is not considered as *sykarikon* (and the lands therein are therefore not to be considered as stolen lands for those in possession of them). Which cases does this refer to? To those who were killed prior to the war, but for those killed during the war and after, it will be considered as *sykarikon*. Galilee is always subject to the law of *sykarikon*. (*T. Gitt.* 3:10)

The fact that the original owners of land expropriated during the war in the Judean areas had despaired of receiving their lands back served as a basis in Jewish Law for the limitation of the rule that expropriation is by definition theft, thus removing the need to restore the lands to the original owners and facilitating the settlement of the land. On the other hand, in Galilee, where expropriation was not so widespread, such expropriation was treated in accordance with Jewish Law, and the original owners were permitted to repossess their lands.

C. Tax Collection and other Roman decrees

The Rabbis reacted in a similar manner to the various taxes levied by the Roman Government. On the one hand it was viewed as robbery, and as such different methods developed for making the evasion of such taxes permissible under Jewish Law:

> One may make a (false) vow to the extortioners or to the oppressors or to the tax collectors (all acting for the Roman Government) that the extorted property is a priest's due or belongs to a non-Jew or to the Royal House. (*T. Ned.* 2:2)

On the other hand, when there was no reason not to pay the taxes, Jewish Law accorded them priority in debt collection:

> Rabbi (Rabbi Judah the Prince) determined that municipal taxes, head taxes and other taxes were to have the status of those of Ben Nanas [i.e. with the same status as a debt under the debt of the *ketubah* (marriage contract), with priority over other debts]. (*Y. Ket.* 34a)

Thus Jewish Law retained its autonomy while at the same time bowing to the realities forced upon it by the primacy of the foreign Government. A similar approach was adopted by Jewish Law in dealing with decrees that were issued by the Government as a result of the political situation in the country. For example:

> If a bill of divorce (*get*) was issued without a *ketubah*, she collects what her husband is obliged to pay her under the marriage contract; if she seeks the value of her marriage contract without issuing the bill of divorce ... in such cases she is not entitled to be paid. Rabbi Shimon the son of Gamliel said: From the time of the danger (the Hadrianic decrees) onwards, she collects what her husband is obliged to pay her under the marriage contract without the bill of divorce. (*M. Ket.* 9:9)

Since the Romans had forbidden Jewish legal practice, it was dangerous to hold a bill of divorce. The Rabbis here sought to give the wife the financial protection of the marriage contract without endangering her by possession of a Jewish bill of divorce.

These various sources show that Jewish Law in this period reflects the realities of the age, and appears to have enjoyed very considerable autonomy in practice, even in those areas where there was parallel Roman legislation.

2. *Sources of Law*

A. Introduction: *Halakhah* and *Ma'aseh*

As we have already noted, the tannaitic period is the period of the formation of the *halakhah*. In tannaitic jurisprudence, the term *halakhah* comes to stand in opposition to the term *ma'aseh* (literally, action) which refers to a judgment. It is in this connection that Rabbi Shimon ben Gamliel declared: 'I do not know what the law (*halakhah*) is but there is a judgment (*ma'aseh*) in which ...' (*T. Mikv.* 1:2), meaning — 'there is no positive legal provision, but a ruling has been issued in respect of a particular case'. According to the outstanding scholar Saul Lieberman ('*Sefer Hama'asim — Sefer Hapesakim*', *Tarbiz* 2 (1931), 377), the term *ma'aseh* is drawn from the expression *ma'aseh bet din*: 'And any *ma'aseh bet din* — these are the decisions of the court' (*Y. Shebi.* 39:3). The term *ma'aseh bet din* is later contracted to the term *ma'aseh*, meaning judgment; *ma'aseh* and *pesak* thus become synonymous.

The significance of the distinction between *halakhah* and *ma'aseh* becomes clear from a tannaitic dispute as to whether a certain legal rule is based upon a decision in a specific case or a general statement of the law. According to Jewish Law:

A woman who went overseas with her husband ... and came and said: 'my husband is dead' — may be married. (*M. Yeb.* 15.1)

There is a tannaitic dispute as to the scope of this particular rule:

That is, the House of Hillel say: we have only heard of this [rule according to which a woman's testimony that her husband has died is permissible for the purpose of allowing her to marry another man] in the [specific] case of the woman coming from the harvesting, in that country [in which the event happened, so that a court of law could corroborate her statement], and as happened in that particular case [of the woman who said that her husband was killed by a snake]. The House of Shammai said to them: ... (it was only because) the Sages were speaking (about the facts of) the actual case [that they mentioned the harvesting. That was the case that came before them, but whether the woman had come back from the harvesting or from the picking of olives, or grapes, is irrelevant in the sense that this rule applies to all these cases.] [Therefore] The House of Hillel retracted their ruling and ruled according to the House of Shammai.

The source of the law is initially recorded as a *ma'aseh* — a judgment. Thus the House of Hillel initially teach that the law reflects a decision exclusively within the facts of the initial case, but the House of Shammai argue that the case pronounces a legal norm (i.e. a *halakhah*) which is to be inferred from the judgment and should, therefore, not be limited in application to the facts of that case.

Such a distinction between *halakhah* and *ma'aseh*, however, seems to have developed gradually within the tannaitic period, and may represent the understanding of these concepts in later tannaitic times rather than in earlier periods. Rabbi Ḥananyah, who served as the Deputy of the Priests during the time of the Temple:

> testified regarding a small village that was on the outskirts of Jerusalem, where there was an old man who used to lend money to all the villagers. He would write the bill of indebtedness in his own hand, and others would come to sign as witnesses. The case came before the Sages and they permitted it. From this [later Sages suggested] it may be learned that a woman may write her own *get* (bill of divorce) and a man may write his own receipt, for the document is valid by virtue of the signatures (of the witnesses). (*M. Eduy.* 2:3)

In the previous extract, an argument between the Houses of Hillel and Shammai addressing the possible extent of the application of the precedent (regarding the woman who claimed that her husband was killed) is recorded and provides the reason supporting the outcome. From this last passage, we learn that the Sages elevate a particular practice into an act from which rules of law regarding the authorization of deeds in general could be inferred. The fact that it is the recognized function of the Sages to pronounce the Law renders any distinction between *halakhah* and *ma'aseh* irrelevant and impracticable. In a Qumran text known as the *Miktsat Ma'aseh Hatorah* (see ch.2, pp.33f., above), which contains a list of laws (amongst them laws recorded in the *Mishnah* in the name of the Sadducees) the laws are referred to as *ma'aseh*:

> We have written some of the *ma'aseh* of the *Torah* for you ... and it will be considered as justice when you do that which is honest before him.

Here, according to the understanding of the sect, the normativity of the law is anchored in the fact that a person with spiritual authority determines the law through divine inspiration, as a person deputizing for Moses, of whom it is said:

> You shall come before God for the people, and shall bring their affairs to God, and you shall warn them regarding the laws and statutes, and instruct them concerning the path in which they shall walk [from which the word *halakhah* is derived] and the actions [*ma'aseh*] that they shall do. (*Ex.* 18:19-20, cf. *Num.* 16:28)

The result is that the law comprises only those specific actions that have been mandated by the authorized person, i.e. a *ma'aseh*.

This, then, is the background to the tannaitic innovation of the creation of *halakhah* — a system in which the force of law is given to norms based upon rational deduction from a legal source, without relying upon the institutional authority of the medium through which the law is expressed, even the authority of the Supreme Court.

This is also the guiding perception of those Rabbis who, at the time, refrained from counting decisions in the Supreme Court. Instead they decided cases on the basis of their own discretion and understanding of the sources, even against a specific ruling of the Supreme Court.

> He said to him: if so, let us count (the opinions, in order to enact a binding legal norm) ... and Rabbi Yishmael the son of Yossi did not count together with them. When he left Rabbi (Judah Hanasi) said: Why didn't you count together with us? He answered ... I am afraid of the Supreme Court, they may smash my head (when, afterwards, I deviate from their decision). (*T. Ohol.* 18:18)

This, then, is the method by which the Tannaim laid the foundation of the jurisprudence of *halakhah,* and gave binding authority to the corpus of law known as 'the Oral Law' which they themselves ruled to be based upon rational scholarship.

We may now proceed to examine the sources of law during the tannaitic period. *Midrash* is directly based upon the scriptures. Custom (*minhag*), enactments (*takkanah*), and instructions (*hora'ah*) are not.

B.   *Midrash*

i.   The methods of *Midrash*

Midrash (derived from the Hebrew root *d-r-sh* — to seek, to demand, e.g. to enquire of God: *Ex.* 18:15) is the principal source of laws that were enacted during the tannaitic period. Words of the same Hebrew root are used in the Bible, shedding light on the purpose of the activity. The root *d-r-sh* is used to describe the work of Ezra (*Ezra* 7:10):

> Ezra prepared his heart to interpret (*lidrosh*) the teachings (*torah*) of God and to do and instruct Israel in law and justice (*hok umishpat*).

Thus, the identification of *midrash* as interpretation of scriptural verses in order to derive laws from them is already found in the Bible.

Midrash is directly based upon the scriptures. It is an activity best described as the interpretation and exposition of the scriptures in that it is founded on two principal presumptions; on the one hand, it is accepted that the biblical text is to be interpreted (by the Sages and Rabbis) in order to resolve legal problems and create new legal material. On the other, it is supposed that any new legal construct arising out of *midrash*, or any solution to a legal problem, is a mere exposition of a newly discovered aspect of biblical law.

From the *midrashim* themselves it is difficult to learn what are the precise exegetical principles for the interpretation and creation of laws. One formulation of these principles is attributed to Hillel the Elder:

> Hillel the Elder would explain the seven exegetical principles for the *Torah* to the Elders of the Sons of Bethyra: *A fortiori* (*kal vahomer*); inference from similarity of words (*gezerah shavah*); application of a general principle (*binyan av*); (inference from the relation between) two passages (*shene ketuvim*); (inference from the relation between) a generalisation and a specification (*kelal uferat*); (inference from) a similar case in a different place (*kayotse vo mimakom aher*); inference from the context (*davar hanilmad me'inyano*) (*Sifra* 3a (*Baraita* of Rabbi Yishmael); *T. Sanh.* 7.11; see also Elon, *Jewish Law*, I. 315)

Further formulations of the principles of exegesis are also produced during the tannaitic period; among the others, notably, that of Rabbi Yishmael. However, the sources also attest an actual dispute between the Sages as to the limitations of *midrash*:

> 'And if the daughter of a Cohen begins to prostitute herself' (*Lev.* 11:9) ... the text is referring to a maiden who is betrothed ... these are the words of Rabbi Yishmael. Rabbi Akiba says: the same applies to both one who is engaged and one who is married ... she is to be burnt ... [in response to an objection from Rabbi Yishmael] Rabbi Akiba said to him: 'My brother, I interpret the "*and* the daughter" (*ubat* — when it would have been sufficient to say 'the daughter') as teaching the inclusion of one who is married.' Rabbi Yishmael said to him: 'and just because you interpret the superfluous (letter) *vav* (in *ubat*), should we take her to be burnt?' (*Baraita, Sanh.* 51b)

Midrash is thus an activity that encourages rigorous, constructive and imaginative study of the scriptures and presupposes their total authority and relevance.

ii. The function of *Midrash*

In the first century B.C.E., Shemayah and Avtalion, the most highly regarded authorities on matters of Jewish Law in their generation (listed as one of the 'pairs' (*zugot*) in *M. Avot* 1:10, and the immediate predecessors of Hillel and Shammai) were later described as (*B. Pes.* 70b):

The two great men of the generation ... who are great Sages and *darshanim*.

The fact that these two heads of the Sanhedrin are particularly recognized as experts in exegetical interpretation [*darshanim*, viz., practitioners of *midrash*) indicates the crucial role of *midrash* as a legal source in this early period. This is attested also from the fact that the 'legislator' in the *Damascus Covenant* is described as *doresh hatorah* (VI:2), and is therefore regarded as the successor of Moses.

Some researchers are of the opinion that these exegeses are no more than literary justifications for laws that were already accepted in the legal tradition. For example:

> 'When a man takes a woman' (*Deut.* 22:13) — this teaches us that a woman is bought with money, for there is no taking except by way of money, as it is said, 'the money for the field take from me' (*Gen.* 23:13). Just as here the taking is by money so too in the other case the taking is by money. (*Midrash Tannaim, Deut.* 24:1)

But a simple reading of these *midrashim* indicates that many of these interpretations are legally creative. For example, the Bible lays down a procedure for determining the case of a wife accused after the first night of not being a virgin:

> 'and they shall spread out the garment' (*Deut.* 22:17), this means that this one's witnesses and this one's witnesses shall come and speak their words before the City Elders. But Rabbi Eliezer the son of Yaakov says — 'the words are meant as they are written.' (*Sifre, Deut.* 237)

There was a dispute as to whether the Biblical requirement that 'they shall spread out the garment' should be taken literally or not. Rabbi Eliezer took it literally, and the Scholion to *Megillat Ta'anit* attributes precisely this opinion to the *Bittusim*: 'They shall spread out the garment before the city elders, the words are as they are written.' It is striking that the opinion attributed to the Sectarians (*Bittusim*) is here identical, not only substantively but also verbally, to that of Rabbi Eliezer in *Sifre*. The Rabbis, on the other hand, derive from the same verse alternative modes of proof: witness evidence as against real evidence.

Another example may be used to counter the argument that this is a form used to justify existing laws:

> Rabbi Judah said: Ben Bukhri testified in Yavneh (in the Sanhedrin): 'Every priest who pays (the half Shekel payment to the Temple) has not sinned.' Rabbi Yohanan ben Zakkai said to him: 'This is not so, rather, every priest who does not pay has sinned, but the Priests have interpreted the Scripture as referring to themselves (i.e. for their benefit), arguing: 'Every gift of the

Priest shall not be totally consumed' (*Lev.* 6:16). If the Omer (sheaf) and two loaves and the Holy bread were provided from our money also (i.e. in shekalim) how could they be eaten (by us) [since they would then need to be burned] ...' (*M. Shek.* 1:4)

From this it may be learned that Rabbi Yoḥanan ben Zakkai is of the opinion that the interpretation of the Priests could not serve as a source for *this specific law*, insofar as it lacks (in his view) a sufficient textual basis (*Ex.* 30:11-16). The implication is that law could in principle be based solely on *midrash:* the objection is to the self-interested nature of this particular interpretation.

We may conclude that *midrash* was the principal manner of developing Jewish Law in the tannaitic period. As opposed to the scribes, who were charged with the preservation of the tradition, the Sages viewed the scriptures as a material which was given to them for the purpose of deriving laws by interpretation. As Rabban Shimon ben Gamliel said: 'Scribes, leave me and I shall read [the scripture] as [if it were made of] clay' (*Sifre Numbers* 8). Even so interpretation *per se* was not binding unless its validity had been established by the Sages:

> Although he (Hillel) sat and interpreted (*doresh*) (the law) all that day, (the sons of Bethyra) did not accept his learning, until he replied: May evil befall me if I have not heard it from Shemaiah and Abtalion. (*Y. Pes.* 33a)

C. Custom (*minhag*)

Custom, as opposed to *midrash*, is the source of those practices which developed over time independently of the scriptures, and which were given obligatory status by the Sages. For example:

> In Judah, the initial practice was for the chaperones to sit in the sleeping place of the Bride and Groom, but this was not the practice in the Galilee. Anyone not adhering to this practice [in Judah] cannot come afterwards with a claim regarding the virginity of his wife (because he is supposed to raise his claim immediately and not wait for the morning). (*T. Ket.* 1:4)

The Sages determined that this custom would have the force of law, even though it lacked firm scriptural foundation in *Deut.* 23:13-21. According to *M. Ket.* 1:1:

> Marriages of virgins are to be held on Wednesdays, so that the husband who wishes to make such a claim may 'go immediately in the morning to the court'

since the court sat on Thursdays.

D. Enactment (*takkanah*)

Enactments (*takkanot*) are the legal source for those laws that the Sages sought to initiate for reasons based on societal conditions. Usually it was the *Nasi* who made such enactments, since he was recognized as having overall judicial authority (usually combined with political authority). There were cases in which the enactments contradicted the accepted law, even a law grounded in the scriptures themselves:

> In the beginning he [the husband] would convene a court elsewhere [from where the wife was] and cancel it [the *get* (writ of divorce) that he had sent to his wife]; Rabban Gamliel the Elder issued an enactment that this practice should cease, for the public benefit. (*M. Gitt.* 4:2)

In the *Tosefta,* the validity of a cancellation made despite the *takkanah* is disputed:

> If he cancelled it, the *get* is void, in the opinion of Rabbi (Judah the Prince). Rabban Shimon ben Gamliel says, 'he is unable to cancel it, nor may he add to his condition.' (*T. Gitt.* 3:3)

It seems that Rabbi Judah did not endorse the authority of any such *takkanah,* because it contradicted the accepted law of the *Torah*, that the husband may cancel the *get* at any time before the wife received it. However, this argument against the validity of the *takkanah* did not prove decisive. Rabban Shimon ben Gamliel did not reply, and impliedly adhered to the enactment which invalidated the husband's cancellation of the *get.*

E. Instruction and Precedent (*hora'ah*)

'Instruction' (*hora'ah*) is the legal source for those laws that the Supreme Court established as the result of its own legal scholarship or interpretation (*midrash*) as a precedent or instruction (i.e. either as a result of a case or on the basis of teaching promulgated by the court not in the context of a particular case).

> The instruction has an element of severity which does not exist in the Capital Laws ... for the instruction must be issued by the court in the Hall of the Hewn Stone (i.e. the Supreme Court of 71 judges), whereas there is jurisdiction for capital laws in all places (i.e. local courts of 23 judges). (*T. Hor.* 1:3,4)

The validity of the instruction may be inferred from the following story:

> All the time that Rabban Gamliel [who was then the *Nasi*], was alive, the *halakhah* was practised according to his rulings but after the death of Rabban

Gamliel, Rabbi Joshua attempted to revoke his rulings. Rabbi Yoḥanan b. Nuri got up on his feet and said: 'I see, after the head all the body goes [i.e. the *Nasi*'s authority gives it the status of a precedent: see *M. Eduy.* 1:5 below]; so long as Rabban Gamliel was alive, the law followed his opinion. Now that he has died, do you want to nullify his opinion?' He said to Rabbi Joshua: 'We shall not listen to you! The *halakhah* was determined according to (the rulings of) Rabban Gamliel and nobody (then) contested his rulings.' (*T. Taanit* 2:5).

This means that the ruling of the Supreme Court (over which Rabban Gamliel, as *Nasi*, will have presided) is vested with the status of a binding precedent. It was only another Supreme Court that was vested with the authority to repeal a ruling, and even then only under very special circumstances:

For another *Bet Din* cannot revoke the ruling of its collegiate *Bet Din*, unless it is greater than it in wisdom and numbers. (*M. Eduy.* 1:5)

In fact, it was Rabbi Joshua himself who in relation to a number of laws said: 'The Scribes have initiated something new and I am unable to contest it' (*M. Kel.* 13:7).

This rule of precedent was the basis for accepting a ruling of Rabbi Yoḥanan:

The Rabbis taught: Once it happened that Rosh Hashanah began on a Shabbat, and all of the cities gathered [to the Supreme Court in Yavneh, to hear the blowing of the *shofar*]. He [Rabbi Yoḥanan ben Zakkai] said to the Bene Bethyra: 'We shall blow [the *shofar*].' They said to him: 'We should discuss it.' He said to them: 'We shall blow and then we shall discuss it.' After they had blown, they said to him, 'Let us now discuss it.' He said to them. 'The horn has already been heard in Javneh, and one does not contest the issue after the act. (*B. R.Sh.* 29b)

It was necessary to ensure the status of the *halakhot* decided in this way by the Sages. In order to reduce the possibility of violation of these *halakhot* (termed *divre sofrim*, i.e. lacking biblical support) which derived purely from the authority of the Sages, special sanctions were sometimes imposed. For example:

Why did they rule that those engaging in incestuous relations in the second degree, thus forbidden only by scribal decision, *divre sofrim*) shall not be entitled to a *ketubah*? Since both he and she are strictly (according to the *Torah*) legally competent (to marry each other), they penalized her, by denying her a *ketubah*, in order to make it easy for him to divorce her. Rabbi Meir says: ... the teachings of the *Torah* do not require reinforcement. But this ... is prohibited by reason of the teachings of the scribes, and the teachings of the scribes do require reinforcement. (*T. Yeb.* 2:4)

To conclude, we may summarize the distinctions between the different sources of law in this period as follows: *ma'aseh* is a judgment made in a case but not based on any explicit rule; *takkanah* is an enactment made by the Rabbis but inferred neither from a biblical verse nor from a decided case; *hora'ah* is an instruction or precedent of the Supreme Court, made either in court (*hora'ah lema'aseh*) or on the basis of teaching (*midrash*). The term *halakhah* means a law or rule based on any of the sources of law.

3.   *The Literary Sources*

A.   Introduction: The Writing Down of the Oral Law

The literary sources of Jewish Law during this period are referred to as the Oral Law, since the act of writing down the law was originally forbidden. As a result the laws were taught and repeated orally until this period. The verse in Exodus 'for according to these words ...' (*Ex.* 34:27) is interpreted as follows: 'words that you have been taught orally — you are not permitted to recite them from writing' (*B. Gitt.* 60b). This is also the source of the name *tanna*, which means one who recites orally. This particular tradition also set the Sages apart from the approach of the Sadducees, as becomes clear from an early interpretation (Scholion) to *Megillat Ta'anit*, a calendar of important dates that are celebrated during the times of the Temple:

> A book of decrees has been written and promulgated by the Sadducees, in which it was written: 'These shall be stoned, these shall be burnt, these shall be killed and these shall be strangled.' And when they sat down and a person posed a question (about these matters), he was shown the book. If he asked 'what is the source ... ?', they were unable to bring him proof from the *Torah*. The Sages said to them: Isn't it written 'according to the law that they instruct you (i.e. orally) ...' etc. (*Deut.* 7:11). From here we learn that laws are not to be written in a book.

The existence of this dispute is further substantiated by the documents discovered in Qumran, in which the laws are written down by the 'Legislator':

> And the legislator (*hamehokek*, the title of Moses) — he is the one who interprets (*doresh*) the *Torah* ... (i.e.) the statutes that the legislator enacted. (*Damascus Document* VI:2)

The result is that these laws laid down by the *mehokek* became binding upon the Qumran community together with the *Torah*. This was justified as being an act of interpretation of the written law (*doresh hatorah*). In the Temple Scroll, the same verse from which the Sages derive their capacity to develop the Oral Law (*Deut.* 17:10) is quoted to prove that the enactments of the Lawmaker in Qumran have independent validity:

> Then you shall do according to the law that they declare to you and according to what they say to you from the book of the Law (*Torah*), which they declare to you in sincerity. (56:3-4)

Whereas the intention in Qumran is to prove that the enactments of the Lawmaker are to have independent validity because they are set by the *meḥokek*, the rabbinic Sages conclude that only a law which had been orally learned, in the sense that it had been derived through the processes of explicit discussion of the text of the *Torah*, could be legally binding.

As noted above (Scholion to *Megillat Taʿanit*), the original context of the ban on writing down the Oral Law was the view that the Sadducees 'were unable to bring proof from the *Torah*'. Such reasoning was pertinent with regard to statutes formulated independently of the written *Torah*. The prohibition was, however, then expanded to include the *midrash,* the very interpretation of the text — probably as a means by which the early Rabbis (the Pharisees) sought further to distinguish themselves from the Sadducees. The latter, as seen in the passage above from the Scholion to *Megillat Taʿanit,* wrote down laws for which 'they were unable to bring ... proof from the *Torah*'. The Sages, at this time, were probably concerned to avoid the impression that *any* laws, even if they were clear interpretations of the written *Torah* (the result of *midrash*), lacked biblical support, through association with the Sadducean genre of written law.

The sources of Jewish Law are, therefore, based upon processes of biblical exegesis (the Oral Law) and not on the independent redaction of legal collections. As a later authority put it:

> Rabbi Zeira said in the name of Samuel: One learns [a law] neither from the laws [*halakhot* i.e. the *Mishnah*], nor from traditions [*haggadah* i.e. *Midrashe halakhah*], nor from the additions [to the *Mishnah,* i.e. the *Tosefta* and the *Baraitot*], but rather from learning [*talmud* i.e. the oral process]. (*Y. Peah* 17a)

After the destruction of the Temple, it was said that there was a need to collate the collections of *halakhot* from various academies and to produce a standardised version of the Law. The beginning of this process is described in the *Tosefta*:

> When the Sages gathered together in the vineyard at Yavneh they said: There will be a time in the future when people will search for teaching of the *Torah* and will not be able to find it; a teaching of the scribes ... and will not find it, ... 'they shall seek ... the word of the Lord, but they shall not find it' (*Amos* 8:12). They said, let us begin [the compilation] from Hillel and Shammai! (*T. Eduy.* 1:1)

The canon of Jewish Law compiled during the tannaitic period includes collections of *halakhot* (laws) in the *Mishnah* and the halakhic interpretations of the Bible (*Midrashe Halakhah*), both sharing equal status as part of the Oral Law, then known as *talmud*. The term *midrash,* from this period onwards, is used both to describe the act of interpreting the scriptures and as a name for the written collections of these interpretations. The difference between the *Mishnah* and the halakhic *Midrash* resides only in their literary form.

B. The *Mishnah*

The *Mishnah* is used as the name of the codex of laws compiled at the end of the tannaitic period by Rabbi Judah the Prince (R. Judah Ha-Nasi), and which comes to be recognised as an authoritative statement of the 'Oral Law'.

The term *mishnah* comes from the root *sh-n-h* — to recite the law orally, as seen in *M. Avot* 3:8, which speaks of

> ... a man [who] was walking by the way and reciting (*shoneh*) and he ceased his *mishnah* and said, 'How fine is this tree!'

Over a period of generations these *halakhot* were compiled in academies of the *tannaim* where the *tanna* recited (*shoneh*) the law before the assembled scholars, transmitting it as he had received it from his teacher:

> When Rabbi Akiba would present the laws [teach *Mishnah*] to the students, he said: 'Every person who has heard an explanation ... shall come forward and present it' ... Rabbi Eleazar ... replied to him ... Rabbi Shimon replied to him ... Rabbi Akiba again began reciting in accordance with the words of Rabbi Shimon. (*T. Zab.* 1:5-6)

The picture before us is of Rabbi Akiba bringing his own version of the *Mishnah* before his students. This version includes the traditions of the Houses of Shammai and Hillel (*T. Zab.* 1:1); other scholars would then present him with the versions of those debates that they had received from their own teachers. Rabbi Akiba would then adopt into his written *Mishnah* the opinion he would find most acceptable to him. It is in this manner that extra layers would include new interpretations and come to be treated as part of the original version. The new *Mishnah* thus compiled in the academies of that generation would then be published in the 'Oral-Law' book for the students, and become part of the public instruction of the *Torah*.

These new additions to the *Mishnah* would become legally binding by virtue of the authority vested in the particular Sage who had been teaching the *Mishnah* in a particular academy. This is the background to the talmudic statement: 'Any *Mishnah* that was not introduced into the study group is not to be relied upon.' (*Y. Eruv.* 9:2).

The arrangement of these collections of *halakhot* by subject, their classification, and the determination of their order by content is considered to have been achieved already before the destruction of the Temple. We learn:

> [The rules about] vows, ... laws of the Sabbath, Festive sacrifices and sacrifices for sacrilege are as mountains hanging by hair, for [teaching of] scripture [thereon] is scanty and the rules many; the civil laws and [the laws] about Temple Service, about purity and impurity, forbidden degrees, and monetary vows are all well substantiated — these are basic parts of the *Torah.* (*M. Hag.* 1:8)

This particular tradition of studying the *halakhot* received its final crystal-isation in the official version of the *Mishnah* which was compiled by Rabbi Judah the Prince around 200 C.E. Any individual laws (*mishnayot*) that are not included in it are thereafter referred to as *baraitot* (meaning 'external'); they are found in different compilations of *Midrashe Halakhah* (below) in one or other of the *Talmudim* and in the *Tosefta* (which means an 'addition', viz., to the *Mishnah*), a collection of such exteɩnal *mishnayot* not included in the *Mishnah*.

The result of Rabbi Judah's work was that his collection preserved some of the earliest *mishnayot* in their original format: in the talmudic phrase, 'the *Mishnah* has not moved from its place' (*B. Hull.* 32b). Even those early *mishnayot* gradually came to be legally binding as a result of their inclusion in the collection of Rabbi Judah the Prince. Subsequent to his compilation of the *Mishnah*, it was no longer possible to determine a law without taking the *Mishnah* into account, even though it was still possible to argue and disagree, just as argument and difference had been legitimate in the days of Rabbi himself.

Though the *Mishnah* of Rabbi was considered to be the primary source for the learning of the Law, with priority over other sources (as may be inferred from the order of the words of Rabbi Zeira, quoted at p.115 above), even after it had become the standard and accepted version, the *halakhah* was still determined for practical purposes by way of the learning process in the academy, and not by reliance upon single legal sources (see, for example, the dictum of Samuel on *M. Shab.* 22:5 at *Y. Shab.* 6a).

The *Mishnah* of R. Judah is divided into six 'orders' (*sedarim*), each representing a general area of law, within which particular topics are accorded their individual 'tractates' (*masekhtot*). Each *masekhta* is divided into chapters and the chapters into individual *mishnayot*. Conventionally, the *Mishnah* is cited (only) by *masekhta*, chapter and *mishnah* (e.g. *M. Sanh.* 9:6). Since the *Babylonian Talmud* (the *Gemara*) is organized as a running commentary on the *Mishnah*, with each *mishnah* printed in its body, traditional literature often cites the *Mishnah* itself by the folio on which it is quoted in the standard edition of the Gemara. In this volume, the former method of citation is used.

The arrangement of the *Mishnah* formed the basis of the systematics of the Oral Law for many centuries. Though topical, and independent of the arrangement of material in the Bible (unlike the genre of *midrash*), the Biblical sequence is sometimes reflected internally within particular tractates. A valuable study, in relation to the order of the civil law, is D. Daube, 'The Civil Law of the Mishnah: The Arrangement of the Three Gates', *Tulane Law Review* 18 (1944), 351-407, reprinted in Collected *Works of David Daube, Volume I: Talmudic Law*. ed. C.M. Carmichael (University of California at Berkeley: The Robbins collection, 1992), 257-304,

The content of the *Mishnah* is as follows (the tractate abbreviations, used throughout this volume, follow those of H. Danby, in his translation of the *Mishnah*):

FIRST ORDER, *ZERAIM* ('SEEDS': largely agricultural law, relevant only to the cultivation of land in Israel)

Berakoth ('Benedictions'), abbr. *Ber.*
Peah ('Gleanings'), abbr. *Peah*
Demai ('Produce not certainly tithed'), abbr. *Dem.*
Kilaim ('Diverse Kinds'), abbr. *Kil.*
Shebiith ('The Seventh Year'), abbr. *Shebi.*
Terumoth ('Heave-offerings'), abbr. *Ter.*
Maaseroth ('Tithes'), abbr. *Maas.*
Maaser Sheni ('Second Tithe'), abbr. *M. Sh.*
Hallah ('Dough-offering'), abbr. *Hall.*
Orlah ('The Fruit of Young Trees'), abbr. *Orl.*
Bikkurim ('First-fruits'), abbr. *Bikk.*

SECOND ORDER, *MOED* ('FEASTS': religious festivals)

Shabbath ('The Sabbath'), abbr. *Shab*
Erubin ('The Fusion of Sabbath Limits'), abbr. *Erub.*
Pesahim ('Feast of Passover'), abbr. *Pes.*
Shekalim ('The Shekel Dues'), abbr. *Shek.*
Yoma ('The Day of Atonement'), abbr. *Yom.*
Sukkah ('The Feast of Tabernacles'), abbr. *Sukk.*
Yom Tob or Betzah, ('Festival-days'), abbr. *Betz.*

Rosh ha-Shanah ('Feast of the New Year'), abbr. *R. Sh.*
Taanith ('Days of Fasting'), abbr. *Taan.*
Megillah ('The Scroll of Esther'), abbr. *Meg.*
Moed Katan ('Mid-Festival Days'), abbr. *M. Kat.*
Hagigah ('The Festal Offering'), abbr. *Hag.*

THIRD ORDER, *NASHIM* ('WOMEN': including much of family law)

Yebamoth ('Sisters-in-law'), abbr. *Yeb.*
Ketuboth ('Marriage Deeds'), abbr. *Ket.*
Nedarim ('Vows'), abbr. *Ned.*
Nazir ('The Nazirite-vow'), abbr. *Naz.*
Sotah ('The Suspected Adulteress'), abbr. *Sot.*
Gittin ('Bills of Divorce'), abbr. *Gitt.*
Kiddushin ('Betrothals'), abbr. *Kidd.*

FOURTH ORDER, *NEZIKIN* ('DAMAGES': including much of the civil law,
criminal law, and procedure)

Baba Kamma ('The First Gate'), abbr. *B.K.*
Baba Metzia ('The Middle Gate'), abbr. *B.M.*
Baba Bathra ('The Last Gate'), abbr. *B.B.*
Sanhedrin ('The Sanhedrin'), abbr. *Sanh.*
Makkoth ('Stripes'), abbr. *Makk.*
Shebuoth ('Oaths'), abbr. *Shebu.*
Eduyoth ('Testimonies'), abbr. *Eduy.*
Abodah Zarah ('Idolatry'), abbr. *A. Zar.*
Aboth ('The Fathers'), abbr. *Ab.*
Horayoth ('Instructions'), abbr. *Hor.*

FIFTH ORDER, *KODASHIM* ('HALLOWED THINGS': principally the law relating
to Temple dues)

Zebahim ('Animal-offerings'), abbr. *Zeb.*
Menahoth ('Meal-offerings'), abbr. *Men.*
Hullin ('Animals killed for food'), abbr. *Hull.*
Bekhoroth ('Firstlings'), abbr. *Bekh.*
Arakhin ('Vows of Valuation'), abbr. *Arak.*
Temurah ('The Substituted Offering'), abbr. *Tem.*
Kerithoth ('Extirpation'), abbr. *Ker.*
Meilah ('Sacrilege'), abbr. *Meil.*
Tamid ('The Daily Whole-offering'), abbr. *Tam.*
Middoth ('Measurements'), abbr. *Midd.*
Kinnim ('The Bird-offerings'), abbr. *Kinn.*

SIXTH ORDER, *TOHOROTH* ('CLEANNESSES': laws relating to the purity of
persons, things and places)

Kelim ('Vessels'), abbr. *Kel.*
Oholoth ('Tents'), abbr. *Ohol.*
Negaim ('Leprosy-signs'), abbr. *Neg.*

Parah ('The Red Heifer'), abbr. *Par.*
Tohoroth ('Cleannesses'), abbr. *Toh.*
Mikwaoth ('Immersion-pools'), abbr. *Mikw.*
Niddah ('The Menstruant'), abbr. *Nidd.*
Makshirin ('Predisposers'), abbr. *Maksh.*
Zabim ('They that suffer a flux'), abbr. *Zab.*
Tebul Yom ('He that immersed himself that day'), abbr. *Teb. Y.*
Yadaim ('Hands'), abbr. *Yad.*
Uktzin ('Stalks'), abbr. *Uktz.*

C. The *Tosefta*

The *Tosefta* is the second book of laws of the tannaitic period, having been edited mainly during the generation after Rabbi Judah the Prince. Its title and structure bear testimony to the fact that it was in essence a complementary collection to the *Mishnah*. The *Tosefta* is a completion of the *Mishnah* in a number of different ways:

a.   It adds laws or problems that are not found in the *Mishnah*.
b.   It adds laws from the period subsequent to the compilation of the *Mishnah*.
c.   It quotes different sources or versions of the laws from those in the *Mishnah*.
d.   It provides interpretations of the *Mishnah*.

Such additional material is arranged in the *Tosefta* according to the chapters of the *Mishnah*, but quite often the order of laws within chapters is different from that presented in the *Mishnah*.

Functions (a) and (d) above are exemplified from the opening *halakhot* of *Mishnah* and *Tosefta Kiddushin*. The former states the basic rule:

> The woman is bought in three ways ... with money, a writ and with intercourse. (*M. Kidd.* 1:1)

The *Tosefta* quotes this *Mishnah* and explains:

> *With money.* How? If he gave her money and said to her 'You are hereby sanctified (= bought) to me' ... then this woman has been validly sanctified, but if she gave him money and said to him ... 'Behold I am sanctified to you' ... then she is not validly sanctified. *And with the writ* ... Even if he wrote it on a piece of clay and gave it to her ... *And with intercourse*: by any intercourse with the purpose of marriage ... she is sanctified but if not for the purpose of marriage, she is not sanctified. (*T. Kidd.* 1:1-3)

The *Tosefta* then adds a further rule, not found in the *Mishnah*, which may be viewed as a reaction against a rule known from Qumran:

> A man shall not marry a woman before his niece has grown up ... (*T. Kidd.* 1:4)

The absolute character of the formulation of the prohibition of any other marriage indicates that it is a reaction against a deviant Qumran opinion, since such uncle-niece marriages had been explicitly prohibited at Qumran, where we read in the *Damascus Covenant* (*CD* V:7-11):

> They defile the sanctuary ... marrying the daughter of brother or sister. Yet Moses said: 'You shall not approach your mother's sister, for she is akin to your mother.' The law of incest is written in terms of males, but it is the same for women, so that a brother's daughter should not have intercourse with the brother of her father, for he is akin (to her father).

There is no substantive reason for the non-inclusion of parts of the *Tosefta* in the *Mishnah*, nor is it clear why *baraitot* and other additional tannaitic laws now found in collections such as the *Midrashe Halakhah*, are not themselves included in the *Tosefta*. The *Tosefta* should be seen as a complementary book, edited by Tannaim, which supplements the *Mishnah* (the authoritative canon of tannaitic law) and not as a rival *Mishnah* deriving from another academy and not accepted by Rabbi Judah the Prince. There is no evidence of any legal distinction between the laws appearing in the *Mishnah* and the *Tosefta*; both books were treated as halakhic sources from the time of the Tannaim.

D. *Midrashe Halakhah*

While *midrash* primarily stands for a set of methods of interpretation (see pp.108-111 above), it has also been collected and compiled, and reduced to writing. A number of these compilations of *midrashim* interpret biblical texts of legal significance — from which *halakhah* is derived. The *Midrashe Halakhah* are collections of exegetical derivations of laws from the books of *Exodus*, *Leviticus*, *Numbers* and *Deuteronomy*. They were compiled during the tannaitic period in the academies of Rabbi Akiba and Rabbi Yishmael. Those which have survived to modern times are:

— the *Mekhilta of Rabbi Yishmael* and the *Mekhilta of Rabbi Shimon Bar Yoḥai* on the book of *Exodus*;
— *Sifra* on the book of *Leviticus*;
— *Sifre* and *Sifre Zutta* on *Numbers*;
— *Sifri* and some fragments of the *Mekhilta of Rabbi Yishmael* on

Deuteronomy.

The study of Jewish Law by way of legal exegesis of the verses of the Bible continued throughout the Second Temple period. But unlike the biblical commentary scrolls of Qumran (called *pesharim*), where the exegesis was immediately committed to writing, the Sages approached commentary in the same way as they studied the *mishnayot*; originally, it was a form of oral teaching, for the same reasons that the *halakhot* were not written down (pp. 114-16, above). Only later, during the tannaitic period, were the *Midrashe Halakhah* compiled.

As we noted above, the difference between *mishnah* and halakhic *midrash* is not in their legal status but in their literary form. The following example illustrates the difference. In the *Mishnah* it is said:

> The woman is acquired in three ways ... with money, and writ, and with intercourse. (*M. Kidd.* 1:1)

In *midrash*:

> 'If a man takes a woman' (*Deut.* 24:1) — this teaches us that the woman is acquired with money; 'and had intercourse with her' (*ibid.*) — this teaches us that a woman may be acquired with intercourse; from where do we learn that (she may be acquired) even with a writ? For it is taught 'and he shall write her a writ of divorce' (*ibid.*). Her entrance to marriage is here parallel to her exit (from marriage, i.e. by divorce): just as her exit from him is made by a writ, so too is her entrance to the other made by a writ. (*Sifre Deut.* 268)

On the other hand, some *Midrashe Halakhah* include the reactions of the Tannaim to the exegesis of the early Sages. For example on *Lev.* 15:33, 'This is the law for the woman suffering her menstruation (*benidata*)':

> ... the early Sages have said: 'she is forbidden to make up or decorate herself in her impurity (*benidata*)', until Rabbi Akiba came and taught, 'he will come to hate her and will want to divorce her!' How then do I interpret the verse ...? It means that she shall remain impure (*benidata*: in her impurity) until she has immersed herself in water. (*Sifra, Metsia*, 9: 12)

We also find in the *Midrashe Halakhah* exegeses in which the Sages react to the opinions of other sects. For example (in relation to the ceremony whereby a childless widow is released from marriage to her deceased husband's brother, the 'levir'):

> 'And she shall spit in his face' (*Deut.* 22:9). Does this mean really in his face? The verse says: 'in the eyes of the elders', to teach us only that the spit must be seen by the Elders. (*Sifre, Deut.* 291)

This particular exegesis opposes the view attributed in the Scholion to *Megillat Ta'anit* to the decrees of the *Bittusim* (thought to be the Essenes):

'and she shall spit in his face — that she should (actually) spit in his face'. Such an interpretation is also mentioned in the *Testament of the Twelve Tribes*:

> For so it is written in the book of Enoch ... anyone not willing to establish the seed of his brother and they shall take his sandal off and spit in his face ... for he too has spat at them. (*Testament of Zevulun* 3:4-7)

We find the rabbinic *midrash* on this matter incorporated into the *Mishnah*: 'And she shall spit in his face — spit that can be seen by the judges' (*M. Yeb.* 12:6)

Translations of the Bible made during the tannaitic period also incorporate exegeses (often known from other tannaitic sources) of the scriptural text. For example, *Lev.* 19:20 deals with a sexual offence committed with a slave girl assigned to another man and to whom 'freedom has not been given to her'. The latter phrase is translated by Onkelos (the translator of the Pentateuch into Aramaic) as 'her freedom was not given to her *by a document.*'

It would seem that the halakhic *midrashim* were compiled in the Land of Israel *after* the compilation of the *Mishnah* of Rabbi, given that they quite frequently quote the *Mishnah*. Nonetheless, it is clear that they reflect studies that took place in the academies during the tannaitic period. The internal relations between the academies are reflected in a passage such as the following:

> For the sages have already communed in Yavneh and Rabbi Joshua was not there. When the students came to him, he would ask: 'What did you hear today in Yavneh?' They said to him: 'After you, Rabbi' (i.e., we are your students, and we only have your *Torah*). He asked: 'And who was sitting there?' They said to him: 'Rabbi Eliezer the son of Azariah.' He said to them: 'Is it possible that Eliezer the son of Azariah sat there and did not say anything new?' They said to him: 'He interpreted the following principle ...' He said to them: 'What other new thing did he say besides that ... the generation is not orphaned if Rabbi Eliezer is present with it.' (*Mekhilta of Rabbi Yishmael, Bo, Piska* 16, *T. Sot.* 7:9)

The *midrashim* also reflect external relations between the academies and the Government:

> Rabbi Nathan says: 'and to those who love me and observe my commandments' — these are those of Israel who sit in the Land of Israel and devote their whole beings to the Commandments. What difference does it make if the person is to be killed by the sword for having circumcised his son, or is to be burnt because of studying the *Torah*, or is to be crucified for eating *matza* or is to be lashed for holding a *lulav*? (*Mekhilta, Jethro, Bahodesh*, 6)

The context of these comments was the Hadrianic Decrees (section 1 above)
and the attitude of the Rabbis towards them.

The halakhic *midrashim* were thus supplementary sources of law.
Indeed, the *Tosefta*, commenting on *M. Hag.* 1:8 (quoted above, p.117) —
in which four areas of law where many laws were inferred by *midrash* from
little biblical text were contrasted with four further areas where the many
laws were based on abundant biblical texts — observes that 'these eight
topics of the *Torah* constitute the essentials of the law' (*T. Hag.* 1:9), thus
without any legal distinctions between them.

4. *Judicial Institutions*

A. Introduction

During the tannaitic period, legal institutions went through substantial
changes as a result of the political and social circumstances obtaining in the
land of Israel, amongst them the Great Rebellion of 66-70 C.E., the
Destruction of Jerusalem and the Temple (70 C.E.), and thereafter the
Rebellion of Bar Kochba (132-135 C.E.). The existing sources make any
accurate description of the judicial institutions and their infrastructure
difficult. For example, with respect to the authority to appoint the judges
after the Destruction, the following description appears:

> Rabbi (A)ba said: At first everyone would appoint his pupils, Rabbi Yoḥanan
> ben Zakkai appointed Rabbi Eliezer and Rabbi Yehoshua ... later on they
> turned (= began) to give honor to this house (i.e. that of the *Nasi*) and they
> said that a court that appoints a candidate without the permission of the
> *Nasi* — the appointment is not valid, but a *Nasi* who made an appointment
> without the permission of the court, his appointment is valid. Later they
> turned and changed their view: that the court should not make any appoint-
> ment that was not permitted by the *Nasi*, and that the *Nasi* should not make
> any appointment that was not permitted by the court. (*Y. Sanh.* 15:1, 19a)

But we possess no indication as to the source of the original norms, the
justifications for these changes, or who it was that promoted the changes and
gave them their validity.

B. *Ṣemikhah* (Ordination)

A primary feature characterizing the legal institutions of the period is the
fact that all the Sages functioning within the judicial institutions had received
ṣemikhah. In this period *ṣemikhah* meant that the recipient was authorized to

preside over a trial:

> And there were three rows of Student-Sages, sitting before them (the
> judges) ... if the judges had to ordain, they would begin from the first row ...
> (*M. Sanh.* 4:4)

The Sage who was appointed as a judge was called 'a person sitting in the
meeting' of the court (e.g., 'Rabbi Yoḥanan ben Nuri and Rabbi Eliezer ben
Ḥasma were brought in to sit by Rabban Gamliel in the meeting of the
court; in the evening they left (the meeting) and sat with the students ...'
Sifre, Deut. 16).

Ordination is a declaration that the Sage is an expert (*mumḥeh*) for the
court, and thus that his verdicts have the authority of a binding judicial
decision. Therefore, even where the court is sitting as a court of arbitration,
where one of the litigants chooses a *dayan mumḥeh* (expert judge), then the
other side is unable to disqualify him from presiding over the case (*M. Sanh.*
3:1). Ordination by the *Bet Din* also had the effect of investing the *mumḥeh*
with immunity against a claim in tort:

> If he (one who isn't a *mumḥeh*) presides over a case, and he acquitted the
> guilty and convicted the innocent ... what he has done remains, but he pays
> indemnity from his property, but if he was an expert for the Court he is
> exempt from payment. (*M. Bekh.* 4:4)

Ṣemikhah had the further consequence of conferring authority to create
precedents: the laws that the *mumḥeh* creates, whether through interpretation
of the text or based on his own opinion, attained the status of a *hora'ah* (a
binding provision) in Jewish Law thereafter. The decision of the *mumḥeh*
possessed this authority provided that he stated expressly that it was *halakhah
lema'aseh* (binding law), either in the academy, or while presiding in a trial
in his capacity as a judge.

> The Rabbis taught: one does not learn the *halakhah* from the *Talmud* (from
> academic learning) and not from *ma'aseh* (i.e. *ma'aseh bet din*, the judicial
> decision of a court, pp.106-108 above), unless it has been expressly deter-
> mined as *halakhah lema'aseh*. (*B. Baba Batra*, 130b)

The Rabbis regarded this function of ordination as having been established by
the ṣemikhah of Joshua bin Nun by Moses:

> 'And you shall lay your hands upon him' (*Num.* 27:18). And he [God] said to
> Moses: 'Moses, appoint for Joshua an interpreter, to enquire and interpret
> and instruct what laws are binding.' (*Sifre, Num.* 140)

Ṣemikhah thus involved the authority to instruct the people in the general
legal norms binding upon them. The ambit of such 'academic freedom' was

defined by the law of the 'rebellious Elder' (*zaken mamre*) — a capital
offence derived from *Deut.* 17:12. This was taken to refer to an ordained
Sage who refused to accept the authority of the Supreme Council of Elders:

> If he [the Elder] returned to his city, and continued to learn and teach
> according to the way he taught previously, he is exempt; but if he gave a
> decision concerning what should be done (*halakhah lema'aseh*), he is
> liable ... If a (non-ordained) student gave a decision concerning what should
> be done, he is exempt. (*M. Sanh.* 11:2)

Hence the discipline imposed by the law of the 'rebellious Elder' is applied
only to those who had received *semikhah,* and not to a student, even though
the *Mishnah* elsewhere (*M. Hor.* 1:1) regards as culpable a non-ordained
'disciple who was himself fit to give a decision' who acts on the decision of
a court which he knows has erred in law.

The concept of *semikhah* reflects the nature of the Sages' conception of
Jewish Law as a system of Divine Law. As observed below, both in the
Qumran writings and elsewhere, it was the divine inspiration of the person
interpreting the Bible that gave the norm its validity. In the Community
Rule of Qumran, prophecy is still accepted as a recognized form of revelation
of divine will. The text understands *Isa.* 40:3 as referring to:

> The interpretation of the *Torah* (*midrash hatorah*) [which] was commanded
> through Moses to do everything that was revealed from time to time, and as
> the prophets had revealed through the Divine Spirit. (*Serekh Hayahad* 8:15-
> 16)

The concept guiding the Sages' perception of revelation was different, as may
be seen from their interpretation of the verse: 'These are the Commandments
which God commanded Moses for the people Israel at Mount Sinai' (*Lev.*
27:14):

> From hereinafter the prophet is forbidden to decree anything new. (*Sifra,*
> *Behukotai* 13:7)

Thus from Moses onwards the ordained Sages are seen to be the only ones
authorized to create new interpretations of the *Torah.* As such, the status of
the Law of Moses as given from Sinai is attributed to the words of the
ordained Sages themselves.

> And when Yossi the son of Dormeskit came to Rabbi Eliezer in Lod, the latter
> asked him: 'What novel matter was said in the Academy today?' He (Yossi)
> replied: 'They gathered and decided: [the land of] Ammon and Moab are liable
> for the second tithe during the Sabbatical year.' Rabbi Eliezer cried and said:
> *'The secret of God is with those who fear him and his covenant he shall make*
> *known to them* (*Ps.* 25:14). Go and tell them: do not be anxious about your

decision; for I have a tradition from Rabbi Yoḥanan ben Zakkai, who received it from his Rabbi, and his Rabbi received it from his Rabbi, that it is a Law of Moses from Sinai, that Ammon and Moab give a second tithe during the Sabbatical year.' (*M. Yad.* 4:3)

R. Eliezer thus claims an unbroken tradition from Sinai for a rule which clearly derived from a new interpretation made by the Sages. The halakhic authority of the legal institutions was thus based upon the recognition of the status of Sages possessing *ṣemikhah*.

During the tannaitic period the Ordained *Bet Din* was supplemented by a Layman's *Bet Din* (*M. Sanh.* 3:1), a *Bet Din* of the Priests (*M. Ket.* 1:5) and at one time even a *Bet Din* of the Jewish Monarchy (*T. Sanh.* 4:6). Without doubt, the authority of the *Bet Din* of the Priests, and perhaps that of the other courts too, was based upon Jewish Law. The *Mishnah* states:

> There were two judges for the issuing of edicts (*dayyane gezerot*) in Jerusalem, Admon and Ḥanan the son of Abishalom ... whoever goes overseas and his wife demands her maintenance payments, Ḥanan said: 'Let her swear an oath at the end and not at the beginning.' The Sons of the Priests argued with him, and said: 'Let her swear an oath at the beginning and not at the end.' Rabbi Dossa b. Hyrcanus agreed with them, Rabbi Yoḥanan ben Zakkai said: Ḥanan has spoken well, Let her swear an oath only at the end. (*M. Ket.* 13:1)

But whatever the authority attributed to these courts under the *halakhah*, the *Mishnah* here records them together with such endorsements as they received from ordained Rabbis.

C. *The Bate Din* (Rabbinical Courts)

The tannaitic sources present a picture of an organized network of *Bate Din*. The Supreme Court stands at the head of the system:

> From where do we know that a Supreme Court is to be appointed for the whole of Israel? It is taught, 'you shall appoint Judges' (*Deut.* 16:18) ... And from where do we learn that a *Bet Din* is to be appointed for every city? It is taught 'in all your gates' ... And from where do we learn that a *Bet Din* is to be appointed for every Tribe? It is taught 'Judges for your tribes'. (*Sifre Num.* 145)

A different number of judges was to sit in each court: 'The Supreme Court of seventy one sat in the Hall of the Hewn Stone (by the Temple), and the other Courts of twenty three were in the cities of the Land of Israel' (*T. Ḥag.* 2:9). The Supreme Council of seventy one was to preside over matters regarding the totality of the nation, for example the laws of the High Priest (*M. Sanh.*

1:2); the Court of twenty three was authorized to deal with capital matters (*M. Sanh.* 1:4) and monetary matters came under the jurisdiction of any court of three (*ibid.*).

The members of the Supreme Court were judges who had previously served in lower courts: an elder was not to be appointed to the Hall of the Hewn Stone unless he previously had been a judge in his own town (*T. Shek.* 2:2). This court had functioned as the final authority whose decisions were legally binding:

> If one of them (a court of three) needed to know what is the law ... he would go to the ordained court (*bet din haṣamukh*, i.e. of twenty-three) in his town. If they had heard [the solution], they told him, and if not he and the most distinguished member of the court would go to the *Bet Din* at the Temple Mount. If they had heard [the solution], they told him, and if not he and the most distinguished member of the court would go to the *Bet Din* on the Rampart. If they had heard [the solution], they told him, and if not he and the most distinguished member of the court would go to the Great *Bet Din* in the Hall of the Hewn Stone ... If they had heard it they told them and if not they would rise to take a vote: if those who ruled that it was impure were the majority, it was impure, and if those who ruled that it was pure were the majority, it was pure. (*T. Hag.* 2:9)

From this description of the hierarchy of judicial decision-making, it is clear that the sources reflect a real, living situation (cf. *M. Peah* 2:6). This view is substantiated by the records of laws that relate to the activities of the *Bet Din*. For example, we hear of a regulation that the *Bet Din* in Usha enacted that 'A President of Court who sinned — is not excommunicated' (*B. M. Kat.* 17a); or that 'a forced act of *ḥalitsah* (release from the levirate) in the *Bet Din* is valid, but in a non-Jewish court is invalid' (*T. Yeb.* 12:13); and of rules regarding matters which are brought to the court during the intermediate days of Festivals (*Ḥol Hamo'ed*) (*T. M. Kat.* 2:11).

It would appear that the *Bet Din* was conducted according to accepted rules, for example:

> The *halakhah* is always determined according to the majority opinion, and minority opinions are only mentioned for the purpose of their negation. Rabbi Judah says ... perhaps an occasion will arise when it will have to be relied upon ... (*T. Eduy.* 1:3)

Or the principle noted by Rabbi Joshua:

> Rabbi Joshua ben Karḥa says: In matters that are derived by interpretation from the biblical text, we follow the stricter opinion; in matters which derive from the 'words of the scribes' (i.e. rabbinic enactments), we follow the more lenient opinion. (*T. Eduy.* 1:5)

It is difficult to imagine that the extremely well developed *halakhah* found in the tannaitic sources is purely the result of academic study in the academies, and does not contain the law as it was actually practised. Similarly, it is impossible to understand that the *halakhah*, as a practical legal system, did not function according to accepted rules.

The degree of reality reflected in the sources is particularly well illustrated in something which at first glance appears out of place. During the tannaitic period the *Bate Din* were also known as *Sanhedrin*: 'There was a large Sanhedrin of seventy one and a small one of twenty three' (*M. Sanh.* 1:6). However, from the historical writings of the time (especially Josephus) it is also evident that the Sanhedrin was the central political institution at the end of the period of the Second Temple. How could both of these institutions have used the same name? One might argue that there were indeed two separate institutions, and that the sources of Jewish Law gave the name Sanhedrin to the Supreme Court in order to explain that political authority which we know the Sages came to possess. But it is precisely this attribution of the name Sanhedrin that seems to indicate that at the time of the compilation of the sources there was already in existence a Sanhedrin that functioned as the supreme political body. Hence the Jewish legal sources could not deviate from what was known in reality. A second, and more plausible, possibility is that there was a connection between the Supreme Court and the political institution, in that the principal Sages were members of what was really a single institution. When the term is used in the historical writings, it refers to those meetings which were not connected to halakhic matters. It was this connection between the political and legal roles of the Sanhedrin which gave rise also to the use of the title 'Prince' (*Nasi*, often rendered 'Patriarch'). This was the title granted to the person standing at the head of the Sanhedrin.

A political role of the office of *Nasi* is well illustrated from the fact that 'Bar Kokhba' is himself referred to as *Nasi*, in the letters discovered near the Dead Sea. Indeed, the title *Nasi* had already had a political connotation in the Pentateuch. It may well be this political power which gave the *Nasi*, as Head of the Sanhedrin, the power to enact changes in the law. The connection between the political and juridical roles of the *Nasi* receives its most complete expression in the personage of Rabbi Judah the Prince, as will be seen presently.

5. The Principal Authorities

A. Hillel

Normally referred to as Hillel the Elder, Hillel was the holder of the highest legal post, that of the Head of the Supreme Court, at the end of the first century B.C.E. and the beginning of the first century C.E. Hillel can be considered as the Sage who initiated the tannaitic period, since it was he who established the system of *Torah* learning in the academy (the *Bet Midrash*).

> It happened once that the 14th [of Nissan] fell on the Sabbath. They asked Hillel the Elder: 'Does it [the *Pesach* Sacrifice] override the Sabbath?' He said to them: 'Do we only have one *Pesach* that overrides the Sabbath? We have more than three hundred *peṣaḥim* (sacrifices of the community) all of which override the Sabbath. ... Regarding the *Tamid* [the daily whole-offering], it says 'At its appointed time' and regarding the *Pesach* it says 'at its appointed time'. Just as the *Tamid* overrides the Sabbath, so too the *Pesach* overrides the Sabbath. Moreover, there is an *a fortiori* (*kal vaḥomer*) argument. If the *Tamid*, for failure to bring which one is not liable for *karet* [extirpation], nevertheless overrides the Sabbath, how much more so must the *Pesach*, for which one *is* liable to *karet*, override the Sabbath ...' And furthermore, I have also received this tradition from my masters ... On that same day they appointed Hillel as the Patriarch, and he taught them the laws of *Pesach*. (*T. Pes.* 4:13-14)

Today we also know from the Scrolls of Qumran that the question whether the sacrifices of the festivals were to be brought on the Sabbath was the subject of an extensive controversy between the members of the sect and the Sages. It was consequently necessary firmly to establish the *halakhah* on a matter regarding which there was opposition on the part of the sects. An echo of the controversy is hinted at in another rabbinic version of the dispute:

> And even though he (Hillel) sat before them explaining all day long, they did not accept his words, until he said to them, 'may it come upon me [i.e. a form of oath] ... This is what I learned from Shemayah and Abtalion.' (*Y. Pes.* 33a)

Thus the Sages were initially unwilling to accept Hillel's teaching of the law until he finally anchored it in tradition. Later on, however, the development of the interpretative rules of derivation of law from Scripture (the *middot*, used in *midrash halakhah*) were attributed to Hillel. Indeed, those attributed to him commence with the two forms of argument used in *T. Pes.* 4:13-14 (above) regarding the Passover sacrifice:

> Hillel the Elder expounded (*darash*) seven exegetical rules before the Elders of Bethyra: *kal vaḥomer* (inference *a fortiori*), *gezerah shavah* (inference from

the similarity of words or phrases) ... (Baraita d'Rabbi Yishma'el, *Sifra Lev.* 1:7, *T. Sanh.* 7.11; cf. Elon, *Jewish Law*, I.315f.)

Consequently, at the initial stages of the editing of the *Mishnah* after the Destruction of the Temple it is related (*T. Eduy.* 1:1): 'They said: Let us begin from Hillel and Shammai.'

Shammai the Elder was Hillel's disputant, and their disputes were carried over to the coming generations in debates between their Academies. After a few generations the Law was unanimously determined to follow the rulings of the House of Hillel, and Hillel's descendants continued to serve as the princes of the High Court during the tannaitic period. Hillel's various *takkanot*, on the other hand, were already accepted in his own generation, even though they were in conflict with the then accepted *halakhah*. A famous example is Hillel's *prozbul'* (a device whereby the cancellation of debts in the sabbatical year might be evaded, by signing a declaration before the court (Greek: *pros boule*).

> This is one of the matters enacted by Hillel the Elder. When he saw that people had stopped lending to one another, and were thereby transgressing the Commandment of the *Torah, Beware that there be not a base thought in your heart* (*Deut.* 15:9), he enacted the *Prozbul*. This is the text of the *Prozbul*: 'I hereby affirm to you _____ and you _____, honourable judges of the place of _____, that as regards any debt owing to me that I may collect it at any time that I wish.' And the judges sign below, or the witnesses. (*M. Shebi.* 10:3-4)

B. Rabbi Yoḥanan ben Zakkai

Rabbi Yoḥanan ben Zakkai was the most prominent of the early *Tannaim*, second only to Hillel the Elder. His Academy was established in Javneh after the destruction of Jerusalem. Already during Temple times he had established his own independent standing, not dependent on the *halakhah* as determined by the institutions. On the one hand, he took issue with those advocating what was known as the *halakhah* of the Sadducees, and who had attained key positions in the Rabbinical hierarchy:

> It happened that there was a Sadducee, for whom the sun had set (termination of the period of impurity) and he came to burn the [red heifer], and the matter became known to Rabbi Yoḥanan ben Zakkai, and he came and placed both of his hands upon him [to make him impure] ... (*T. Par.* 3:8).

Rabbi Yoḥanan did not accept the Sadducean rule that impurity terminated only at sunset. The antiquity of this dispute is evidenced by the Qumran

scroll, *Miktsat Maʿaseh Hatorah* (B13-16), where the same view as that of
the Sadducees is found.

> And concerning the purity-regulations of the cow of the purification-offering
> [the red heifer]: he who slaughters it and he who burns it and he who gathers
> its ashes and he who sprinkles the [water of] purification — it is at sun[se]t
> that all these become pure.

On the other hand, Rabbi Yoḥanan ben Zakkai also disputed the laws of the
priests, who in general adhered to the Sages' own approach to the *halakhah*.
Furthermore, his *takkanot* were also in opposition to the accepted *halakhah*,
and were accepted despite initial opposition to them:

> Rabbi Joshua and R. Judah b. Bethyra testified, with regard to the widow
> who belonged to a family of doubtful purity, that she was eligible to marry a
> Priest ... Rabban Shimon ben Gamliel said: we have accepted your testi-
> mony [in the Supreme Court], but what shall we do, for Rabban Yoḥanan ben
> Zakkai decreed not to have courts presiding over these matters ... (*M. Eduy.*
> 8:3)

Rabbi Yoḥanan ben Zakkai issued a number of enactments after the
destruction of Jerusalem, with the aim of establishing the hegemony of the
halakhah, independent of the Temple. He is said to have ordained his students without requesting the authorization of the Supreme Court, or that of
the *Nasi* (*Y. Sanh.*, 19a). He also issued enactments aimed at abolishing the
dependence of the *halakhah* on institutions (like the Sanhedrin or the *Nasi*),
and it was the introduction of this feature that characterized the entire
subsequent tannaitic period.

C. Rabbi Akiba

Rabbi Akiba was the most prominent Sage of the first half of the second
century C.E. Notwithstanding the fact that he did not attain the position of
Nasi, his stamp is clearly imprinted on all the tannaitic *halakhah*:

> And isn't it clear that if Ezra had not been there during his time, and Rabbi
> Akiba in his time, that the *Torah* would have been forgotten by Israel? (*Sifre,
> Deut.* 48)

He was executed by the Romans after the 'Bar Kochba' rebellion (132-135
C.E.), of which he was one of the leaders.

Rabbi Akiba stood at the head of a project of compilation of all of the
halakhic literature, including the *Midrashe Halakhah*. He compiled all of the
early *mishnayot* and added his own traditions, or those of other sages whose
views he had accepted (e.g. *M. Sanh.* 3:4, *M. Taan.* 3:4). In fact, the com-

pilation of all the halakhic literature was attributed to the students of Rabbi Akiba's academy (*B. Sanh.* 86a).

Of all the Sages, it was Rabbi Akiba who made the most significant contribution to the *halakhah*, both by the introduction of new *halakhot* and by way of creative interpretation (*Y. Shek.* 48a). For example:

> If she drew off the shoe and pronounced the words but did not spit, according to Rabbi Eliezer her *halitsah* is invalid, but according to R. Akiba it is valid. Rabbi Eliezer said: 'It is written: So shall it be done ... (*Deut.* 25:9), hence everything that is a deed is necessary.' Rabbi Akiba said to him: 'My proof is from the same verse. "So shall it be done *to the man*." Thus, only actions to be performed on the man are necessary.' (*M. Yeb.* 9:3)

The specific innovation of Rabbi Akiba (eliminating the necessity for spitting from the biblically-prescribed ceremony releasing the sister-in-law from the obligation to marry the brother of her deceased husband) involved a radical reinterpretation of the verse. Sometimes he went further, in attaching significance to tiny grammatical details.

> Rabbi Judah said in the name of Rav: 'When Moses went on high, he found the Lord sitting and fastening crownlets to the letters of the *Torah*. Moses said to him 'Master of the universe, why are you delaying [the giving of the *Torah* by fastening crownlets]?' God responded, 'There will be a man who will live many generations from now, whose name is Akiba, son of Joseph, who will deduce myriads of law from every jot and title of every letter.' Moses said to God, 'Master of the universe, allow me to see him.' God replied, 'turn around.' He [Moses] went and sat behind eight rows [of students] and did not understand what was being said, and he felt faint. But when the discussion reached the question [of the source of the law], R. Akiba's students said to him, 'Rabbi what is your authority?' R. Akiba answered, 'It is a law given to Moses at Sinai.' Then Moses was at ease. (*B. Menahot 29b*)

This method of interpretation proved not to the liking of Rabbi Yishmael, a contemporary and frequent disputant of Rabbi Akiba. Rabbi Yishmael had adopted the rule that 'The *Torah* speaks in the language of men' (*B. Sot.* 3a), a less esoteric exegetical approach.

Rabbi Akiba also innovated with respect to legal argumentation, formulating new legal principles — for example: the rule that one must be strict in matters of *issurin* (prohibitions). Thus, in the context of relations forbidden to an *agunah* (abandoned wife):

> 'A woman who went overseas together with her husband, and came back and said: "My husband is dead", she may marry again ...' These are the words of Rabbi Tarfon. Rabbi Akiba said: 'This is not the way of ensuring her avoidance of sinning: she may not remarry ...' (*M. Yeb.* 15:6)

It was this interpretive approach of Rabbi Akiba which became the basis for many innovations in the interpretation of the *halakhah* (e.g. *T. Zeb.* 1:8). Indeed, we find the following endorsement of the importance attached by R. Akiba to scholarly interpretation as a source of law:

> Rabbi Tarfon (one of Rabbi Akiba's teachers) and the Elders were sitting in the attic of the house of Nitza in Lydda, and they were asked the following question: 'Which is greater: study (*talmud*) or judgment (*ma'aseh*)?' Rabbi Tarfon answered: judgment. Rabbi Akiba answered: study. They all answered together and said: Study is greater, for study leads to judgment. (*B. Kidd.* 40b)

D. Rabbi Judah the Prince (the *Nasi*)

Rabbi Judah the Prince was the editor of the *Mishnah* and is consequently referred to simply as 'Rabbi'. He lived during the second half of the second century and the beginning of the third century C.E. Jewish Law during his time was characterized by the fact that all of the institutional powers were concentrated in the hands of the *Nasi*. This was the result of a number of factors: the political standing acquired by the office of *Nasi* with the Government in Rome; the status of the *Nasi* in the eyes of the people as a national leader; and his standing in the eyes of the Sages as a *Torah* scholar of outstanding stature.

This variety of qualities is reflected in the various *takkanot* enacted by Rabbi, all of which attest to the force of his authority. As observed at p.105 above, Rabbi determined that the various tax obligations would have the status of preferred debts as against other claims against the property of the debtor (*Y. Ket.*, 34a). In order to strengthen Jewish autonomy, he gave a more limited interpretation to the law of *sykarikon* (p.104, above):

> Rabbi convened a *Bet Din* and they determined that if it [the field] had been in the hands of *sykarikon* for twelve months then whoever took possession of it first would be entitled to it, but the original owners had the right to a quarter. (*M. Gitt.* 5:6)

In these particular laws, Rabbi was in essence following in the footsteps of previous rulings, yet in other cases he did not hesitate to issue new enactments in order to strengthen Jewish autonomy. For example, he released Jewish residents from the obligation to observe the sabbatical year in areas in which most of the residents were non-Jews, in order to strengthen their economic position (*Y. Dem.* 22c), thereby strengthening the authority of the Rabbis amongst Jews living in such areas.

As *Nasi*, Rabbi enjoyed an unprecedented degree of respect by comparison with his predecessors. During his time, ordination of Sages (*semikhah*) could not be performed without his authorization (see *Y. Sanh.* 15:1, 19a, quoted at p.124 above). Rabbi was authorized to prevent the ordination even of persons who had been found suitable for such appointment by the *Bet Din*, and he was also able temporarily to delay an appointment.

Rabbi's main influence on Jewish Law was the editing of the *Mishnah*. The *Mishnah* of Rabbi became the binding version of the *Mishnah* and this was primarily due to his authority and stature as a great scholar of the *Torah*. Rabbi's stature is especially reflected in the vast number of laws in his name, primarily in the *Tosefta* and the *Baraitas*. For example, the *Mishnah* presents a list of prayers which could be said in all languages (*M. Sot.* 7:1), but the *Tosefta* states:

> The Blessings, *Hallel*, *Shema*, and the *Amidah* (18 blessings) may be said in all languages. Rabbi says: 'I say that the *Shema* may be said only in the Holy Language, for it is said: "And these words". (*Num* .6:6)' (*T. Sot.* 7:7)

Rabbi was even known to have argued with his father:

> The Rabbis taught: 'If he revoked the *get*, it is considered invalid.' These are the words of Rabbi. Rabbi Shimon b. Gamliel said: 'He may not revoke or add to his condition, for if he is allowed to, then what power does the *Bet Din* have?' (*B. Gitt.* 33a)

It was Rabbi's editing of the *Mishnah* that laid the basis for the development of Jewish Law over the generations.

6. Betrothal and Marriage in the Law of the Tannaitic Period

The legal sources of the tannaitic period are not limited to the law that was actually practised at that time; rather, they preserve both earlier sources and sources which may have been of purely academic value. Nonetheless, we can assume that if they were actually studied in the academies, and if they were included in the compilations of the *halakhah* of the period, then they must have been thought to possess some kind of practical significance. In the absence of this assumption it is difficult to explain the reason for their inclusion in the books of learning, together with the sources of the practical law. But given the lack of historical documentation and the current state of research, this must be viewed as a working assumption only. On the other hand, it is precisely this working assumption that helps us to elucidate the sources and increase our understanding of them, in terms of their legal purpose and meaning. It is with this assumption that the following hypotheses on the development of aspects of Jewish family law during this period are presented.

The tannaitic law relating to betrothal and marriage reflects the understanding, at the time, that these acts were in many of their aspects essentially property transactions. The betrothal is an act of acquiring in which the husband appropriates his wife. Generally, before a woman was betrothed, it was her father who held property rights in her. The father's rights in his daughter are described in the *Mishnah*:

> He is entitled (*zakai*) to any lost property found by her, to the fruits of her labour, to set aside her vows, and he shall receive her bill of divorce (*get*). (*M. Ket.* 4:4)

The term 'entitled' (*zakai*) used in the *Mishnah* is taken from the language of property rights (*zekhut, zekhiyah*): the father has property rights in his daughter and, hence, is entitled to something in exchange for them. It is, for this reason, the father who betroths his daughter and grants rights in her to her husband in consideration for money. It is therefore also he who holds the marriage contract (*ketubah*).

An ancient *mishnah* at the beginning of the Tractate *Kiddushin* states:

> A woman is acquired in three ways — by money, a writ, and intercourse (*M. Kidd.* 1:1, *T. Yeb.* 21:1; see also p.122 above).

Following the act of acquisition — the betrothal — the woman was already considered 'a married woman'. This was also reflected in the penal law (of adultery, for example). The full marriage, however, occurred in two stages. It was only after the betrothed woman left her father's house for her husband's that the marriage was complete and marital relations commenced. The transfer of the woman from her father's house to her husband's for the purpose of the marriage, then, completes the betrothal, or the transaction.

> She shall remain in the domain (*reshut*) of her father [during the betrothal period], until she enters the domain of the husband for marriage. (*M. Ket.* 4:5)

Betrothal may be regarded as a form of inchoate marriage: though relations between the parties are not yet those of full marriage, relations between the woman and other men are strictly forbidden.

In terms of the property relations between the parties, betrothal also has a special nature. With regard to maintenance, for example, an early *mishnah* (*M. Ket.* 4:5:2, *T. Ket.* 5:1, *Sifre Num.* 117) states that the husband was required to maintain his wife already by virtue of the betrothal. If the woman were betrothed to a priest, he was also entitled to support her from his tithe income-in-kind. In a later *mishnah* (apparently from the time of Rabbi Akiba and Rabbi Tarfon) the Sages ruled that a woman betrothed to a priest may not eat from the tithes until her husband asks to marry her. Then she goes through a waiting period of 12 months after the betrothal. In the latest version of the *mishnah* it is determined that 'the woman shall not eat of the *terumah* (the heave offerings owed to the priests) until she goes under the (marital) canopy' (*M. Ket.* 5:3). It appears as if the Sages come to the view that it is only when the initial (merely proprietal) connection of betrothal is transformed into full marriage that the woman is entitled to eat of the tithes.

The legal consequences of betrothal are further illustrated by the law of inheritance. Even if the husband has been alone with his fiancee (and may have engaged in conjugal relations) prior to her entering the canopy, he does not inherit from her:

> [In the case of a betrothed woman] who came under the canopy not for the sake of marriage and died, even though her *ketubah* is situated with her husband, her father still inherits her ... If she came under the canopy for the purpose of marriage, and then died, even though her *ketubah* is still situated with her father, her husband will inherit from her. (*T. Ket.* 4:4)

Thus, it is the entrance of the bride to the house of the husband which accomplishes the act of the marriage.

From the concluding words of this *tosefta* it is apparent that at the stage of the betrothal the father of the bride receives the money of the *ketubah,* in addition to the money he has provided for the dowry. This is reflected in another passage of the *Tosefta* regarding the very early law:

> At the beginning when the *ketubah* money was with her father, it was easy for him to divorce her. Shimon ben Shetaḥ therefore enacted that the *ketubah* money would remain with the husband; and that he would write to her: 'All of the property that I have is in lien and mortgaged to your *ketubah.*' (*T. Ket.* 12:1)

Termination of a betrothal would normally require a bill of divorce (*geṭ*). There is evidence of a law allowing one to make a condition under which the betrothal could be cancelled retroactively without the necessity of a *geṭ*.

> When the people of Alexandria betrothed women, and then someone came from the market and stole her [and married her], and the matter came before the Sages, they considered declaring the children bastards (*mamzerim*). Hillel the Elder said to them: 'Bring me the *ketubah* of your mothers'. They showed them to him, and it was written, 'When you enter my house you will be my wife according to the custom of Moses and Israel.' (*T. Ket.* 4:9)

Thus, by virtue of the conditions laid down in the *ketubah*, the acquisition made by the betrothal was cancelled without the requirement of a *get*, even though the act of betrothal did result in the creation of the status of 'married woman'.

Let us now look more closely at the nature of the institution of the *ketubah*. The *ketubah* has been regarded as being derived from Scripture:

> Rabbi Yishmael taught: 'He shall weigh money as in the dowry for the virgins' (*Ex.* 22:16). This tells us that he [the groom] makes it for her as a dowry, and a dowry is none other than a *ketubah*, as it is said (*Gen.* 34:12): 'Give me a large *mohar* and present.' (*Y. Ket.* 24:4)

Even the sum of the *ketubah* was based upon the same verse:

> Just as this one was for fifty pieces of silver, so [the *ketubah* of] all virgins is for fifty pieces of silver. Rabbi Shimon ben Gamliel says: 'The *ketubah* of the woman has no limitation from the *Torah*!' (*Mekhilta de Rashbi*, ad *Ex.* 22:16).

According to this approach, the *ketubah* is a part of the contract of betrothal by force of the law of the *Torah* itself. On the other hand, according to the approach attributed to Shimon ben Shetaḥ, the *ketubah* is an enactment of the Sages. This question of the status of the institution has practical consequences. If it is biblical, then the giving of the *ketubah* is dependent on the consent of the father of the bride and the groom (since the whole institution of betrothal in the Bible is dependent on the will of the parties, rather than general rules of law). But if it is an enactment of the Sages, as Shimon ben Shetaḥ maintained, it is not dependent on such consent. Hence,

> If he did not write her a *ketubah* — a virgin is nonetheless entitled to 200 *denars* [50 pieces of silver = 200 *denars*] ... for this is a condition set by the *Bet Din.* (*M.Ket.* 4:7)

Thus the Sages converted the marital contract of the *ketubah* into a legally mandated requirement not based on the consent of the sides.

This particular approach is consistent with the later understanding according to which the document itself came to function as the primary form of betrothal, in place of monetary consideration. Indeed, the money itself came to be purely symbolic:

> 'By money' — The House of Shammai say: by a *denar* (a coin, the *denarius*) or a *denar*'s worth; The House of Hillel say: by a *perutah* (the smallest copper coin) or a *perutah*'s worth ... [a *denar* was worth 196 perutahs].

This explains the change from the older terminology of 'a woman is acquired' (*niḳnit*) to that of 'a woman is sanctified' (*meḳudeshet, M. Kidd.* 2:1), i.e.

(normally) through this common agreement, *T. Yev.* 2:1).

Our review of this area of Jewish Law during the tannaitic period demonstrates that the *halakhah* was not a homogenous system and that a number of different traditions existed simultaneously. The different legal approaches were based on ancient traditions or on enactments of the Sages. Jewish Law during the period reflected a legal theory according to which the *halakhah* was not dependent on a particular legal or political institution, but rather on scholarship that conferred validity on the different laws. Despite the differences between the divergent strands, a fundamental sense of unity was preserved.

> A person should not say: 'Since some prohibit and some permit, why should I study?' But it is written: '(the words of the Sages) have been given by a single Shepherd ...' (*Eccles.* 12:11). (*T.* Sot. 7:12)

Moreover, such scholarly differences did not generate sectarian division. It was said of the House of Shammai and the House of Hillel:

> Even though these prohibit and these permit, these negate and these affirm, the House of Shammai did not refrain from marrying women belonging to the House of Hillel, nor did the House of Hillel refrain from marrying the women of the House of Shammai. (*M. Yeb.* 1:4)

7. *Bibliography*

Alon, G. *Jews, Judaism and the Classical World* (Jerusalem: Magnes Press, 1977).

Elon, M., *Jewish Law: History, Sources, Principles*, trld. B. Auerbach and M.J. Sykes (Philadelphia and Jerusalem: Jewish Publication Society, 1994), chs.8, 9, 15, 27-28.

Falk, Z.W., *Introduction to Jewish Law in the Second Commonwealth* (Leiden: E.J. Brill, 1978).

Grabbe, L.L., *Judaism from Cyrus to Hadrian* (London: SCM Press, 1994).

Halivni, D.W., *Midrash, Mishnah and Gemara* (Cambridge MA.: Harvard University Press, 1986).

Halivni, D.W., *Peshat and Derash* (New York: Oxford University Press, 1991).

Mantel, H., *Studies in the History of the Sanhedrin* (Cambridge MA.: Harvard University Press, 1961).

Neusner, J., *Development of a Legend: Studies on the Traditions Concerning Yohanan ben Zakkai* (Leiden: E.J. Brill, 1970).

Neusner, J., *Eliezer ben Hyrcanus: The Tradition and the Man* (Leiden: E.J. Brill, 1973).

Rakover, N., *The Multi-Language Bibliography of Jewish Law* (Jerusalem: The Library of Jewish Law, 1990).

Safrai, S. and Stern, M., eds., *The Jewish People in the First Century* (Assen: Van Gorcum, 1974-76, 2 vols.).

Safrai, S., ed., *The Literature of the Sages*, First Part (Assen/Maastricht: Van Gorcum and Philadelphia: Fortress Press, 1987), bibliography: pp. 415-431.

Talmon, S., ed., *Jewish Civilisation in the Hellenistic-Roman Period* (Sheffield Academic Press, Sheffield, 1991).

Urbach, E.E., *The Halakhah, Its Source and Development* (Jerusalem: Massada Press, 1986).

Urbach, E.E., *The Sages, Their Concepts and Beliefs* (Jerusalem: Magnes Press, 1975).

Weisbard, P.H. and Schonberg, P., *Jewish Law: Bibliography of Sources and Scholarship in English* (Littleton: Rothman, 1989).

6

JEWISH AND ROMAN
JURISDICTION*

by

ALFREDO MORDECHAI RABELLO
Hebrew University, Jerusalem

1. *Introduction*

In this chapter we shall discuss the extent to which the Roman authorities (who conquered all the Mediterranean lands, including Palestine —
known to the Jews as *Erets Yisrael*, 'the Land of Israel') permitted the Jews
to keep their own civil law as the binding law in their relations amongst
themselves. From the perspective of the Roman sources, it is a question of
jurisdiction.[1]

The problem of jurisdiction is a particularly complex one; its difficulties
vary according to the different sources and the different periods. There is a
distinction between the problems of civil jurisdiction — which deals with
private law (e.g., family law, contract law or property law) — and those of
public jurisdiction which includes criminal law. Moreover, what were the
characteristics of the court which exercised jurisdiction over Jews in civil and
criminal matters? Was it a Jewish court or a Roman court? Did Jewish
courts and Roman courts have any kind of contact with one another?
According to which legal system were the Jews judged? Other questions
concerning this issue emerge: did Roman law give the Jews the right to hold
their own courts with legal authority to judge matters between Jews? Could
these Jewish courts give judgments which would be recognized by the
Roman Government as judgments that could turn into a *res iudicata*, so that
these cases would not be brought again before a Roman court? Were the
judgments of the Jewish courts executable and who was to implement

* This study is dedicated to the blessed memory of the great Talmudist, Scholar,
Teacher and Friend, Professor Ephraim Urbach ל׳ז with gratitude and love.

them — the Jewish authorities or the Roman authorities?

Closely implicated in these questions is the issue of citizenship. What was the civil status of the Jews under Roman rule? Did they continue to have a recognized citizenship, or was their status so reduced that they no longer enjoyed any civil rights? If the answer to this latter question is affirmative, it will have a major impact on the question of jurisdiction, because it is not possible that people with low civil status will enjoy high jurisdictional status and other privileges. Our treatment of each period therefore commences with some remarks on *status civitatis*.

The problem of civil status arises also in respect of Diaspora Jews. In many places these Jews received political rights locally; in others they acquired Roman citizenship. Any serious discussion of this subject must draw distinctions according to the various provinces and the different periods.

Here, we shall discuss principally those questions which relate specifically to Jewish civil jurisdiction[2] in Palestine, reviewing the evidence for each major period in turn (sections 2-5); we then turn to the Diaspora (section 6), and conclude with some questions concerning family law (section 7).

2.   *Jewish Jurisdiction in Palestine until the End of the First Jewish War (63 B.C.E.-70 C.E.)*

Those Jews who had local citizenship in Palestine were considered by Roman law as *peregrini* in consequence of treaties between Judaea and Rome. As far as Greek cities were concerned, Jews were aliens of Jewish nationality. They could become either 'aliens without the right of local residence' (ξένοι) or, the more common case 'aliens with the right of domicile' (*incolae*).[3] In neither case, however, could they obtain the right of citizenship.

Furthermore, a large number of Jews enjoyed some local civic rights.[4] Those possessing Greek citizenship were exempt from having to worship the local gods, a circumstance which often led to riots on the part of the local population. There were in addition Jews who were Roman citizens (*cives Romani*). Such were either slaves freed by a master who was himself a Roman citizen (by *manumissio*), or freemen who had won Roman citizenship as a grant from the Government. Finally, there were Jewish slaves (*servi*).

We have many sources — both documents and the Palestinian rabbinic sources — which show that Jews regularly used to arrange their own affairs before Jewish judges. But was this practice accepted legally?

At the beginning of the occupation, Rome was well aware of how highly the Jews of Palestine valued their traditions (the customs of the fathers), which were, above all, of religious importance. Rome had no desire to involve itself in internal institutions, other than the determination of who would be responsible to Rome for providing internal order. More extreme intervention would have brought negative reactions and could, they realized, lead to a revolt. Thus Pompey (who in 63 B.C.E. overthrew the Hasmonean kingdom and established a new order in Palestine[5]) left Judea under the rule of Hyrcanus II (the last member of the Hasmonean dynasty), as Ethnarch (the highest Jewish official in Palestine) and High Priest;[6] after the difficult governorship of Gabinius, Julius Caesar restored Hyrcanus II to his position (47 B.C.E.). His duties were primarily religious, and related to the Temple in Jerusalem. Hyrcanus was subordinated to the supervision of the Roman ruler of Syria. What is worthy of note is that Hyrcanus retained the right to administer justice to the nation on an internal basis according to the 'customs of the fathers';[7] the principle of judicial autonomy was thus preserved.[8]

In general, as far as civil law goes, King Herod (37-4 B.C.E.) too did not interfere overtly by changing the 'laws of the fathers'. Local courts continued to function in accordance with traditional norms.[9] Clearly the internal conflicts between classes and sects, particularly between Sadducees and Pharisees, bear no connection at all to the question of whether Rome allowed autonomy of civil justice to remain, as it apparently did.

In the year 6 C.E., Judaea became a Roman *provincia*,[10] and the Roman ruler became the highest authority in both criminal and civil law. The same rules which were applied in other countries subordinated and attached to the Roman Empire by alliance, appear to have applied also in Palestine. Jewish courts (i.e. 'local courts') had the authority to execute judgments in civil cases involving Jews (*iudaei*), whether they were cases of conflicts among Jews or cases involving Jews and non-Jews. However, a case involving a Roman citizen could be brought before a Roman magistrate.

One of the responsibilities of the Jewish court was the appointment of guardians, at least when the matter concerned a non-Roman citizen. In the case of Roman citizens, members of the family were automatically appointed, in the absence of guardians appointed by will. Roman law required both children under 14 and women to have their dealings, including litigation, authorized by guardians. The Jewish practice may have been prompted by the needs of Jews who were non-citizens to seek access to Roman courts in property matters (as in the case of Babatha, ssee p.146 below). The very term for guardian, *apotropos*, suggests a Hellenistic source for the institution in Jewish law.

Alongside the courts, it seems that archives existed in Greek towns (i.e. the towns with a longstanding population of Hellenistic origin, such as Caesarea, Gaza and Scytopolis[11]) and other places; these archives helped in confirming and validating various kinds of legal document.

Roman provincial governors also had in theory authority to involve themselves in civil judgments; however, following the custom of Rome, they preferred, in this period, not to intervene. There was, however, no universal practice in such matters throughout the Empire.[12] Yet even after Judea became a Roman *provincia*, the governor maintained the principle of leaving civil justice to the local Jewish institutions. Rome defined autonomy as the right to live according to independent laws (*suae leges*), 'autonomy in the broad sense of independent civil justice'.[13]

I believe that Judaea was among those states that had their own law restored to them — *leges suas reddere*.[14] The residents had the status of foreigners enjoying their own law (*peregrini qui suis legibus utuntur*), and thus living 'in accordance with local law' (*secundum propriae civitatis iura*). Thus it is possible to establish that Jewish courts in Palestine were able to judge conflicts between Jews, just as in other places conflicts between local residents were decided by local courts or by *iudex peregrinus*.

As for criminal law, we cannot be certain as to the limits which Rome placed on the competence of Jewish courts to enjoy jurisdictional autonomy. The issue is discussed in an earlier chapter, in the context of the trial of Jesus (ch.2, p.38, above). One special problem relates to the capital punishment of a stranger who entered the Temple of Jerusalem. Jean Juster believed that the Sanhedrin had the authority, with the backing of the Roman law, to execute every stranger (even if he were a Roman citizen) who had entered the forbidden grounds of the Temple. His belief was based on a dubious paragraph in Josephus' *War*, 6,2,4, which stands in contradiction to other sources. There is no other source, either Jewish or Roman, that can verify the assumption that the Roman administration recognized the Sanhedrin's power to pronounce death verdicts on Roman citizens. In fact, the 'capital punishment' here may well be extra-judicial, a form of popular justice (or self-help) rather than an act of government or the judicial system.[15]

3. *Between the Two Jewish Revolts (70-135 C.E.)*

A. Citizenship

According to the theory of Mommsen,[16] after the war which ended in the destruction of their State in 70 C.E., all the Jews in the Empire lost the autonomy they had formerly enjoyed. Those who had remained free became *peregrini dediticii*:[17] According to Mommsen Judaism was no longer the national cult of the Jewish people. It became a 'tolerated cult', a *religio licita*. Juster vehemently rejects this view. In his opinion, the war which destroyed the Jewish State had no effect on the *status civitatis* of the Jews in the Empire. They continued to be regarded as a people (*natio*) even after 70 C.E., and in a certain sense they enjoyed a number of privileges. This was due to the respect for religion which the Romans had acquired and to the close link which existed between the Jewish religion and the Jewish Law.[18] Juster's criticism of Mommsen's theory opened the door for recent studies, which proved that the legal status of the Jews was much more diversified, not only in different places but also at different periods; therefore, it would be wrong to generalize. In particular with regard to the Jewish community in Palestine, one must make distinctions according to the different types of relationship which could exist with Rome. In theory, conquered communities could be deprived of all civil rights, being relegated to the status of *dediticiae*. This does not appear to have occurred in Palestine;[19] rather, it appears that here as elsewhere there is 'decisive proof that local laws were applied in the Roman provinces for regulating the relations between private persons' (Volterra).[20]

B. Roman Courts

i.   The application of Jewish Law by Roman courts in Palestine (70-132 C.E.)

Each province had its own special law (*lex provinciae*); we do not however have any evidence concerning the special law of Syria-Palestine. Therefore, we must try to draw a picture of the situation from what evidence we do have, which are rabbinic sources on the one hand, and Roman sources from other provinces on the other hand.

In civil cases involving Jews only,[21] the Jewish courts had authority to pass judgments, but this authority was no longer exclusive, as it had been before the War; it was concurrent with the authority of Roman courts. But even these Roman courts might apply Jewish Law, as the Jewish sources themselves indicate. Rabbi Eleazar ben Azariah (end of the first century and one of the greatest Sages of Yavneh), reports:[22]

Now suppose the gentile courts judge according to the laws of Israel. I might

understand that their decisions are valid. But Scripture says: 'And these are
the ordinances which thou shalt set before them.' You may judge their cases
but they are not to judge your cases.

On the basis of this interpretation of 'And these are the ordinances which
thou shalt set before them' (*Ex.* 21:1), the Rabbis argued (*ibid.*):

A bill of divorce given by force, if by Israelitish authority, is valid, but if by
gentile authority, it is not valid. It is, however, valid if the Gentiles merely
bind the husband over and say to him: 'Do as the Israelites tell thee'.

Thus we understand from Rabbi Eleazar's words that non-Jews (i.e. Roman
courts) were indeed allowed to judge Jews. According to which law did the
Roman courts judge the Jews? The answer to this question can also be found
in Rabbi Eleazar ben Azariah's words: generally they had to pass judgments
according to the local law, i.e. in this case the national laws of the Jews
(*iudaei*): 'The non-Jews passed judgments according to the laws of Israel'.

There is a great importance in Rabbi Eleazar's words, since we know that
at a certain period he served as Patriarch (*Nasi*) instead of Rabban Gamliel
(after the latter's temporary expulsion): the Patriarch, as Head of the
Sanhedrin (see pp.44f., 127ff., above) was the Jewish leader of *Eretz Yisrael*,
and was regarded by the Diaspora Jews as the leader of all Jewry, a sort of a
national leader. According to the Jerusalem Talmud, Rabbi Eleazar was
appointed President of the Court (*Av Bet Din*) after the return of Rabban
Gamliel to his previous position of Patriarch; moreover, Rabbi Eleazar was
in Rome with the delegation of Rabbis from Yavneh.[23]

ii.   The application of Roman Law to Romans and non-Romans in Roman
      courts: the case of Babatha

It is clear that in Palestine, as in other provinces, the Roman governor
had judicial authority concurrent with that of the local courts. The authority
of justice (*iurisdictio*)[24] — both civil justice[25] and criminal justice — was
among his most important responsibilities. He exercized this authority in
the courts that were established in various areas, the *conventus*. The governor judged civil cases primarily between Roman citizens, with authority
similar to that of the *praetor urbanus* at Rome. He upheld the norms of
provincial decrees (*edicta*) and the norms established by the law of the
province (*lex provinciae*). We must not forget that at this time there were
many Roman citizens in Palestine. They were members of the provincial
government, soldiers, newly created Roman citizens (such as Herod's family),
former slaves who were freed by Roman masters,[26] or non-Jewish citizens

living in Palestine. The Roman Judge had to judge cases involving Roman citizens, at least when the citizens were the defendants.

Recently, in 'the Cave of Letters' at Ein Gedi (near the Dead Sea) the Archive of Babatha, the daughter of Simon, was discovered. It includes documents of great interest.[27] Babatha, who lived in Maoza (in the recently established province of Arabia [Petraea]) preserved documents from the period between 93-94 and 132 C.E.;[28] three of the papyri discovered, from 124-125, directly concern our problem: they deal, for example, with her dispute with the guardians of her orphan son, Yeshua Ben Yeshua. Though Babatha does *not* appear to have had Roman citizenship, she sues in the court of the Roman governor at Petra. Some deeds of gift in the archive, designed to advance the financial interests of daughters and wives, appear to presuppose a law of succession in some respects different from that of Jewish law.[29] There is also evidence of Jews registering their ownership of land in Greek declarations which include oaths by the Roman Emperor.[30]

One of the Greek texts is a translation of the praetor's formula reported in Gaius' *Institutes*, IV.7.[31] A non-Roman citizen was thus submitting to a Roman jurisdiction applying Roman law, and the Roman jurisdiction was available to such a non-citizen. But in order to get a more balanced picture it should be remembered that the period concerned was a particularly hard one (between the revolt which had just ended in 117 and the revolt which was about to occur in 132). It should also be taken into account that Babatha was a widow who wanted to secure her position and that of her son, and who wanted her document to be recognized throughout the land, e.g. in the new province of Arabia. I would not therefore derive from this any general conclusion regarding the extent of exercise of Roman jurisdiction over Jews, although the phenomenon of the use of Roman, or Roman-Hellenistic, Law in different aspects of Jewish life could not have been marginal. The Jews were well aware of all the dangers to Jewish Law concealed in the power of the laws of the conquerors.

C. Jewish Courts

i. Jewish courts in Palestine before Bar Kochba's revolt, 132 C.E.

We have noted already the comments of Rabbi Eleazar on the possibility of Roman application of Jewish Law (pp.145f., above). The comment indicates the possibility that a Jew would not wish to be judged according to a completely unfamiliar law (Roman Law), but might agree to be judged in a

Roman court if it were to pass judgments according to the 'Jewish Law'. On account of this potential danger to the integrity of the Jewish system, Rabbi Eleazar forbids Jews to have recourse to Roman courts. It must follow that in this period — between the First Jewish Revolt and that of Bar Kochba's— the Jews of Palestine did have (concurrent) juridical autonomy.

Other Rabbinic sources lead to similar conclusions. For example, *B. Gitt.* 88b:[32]

> Rabbi Tarfon used to say: in any place when you find Heathen law courts (*Agoraiot*), even though their law is the same as the Israelites', you must not resort to them ...

Attention should be paid to the word *Agoraiot*: the *agora* was the place where public meetings and trials took place, but here the Greek term is the translation of the Latin term *conventus*, and refers to public meetings in provinces for the purpose of passing judgments.

Recent research on the Roman provinces helps us to understand better the Sages' fears. In the provinces there was a juridical system which was divided into three: first, there was the Roman Law, the one which was implemented in Rome, and which was also applied to Roman citizens in the provinces; second, there was the local law, the national law which existed in the area prior to the Roman occupation (including Jewish Law, Greek Law and Egyptian Law); third, there was the Provincial Law — in reality the local law, but subject to such changes as the rulers wished to introduce as a part of the local law according to the Roman spirit. This triple juridical system meant that judgment varied from place to place. Thus, even where Roman courts purported to apply 'local' (here, Jewish) law (pp.145f., above), it would be in the sense of 'Provincial Law', and thus subject to modification in the light of Roman directives and principles.

Greek writers from the Flavian period such as Dio Chrysostomus (from Bytinia) and Plutarch also considered legal autonomy as a serious problem.[33] These writers emphasize the subordination of the Greek magistrate to the Roman magistrate. They also stress the importance of bringing their cases before local judges (i.e. in this case Greek judges) and not before the Roman proconsul. If we take into account the fact that these sentiments were uttered by writers who thought that the cultures of Greek and Rome could coexist, we will be able to understand better the Jewish Sages' position on this matter. It was in the very procedure which apparently made Jewish Law applicable in Roman courts that the Sages of Palestine foresaw the greatest danger to the independence of the Jewish Law.

The Sages of Israel understood that the common people could have innocently thought that they were presented with a *Torah* judgment in Roman courts too, because that could have been the way matters appeared. But they realized that *Torah* judgment could not possibly remain autonomous if it was applied by non-Jewish judges and mixed with other laws which could have appeared as 'more human' or more correct in the view of Roman judges. The integrity of Jewish Law depended not merely on its being applied as law, but also on its being applied by its own justices.

Indeed, just as we hear of a Roman judge in Egypt who negated the local law because it appeared 'inhuman' to him,[34] so too do we hear in *Erets Yisrael* of delegations that came from Rome to Yavneh in order to check the laws of the Jews. The Romans thus sought to control local legislation in addition to the local courts. They noted with disapproval the existence of a number of laws which discriminated against foreigners in matters concerning tortious responsibility for animals, although it seems that this inspection never brought practical results.[35]

The presence of Roman rule was already profoundly felt in Palestine and several ways of opposing it were considered, but the Sages and the Patriarch could not always agree on which to choose. The Patriarch wished to strengthen his institution in order to create a spiritual and political centre which could guide the people both in domestic and in foreign affairs. 'The Patriarchate institution saw itself,' writes Urbach, 'as an institution which was to organize the jurisdiction in towns and provinces and to create an attachment between the towns and the centre.'[36] The story of Rabban Gamliel, who went 'to ask permission from the *hegemon* of Syria',[37] may be understood against this background. Hence, too, the strictness of the rule the Patriarch established, in his relations with the Sages, which allowed him to make nominations of judges on his own, and furthermore to prevent courts from making such nominations unless they had his permission.

In this period there were clearly elements in the community who were not satisfied with the system of Jewish jurisdiction. They used to approach the authorities and complain about certain legal proceedings, as in the case of the denunciation of the 'too simple judgment' of Rabbi Bana'a,[38] but the authorities allowed him to carry on passing judgments. It is obvious that the judges of Israel had to pass fair judgments and to do their jobs the best way they could; they not only had to consider the amount of evidence, but also had to make sure that no one would suspect them of light-mindedness or judging for reward. We can now understand Yossi Ben-Elisha's words: 'If you saw a generation which suffered great distress, go and check the cause for it with the judges of Israel.'[39]

ii.   Jew and gentile before a Jewish court

A particular problem was that of a civil judgment involving a non-Jew before a Jewish court. A passage reported in the Babylonian *Talmud* introduces us to the problem:[40]

> Our Rabbis taught: The Government of Rome had long ago sent two commissioners to the Sages of Israel with a request to teach them the Torah. It was accordingly read to them once, twice and thrice. Before taking leave they made the following remark: We have gone carefully through your Torah, and found it correct ['*ve'emet hu*'] with the exception of this point, viz. your saying that if an ox of an Israelite gores an ox of a Canaanite there is no liability, whereas if the ox of a Canaanite gores the ox of an Israelite, whether *Tam* [uncertified as dangerous] or *Mu'ad* [certified as dangerous], compensation has to be paid in full ... We will, however, not report [*modi'im*] this matter to the Government.

The problem is examined also in another passage from the tannaitic period:[41]

> Listen to your brothers: This was the practice of R. Ishmael: when a Jew and a Gentile came to him for judgment, if it was according to the laws of Israel, he would justify the Jew, and if it was according to the laws of the heathen, he would justify the Jew. He said: What is it to me, did not the Torah say, Listen to your brothers? R. Simon b. Gamliel said — it is not so — if they came to be judged according to the laws of Israel, he judged according to the laws of Israel; if according to the laws of the heathen, he judged according to heathen law.[42]

I think that for a better understanding of this problem we have to compare the situation with the principles of Roman Law in other provinces. In a case of judgment between a local resident and a Roman citizen it would seem that the *lex Rupilia* applied. This law from 111 B.C.E. required that the judge and the defendant be of the same nationality, and that the law in effect be that of the plaintiff.[43] A letter from Octavius to Rhosos apparently refers to this principle: in it citizenship is granted to Seleucus and his relatives along with the right to choose the manner of justice should he be a defendant; however, as a plaintiff he would be required to follow the local law.[44] Thus, the principle of choosing the better law for the citizen was not strange to Roman Law either!

4.   *Palestine from Bar Kochba's Revolt (135 C.E.) to the Christianization of the Empire*

The abolition of Jewish jurisdiction in Palestine may be regarded as one of the many terrible consequences of the Bar Kochba revolt.[45] Roman authorities probably continued to deny recognition of rabbinic jurisdiction for years after the end of the revolt. This may explain the dark picture painted by some contemporary scholars.[46] But Roman policy changed soon after, during the second half of the second century, at the end of the Antoninian dynasty and the beginning of the Severian dynasty (second half of the second cent C.E.), when the Emperor and the Patriarch reached a *modus vivendi* which included, *inter alia*, the permission for Jews to pass judgments according to their own laws. This period was blessed by the exceptional character of Rabbi Judah the Patriarch, the compiler of the *Mishnah*. The bitter experience of severe persecution in the Hadrianic period and the desire of several Sages not to be totally subordinated to the Patriarch, prompted the Sages to decide to develop the institution of arbitration and compromise, an institution which was recognized by Roman law too.

A major change in citizenship occurred in the middle of this period, close to the time of the compilation of the *Mishnah*. In the year 212 C.E. the *Constitutio Antoniniana* of the Emperor Antoninus Caracalla granted Roman citizenship to all inhabitants of the Empire by the *Constitutio Antoniniana de civitate*.[47] A question to which no agreed solution has yet been reached is whether the Jews — now Roman citizens — also retained citizenship of the political communities to which they had previously belonged? Scholars are divided on this issue. Luzzatto and Arangio-Ruiz maintain that there is no basis in the sources for 'dual citizenship'. They claim that foreigners, after receiving Roman citizenship, remained under the jurisdiction of their local law, under the principle of 'the personality of the laws'. Local officeholders, in practice, applied both Roman law and local law to such citizens: this practice led to the formation of 'Vulgar Law', a composite legal system which ultimately came to be regarded as normative Roman Law.

It seems that this new political reality did not have a major impact on the status of Jewish Law, since the basis of adherence to Jewish Law had always been national-religious, rather than a matter of citizenship. Nevertheless, at a time when the Roman Empire was striving for centralization, it is clear that there was always a danger that the autonomy of a local legal system could be cancelled.

Let us sum up the situation with the words of Juster:

> After the fall of Jerusalem, as before it, the Jews brought their law suits not only before Jewish judges — who might possibly be considered as arbitrators — but also before true Jewish courts empowered to dispense justice in accordance with Jewish law, and they were authorized by the Romans to do so. That is to say, a Jewish court of law was constituted [as a

recognized tribunal]; this court then had authority over the defendant; it could summon and compel him to appear before it or convict him by default, subsequently carrying out the sentence by whatever means it had. The Roman government recognized that the verdict was founded on legitimate judicial authority. Nevertheless, as in other parts of the Empire, it seems that Roman rule provided some kind of supervision over the moral standards and professional competence of the Jewish Judges.[48]

With regard to the period in which the Jewish jurisdictional autonomy was still recognized, the following question must be asked: who exercised this jurisdiction which was recognized by the Roman Government? It is possible that we may be able to find the answer to this question in a rescript by Diocletian (Emperor from 284-305 C.E.) which was included in Justinian's Code (C.3.13.3). The Emperor's answer was sent to one Iuda[49] — the only time that this name appears in Roman legal sources. He says:

> The agreement of the private [people] (*privatorum consensus*) cannot appoint as a judge a person who does not hold the position of Head of a court, and whatever judgment he makes, it will not have the effect of a court judgment (*res iudicata*).

I believe that this rescript was composed as Diocletian's response to the Patriarch regarding the Patriarch's conflict with the Rabbis regarding the power of judicial ordination. I interpret the rescript as a reaffirmation by Diocletian to the Patriarch that the Rabbis hold the status of *privati*, that though they play an important role in the public life of the Jewish people, they have no recognized standing in Roman Public Law.[50] Only the Patriarch, recognized as an institution by Roman Public Law, may appoint Judges.

From the historical perspective, the meaning of the rescript would be as follows: Roman Law does not recognize a judge appointed by private individuals (note the distinction between *privati*, private individuals, and *partes*, parties to a dispute). To be a judge, that person must stand at the head of a court of law. For that purpose a judge must be appointed by the competent authority — in our case, the Patriarch, who, after the destruction of the Temple and the loss of Judean political independence, assumed ever-increasing importance as a political leader, until he was eventually recognized as such by the Roman administration. Moreover, whenever the parties turned to judges appointed only by the Rabbis (private individuals by the Roman Law), the decisions of these judges would not have been recognized in Roman Law as *res iudicata* (a judgment passed by a judge). This reality represented a threat to the integrity and independence of Jewish Law, since all judicial appointments would be in the hands of an official himself requiring the recognition of the Roman power.

Only after the Roman Emperor had explained the position of Roman Law was a compromise reached between the Patriarch and the Sages, namely that judges ought to be appointed with the agreement of both the Patriarch and the Rabbis. An echo of these disputes and of the subsequent agreement can be found in a passage of the Palestinian *Talmud*, *Sanhedrin* 1, 4(5), 19a:

> Rabbi Abba said: At first everyone used to ordain his own students like Rabban Yoḥanan ben Zakkai (who) ordained R. Eliezer and R. Joshua, and R. Joshua (who ordained) Rabbi Akiva, and Rabbi Akiva (who ordained) Rabbi Meir and R. Simeon. He (R. Akiva) said: Let R. Meir sit first. R. Simeon became distraught. Said R. Akiva to him: Enough — I and your creator recognize your worth. They returned to their original practice of honouring the Patriarchate (granting honour to this house, i.e. Patriarchate). They said: A court which ordains against the will of the Patriarch — its ordination is invalid. A Patriarch who ordains against the will of the court — his ordination is valid. Once again they changed their position and laid down that a court should not ordain against the will of the Patriarch and that the Patriarch should only ordain in accordance with the will of the court.

In any event, the decisions of the Sages accepted by the parties were recognized by the Roman authorities as valid arbitrations.

5. *The Christian Period (313-565)*

The Christian Emperors treated the Jews harshly in matters of political and civic status, but the Jews still continued to be *cives Romani: Iudaei Romano et communi iure viventes,* as the fifth century Theodosian Code, 2.1.10, put it. However, there was a real change in jurisdiction: with the promulgation of Arcadius' and Honorius' famous Constitution of 398, Jewish jurisdictional autonomy was abolished and the recognition of its courts was withdrawn. The constitution reported in the Theodosian Code (*C.Th.* 2,1,10) thus:

> The same Augustuses to Eutychianus, Praetorian Perfect. Jews who live under the Roman and common law shall approach the courts in the customary manner in those cases which concern not so much their superstition as their forum, the statutes and the law; and they shall bring and defend all actions according to Roman law; in fine, they shall be subject to Our laws. Certainly, in the case of civil suits only, if any Jews should suppose that, by a mutual promise to abide by the decision in accordance with the agreement of both parties, they should litigate before Jews or Patriarchs as though before arbitrators, they shall not be prohibited by public law from choosing the judgment of such men. The judges of the provinces shall execute their

sentences as if such arbitrators had been assigned by a judge's decision. — Given on the third day before the nones of February at Constantinople in the year of the fourth consulship of Honorius Augustus and the consulship of the most Noble Eutychianus. — 3 February, 398. (Pharr's translation)

As we can see, in this Constitution jurisdictional distinctions were made relating to subject-matter: purely religious matters remained in the authority of the Jewish (rabbinic) courts alone; criminal cases were to be dealt with in Roman courts alone; civil matters were also passed on to Roman courts, but the litigants — through a mutual agreement (*compromissum*) — were permitted to bring their cases before rabbinic courts acting as arbitrators. Nevertheless, as far as the Roman administration was concerned, Jewish jurisdictional autonomy ceased to exist. Jewish jurisdiction had changed its status from that of a recognized jurisdiction in competition with Roman jurisdiction, to that of arbitration, whose existence was now dependent upon the good will of the parties to settle their disputes.

Even the autonomy of the rabbinic courts in religious matters ceased to exist in the days of Justinian (early sixth cent C.E.), — who changed the meaning of the constitution by the simple expedient of omitting the word *non* (Justinian Code 1,9,8, cf. also Novella 146 of Justinian, 553 C.E.). Nevertheless, even during the Christian period the Jews retained the right to keep the Shabbat and not to be judged on that day (*C.Th.* 2.8.26), a right that was confirmed also by Justinian (Justinian Code 1.9.13).

6. *The Diaspora*

A. Egypt and Other Provinces

The information we have from other provinces helps us to confirm that Palestine (pp.145ff., above) was not exceptional in having local law applied by Roman officials. We have protocols of several trials which took place in the Roman province of Egypt, preserved in Greco-Egyptian papyri. In these trials, the Roman official (*procurator*) refers to *Nomos ton Aiguptíon* (literally, the custom of the Egyptians[51]); in his judicial role he was assisted by the *Nomikoi* (*iurisprudentes*) who were, it seems, experts in local laws (mainly unwritten laws).[52] In Egypt 'local law' means, of course, Greek and Egyptian Law. According to Lieberman, Moses appeared as *Nomike* in some Jewish and Samaritan sources, and this proves that such a role (i.e. an expert on local law) existed in Palestine too (where, of course, the expert had to be familiar with Jewish Law).[53]

From the exchange of letters between the Roman writer Pliny, who was Governor of the Roman Province of Bitynia, and the Emperor Trajan, we learn much about the normal procedure in another province and in Roman provinces in general.[54] From them, it appears that in the provinces, Roman magistrates and local officers did not apply the Roman Law (i.e. the law valid in Rome and Italy) to private individuals; they applied only the local laws (those which existed before the Roman occupation) of that province, with such specific changes as were made for each province by governors or Emperors.

B.   Jewish Jurisdiction in the Diaspora

The problem of Jewish jurisdiction was common also in the Diaspora. Some scholars have maintained that a distinction should be drawn between the Eastern part of the Empire, where autonomy of Jewish jurisdiction did exist, and the Western part, where it did not. Others dispute this. In my view, each place in the Empire ought to be thoroughly examined independently. Nevertheless, there seems to be an agreement on one fact: many Jews continued to bring their cases before local Jewish judges. It is also clear that *C.Th.* 2.1.10 (pp.153f., above) refers also to the Jews of the Diaspora, and thus that from 398 the Jews had to bring their cases before Roman courts — unless they agreed that their cases be brought before a rabbinic court recognized by the Roman authorities as an arbitration institution.[55]

Among the privileges which the Jews enjoyed during the Christian period was the right not to appear in court on Shabbat, Shabbat Eve or holidays; even Justinian did not deny the Jews this privilege. However, it was in the days of Justinian that the position of the Jews worsened: while it was forbidden for a Jew to testify *against* an Orthodox Christian, a Jew's testimony would count if he testified in *favour* of a Christian. There was discrimination against Jewish testimony in most cases — apart from cases in which he testified in favour of the Government.[56]

7.   *Some Questions Concerning Family Law*

Many questions arise concerning the application of family law by the Jews under the Roman Empire.[57] We shall discuss a few relating to marriage and divorce.

(1) There is the question of the validity of marriages between Jews of a

different civil status (*status civitatis*): does legal competence for marriage (*connubium*) exist between them? It seems that a positive answer would have been given according to Roman Law. Take, for example, a Jew from Palestine who has the status of *peregrinus* (a foreigner, a citizen of a State other than Rome) who wants to marry a Jew from Rome who has the status of Roman citizen (*civis romana*): it is clear that this kind of marriage is permitted according to Jewish Law, but I believe that the man has the competence to marry the woman legally according to Roman Law too.

(2) Are Jews allowed to be married to two or more wives though Roman Law forbids and punishes bigamy? It appears that originally the Roman authorities tolerated Jewish polygamy *de facto*, especially in Palestine, but from 393 C.E. it was explicitly forbidden.[58]

(3) What authority does a father who is a Jewish Roman citizen have over his sons: does he enjoy the father's authority (*patria potestas*) as a Roman father or must he go by Jewish Law? I believe that in cases of *iustum matrimonium*, a father may exercise his Roman *patria potestas*. Generally, in Roman Law a father had a dominant position in his family, but in cases of mixed marriages (i.e. a marriage between a Jew and a Christian), the Christian Empire always preferred the Christian parent, despite the *patria potestas* rules.

(4) In inheritance matters there was special legislation in the days of Constantine which maintained the right of a Jew who was converted to Christianity to succeed his Jewish parents, even against their will (the Christian faith thus being accorded priority over general rules of freedom of testation); additionally, a law was passed guaranteeing the freedom of worship of Christian slaves inherited by Jews.

(5) As for divorce, we know that in the period of classical Roman Law (first-third centuries C.E.) both Roman and Jewish Law permitted divorce; there existed, however, numerous differences between them, both substantive and formal. In the first place, in Jewish Law, as opposed to Roman Law, the woman could not renounce her husband directly: divorce remained a unilateral act, even if one accords importance to the fact that the *get* (*libellus repudii*) had to be accepted by the woman. In some specific cases the wife could have recourse to a Jewish tribunal for a decision. However, such a decision could not of itself dissolve the marriage bond. That could have been done only by pressure on the husband to consent personally to a divorce; if he declined, the

Roman authorities could exert pressure to convince him to grant the divorce. *M. Gitt.* 9:8 states the rule:

> A bill of divorce given under compulsion is valid if it is ordered by an Israelitish court, but if by a gentile court it is invalid; if the gentiles beat a man and say to him: 'Do what the Israelites bid thee', it is valid.

The text demonstrates clearly that in this period the Roman Government recognized the decisions of Jewish tribunals in matters of personal status and was ready to utilise enforcement mechanisms in order to give practical effect to such decisions. This assumes that the wife has approached a Jewish court first; perhaps 'if by a gentile court' refers to a woman who approaches the Roman court directly (Babatha-like!, but in a different case). The situation is further clarified in a passage of the Palestine *Talmud* which follows the above *Mishnah* passage:

> R. Yirmiyah says in the name of Rav: A divorce given by a Jew under the compulsion of gentiles is invalid. This refers to the case where the husband tells the wife: I do not wish to give you maintenance. R. Ḥiyyah taught: But if the gentiles issued their ruling in accordance with Jewish practice, it is valid even if the husband tells the wife: I do not wish to give you mainten-ance. R. Jose says: the *mishnah* says so explicitly: the gentiles beat him and say to him 'Do what the Israelites tell you to do.' R. Ḥiyyah bar Ashi said in the name of Isi: In the case of one who says: I do not wish to give you maintenance, we compel him to give a divorce.

From these texts it appears that in the case of two Jewish *peregrini* in *Erets Yisrael* and, almost certainly, in other parts of the Empire, Jewish Law was applied, whatever tribunal the parties had recourse to, even if Roman Law ignored the possibility of decisions which obliged the husband to divorce; for its part, Jewish Law recognized only the decisions of Jewish tribunals, even if it was admitted that there could be external coercion to ensure their application.

Coming now to examine the situation of those Jews who were also Roman citizens, based on some passages of Josephus (*Vita*, 75, 414-15), we can assert that if the parties preferred to rely on their status as Roman citizens, they could do so, and in that case the divorce would be valid only according to Roman Law and not Jewish Law; it is clear therefore that in Roman Law Jewish Roman women could have validly divorced their husbands — even against the will of the latter. Nonetheless, if the spouses preferred to conduct themselves according to Jewish Law, then whenever the divorce was desired either by both parties or by the husband alone, there ought to have been no difficulty in Roman Law. Very likely, in order to avoid difficulties of interpretation, Jewish spouses would have preferred to

have both a 'Jewish' and a 'Roman' divorce and thus satisfy the rather rigid
Jewish norms, as well as the Roman ones.[59]

A more complicated case arises with a *iustum matrimonium* (marriage
valid according to Roman civil law) in which the two spouses were Roman
Jews or in which the husband was Roman and the wife a foreigner. What if,
in such a case, it was the wife who desired a divorce? In such cases the
woman could have divorced freely according to Roman Law, but it is difficult
to assume that the Roman authorities would collaborate with a Jewish
tribunal which decided that the husband must concede the divorce according to
Jewish rules. In cases of a Roman woman married to a foreigner, one may
assume that the Roman authorities would have assisted the woman seeking
divorce;[60] this would be consistent with the Roman principle of freedom of
marriage and divorce. The situation changed, probably during the Christian
period.

In general, we may conclude that Jewish private law remained in effect
for the Jews in the Roman Empire, even after they were granted Roman
citizenship. Roman Law was willing to tolerate a number of exceptions in
the field of marriage and divorce. In this field too the important limitations
appeared only when Christianity became the recognized and preferred religion,
and especially in the days of Justinian.

8. *Bibliography*

Albeck, S., *Law Courts in Talmudic Times* (Jerusalem: Bar-Ilan University
    Press, 1980, in Hebrew).
Alon, G., *Jews, Judaism and the Classical World* (Jerusalem: Magnes Press,
    1977).
Alon, G., *The Jews in their Land in the Talmudic Age* (Jerusalem: Magnes
    Press, 1980-1984, 2 vols.).
Bammel, E., 'The Organisation of Palestine by Gabinius', *Journal of Jewish
    Studies* 12 (1961), 159-162.
Colorni, V., *Legge ebraica e leggi locali* (Milano: Giuffrè, 1945).
Daube, D., 'Jewish Law in the Hellenistic World', in *Jewish Law in Legal
    History and the Modern World*, ed. B.S. Jackson (Leiden: E.J. Brill,
    1980), 45-60.
Elon, M., ed., *The Principles of Jewish Law* (Jerusalem: Encyclopaedia
    Judaica, 1975).

Friedman, M.A., *Jewish Marriage in Palestine — A Cairo Geniza Study* (Tel Aviv and New York: Jewish Theological Seminary of America, 1980, 2 vols.).

Jackson, B.S., 'On the Problem of Roman Influence on the Halakhah and Normative Self-Definition in Judaism', in E.P. Sanders, ed., *Jewish and Christian Self-Definition* (Philadelphia: Fortress Press, 1981), II, 157-203 (text), 352-79 (notes).

Jolowicz, H.F., *Historical Introduction to the Study of Roman Law* (Cambridge: Cambridge University Press, 1961).

Juster, J., *Les Juifs dans l'Empire Romain. Leur condition juridique, économique et sociale* (Paris: P. Geuthner, 1914, 2 vols.).

Katzoff, R., 'Responsa Prudentium in Roman Egypt', in *Studi in onore di Arnaldo Biscardi* (Milano: Giuffrè, 1968), II, 523-535.

Levine, L.I., *Caesarea under Roman Rule* (Leiden: E.J. Brill, 1975).

Levine, L.I., *The Rabbinic Class in Palestine during the Talmudic Period* (Jerusalem: Yad I. Ben-Zvi Institute, 1985), in Hebrew.

Lieberman, S., *Hellenism in Jewish Palestine* (New York: The Jewish Theological Seminary of America, 1962, 2nd ed.).

Lieberman, S., 'Palestine in the Third and Fourth Centuries', *Jewish Quarterly Review* 36 (1946), 329-370; 37 (1947), 31-54.

Lieberman, S., *Studies in Palestinian Talmudic Literature*, ed. D. Rosenthal (Jerusalem: Magnes Press, 1991), in Hebrew.

Lifshitz, B., 'The rules governing conflict of Laws between a Jew and a Gentile according to Maimonides', in *Mélanges M.H. Prévost* (Paris: Presses Universitaires de France, 1982), 179-89.

Rabello, A.M., 'The Lex de Templo Hierosolymitano prohibiting gentiles from entering Jerusalem's Sanctuary', *Christian News from Israel* XXI/3 (1970), 28-32; XXI/4 (1970), 28-32.

Rabello, A.M., 'On the paternal power in Roman and Jewish Law', *Diné Israel* 5 (1974), 85-153 (in Hebrew).

Rabello, A.M., 'The Responsibility of Minors in Jewish Criminal Law', *Acta Juridica* (1977), 309-36 (Essays in Honour of Ben Beinart).

Rabello, A.M., *Effetti personali della Patria Potestas* (Milano: Giuffrè, 1979).

Rabello, A.M., 'The Legal Condition of the Jews in the Roman Empire', *Aufstieg und Niedergang der Römischen Welt* (Berlin-New York: de Gruyter, 1980), II, 13, 662-762.

Rabello, A.M., 'Divorce of Jews in the Roman Empire', *The Jewish Law Annual* 4 (1981), 79-102.

Rabello, A.M., 'Les Effets personnelles de la puissance paternelle en droit hébraïque, à travers la Bible et le Talmud', in *Mélanges M.H. Prévost* (Paris: Presses Universitaires de France, 1982), 85-101).

Rabello, A.M., 'On the Relations between Diocletian and the Jews', *Journal of Jewish Studies* 35 (1984), 147-67.

Rabello, A.M., *Giustiniano, Ebrei e Samaritani alla luce delle fonti storico-letterarie, ecclesiastiche e giuridiche* (Milano: Giuffrè, 1987-88, 2 vols., Monografie del Vocabolario di Giustiniano).

Rabello, A.M., 'Herod's Domestic Court? The Judgment of Death for Herod's Sons', *The Jewish Law Annual* 10 (1991), 39-56.

Rabello, A.M., 'Civil Justice in Palestine from 63 B.C.E. to 70 C.E.', *Classical Studies in honor of David Sohlberg*, ed. R. Katzoff, J. Petroff and D. Schaps (Ramat Gan: Bar- Ilan University Press, 1996, forthcoming).

Schürer, E., *The History of the Jewish People in the Age of Jesus Christ (175 B.C.- 135 C.E.)*, ed. G. Vermes & F. Millar (Edinburgh: T. & T. Clark, 1973), Vol. I.

Smallwood, E.M., *The Jews under Roman Rule from Pompey to Diocletian* (Leiden: E.J. Brill, 1981).

Urbach, E.E., *The Halakhah: Its Sources and Development* (Ramat-Gan: Massada, 1986).

Urbach, E.E., *The Sages, Their Concepts and Beliefs* (Jerusalem: Magnes Press, 1975).

Urbach, E.E., *The World of the Sages. Collected Studies* (Jerusalem: Magnes Press, 1988), in Hebrew.

Notes:

1   On the legal situation of the Jews in the Roman Empire and the problem of jurisdiction, see A.M. Rabello, 'The Legal Condition of the Jews in the Roman Empire', *Aufstieg und Niedergang der Römischen Welt* (Berlin-New York, de Gruyter, 1980), II, 13, 662ff.; see also A.M. Rabello, *Giustiniano, Ebrei e Samaritani alla luce delle fonti storico-letterarie, ecclesiastiche e giuridiche, Monografie del Vocabolario di Giustiniano* (Milano: Giuffrè, 1987-88), 2 vols., and see the bibliography in section 8, above; J. Juster, *Les Juifs dans l'Empire Romain. Leur condition juridique, économique et sociale* (Paris: Geuthner, 1914), II.94; B.S. Jackson, 'On the Problem of Roman Influence on the Halakhah and Normative Self-Definition in Judaism', in E.P. Sanders, ed., *Jewish and Christian Self-Definition* (London: SCM Press, 1981), vol.II, 157-203 (text), 352-79 (notes), at 159ff.

2   A. Berger, *Encyclopedic Dictionary of Roman Law* (Philadelphia, The
     American Philosophical Society, 1953), s.v. *'Iurisdictio'*.

3   See *Digesta* 50.16.239.2. See V. Colorni, *Legge ebraica e leggi locali*
     (Milano: Giuffrè, 1945), 13ff.; S. Applebaum, 'The Legal Status of the
     Jewish Communities in the Diaspora', in *Compendia Rerum Judaicarum ad
     Novum Testamentum*, ed. S. Safrai and M. Stern (Assen: van Gorcum, 1974),
     Vol. I, Pt.1, 455ff.

4   It is not possible to deal here with the many places which have been treated
     in great detail (in Asia and especially Antioch, Caesarea, Tiberias; in Africa
     and especially Alexandria and Cyrene). For a detailed discussion see
     Applebaum, *supra* n.3, at 420ff.; and E.M. Smallwood, *The Jews under
     Roman Rule from Pompey to Diocletian* (Leiden: E.J. Brill, 1981), *passim*.

5   This was not the first appearance of the Romans in Jewish political history.
     A treaty of friendship had been signed between Rome and Judah the
     Maccabee: *I Mac.* 8, Josephus *Ant.* xii, 414-19; see further E. Schürer, *The
     History of the Jewish People in the Age of Jesus Christ* (175 B.C.- A.D.
     135), ed. G. Vermes & F. Millar (Edinburgh: T. & T. Clark, 1973), Vol.I,
     171. Perhaps it was the memory of this that later prompted the Romans (with
     the notable exception of the period of Hadrian) to permit the Jews to use their
     own laws (*suis legibus uti*).
        From a legal perspective the new order established by Pompey cannot be
     called a *provincia*, as did Ammianus Marcellinus, in his *Res gestae*; see M.
     Stern, *Greek and Latin Authors on Jews and Judaism*, (Jerusalem: Israel
     Academy of Sciences and Humanities, 1976-1984), Vol. II, No. 505. Rather
     it constituted an intermediate situation, differing both from a *provincia* and
     from a state in alliance with Rome. On the basis of statements of Josephus,
     it may have been incorporated into the Roman province of Syria, under
     Gabinius' governorship of that province (57-55 B.C.E.): see Schürer, *supra*
     n.5, at Vol.I, 267. In any event, institutions of government and national
     laws were preserved. See A.M. Rabello, 'Civil Justice in Palestine from 63
     B.C.E. to 70 C.E.', *Classical Studies in honor of David Sohlberg*, ed. R.
     Katzoff, J. Petroff and D. Schaps (Ramat Gan: Bar-Ilan University Press,
     forthcoming).

6   Smallwood, *supra* n.4, at 32ff.; Schürer, *supra* n.5, at Vol.I, 267-80 (on
     Hyrcanus II, 63-40 B.C.E.).

7   Z.W. Falk, *Introduction to Jewish Law of the Second Commonwealth* (Leiden:
     E.J. Brill, 1972), I, 88ff.('The Town Court').

8   One possible objection may be derived from a text of the Palestinian Talmud,
     Sanhedrin 1:1:

     It was taught: Forty years before the destruction of the Temple the right
     to judge capital cases was withdrawn, and it was in the days of Shimon b.
     Shetaḥ that the right to judge property cases was withdrawn. Said R.
     Shimon b. Yoḥai, 'Blessed be the All merciful that I am not a sage
     required to make court decisions' (translation of J. Neusner, *The Talmud*

of the Land of Israel, vol. 31 Sanhedrin 1,1 p.12, III [A], [B].)
Shimon b. Shetah dates from the 1st century B.C.E. and is thought to have been a contemporary of Alexander Jannaeus, while Rabbi Shimon b. Yohai was a scholar from the 2nd century C.E. Although, the period in the days of King Jannaeus and Shimon b. Shetah (before Pompey's conquest) was complicated, I do not believe that traditional Jewish civil law was cancelled. We should notice that the reading is not certain; in the parallel text in *Sanhedrin* 7:2 instead of Shimon b. Shetah, Shimon b. Yohai appears. Neusner ignores this difference. The reading Bar Yohai corresponds with the continuation of the talmudic text and it seems to correspond with the historical period (in the days of the Emperor Hadrian and Bar-Kochba's Revolt). This reading is accepted by A. Büchler and G. Alon; see also Jackson, *supra* n.1, at 159ff.

9   B. Cohen, 'Arbitration in Jewish and Roman Law', in his *Jewish and Roman Law* (New York: Jewish Theological Seminary of America, 1966), II, 651ff.

10   A. Momigliano, 'Judaea becomes a Roman Province', *Cambridge Ancient History*, X, p.337ff.; M. Stern, 'The Province of Judaea', in *Compendia*, *supra* n.3, at Vol. 1 Pt. 1, 308ff.

11   A.H.M. Jones, *The Cities of the Eastern Roman Provinces* (Oxford: Clarendon Press, 1937), 227ff.; Z.G. Downey, The Later Roman Empire (New York: Holt, Rinehart and Winston, 1969); Y. Dan, *The City in Eretz-Israel During The Late Roman and Byzantine Periods* (Jerusalem: Yad Ben-Zvi, 1984, in Hebrew); on Caesarea, see L.I. Levine, *Caesarea under Roman Rule* (Leiden, E.J. Brill, 1975); on Gaza: M. A. Meyer, *History of the City of Gaza* (New York: Columbia University Press, 1907); G. Downey, *Gaza in the Early Sixth century* (Norman: Oklahoma University Press, 1963); on Scytopolis: G. Fuks, *Scytopolis — a Greek City in Eretz-Israel* (Jerusalem: Yad Ben-Zvi, 1983, in Hebrew).

12   Like Judea, other nations sought autonomy. Cicero tells us of the decree he made as ruler of Cilicia, in which he permitted local judges to continue to perform their function: *Ad Atticum,* VI, 1.15. F. De Martino, *Storia della Costituzione Romana*, Napoli, Jovene, 1960, Vol. II, 316ff., observes: 'There was no firm standard principle requiring preservation of national norms ... We must remember that Roman policy adapted itself to different situations. In a few cases local law and national institutions were indeed preserved with unsure status, always subject to suspension by the ruler. In other cases even these were changed, or otherwise, national institutions were changed fundamentally, Roman judges and Roman courts were imposed, and the traditional norms of the subjugated people were not honoured.' (Translation of AMR.)

13   See R. Martini, *Ricerche in tema di Editto provinciale* (Milano: Giuffrè, 1969), 48: 'This recognition in the autonomy of the citizens had seemed to the citizens of the provinces, first of all, as a possibility, which was derived

from this autonomy, to use the local judges'. See my examination of the situation in 'Civil Justice ...', *supra* n.5.

14 Inferred from Cicero, *Ad Atticum*, VI, 1.15.

15 See further A.M. Rabello, 'The *Lex de Templo Hierosolymitano* prohibiting gentiles from entering Jerusalem's Sanctuary', *Christian News from Israel* XXI/3 (1970), 28-32; XXI/4 (1970), 28-32.

16 Th. Mommsen, 'Der Religionsfrevel nach roemischen Recht', *Historische Zeitschrift* 64 (1890), 389ff.; *idem, Römisches Strafrecht* (Leipzig: Duncker, 1899), 573.

17 Berger, *supra* n.2, at 427: 'The citizens of a foreign state or community, who were vanquished in a war with Rome, surrendered to the power and protection of Rome (*deditio*). They constituted a specific group of the Roman population; they were free but lacked any public rights and citizenship (*nullius civitatis*). Their legal status as *peregrini dediticii* could be improved by unilateral concessions granted by Rome to individuals or groups. But even the general grant of Roman citizenship to peregrines by the constitution of the Emperor Caracalla excluded the *dediticii*. The status of *dediticii* termed by Justinian *dediticia libertas*, was abolished by him (C.J. 7.5.1).' *Dediticii* were not allowed to reside within 100 miles of Rome.

18 Juster, *supra* n.1, at II, 19-23: 'Since the Jews continued to enjoy their privileges ... they could do so as members of a nation ... The exercise thereof was therefore permitted only to the members of the Jewish nation.'

19 See also Colorni, *supra* n.3, at 16: '... in whatever way the question should be solved as regards Palestine, scholars agree with Juster's certain belief that the Jews of the Diaspora were subjected to no reprisals for the events of the year 70.' See also Applebaum, *supra* n.3, at 420ff.

20 This is on the basis of documentation discovered at Murabba'at. See E. Volterra, 'Nuovi documenti per la conoscenza del diritto vigente nelle provincie romane', *IURA* 14 (1963), 29ff.; E. Volterra, 'I diritti locali', in *I diritti locali nelle provincie romane con particolare riguardo alle condizione giuridiche del suolo* (Rome: Accademia Nazionale dei Lincei, 1974), 55ff.: '... it must have been extremely difficult for the Roman authorities to abrogate these norms and institutions as well as local customs. And yet, it is most likely that, in Palestine, the local laws and customs, especially in certain matters, must have been preserved for a long time ... The victorious nation did not impose its private law upon the vanquished, but allowed them to keep their own local law, customs and often even their own local administration. In contrast to the modern idea of unity of private law in every State, it was considered quite normal in the ancient world, that, among the subjects submitted to the same sovereignty, there could be different laws applicable simultaneously' (at 64).

21 Ultimately, in 398 C.E., Jewish legal autonomy was drastically limited by the famous Imperial Constitution of Theodosius II (reported in the Theodosian Code, 2.1.10). In 1899, Chajes argued that during the whole period from 70-

398, Jewish courts functioned merely as arbitral bodies, but most scholars now think that the Jewish courts did have authority to pass judgments. See H.P. Chajes, 'Les Juges Juifs en Palestine de l'an 70 à l'an 500', *Revue des Etudes Juives* 39 (1899), 39ff.; see also Sh. Albeck, *Law Courts in Talmudic Times* (Jerusalem: Bar-Ilan University Press, 1980, in Hebrew). See further section 3Ci.

22 *Mekhilta deRabbi Ishmael* ('Mishpatim' section, Exodus, 21), quoted from the English translation of Jacob Z. Lauterbach, *Mekilta de-Rabbi Ishmael* (Philadelphia: Jewish Publication Society of America, 1933), Vol. III, 1-2.

23 Groups of Sages used to come from Palestine to Rome to discuss the relations between the Jews of Palestine and the Roman Government. On the delegation to Rome see G. Alon, *The Jews in their Land in the Talmudic Age*, (Jerusalem: Magnes Press, 1980), I, 124ff.; M.D. Herr, 'The Historical Significance of the Dialogues between Jewish Sages and Roman Dignitaries', *Scripta Hierosolymitana XXII* (Jerusalem: Magnes Press, 1971), 123ff.

24 Stern, *supra* n.10, at 336ff.; S. Safrai, 'Jewish Self-Government', in *Compendia Rerum Judaicarum ad Novum Testamentum*, ed. S. Safrai and M. Stern (Assen: van Gorcum, 1974), Vol. 1 Pt. 1, 397ff.

25 Justinian *Digest*, 1.16.7.2; 1.18.10.12.

26 Rabello, 'Legal Condition', *supra* n.1, at 725ff.

27 See the text of these documents in N. Lewis, Y. Yadin and J.C. Greenfield, eds., *The Documents from the Bar Kochba Period in the Cave of Letters. Greek Papyri and Aramaic and Nabatean Signatures and Subscriptions* (Jerusalem: Israel Exploration Society, 1989); the texts to which we refer are at 118ff. See also N. Lewis, 'The World of P. Yadin', *Bulletin of the American Society for Papyrology* 28 (1991), 35-41; H. Cotton, 'The Guardianship of Jesus Son of Babatha. Roman and Local Law in the Province of Arabia', *Journal of Roman Studies* 83 (1993), 94-108; B. Isaac, 'The Babatha Archive. A Review Article', *Israel Exploration Journal* 42 (1992), 62-75.

28 The archive (mostly in Greek) of a second Jewish woman, also from Maoza, dating from between 125 and 131, has also now been published. See H. Cotton, 'The Archive of Salome Komaise Daughter of Levi: Another Archive from the "Cave of Letters"', *Zeitschrift für Papyrologie und Epigraphie* 105 (1995), 171-207. She concludes that the marriage contract in it (*P. Yadin* 37) reflects the Hellenistic *agraphos gamos*.

29 See H.M. Cotton and J.C. Greenfield, 'Babatha's Property and the Law of Succession in the Babatha Archive', *Zeitschrift für Papyrologie und Epigraphie* 104 (1994), 211-224, esp.220. Cotton takes the view, in general, that the papyri from such Jewish archives show little awareness of Jewish law, but indicate considerable assimilation into a Roman-Hellenistic legal environment not dissimilar from that of Egypt. See H. Cotton, "A Cancelled Marriage Contract from the Judaean Desert (*XHev/Se Gr.2*)", *Journal of Roman Studies* 84 (1994), 65-86, esp. 81-85, reviewing evidence

from eight marriage contracts (including two written in Greek) from various sites in the Judaean desert;

30 H.M. Cotton, 'Fragments of a Declaration of Landed Property from the Province of Arabia', *Zeitschrift für Papyrologie und Epigraphie* 85 (1991), 263-267; *idem*, 'Another Fragment of the Declaration of Landed Property from the Province of Arabia', *Zeitschrift für Papyrologie und Epigraphie* 99 (1993), 115-121.

31 See the following studies: H. J. Polotsky, 'Three Greek Papyri from the Cave of Letters', *Israel Exploration Journal* 12 (1962), 258ff.; *idem*, 'Three Greek Documents from the Family Archive of Babatha', *Eretz Israel* 8 (1967), 46ff.; M. Lemosse, 'Le procès de Babatha', *The Irish Jurist* 3 (1968), 363ff.; A. Biscardi, 'Nuove testimonianze di un papiro arabo-giudaico per la storia del processo provinciale romano', *Studi in onore di G. Scherillo* (Milano: Giuffrè, 1972), I, 111ff.; *idem*, 'Sulla identificazione degli "Xenokritai" e sulla loro attività in P.Oxy. 3016', *Festschrift für E. Seidl*, ed. Huebner (Cologne: P. Hanstein, 1975), 15ff.; Jackson, *supra* n.1, at 164f.

32 In parallel texts we find the names of Rabbi Shimon and Rabbi Meir (from a later period than Bar-Kochba's revolt). See Alon, *supra* n.23, at II, 537f.

33 See Dio Chrysostomus, *Orationes* 40, 509-12 and Plutarch, *Moralia, De reipublicae gerenda*, 19.

34 P. Oxy. II, 237; see J. Mélèze-Modrzejewski, "La loi des Egiptiens: le droit grec dans l'Egypte romaine", in *Droit impérial et traditions locales dans l'Egypte romaine* (Aldershot: Variorum, 1990), 383-399.

35 *B.B.K.* 38a, quoted below at n.37, in the discussion of Jew and Gentile before a Jewish court, section Cii *infra*.

36 E.E. Urbach, *The World of the Sages. Collected Studies* (Jerusalem: Magnes Press, 1988), 306ff. (in Hebrew).

37 *M. Eduy.* 7:7. According to Alon, *supra* n.23, at I, 121: 'Rabban Gamaliel went to get an official appointment as Patriarch and leader of the Jews.'

38 A Palestinian *Tanna* from the 3rd century, *B.B.B.* 58a. See Alon, *supra* n.23, at I, 216.

39 *B. Shab.* 139a. Cf. Alon, *supra* n.23, at II, 674. See also n.8, *supra*.

40 *B.B.K.* 38a, Soncino translation. Other versions are found at *Y.B.K.* 4.3 (4b) and *Sifre Deut* 344 (Finkelstein, 401). See recently: Jackson, *supra* n.1, at 168; B. Lifshitz, 'Conflict of Laws between a Jew and a Gentile', *Mélanges M.H. Prévost* (Paris: Presses Universitaires de France, 1982), 179ff.

41 *Sifre Deut.* 16 (Finkelstein, 26).

42 This dispute appears in a somewhat different format in Babylonian *Talmud*, *B.K.* 113a: 'Where a suit arises before you between an Israelite and a heathen, if you can justify the former according to the laws of Israel, justify him and say: "This is our law"; so also if you can justify him by the laws of the heathens justify him and say (to the other party): "This is your law"; but if this cannot be done, we use subterfuges to circumvent him. This is the view

of R. Ishmael, but R. Akiba said that we should not attempt to circumvent him on account of the sanctification of the divine Name.' See also *T.B.K.* 4:2, *Y.B.K.* 4:3 (4b); Lifshitz, *supra* n.40, at 184.

43 In other cases, the case could be tried before a Roman court (*ex conventu civium romanorum*) or a local court.

44 CIL, XVI, No. 11; S. Riccobono, *Fontes iuris romani antiqui* (Florence: Barbera, 1941), I, 308ff., line 53ff.

45 *Y. Sanh.* 1:1, and see n.6 above.

46 M. Goodman, *State and Society in Roman Galilee A.D. 132-212*, (Totowa, New Jersey: Rowman and Allenheld, 1983), esp. pp.93ff., 119ff., 155ff. (note that this study is limited to Galilee); see also D.M. Goodblatt, *Rabbinic Instruction in Sasanian Babylonia* (Leiden: Brill 1975).

47 See Berger, *supra* n.2, at 409: 'A constitution of the emperor Caracalla by which all inhabitants of the Empire, organized in *civitates* with local autonomy, were granted Roman citizenship, except the so-called *peregrini dediticii*.' On the other hand, Colorni, *supra* n.3, at 17ff., maintains that citizenship was extended without any discrimination (i.e. even to *peregrini dediticii*). On the effect of the constitution, H.F. Jolowicz and B. Nicholas, *Historical Introduction to the Study of Roman Law* (Cambridge: Cambridge University Press, 1972, 3rd ed.), 347, comment: 'From the point of view of private law, however, it was more important, though rather for its indirect effect on the character of the law itself than for its direct impact on the new citizens. For though, on the generally accepted view, large numbers of provincials who previously had lived by their own laws, were now expected to adapt themselves to Roman law, the immediate result, as we shall see, was often no more than the adoption of the forms of Roman law as clothing for the unchanged substance of local law.'

48 *Supra* n.1, at vol.II, p.96.

49 Perhaps Rabbi Judah III, who was the Patriarch from 290 to 320, i.e. at the time of Diocletian. If so, we may assume that he himself petitioned the Emperor. For a full discussion, including the implications of the passage for the jurisdictional situation after 70 C.E., and its relationship to *C.Th.* 2,1,10 (discussed below), see A.M. Rabello, 'On the Relations between Diocletian and the Jews', *Journal of Jewish Studies* 35 (1984), 147-167.

50 See further Rabello, *ibid.*, at 164-65 and sources there quoted.

51 Actually, Greek law practiced by the "*Aegyptii*": peregrines who are neither Roman citizens nor citizens of a Greek city of Egypt (Alexandria, Ptolemais, Neucratis). See Mélèze-Modrzejewski, *supra* n.34.

52 On the *nomikos* in Egypt see R. Katzoff, 'Responsa Prudentium in Roman Egypt', *Studi in onore di Arnaldo Biscardi* (Milano: Giuffrè, 1968), II, 523ff.

53 On the *nomikos* in Palestine, see S. Lieberman, *Hellenism in Jewish Palestine* (New York: Jewish Theological Seminary of America, 1962), 81f

54 On Pliny's letters see A.N. Sherwin-White, *The Letters of Pliny. A Historical*

and Social Commentary (Oxford: Clarendon Press, 1966).

55 Rabello, *Giustiniano*, *supra* n.1, at Vol. II, pp.751ff.

56 A.M. Rabello, 'L'Observance des fêtes hébraïques dans l'Empire Romain', *Aufstieg und Niedergang der Römischen Welt* (Berlin-New York: W. de Gruyter, 1984), Vol. II, 21, 2, pp.1288-1312.

57 See further A.M. Rabello, 'Divorce of Jews in the Roman Empire', *The Jewish Law Annual* IV (1981), 79ff.

58 In a constitution reported in Code of Justinian, 1.9.7

59 After the *Lex Iulia de adulteriis*, Roman law required the observance of various formalities in divorce, in order to avoid penal sanctions.

60 Juster, *supra* n.1, at II.59. On the problem in general from the point of view of Roman Law see M. Kaser, *Roman Private Law* (London: Butterworths, 1968), 238ff. On problems of citizenship, see A.N. Sherwin-White, *The Roman Citizenship* (Oxford: Oxford University Press, 1939). See also A. Linder, *The Jews in Roman Imperial Legislation* (Jerusalem: The Israel Academy of Sciences and Humanities, 1987).

7

THE AGE OF THE TALMUD

by

BERACHYAHU LIFSHITZ

Hebrew University of Jerusalem

The great halakhic works, which constitute the basis for all later halakhic literature, were created during the three centuries following the redaction of the *Mishnah* by R. Judah the Patriarch (220 C.E.). These works are the Jerusalem (Palestinian) *Talmud* created in the Land of Israel (and completed — insofar as it is complete — in the fifth century C.E.), and the Babylonian *Talmud* which was edited and redacted in Babylonia, and completed there in the sixth century C.E.). Their primary aim was the clarification and interpretation *of* the *Mishnah* of R. Judah the Patriarch. The term *Talmud* means 'teaching' or 'study'; the two *Talmudim* were compiled through the process of teaching and study of the earlier halakhic literature, particularly the *Mishnah*. Whereas the form of the *Mishnah* is that of an organised collection of concisely-stated rules, the form of the *Talmudim* is that of a discursive scholarly commentary on the *Mishnah*.

1. *Political and Juridical Background*

A. The Land of Israel

In both the Land of Israel and Babylonia (Mesopotamia) — the two great centres of Jewish life — the Jews were subjected to foreign domination. The Romans effectively ruled in the Land of Israel since its conquest by Pompey in 63 B.C.E., and eventually the country became a Roman province in the full sense (see Ch.6, above). The character of many cities changed as foreigners gained a foothold in them, while other cities were founded entirely by foreigners. Most of the land changed hands from Jewish to Roman landlords, though Jews went on to cultivate it as tenant farmers. Taxation was heavy, in addition to the 'Jews' tax' (*fiscus iudaicus*) which Jews had to pay throughout the empire.

The third and fourth centuries were critical times for the Roman Empire. Internal security was unstable, the value of money declined, and the burden of taxes increased. In the Land of Israel, hopes did not cease for political independence, and when it was thought opportune, Jews rose to yet another unsuccessful revolt (against Gallus, 351 C.E.).

From the internal, spiritual aspect we need to take account of the internecine Jewish-Christian antagonism. The new sect was bidding for recognition — which ultimately it received from Rome during the reign of Constantine (early fourth century), first as a tolerated religion then as the official religion of the State. There was also the rivalry between Jews and Samaritans who claimed that their tradition represented the authentic Judaism.

In spite of the struggles and difficulties on all these levels, this was a period of cultural and communal flourishing, a period of intensive activity on the part of the Jewish spiritual leadership (the Sages), in which the majority of the tannaitic and amoraic literature in the Land of Israel was redacted: the *Mishnah*, the *Tosefta* and the Jerusalem *Talmud*.

Most of the intellectual activity took place in two main centres, Yavneh and Usha, under the aegis of the Patriarch and his court, and at independent Academies headed by prominent scholars in various cities. There was some tension in the relationships between these two centres.

The power of the Patriarch was delegated to him by the Roman authorities, and he could bestow benefits on various interested parties, either by appointments to positions of influence or by offering exemption from obligations — the most important of which was exemption from taxes. But the Patriarch held also a religious-juridical authority, as one of the Sages in his own right, and he used this authority on both judicial and legislative levels. In this, he encroached, so to speak, on the territory of the Sages — who themselves lacked administrative powers.

It has to be remembered that the statement of R. Yoḥanan B. Zakkai 'Give me Yavneh and its scholars' expressed a trend towards religious-legal rather than political authority, and a preference for the former over the latter. Concentration of both kinds of power in the office of the Patriarch contradicted, to a certain extent, the policy of rehabilitation of the Jewish nation along religious lines after its loss of political independence.

One of the most important prerogatives of the Patriarch was the appointment of judges (see Ch.5, pp.124-27, above). This appointment had an economic aspect too, for public officials enjoyed various tax-exemptions, and therefore their number was limited. It was claimed that R. Yohanan and R. Joshua b. Levi (third century) were commissioned to appoint judges, and given further administrative powers, because of their good relationship with the Patriarch.

Judges administered civil law and also had means of law-enforcement, such as the Patriarchal Police (the patriarch used his slaves for this purpose: *Y. Ket.*, 9:2, 33a), the authority to fine litigants (*Y. Kil.* 7:4, 31a; *B.K.* 8:6, 6c), and to proclaim bans and excommunication to enforce the authority of courts and of the Sages on those who had to be disciplined, e.g. for not obeying their rulings. It may be assumed that those judges who were qualified for their office (for there were such who purchased their appointment: *Y. Bikk.* 3:3, 65d) ruled according to the law of the *Torah*, and traditional rules of legal decision, pertinent to the circumstances of each case.

The nature of the relationship between the centers of learning such as the Academies and halls of study, and the courts, remains an unsolved question We do not know whether the Sages of the Academies acted as independent judges, or whether the Heads of the Academies were appointed by the Patriarch. It may be assumed that litigants appeared by their own volition before renowned Sages even if those Sages did not hold a commission from the authorities. The Sages, in their sermons, encouraged them to do so, to make sure that they would not go to the courts of foreigners which were also available (see further Ch.6, pp.145f., 154f., above).

B.   Babylonia

The Jewish settlement in Babylonia had commenced soon after the destruction of the First Temple (586 B.C.E.) by Nebuchadnezer, and the subsequent exile of the Jews there (cf. Ch.1, pp.3f., above). Even after the return from exile (538 B.C.E.) many Jews remained in Babylonia. We lack reliable information about the events of that period. Though we have the books of *Ezekiel, Esther, Daniel*, and *Tobit*, which relate to Babylonian Jewry in the Second Temple period, and cast some light on the life of this Jewish community, the picture of their society and institutions is not clear and many details are missing.

Some scholars draw attention to the indirect reference to Jewish learning in Mesopotamia, as implied by the biography of Hillel the Babylonian, who came to the Land of Israel toward the end of the first century B.C.E., and became Patriarch after winning a legal dispute with the incumbent *Bene Bethyrah*, who themselves apparently were from Babylonian-Jewish descent. Others argue, however, that this information is derived from sources edited in the Land of Israel, which do not reflect the life of Jews in Babylonia itself.

Only toward the end of the Parthian period (second century B.C.E.), still during the period of the Second Temple, is there a specific mention of a Babylonian Sage, R. Judah b. Bethyra (*B. Pes.* 3b), who lived in Nezivin.

Josephus mentions an independent state established by the outlaw brothers Hasinai and Hanilai in Babylonia (20-35 C.E.). He also records the conversion of the kings of Adiabene to Judaism, and comments on the vast number of Jews who lived in Mesopotamia (*Ant.*, xx.17ff.).

After the destruction of the Second Temple, we have more information about the connections between the two communities, and especially about the emigration of some Sages from the Land of Israel to Mesopotamia. For example, R. Akiba tells us about Nehemiah of Bet Deli in Nehardea who knew of a traditional dictum attributed to Rabban Gamaliel the Elder (*M. Yeb.* 16:7). There is also information about R. Hananiah the brother of R. Joshua, who claimed the right to intercalate the new year, a prerogative of the Patriarch in the Land of Israel. The *Talmud* (*B. Sanh.* 32b) describes the court of R. Hananiah as 'a worthy court in the Diaspora'.

Conversely, in the generation of the Usha synod (c. 140 C.E.), R. Nathan the Babylonian, son of the Exilarch, came to the Land of Israel, and was appointed Chief Justice (*Av Bet Din*) by the Patriarch R. Simon b. Gamaliel (*B. Hor.* 13b). Though the issue is regarded with some scepticism, R. Nathan apparently held a halakhic tradition which indicates the existence of an independent halakhic tradition in Babylonia. He and R. Judah the Patriarch are regarded as the last mishnaic Sages (*B. B.M.* 86a). So Babylonian tradition already appears to have merited an honorable place beside that of the Land of Israel.

Information is more extensive about the transitional period between the *Mishnah* and the *Talmud*. We know about a compendium of *baraitot* (tannaitic *dicta* which were not included in the body of the *Mishnah*) in the possession of the third century C.E. Babylonian Sage Karna (*B. B.K.* 47b), 'the Judge of the Diaspora' (*B. Sanh.* 17b). In the same period, we know that the father of Mar Samuel was a scholar in Babylonia (*B. Meil.* 9a etc.). R. Yohanan was told that the Head of the Row (in the study hall the students used to sit in rows, each one with its head) in Babylonia was R. Shelah of Nehardea. This institute was apparently an Academy. Rab, who is regarded as the first Babylonian Amora, served the same R. Shelah as a lecturer, and succeeded him as the Head of the Row (*B. Hull.* 137b).

All this confirms the existence in Babylonia of organized learning and a spiritual leadership. Such institutions are not established in a day, nor do they change their nature overnight. So there is reason to accept the geonic tradition which claims that the Academies in Babylonia had existed long before they were specifically mentioned — which does not mean, of course, that their organizational structure and procedures remained unchanged throughout that period.

Similarly, with regard to the political leadership, it is reasonable to suppose that it was not created suddenly, nor was it subject to rapid changes. *Seder Olam Zuta* (ed. Neubauer, 73-75) states that the first Exilarch was King Jehoiachim exiled to Babylonia (596 B.C.E.), and even notes the names of some of his successors. Although this list is a fiction, it reflects nevertheless a reasonable reconstruction. The tradition of Rav Sherira Gaon (below, p.198) in his famous Letter (986 C.E.) is substantially identical.

The *Talmudim* relate that R. Judah the Patriarch (end of second century C.E.) acknowledged the superiority of Rav Huna, the first Exilarch known to us by name, because he descended from the tribe of Judah by the male line, whereas R. Judah himself descended from the female line of Benjamin (*Y. Kil.* 9:3, 32c). We have already mentioned R. Nathan the Babylonian at the time of the Usha synod, who according to an interpretation of the *Talmud* (*B. Hor.* 13b) was the son of the Exilarch.

Altogether, the names of four Exilarchs are known to us from the *Talmud* (Rav Huna, Mar Ukba, Ukban b. Nehemiah, Rav Huna b. Nathan), though it is certain that there were many more during the seven generations of the amoraic period (cf. *B. Ber.* 46b; *B. A.Zar.* 72b, etc.). These four are mentioned in the context of anecdotes praising their erudition and noble deportment (*B. Meil.* 9a; *B.B.* 55a; *Gitt.* 59a, etc.).

The authorities of the Sasanian dynasty in Babylonia (which came to power in 224 C.E.) recognized the institution of the Exilarch, and granted it various administrative prerogatives. This recognition added to the Exilarch's recognition by the Jews themselves — both in Babylonia and in the Land of Israel — enabled the Exilarch to assume a central, decisive role in the affairs of the Jews in Babylonia. He could appoint officials to supervise commerce and the economy, and had the means and authority to enforce the law, though it is not certain that this authority extended also to capital cases.

Within the autonomy allowed by the Sasanian authorities to minorities, we find also Jewish law courts operating, with various changes, throughout the talmudic period, against a background of periodically deteriorating relationships between the ruling Sasanians and Jews, and intermittent persecutions. These courts certainly judged on the basis of the *halakhah*, and many of their rulings are extant. Nevertheless, it is likely that some litigants turned to the Sasanian courts. As in the Land of Israel, so in Babylonia, there was interaction between the Exilarch and the Sages, who stood at the head of the various Babylonian academies.

The Exilarch had his own court, and if he was a learned man, like Mar Ukba (of whom it is said that Mar Samuel sat before him at a distance of four cubits out of respect), he would preside over it himself (*B. Kidd.* 44b). Sages with close relationships to the court of the Exilarch, with its extensive legal activity and a first-hand knowledge of applied law, gained an advantage over theorists, and this could tip the balance of legal arguments in their favour (*B. B.B.* 65a). Theoretical and practical *halakhah* thus mutually enriched each other.

Despite the debate about the comparative legal, educational and spiritual merits of study and practice (*B. B.B.* 130b), great importance was attributed to court rulings. It is not always clear, in the Babylonian *Talmud*, whether a particular passage reflects actual rulings or theoretical studies, due to the peculiar method of editing material which was used (see below). However, it has been shown that some apparently abstract propositions originate from actual court cases (E.E. Urbach, *The Halakhah, its Origins and Development* (Cambridge: Harvard University Press, 1987), 77; Hebrew ed., 59).

The Exilarch had the authority to appoint judges. These had a distinct advantage over independent judges because they enjoyed immunity; they could not be sued if they erred in judgment (*B. Sanh.* 4b). Furthermore, the jurisdiction of independent judges was sometimes questioned. For example, in a case in which the litigants appeared in turn before R. Sheshet (who was Head of the Academy) and R. Nahman, the latter argued that R. Sheshet did not have the prerogative of the 'discretion of judges' because he was not an officially appointed judge, while he, R. Nahman, was (*B. Ket.* 94b).

Further arguments about authority clearly indicate the existence of another juridical system, administered by judges appointed by the Academies rather than by the Exilarch (*B. Sanh.* 5a). Moreover, there were sessions before judges who acted by the mutual consent of the litigants. There was also the possibility of presenting the case before the Head of the Academy while studies were in progress (*B. B.K.* 50b; *Shab.* 55a; etc.).

We do not know the identity of the Sages from the Academies who were appointed as judges by the Exilarch. Therefore, it is hard to know whether their recorded actions of enforcement and punishment, (fines, subpoena, incarceration, flogging, ban, perhaps even capital punishment) were delegated by the authority of the Exilarch, or by the independent authority of the Sage and his court. If the first alternative is true, then the difference between the two kinds of court is smaller than on the latter hypothesis.

In any case the role of the Academy was two-fold. It was a place of study for the individual and for the public (at the *Pirka* and *Kallah* sessions), a place for establishing the theoretical *halakhah* (i.e. exegesis, clarification, elaboration and harmonization of the early sources, unrelated to actual decision-making) and also a court of law which ruled in small and great matters on the practical level. The mutual linkage of these two roles is also expressed by the study of precedents by various Sages at the Academy, who analyzed them in the context of the theoretical *halakhah* for contradictions or for supporting arguments.

As observed above, the existence of courts in which the Sages officiated under the auspices of the Exilarch ensured a connection between theoretical and practical law, as administered in that court and later discussed in the Academy. It is to be noted that this dual function was instrumental in reviewing earlier *halakhot* in a new context and their interpretation in the light of experience.

2. *The Literary Sources of the Halakhah — The Two Talmudim*

The most important halakhic works of this period are the two *Talmudim*, the Babylonian and the Jerusalem, produced by the learning of the talmudic Sages (Amoraim, from a-m-r, to say) at the Academies in the Land of Israel and in Babylonia. Any attempt to describe the *Talmud* meets with serious difficulties. In fact, we do not know exactly the method, stages and time of its editing, the identity of the editors, their aims and the guiding principles of their work or the legal validity attributed to it by them. Since the *Talmudim* do not reveal these matters about themselves, we can only arrive at conclusions indirectly, or by relying on traditions in the post-talmudic sources.

Most of the *Talmud* deals with the *Mishnah* and its interpretation by the Amoraim, and the laws inferred from it. But there are quotations from other early (tannaitic) sources too (*baraitot, halakhic midrashim*), legal precedents, records of decrees and enactments, lore and fables which were integrated into the main body of discussion by various means, whether they were strictly pertinent or only vaguely tangential to the matter under notice. The interpretation of the *Mishnah* is as a whole termed *Gemara* (from *g-m-r*, to learn traditional material). The *Talmud* is the combination of the *Mishnah* and the *Gemara*. Indeed, the Babylonian *Talmud* is often referred to colloquially as the *Gemara*.

The language of the Jerusalem *Talmud* is Western Aramaic and that of the Babylonian *Talmud* Eastern Aramaic (Babylonian).

A. The Scope of the *Talmudim*

The 63 tractates of the *Mishnah* are represented in the Jerusalem *Talmud* by only 39 extant tractates — those discussing the first four Orders: Agriculture (*Zera'im*), Appointed Times (*Mo'ed*), Women (*Nashim*) and Torts (*Nezikin*), the latter with the exception of the tractates on Testimonies (*Eduyot*) and Sayings of the Fathers (*Pirke Avot*). There was no *Talmud* on the Order of Holy Things (*Kodashim*) and Purities (*Toharot*), although it is possible to prove the existence of a *Talmud* on the Tractate *Niddah* in the latter Order.

Nevertheless, it is evident that the Amoraim in the Land of Israel studied all the mishnaic Orders with equal diligence. Even if we assume that at a certain stage the now missing tractates of the Jerusalem *Talmud* were edited, these were lost at a very early period and forgotten.

The Babylonian *Talmud* presents a different picture. There is no *Talmud* on the Order of Agriculture except for the Tractate of Benedictions (*Berakhot*), nor for the Order of Purities except tractate *Niddah*. There is *Talmud* for the remaining four Orders with the exception of five tractates (*Shekalim*, *Eduyot*, *Pirke Avot*, *Middot*, and *Kinnim*). There are altogether 369 chapters of *Talmud* corresponding to the 523 chapters in the *Mishnah*.

There is no doubt that the Babylonian Amoraim knew all the mishnaic Orders, and studied them intensively. The *Talmud* tends to expand the discussion of *mishnayot* from the Orders of Agriculture and Purities when quoted in the context of the debate on *mishnayot* from other Orders. If so, why is there no *Talmud* on them? The omission could be attributed to the lack of organized study of these Orders in the curriculum of the Academies, and therefore to the absence of a core for the development of later pericopes. It could also be attributed to a decision of the editors not to make a final redaction of the material which they had on Agriculture and Purities. In any event, the Babylonian *Talmud* in its present form is to be regarded as a completed work from which there are no parts missing.

B. The Sources and their Redaction

The *Talmudim* as we know them cannot be regarded as homogeneous units, since their final recension is based on material gathered from many sources. An analysis of this material reveals that it is composed from different books. It may be stated that each tractate is a separate work in its own right, which does not necessarily correlate with other tractates, and the times of the various recensions of tractates is not identical.

Furthermore, even within the tractates, some pericopes contradict each other. The accepted assumption is that they originated in different Academies or centers of learning. This might also explain why sometimes the teachings of Babylonian Sages are quoted by the Jerusalem *Talmud* but do not appear in the Babylonian *Talmud*. Conversely, material from the Land of Israel some-times appears in the Babylonian *Talmud* but is absent from the Jerusalem *Talmud*, or is quoted there in a different manner. It could be assumed, that there were various *Talmudim* and learning traditions, but we only know the extant version.

It is possible to regard the *Talmud* as an integration of two distinct sources: on the one hand, the statements of the Amoraim, on the other the anonymous narrator of the *Talmud* (i.e. the anonymous explanations, linking phrases, and discussions not attributed to a particular Sage). This duality is conspicuous in the Babylonian *Talmud*, particularly when juxtaposed with the Jerusalem *Talmud*, where quite often the amoraic statement on a *mishnah* is quoted without any discussion, explanation, query or reply — all of which are typical of pericopes in the Babylonian *Talmud*. This difference indicates a higher level of editorial involvement in the Babylonian *Talmud*, which renders it more understandable than the Jerusalem *Talmud*. There is a tendency to attribute this difference to the difficult political conditions in the Land of Israel relative to Babylonia (pp.169-175, above), which did not facilitate the orderly and thorough treatment of the material.

These conditions also prompted the premature redaction of the Jerusalem *Talmud* towards the end of the fourth century, preceding by about 200 years that of its Babylonian counterpart, though the editing of the latter is also imperfect and in some parts incomplete. Indeed, it is difficult to determine with certainty when the Babylonian *Talmud* was edited and redacted. *Rashi* (p.313, below) says (*B. B.M.* 86a) that the process of editing the *Talmud* did not commence until the end of the fifth century when Rabina and R. Ashi 'arranged the amoraic statements on each topic and fixed the order of tractates' and also decided the *halakhah*. Rav Sherira Gaon (ninth century) says that each generation had its own *Talmud*, i.e., exposition to the *Mishnah*, which was added to the already extant expositions, and the *Talmud* as we know it is a record of these accumulated interpretations. Other opinions attribute the editorial work to the generation of Abbaye and Raba (p.183, below) and limit the role of Rabina and R. Ashi (p.184, below) to the final recension. Others still are of the opinion that the editorial work commenced after the generation of Rabina and R. Ashi (p.184, below) and continued until the eighth century (thus into the geonic period).

The three centuries (approximately) between the Babylonian *Talmud* and the Geonim is called the Period of the *Saboraim* (from *s-v-r*, to reason), most of whom are anonymous; there is little information about their activities. If indeed editorial work on the Babylonian *Talmud* did not commence until after the generation of Rabina and R. Ashi, then the *Saboraim* have the decisive role in determining the form of the Babylonian *Talmud*. In any event, there is unanimous agreement that some additions (such as the general rules for determining the *halakhah*, together with decisions on a number of issues) and even entire pericopes are the work of the *Saboraim*. It should be remembered that the *Talmud* was normally taught and studied orally even after its recension, which led to slight sequential and textual variations. Some errors in the transmission of the text could account for substantial differences in meaning.

Furthermore, for a long time the Babylonian *Talmud* was regarded as an 'open' book which might be changed and emended. The changes were made to correct or improve the existing text and it is difficult therefore to detect them. In the Jerusalem *Talmud*, on the other hand, most of the textual variations are the result of scribal errors and are therefore easier to spot.

In any case, the problem of errors will not be solved until the publication of scientific, critical editions of the *Talmudim*, which has yet to be undertaken.

C.   The Pericope (*Sugya*)

If a discussion of the editing of the Babylonian *Talmud* (or of each tractate) is important, a discussion of the design of the pericope (*sugya*), the basic literary unit of the *Talmud*, is essential.

The text is presented dialectically, as a dialogue of negotiation, give and take, proof and rejection, question and answer, with a special terminology (different in the two *Talmudim*) to mark the different parts of the *sugya*, such as the presentation of sources, queries, solutions etc. Owing to this predilection for dialectic presentation, the content is sometimes subordinated to stylistic considerations.

We have already mentioned the 'anonymous narrator' of the *Talmud*, who provides context for the sources ascribed to tannaitic and amoraic authorities. On removal of the narrative layer, the other sources stand on their own. Frequently it is possible to detect a different opinion in the sources from that advocated by the narrator.

Some *sugyot* have been proved to be fictitious. Such a *sugya* looks as if it has evolved around a particular *mishnah*, but this it is not so. The *sugya* has been moved from elsewhere and was changed stylistically in order to fit its new location. This was done in order to give the information regarding the *mishnah* in its proper location, even though the original discussion arose around another *mishnah*.

D.   The Aim of the *Talmud*

It is reasonable to ask what the relationship is between its literary form and its legal content — from which conclusions are drawn according to the traditional dogmatics of Jewish law, in which literary research plays but little if any role.

It is a most important point whether the 'author' of the *Talmud* intended it to be a legal codex or simply as a commentary on the *Mishnah*, which itself is the legal codex. In spite of the peculiar dialectics of the talmudic narrative, there are indications of the editors' wish on occasions to decide the *halakhah*.

In any event, the Geonim asserted the proposition that the law must be decided according to the Babylonian *Talmud* (even when it contradicted the Jerusalem *Talmud*) and Maimonides (twelfth century; see pp.288f. below) sustains the proposition with the declaration that it is the duty of every Jew to follow the course set by the *Talmud* 'because all Israel submitted to it' (Prologue to Code of Maimonides). Since the time of Maimonides, there has been an endeavour to base every legal ruling on the *Talmud*, which — with its questioning, pluralistic structure — opens almost unlimited horizons for various possible decisions.

For this reason, the Babylonian *Talmud* became the most extensively studied standard reference work for halakhic scholars, who elucidated it with notes and commentaries; the relatively obscure Jerusalem *Talmud*, lacking supporting literature, has remained more difficult to master.

E.   Characteristic Attributes of the *Talmud*

As already observed, the Amoraim mainly occupied themselves with the study of the *Mishnah*. Their aim was to clarify its contents, and to infer additional implicit *halakhot*. The early Amoraim did not regard the *Mishnah* as an immutable text in its phraseology or (sometimes) even in its content, and their approach is more critical than that of their successors. They emended certain *mishnayot*, rejected others which contradicted the *halakhah* as they knew it, and distinguished apparently general laws as applying only to a particular, unique set of events, thus effectively limiting their scope. This procedure is called *okimta*, and it was also used as a means of harmonizing contradictory sources, or of settling the *halakhah* according to the rationale of the Amoraim.

The later generations of Amoraim, however, regarded the *Mishnah* as a final, (quasi)-canonical text, and subjected it to painstaking analysis in order to justify its contents.

It is characteristic of talmudic methodology to juxtapose texts from various legal spheres, for their mutual clarification. Since the *Mishnah* employs the casuistic method, these comparisons draw attention to under-lying legal principles. The tendency of the *Talmud* is to formulate abstract legal concepts (on such matters as retrospective designation, despairing of the recovery of lost property, promise, unintentional outcomes, etc.). These influence the evolution of the law, and the interpretation of the tannaitic sources. Another method of the *Talmud* is to propose patently impossible cases, the purpose of which is to express the pure, abstract principle, in order to overcome the difficulty of identifying relevant factors in the determination of a particular *halakhah* (e.g. *B. B.K.* 27a, *B. B.K.* 143a; M. Silberg, *Talmudic Law and the Modern State* (New York: Burning Bush Press, 1973), 20f.).

3.   *Some Prominent Sages*

As a rule the biography of a talmudic Sage consists of his collected statements, by which he is remembered. The *Talmud* has no intention to tell the life stories of the Sages. Biographical notes appear either incidentally or if they are pertinent to a teaching in his name. We can, however, list the prominent amoraic figures in both centers in a chronological order. The traditional division by 'generations' is merely for convenience. The 'genera-tion' only indicates in general terms the period in which a particular group of Sages, as a group, flourished. Some authorities were older contemporaries of the following generation, their teachers, etc., and some were also younger contemporaries of the previous 'generation'.

A.   The Land of Israel

i.   The First Generation (220-250 C.E.)

This is the transitional generation between the tannaitic and amoraic periods. One of the first representatives of this generation is R. Ḥiyya, who came with his sons from Babylonia to study with the redactor of the *Mishnah* — R. Judah the Patriarch. For this reason interpretations of the *Mishnah* by R. Ḥiyya are authoritative. He himself edited anthologies of *baraitot*. His contemporaries, Bar Kappara and Levi also made similar anthologies. Other notable figures of the same generation are R. Jannai and R. Hoshea, the teachers of R. Yoḥanan (see below). R. Jannai taught in the Galilean town of Akhbara, while R. Hoshea became head of the Academy in Caesaria. He is also the editor of an anthology of *baraitot*, comparable to that of R. Ḥiyya, and dealt with many problems of great profundity.

ii.   The Second Generation (250-280 C.E.)

In this generation the foundations of the Jerusalem *Talmud* were laid in the Tiberias Academy by R. Yoḥanan b. Naphah (a disciple of R. Judah the Patriarch), R. Jannai and R. Hoshea. The opinions of R. Yoḥanan are widely quoted in both *Talmudim*. He was highly esteemed also in Babylonia, to the extent that his opinions gained precedence over those of Rab, the first Babylonian Amora. His method of harmonizing inner controversies within the *Mishnah* was to distinguish their different sources. He is known also for his propensity to identify abstract rules in the *halakhah*.

R. Yoḥanan was assisted by his brother-in-law, R. Simon b. Lakish (Resh Lakish), an erstwhile prize-fighter and gladiator in Roman service who graduated from being a disciple of R. Yoḥanan to serving as his colleague. They came to be called 'the two great men in the world'. Resh Lakish repeated the lectures of R. Yoḥanan for the students, and his analytical approach facilitated the clarification of R. Yoḥanan's opinions.

Another great colleague of R. Yoḥanan, Ilfa, left his studies to become a businessman. He claimed that he could show the mishnaic source of every *halakhah* which appeared in the *baraitot*.

iii.   The Third Generation (ca. 280-330 C.E.)

The outstanding disciple of R. Yoḥanan was R. Abbahu, who lived in Caesaria, in the Academy of which he apparently redacted the Order of

Nezikin of the Jerusalem *Talmud*. R. Abbahu enjoyed a good relationship with the Roman authorities, was well versed in Greek and mathematics, and participated in public debates with the Christians, opposing their interpretation of Scriptures. Another disciple of R. Yoḥanan was R. Elazar b. Pedath, who came from Babylonia. Where his dicta are unattributed, they are believed to derive from R. Yoḥanan.

Further disciples are R. Ammi and R. Assi, who closely collaborated. They were regarded as the most important *kohanim* (which is an incidental courtesy title) and 'The Judges of the Land of Israel'.

iv.   The Fourth Generation (320-360 C.E.)

Among these must be mentioned R. Zeira (Zera), who came from Babylonia and became the teacher of R. Jonah and R. Jose b. Zevida, two companions from the Tiberias Academy who are often quoted by the Jerusalem *Talmud*. Another Babylonian scholar who came to the Land of Israel was R. Jeremiah, famous for his questions about the nature of the arbitrary quantities and measures determined by the Sages.

v.   The Fifth Generation (360-400 C.E.)

This generation marks the end of the redaction of the Jerusalem *Talmud*. The notable figures of this generation are R. Mana and R. Jose b. Abin (Boon).

B.   Babylonia

i.   The First Generation (200-250 C.E.)

The most prominent authorities of this generation are Rab and Mar Samuel. Rab founded the Sura Academy, and Mar Samuel was the head of the Academy in Nehardea. The talmudic rule used to resolve disputes between them is that the opinion of Rab is accepted on questions of religion and that of Mar Samuel on Civil Law, but in their own localities during their lifetimes they enjoyed unimpaired jurisdiction. They are the only Babylonian Amoraim who systematically taught the Orders of Agriculture and Purities.

ii.   The Second Generation (250-280 C.E.)

These are the disciples of Rab and Mar Samuel. One of the most prominent of them was Rav Huna, successor of Rab as Head of the Sura Academy, who was recognized as the leading authority, and even superior to his contemporaries in the Land of Israel — R. Ammi and R. Assi. Another important disciple of Rab and Mar Samuel was R. Judah b. Yeḥezkel. He was the head of the Pumbedita Academy and known for his brilliance.

iii.   The Third Generation (280-310 C.E.)

On the demise of R. Judah b. Yeḥezkel, R. Ḥisda was elected to the head of the Sura Academy, which became the predominant centre of learning. R. Ḥisda was also a disciple of both Rab and Mar Samuel, was known for his sharp epigrammatic sayings and as a dialectician. The place of R. Judah at the Pumbedita Academy was taken by Rabbah b. Naḥmani (Rabbah), a position he held (it is said that he 'reigned') for 22 years. He was succeeded by R. Joseph. The latter was called 'Sinai', for his great erudition in the *Mishnah* and *baraitot* and for his great ability to interpret and translate the Scriptures.

Of the same generation were also R. Naḥman b. Jacob, a son-in-law of the Exilarch and chief justice of his court, who specialized in civil law, and R. Shesheth, who lived in Nehardea and was known for his wide knowledge of *baraitot*, which enabled him to solve many difficult problems. He was known as 'wise and sharp who cuts cases clear as an iron [knife]'. Also of this generation was Ulla, the 'flying Amora', who made many trips from Babylonia to the Land of Israel and was thus instrumental in the exchange of ideas between them.

iv.   The Fourth Generation (310-340 C.E.)

The prominent Amoraim of this generation are Abbaye and Raba, whose sayings, interpretations and disagreements are so numerous that it is has been suggested (see p.177, above) that it was they who commenced the recension of the Babylonian *Talmud*. Abbaye, who was a nephew of Rabbah, was appointed to the head of the Pumbedita Academy following the demise of R. Joseph, and held this office for about 14 years.

His colleague and opponent in many disputes was Raba. In order to resolve those many disputes, the *Talmud* laid down that the *halakhah* should follow the view of Raba in every disagreement except for six, where the view of Abbaye prevails. Raba lived in Mehoza, where he headed the local Academy. After Abbaye's death R. Naḥman b. Yitzḥak became the head of the Pumbedita Academy, and it is quite possible that he too worked on the editing of the *Talmud*.

There were also two famous 'flying Amoraim' in this generation, R. Dimi and Rabin, who travelled a number of times from Babylonia to the Land of Israel and facilitated close relations between the two centres.

v. The Fifth Generation (340-380 C.E.)

R. Papa, a disciple of Raba, is the chief figure of this generation. He lived in Naresh near Sura. His colleague was R. Huna b. R. Joshua. Both of them combined study with commerce. R. Papa aspired to harmonize all the different views concerning customs and religious rites and to minimize outstanding disagreements.

Another famous disciple of Raba was Rabina, who later debated the *halakhah* with R. Ashi. Ashi and Rabina were characterized in the *Talmud* by the cryptic statement (*B. B.M.* 86a) 'they are the end of instruction'. The real sense of that statement is unknown.

vi. The Sixth and Seventh Generations (380-500 C.E.)

Here the figure of R. Ashi rises above all. Of him, it is said: 'Since the days of R. Judah The Patriarch until R. Ashi we never found *Torah* and greatness at the same place.' Even the Exilarch was subordinated to him (*B. Gitt.* 59a). His Academy was located at Mattah Mehasya, near Sura, and there, according to many learned opinions, he edited the Babylonian *Talmud* with the assistance of the board of scholars, aided especially by Rabina and Amimar.

His son Mar b. R. Ashi is the most important Amora of the seventh generation, among whom we may additionally note R. Aha, Rabina (II), Marimar (the teacher of Rabina II), and Rafram.

4. *Legal Practice: the Courts*

The period under discussion was characterized by the absence of Jewish self-rule. It was therefore primarily the concern of the ruling government, whether the Roman Government in *Erets Yisrael* or the Sasanian Government in Babylonia, to establish a judiciary system of courts and enforcement institutions whose authority extended to the Jews.

Obviously, there is an important difference between the two situations. The Romans came (ultimately) as conquerors in a land where, prior to its conquest, justice had been administered by the local inhabitants themselves, whereas the Jews who were taken to Babylonia came to a foreign land which had its own laws and institutions.

Rome traditionally allowed the local institutions in the provinces which it had captured to continue operating, and this was initially the case in *Erets Yisrael*. But already in mishnaic times, legislation gradually reduced the authority of these local institutions (see Ch.6, above). However, this reduction of authority applied only to the power of enforcement enjoyed by Jewish courts of law. It did not apply to their capacity to adjudicate by virtue of mutual consent (as arbitrators), nor to the exercise of communal coercion (using socio-religious sanctions) nor did it affect the Sages' moral and religious authority. Given the opposition of many Jews to Roman rule and its symbols, and the importance which they attached to Jewish law, we can assume that Jewish courts of law continued to operate throughout this entire period. Those Jewish authorities who sought to impose a total ban on recourse to a gentile legal system (*B. Gitt.* 88b) had to offer an alternative form of litigation.

Indeed, there is evidence regarding the existence of courts of law which operated in *Erets Yisrael*, and even the existence of a judicial hierarchy. For example, there is mention of courts of law in Tiberias and Zippori (Sepphoris); litigants could choose to select the venue of the lawsuit in the dispute between them, but as between creditor and debtor the creditor had priority of choice. The venue of preference was the 'Place of Assembly' and it could be demanded that a case be tried there (*B. Sanh.* 31b). In the same context, the possibility that one of the litigants may compel the other party to attend the court in his own town, rather than travel to another city for litigation, is discussed. Indeed, we know of correspondence between the courts of law in Tiberias and Babylonia regarding a Babylonian Jew, resident in Israel, who had a lawsuit against a Jew in Babylonia. The Tiberian court asked the Jewish authorities in Babylonia (Mar Ukba) to adjudicate (though R. Ashi suggests that this was out of respect; the Babylonian court lacked authority to judge cases of 'fines': ḳenaṣ): if the defendant would heed his local, Babylonian court, fine; if not, the Babylonian authorities were asked to force him to go to Tiberias and submit to the court there (*B. Sanh.* 31b).

Babylonia had its own courts of law. Those at Sura and Nehardea were regarded as 'expert courts of law' (*B. Sanh.* 23a), which differ from lay courts in that they had power to insist that a lawsuit be heard locally, rather than troubling the parties to litigate in another city.

According to Jewish law, a court of law (composed of three men) is required not only for litigation involving monetary disputes, but also for other judicial processes in the realm of *halakhah*, such as divorce, levirate marriage etc. These courts of law do not necessarily have to be permanently established courts, but can be convened on an *ad hoc* basis. It stands to reason, however, that such bodies eventually become established institutions and served as the foundation for a formal, established judicial system.

These courts of law, however, had purposes beyond that of formal adjudication. The *Talmud* refers to the court of R. Ammi and R. Assi in *Erets Yisrael* as an 'important court of law'. The *Talmud* (*B. Shab.* 10a) describes the activities of these two sages thus:

> Rabbi Ammi and Rabbi Assi were sitting and studying between the pillars (on which the academy rested— Rashi) and every now and then they knocked on the side of the door and said, 'If anyone has a lawsuit, let him enter and come in.'

The relationship between the court of law and the Academy, the Babylonian talmudic college, is not entirely clear. The *Talmud* often mentions litigants who applied to the head of the Academy in the middle of a study session. Study would be interrupted and litigation would begin. The litigation between the two sides does not appear to have been orderly in every case, but the lack of an accurate account of what actually took place, apart from the ruling (preserved in the *Talmud*) that was derived from the litigation, prevents us from determining precisely what happened.

Overall, however, we do gain the impression that the courts of law functioned in an established, orderly fashion. From random discussions in the Babylonian *Talmud*, we know of Sages who went out of their houses to hear cases; about messengers of a court of law (*shaliaḥ bet din*) who delivered legal summonses (*B. M.Kat.* 16a, *B.K.* 112b); about fixing a date for a person to appear in court (*B. B.K.* 113a); about the judges' scribes (*B. B.B.* 167a), etc. Moreover, the courts of law were conscious of their status, and mention is made of accusations of contempt of court (*B. Ket.* 26b). From a discussion about deviating from court procedures in a case involving violent litigants, we may infer that there were fixed court procedures for conducting trials and for obtaining evidence (*B. Gitt.* 88b, *B.K.* 92b, *B.M.* 39b).

Reference is made to the giving of prior consideration to the plaintiff when the defendant brought a counter-claim (*B. B.K.* 46b), and to the question of whose case is heard first when there are several lawsuits (*B. Sanh.* 8a). The *Talmud* generally required the personal presence of the litigants, and therefore there is no mention of written pleas (the records of pleas referred to in *B. B.B.* 168a are the summaries of the litigants' pleas *after* they had been heard). The court summons was of great importance, and a person who refused to appear in court was threatened with excommunication (*B. B.K.* 114a).

Judgment was also generally handed down orally, unless the court was required to explain its verdict (*B. Sanh.* 30a), or if a written judgment was required for purposes of execution.

The existence of a well-developed judicial system indicates that the Jews had considerable need for a judicial system administered by their own people. Indeed we read that R. Ḥisda and Rabba bar R. Huna used to sit in judgment all day until their hearts grew faint (*B. Shab.* 10a). Perhaps it was the need to avoid judicial exhaustion that led R. Sheshet to rule: 'Until when must [the judges] sit in judgment? Until the time of the [main] meal [of the day].'

The abolition of *semikhah* in *Erets Yisrael*, probably in the mid-second century C.E. (see Ch.5, pp.124-27, above), and with it the power — as recognized by Jewish law itself — of the judge to enforce his sentence, raised special problems. In Babylonia, the right to judge was conferred by the Exilarch, in *Erets Yisrael* by the Patriarch, and the *Talmud* (*B. Sanh.* 5a) deals with the jurisdiction of a judge from one country with regard to the other (concluding that the Babylonians had jurisdiction over Israel, but not vice versa). In any event, it was claimed by Babylonian scholars that they were, in a manner of speaking, carrying out the commission of the 'early sages' in *Erets Yisrael* (*B. Gitt.* 88b, *B.K.* 84b) — but not in all types of case. Thus, for example, the consensus was that Babylonian courts of law were *not* authorized to deal with matters of a penal nature (*B. Sanh.* 14a, *B.K.* 84b), and there was some doubt with regard to cases of larceny (which in Jewish law gives rise to multiple compensation, rather than a fine or some form of corporal penalty) and bodily injuries (*B. Gitt.* 88b, *B.K.* 84b and *Tosafot* in both sources).

In this respect the *Talmud* also considers the number of judges required to adjudicate a case. Mar Samuel discusses whether a judgment of two judges can be valid (*B. Sanh.* 2a), and R. Naḥman regarded himself, because of his great expertise, as of sufficient standing to adjudicate alone in monetary cases (*B. Sanh.* 5a).

There appears to be little reason to doubt that these courts were generally conducted according to Jewish law, which circumstance also furthered its development. Thus, for example, a special oath was imposed on a defendant who denied a claim *in toto* — contrary to Pentateuchal law, which imposes an oath only when the defendant admits part of the claim (*B. Shebu.* 40b).

In a famous dictum (*dina demalkhuta dina*), Mar Samuel held that the law of the land is binding (*B. Gitt.* 10b), but it should not be inferred from this that Babylonian law was generally applied in Jewish courts, but rather that it was applied only in particular instances (on the details of which, there is considerable scholarly debate). Even the existence of certain penal powers, which the Babylonian authorities apparently conferred on the Exilarchs and other distinguished Sages, does not alter this conclusion.

The numerous talmudic discussions cannot be viewed merely as theoretical commentaries on the *Mishnah*, but as discussions of actual proceedings. That Jewish law was indeed implemented and practised is indicated by the many judgments contained in the *Talmud*, by the legal documents preserved there (whose content generally comply with Jewish Law), and by the existence of scribes who were familiar with the phraseology of these documents (quotations from which were collected by A. Gulak, *Otsar Hashtarot*, Jerusalem: Yanovitz, 1926).

5.   *Some Features of the Halakhot of the Period*

A   Sources of Law

As we have seen, the Sages of the *Talmud* essentially regarded their role as being that of commentators on the *Mishnah* and other tannaitic sources, and as a rule they felt bound by the *halakhot* in these texts. Nevertheless, there can be no commentary without effecting some change, and sometimes the interpretation caused the law to differ from its original intention. It has also been noted that the integration of legal precedents into the studies at the Academies brought about some limiting or expansion of the scope of particular *halakhot*.

In addition to their role in the Academies, the Sages also had some powers of legislation (by *takkanot* and *gezerot*), and they enacted laws in all spheres — as their predecessors, the *Tannaim*, had done before in the mishnaic period. These enactments changed the then current *halakhah*, but unlike changes brought about by interpretation, they were declared as intentional.

In the following subsections, we note some of the more prominent topics on which the *halakhah* underwent change in the talmudic period. One of these depends on interpretation, and has an important role in civil law; the others were effected by legislation.

B. Contracts

A controversial issue from tannaitic times was the validity of a promise to transfer ownership of property in the future and more generally to do something in the future. This topic has far-reaching ramifications, because it raises the problem of the validity of any promise concerning a future action. Some were of the opinion that such a promise had no legal validity; they enforced only legal transactions which were effective at once, even though they praised those who did not break their word, and condemned those who did. The following *Mishnah* illustrates this controversy (*B. B.B.* 10:5):

> A man paid a part of his debt, and deposited the bond with the instruction: 'If I do not pay the balance by a certain date, give the creditor his bond.' The date arrived and he did not pay. R. Jose says: He shall give it. R. Judah says: He shall not give it.

The *Talmud* (*B. B.B.* 168a) explains the reason for this difference of opinions:

> What is the point of their argument? R. Jose holds that a mere promise (*asmakta*) conveys property, and R. Judah holds that a (mere) promise does not convey property.

The argument about the validity of a bare promise appears a number of times, and it was a subject of fierce controversy among the Amoraim both in the Land of Israel and in Babylonia. Some, who were of the opinion that a promise is legally binding, had changed their mind without giving any reasons. We learn in the same *sugya* (*B. B.B.* 168a):

> R. Nahman in the name of Rabbah b. Abbuha in the name of Rab said: The *halakhah* is according to R. Jose. When such a case came before R. Ammi, he said. 'Since R. Yohanan has taught us more than once that the *halakhah* is according to R. Jose, what can I do? Nevertheless, the *halakhah* is not according to R. Jose.'

This problem can be seen in other *sugyot* too. An original attempt to harmonize the different views was made by R. Papa (Babylonian Amora of the fifth generation). He tried to distinguish between cases in which there is corroborative evidence that the promise was not meant to be kept and cases in which such evidence is to the contrary. This distinction is diametrically opposed to the position held by Raba, the teacher of Rav Papa. In spite of the opposition to this distinction when it was first proposed, it has become a decisive consideration in the *halakhah* and exerted a great influence on the evaluation of obligations in Jewish law ever since.

C.   'And You Shall Do that which Is Right and Good'

The *Talmud* (*B. B.M.* 108a) mentions an enactment (*takkanah?*) by the Sages, with regard to the sale of land. When land is sold, the holder of the neighbouring property has first option to purchase it. If the land was sold to a third party, without letting the neighbour make an offer, it is the right of the latter to redeem this land from the new buyer at the purchase price. This enactment is based on the Biblical verse 'and you shall do what is right and good' (*Deut.* 6:18), because it is right that the neighbour should have a bigger parcel of land if the vendor suffers no loss. This enactment is called the 'law of pre-emption'.

Since the enactment is based on a Biblical principle, it governs all transactions of land, and it is decisive in determining which cases are subject to the law of pre-emption. The *Talmud* (*ibid.*) lists a number of cases:

> A gift is not subject to the law of pre-emption ... When one sells all his land to one person the law of pre-emption does not apply. If the land is sold back to its original owner the law of pre-emption does not apply ... When the property is sold for poll tax, alimony, or funeral expenses, the law of pre-emption does not apply ... If one offers well minted coins and the other offers bullion, the law of pre-emption does not apply.

In all these cases the decision is made on the basis of a whole set of considerations as to when the ultimate aim of doing 'the right and good' is best served.

Another enactment (*takkanah*) based on the same principle is 'an assessment returns to its erstwhile owner' (*B. B.M.* 35a):

> The Nehardeans said: An assessment (expropriation in lieu of a debt) is returnable up to twelve months. Amemar said: Though I am of Nehardea, I hold that an assessment is always returnable, because it is said: And you shall do what is right and good.

This enactment is in favour of debtors who could not meet their obligations and therefore their property was 'assessed' and given to the creditor. According to ordinary law this procedure is regarded as a sale of the property to the creditor in exchange for the loan, and, like any other transaction, it is irreversible except with the agreement of both parties. After the enactment, the debtor, once he raised the funds, was in a position to reverse the sale and redeem his property from the creditor, with no time limit. As to the reason, the *Talmud* says that the creditor never really intended to acquire the property, but wanted to get his money back, which he does in any case. If, however, the creditor sold the property, or bestowed it as a gift on a third party, the debtor is in no position to reverse the sale, because the third party surely intended to acquire the property and it is 'right and good' that it should remain in his possession. Conversely, if the creditor owed money to a third party, who expropriated the newly acquired land, it is within the right of the original owner to redeem it from the second creditor, because the latter never intended anything other than to get his money back.

D. Family Law

The Sages made a number of enactments in the sphere of family law.

1. Rab enacted (*B. Kidd.* 12b) that a man who betroths a woman without a prior agreement to marry is to be flogged.

> A man betrothed a woman with a myrtle branch in the market place. R. Aha b. Huna sent for the opinion of R. Joseph: 'What is to be done?' R. Joseph said: 'Order him to be flogged, according to [the edict] of Rab, but she must be properly divorced, according to Mar Samuel' (i.e., the betrothal is valid).

Betrothal is regarded by Jewish law as a private act, and a man may betroth a woman privately before two witnesses. But such an act may be a source of all kinds of difficulties if it was performed without a previous agreement — a 'match' (*shidukhin*) arrangement. The intention of Rab was to prevent such difficulties. This was just one of a number of cases where Rab ordered a flogging in circumstances where the behavior so sanctioned was permitted by the previous law:

> One who betroths a woman in the market place, one who betroths by intercourse, one who betroths without a previous agreement (*shidukhin*), one who cancels his own letter of divorce, one who queries the validity of a letter of divorce, one who makes trouble for the bailiff, one who was excommunicated for thirty days or more, and one who lives with his mother-in-law (*B. Kidd.* 12b).

Rab also ruled that 'a man may not betroth a woman without seeing her first, and a father must not betroth his minor daughter [but waits] till she comes of age and says 'I want so-and-so.'

2. An enactment to prevent the status of a 'deserted wife' (*agunah*).

Suppose that a husband has already agreed to a divorce, but has ordered the bill of divorce (*get*) to be written in the presence of many people. In such a case some might argue that the bill is invalid until *all* those present have signed, since the husband has insisted on their presence. The amoraic enactment states that either all of them or some of them suffice to sign the bill. Indeed, some say that in such a case the husband must explicitly stipulate that the intention was for all of them to sign, otherwise any two may sign and any one may deliver the bill of divorce to the woman (*B. Gitt.* 67b).

3. A further enactment to prevent the status of 'deserted wife' enables the woman to pay the fees of the scribe. This payment was originally the duty of the husband, and it led to delays because he was not always willing to pay.

> And why is this [payment by husband] not done at the present time? The Sages imposed it on the woman so that he might not cause her delay. (*B. B.B.* 168a)

If the husband had to pay the scribal fees, he could delay the divorce by claiming reimbursement for his expenses. Hence the enactment, which places the obligation on the woman.

4. In the amoraic period we find delegation of authority to the Sages to annul and make void marriages retroactively when the case so warranted. This authority was exercised in two types of case.

One group includes the *Talmud*'s explanation of the enactment of R. Gamaliel the Elder, concerning a bill of divorce sent by a messenger. By this enactment, the bill is valid, even if the husband revoked it before the wife could have taken possession of it (*M. Gitt.* 4:1-2). This enactment contravenes scriptural law, according to which the bill of divorce is indeed void, and the woman cannot marry another person. If she did unwittingly marry, because she had received the bill of divorce and was unaware that her husband had revoked it, she is a bigamist and her children from the second 'marriage' are *mamzerim*. The enactment of R. Gamaliel aimed to prevent such a mishap on the principle of 'the betterment of the world'.

In the talmudic discussion of this *mishnah* (*B. Gitt.* 33a), it is concluded that the Sages have the authority to annul a marriage by making use of their authority of expropriating property. They could in fact retroactively expropriate the betrothal coin from the groom, so that the betrothal did not take place at all. The *Talmud* there asks the obvious question: what if the betrothal was effected by intercourse? This question is dismissed with 'the Sages regard this communion as an act of lechery.' And the *Talmud* concludes: 'All who marry do so subject to the approval of the Sages, and the Sages made the betrothal void.'

This authority to annul a marriage is mentioned also in a case where a person gave a bill of divorce, subject to the fulfilment of conditions which he could not meet due to *force majeure* (*B. Ket.* 3a). Usually, such an event exempts from all obligation, but in this case the Sages annulled the marriage. The Sages did not here validate the bill of divorce, which was not in their power; rather, they chose annulment as the means of freeing the woman from the marriage (*B. Gitt.* 73a).

The second group comprises those cases in which it is impossible to say that 'he married subject to the approval of the Sages', because it is clear that he did not. In these case the annulment is effected without any rationalization of 'All who marry do so subject to the approval of the Sages'. An example of this group includes a case in which a man held a woman under duress until she agreed to marry him. The marriage, though valid because it took place with the (notional) agreement of both parties, was not ratified by the Sages. 'He acted without propriety, therefore we deal with him without propriety' — said the Sages, and annulled the marriage (*B. B.B.* 48b).

The same ruling was given in another case in which a man kidnapped a girl and betrothed her. The girl had earlier betrothed herself to another man, but that act had no validity, since the girl had been a minor. The betrothal effected by the kidnapper ought therefore to have been binding. Nevertheless the Sages annulled the marriage because the kidnapper had acted without propriety, and therefore should be dealt with likewise (*B. Yeb.* 16a).

5. The following enactment was made in order to safeguard domestic peace.

According to law, a housewife had the status of a hired labourer as regards her liability for breakage of and damage to household goods. She was only exempt if such damage was incurred by an 'act of God'. She was regarded as a paid labourer because she received food and lodging from her husband. So, in the strict legal sense, the woman was responsible for most of the damage to household property during her daily tasks. However, the Sages enacted: 'She is not liable even to the extent of the responsibility incumbent on an unpaid watchman (*shomer ḥinam*). Otherwise there would never be peace in the household' (*Y. Ket.* 9:4, 33a). Maimonides later commented as follows (*The Laws of Matrimony* 21:9):

> The woman who broke household utensils in the course of her household chores is exempt. This is not the (strict) law, but an enactment, for if it were not so, there would never be peace in the household, because she would take excessive care and refrain from doing most of her household tasks, which would inevitably lead to quarrels.

Accordingly, she is exempt even if she was negligent, because an 'unpaid watchman' is only liable for gross negligence and wilful damage.

6. *Bibliography*

1. On the Political and Juridical Background and the Rabbinic institutions of the period:

Ackroyd, P.R., *Israel under Babylonia and Persia* (Oxford: Oxford University Press, 1970) (for the pre-talmudic period).
Encyclopedia Judaica, s.v. 'Babylonia', Vol.4, cols. 34-43.
Goodblatt, D.M., *Rabbinic Instruction in Sasanian Babylonia* (Leiden: E.J. Brill, 1975).
Neusner, J., *A History of the Jews in Babylonia* (Leiden: E.J. Brill, 1965-1970, 5 Vols.).
Weidengren, G., 'The Status of Jews in the Sasanian Empire', *Iranica Antiqua* I (1963), 117-162.

2. On The Literary Character and History of the Talmudim:

Bokser, B.M., 'An Annotated Bibliographical Guide to the Study of the Palestinian *Talmud*', in *Aufstieg und Niedergang der Römischen Welt* (Berlin-New York, de Gruyter, 1979), II, 19, 2, 139-256.
Elon, M., *Jewish Law: History, Sources, Principles*, trld. B. Auerbach and M.J. Sykes (Philadelphia and Jerusalem: Jewish Publication Society, 1994), Vol. III ch.29 ('The Literary Sources in the Amoraic Period').
Encyclopedia Judaica, s.v. 'Talmud', 'Talmud, Babylonian', 'Talmud, Jerusalem', vol. 15, cols. 750-779.
Goldberg, A., 'The Babylonian Talmud', in S. Safrai, ed., *The Literature of the Sages, First Part* (Assen: Van Gorcum, 1987), 323-345.
Goodblatt, D.M., 'The Babylonian Talmud', in *Aufstieg und Niedergang der Römischen Welt* (Berlin-New York: de Gruyter, 1979), II, 19, 2, 139-257.
Jacobs, L., *Studies in Talmudic Logic and Methodology* (London: Shapiro Vallentine, 1961).
Jacobs, L., *The Talmudic Argument* (Cambridge: Cambridge University Press, 1984).

Jacobs, L., *Structure and Form in the Babylonian Talmud* (Cambridge: Cambridge University Press, 1991).

Kaplan, J., *The Redaction of the Babylonian Talmud* (N.Y.: Bloch Publishing Co., 1933).

Kraemer, D., *The Mind of the Talmud* (New York: Oxford University Press, 1990).

The Talmud, ed. I. Epstein (London, Soncino, 1935-1952), 35 vols. (English translation of the *Babylonian Talmud*)

Weisbard, P.H. and Schonberg, D., *Jewish Law: Bibliography of Sources and Scholarship in English* (Littleton: Rothman & Co., 1989), 13-15.

Weiss-Halivni, D., *Midrash, Mishnah and Gemara* (Cambridge MA: Harvard University Press, 1986).

3. On Prominent Sages

Strack, H.L, *Introduction to the Talmud and Midrash* (Philadelphia: The Jewish Publication Society of America, 1931), ch.13.

4. On the Court system

Albeck, Sh., *Law Courts in Talmudic Times* (Jerusalem: Bar-Ilan University Press, 1980, in Hebrew).

5. On *halakhot* of the Period, particularly those created by *takkanah*:

Elon, M., *Jewish Law: History, Sources, Principles*, trld. B. Auerbach and M.J. Sykes (Philadelphia and Jerusalem: Jewish Publication Society, 1994), Vol. II ch.16 ('Legislation in the amoraic Period').

Ginzberg, L., *Jewish Law and Lore* (Philadelphia: The Jewish Publication Society of America, 1955), 3- 57.

Rakover, N., *The Multi-Language Bibliography of Jewish Law* (Jerusalem: Library of Jewish Law, 1990), 25-32, 65-73, 218-261.

Silberg, M., *Talmudic Law and the Modern State*, trld. B.Z. Bokser (New York: Burning Bush Press, 1973).

8

HALAKHAH AND LAW
IN THE PERIOD OF THE GEONIM

by

GIDEON LIBSON
Hebrew University of Jerusalem

1. *Historical, Political and Juridical Background*

In the commonly accepted periodization of Jewish Law, the five centuries between the compilation of the *Talmud* (sixth century C.E.) and the advent of the authorities known as *rishonim* (the 'early' or 'first' scholars, eleventh century C.E.), are known as the geonic period. The name is derived from the title *ga'on* ('Excellency') given to the Sages who, at the time, headed the Academies of Sura and Pumbedita in Babylonia. For the purposes of this discussion, the period will include the so-called saboraic period, which began at the end of the talmudic period, placed by most scholars at the beginning of the sixth century. There is no agreement, however, among scholars as to the borderline between the saboraic and geonic periods: estimates vary from as early as the end of the sixth century to the mid-eighth century.

The indeterminacy is due primarily to the similar, sometimes even identical, nature of the activities of the Saboraim and the Geonim; it is compounded by the lack of any prominent event, historical or literary, that might mark the distinction. Although the Muslim conquest of the Middle East in the middle of the seventh century more or less coincided in time with the end of the saboraic period (Ch.7, p.178, above), it had little immediate effect on literary activity *per se*. Yet another complicating factor is that many saboraic elements filtered into talmudic literature, so much so that the Geonim discuss saboraic glosses as if they were an integral part of the Babylonian *Talmud*; conversely, saboraic material made its way into the works of the Geonim as well.

The end of the geonic period is generally marked by the death in 1038 of Rav Ḥai, Gaon of Pumbedita, 'the last of the Geonim in time and the first in importance'. During his lifetime, other centres emerged in addition to those already existing in North Africa, Spain and Italy, namely those of France and Germany, and Babylonia/Iraq lost its hegemony to a significant degree. Some scholars nevertheless extend the period for another two and a half centuries, up to the last quarter of the thirteenth century, arguing that the influence of the Babylonian Geonim had not waned, despite the rise of other centres.

Our knowledge of the geonic period derives from four principal literary sources: the *Epistle of Rav Sherira Gaon*; the *Story of Nathan haBavli*; letters written by the Geonim, which contain much historical material; and documents and notes (*shtarot*), mostly from the Cairo Genizah.

Rav Sherira's Epistle, written in 987 in response to an inquiry from the Jews of Kairouan, North Africa, was based on records written by earlier Geonim. In addition to chronological lists and dates of special events, the epistle describes the traditions of study in the Babylonian Academies.

The Story of Nathan haBavli, composed in the first half of the tenth century, purports to describe the organization and study methods of the Academies, as well as the positions of Exilarch and heads of the Academies. The author's object was to stress the continuity of tradition up to the Babylonian Academies and thus to justify their leading position in the Jewish world.

The Geonim corresponded extensively with Jewish communities the world over, to solicit contributions and provide encouragement to them; scores of their letters have been preserved. Documents and other material from the Genizah testify, among other things, to the multifaceted economic and commercial activity of the times.

The halakhic work of the Geonim is unique in all respects — in its literary character, the variety of topics with which it dealt, its volume and its innovation. Among the factors that shaped the form and content of geonic legal literature were the economic, social and political changes that were then taking place. The principal change was political: Sasanian Persia fell to the Muslims (637 C.E.), bringing all Jewish communities in the Near East, including those of Iraq and Palestine, under a single, Islamic régime. Toward the end of the tenth century, with the rise of the Fatimids in Egypt and its vicinity and the consequent fragmentation of the Muslim Empire, new Jewish centres emerged in North Africa and Egypt, deriving their authority both from the Muslim authorities and from the local communities.

It is highly significant that the Geonim, and the communities they served, were subject to Muslim rule, hence automatically to the law of Islam. Accordingly, Islam exerted considerable influence on geonic activities, including halakhic decisions and innovations. One obvious effect of the Muslim occupation and the receptivity of the Geonim to Arab culture was their use of the Arabic language, beginning from the time of Rav Saadya Gaon, as an acceptable language of legal literature — certainly for halakhic treatises, less so in responsa. Legal notes and documents, however, continued to be written in Aramaic. Economic terms common in geonic writings (such as *nisaya*, *abas*, *suftaja*, etc.) were also borrowed from the parlance of Arab traders. Muslim rule was also partly responsible for the competition between the Geonim and the Exilarch, who generally enjoyed the backing of the secular régime — the Muslims recognized the institution of the Exilarch and even increased his powers. Exilarchs played political, economic and legal roles; but their standing varied at different times during the geonic period.[1]

The Geonim were fully aware of the implications of Muslim rule, respecting and fearing it at one and the same time. An echo of their attitude to the Muslim authorities may be discerned in a geonic responsum concerning obedience to the secular Government:

> The new [Government has acquired possession] over the whole land and none can come and say, this land was mine ... for the victorious Government has acquired absolute possession.[2]

Geonic acceptance of the benefits of Muslim rule is obvious in such assertions as: 'These Muslims are most solicitous for our good and protect us to a high degree.' Nevertheless, there was a measure of fear, which may be detected in various responsa. An anonymous Gaon opined that the prohibition on selling houses to three gentiles (lest they establish a 'neighbourhood') is not absolute, but only meritorious, 'and in order not to provoke enmity we do not reveal this [prohibition] to the authorities.'

In view of this reality, the Geonim were not infrequently obliged to take Islamic Law and religion into consideration. Such apprehensions often prompted a forced exegesis of talmudic law, sometimes even departure from it. The Muslims, for their part, granted the Jewish community legal autonomy, as part of the Islamic attitude in general towards the 'protected nations,' *ahl al-dhimma*, or 'nation of the book,' *ahl al-kitab*, as we shall see. The legal status of the Jews under Muslim religious law was probably first defined in the time of the Umayyad khalif 'Umar ibn 'Abd al-'Aziz, in the first quarter of the seventh century. However, this positive attitude was not enough to ensure the absolute independence of Jewish Law or to discourage Jewish litigants from appealing to Muslim courts. Such appeals constituted a constant threat to Jewish legal autonomy and indirectly influenced the evolution of the *halakhah*, both substantially and procedurally.

In the social realm, contacts with Muslim society at various levels brought about some degree of conversion to Islam, though the exact dimensions of the phenomenon are hard to gauge. At any rate, it is widely attested in geonic responsa dealing with matters involving converts to Islam.

The most important economic change was the transition from an agricultural society to a commercial one in which, besides local trade, international commerce also occupied a fairly prominent place. There are numerous testimonies in geonic literature to landless Jews, though some Jews were nevertheless engaged in agriculture (explaining why one still finds cases of lien over land belonging to debtors). The shift to an emphasis on trade — which occurred quite widely and rapidly, increasing the mobility of Jewish society and enhancing the power of money — could not but influence the development of *halakhah*. Economic changes and constraints provided an impetus for halakhic innovation, particularly through the legal institutions of *takkanah* (enactment), and *minhag* (custom or usage), affecting such areas as the laws of purchase, agency and legal procedure. At times they also influenced areas not directly linked with economic affairs, such as family and society.

Among the more impressive manifestations of the new economic emphasis were the frequent use of credit and the emergence of chattels, rather than real estate, as the central object of trade. The new situation provided fertile ground for deception and fraud, a complaint occurring frequently in geonic responsa being 'now that liars have multiplied ...'. The Geonim met this challenge, too, by having recourse to *takkanah* and *minhag*. All this halakhic initiative was designed to facilitate free trade; geonic sources frequently cite such motivations as the need to enhance the security offered by notes or to safeguard creditors' rights, so that there would be no obstacles to borrowing.

Jewish communities were now scattered all over the Mediterranean Basin and the Near East, with an important concentration in North Africa. The centre of the stage was still held by the Babylonian Academies of Sura and Pumbedita, which moved to Baghdad at some time in the tenth century. The relationships between the centre and the Diaspora were still plagued by the competition between the Babylonian and Palestinian centres and the differences between them in *halakhah* and religious custom. During the geonic period, particularly toward its close, the Palestinian centre came to be increasingly influenced by the now well-established Babylonian hegemony.

This geographical fragmentation was complicated by a division of the Jewish world into three distinct spheres of influence (the Hebrew term used in contemporary historiography is *reshuyot*, domains), depending on which of the leading Academies' rulings were considered binding: these were the Academies of Sura and Pumbedita and that of the Exilarch, each extending its authority over nearby districts. Remote communities remained outside this triple framework.

The Sura Academy maintained ties with the Academy of the Exilarch, and the two were known collectively as 'the two Academies.' There was some competition between the Academies of Sura and Pumbedita, owing partly to the desire for recognition as well as for financial support from the Diaspora communities. This was one of the reasons for the numerous controversies and tensions among the Geonim. Emigration, mainly from east to west, did not ease the controversies and sometimes even deepened differences between the Academies, on the one hand, and the communities, on the other.

In order to improve relationships between the Academies and the communities and encourage financial support, members of the communities were requested to address their halakhic questions to the Geonim of the Academy, while the latter, for their part, would dedicate their halakhic works to certain community notables. However, although the communities and their leaderships voluntarily accepted the legal authority of the Babylonian Geonim, they nevertheless maintained a certain measure of judicial independence, and there were unmistakable signs of the onset of decentralization.

Yet another social phenomenon was the emergence of various movements and sects, most notably the Karaites, who made their appearance around the middle of the ninth century (see Ch.9, below). The mainly halakhically motivated Karaite 'rebellion' exerted influence on the halakhic positions of the Geonim and may have perhaps added impetus to the legal creative process.

These three factors — political, economic and social — all had their effect on modes of halakhic creativity, on the authority of the Academies and the Geonim who headed them, and on the evolution of the *halakhah* itself, both on the theoretical level of halakhic thought and on the practical level of positive law. They strongly influenced such sources of law as *takkanot*, *minhagim* and judicial decisions in all areas, including family and personal law.

Internal Muslim politics also affected the development of the *halakhah*, particularly in Palestine. In the wake of the division that split the Muslim world from the early tenth century onward, Egypt became an independent kingdom under the Fatimids, no longer subordinate to the khalifate in Baghdad. The fact that Palestine and Egypt were now governed by the same power reinforced the jurisdiction of the Jerusalem Academy *vis-à-vis* the Jewish communities in its sphere of influence, including that of Egypt. Circumstances thus strengthened the influence of Palestinian practices in those communities, sharpening the competition for spiritual hegemony between the two major centres, especially in countries, like Egypt and Palestine, where there were sizeable communities of Babylonian Jews. The Jewries of those countries now sought to establish their legal independence and institute their own system of autonomous Government; thus, the title *Naggid* made its first appearance in Egypt in the middle of the eleventh century.

There were contacts between the Palestinian centre and the communities in Egypt and North Africa, which observed some Palestinian practices. The Jews in Palestine, like their Babylonian brethren, enjoyed legal autonomy by virtue of their position as 'protected people' under Muslim rule, though the laws governing this special status were apparently not maintained in all their stringency. However, our information concerning *halakhah* and legal matters in Palestine and the legal autonomy of the Palestinian community during most of the geonic period is sparse. It is thanks only to the Genizah that we are somewhat more knowledgeable with regard to the end of the period.

Though the Jews of Palestine enjoyed a measure of legal autonomy, it is clear from documents attesting to threats and sanctions, including excommunication, imposed upon Jews having recourse to gentile courts, that the intervention of the Muslim authorities, who of course wielded supreme legal power, was not infrequently requested. Such appeals, though quite consistent with the usual relationships between protected subjects and the Muslim rulers, were clearly frowned upon as endangering the autonomy of the community.

Owing to the difficult conditions then obtaining in Palestine, *halakhah* and halakhic institutions did not develop as freely as they did in Babylonia. The Palestinian Academy (sometimes referred to as the Great Sanhedrin), the central religious institution, sat first at Tiberias, later at Jerusalem and finally, toward the end of the eleventh century, at Tyre and later Damascus. It was headed by a Gaon and an *Av Bet Din*, under whom were an additional five scholars of the Academy. The Gaon was recognized by the Muslim authorities, who confirmed his supreme legal authority in a special letter of appointment. This authority concerned, inter alia, the areas of personal law, divorce and marriage. The Gaon presided over the local judiciary system and was also empowered to appoint officials in the various communities. He handed down decisions in halakhic matters, also writing responsa.[3] Some Palestinian Geonim also produced halakhic literature.[4]

In Palestine, as in Babylonia, *herem* (banning) was the main instrument available to the Gaon to enforce his rule and discipline offenders. Though the surviving written evidence of Palestinian judicial activity is rather meagre, it includes notes, verdicts, documents relating to inheritance, and other similar court-related material. Some of the documents and notes seem to follow Babylonian practice and betray Babylonian influence,[5] perhaps because they relate in part to commercial customs, which were the same everywhere — and some of the main trade routes passed through Palestine. Thus we find the institution of conditional divorce,[6] extensive use of *suftaja*,[7] appointment of representatives,[8] and the writing of documents and deeds of guardianship, compensation, partnership, among others.[9] Babylonian influence is also occasionally felt in the style of Palestinian marriage contracts.

2. *Halakhic Literature*

The halakhic literature of the Geonim falls into four main categories: (A) commentaries on the *Talmud*, introductory works, and theoretical theological-legal literature; (B) codificatory works (the literary categories known in Hebrew as books of *halakhot* (laws) and books of *pesakim* (rulings) — terms for which there are no exact equivalents in English);[10] (C) responsa; (D) halakhic monographs and collections of notes, including those found in the Cairo Geniza.

A. Commentaries on the *Talmud*, Introductory Works, and Theoretical Theological-Legal Literature

The Geonim composed commentaries on a number of talmudic tractates, most of which were in response to requests on specific words or *sugyot* and simplistic in their quality. It seems that the commentaries were part of the Geonic attempt to spread the study of the Babylonian *Talmud*. The most important one, which survived completely, is the commentary on the Order of *Tohorot*. The Geonim also composed works of methodology to facilitate the study of *Mishnah* and *Talmud*. The most important one is the *Introduction to the study of the Mishnah and Talmud* by Rav Samuel ben

Hofni Gaon. Among the topics included in the book are: the nature of tradition, differences of opinion among Tannaim and Amoraim, technical terms,
and so on. Beside commentaries and introductions, Rav Saadya and Rav
Samuel ben Hofni composed treatises on legal theory like Rav Samuel's
book on the *Treatise on the Commandments* or his treatise on ten questions,
most of which deal with the theory of law.[11]

B. Codificatory Works

Two important codificatory works were written in the early part of the
geonic period, around the mid-eighth century: the *She'iltot* and *Halakhot
Peṣuḳot*. Both works, despite their differences, continue the oral tradition of
the *Talmud* and provide yet another building block for the body of material
on which the Geonim based their decisions, although explicit quotations
from the *She'iltot* and *Halakhot Peṣuḳot* in geonic works are rare. They also
largely represent talmudic traditions found not in the *Talmud* itself but only
in geonic literature. One motive for the composition of such works, and of
Halakhot Peṣuḳot in particular, was pointed out somewhat later, in a
responsum from the time of Rav Palṭoi Gaon:[12]

> Which is preferable and desirable, to delve into [the *Talmud*] or to study
> abridged *halakhot*? We have asked this question because a majority of the
> people incline to abridged *halakhot*, saying: Why should we be occupied
> with the complexity of the *Talmud*?! He answered, they are doing something
> undesirable, and it is forbidden to do so, for they detract from the *Torah* ...
> Moreover, they cause the study of the *Torah*, Heaven forbid, to be forgotten.
> [Abridged *halakhot*] have been compiled not [in order to be studied
> intensively], but rather so that they may be referred to [by those who have
> studied the whole of] the *Talmud* and experience doubt as to the proper
> interpretation of anything therein.[13]

i.   *She'iltot*

The work known as *She'iltot*, written by Rav Aḥa of Shabḥa (fl. mid-
eighth century), is unique for its arrangement according to the order of the
weekly portions of the *Torah*, incorporating both aggadic and halakhic
material, with a tendency towards definite rulings. Rav Aḥa interweaves the
Oral and Written Law in a creative manner, usually taking up a halakhic
topic in a portion of the *Torah* where it occurs in a narrative passage, rather
than in the portion that features it explicitly in a legal context.

We do not know whether Rav Aḥa wrote the *She'iltot* himself or only collected them. The book was long considered a kind of popular codex, each section concerning itself with one particular law of a given topic, rather than with a complete exposition of all its legal details. In keeping with the writer's educational goal, therefore, the key words of a halakhic decision, 'And thus is the law' (*vekhen halakhah*), are missing in many cases.

Unlike *Halakhot Peṣuḳot* (see below), the *She'iltot* is not often referred to by the Geonim. Rav Ḥai mentions it in his responsa only once, and it is occasionally mentioned by other Geonim. Actual quotations from the book may be found in the later *Halakhot Gedolot*, and numerous parallels have been pointed out between it and *Halakhot Peṣuḳot*. However, it would seem that the author of the latter work did not copy his material from the *She'iltot*, but rather that both authors drew from the same sources. It was therefore seen by the early halakhic authorities as a work continuing the traditions of the Saboraim.

The major importance of the *She'iltot* is the information they provide regarding parts of talmudic discussions not found in our text of the *Talmud*. Accordingly, a question that has occupied scholars is whether the *She'iltot* attest merely to a variant reading of the *Talmud*, or to a different version. The technical terms utilized in the work are not specific to the *She'iltot*, but they may be found in all of the contemporary literature. The work has reached us in fragmentary form: many sections are still extant only in manuscript form and were not included in the collections currently available.

ii. *Halakhot Peṣuḳot*

Unlike the *She'iltot*, *Halakhot Peṣuḳot* is a codificatory work proper, retaining almost nothing of the talmudic debate underlying the legal decisions. The author was Rav Yehudai, Gaon of Sura in the mid-eighth century, whose composition of the book essentially ushered in a new period. The work was attributed to Rav Yehudai because of the many legal decisions contained in it that are delivered in his name. Some scholars, however, believe that the book was authored not by Rav Yehudai himself but by his disciples.[14]

Scholars disagree as to the reason for the composition of the book. Some suggest that the impetus was provided by the emergence of Karaism, but this is only a hypothesis. Other scholars point to political factors and the needs of the times; still others place emphasis on the personality of Rav Yehudai. Most probably not one but several factors were responsible.

The author drew on many sources. Among other things, Rav Yehudai's book contains teachings of the Saboraim; many teachings cited in their name may be found in *Halakhot Peṣuḳot*, in addition to other sources not found in the *Talmud*. Rav Yehudai frequently based himself on early traditions, as his disciple Pirkoi b. Baboi reports in his name:

> Never have you asked me anything, nor have I told you anything, except it has proof from the *Talmud* or I learned its practice from my master and my master from his master ... [15]

Early talmudic sources of all kinds are used: *Halakhic Midrash*, *Tosefta* and the *Jerusalem Talmud*. In addition, as already stated, the book includes passages that have parallels in the *She'iltot*, the two authors presumably relying on a common source.

Halakhot Peṣuḳot gave rise to a large body of literature, mainly abbreviated versions published under a variety of titles: *Halakhot Ḳetu'ot*, *Halakhot Ḳeṭanot*, and so on. As a result, the works became more popular than the *Talmud* itself, resulting inter alia in the question addressed to R. Palṭoi Gaon (see above). The original, written in Aramaic, was translated into Hebrew; the latter version became known as *Hilkhot Re'u*, though there are differences (including additions and lacunae) between the Aramaic and Hebrew works as we have them today. It was also translated into Arabic.

The book is not arranged according to the tractates of the *Talmud*, but by topics relevant to contemporary halakhic practice; for that reason, laws not relevant to the post-Temple period or to the Diaspora are not included.

iii. *Halakhot Gedolot*

The third important book of the geonic period is *Halakhot Gedolot*, authored by Simeon Kayyara, who probably flourished toward the end of the ninth century or at the beginning of the tenth.[16] Though the author's dates have not been fixed with any confidence, any doubt as to his identity is removed by Rav Ḥai's explicit statement: 'Our master Simeon of Bozrah, who composed *Halakhot Gedolot*, did not ascertain the reasons of our master Rav Yehudai or of these Sages.'[17]

Halakhot Gedolot is based on Rav Yehudai's *Halakhot Peṣuḳot* but also draws on other sources, such as the *She'iltot*, saboraic traditions and perhaps also the book known as *Ma'asim livne Erets Yisra'el* (see p.214, below). The title *Halakhot Gedolot* (Great Laws) was apparently intended to differentiate it from the more limited *Halakhot Peṣuḳot*.

The main body of the work is a summary of *halakhah* in the Babylonian *Talmud*, arranged in the order of the tractates of the *Talmud*. It also deals with certain topics no longer relevant in the post-Temple era, such as laws of sacrifices. Because of the large number of sources, there are occasional duplications. The Geonim — at least from the time of Rav Saadya — frequently quote from the work, and generally cite it in their rulings. Thus Rav Samuel b. Hofni states of the author of *Halakhot Gedolot*:

> And we rely on what the author of *Halakhot* said, for he was learned in matters of *halakhah* and his intentions were for the sake of heaven.[18]

Rav Hai, too, utilizes *Halakhot Gedolot*, but only rarely rules in accordance with the book, sometimes even opposing its view, as in a responsum concerning the question of whether a creditor's heirs may sue the debtor:

> Therefore this ruling as found in the *Halakhot* is not in accordance with the law; you should not rely on it, and it is a common occurrence that notes come before us in which the creditor's heirs sue the debtor and the loan is collected. No-one has ever taken this ruling into consideration in the two Academies.'[19]

Referring to this responsum, an anonymous Gaon wrote:

> Our Master R. Hai wrote in a responsum that one should not rely on Rav Sar Shalom or on R. Simeon Kayyara, who stated the earlier view.[20]

Most probably, Rav Hai's attitude to *Halakhot Gedolot* depended on the context and situation.[21]

C. Responsa

Another major source for the geonic period — perhaps the richest and most comprehensive — is the responsa literature. The responsa reflect the entire legal reality of the times, with all its problems and complexities, showing how the Geonim actually answered questions brought before them. We find in this category a huge volume of legal material: *takkanot*, *minhagim*, documents and legal judgments, constituting an invaluable contribution to our understanding of *halakhah* and its development in the geonic period.

Questions were addressed to the Geonim in almost all areas of Jewish life: interpretation of biblical or talmudic passages; explanations of words; problems of theoretical or practical import. They reached Babylonia from the centres of Jewish life in most of the world. Most originated in the *Maghreb* (North Africa), with a small number coming from Spain and Egypt, as well as Italy, the south of France and Palestine — clearly attesting to the leading role of the Babylonian Academies in contemporary Jewry. The Geonim themselves encouraged the Jews of the Diaspora to send their questions, considering the responsa one way of maintaining their position and authority — as well as their material welfare.

The questions were sent in collections (*kevatsim*) or booklets (*kuntresim*) and were answered in the same way; a collection was generally named for the first responsum it contained. Copies were kept by the Geonim in their archives — some of the responsa collections were preserved in this way. It was customary to put together several booklets to form a collection; in addition, indices were sometimes made, listing the items by subject or the name of the responding Gaon. These indices no doubt promoted the dissemination of the responsa: we know of collections of geonic responsa that reached as far as Central Europe. One which reached Germany is attested by the following remark:

> The Lord granted me good fortune, and there came into my hands responsa brought from the African lands, a great book, consisting of responsa of the Sages of Africa, asked of the Babylonian Geonim ...[22]

Not all the geonic responsa have survived in the original collections; many of them appear in more than one. Identification of the person who sent or received a specific collection will sometimes help to determine the respondent's identity, which is not always known. Another aid to identification is the fact that almost every Gaon had his own style or characteristic phraseology which sometimes helps to identify the authors of responsa.

Unlike monographs, which were written in Arabic, responsa were also written in Aramaic, although queries addressed to the responder in Arabic were also answered in Arabic. Out of caution, the Gaon would repeat the question at the beginning of his reply.

There exist today many collections of geonic responsa, some of which were not originally independent collections but were anthologized at a later date, such as *Teshuvot haGe'onim* of Lyck and *Sha'are Teshuvah*, both anthologies culled from R. Judah Al-Bargeloni's *Sefer Ha'Ittim*. The most important collection of responsa currently extant is that published by A. Harkavy in 1887, which actually preserves the original forms of some of the booklets, including opening and closing passages of the responsa. In 1928, Benjamin Menashe Lewin started a monumental work, *Otsar Hageonim*, in which he collected geonic responsa and commentaries according to the order of the talmudic tractates. At the time of his death in 1944 he had published 13 volumes through the middle of *Baba Metsia*. In 1967, H. Taubes published *Otsar Hageonim* on tractate *Sanhedrin*.

Most of the responsa in our hands today — only a small fraction of the total number written by the Geonim — are attributed to Rav Sherira and Rav Ḥai. A further large group comprises those written by Rav Natronai. We also possess a few dozen responsa of Rav Saadya, Rav Palṭoi, and other Geonim. Geonim were sometimes asked questions concerning responsa of earlier Geonim; conversely, they sometimes quoted or referred to their predecessors' responsa.

A number of factors had a deleterious effect on the authority and reputation of the responsa: the fact that they sometimes survived only in abbreviated versions; the omission of the names of the questioners and the respondents; changes in the opinion of the responding Gaon; forgeries and misattribution of responsa. Such questions arose during the geonic period itself, as Rav Sherira writes:

> We see that these things are forged [and wrongly attributed] to our Master Saadya Gaon, of blessed memory, for he was a great scholar and would not have overlooked an entire section of our *Mishnah*.[23]

Sometimes, however, the accusation of forgery appears to have been used merely as an excuse for rejecting a Gaon's ruling.

One can discern a certain evolution in the written style of the responsa, from succinct, briefly worded answers at the beginning of the period, to more elaborate discussions at its end. At times the Geonim seem to have discoursed at considerable length as a rhetorical device, to stress their authority and influence.

The personal standing of the Gaon and the community's readiness to accept his rulings largely determined the legal status accorded his responsa. This may well be the reason for the vehement objections of some Geonim to the practice, common at the time, of addressing the same question to two different Geonim — for the responsum was considered a binding judicial decision, not merely a legal opinion that could be obtained from more than one authority. Hence Rav Naḥshon Gaon's harsh words:

> You have committed a grave offence by asking a question of four principals of Academies; you are thereby initiating controversy in Israel, that will never die down ... [24]

Where two Geonim handed down the same decision but proffered different arguments, the problem was serious enough; where they gave different decisions, the problem was greater still. Rav Sherira and Rav Ḥai wrote:

> But when the case cannot be raised before the Great Court and two Geonim give two answers, the judge should do as he sees fit and whatever his heart decides, for he can only rely on the sight of his eyes ... [25]

R. Meir b. Barukh of Rothenburg laid down the following rule for cases in which two Geonim had delivered conflicting decisions:

> Wherever there is a disagreement of Geonim, no property should change hands.[26]

The basis for the view that a responsum constitutes a legal decision may already be found in a responsum of Rav Yehudai Gaon, who was asked about a person who requested a judge's opinion, rather than a verdict proper:[27]

> It is forbidden to discuss the case with him at all, or to give him any opinion concerning the case, for that is the practice of gentile courts, who are required to judge a case and offer an opinion.

In other words, R. Yehudai condemned the practice for the sole reason that the appellant had requested only an opinion; there would have been no complaint had he accepted the judge's jurisdiction and requested a legal decision proper. Conversely, I believe, one should equate the binding legal authority of the responsum to that of a judicial verdict, since the questioners considered the respondents to be judges handing down a verdict. An echo of this idea may be discerned in a question addressed to Rav Sherira and Rav Ḥai:

> As to your question, why did R. Yoḥanan say this? Surely, he is the principal of an Academy and all laws are decided according to him ... [28]

A further indication of the legal status of responsa is the fact that they were read and written down in a quasi-formal assembly of the scholars and heads of the Academy, as described by R. Natan haBavli (cited in many geonic responsa). The careful deliberation and profound study of the questions gave in this forum gave it the standing of a court, bearing collective responsibility for the content of the responsum, enhancing its formal dimension and its importance.

In the later phase of the geonic period this element of joint responsibility was somewhat diminished; instead, emphasis was laid on the personal responsibility and authority of the responding Gaon. A result of this shift was a transition to the writing of halakhic literature besides responsa. Undoubtedly, the personalities of the Geonim from Rav Saadya onwards, especially Rav Saadya himself and, later, Rav Samuel b. Hofni, were partly responsible for this changed emphasis.

D. Halakhic Monographs and Books of Notes

A special category in geonic literature comprises halakhic monographs, the earliest of which date to the time of Rav Saadya Gaon, and books of notes, which were apparently current even before Saadyah's time.[29] If Rav Yehudai's *Halakhot Pesukot* ushered in a new period in codificatory literature, Rav Saadya initiated a new departure in his composition of halakhic treatises, apart from his being the major authority of his time on halakhic matters. The trail blazed by Rav Saadya was later followed by Rav Samuel b. Hofni and Rav Hai, and the latter in fact acknowledges his debt to Rav Saadya in several places.

The Geonim did not write comprehensive halakhic treatises but only monographs limited to specific topics — though combination of several such monographs could serve as a foundation for a comprehensive code; perhaps that was the purpose of the various authors. These works, taken together, may be considered as having prepared the ground for Maimonides' great code, *Mishneh Torah* (below, Ch.10, pp.277-279). One should not try to attribute the composition of these geonic works to deeper motives, such as the challenge of Karaism, the fear that the *Torah* might be forgotten, the need to facilitate study of the *Talmud*, and similar motives. Such explanations are upheld neither by the historical background nor by the monographs themselves or their structures. A better suggestion is that of Goitein, that the works may have originated as lectures to students at the Academy.[30]

Whatever the origin, the principal purpose of these monographs was to serve as practical guides for judges or even laymen, in order to preserve halakhic and talmudic tradition, and to help bond together the Jewish people by strengthening ties between the Babylonian Academies and the Diaspora communities. Support for this last motive comes from the Arabic language of the monographs and the dedication of some of them, in particular from the time of Samuel b. Hofni and later, to prominent persons with whom the Geonim were in contact. That the purpose was also practical may be inferred, for example, from the introduction to Rav Saadya Gaon's *Book of Notes*, where we read:

> I realize the great need of the nation for it and I know the considerable benefit that they will derive therefrom ...

— a motif that recurs several times both in this and in other works of Saadya.[31] Emphasis is placed upon the fact that these works were explicitly written for beginners, lacking a talmudic background, sometimes at their express request; such were, e.g., Rav Hai's *Mishpete shevu'ot* and Saadya's *Sefer hapikadon*. The Geonim were influenced to a large degree, both in the actual composition of these works and in their form, by the literary work of their neighbours, the Muslim jurists, who also wrote treatises of law and books of documents.

The geonic works, without exception, list laws together with proof-texts from the *Mishnah* and the *Talmud*, arranged in chapters by topic, in a logical sequence. In each topic, the relevant concepts are clearly defined. Though the names of many such monographs are now known, thanks to book lists found in the Genizah, few of the works themselves have survived in their entirety; others have reached us in a fragmentary form, while still others, known to exist in the Genizah, await publication.

The only complete surviving work from the pen of Rav Saadya Gaon is his *Treatise on Inheritance*; in addition, most of his *Book of Notes* has been discovered. Perhaps the most prolific Gaon was Rav Samuel b. Hofni, who wrote more than forty halakhic treatises, covering all areas of *halakhah* (see below, pp.231f.). Of Rav Hai's compositions, we know of his treatises on oaths, laws of sale and purchase, abutters' rights, loans and judges' duties, a book of note, and perhaps also a treatise on the laws of conditions.

The content of these monographs is not associated with one Academy or the other; they reflect talmudic law as a whole. The Geonim generally refrain from citing geonic literature, unless questions were posed directly on that point.

Mention may also be made of further works written during the geonic period or towards its end, such as *Halakhot deR. Abba, Ṣefer Hefez, Ṣefer Metivot* and *Ṣefer hamiktso'ot* (the geonic authorship of the latter is dubious).

Our knowledge of Jewish Law in this and the following period has been considerably enhanced by the texts discovered in the Cairo Genizah at the end of the nineteenth century. A Genizah is a room, often in the precincts of a synagogue, where superseded manuscripts are archived. The practice may derive from the ban on destroying *Torah* scrolls, bearing as they do the name of God. A myriad of diverse documents was discovered in the Genizah of ancient Cairo, dating from the second half of the tenth to the second half of the thirteenth century, thus overlapping the second half of the geonic period and the first part of the period of the *rishonim*. These texts have since found their way to libraries all over the world: the largest concentration is the Taylor-Schechter Collection at Cambridge; other important collections are those at Oxford, Leningrad and New York.

Halakhic literature discovered in the Genizah has made a major contribution to halakhic research. The finds include fragments of the *Talmudim* and *Midrashim*; geonic halakhic works and responsa. Of no less importance is the tremendous volume of documents: letters and notes, court records of deliberations, testimony, charitable endowments, and the like, which give us a graphic picture of legal practice and reality during the period. These treasures attest to a sophisticated network of international contacts and to the Jews' relationship to the culture of the times. A major result of Genizah studies has been the realization that the legal traditions and institutions of Palestine were still active during the Genizah period.[32]

The Genizah has supplied material for studies in a variety of legal fields: marriage contracts (*ketubot*), marriage and women's status in general, charitable endowments, partnerships, wills and more. A striking point is the absence of certain categories of documents, such as legal enactments (*takkanot*) or decrees (*gezerot*) and appointments. Although the finds from the Genizah are fragmentary and random, and far from all of them have been investigated, they undoubtedly provide a faithful picture of reality during the period.

The legal status of the Jews at this time has been more clearly defined thanks to Genizah material; it, too, represents continuity rather than change. This is the message from a letter of authority found in the Genizah, which details the powers of the principal of the Jerusalem Academy in religious and legal affairs, appointment of judges, imposition of penalties (*ḥerem*), marriage and divorce, supervision of services, and so on.

The Genizah material may be the first surviving evidence of early traditions that for some reason had not been committed to writing till then (such as *ketubot*); alternatively, it may represent social phenomena which, though present in earlier periods, had not received sufficient emphasis through lack of adequate documentation. Examples of these are polygamy, conjugal relations with slave-girls, divorce initiated by the wife, and so on.

Nevertheless, Genizah finds do sometimes represent genuine differences between the Geonim and various Diaspora scholars, e.g., in the field of legal precedents. The Geonim, as might be expected given their powers, composed lengthy, well-reasoned responsa, based on proofs and citations from talmudic sources. On the other hand, little has come down to us through the Genizah of legal decisions handed down in ordinary court proceedings; what we do possess is more concerned with arbitration, mainly the factual descriptions and final decisions. Another difference is the prominent place given among Egyptian *halakhah* scholars to Palestinian halakhic traditions, far more than was common during the geonic period — evidence of the major importance of the Jerusalem Academy in the Fatimid kingdom.

E. *Erets Yisrael: Ḥillukim* and *Ṣefer haMaʿasim*

Particularly important in Palestine were the genres of *Ḥillukim* and *Maʿasim*. The *Ḥillukim* ('differences' in halakhic practice between Babylon and Palestine) probably date to the early phase of the Muslim occupation of Palestine. A most important literary legal source, written in approximately the same period, is the book known as *Ṣefer haMaʿasim liVene Erets Yisrael*. This work, discovered more than 50 years ago, has recently been discussed by M.A. Friedman, who believes that it may have been not a single, continuous work, as implied by the term '*Ṣefer*' ('book') in the title, but rather a compilation of '*maʿasim*,'[33] 'decisions' — a term that does not necessary denote legal verdicts, but may stand for halakhic rulings. The '*maʿasim*' in this book were probably some kind of responsa, mostly reflecting Palestinian law and its early traditions.

In content the *maʿasim* generally accord with the Jerusalem *Talmud* and early Palestinian customs, sometimes directly counter to the Babylonian *Talmud*. It is not surprising, therefore, that the work was sometimes referred to as Responsa *of Erets Yisrael*.[34] It is generally dated to the beginning of the seventh century, the early phase of the Muslim occupation. The work (or the works from which it was compiled) was known (at least by hearsay) to the Babylonian Geonim, as we hear from Rav Ḥai: 'For we have heard that these matters may be found in *Maʿasim liVene Erets Yisrael* and it is there that they were formulated.'[35] It may even have been used by the Babylonian Geonim.[36] Some of the *maʿasim*, as well as later anthologies culled and abbreviated from them, found their way into geonic responsa and halakhic literature, such as the collections of responsa in *Shaʾare Tsedek*, *Teshuvot haGeʾonim*, ed. N. Coronel (Wien: Holzwarth, 1871), and *Halakhot Gedolot*. They may also be found in halakhic works from Germany and France: *Ṣefer haPardeṣ, Ṣefer Maʿaseh haGeʾonim* and others. Many of the laws dealt with in the *maʿaseh* literature pertain to the areas of matrimony and personal law.

3. *Sources of Law*

A. The *Talmud* and Tradition

As stated previously, it was the Geonim who maintained talmudic tradition, both in theory and, to a considerable extent, in practice. We refer here particularly to the tradition of the Babylonian *Talmud* — the basis for the codificatory literature of the Geonim and the main pillar of their teachings, commentaries and responsa in matters of *halakhah*. The main talmudic traditions of the Geonim were oral, as attested by the Geonim themselves. Thus, Rav Sherira writes in his celebrated epistle: 'The Rabbis take care to teach orally, not from a written text';[37] nevertheless, the written text was certainly not ignored, as Rav Ḥai writes: 'But now that understanding has diminished, it is necessary to refer to written texts.'[38] Similarly, we read somewhat later of a tradition current in Spanish Jewry, according to which:

> the elders received [the tradition] from Prince Natronai [Gaon] bar Hakhinai and it was he who wrote the *Talmud* for the people of Spain, *by heart, not from writing.*[39]

For much of the period, the *Talmud* continued as an oral work, though by that time it had already been committed to writing. Characteristic of the times was a certain ambivalence toward the written text, a definite tension between oral and written cultures. The Geonim did not possess a uniform text of the *Talmud*, and oral tradition presented a fertile ground for the emergence of variant readings, as a result of which it was not always easy to determine a 'correct' version. Thus, it was not infrequently necessary to declare one particular tradition superior to another, and we read of cases in which:

> All the rabbis and students are hereby admonished to read thus, to avert the possible occurrence — Heaven forfend! — of some mishap.[40]

This situation had two important implications. On the one hand, the oral nature of talmudic tradition brought about the inclusion of many geonic glosses, comments and even legal decisions in the text of the Babylonian *Talmud*. We sometimes find late authorities basing their own halakhic rulings on a geonic gloss to the *Talmud*, rather than on the *Talmud* itself. Only a careful scrutiny of geonic phraseology can help to distinguish the original talmudic text from such accretions. On the other hand, the Geonim sometimes cite ancient traditions, going back, they claim, to the Babylonian Amoraim and even earlier, which for some reason did not enter the *Talmud* itself. As a consequence, it is sometimes difficult to determine the history of certain legal institutions during the geonic period. Nonetheless, many of the Geonim considered themselves guardians of the true version of the *Talmud*, avoiding emendations even when the text seemed obscure. Thus, Rav Ḥai rules in a responsum: 'We are not permitted to emend the *mishnayot* or the *Talmud* because of some difficulty that we find.'[41] This attitude is quite different from what we find among Ashkenazi scholars. The continuity of talmudic tradition was of paramount importance for the Babylonian Geonim, as they stress repeatedly.

The Geonim should also be credited with consolidating the rules of legal decision. While most of these rules may already be found in the *Talmud* itself, some are first mentioned in geonic literature, such as the rule that 'The law is decided according to the latest authorities'; or that the law should not be decided in accordance with a disciple's view contrary to that of his master; and the like.[42]

Perhaps the most important principle of legal decision in the history of *halakhah* is the crucial and binding role given to the Babylonian *Talmud*, which the Geonim considered the central pillar binding *halakhah*, preferring it to the Jerusalem *Talmud* whenever the two differed. This principle is enunciated in several responsa of Rav Hai Gaon:

> We rely on our *Talmud*, and accept whatever is ruled here [the Babylonian *Talmud*], without regard for what is stated there [the Jerusalem *Talmud*]. Of course, if it is a question of clarifying something that is obscure here, or not made explicit here, and if there is no contradiction, we rely on it too. Similarly with regard to a matter of exegesis.[43]

And, elsewhere:

> Whatever we find in the Palestine *Talmud* that is not disputed in our *Talmud*, or if it is explained with good reason, we hold to it and rely upon it, for it is no worse than the commentaries of the early scholars. However, whatever is at variance with our *Talmud* — we reject.[44]

Rav Hai's reasoning in this matter is not based on the principle that 'the Law is decided according to the latest authorities,' found later in Alfasi's code (p.277, below), but on the political turmoil in Palestine during the talmudic period, which led to a cessation of Academic activities and a decline in *Torah* study; this reason was cited long before by Pirkoi b. Baboi.[45]

Recognition of the superiority of the Babylonian *Talmud* did not mean that the Geonim entirely ignored the Jerusalem *Talmud*. On the contrary, we have evidence that the Geonim — at least, from Saadya Gaon's time on — studied the Jerusalem *Talmud* and in fact utilized it in their halakhic work, according to the decision-making rule they had formulated. Thus, Rav Sherira writes:

> This statement of Rav Amram, though not explicit [in the Babylonian *Talmud*] but only a tradition, was stated explicitly in the Palestine *Talmud* ... In the same way as this matter presently before us, it is a common occurrence that one derives support from the *Talmud* of Palestine, for it is dependable.[46]

In addition to their use of talmudic literature and its interpretation, the Geonim also made use of analogies between scriptural verses as a legal source for the derivation of new laws. However, they rarely had recourse to homiletical exegesis of the Bible, and they never based a decision on aggadic material. This last-named limitation is stressed in some passages of geonic works. Thus, Rav Sherira states:

> One does not rely on the aggadah as proof-text, as our Sages said, One should not learn from aggadic sources.[47]

and R. Samuel b. Hofni, in a famous couplet, writes:

> We have indeed paved other ways
> to the writing of laws and legal traditions;
> these are the finest sifted white flour,
> but aggadot are the leavings.[48]

As we have seen, the Babylonian Geonim relied as a matter of course on the *Talmud*, referring only rarely to post-talmudic literature, that is, to already extant codificatory works — *Halakhot Gedolot, Halakhot Pesukot* and the *She'iltot* (the latter least of all). They also made use of traditions current in the Academies, saboraic and quasi-talmudic, and sometimes also of ancestral traditions. The traditional element frequently receives considerable emphasis in geonic writing, both on the theoretical level of sources of law and on the practical plane in discussions of specific laws. Two passages will suffice to illustrate this general tendency. The first is attributed to Rav Yehudai's disciple Pirkoi b. Baboi:

> From this you learn that the oral law in the hands of the scholars in the Academy in Babylonia and the minutiae of the commandments as held by the scholars — they did not learn them by logic, nor from their own wisdom, but from the *Talmud* and practice that they acquired from their masters and their masters from *their* masters, all the way to our Master Moses, as Law given to Moses at Sinai.[49]

The second is from a responsum of R. Zemah Gaon about Eldad Hadani:

> For the most important scholars and prophets were exiled to Babylon, and they established the *Torah* and set up an Academy on the Euphrates ... They were the chain of wisdom and prophecy and from them did *Torah* issue to the whole world. And we have already told you that all drink from one spring.[50]

The element of oral transmission is also much emphasized in geonic responsa and other works, and the expression 'This is our custom, by tradition received from our fathers' and the like are common in geonic literature.[51] At this transition from the chain of tradition to codified *halakhah*, the Geonim generally preferred oral tradition to written texts; we have already seen that even when referring to rulings from *Halakhot Pesukot* and the

She'iltot, the Geonim claimed to be transmitting traditions. Moreover, the fact that the two most important works composed up to the time of Rav Saadya Gaon, *Halakhot Peṣuḳot* and *She'iltot*, were not written by the Geonim of the Academies may have contributed to their relatively low status in comparison with oral tradition — despite the fact that both works in fact reflect that tradition. In general, the geonic attitude to written versus oral sources was somewhat ambivalent.

B. Agreement, *Taḳkanah* and *Minhag*

The talmudic tradition, however, could not fully satisfy the demands raised by the new realities of the times. The Geonim were obliged to seek solutions through the use of additional legal tools. The most important of these tools were *taḳkanah* (enactment) and *minhag* (custom, usage or practice), the latter usually referred to as 'custom of the Academy' or 'of the Academies'. It was these two sources of law that enabled the Geonim to modify and revitalize the law, and thus to bridge the gap between *halakhah* and reality.

Another legal tool used by the Geonim, 'agreement' (*haṣkamah*), meaning general agreement, whether of the whole of Jewry or of the scholars, also came to be treated in the geonic period as a kind of source of law; however, it was usually invoked only in conjunction with tradition and could not really be considered a valid, independent source of law.

The question of the relationship between *taḳkanah* and *minhag* in the geonic period is a rather difficult one. Suffice it to mention the interchangeability of the two terms in geonic sources, which further obscures the distinction between them. The difficulty is compounded by the fact that many laws stemming from the Geonim and accepted by later generations as *taḳkanot* had their origins in *minhag*. This makes the number of *taḳkanot* now attributed to geonic enactment smaller than what was originally believed.[52] It would seem that during the period in question *taḳkanah* as a source of law gradually yielded to *minhag*, the most important geonic *taḳkanot* dating to the early phase of the geonic era.

Taḳkanah and *minhag* share the feature that both clash with some element of talmudic literature; they differ mainly as to the motivation for their emergence. A *taḳkanah* was enacted in deliberate reaction to some major, overall change in living conditions; and since it was not a response to specific circumstances, its enactment was apparently subject to certain set rules. *Minhagim*, customs, by contrast, generally owed their beginnings to popular pressure, a matter entirely beyond the control of the Geonim; they generally reflect a solution after the fact. Some customs arose as legal precedents handed down in geonic law courts, evolving in time into an accepted practice and generally touching on a specific situation. An example is the practice of excommunicating a person liable for inflicting bodily harm until he compensated the injured party.

Besides the customs of the Academies, there were also local customs, sometimes conflicting with those of the Academies. Other customs pertained to special groups, such as traders' customs, which constituted a category apart and were generally at variance with Rabbinic Law.

The Geonim almost never discussed the theoretical aspect of the use of *minhag* as a source of law, although this source became quite prevalent in their times — perhaps because it was already recognized in talmudic literature as a legal source. Illustrations of the relationship between *takkanah* and *minhag* are discussed in sections 6A-B (pp.234-39) below.

Various local customs emerged in connection with personal status, such as the practice of betrothing a woman before writing the *ketubah* or the writ of betrothal, or the practice of a father marrying off his adult daughter. Many such practices were condemned by the Geonim; some were finally accepted, sometimes not very willingly.

4. *Courts and Legal Practice*

Halakhic and judicial activity during the geonic period revolved around the Babylonian Academies and the Geonim who headed them. The Academies demanded recognition of their position as the supreme judicial authority. Unlike the situation in France and Germany in the medieval period, where the lay community, the *kahal*, wielded considerable power, including the right to enact *takkanot*, in Iraq the *bet din*, court, of the Academy was the major authority. It alone was privileged to enact *takkanot*, to confirm the validity of customs and oversee the dispensation of justice; only in rare cases was some measure of power delegated to the community and its representatives. The court was an integral part of the Academy's activities; the judicial power that it commanded was inextricably bound up with its religious authority. The notion that the court, rather than the community, was the central legal institution is expressed in a responsum delivered by an anonymous Gaon, concerning the commonly accepted right of a plaintiff to suspend prayers in the synagogue:

But in Iraq this is not known, for there the community does not exercise supervision over law and justice, that being the task of the court. The community must obey what the court commands, such as to impose upon the defendant a warning, or excommunication or a ban. Similarly, wherever there is a duly appointed judge, the plaintiff is not entitled to present his case to any but him, and not to the community.[53]

Although this ruling concerns a specific custom, it reflects the broad powers commanded by the Babylonian Geonim and their courts.

The Geonim derived their authority in great measure from their social status and scholarly reputation, rather than from the sanctity of the Academy or from any formal commitment on the part of communities outside Babylonia. Lineage was also a factor in determining the status of a Gaon and the hierarchical ranking of scholars in the Academy.

On the one hand, the geonic Academy — by which we mean all its institutions, including the court and other offices — was an extension of the amoraic Academy; on the other, it also most probably reflected changes that took place during the geonic period. The organization of the Academy and its institutions, particularly its court, is known to us primarily from *The Story of Nathan haBavli*, though one can also glean important details from geonic responsa. For example, Rav Amram Gaon, in a responsum to the Jews of Barcelona, describes the hierarchy of scholars in the Academy as follows:

> Greetings from myself and from our master Rav Zemaḥ, *dayyana debava* (lit.: 'judge of the gate'), from *reshe dekallah* (lit.: 'leaders of the *kallah*,' scholars of the semiannual general assemblies), and from all the ordained scholars, who are in place of the *Great Sanhedrin*, and from *bene kiyyume* (read: *bene siyyume*, unordained scholars whose task was to sum up the day's deliberations), who are in place of the *Small Sanhedrin*, and from all the other scholars and *tannaim* and learned persons in the entire Academy ... We commanded that the questions that you addressed to us be read before us in the presence of the *Av Bet Din* (president of the court) and the *Alufim* (lit.: 'chiefs') and *Ḥakhamim* (Sages) and all the students.[54]

The sources refer to other functionaries as well: *rashe midreshe* ('leaders of the schools'), *rashe pirke* ('leaders of the sections'), *rabbanan dedara* ('rabbis of the row'). In addition, the Academy employed a scribe (*sofer hayeshivah*), who played an important role in the organization and administration of the Academy; among other things he wrote notes and other documents.[55] Some later sources also refer to *rosh haseder* (lit.: 'leader of the order') as empowered to rule in halakhic questions alongside the Exilarch and the *dayyana debava*; the role of this functionary, however, is not adequately clear, and the term may be simply a synonym for 'leader of the *kallah*'.

It is doubtful whether all the terms listed above reflect a real situation, or just preserve talmudic designations, some of which had become meaningless long before the geonic period. Neither do we know the precise definitions of the functions that some of the persons named fulfilled in the Academy, although they are well described by R. Nathan haBavli. At any rate, there survive many halakhic rulings and explanations that were delivered during the 'months of *kallah*', during which the 'leaders of the *kallah*' played a special role.

A particularly important post was that of the *av bet din* or *dayyana debava*, who presided over the Academy *bet din* and sometimes also deputized for the Gaon himself in responsa; he was generally the natural candidate to succeed to the Gaonate. And indeed, several Geonim, such as R. Samuel b. Hofni, Rav Sherira and Rav Hai, served in this capacity before their accession, in fact writing some of their works during that term of office. The position existed in the court of each of the two Academies, as well as in the Exilarch's court.

Although there were certain differences in customs and laws from one Academy to the other, neither of them should be considered a fully self-reliant institution, with an independent legal tradition. Not every dispute between the Geonim of the two Academies necessarily reflects a conflict of Academy traditions. Sometimes the conflicting tradition may be that of only one dynasty within the Academy; and scholars of the same Academy might also disagree with one another. There was no formal relationship between the courts of the two Academies; nevertheless, it appears that rulings decided in the Exilarch's court required ratification by those of the 'two Academies'.

The decision-making and judicial activities of the Geonim followed two separate paths. One of these was conventional judicial practice within the court. The other was the issuing of responsa to questions addressed to them by community rabbis and judges, extending over a broad spectrum of topics, including requests for legal verdicts in the strict sense of the word. Despite the distinction between the roles of judge and respondent,[56] it would appear that in practice the Geonim combined the two, considering responsa to be part of their judicial function as a court: ruling on matters of law was equivalent to delivering a verdict, a fact not infrequently reflected by the phraseology in which responsa were couched.

The Geonim equated their courts to the Sanhedrin, or to 'the Great Court of all Israel'; both terminologies occur frequently in responsa and letters. Thus, Rav Hai writes in a letter:

This form is in place of the Sanhedrin and its Head is in place of our Master Moses, and the customs (*minhagot*) of the Sanhedrin issue from it.[57]

The notion also received formal expression in the seating arrangements of the geonic Academies, as described by R. Nathan haBavli, which were modelled on those of the Sanhedrin. Correspondents who addressed questions to the Geonim also referred to them as the 'Great Court'.[58] However, such turns of speech are not expressions of the binding, official, formal status of a High Court, so much as mere rhetoric, reflecting a desire on the part of the Geonim to maintain the Academy's superiority, especially in relation to the centre in Palestine, as well as a reminder to obey their rulings. Questioners, for their part, resorted to such phrases as expressions of respect and apprecia- tion.

The Geonim encouraged and even solicited questions; local justices willingly complied. But as the requests from the Geonim were essentially unofficial, it appears that the communities generally requested advice and guidance, e.g., on matters that had not been solved or settled to the litigants' satisfaction, rather than a legal decision proper.

Nonetheless, it is clear from the wording of many responsa that the Geonim expected their decisions, once solicited, to be honoured. They prob- ably considered themselves in this respect as a court of appeals, whose verdict was final and binding. In other words, local courts were, on the one hand, independent and free to hand down their own legal decisions, based on the local judges' reasoning; there was no obligation to appeal to the 'Great Court'. However, once the appeal had been made and the question answered, the Geonim argued, the decision was binding. Intimations to that effect are occasionally heard from the Geonim themselves. For example, Rav Nahshon Gaon, referring to a disagreement among Geonim as to whether a husband may, after his wife's death, seize property of the category known as *nikhse melog*[59] which she had sold without his agreement, writes:

> If there are rabbis in your community who say, 'He must pay,' and they rule thus, what need have you of these Academies? Let the rabbis who are there rule on the question![60]

That the Academy courts had no formal authority over the local courts also follows from the procedure for the appointment of judges in the communities, which points to a decline in the authority of the Academies and a greater measure of local independence. At first, so we are told in a geonic responsum, judges were appointed in the same way as in Babylonia:

> None was considered a qualified judge (*mumheh*) save he received authorization from the president (*Nasi*) or the principal of the Academy.[61]

Later, however, the definition was not formal but dependent on the judge's personality.

Rav Ḥai differentiates between judges appointed in Babylonia and those appointed in remote localities:

> The custom in Babylonia is that the Great Court appoints judges in each and every district, and provides each judge with a letter of authorization, known in Aramaic as *yapteka dedayanuta*. And thus it is stated [in the letter of authorization]: We have appointed so-and-so son of so-and-so judge in such-and-such a place. And we have given him authorization to hold court and to consider all matters of [religious] commandments, and what is forbidden and what is permitted, and whatever is pleasing to Heaven. And whosoever does not accept [the court's] authority, [the court] is entitled to deal with him as it sees fit, as required by heavenly Law ... But the courts in remote places, that are not appointed by the Great Court ... [62]

In addition to the formal status of the court in matters of legal import and judgment, it had standing on ethical questions and borderline issues between religious observance and moral rectitude; they thus acted, so to speak, as guardians of public morals and reprovers. For example, they took measures to prevent leaven being hidden away during Passover:

> They sought after whosoever did so, for we and the authorities have long been accustomed to send agents and emissaries and to check whosoever should hide something... [63]

Or,

> In connection with persons who have left their wives without their permission, the court is entitled to admonish them and instruct them to return to their homes. [64]

Again, the court was expected to care for the needs of orphans:

> For the court is obligated to seek a favourable judgment for orphans as far as possible, particularly when the orphans are minors and some time will pass till they attain majority. [65]

If necessary the court would even appoint guardians. [66]

The local courts were not of one piece. While some were permanent institutions and appear as addressees in notes issued by Geonim, [67] others possessed an *ad hoc* nature. Certain courts were considered equivalents of the Great Court for a specific district. Such courts were generally constituted of three magistrates, though in some cases a single professional judge was sufficient. [68]

The local courts dealt with a host of topics: confirmation of new procedures and new formulae for notes; letters of appointment for various agents of the court, and the like. They were also empowered to enforce their decisions. Some of the functions of the local courts, such as confirmation of notes and administration of oaths, invested them with a special status in their regions of jurisdiction.

The Geonim upheld the status of the local courts; accordingly, any criticisms that they had of the latter's decisions were generally quite moderate.[69] They assessed judges on the basis of personality and social position. Only rarely did they express sharp disapproval of judges, sometimes, however, going so far as to refer to them as 'judges of Sodom' who acted in ignorance and violated talmudic law; the Gaon in question called for the judges' dismissal.[70] The sources in fact provide examples of incompetent judges, sometimes even committing outright legal errors.[71] But the Geonim did not have the power to dismiss local judges.

The local court was not the only judicial institution in the community. Indeed, we sometimes find alternative institutions, perhaps easier to appeal to insofar as they did not follow a formal legal procedure. Such were traders' tribunals or centres of arbitration. Laymen at times served as lay magistrates or arbitrators.[72] Many geonic responsa refer to the 'elders' (zekenim) or to 'important members of the community' (hashuve hakahal), but the status of these officials was apparently not the same in all parts of the Jewish world. While in Egypt they were considered a judicial institution, in North Africa they seem to have possessed no independent judicial status, at least not until a later period. Rather, they fulfilled an auxiliary function, providing the local magistrates with various services (such as legal opinions).[73]

The main alternative open to the Jews during the geonic period was recourse to the gentile authorities, in particular the Muslim courts. In some cases the appeal was indirect, e.g. a plea entered before a Jewish court to confirm or validate a legal document issued by a Muslim bench. Almost all the Geonim who dealt with such questions limited the validity of documents issued in Muslim courts to cases in which the document served as evidence of some transaction, such as a loan or a sale; documents that were constitutive, i.e. were in themselves legal instruments, such as writs of divorce or manumission, deeds of gift, and the like, were unacceptable. The truth is, however, that this distinction was not based on the real character of the documents concerned, but rather on a formal decision-making principle, according to which the Geonim founded their halakhic rulings on the most recent acceptable interpretation of the relevant talmudic discussion (B. Gitt. 11a).[74] This principle automatically placed deeds of gift, for example, within the scope of the prohibition on recourse to gentile courts, and this was the understanding of almost all the Geonim — with the exception of Rav Hananyah Gaon, who ruled in accordance with the earlier formulation in the talmudic discussion and allowed deeds of gift.[75]

On the whole, therefore, the Geonim accepted documents issued by Muslim courts and recognized the authority of the governing power to validate a document. This recognition, though somewhat restricted, permitted normal commercial relations between Jews and Muslims.

The situation was far more serious when a Jew actually initiated the appeal to a Muslim court, as such action in itself constituted an infringement of a strict prohibition of talmudic law. It would seem, however, that the talmudic prohibition did not prevent such appeals from being made, even though the Jews enjoyed a measure of legal autonomy. The constant contacts between Jews and non-Jews in all possible legal areas — partnership, rental, loans, etc. — made it difficult to refrain from the use of Muslim courts.

A number of legal measures instituted by the Muslims encouraged Jewish use of their courts. As already noted, it took only one party to appeal to the Muslim court to found jurisdiction. Moreover, Muslims and non-Muslims enjoyed equal status in all areas of civil law, so that the 'protected peoples' were encouraged to enter their pleas in Muslim courts. These two measures undoubtedly made recourse to Muslim courts more advantageous, and increasing numbers of Jews seized the opportunity to seek legal remedies not provided by the Jewish legal system. Moreover, the Muslim court (or Muslim Government) was the only instrument for the execution of verdicts delivered in Jewish courts.

I believe that the increasing popularity of the Muslim courts among Jews was the underlying motive for many innovations introduced by the Geonim. They must have realized that the only way to combat or limit it as far as possible was, on the one hand, to exercise greater flexibility in allowing appeals to gentile courts (somewhat moderating the talmudic prohibition); and on the other hand, to make the same legal remedies obtainable in Muslim courts available in some cases within the system of Jewish Law, thus eliminating the very motive for infringing the prohibition. The Geonim sometimes turned to the Muslim courts on their own initiative, in order to execute verdicts handed down by the Jewish courts, when the legal instruments at their disposal were insufficient or had been exhausted to no avail. This flexibility won the Geonim two advantages: first, they maintained their authority; second, they did not relinquish their control of Jewish recourse to gentile courts.

The shift in the attitude toward Muslim courts occurred during the Gaonates of Rav Paltoi and Rav Natronai. Thus, Rav Paltoi rules that if one litigant refuses to bring his case before a Jewish court, he may be sued in a gentile court.[76] Further confirmation for this dating may be derived from writs of execution (*adrakhta*) from this period, which state that the procedure for collection of loans, should the debtor refuse to defray his debt, involves an appeal to the Muslim tribunal.[77] This trend continues into the times of Rav Sherira and Rav Hai, who permit the magistrates or community leaders to testify in Muslim courts when the defendant refuses to comply with the verdict. On the one hand, they dictate certain restrictions on such an appeal, mainly that all measures possible in a Jewish court be taken first and that an appropriate tribunal be selected. On the other, Rav Sherira instructs the judges to testify before the Muslim court to enable it to carry out the verdict:

> Thus we have seen that they have permission and it is meritorious to do so. ... And we too always instruct the judges to do so with regard to a person who defies the court and is undaunted by a rabbinical excommunication.[78]

Geonic flexibility in allowing recourse to Muslim courts accords with what we know from contemporary Muslim sources, which actually encouraged such appeals on the part of Jews.[79]

In Muslim eyes, the Jewish courts were simply a constituent part of the juridical system of the Muslim State, which respected the needs of the various religious communities under its rule by granting them legal autonomy. However, that autonomy was restricted, in that it did not confer powers of capital punishment and (civil) execution, which were retained by the Government. In consequence, *herem* (ban) and *niddui* (excommunication) become central instruments of punishment during the geonic period, alongside flogging. Although Jewish magistrates were also empowered to impose temporary imprisonment (until appearance in court) or to order that the accused's hair be shaved, the references to these measures in geonic responsa are so rare as to imply that they were not frequently used.[80]

The use of excommunication was considerably expanded in comparison with talmudic practice. It was used both as a punitive measure, mainly in offences of a religious or moral nature, and as a means of enforcement, to compel litigants to appear at court or to comply with a verdict. Thus, on the one hand, it replaced the death penalty, insofar as a court was not empowered (according to Jewish Law) to deliver death sentences during the Exile; on the other, it enabled the judges to circumvent the principle that fines could not be imposed in the Diaspora, since it forced, for example, a tortfeasor to pay the injured party compensation — an innovation attributed to Rav Zemah Gaon. Geonic responsa show that the ban and excommunication were imposed for a wide variety of offences; as an enforcement measure it was applied mainly in cases involving money.[81] Among the religious offences punishable by excommunication (or the threat of such) were practices that betrayed leanings toward Karaism.

From the mid-ninth century, one discerns the first indications of the use of the excommunication and ban also to enforce *takkanot*, a trend which becomes stronger somewhat later. Rav Naḥshon replied thus to a query as to how to excommunicate a person who had infringed a *takkanah* or decree issued by the community:

> One decrees a 'blessing' (curse) upon the communities, that they should not speak to him, nor pray with him. But if he should agree to comply with the community *takkanah* that he violated, he is excommunicated for seven days.[82]

Besides ban and excommunication, which were social/sacral sanctions, extensive use was made, as we have mentioned, of flogging. The Geonim of the two Academies apparently administered both legal modes of flogging: punitive flogging, in cases dictated by biblical law; and disciplinary (i.e. rabbinically ordained) flogging (*makkot mardut*), which was a rabbinic measure. This follows from the considerable number of geonic responsa that refer to flogging, though there are differences and even contradictions among the sources with regard to the mode of flogging, the number of lashes and the offences for which it was administered. Opinions differed among the Geonim on this question, some allowing no more than disciplinary (rabbinic) flogging. Thus, for example, Rav Natronai states:

> Biblical flogging is not customary today, only disciplinary flogging. While biblical flogging involves forty lashes minus one, disciplinary flogging is not so, but one flogs [the offender] until he obeys or until his soul leave his body ... [83]

Nevertheless, one modern scholar sums up his study of the subject as follows:

> Throughout the geonic period the Geonim of both Sura and Pumbedita ... administered the biblical punishment of forty lashes. Moreover, they in fact expanded the scope of the flogging punishment, applying it even for offences that were not punishable with flogging by either biblical or talmudic law.[84]

The geonic courts played a major role in the institution of new legal and court procedures, formulae of notes and similar innovations in many areas, largely associated with civil execution and collection of debts, agency and legal enforcement. In such areas one clearly senses a response to needs engendered by contemporary economic realities. A large quantity of notes and note collections has reached us from the geonic period. While some are already mentioned in the *Talmud*, many notes and formulae appearing in the geonic literature but not found in the *Talmud* may probably be dated to the time of the early Geonim, some in fact receiving their definitive formulation at the hands of the Geonim themselves. As early as the ninth century one finds set formulae for notes concerning numerous topics.

The frequent use of notes provided the impetus for Rav Saadya's anthology of notes, *Sefer ha'edut vehashetarot* (*Book of Testimony and Notes*), which was intended to facilitate and direct commercial activities. Later Rav Hai composed a similar work.

The writing of notes became so deeply rooted in legal practice during the geonic period that a loan transacted orally, without a note, was termed by one questioner 'highly improper' (Heb. *pesha*).[85] But despite the various devices adopted to validate notes, practical developments ultimately produced a situation in which mere correspondence could serve, so to speak, as a 'substitute' note. The measures we have described were intended to facilitate and stabilize commerce; correspondence without notes was just one further step in that direction.

The geonic period also witnessed innovations in the organization of legal proceedings. The most important of these were the *gezerta*, the replacement of oaths proper, i.e. those which used the divine name or one of the divine attributes, by imprecation oaths (a curse not involving use of the divine name or attributes),[86] and the institution of *herem setam* ('anonymous ban': the threat that a ban would be pronounced against *any* offender, whoever he might be), both of them being legal measures designed to settle doubtful cases when no real evidence was forthcoming and an oath was undesirable or impossible.[87] Similarly, the Geonim introduced a new oath, known as *shevu'at eyn li* (oath of destitution), whose purpose was to ascertain whether a defendant had assets. New practices were also introduced in court procedures, such as the requirement that litigants clarify their arguments in greater detail while taking an oath.

5. Biographies of Some Selected Geonim

Of the many Geonim who headed the two Babylonian Academies, some achieved renown for special innovations, others through written works, and still others by strong leadership and the central role they played in contemporary events. I would like to dwell briefly on four of the most celebrated Geonim, who left an indelible mark both on their own era and on later generations; the differences among these four personalities also reflect the changes that took place over the geonic period.

A. Rav Natronai Gaon

Rav Natronai bar Rav Hilai Abba Mari was Gaon of the Sura Academy for some 8 years (854/5-862/3). We know very little about his life prior to his appointment to the Gaonate. His father Hilai had also been Gaon (though many years before) and the son was later to serve in the same position. His term of office parallels those of Rav Mattityah and Rav Paltoi as Geonim of Pumbedita. Consequently, his name is confused with Rav Paltoi's in many responsa, among other things because they not infrequently received identical questions. The same responsa are sometimes attributed to Rav Natronai and Rav Hai.

Rav Natronai maintained contacts with many communities in Spain and North Africa. One of his correspondents in Spain was Rav Eleazar Aluf demin Aspamya ('of Spain'), who addressed several questions to him and may also have met him in person. In North Africa, Rav Nathan b. Hananyah and Rav Judah bar Shaul were among his correspondents.

Though he wrote many responsa, he did not compose halakhic works or biblical exegesis as did some of his successors. The number of surviving responsa ascribed to him reaches some five hundred, of which one-third deal with halakhic matters.

B. Rav Saadya Gaon

Rav Saadya Gaon's term of office as Gaon of Sura lasted some 14 years (938-942). He was born in Egypt and spent his formative years in the cultural environment of Egypt, Syria and Palestine. Aware of the special needs of Jewish society in a Muslim milieu, Rav Saadya realized that the best way to meet the challenge of the cultural crossroads was to integrate the Jews as far as possible in their host societies, so as to mitigate the clash of the two cultures, in effect to create a synthesis between them. From his time on, Arabic became not only the language of everyday affairs in the Jewish communities, but also the principal tool of intellectual creativity in the Babylonian Academies. One might say that Rav Saadya Gaon was the founder of Judaeo-Arabic culture in many areas: philosophy, language, biblical commentary and *halakhah*.

The historical context of Rav Saadya's times — particularly, his struggle against the Karaites and the crisis in the status of the Academies — made it somewhat easier for him to achieve his goal of integrating the tradition of the Academies and their scholars in their cultural environment. This principle of integration guided the composition of his halakhic and philosophical works, as well as his commentaries, all of which were designed to buttress religious faith and the foundations of Jewish Law. One can thus place such disparate works as his philosophical treatise, *Sefer haEmunot vehaDe'ot* (*The Book of Beliefs and Opinions*), and his biblical exegesis and translations, written to underpin the textual basis of faith, in a single context; alongside these were his writings in talmudic commentary and *halakhah*.

In several of the introductions to his works Rav Saadya stresses the nation's need for cultural integration. In this respect he was in effect strengthening the Academy's authority, as well as the position of the Geonim. As the first scholar to engage in the composition of halakhic monographs, he was blazing a trail later followed by R. Samuel b. Hofni and Rav Hai.

Rav Saadya's activities and leadership placed him squarely in the forefront of several controversies. The first and perhaps best known of these was his dispute with the Gaon of the Palestinian Academy over the calendar, which ended in the victory of Rav Saadya and with him of the Babylonian centre in general. Rav Saadya also feuded with the Exilarch, David b. Zakkai, probably over the distribution of power between the Gaon and the Exilarch in general.

One of Rav Saadya's major battlegrounds was his struggle against contemporary heretics, especially the Karaites; several of his works were explicitly devoted to that end. Although a previous Gaon (Rav Natronai) had already issued responsa concerning the status of heretics, Rav Saadya devoted a special book to the subject, known as *Rav Saadya's Answers to the Questions of Hiwi haBalkhi*, as well as a work entitled *Sefer haHokhahah* (*The Book of Proof*), which treats the phenomenon of heresy in general.

The dispute with the Karaites was probably one of the factors which defined Rav Saadya's approach to the sources of Jewish Law. Whether in his compositions or in his responsa, he emphasizes talmudic sources and tradition, assigning to the latter a major position, while almost completely ignoring *minhag* as a source of law. He similarly limits recourse to the thirteen hermeneutic rules (*middot*)[88] for the interpretation of the *Torah*, arguing that they were never meant to create new laws, not already part of tradition. For Saadya, Written and Oral Law constitute a single, integrated unit, and in many cases he strives to trace the sources of laws created in his time to Scripture.

Rav Saadya may be considered a pioneer in several other areas. He was the first author of a book on the commandments, and probably the first to divide the commandments into the two categories of rational (*mitsvot sikhliyot*) and traditional (*shim'iyot*). This classification guided other Geonim and scholars, first and foremost R. Samuel b. Hofni, and later also Maimonides. Following the lead of Rav Amram Gaon, Rav Saadya also compiled a prayer-book.

Rav Saadya's major innovation was the composition of halakhic monographs. Of these, special mention should be made of the *Sefer hayerushot* (*Book of Inheritance*), which has survived complete, and his book of notes, *Sefer ha'edut vehashetarot* (*Book of Testimony and Notes*), which also exists almost in its entirety. Other works are *Sefer hapikadon* (*Book of Deposits*), and probably also monographs on the laws of gifts, purchase and sale, interest and purities. Because of Saadya's special affinity with Palestinian tradition, he was apparently the first Gaon to make use of the Jerusalem *Talmud*, this being an indication of his independent approach to legal decisions. In addition to these halakhic works, there are a few dozen surviving responsa, which were collected and published by Müller.[89] He also corresponded with various communities, including that of his Egyptian homeland.

C. Rav Samuel ben Hofni

Rav Samuel b. Hofni, Gaon of Sura, also came from a family of Geonim which was involved in various intrigues and splits in the Pumbedita Academy, to which Rav Samuel himself was no stranger. Possibly to alleviate the tension, it was decided to reopen the Academy of Sura, which had closed down shortly after Rav Saadya Gaon's death. Some time later, in 997, Rav Samuel b. Hofni was appointed Gaon of Sura, continuing to serve in that position till his death in 1013. During his term of office his son Israel, later to succeed Rav Saadya Gaon's son Dosa as Gaon, was scribe of the Academy.

One of Rav Samuel's main tasks was to assure the resumption of material support from the Jewish communities. In his lifetime the two Academies concluded an agreement concerning a redistribution of funds sent to both of them jointly. The tension between the two Academies declined somewhat, though it did not entirely disappear. One reason for the better relations was a family bond — Rav Samuel b. Hofni's daughter became the wife of Rav Sherira's son Rav Ḥai.

Like Rav Saadya Gaon before him, Rav Samuel wrote halakhic literature ranging over a broad spectrum of literary patterns; in extent, his monographic works far surpassed those of any other Gaon, before or after him. Apart from the dozens of responsa that have survived from his pen, which are scattered in collections of geonic responsa and in rabbinic literature, he wrote dozens of halakhic works, mostly monographs, a smaller number of treatises on legal theory and a *Treatise on the Commandments*. His halakhic books include theological comments, just as his works of biblical exegesis incorporate remarks on *halakhah*. He also wrote commentaries to the *Talmud*, none of which has survived. His most important extant work is an Introduction to the *Talmud*, in which he was concerned primarily with talmudic tradition, its transmitters and its terminology.[90] In addition to the aforementioned, Rav Samuel also wrote commentaries on some books of the Bible (*Genesis, Exodus, Deuteronomy*), thus continuing in the same vein as his illustrious predecessor Rav Saadya Gaon.

Fragments have recently come to light in Genizah material of Rav Samuel's works on legal philosophy and theory, as well as works on various aspects of the commandments, including a treatise 'On the Abrogation of the Law' and the already mentioned *Treatise on the Commandments*. In addition, there are about a dozen letters.

Rav Samuel b. Hofni's methodology was unique and independent. He was influenced inter alia by the culture of his environment far more than his predecessors: receptive to Arab culture, he was probably well versed in the non-Jewish literature of his time. This element is perhaps responsible for his departures from the established tradition of the Academies, emphasizing his own authority in halakhic matters, as he writes

> By this shall you know our power and the difference between us and our peers, and you shall know our strength in the Lord's *Torah*.[91]

It accounts, too, for his rational philosophy, which bespeaks an acquaintance with the thought of the Mu'tazilites.

Indeed, Rav Samuel's rationality is apparent both in his works on legal theory and in his halakhic treatises. In both he adopts the structure and style of Arabic literature, more in theology and less so in legal writing. Occasionally, such influence is apparent also in content. This finds expression in his biblical exegesis, where he adopts interpretative terminology used by the Muslims in their exegesis of the Koran.

D. Rav Hai Gaon

Chronologically the last of the Geonim, Rav Hai is generally considered
the first in importance — 'the greatest of them all,' as Samuel haNagid
called him. Rav Hai headed the Academy of Pumbedita for close to 35 years
(1004-1038). He was fourth in a line of Geonim: his great-grandfather Rav
Judah b. Samuel (906-917), grandfather Rav Hananyah b. Judah (938-943)
and father Rav Sherira b. Hananyah (968-998) all officiated as Geonim.
Before his accession to the Gaonate he served as *Av Bet Din* under his father,
and was appointed Gaon during the latter's lifetime.

Rav Hai's halakhic activity as a Gaon was concentrated in three main
areas: responsa, halakhic treatises and commentaries to the *Talmud*, mostly
written in Arabic. Rav Hai Gaon wrote more responsa than any other
Gaon — more than a thousand, though some were written in collaboration
with his father. While some of the responsa deal with practical matters,
others constitute explanations of talmudic passages. Of his commentaries of
the *Talmud*, we know of those to the following tractates: *Berakhot*, *Shabbat*,
Hagigah, *Baba Batra*, *Avodah Zarah*, *Hullin*. He probably wrote commentaries to parts of Order *Nashim*, including tractates *Ketubot* and *Gittin*. Of
his halakhic works, two have reached us in Hebrew translation: *Sefer
hamikkah vehamemkar* (*Book of Purchase and Sale*) and *Sefer Mishpete
Shevu'ot* (*Book of Laws of Oaths*), quotations of which exist in the original.
His *Book of Notes* has also survived. Also extant are quotations from other
books, among them works about abutters' rights, judicial ethics, loans and
others, occasionally cited in works by the early halakhic authorities. Some
fragments from these works are known to be among the as yet unpublished
documents from the Cairo Genizah. In addition to these halakhic works, Rav
Hai Gaon wrote letters, liturgical poems (*piyyutim*) and a talmudic-biblical
dictionary.

In his halakhic treatises and monographs Rav Hai generally presents the
talmudic law systematically, as did previous Geonim. In his responsa,
however, while he cites the *Talmud* and relies on various rules of decision-
making, whether talmudic or of geonic origin (such as the principle,
mentioned in Rav Hai's responsa, that the law may not be decided in
accordance with the opinion of a disciple against that of his teacher), he also
leans on early traditions, on halakhic rulings of saboraic or even geonic
origin, and sometimes on what he calls his ancestors' traditions. Only very
rarely does he cite a specific work of the geonic period. In addition, he may
appeal to scholarly consensus, custom and logical analogy, or extend existing

talmudic principles to additional situations.

Rav Hai's recourse to *minhag*, custom, is quite frequent; he sometimes treats it as the most authoritative source of law, even basing his exegesis of the talmudic text upon it. He uses various principles of halakhic decision, such as the rule that the law is decided according to the latest authority. He does not, however, accept *aggadah* as a reliable source; neither does he rely on biblical exegesis as a basis for halakhic innovation.

In many cases we find Rav Hai, in his responsa, retracting a ruling recorded in his written works. Thus, after originally stipulating that assets of doubtful ownership should be divided equally among the disputants, he reconsiders his position:

> Anything that stands in doubt should be decided according to the lenient alternative, in the sense that one is stringent toward the plaintiff and lenient toward the defendant.

His works, especially his responsa, became part and parcel of the halakhic literature of the *rishonim*, who frequently quote him and rely on his rulings. His contribution to the development of *halakhah* was thus of major import.[92]

6. *Characteristic Features of the Law of the Period*

As a general statement, the basic feature of the period in all fields of law, private and public, was the continuity of geonic and talmudic tradition, rather than innovation. This is the case in all areas for which we have evidence of legal activity during the period: in penal law, we find extensive use of banning and excommunication; in personal status, polygamy is sanctioned; in private law, we find various traders' customs, including the admissibility as evidence of handwritten material, letters and account books; *suftaja* is also used (*diyokne* in the *Talmud*: an order of payment issued by one merchant to another located in a remote place after the former received the agreed-upon sum of money[93]). In legal procedures we find the 'anonymous ban' (*herem setam*), which served as the prime instrument to prevent the litigants from entering any false plea or claim and to force them to admit the truth in cases where there was not a legal ground for the imposition of an oath or the litigants refused to take an oath. In court practice, there was appeal to gentile courts (mainly owing to clashes between Jewish and Islamic Law) and lay judges alongside professional jurists. In the commercial field, acquisition of movables as 'incidental' to real estate (*kinyan agav*) was allowed: here one transfers to another land of any size and incidental to the transfer he also transfers movables (situated elsewhere) in order to overcome the normal requirement of Talmudic Law that movables be actually present at the act of acquisition. The geonic innovation was that movables can be transferred incidental to land even when the seller does not own any land. This was done in order to facilitate transfer of movables when people did not own land. A similar continuity characterizes relations between slaves and masters, including property linkage between manumitted slaves and their former masters. Formulae of notes adhering to the models laid down by the Geonim were utilized in practice.

In this period, Arabic was the *lingua franca*, and considerable use was made of Muslim legal terms, though not always with precisely their original connotations. Some Muslim influence continued to make itself felt in such areas as economics, inheritance and family law, as well as legal organization. The Jewish judge was seen as representing the Principal of the Academy, in the same way as the Muslim *qadi* was the representative of the Government; other points of affinity were the existence of officials who could provide legal opinions (*muftis*), and scholars' reluctance to serve as judges.

Nevertheless, in some areas the Jewish and Muslim legal systems showed essential differences, due more to adherence to earlier Jewish traditions than to rejection of Muslim influence. An example is the status of courts constituted of three judges, as evidenced by legal documents discovered in the Genizah, signed in the presence of three judges. In Islamic Law, however, a single judge could preside over legal proceedings. A similar manifestation of Jewish tradition was the continued practice of convening courts in some localities on Mondays and Thursdays, as was the custom in Palestine. Such cases demonstrated that the power of tradition still exceeded that of the milieu in which the Jews found themselves.

Two aspects of the law of the period relevant to the status of women merit more detailed consideration.

A. The *Takkanah* of the Rebellious Wife

The first geonic *takkanah*, one of prime importance, enacted in the middle of the seventh century (650/1 C.E.), was the so-called '*takkanah* of the rebellious wife'. It stated that if a woman entered a claim against her husband to the effect that she could not bear to live with him ('He is repulsive to me'), her husband could be coerced to grant her an immediate divorce, on condition that she relinquish most of her financial privileges. According to some Geonim she would have to give the statutory portion of the marriage money (*ikkar ketubah*), the incremental payment (*tosefet ketubah*) and apparently also whatever parts of her husband's property she had seized. This was a considerable departure from talmudic law, and since the talmudic text itself could not be easily interpreted and the details of the *takkanah* itself were not known, the interpretation became a matter of controversy among the Geonim themselves. It is therefore difficult to determine the *takkanah*'s precise degree of deviation from talmudic law proper. To clarify matters, we may cite from a responsum in which Rav Sherira Gaon describes the background to the enactment of the *takkanah*, though his interpretation does not necessarily correspond to the core of the original *takkanah*:

> As to your question, concerning a woman living with her husband, who says to him, 'Divorce me! I do not wish to live with you!' — is he required to give her something from her *ketubah* or not? Is such a woman considered rebellious or not? We have seen that, by the letter of the law, we do not oblige the husband to divorce his wife when she sues for divorce, except in those cases where our Sages stated that it is incumbent on him to divorce her (*M. Ket.* 7:10) ...
>
> Later they enacted another *takkanah*, that the court should issue a proclamation concerning her for four consecutive weeks, and the court should admonish her: 'Know that even if your *ketubah* amounts to one hundred *maneh*, you have forfeited it ... '
>
> Finally, they enacted that the proclamation be issued for four weeks and she forfeits everything; nevertheless, the husband was not obliged to grant her a divorce ...
>
> It was then enacted that she should be kept waiting for twelve months without a divorce, in the hope that she might be placated. But after twelve months, the husband is forced to grant her a divorce. Later, our Sages the *Saboraim* realized that the daughters of Israel were appealing to the gentile courts to obtain a coerced divorce from their husbands, and some were divorcing their wives under duress, resulting in doubts concerning the validity of such a divorce, creating a calamitous situation. Accordingly, in the time of Mar Rav Rabbah [and] Mar Rav Hunai, may they rest in peace, it was enacted that a rebellious wife suing for divorce should receive intact all the 'property of iron sheep'[94] that she had brought with her, and that the husband should make good all destroyed or lost property. But whatever he himself undertook to bestow upon her, whether yet extant or not, he need not pay her, and if she should seize any such assets [the court] will confiscate them and restore them to the husband. As to the husband, we force him to write her an immediate writ of divorce, and she is entitled to the [statutory payment] of 100 or 200 *zuzim*. This has been our custom now for more than three hundred years, and you, too, should do so.[95]

Rav Sherira describes two principal aspects of the *takkanah*. One is universally accepted by the Geonim: the husband is obliged to grant a divorce immediately. This apparently applies only to a woman pleading that her husband is repulsive to her, though this is not stated explicitly. Rav Sherira holds — and this seems to be the view of all the Geonim — that the compulsory nature of the divorce had already been laid down in the *Talmud*, the only new element in the *takkanah* being the stipulation that divorce be granted forthwith, without delay.

However, Rav Sherira's ruling that the wife is entitled to receive the statutory portion of the marriage money, in apparent agreement with the interpretation of his predecessors at Pumbedita, was not generally accepted; other Geonim, presumably those of Sura, interpreted the *takkanah* differently, and ruled that the wife forfeited the statutory payment. Quite possibly, the latter interpretation is closer to the original intent of the *takkanah*, which deprived the wife of the statutory amount of her *ketubah*. The reason why Rav Sherira may have departed from the original interpretation will appear presently. Moreover, according to Rav Sherira the woman is also entitled to the original value of the property that she had brought with her upon entering into the marriage, whether still extant or not. This, too, was disputed by some Geonim.

It is not inconceivable that the unclear wording of the original *takkanah* was responsible for the differing views. On one count, at least, there was universal agreement: the woman was not entitled to receive the incremental payment specified in the *ketubah*: 'But whatever he himself undertook to bestow upon her, whether yet extant or not, he need not pay her' — even what she had already taken of her own accord.

Rav Sherira's explanation of the purpose of the *takkanah* is most instructive:

> The daughters of Israel have recourse to the gentile courts to obtain a coerced divorce from their husbands ... creating a calamitous situation. ... It was enacted for a rebellious wife, if she should sue for divorce ...

According to Rav Sherira, the Geonim who introduced this *takkanah* were troubled by the prospect of 'coerced divorces' in violation of Jewish Law (i.e., divorces awarded in gentile courts). Their purpose was to neutralize the danger by instituting a mode of coerced divorce that accorded with *halakhah*.

Rav Natronai Gaon proposes a different motivation for the *takkanah*: '... lest the daughters of Israel fall into bad ways.'[96] The background to the enactment of the *takkanah* may be the fear of apostasy, for according to Islamic Law conversion to Islam annulled a woman's previous marriage, so that she was automatically released from the bonds of marriage.

To my mind, the mere possibility that wives might appeal to Muslim

courts was motive enough for the enactment of this *takkanah*. For according
to contemporary Islamic Law, the appeal of only one litigant to a Muslim
court gave it jurisdiction over both parties, and also entailed the real
possibility that the court could itself dissolve the marriage without requiring
the husband to grant the divorce. This, then, was the principal motive for
the preventive measure embodied in the *takkanah* of the rebellious wife.
Despite the short time that elapsed from the Muslim conquest to the enactment of the *takkanah*, Islamic Law was already a highly influential element,
contrary to some recently published views that, at the time, Islamic Law in
Iraq was still largely in a state of flux.[97]

The history of the *takkanah* of the rebellious wife is instructive.
Although it was recorded in geonic codificatory works, such as *Halakhot
Pesukot* and *Halakhot Gedolot*, it did not win acceptance in later rabbinic
literature — a fate similar to that of many other *takkanot* and customs from
the geonic period.[98]

B. The Examination of Women Witnesses

Our second example, which relates to the use of *minhag* in the geonic
courts, has a bearing on women's status *vis-à-vis* court procedure. The practice in question, far from being accidental, reflects a sensitivity towards
women's honour and modesty; it also indicates that women's legal status in
the geonic period had already reached a level of development such as to foster
a willingness to depart from talmudic law, as seen already in the previous
example. We read in a geonic responsum:

> Where a married woman is obligated to take an oath, we impose it upon her.
> However, in these matters all courts have a custom when a man says of a
> married woman, 'Summon her!' They investigate in the neighbourhood and
> of those familiar as to whether she is accustomed to go out and buy and sell
> and speak with men and similar habits. If she is accustomed to this, she is
> summoned and judged as required by law, except that she is secluded (in
> court), so that she not be insulted and disgraced, in accordance with the
> respect due her. If she is not accustomed to this but is modest and sits inside,
> the claimant against her is questioned concerning his dealings with her and
> what his claim against her is. Even though our rabbis have said [*B. Shebu.*
> 31a], 'Hear out your fellow men' [*Deut.* 1:16] and from these words of the
> *Torah* a warning was derived that a judge should not hear the words of one
> litigant before the other litigant comes, nevertheless for the sake of this
> character trait [modesty] which is of great benefit, this is done [counter to the
> explicit injunction of the *Torah*]. Similarly, in the case of two litigants
> [*B.Sanh.* 31b], one of whom says, 'Let us deliberate here,' while the other
> says, 'Let us go to the Place of Assembly,' if it is customary in that locality

to go to the Place of Assembly, they are summoned and questioned and investigated concerning the subject of the claim, to see whether proofs exist or not, and if the claim is being made confidently, and so on — all this they are required to bring to the Place of Assembly ... Here, too [i.e. the case of the married woman] the claim is examined, and they say: 'How did you spend the money? And how did you give to her? And why did you give (something) to a married woman?' They weigh his words, and if they consider the matter to have any foundation, she is summoned to appear with him, as we have explained. But if they consider the claim to be unlikely but only a pretext, she is not summoned to appear with him; and she is not disgraced. This is done not only for a married woman but also for a virgin in her father's house who is not accustomed to come and go. While these things are not found expressed in the words of our rabbis, it is nevertheless the practice of all courts. It is proper to act accordingly, for otherwise anyone who hates another would disgrace his wife, because rumours are easily spread ... So is our custom and so we practice. Likewise you act accordingly, with a pure mind. Stray not from this.[99]

The most striking element in this responsum is that although the custom — in this case an accepted practice of Jewish courts — explicitly contradicted the rabbinic exegesis of Scripture not to hear one party in the absence of the other, consideration of the woman's personal standing sustained the practice nonetheless. It seems, moreover, that the practice was not an innovation initiated by the Geonim themselves, but a custom that emerged from popular usage, or, at least, a practice learned from the Muslim host society (there is indeed a similar procedure in Islamic Law). It is true that the respondent appeals to logic: 'It is proper to act accordingly ...' and also tries to adduce a proof-text from the *Talmud*: 'Similarly, in the case of two litigants, etc.' The proof-text in question, however, is not really relevant, and one senses a rather artificial, forced attempt to justify a prevalent practice: the Geonim acquiesced and legitimized the custom in order to equate the Jewish woman's legal status to that of her Muslim counterpart.

7. The Status of Geonic Rulings in Later Rabbinic Literature

Although the teachings of the Geonim ultimately became an integral part of the fabric of later halakhic literature, making a major contribution to the evolution of Jewish Law, their rulings and doctrines were not always universally accepted as binding. While some authorities accepted their rulings as law, others contested their *takkanot* and customs.

Maimonides, for example, was quite reserved in his attitude, denying the power of the Geonim to enact *takkanot*. In his view, the mere fact that some

decision had been issued by geonic authorities, even as a full-fledged
takkanah, did not guarantee its immediate validity; its force depended on the
degree to which it had gained popular acceptance. Thus, Maimonides rejected
the *takkanah* of the rebellious wife. Moreover, if he considered the institution (or acceptance) of some geonic custom to be erroneous, he denied its
validity despite that acceptance. His objections are sometimes so vigorous
that he may entirely ignore a geonic innovation; this was the case with regard
to the *gezerta* oath. At other times, he may explicitly challenge the
innovation, as he did in the case of the principle of acquisition 'through four
cubits of land in Palestine', remarking: 'These things are extremely light and
precarious.'[100]

Other *rishonim*, too, challenged the authority of the Geonim. Thus,
R. Elijah Mizrahi (1450-1526) wrote in a responsum:

> For, as you know, several things that the Geonim said have been rejected,
> since it is apparent that those things were not properly founded according to
> the principles of the *Talmud*, despite the fact that the Geonim are of very
> high standing and we accept their authority and that of their teachings.

He proceeds to substantiate his complaint with several examples.[101]

Other authors, on the contrary, saw fit to follow the Geonim in many
respects, though not necessarily systematically. Thus, R. Abraham
b. David of Posquières (Provence, 1125-1198) writes:

> It is not for us to dispute the view of the Gaon, other than with a well-known
> argument. But that is rarely possible [lit.: 'that is glue that is hard to come
> by'].[102]

A similar statement is made by R. Moses b. Nahman (Spain, 1194-1270):

> ... But since the Geonim testify and say that never was such a thing done in
> the Academy ..., we have no choice in the matter but to accept their
> testimony. For the Geonim received their tradition from our masters the
> Saboraim and our masters the Saboraim from our masters the Amoraim ... [103]

R. Solomon b. Adret (Spain, 1235-1310), too, expresses himself with the
utmost respect:

> At any rate, as far as the final law is concerned, we accept the authority of the
> Geonim, of blessed memory, and their mere conversation is like *Torah*, how
> much more so their teachings ... [104]

One question of great interest regarding the Geonim was whether a
scholar who cited them erroneously was considered as having erred 'on a
point of *mishnah*' and was therefore required to retract; or whether he was
deemed to have erred on a point of reason and so could not retract. Some

scholars, like R. Abraham b. David of Posquières, held that their teachings were equivalent (in this sense) to the *mishnah*, while others, like R. Zerahiah Halevi (Provence, twelfth century), contested this view. Still others, such as R. Asher b. Yehiel (Germany, Spain, 1250-1328), took what in some senses might be termed an intermediate path, agreeing in general with R. Abraham b. David but allowing greater leeway for departures from geonic rulings should a later judge insist on rejecting them.[105]

In some cases we in fact find judges and respondents following the first approach: 'At any rate, as far as the law in practice is concerned, ... we believe the view of the Geonim should be followed.'[106] Some even refer to the geonic teachings as 'tradition'.[107] A greater number, however, take the negative view, disputing geonic practice, sometimes referring derogatorily to the teachings of the Geonim as 'words of prophecy'.[108] Rejections of geonic rulings are more common among Ashkenazi scholars, who allowed themselves more latitude in legal decisions than the Sephardim. Quite frequently, authors felt constrained to explain their objections to geonic decisions by suggesting that some error had crept into the original teaching of the Gaon, that what was reported in his name had never actually been said or written by him. It would seem, however, that such arguments were not always justifiable and were adduced solely out of respect for the Geonim.[109] Despite these reservations, however, geonic literature ultimately became an integral constituent of the world of *halakhah*, both in Spain and in Ashkenaz (northern and central Europe); it was to exert considerable influence on the evolution of *halakhah* in the following generations.

8. Postscript: Ashkenazim and Sephardim*

According to most authorities, the geonic period ended in the eleventh century. From that time on historians of Jewish Law and of Jewish life in general, recognize two simultaneous and parallel streams of development: the Ashkenazi and the Sephardi, which had begun to emerge in the tenth century. The terms Ashkenaz and Ashkenazi, in rabbinic literature refer to Jewish life and settlements in Northwest, Central and eventually Eastern Europe. The terms Sepharad and Sephardi in rabbinic literature refer to Jewish life and settlement in the Iberian Peninsula and parts of North Africa adjacent to it. The two groups differ in cultural and ritual tradition, liturgy, and various other matters. The Sephardim are often called 'Spanish' Jews and the Ashkenazim 'German' Jews, but this quick identification is often misleading. After the expulsion from Spain in 1492, Sephardi Jews re-established communities in the Ottoman Empire and elsewhere, and thus became Greek, Turkish, and Macedonian Jews as well. As already noted, Ashkenazim spread abroad from Germany into Poland, the Baltic region, Belarus, Ukraine, Hungary, etc. For the most part, Ashkenazi communities grew and developed within the Roman Christian Society of Northern Europe, while Sephardi communities grew and developed first in the Moslem context of the Iberian Peninsula, and later in Roman Christian Spain until 1492, and then in the Muslim and Eastern Orthodox world of the Eastern Mediterranean.

Although the Ashkenazi and Sephardi legal traditions did not remain entirely separate, and indeed became amalgamated in codes, responsa, and other rabbinic legal literature during and after the fourteenth century, the two traditions retain their identity to this day.

Sephardi communities have appeared in Western Europe, notably Amsterdam, in the seventeenth century. Jews of Ashkenazi heritage organized the first Jewish resettlements of the modern State of Israel when it was still part of the Ottoman Empire. The original rather strict geographical distinctions as between Ashkenazim and Sephardim no longer apply. The ritual and cultural differences, however, are often maintained with punctilio.

9.   Bibliography

Historical, Political and Juridical Background

Cohen, G.D., 'The Reconstruction of Gaonic History', in *Studies in the Variety of Rabbinic Cultures* (Philadelphia, The Jewish Publication Society, 1991), 99-155.

Goitein, S.D., "New Sources on the Palestinian Gaonate," in *S. Baron Jubilee Volume,* ed. S.Lieberman and A. Hyman (New York: Columbia University Press, 1974), 503-537.

Goitein, S.D., 'The Interplay of Jewish and Islamic Laws', in *Jewish Law in Legal History and the Modern World,* ed. B.S. Jackson (Leiden: E.J. Brill, 1980), 61-77.

Libson, G., 'Islamic Influence on Medieval Jewish Law? Sefer Ha'Arevuth ('Book of Surety') of Rav Shmuel ben Hofni Gaon and its Relationship to Islamic Law', *Studia Islamica* 73 (1991), 5-24.

Mann, J., 'The Responsa of the Babylonian Geonim as a Source of Jewish History', *Jewish Quarterly Review* (n.s.) 7 (1916/1917), 457-90; 8 (1918), 339-66; 9 (1918/1919), 139-74; 10 (1920), 121-

53, 309-66; 11 (1920/1921), 433-71. Reprinted in his *Collected Articles*, II (New York: Arno, 1973 and Gedera: M. Shalom, 1971).

Mann, J., 'The Last Geonim of Sura', *Jewish Quarterly Review* (n.s.) 11 (1920-1921): 409-22 = *Collected Articles*, II (New York: Arno, 1973 and Gedera: M. Shalom, 1971), 293-306.

Halakhic Literature and Sources of Law

Altmann, A., *Saadya's Conception of the Law* (Manchester: John Rylands Library, 1944, John Rylands University Bulletin).

Aptowitzer, V., 'Formularies of Decrees and Documents from a Gaonic Court', *Jewish Quarterly Review* 4 (1913/1914), 23-51.

Elon, M., *Jewish Law: History, Sources, Principles*, trld. B. Auerbach and M.J. Sykes (Philadelphia and Jerusalem: Jewish Publication Society, 1994), chs.17, 30-31.

Groner Z., *The Legal Methodology of Ḥai Gaon* (Chico, CA: Scholars Press, 1985); reviewed by R. Brody in *Jewish Quarterly Review* 76 (1986), 237-45.

Ginzberg, L., *Geonica* (New York: Hermon Press, 1968, 2nd ed.)

Libson, G., '*Halakhah* and Reality in the Gaonic Period: *takkanah*, *Minhag*, Tradition and Consensus. Some Observations', Paper delivered at University College, London 1992, in press.

Courts and Legal Practice

Libson, G., 'The Use of a Sacred Object in the Administration of a Judicial Oath', in *Jewish Law Association Studies I: The Touro Conference Volume*, ed. B.S. Jackson (Chico, CA: Scholars Press, 1985), 53-60.

Biographies of Geonim

Malter, H., *Saadia Gaon. His Life and Works* (Philadelphia: Jewish Publication Society of America, 1921).

Features of the *Halakhah* of the Period

Friedman, M.A., *Jewish Marriage in Palestine* (Tel Aviv and New York: Jewish Theological Seminary of America, 1980, 2 vols.).

Goitein, S.D., *A Mediterranean Society* (Berkeley, CA: University of California Press, 1971).

Wacholder, B.Z., 'The Halakah and the Proselyting of Slaves During the Gaonic Era', *Historia Judaica* 18 (1956), 89-106.

The Status of Geonic Rulings in Later Rabbinic Literature

Brody, R., "Maimonides' Attitude towards the Halakhic Innovations of the Geonim," in *The Thought of Moses Maimonides*, ed. I. Robinson, L. Kaplan & J. Bauer (Lewiston NY: The Edwin Mellen Press, 1990), 183-202 (Studies in History of Philosophy 17).

Notes

1 See A. Grossman, *The Exilarchy in Babylon during the Period of the Geonim* (Jerusalem: Merkaz Zalman Shazar, 1984, Hebrew).

2 B.M. Lewin, *Ginze Ḳedem* (Jerusalem: Ginze Ḳedem, 1931), Vol. V, p.121.

3 See M. Gil, *Palestine in the First Muslim Period* (Tel Aviv: A.D. Alkalai, 1983), at I, 558, 572, 597, 606, 621 (Hebrew).

4 Gil, *ibid.*, at 583 n., 596-99.

5 Gil, *ibid.*, at 443, 597, 598 n.896.

6 Gil, *ibid.*, at 504.

7 Gil, *ibid.*, at 210, 497.

8 Gil, *ibid.*, at 554.

9 *Ibid.*, at 210, 559n., 576, 606, 617, 625.

10 See M. Elon, 'Codification of the Law', *Encyclopaedia Judaica* (Jerusalem: Keter, 1971), 5:634f.

11 D.E. Sklare, 'The Religious Thought of Samuel ben Hofni Gaon. Texts and Studies in Cultural History' (Dissertation, Harvard University, Cambridge, MA, 1992), 245, 355.

12 It is not surprising that questions were addressed to Rav Palṭoi concerning *Halakhot Peṣuḳot*, for the work first appeared some 100 years after the death of its author Rav Yehudai, i.e., during Rav Palṭoi's lifetime.

13 *Ḥemdah Genuzah*, ed. Z. Wolf & S.Z. Schneerson (Jerusalem, 1863), no.110; S. Assaf, *Teshuvot haGe'onim* (Jerusalem: Darom, 1928), p.81. This responsum has been widely discussed in the scholarly literature.

14 For a comprehensive study see N. Danzig, '*Halakhot Peṣuḳot (Hilkhot Rav Yehudai Gaon)*', Dissertation, Yeshiva University, New York 1984 (recently published as a book, *Introduction to Halakhot Peṣuḳot with a Supplement to Halakhot Peṣuḳot* (New York: Bet Hamidrash Harabanim beAmerika, 1993), which unfortunately reached me too late to be referred to in this study).

15 See *Ginze Schechter*, II, 558.

16 Several recensions of *Halakhot Gedolot* are extant, of which two are superior.

One, known as the Babylonian recension, was first printed in Venice, 1548, and later in Warsaw 1874 with place references and notes by A.S. Traub. The other, so-called Spanish recension, was published by A. Hildesheimer on the basis of a Vatican MS in 1888. There are differences between the recensions, mainly in connection with rulings by Geonim who flourished after the author's time, which were incorporated in the Spanish recension but are missing in the Babylonian. Pointing to these additions, Epstein conjectured that the Spanish recension originated in Spain or West Africa. However, the later additions in the Spanish recension do not necessarily imply that this was indeed the later version (as already supposed by Danzig, Dissertation, *supra* n.14, at 32 note).

17 *Teshuvot Ge'onim Kadmonim*, ed. D. Kassel (Berlin, 1848), No.87; S. Assaf, *Responsa Geonica* (Jerusalem: Mekitse Nirdamim, 1942), no.37.

18 A. Harkavy, *Teshuvot haGe'onim* (Berlin: Mekitse Nirdamim, 1887), no.312.

19 *Teshuvot haGe'onim* (Harkavy, *supra* n.18), no.232 (end).

20 *Otsar haGe'onim, Ketubot,* no.674.

21 See Abramson, *Inyanot*, 184.

22 *Responsa of R. Meir b. Baruch,* ed. M. Bloch (Berlin: Itzkowski, 1891, repr. Jerusalem: Mekitse Nirdamim, 1968), no.99.

23 *Sha'are Tsedek* 17b, no.11.

24 See S. Assaf, 'Polemical Arguments of an Early Karaite' (Hebrew), *Tarbiz* 4 (1933), 198; and cf. Abramson, *Inyanot*, 38.

25 *Teshuvot haGe'onim* [Harkavy, *supra* n.18], no.347.

26 *Or Zarua,* no.53 [p.16].

27 For Rav Yehudai's responsum see Rashi's commentary to *Mishnah Avot* 1:8. Cf. *Otsar haGe'onim, Ketubot,* no.349; B. Lifschitz, 'The Legal Standing of the Responsa Literature' (Hebrew), *Shenaton hamishpat ha'Ivri* 9-10 (1982-83), 270.

28 *Otsar haGe'onim, ibid.,* no.348.

29 See V. Aptowitzer, 'Formularies of Decrees and Documents from a Gaonic Court', *Jewish Quarterly Review* 4 (1913-14), 23-51. The prayer-book of Rav Amram Gaon also appears to pre-date Saadya.

30 S.D. Goitein, *Sidre Hinnukh* (Jerusalem: Makhon Bet Zvi, 1962), 154-55.

31 M. Ben-Sasson, 'Remnants of Rav Saadyah Gaon's Book of Testimony and Documents' (Hebrew), *Shenaton hamishpat ha'ivri* 11-12 (1984-86), 163; Sklare, *supra* n.11, at 137.

32 For a review of legal activity in Palestine at this time see S.D. Goitein, *A Mediterranean Society* (Berkeley: University of California Press, 1971), II, 311-345.

33 See M.A. Friedman, 'Laws of Matrimony in Light of *Sefer haMa'asim livene Erets-Yisra'el*' (Hebrew), *Tarbiz* 50 (1981), 209; cf. the list of fragments

ibid., 210 n.2. In addition to this work there exist several others referring specifically to Palestinian practices, such as *Halakhot deR. Abba* and *Ṣefer vehizhir*. In this connection mention should be made of the Hebrew translation of *Halakhot Peṣuḵot,* known as *Hilkhot Re'u.*

34 See, e.g., S. Assaf, *Teḵufat haGe'onim veṣifrutah* (Jerusalem: Mosad Harav Kook, 1955), 116; Gil, *Palestine, supra* n.3, at I, 412n.

35 *Ṣefer haMakhria'*, no.36; see Friedman, *op. cit.*, n.7.

36 See J.N. Epstein, '*Ma'asim liVene Erets Yisra'el*' (Hebrew), *Tarbiz* 1/B (1930), 38.

37 *Iggeret Rav Sherira Gaon*, ed. B. Lewin (Frankfurt-a-M: Association for Jewish Literature, 1921; repr. Jerusalem: Makor, 1972), 71-72 (French version).

38 *Otsar haGe'onim, Shabbat*, no.310.

39 R. Judah al-Bargeloni, *Ṣefer ha'Ittim*, 267; cf. S. Abramson, *Tractate 'Abodah Zarah' of the Babylonian Talmud* (New York: Jewish Theological Seminary of America, 1957), xiii n.1.

40 *Otsar haGe'onim, Ketubot*, p.4.

41 *Otsar haGe'onim, Ketubot*, 207.

42 For geonic rules of legal decision, see Assaf, *supra* n.34, at 223.

43 *Teshuvot haGe'onim* (Lyck), no.46.

44 *Ṣefer haEshkol*, II, 49. For further responsa in this vein see *Teshuvot haGe'onim* (Assaf, 1928, *supra* n.13), 125; *Teshuvot haGe'onim* (Harkavy, *supra* n.18), no.434.

45 See *Teshuvot haGe'onim* (Assaf, 1928, *supra* n.13), *ibid.*

46 *Teshuvot haGe'onim* (Harkavy, *supra* n.18), no.434; cf. also *ibid.*, nos. 36, 208, 247, 259, 261, 349. Cf. also the responsa discussed by M. Friedman, *Polygamy in Israel* (Hebrew), Jerusalem, 1986, 344. And there are other examples. For the geonic use of the Jerusalem Talmud, see J. Sussman, 'The Study Tradition and Textual Tradition of the Jerusalem Talmud' (Hebrew), in *Meḥkarim baṣifrut hatalmudit*, Jerusalem, 1983, 18; M. Ben-Sasson, 'The People of the Maghreb and their Ties with Eretz-Israel in the 9th to 11th Centuries' (Hebrew), *Shalem* 5 (1987), 43; and cf. Danzig's comment in his dissertation (*supra*, n.14), 84 n.345 and bibliography cited *ibid.*

47 *Otsar haGe'onim, Hagigah*, 60.

48 Assaf, *Teḵufat haGe'onim, supra* n.34, at 283 (the original Hebrew is rhymed). See also Rav Sherira's responsum in *Teshuvat haGe'onim* (Harkavy, *supra* n.18), no.251.

49 See S. Spiegel, "On the Polemical Episode of Pirkoi ben Baboi" (Hebrew), in *H.A. Wolfson Festschrift* (Jerusalem and New York: American Academy for Jewish Research, 1965), 243.

50 See A. Epstein, '*Ṣefer Eldad Hadani*' (Hebrew), in *Kitve A. Epstein*, I (Pressburg: A. Alkalai, 1891; Jerusalem: Mosad Harav Kook, 1950), 40.

51 See, e.g., *Teshuvot haGe'onim* (Harkavy, *supra* n.18), no.228.

52 See G. Libson, '*Halakhah* and Reality in the Gaonic Period: *takkanah, minhag*, Tradition and Consensus. Some Observations', Paper delivered at University College, London 1992, in press, and sources cited therein.

53 *Teshuvot haGe'onim* (Assaf, 1942, *supra* n.17), p.108 .

54 *Otsar haGe'onim, Berakhot*, 100.

55 Lewin, ed., *Iggeret Rav Sherira Gaon*, xxiv; Aptowitzer, *supra* n.29. For the role of the scribe see H. Soloveitchik, 'A Deed in *Sefer ha'Ittur*', *Tarbiz* 41 (1972), 324 (Hebrew).

56 See M. Elon, *Jewish Law: History, Sources, Principles*, trld. B. Auerbach and M.J. Sykes (Philadelphia and Jerusalem: Jewish Publication Society, 1994), Vol. III, pp.1466-67.

57 Lewin, *Iggeret Rav Sherira Gaon, Likkutim*, 27.

58 *Teshuvot haGe'onim* (Harkavy, *supra* n.18), nos. 198, 200; *Teshuvot haGe'onim* (Assaf, 1942, *supra* n.17), 102.

59 That is, property whose principal remains in the wife's ownership, while the husband has the usufruct.

60 Abramson, *Inyanot*, 38-39; and cf. R. Brody, 'Halakhic Responsa of Rav Natronai bar Hilai Gaon' (Dissertation, Jerusalem, 1981, in Hebrew), 320; *Ginze Schechter* 2, 62; *Teshuvot haGe'onim* (ed. Assaf, 1928, *supra* n.13), 24; M. Ben-Sasson, 'Society and Leadership in the Jewish Communities of North Africa in the Middle Ages' (Dissertation, Jerusalem, 1983), I, 230 (Hebrew); Aptowitzer, *supra* n.29, at 32; and cf. a responsum of Rav Aaron Gaon instructing the local elders to heed his counsel (*Hemdah Genuzah, supra* n.13, no.37).

61 *Teshuvot haGe'onim* (Assaf, 1928, *supra* n.13), 24, no.69. For the definition of *mumheh* see *Sha'are Tsedek* 91a, no.35; 91b, no.37; and cf. *ibid.*, no.40, and Assaf, *ibid.*, n.11.

62 *Teshuvot haGe'onim* (Harkavy, *supra* n.18), no.180. For parallels see *Otsar haGe'onim, Sanhedrin*, 39.

63 *Sha'are Teshuvah*, no.270

64 *Hemdah Genuzah, supra* n.13, no.81

65 *Teshuvot haGe'onim* (Harkavy, *supra* n.18), no.178.

66 *Gaonica* 2, 101.

67 See, e.g., Aptowitzer, *supra* n.29, at 26.

68 See, e.g., *Otsar haGe'onim, B.M.*, 58.

69 *Teshuvot haGe'onim* (Assaf, 1928, *supra* n.13), 24.

70 *Sha'are Teshuvah*, no.86.

71 Ben-Sasson, 'Society and Leadership', *supra* n.60, at I, 211; II, 125 n.3.

72 *Teshuvot haGe'onim* (Harkavy, *supra* n.18), no.554; Goitein, *A Mediterranean Society, supra* n.32, at II, 327-28; *Teshuvot haGe'onim* (Harkavy,

supra n.18), no.235 (also illustrating the constitution of traders' tribunals).

73 See S.D. Goitein, 'On the History of the Palestinian Gaonate', in *Palestinian Jewry in Early Islamic and Crusader Times* (Jerusalem: Yad Yitshak Ben Zvi, 1980), 109-111; *Sha'are Tsedek*, 84b, no.4; *Teshuvot haGe'onim* (Harkavy, *supra* n.18), nos. 178, 182, 233, 346; *Hemdah Genuzah, supra* n.13, no.37 (= *Otsar haGe'onim, Nedarim*, 44).

74 See *Teshuvot haGe'onim* (Assaf, 1942, *supra* n.17), no.66.

75 See *Teshuvot haGe'onim* (Harkavy, *supra* n.18), no.82; for Rav Hananyah's responsum see *Sha'are Tsedek* 26a, no.24.

76 R. Asher b. Yehiel, *B.K.*, ch. 8, para. 17; *Sefer Mesharim*, path 1, pt. 12.

77 Aptowitzer, *supra* n.29, at 27; Nahmanides, *Responsa*, no.63.

78 *Sha'are Tsedek*, 84b, no.4 (Rav Sherira); *Teshuvot haGe'onim* (Harkavy, *supra* n.18), no.233 (Rav Hai).

79 See G. Libson, 'Jurisdiction over Jews in Muslim Courts during the Gaonic Period', in press.

80 For imprisonment see, e.g., a responsum of Rav Paltoi, *Sha'are Teshuvah*, no.182; *Halakhot Pesukot,* para. 135; and a responsum of Rav Sherira cited in *Ge'one Mizrah uMa'arav*, no.146. For shaving the hair see *Toratan shel Rishonim*, I, 29; II, 20.

81 For excommunication as a punishment for religious lapses, see *Sha'are Teshuvah*, no.116; *Hemdah Genuzah, supra* n.13, no.15; *Sha'are Tsedek*, 91b, no.38; etc. For excommunication as an enforcement measure, see *Ge'one Mizrah u-Ma'arav*, no.42; *Gaonica* 2, 154; etc.

82 M. Hershler, 'Responsa and Enactment of Geonim and Early Authorities, from a Manuscript' [Hebrew], *Sinai* 66 (1970), 175. Cf. a responsum of Rav Hananyah, *Sha'are Tsedek*, 57a, no.16, and also *ibid.*, no.17: 'And several times it was necessary to excommunicate anyone who gives too much for his daughter's gift and dowry.'

83 *Sha'are Tsedek* 91b and parallels. Cf. also Rav Natronai's responsum in *Hemdah Genuzah, supra* n.13, no.20, though he too seems to have delivered conflicting decisions. Cf. responsum of Rav Hai, *Teshuvot haGe'onim* (Harkavy, *supra* n.18), no.440, which stipulates thirty-nine lashes. For a detailed discussion see V. Aptowitzer, 'Flogging and Disciplinary Flogging in Geonic Responsa', *Hamishpat Ha'Ivri* 5 (1937), 33-104 (Hebrew), who tries to resolve the contradictions and suggests a systematic approach.

84 Aptowitzer, *op. cit.*, 103.

85 *Teshuvot haGe'onim* (Harkavy, *supra* n.18), no.215.

86 The Geonim abandoned completely the use of either the Divine Name or the attribute-Name oath and limited themselves to the imprecation oath alone which was generally termed *gezerta.* Although the basic rules and regulations regarding the administration of oaths did not change, the fact that the only type of oath now administered was the less severe form of *gezerta* gave them room for broadening the use of *gezerta* to areas where heretofore oaths in

general were not required.

87 On *gezerta* and *ḥerem ṣetam* see G. Libson, '*Gezerta* and *Herem Setam* in the Geonic Period and the Early Middle Ages' (Dissertation, Jerusalem, 1980, Hebrew).

88 See Ch.5, section 2Bi above.

89 J. Müller, *Traité des Successions* (Paris: E. Leroux, 1897, repr.: Jerusalem, 1968).

90 See recently S. Abramson, *Chapters from R. Samuel ben Hofni Gaon's Introduction to the Talmud* (Jerusalem: Mekitse Nirdamim, 1990, Hebrew).

91 Assaf, *Teḳufat haGe'onim*, *supra* n.34, at 284.

92 For a comprehensive account of Rav Hai see Z. Groner, 'Rav Hai Gaon and his Halakhic Method' (Dissertation, Jerusalem, 1974, Hebrew). Most of the topics referred to here were discussed by Groner.

93 S.D. Goitein, 'The Interplay of Jewish and Islamic Laws', in *Jewish Law in Legal History and the Modern World*, ed. B.S. Jackson (Leiden: E.J. Brill, 1980), 65.

94 A term in talmudic law denoting that part of the wife's property under the husband's responsibility, i.e., subject to his undertaking, recorded in the *ketubah*, to restore it to her upon dissolution of the marriage.

95 *Otsar haGe'onim*, *Ketubot*, no.478.

96 *Otsar haGe'onim*, *Ketubot*, no.471.

97 See M. Gil, *Palestine in the First Muslim Period* (Tel Aviv: University of Tel-Aviv, 1983), I, 136 (Hebrew).

98 On attitudes to this *takkanah* in the literature of the *rishonim* see Elon, *supra* n.56, at Vol. II, 661-665.

99 S. Assaf, *Teshuvot haGe'onim* (Jerusalem, 1927), no.3. On this responsum see also M. Friedman, 'The Ethics of Medieval Jewish Marriage', in S.D. Goitein, ed., *Religion in a Religious Age* (Cambridge, MA: Association for Jewish Studies, 1974), 93-94 (whose translation is here followed with minor adaptations).

100 Maimonides, *Mishneh Torah*, *Hilkhot Sheluḥin veshutafin* 3:7.

101 See Elijah Mizraḥi, *Responsa*, no.76, 248.

102 *Katuv Sham*, *Sanhedrin*, ch. 4.

103 Naḥmanides, 'Sermon for the New Year', in *Kitve haRamban*, ed. H.D. Chavel (Jerusalem: Mosad Harav Kook, 1964), I.248 (Hebrew).

104 R. Solomon b. Adret, *Responsa*, II, no.21. Sentiments like these and those of Naḥmanides appear in the responsa of many Spanish scholars.

105 *Piṣke haRosh*, *Sanhedrin* ch. 4, para. 6; for a discussion of the question see Elon, *supra* n.56, at I, 233, discussing R. Asher's view in connection with the rule that the law is decided according to the latest authorities; I. Twersky, *Rabad of Posquières* (Philadelphia: Jewish Publication Society of America, 1980), 185.

106 R. Joseph ibn Migash, *Responsa*, no.71.

107 See, e.g., R. Solomon b. Adret, *Responsa*, I, nos. 161, 329; R. Yomtov Ashbili, *Responsa*, nos. 24, 145; etc.

108 See, e.g., R. Isaiah di Trani, *Ṣefer haMakhria'*, no.14; R. Isaac b. Sheshet, *Responsa*, no.168. On *rishonim* rejecting geonic opinions see, e.g., R. Asher b. Yeḥiel, *Responsa*, 32:5; R. Nissim, *Responsa*, no.46; etc.

109 For examples see e.g., R. Abraham b. Maimon, *Responsa*, no.82, 109; R. Isaac b. Sheshet, *Responsa*, no.168; and many more.

*   Contributed by S.M. Passamaneck.

9

KARAITE HALAKHAH

by

MICHAEL CORINALDI

University of Haifa

1. *The Name*

The name of the sect 'Karaites' (in Hebrew *Kara'im, Bne Mikra* or *Ba'ale Mikra* — 'People of the Scriptures') betokens advocacy for a return to the Scripture as the sole source of Divine Law and rejection of the Oral Law in the talmudic-rabbinic sense. The Karaite sect was founded by Anan Ben David (Baghdad, eighth century), who opposed the halakhic authority of the Geonim.

2. *Leading Authorities and Literary Sources*

A. The Early Karaites (eighth-ninth Centuries)

Anan ben David — author of *Sefer Hamitsvot leAnan*[1] — and his followers were originally known as 'Ananites'. Following an initial period under his leadership the sect was fluid in its composition until it became consolidated under the composite guidance, in subsequent periods in Persia, of Benjamin b. Moses Nahawandi (mid-ninth century), and Daniel b. Moses al-Qumisi (end of ninth century). Nahawandi codified a book of rules, *Sefer Dinim Mas'at Binyamin*.[2] Al-Qumisi's best known work is a commentary on the Minor Prophets, *Pitron Sheneim Asar*.[3]

B. The Golden Age of Karaite Literature (tenth-eleventh Centuries)

The greatest Karaite scholar of the beginning of the golden age of Karaite literature was Abu Yusuf Ya'qub al Kirkisani (first half of tenth century, Babylonia), the author of *Kitab al-Anwar Wa-Al-Maraqib* (*Book of Lights and Watchtowers*).[4] The book discusses the Commandments and covers many legal topics, such as succession and incest, with many references to Anan, Nahawandi and other early Karaites.

During this period Karaism spread and many Karaites settled in Palestine, especially in Jerusalem. The leading authority of the Karaite community of Jerusalem was Levi ben Yapheth Halevi (end of tenth century and beginning of eleventh century). His main work, *Sefer Hamitsvot* (*Book of Precepts*), is one of the most important in Karaite *halakhah*. It was originally written in Arabic, but a Hebrew version is extant in manuscript (Ms. Bodleian 21618). The period of effervescence of Karaism in Jerusalem ended with the capture of Jerusalem by the Crusaders (1099), when many Karaites fled to Egypt. Thereafter the community in Egypt, and especially Cairo, became an important centre serving as a bridge between the Karaites and the Rabbis down to the present century.

C. The Byzantium Centre: The Era of the Codifiers of Karaite *Halakhah* (twelfth-sixteenth Centuries)

By the end of the eleventh century the main Karaite centre had moved from Iraq and Persia to Byzantium.

The most important sages and codifiers of Karaite *halakhah* are:

1. Judah b. Elijha Hadassi (Constantinople, mid-twelfth century), who wrote the *Eshkol haKofer*, a basic work of Karaite *halakhah* and theology (first published in Gozlov, 1836).

2. Aaron ben Elijah, known as 'the latter'[5] (Nicomedia and Constantinople, fourteenth century), regarded by the Karaites as the 'Karaite Maimonides', the author of a book of precepts, *Gan Eden* (Gozlov, 1864). He was also one of the greatest Karaite biblical exegetes, as evidenced by his commentary on the Bible, *Keter Torah* (first published, Gozlov, 1867).

3. Elijah ben Moses Basyatchi (Constantinople, fifteenth century), the author of a book of precepts, *Aderet Eliyahu*. He was known as 'the Final Codifier' (*haposek ha'aharon*) in view of the authority attaching to his code in Karaite *halakhah*. From that point of view it is equivalent to the *Shulhan Arukh* of the Rabbis.

D. The East European Centre (sixteenth-twentieth Century)

After the decline of the Karaite centre in Byzantium, the Karaite communities in Crimea, especially Chufut-Kale ('Jews' Castle'), also called also by the Karaites in Hebrew *Sela haYehudim* ('Rock of the Jews'), and Eupatoria became the heart of Karaite literary activity. From the Crimea, the Karaites spread to other East European regions and to towns in Lithuania (Troki, near Vilna, Lutsk and Halicz).

At the end of the eighteenth century all the Crimean and Lithuanian Karaite communities were brought under Russian rule. These East European centres were the seat of remarkable halakhic literary productivity in Hebrew (until the first quarter of the twentieth century), to which we shall refer below.

Religious activity in Crimea was promoted by Simha Isaak Ben Moses Lutski, author of *Or haTsadikim* (1830), a history of the Karaites which contains a list of scholars and their works.

E. The Karaite Centre in Israel, 1950 to the Present Day

After the foundation of the State of Israel, the Karaite centre moved to Israel, where the community, consisting mainly of immigrants from Egypt, settled in various locations, especially Ramla. Today it is estimated that there are some 15,000 Karaites in Israel. The community is regarded as falling within the provisions of the Law of Return.

The community enjoys considerable autonomy in religious matters, although it is not recognized as a 'religious community' under the laws of the State of Israel. Marriage and divorce among Karaites in Israel are governed by specific rules and arrangements (see below, pp.261-64).

3. *Relations between Rabbis and Karaites: Intermarriage*

The Karaites, in spite of their separation from and opposition to rabbinic Oral Law and their vehement debate on this with the Rabbis, remained within the bounds of Jewry, for two significant reasons; to wit: they are of Jewish descent[6] and they observe the Written Law in its plain meaning. As Rabbi Samuel Halevi[7] writes:

> Although ... their ancestors were expelled for challenging our tradition and denying it, these Sadducees[8] were not suspected of not observing any of the Commandments written in the *Torah* or those arising out of rabbinical interpretation, which are close to plain meaning and logic, but retained from their forefathers the view that they were of the seed of Jacob and grew up in performance of the Commandments.[9]

In the early years of Karaism, marriage with its adherents was indeed not rendered void[10] by the rabbinic *halakhah*. Later, even the harshly worded prohibition imposed by the *Rema,* Rabbi Moses Isserles (1530-1572, Poland): 'It is forbidden to marry them, all of them are tainted with bastardy and they are not to be accepted when they wish to return'[11] was limited to central Europe. In Egypt, intermarriage with Karaites was generally permitted; at the beginning of the nineteenth century, it was in fact allowed on condition, as it still is in Israel.[12]

4. *Legal Sources of Karaite Halakhah*

A. The Written Text *(Hakatuv)*

In Karaite *halakhah,* Scripture is the sole holy text, and its interpretation has reached a high and complex level of exposition and analogy, as stated by Anan Ben David: 'Search thoroughly in the *Torah* and do not rely on my opinion'. This rule (first quoted by Japhet ben Eli, tenth century, Jerusalem, in his *Commentary on the Book of Zechariah* 5:8), was widely accepted and became, as stated by Karaite scholars over the generations, the basic principle of the rational approach in Karaite *halakhah.*

According to the great codifier of Karaite *halakhah,* Eliyahu Basyatchi (fifteenth century, Constantinople):

> The written word rests on three matters: the written text itself (*hakatuv*); analogy (*hekkesh*); and the Burden of Inheritance (*sevel hayerushah*). (Introduction to *Aderet Eliyahu*).

The 'written text' means the words of the *Torah* in their plain sense (*mishmah*):

> The interpretation of our divine *Torah* rests on its text and not on any external source, unlike the view of the upholders of tradition who maintain that their tradition constitutes an interpretation of our *Torah,* but in fact is at times in conflict with it (*Aderet Eliyahu, Seder Tefilah,* ch.1, p.85b).

The difference between the 'Burden of Inheritance' (the Karaite tradition; see pp.256f., below) and the rabbinic Oral Law, he explains, lies in the fact

> ... that you rely mostly on the Kabbalah ['tradition', i.e. the Oral Law), giving it Divine sanctity, saying that you have heard and received it from God, whilst we have only our holy father's teachings, and their holiness is like that of law books and the writings of our Sages. A rule in our tradition that is shown to be wrong on the basis of the written text, will not be accepted any more for it is not considered as possessing Divine sanctity.

An example of the difference between the rabbinic and Karaite interpretation of the *Torah* is the rabbinical rule:

> No analogy based on similar phrases (*gezerah shavah*) should be propounded

unless it has been adopted by long tradition. (*B. Pes.* 66a, cf. *Rashi, ad loc.*).

In Karaite *halakhah*, the interpretation of *gezerah shavah* (inference from similarity of phrase, one of Rabbi Ishmael's 'thirteen hermeneutical rules by which the *Torah* is expounded') is not subject to any extraneous authority like the rabbinic tradition, and the Sages are given full freedom to expound the *Torah*. As stated by Eliyahu Kazaz (Crimea, second half of nineteenth century):

> The basic principle of Karaism is that there is freedom to expound the words of the *Torah*, and the rulings of the Sages are not in the nature of divine revelation as is the case with Talmudic rules.[13]

The same view was expressed by the Karaite Bet Din headed by Samuel Panpolof in a decision dated 1880[14] that the authority of Basyatchi (*haposek ha'aharon*, 'the Final Codifier') is not final, since 'there is no such final authority among the Karaites':

> Should someone ask, how can what is forbidden by the 'final authority' be permitted, the reply is that there is no final authority in Karaite *halakhah*, since the Written Law is determinative. Therefore we are called Karaites because our *halakhah* is based on and supported by the *Torah*, which we interpret according to its plain meaning; and we don't appeal to any other authority.

An example of this is found in the Karaite interpretation of the biblical text of *Lev.* 18:18: 'And thou shalt not take a woman to her sister, to be a rival to her to uncover her nakedness, beside the other in her lifetime.' According to the mishnaic rule (*M. Yeb.* 4:13), this means that during the lifetime of one's wife a man may not marry her sister, but after her death such marriage is permitted (and even deemed praiseworthy, since only a sister can show the same affection to the orphaned children). The Karaite rule, based on analogy, is different: the husband's marriage to her was considered incestuous — not only during the wife's lifetime but also after her death.[15] The Karaite *halakhah* interprets the above verse as relating to the question of bigamy — 'sister' in *Lev.* 18:18 meaning 'rival wife' and not wife's sister. In other words, the Karaites allow polygamy if it does not interfere with the husband's duties to his first wife (*Keter Torah*, on *Leviticus, ibid.*)

In the second half of the nineteenth century, however, after much controversy among the Karaite Sages, Samuel Panpolof decided to interpret the verse in its plain sense and to permit a widower to marry his deceased wife's sister (see *Iggeret Nidhe Shemuel,* p.181) and the General Convention of Karaite Scholars (Eupatoria, Crimea, 1910 — known as 'The Last

Synod') favoured the latter decision by issuing a new regulation.[16]

B. Analogy *(Hekkesh)*

Analogy *(hekkesh)* is a complementary source to the interpretation of the written text, which may yield answers to questions which are not clearly dealt with in the *Torah*.

Karaite *halakhah* includes Rabbi Ishmael's thirteen hermeneutical rules, such as argument *a fortiori* (*kal vahomer*, inferences from major to minor). To these it adds various forms of analogy, a detailed account of which is to be found in *Eshkol Hakofer*, sections 168-173, enumerating eighty rules.[17]

C. The Burden of Inheritance *(Ṣevel Hayerushah)*

The third legal source is the Burden of Inheritance (*ṣevel hayerushah*). In the words of Basyatchi:

> There are indeed other precepts on which we have been nurtured since the time of our ancestors ... They are not written in the *Torah*, but have become as part of nature ... and these are termed by the Sages 'the Burden of Inheritance'. (*Aderet Eliyahu*, Introduction)

Ṣevel hayerushah is thus ancestral tradition handed down through the generations; it is also known as *ha'atakah hamishtaleshet*. Large parts of Karaite *halakhah*, such as the laws of ritual slaughtering, circumcision, divorce, the form of the *get* and other matters, are based on this legal source.

Karaite tradition and custom are also referred to among the early Karaites as *edah* or *kibbuts* ('community'), corresponding to the term *ijma* in Islamic Law, i.e. the 'consensus of the community'. As to the relationship between *ha'atakah* or *ṣevel hayerushah* and *edah*, scholars are divided in their opinions. It is clear, however, that at least from the middle of the twelfth century these concepts were unified. As Hadassi says: '*edah* and *ṣevel*, *kabbalah* and *ha'atakah*, all these four terms have one and the same content' (*Eshkol hakofer*, section 169).

The term *ṣevel* corresponds to the term *nakl* in Islamic Law, which means tradition (Kirkisani, *ibid*, p.730). Gotlober[18] explains that 'the Karaites use the root *ṣaval* (to suffer, to bear) in the context of succession, so that heirs are referred to as *ṣovlim*, hence the meaning of *ṣevel hayerushah*, 'the handing down of inheritance'. Zvi Ankori, an Israeli historian, on the other hand, explains the term as parallel to "yoke of the *mitsvot*".[19]

Furthermore, in the words of Basyatchi:

> This handing down (*ha'atakah*) is unlike the rabbinical tradition (*kabbalah*),

since they add to, and remove from, the written text ... whereas the text requires that 'ye shall not add to the word which I command you.' Our Sages have declared that every tradition that does not contradict the written text and does not add thereto and that all Israel acknowledges and that has support in the text is that which is handed down (ha'atakah) and we accept it (Aderet Eliyahu, introduction).[20]

On this legal source we may also quote one of the last great Karaite authorities, Samuel ben Shmaria Pigit (Crimea, second half of nineteenth century), who says:

I will admit further that our Burden of Inheritance is like your Oral *Torah*. Like you (the Rabbis), we also cannot exist without the traditions of our forefathers; no religion or believer, anywhere in the world, would have any standing without the heritage of the forebearers, the ancient traditions and deeds of the predecessors to guide them in the future. (*Hamelitz* XV (1879), 516).

The most famous example of development and change in Karaite *halakhah* is the candle-lighting on Friday evenings, which was forbidden from ancient times (see e.g. *Eshkol haKofer*, section 146), respecting a tradition based on the interpretation of the written text: 'Ye shall kindle no fire throughout your habitations upon the Sabbath day' (*Ex.* 35:3). Basyatchi taught otherwise, and permitted the lighting of candles on Friday evenings (*Aderet Eliyahu, Shabbat*, ch.17-20). His permission was based on a different interpretation of the verses in the Bible; it put an end to the earlier tradition and abolished the prohibition in its entirety.

4. *Other Legal Sources*

Through the centuries, Karaite *halakhah* has known additional legal sources, some of which are controversial amongst Karaite scholars themselves. The scholar Judah Hadassi (*Eshkol Hakofer*, section 168) enumerates in the name of Sahl ben Mazliah (tenth century, Jerusalem) the legal sources of Karaite *halakhah* under four headings: knowledge based on human reason (*hokhmat hada'at*); the plain meaning of the text (*mishmah*); analogy (*hekkesh*); and consensus of the community (*edah*).

Plain meaning, analogy and *edah* (tradition) are the general basic principles in Basyatchi's view, as detailed above, whereas 'knowledge based on human reason', corresponding to 'legal logic' (*sevarah*) in rabbinic *halakhah*, was not accepted by some Karaite scholars and is therefore not included in Basyatchi's dictum.

Human reason as a source of Law and the rationalistic tendency were developed over the centuries and the Hakham Eliyahu Kazaz states explicitly that the halakhic innovations of the Karaites are 'based on common sense and principles of equity',[21] i.e. on a rational approach. For example, Kazaz states that 'the giving of a *get* was restricted by settled rules based on common sense and principles of equity.'[22]

In rabbinic *halakhah*, on the other hand, primary legislation (the Written Law) may not be added to, nor diminished, since it persists in its original formulation. If, however, an addition or diminution appertains to secondary legislation and affirms clearly the original prohibition or permission and states explicitly that it is not intended to change it, but rather to exercise the authority conferred on the Sages by the *Torah*, then the secondary legislation is valid, as it does not purport to be other than it is.[23]

The Hakham Aaron ben Eliyahu 'the latter' regards the question of enacting regulations as central to the dispute between Karaite and rabbinic *halakhah*. He holds that according to the prohibition 'Ye shall not add unto the word which I command you neither shall ye diminish from it' (*Deut.* 4:2 and 13:1), the Sages have no authority to add or remove from the *Torah* even by way of secondary legislation. The text is addressed to all and should be interpreted in its plain meaning (Introduction to *Keter Torah*, p.2a).

Such subordinate legislation is, however, an existing fact in Karaite *halakhah*, at least since the fifteenth century, and Basyatchi happens to recognize its validity:

> Anyone who lays down rules for the public order so as to strengthen religion is not considered to be adding to the *Torah*. The one who adds is the one who declares that God spoke when God did not speak. (*Aderet Eliyahu, Seder Tefilah*, p.3a).[24]

5. *The Development of Divorce in Karaite Halakhah*

Karaite *halakhah* has evolved a number of significant innovations on the status of the wife in divorce law.

In its literal meaning *Deut.* 24:1 ('if she finds no favour in his eyes because he found in her some unseemly thing — *ervat davar*') refers only to the right of the husband to divorce; nevertheless, it prompts also the question of the wife's right to divorce.

Anan ben David (*Book of Precepts, Dine Nashim*, section 56) states simply: 'He shall divorce her if he does not want her or she does not want him', i.e. divorce at the will of either one of the spouses will suffice. An even more radical deviatory innovation is found in the view of the sect of

Abu Isa Al-Isfahini (Persia, eighth century), which assimilated the position of the wife to that of the husband in the reverse direction, prohibiting divorce of the wife even where the husband found in her 'some unseemly thing'. Kirkisani criticizes the sects that hold this view ('the Sadducees, the Christians and the Isunians'), since it contradicts the explicit text.[25]

Anan's innovation, involving as it does a deviation from the text, should not surprise us. Ben Sasson has already shown[26] that the first two leaders of the Karaites (Anan and Benyamin Nahawandi) were not Karaites, in the sense of not being confined to the wording of the text.

Anan's analogy is also the basis of the tendency in Karaite *halakhah* towards equality in the status of husband and wife as far as divorce laws are concerned. It was, however, rejected by Benjamin Nahawandi, who held the view that there was no authority in the *Torah* for divorce at the suit of the wife, except in two cases: the first, where she is deprived of 'food, raiment or matrimonial duty' (according to *Ex.* 21:10-11); the second, where a serious physical blemish in the husband existed before the marriage but only became apparent thereafter.

To coerce the husband to give a *get* is first mentioned in the writings of Nahawandi, but he cites no source. The Karaite codifiers derive this by analogy from the case of the raped woman (*Deut.* 22:28-29: '... she shall be his wife ...'): 'Just as he may be forced to marry against his will, so may he be forced to divorce.'[27]

When the means of coercion at the disposal of the *Bet Din* were of no avail, the Karaite authorities of the tenth century differed in their views. Some thought that the only alternative was to exhaust all possible existing methods of coercion, whereas others took the view that it was possible to effect divorce by judicial decree without the formal necessity of a *get*. There is no explanation in the sources available to us for this latter process, which is in contradiction to biblical prescription. One may assume the judgment of the *Bet Din* serves as a proper bill of divorce in a suit for divorce by the wife, whereas the written text deals only with the case of divorce at the instance of the husband. The debate was settled in the eleventh century in favour of the view that there could be no divorce without a *get* (*Book of Precepts* of Levi ben Japheth) apart from certain instances, such as that of an apostate who is considered dead (The Book of Precepts, *Gan Eden*) and his marriage is thus automatically dissolved. In such cases it was settled that all means of coercion, including resort to non- Jewish authorities, should be used.

Another dispute among the early Karaite authorities related to the interpretation of the verse 'And it shall come to pass that if she find no favour in his eyes, because he found in her some unseemly thing' (*Deut.* 24:1). As against the interpretation of Anan, the emphasis here is on the will of the husband, the majority of later Karaite authorities took the view that divorce by the will of the husband could take place only where there existed 'some unseemly thing'. 'Unseemly thing' constituted two categories: a defect relating to matters of the world to come (*mum bedivre ha'olam habah*, i.e. conduct in transgressions of the Commandments), and a defect relating to matters of this world (*mum bedivre ha'olam hazeh*, i.e. physical defects and defects of behaviour). These terms correspond, generally, to the talmudic *overet al dat Mosheh* (she who transgresses the Law of Moses) and *overet al dat yehudit* (she who transgresses the Jewish religion).[28] The two categories of defects were included in the Karaite codes (*Gan Eden* and *Aderet Eliyahu*) under the concept of 'an unseemly thing'. Following this interpretation, it was also codified that there was to be no divorce except by a *Bet Din*, which would decide on objective criteria whether there existed 'an unseemly thing' or 'an intolerable defect' (*Aderet Eliyahu*).

A significant development of the institution of divorce at suit of the wife took place when Basyatchi succeeded in adapting the status of the wife to that of the husband, based on the analogy of Anan mentioned above. Basyatchi argues: 'Just as the husband may divorce her for some unseemly thing, so may the wife compel her husband by order of a *Bet Din* to divorce her because of some unseemly thing' (*Aderet Elyahu, Nashim*, ch.12).

As for coercion of the husband, it was decided, as noted above, that in every case where the *Bet Din* decides that the husband has 'some unseemly thing' about him, he may be forced to give a *get*. Thus in Karaite *halakhah* no difference existed between the grounds for requiring a *get* and the grounds for imposing a *get* by force. Coercing a *get* was indeed effected in practice, and at times the Karaite *bate din* in Constantinople and elsewhere were aided by the non-Jewish authorities.

At the end of the eighteenth century, however, when the Crimean Peninsula was brought under Russian rule, the problem of divorce of a husband refusing to obey the decree of the *Bet Din* arose once again since, owing to the non-existence of divorce under Russian Law at that time, the Russian authorities refrained from assisting in the enforcement of divorce decrees. One of the greatest of Karaite authorities at the beginning of the nineteenth century, Isaac ben Shlomo of Kale, was active in finding a solution to this problem. Relying on the view which permits divorce by judicial decree, he laid down that a *Bet Din* might effect divorce by a *get* delivered by the *Bet Din* itself. This regulation, which at first aroused considerable controversy among Karaite scholars, was accepted by all Karaite communities in the Crimea and was even subsequently extended to cover all grounds for divorce. Some authorities introduced the system of divorce by judicial decree without a *get* at all.

This practice was later adopted by the Karaite community in Egypt, where divorce by judicial decree was preferred to that of coercion (*Sefer HaMa'amad Ha'Ishi* by Murad 'Beck' Faraj). The Karaite community in Israel also adopts the same system in practice, by delivery of the *get* to the wife through the *Bet Din* (see section 6 below).

A further innovation is represented by the divorce by judicial decree, which was rejected by Karaite authorities until a regulation permitting it was enacted by Isaac Ben Shlomo (early nineteenth century, Crimea). This regulation followed a case which came before the Karaite *Bet Din* at Kale. Isaac ben Shlomo was not deterred by traditional opposition to the idea of divorce by judicial decree. In order to add validity to the regulation, he sought and gained the support of the Karaite Scholars of the Crimea and of Constantinople, and this practice is prevalent to this day among the Karaite community in Israel.

Kazaz sums up the innovations made by Karaite *halakhah* in matters of divorce in the following basic rules:

(a) Prohibition of divorce by the husband without a judicial decree given on the basis of some legally recognized ground for divorce;

(b) Equalization of the status of the wife, who is entitled to divorce on the same grounds available to the husband;

(c) Divorce by *get* through the *Bet Din* in the event of the husband's refusal to give a *get* to the wife.

From the Crimea, the custom of divorce by judicial decree spread to the Karaite community in Cairo. Murad 'Beck' Faraj stated:

> The decree of the *Bet Din* can take the place of a *get* where necessary (*Sefer haMa'amad ha'Ishi*, section 350); Where the husband is obliged by law to divorce his wife or if the wife has the right to a *get* but he refrains from delivering it, the *Bet Din* shall deliver the decree to the wife in place of a *get* (ibid., section 311).

6. *Divorce by Judicial Decree in the Karaite Jewish Community in Israel*

The Karaite Jewish community in Israel, in practice, uses the method of divorce by judicial decree. This is evident from the divorce decree in the *Marzuk* case issued by the *Bet Din* of the Karaite community in Israel in

1964-65.[29] Divorce by a wife was sought from the court on a plea that:

> ... the husband beat his wife mercilessly so as to force her to have marital
> relations with him on the night of the Sabbath, to have unnatural relations
> with him, and to sleep with him even during her period of menstruation.

The decree states that:

> It was proved by his admission that he wished to have marital relations with
> her during her menstrual period and on the Sabbath, and it makes no
> difference that there was no more than an attempt to do so.

The *Bet Din* held that such acts constitute legal grounds for divorce.
Concerning marital relations during the menstrual period, it held that:

> This is strictly forbidden by our holy *Torah*, as is written: 'And if a man shall
> lie with a woman having her sickness, and shall uncover her nakedness, he
> hath made naked her fountain; and she hath uncovered the fountain of her
> blood and both of them shall be cut off from among their people.' (*Lev.*
> 20:18).

Regarding marital relations on the Sabbath, the Karaite *Bet Din* continued:

> As far as relations on the Sabbath are concerned, which we call intercourse,
> while our rabbinic brethren refer to it as *oneg Shabbat* ('a sabbatical
> pleasure'), it is written in the *Torah*: 'Remember the Sabbath day to keep it
> holy' (*Ex.* 20:8); indeed, the sanctity of the Sabbath is mentioned numerous
> times in the *Torah*. It is also written of the woman with whom a man shall lie
> with flow of seed, that 'they shall both ... be unclean until the even' (*Lev.*
> 15:18). Can uncleanliness be identical with holiness? They are after all
> opposing concepts which cannot coincide.[30] It is written 'And thou shalt
> honour it, not doing thy wonted ways' (*Is.* 58:13), meaning that their ways
> include acts which bring about *tum'ah* (defilement), and use things forbidden
> on the Sabbath. This is an activity from which one becomes weary and tired
> and one perspires; and excretion from the man is transferred to the woman,
> resulting in defilement. Why (after all) did the Holy One, blessed be He,
> command Moses our teacher of blessed memory, 'And the Lord said unto
> Moses go unto the people and sanctify them today and tomorrow, and let
> them wash their garments' (*Ex.* 19:10), and again 'And God said ... Be ready
> against the third day, come not near a woman' (*Ex.* 19:15).'

The *Bet Din* accordingly ruled that 'on the basis of these two charges the
husband was obliged to give his wife a *get* , since just as the husband can
divorce his wife for an unseemly thing, so can the wife.' But the husband
refused to obey the decree and after a further warning the *Bet Din* reconvened
to consider execution of its judgment. It held:

> The Religious Council determined finally in accordance with our *halakhah*
> that just as the husband may divorce for an unseemly thing so may the
> woman compel her husband through the *Bet Din* to separate them for an

unseemly thing. And just as the wife may be divorced voluntarily or against her will, so the husband divorces voluntarily or against his will.

In this case, the *Bet Din* ruled that the husband must appear before it and deliver a *get* to his wife, but that it has no power to compel him to do so.

> It is apparent that his desire is to subdue her or to leave her an *agunah* indefinitely. This contradicts justice and fairness as required by the *Torah*. Hence, the *Bet Din* has assumed jurisdiction under our *halakhah* and acted as quoted in *Aderet Eliyahu*, otherwise known as the Book of Precepts of Rabbi Eliyahu Basyatchi, *Ṣeder Nashim*, ch.12. The *Bet Din* itself handed her a bill of divorce, received from her the marriage contract, and cancelled it.

Divorce was thus effected by a *get*, made and written by order of the Karaite Tribunal, against the husband's wishes and in his absence.

It may be noted that here the *Bet Din* based itself on the Book of Precepts, *Aderet Eliyahu*. But, as mentioned above (p.260), the author of that work rules that the husband must be coerced into giving a *get* and that a judicial decree cannot take the place of delivery of the *get* by the husband. Possibly the *Bet Din* adopted the view of Abraham ben Joseph Shlomo Lutzki,[31] namely that the ruling in the *Aderet* relates to a situation where it is possible to coerce the husband to give a *get* by some means or other, as through the non-Jewish authorities, whereas in the case under discussion, as stated in the judgment 'the *Bet Din* has no power of coercing him.'

Accordingly 'it resorted to the method of executing the divorce decree pursuant to the regulation of Isaac ben Shlomo' (although this regulation is not mentioned in the judgment) and according to that which is written in *Ṣefer HaMa'amad Ha'Ishi* of Murad 'Beck' Faraj, i.e., by means of writing a *get* and handing it to the wife through the *Bet Din* itself against the husband's will and in his absence. From the wording of the judgment, however, 'the *Bet Din* has no power of coercing him', one may conclude that the Karaite *Bet Din* was of the opinion that where it can compel the husband to give the *get*, that course is preferable, as laid down in the book *Aderet Eliyahu*, and did not accept the view of Murad 'Beck' Faraj that in the case of an obdurate husband it is not fitting to resort to coercion but the wife can be released from the husband by means of judicial decree.

The Karaite *Bet Din* completed its work in the *Marzuk* case by issuing a certificate of divorce on an official form supplied by the Ministry for Religious Affairs under the Marriage and Divorce (Registration) Ordinance.[32] The husband, who opposed the divorce, applied to the High Court of Justice and petitioned for annulment of the divorce certificate. The petition led to a declaration by the State authorities (the Ministry for Religious Affairs and the Ministry of the Interior) that there was no legal effect to the judgment nor to the certificate of divorce issued by the Karaite *Bet Din*.[33]

7. *Personal Status of the Karaites in Israel*

The basis for the declaration in the *Marzuk* case lay in the fact that the Karaite community was never recognized as a 'religious community'[34] as defined by the Palestine Order in Council, 1922-1947[35] or the Religious Communities Ordinance 1926.[36] Under the laws of the State the Karaite *Bet Din* thus has no jurisdiction over matters of personal status of members of that community.

In 1967, this legal situation was confirmed by a Committee set up under the chairmanship of the former Deputy President of the Supreme Court, Justice Moshe Silberg, to examine the personal status of the Karaites. In its conclusions the Committee stated, inter alia:

> One thing is clear and indisputable. The present situation cannot possibly be allowed to continue, neither in the long nor in the short term. It is intolerable that a large group of persons ... should live without any legal regulation of their personal status, their marriages not being marriages and their divorces not being divorces, there being no one authorized to consider and decide their disputes in matters of family law.[37]

However, the Chief Rabbi of the Karaites in Israel is recognized as a competent 'registering authority' under the Marriage and Divorce (Registration) Ordinance of 1919,[38] for the purpose of registration of marriages between members of the community. Therefore, marriages celebrated in Israel according to the rite of the Karaites are duly registered in the population registry.

As to divorce, in 1976, in the case of *Sihu* v. *Tribunal of the Karaite Community*, the Supreme Court held that:

> The Karaite *Bet Din* functions without any legal basis, and its deliberations and decisions therefore have no legal effect ... There is no mention of such a *Bet Din* in the legislation, enacted since the State was established or beforehand. The Karaite community living in Israel was never recognized as a religious community under the Palestine Order in Council.[39]

But in practice, although the Karaite religious Tribunal has no legal standing, divorce judgments passed in this tribunal with the consent of both spouses are accepted *de facto* and registered by the State.

The Silberg Committee gave an additional reason for the lack of legal effect of a divorce pronounced by the Karaite *Bet Din*, namely, that the Karaites, being a part of the Jewish people, are subject to the Rabbinical Courts Jurisdiction (Marriage and Divorce) Law, 5713-1953, since 'Jews' in that statute 'also includes Karaite Jews'.[40] Consequently:

It is clear that since 1953 (when the Rabbinical Courts Jurisdiction Law came into effect), no Jew, including a Karaite Jew, can perform a marriage or a divorce which will be recognized as valid under the laws of the State, except in conformity with the rabbinic *halakhah*.

A different view was expressed by Justice Landau D.P., in the *Sihu* case. His view was that the Rabbinical Courts Jurisdiction Law does not apply to Karaites, since

... at the time the Statute was enacted (in 1953) there were hardly any Karaites in Israel, and no one at that time had in mind the Karaite practices of marriage and divorce.

Justice Landau D.P. posed the question whether the legislator would have

... imposed rabbinical jurisdiction upon the Karaites against their will and in contradiction to their religious beliefs even though the rabbinic *halakhah* applied by the Rabbinical Tribunal regards all Karaites as potential *mamzerim* [bastards, in the strict sense: a child born to a married woman not fathered by her husband] and disqualifies them as witnesses.

He answers the question in the negative, since, in view of the Karaites' utter denial of the validity of the Oral Law,

... their subjection to rabbinical jurisdiction against their will ... involves a high degree of religious coercion, much more serious than that involved in imposing the jurisdiction of the Rabbinical court on a non-believing Jew of rabbinic origin.

Justice Kahan did not support either of these two conflicting views, but preferred to leave the question, which was in any case an *obiter dictum*, to be decided on some other occasion. The question whether the Rabbinical Courts Jurisdiction Law, 5713-1953, does or does not apply to the Karaites, has been settled, following Justice Landau's opinion in the *Sihu* case, in H.C. *Haine and Karaite Jewry* v. *The Rabbinical Supreme Court* (16.2.95). The Supreme Court of Israel decided, relying on a statement of the rabbinical courts presented to the High Court, that the rabbinical courts have no jurisdiction in matters of marriage and divorce of Karaite Jews, unless the respective couples accept the rabbinical courts' jurisdiction.

8. *Bibliography*

Ankori, Z., *Karaites in Byzantium* (New York: Columbia University Press, 1959, 2nd ed. AMS Press, 1968).

Baron, S.W., *A Social and Religious History of the Jews* (New York: Random House, 1956), vol. V, pp. 209-85 and Index, s.v. Karaites.

Birnbaum, P., ed., *Karaite Studies* (New York: Hermon, 1971).

Corinaldi, M., *The Personal Status of the Karaites* (Jerusalem: Rubin Mass, 1984), Hebrew.

Elgamil, J., *History of the Karaite Jews* (Ramla, 1979-1985, 3 vols.), Hebrew.

Mann, J., *Texts and Studies* (Cincinnati: Hebrew Union College, 1931), vol. II (Karaitica)

Nemoy, L.A., *A Karaite Anthology* (New-Haven and London: Yale University Press, 1952, Yale Judaica Series, VII).

Poznanski, S., *The Karaite Literary Opponents of R. Sa'adiah Gaon* (London: Luzac, 1908).

Schur, N., *History of the Karaites* (Frankfurt-am-Main: Peter Lang, 1992).

Szyszman, S., *Le Karaïsme* (Lausanne: Lage D'Home, 1980).

Trevisan Semi, E., *Ebrei Caraiti tra Etnia e Religione* (Roma: Caruccci, 1984).

Notes

1   A.A. Harkavy, ed. *Zikhron LaRishonim* XIII (1903), St Petersburg.

2   First published by A. Firkovitch as an appendix to the book *Mivhar Yesharim*, Gozlov, 1832.

3   Ed. I. Markon, 1948, 1957.

4   ed. L. Nemoy (New York: 1939-1943), 5 volumes (Arabic, ed. and Eng. tr. by L. Nemoy); *idem*, 'Al Kirksani's Account of Jewish Sects and Christianity', *Hebrew Union College Annual* 8 (1930), 317-97.

5   The designation 'the latter' was to distinguish him from Aaron b. Joseph 'the first' (13th century), author of *Sefer haMivhar* (Gozlov, 1832), a classic Karaite commentary on the Bible.

6   Maimonides, *Mamrim* III, 3; *Resp. Maimonides* (ed. Blau), II, 449 ; *Resp. Radbaz* IV, 219.

7   R. Samuel b. Moses Ibn Hakim Halevi (end of 15th and beginning of 16th century, active in Cairo and Constantinople: see *Enc. Jud.* VII, 1151).

8   In the language of Rabbinic literature, since for Maimonides 'Sadducees' indicates Karaites: Maimonides, Commentary to *Mishnah Avot* I:3.

9   See R. Samuel Halevi's pamphlet, published in M. Corinaldi, *The Personal Status of the Karaites* (Jerusalem: Rubin Mass, 1984), 178, 202 (in Hebrew).

10 S. Assaf, *Be'ohole Ya'aḳov* (1943, in Hebrew) 182 and more extensively Corinaldi, *supra* n.9, at 103.

11 Rema, *Shulḥan Arukh, Even ha'Ezer* 4:37.

12 Corinaldi, *supra* n.9, at 122ff. and 136ff.

13 See his lecture to the Académie Française, published in *Hashiloaḥ* XLII (1904), 13ff.

14 Cited in Samuel b. Shemria Pigit, *Iggeret Nidḥe Shemuel* (St. Petersbourg, 1894), 181.

15 *Levush Malkut* [by R. Mordechai Jaffe, first half 17th century and early 18th century, Kokizov = Krasne Ostrow], 44.

16 See *Ṣefer hama'amad ha'Ishi* [*The Book of Personal Status*] by Murad 'Beck' Faraj, Cairo, first half of the 19th century, section 104, p.20.

17 See Kirkisani, *Kitab al-Anwar*, vol. III, Discourse 6, ch.72, Nemoy ed., p.114.

18 A.B. Gotlober (1810, Staro-Konstantinov (Volhinia)-Bialystock, 1899); Hebrew and Yiddish Writer, author of a critical history of the Karaites, *Biḳoret leToldot HaḲaraim* (1865, in Hebrew). Quotation from p.216.

19 *Karaites in Byzantium* (New York: Columbia University Press, 1959), 231 n. 50. Ḥayyim Hillel Ben Sasson (Israeli historian, 1914-1977) refers to the term as one of abuse by Karaite *halakhah* of the Oral Law: 'the burden of inheritance which cannot be endured any more': *History of the Jewish People* (Tel-Aviv: Dvir, 1969, Heb.), vol.2, p.71. This view is surprising and does not conform with the significance of the handing down of inheritance as part of the legal sources of Karaite *halakhah*.

20 See also Caleb Ben Eliyahu Afendopolo (Constantinople, 1464-1530) in concluding remarks to the book *Patshegen Ktav Hadath* (Ramla: Karaite Jews, 1977), 138.

21 *HaShiloaḥ* XLII (1904), 13.

22 Kazaz in *HaShiloaḥ, supra* n.21.

23 See e.g. Maimonides, *Mamrim* II:9: cf. M. Elon, *Jewish Law: History, Sources, Principles*, trld. B. Auerbach and M.J. Sykes (Philadelphia and Jerusalem: Jewish Publication Society, 1994), vol. II, pp. 496ff. and sources there cited.

24 For various examples of subordinate legislation, see Z. Ankori, 'The House of Basyatchi and their Regulations', in his Introduction to a new Karaite edition of *Aderet Eliyahu*, published in Israel in 1966; the Introduction by Nahamu ben Shlomo Babovich (Crimea, 19th century) to the book by Isaac ben Shlomo (19th century, Chufut-Kale), *Or haLevana* (Zhitani, 1872); and the latest regulations on prohibited degrees of marriage, promulgated at a general convention of Karaite scholars in 1910 at Eupatoria in the Crimea.

25 Kirkasani, *Al-Anwar*, vol. I, Discourse 1, ch.6.

26 'The Early Karaites — Outlines of their Social Theory', *Zion* XV (1950), 42, 54 (Heb.).

27 *Gan Eden, Nashim*, ch.24, p.155b.

28 Cf. *M. Ket*. 7:6.

29 For an outline of the various stages in this case, see H.C. 35/70, *Marzuk* v. *Minister of Religions and Others* (1970) 24 P.D.(2) 628. On the Karaite community's institutions in Israel see Josef b. Ovadia Elgamil, *Toldot haYahadut haKarait* (Ramla, 1979), I, 205ff. (in Hebrew).

30 Prohibition of intercourse on the Sabbath under Karaite *halakhah* originates in the Book of Precepts of Anan, who derived it from the verse 'six days thou shalt work, but on the seventh day thou shalt rest, in ploughing time and in harvest thou shalt rest' (*Ex*. 34:21), interpreting 'ploughing' as marital intercourse. This explanation of Anan is quoted by Ibn Ezra, *Exodus, loc. cit.*, and rejected by him sarcastically. See also *Eshkol hakofer*, Sections 147, 179-180; *Sefer Hamitsvot, Mitsvat Mosheh*, by Mosheh Bagi, Section *Mas'at Moshe*, Question 16, section 'Way of Death' and 'Way of Life'. (This part of the book was printed as an appendix to the book *Pinat Yikrat* of Isaac ben Shlomo, Gozlov, 1834 and 1840.) Karaite *halakhah* severely criticises Rabbanite *halakhah* which considers intercourse on the Shabbat as *oneg shabbat* (Sabbath pleasure). See *B. Ket*. 62b and Maimonides, *Shab*. 30:14.

31 Karaite scholar at Gozlov (1792-1855), known as Aben Yashar. On Lutzki's explanation, see *Iggeret zug venifrad*, Gozlov [1837], 3c.

32 Drayton, *Laws of Palestine*, vol. II, p. 903.

33 H.C. 362/65, *Marzuk* v. *Minister of Religions and others* (the matter was settled without judgment being given, in view of the declaration on the part of the State authorities.

34 The Karaite community is not included in the Mandatory list of recognized 'religious communities' in the Second Schedule to the Palestine Order in Council, 1922-1947, which was added by the Palestine (Amendment) Order in Council 1939 (Palestine Gazette 898 Suppl. 2, p.459), nor was it added by the Israeli legislator. Only the tribunals of such Religious Communities were given jurisdiction in matters of personal status of members of their communities, under Article 51 of the Order in Council 1922-1947. However, under Ottoman rule, in the period before the British Mandate, '[T]he Karaites were separately recognized by the Ottoman Government': G. Young, *Corps de Droit Ottoman* (Oxford: Clarendon Press, 1905), 142. See also A. Galante, *Histoire des Juifs d'Istanbul* (Istanbul: Tyt Husnutabiat, 1941], II, 180 and Corinaldi, *Karaites, supra* n.19, at 143ff. and references therein.

35 Drayton, *Laws of Palestine*, vol. III, p.2569.

36 Drayton, *Laws of Palestine*, vol. II, p.1292.

37 See the report of the Silberg Committee (1967) printed in Corinaldi, *Karaites, supra* n.9, at 226, 239. As a solution to this impasse, the Commi-

ttee recommended enacting a Karaite Tribunals Jurisdiction (Marriage and Divorce) Law, in the form proposed by the Committee. Following these recommendations, the draft Karaite Jews Courts Jurisdiction (Marriage and Divorce) Law, 5731-1971 (*Hatsaot Hok* [Bills of the State of Israel] 923, 5731-1972, p.101) was passed on first reading in the Seventh Knesset (1971), but was voted down in the Eighth Knesset (to which the bill was transferred under the Bill (Continuity of Deliberations) Law, 5724-1964). For comments on this draft law, see M. Corinaldi, 'Draft Karaite Jews Tribunals Jurisdiction law', *Mishpatim* III (1971), 407-13 (Heb.).

38 Drayton, *Laws of Palestine*, vol. II, p.903. See H.C. 35/70, *Marzuk* v. *Minister of Religions and Others*, P.D. vol. 24 (2) 628, 633.

39 H.C. 30/76, (1976) 31 P.D. vol. 31(1), pp.13, 17 *per* Justice Landau D.P.; see also B. Bracha, 'Personal Status of Persons Belonging to a non-Recognized Religious Community', *Israel Yearbook of Human Rights* 5 (1975), 88ff. at 115.

40 This section of the opinion is mentioned in the *Marzuk* case, and see A.C. 450/70, *Rogozinski* v. *State of Israel* (1960) 26(1) 129, 134; A. H Shaki, *Who is a Jew under the Laws of the State of Israel* (Jerusalem, 1977-1978), II, 333 (Heb.). However Justice Shereshewsky disagreed with Justice Landau. He was of the opinion that the 'term Jew in the Rabbinical Courts Jurisdiction Law, 5737-1953, covers everyone who is a Jew, and there is thus no room to distinguish between those who observe the law of the Torah, i.e. the written law and the Oral Law, and those who consider only the written law as binding upon them (i.e. the Karaites).' In view of the clear wording of the statute, in his opinion, the question whether Knesset members did or did not take the Karaites into account when voting for the provision was irrelevant.

10

JEWISH LAW IN SPAIN
AND THE HALAKHIC ACTIVITY
OF ITS SCHOLARS BEFORE 1300

by

ELIAV SHOCHETMAN

Hebrew University of Jerusalem

1. *Introduction*

The focus of this chapter is the status and condition of Jewish Law in Spain prior to 1300, and the general contribution of Spanish authorities to halakhic development. At the start of this period, the greater part of Spain was held by the Moslems who conquered the Iberian peninsula in the eighth century C.E. At the beginning of the eleventh century, however, there was a weakening in the Moslem control of Spain, and conditions allowing the Christian princedoms of Spain to expand and conquer land were created. This process reached its peak at the time of the first Reconquista (1212-1260). The conquests of the Almohads (1146) — Moslem extremists who arrived from North Africa — caused a large scale migration of Jews to the Christian north. The increase of the Jewish population in the Christian part of Spain was also fuelled by the interests of Christian potentates in the settlement of the Jews in their areas. This period in Jewish history is recognized as the Golden Age of Spain.

Some of the scholars discussed below spent their entire lives in Spain; others, e.g. Maimonides (known by his acronym, *Rambam*, from Rabbi Moses ben Maimon), were born there but lived elsewhere; whilst yet others, e.g. *Rif* (R. Isaac Alfasi: see p.287, below), immigrated to Spain from other countries. In terms of their halakhic activity, however, they all belong to the Spanish school. The earliest extant Spanish halakhic material dates from the early eleventh century, hence, the starting point for this chapter is some 300 years before the year 1300.

2. *Historical and Juridical Background: The Judicial Autonomy of Spanish Jewry*

Throughout the period of exile and dispersion, Jewish communities strove to obtain judicial autonomy in the countries in which they lived. Such autonomy enabled them to survive as national entities and not merely as religious sects. The grant of judicial autonomy was, therefore, of inestimable value in preserving the national character of Diaspora Jewry.

The scope of the judicial autonomy granted to a medieval Jewish community varied from place to place and could change over time. The significant feature of the classical period of halakhic development in Spain was the wide scope of judicial autonomy enjoyed by its Jewish communities throughout the period. The extent to which legal systems develop and grow depends largely upon their practical relevance, and in the period dealt with in the present chapter, Jewish courts (under the separate charters accorded to the various communities) enjoyed a large measure of autonomy (sometimes even in criminal law). Judicial autonomy also possesses an internal aspect: it is noteworthy that in this period the prohibition on recourse to non-Jewish courts was strictly enforced, and the disciplinary measures taken against those who ignored this prohibition ensured that breaches only occurred in the rarest of circumstances.

The wide judicial autonomy enjoyed by the Jews of Christian Spain was a continuation of the policy of the Muslims during their domination of the Iberian peninsula. The Muslim Government of Spain had adopted a relatively tolerant attitude towards the members of other faiths, and Jews and Christians alike benefited from privileges which they were not granted elsewhere in the Muslim world. Requests by Muslim theologians to the Spanish administration to apply the discriminatory laws of Omar (laws establishing the status of Jews and Christians as second class citizens in Moslem countries, attributed to the second Khalif Omar, 634-644, but probably only formulated by Omar of the house of Ummayah, 717-720, and reformulated by later rulers) were ignored, and non-believers were permitted to work in the Government service and to build their houses of worship. The leaders of the Jewish and Christian communities bore the sole responsibility for their civil administration, and they reported directly to the central Government.

A unique feature of Jewish judicial autonomy in Spain was the authority to mete out capital punishment, which was not possessed by Jewish communities in other parts of the Muslim world. This authority, which was used in order to punish heretics and informers, was preserved under Christian rule, but was then made subject to the approval of the non-Jewish authorities, who, generally speaking, also carried out the actual death sentence. The first Christian reconquest of Spain began at the end of the eleventh century, and for purely political and economic reasons, it was expedient for the Christians to befriend the Jews, and to use their talents in the areas of administration, diplomacy and finance. The wide judicial autonomy of the Jewish community under Muslim rule was, therefore, preserved throughout the first Christian reconquest.

It has been argued that the scholarly class at this time was not a large one, and hence that the judges in the Jewish courts in Spain were not always experts in the law. Echoes of this state of affairs are found in a responsum of R. Joseph ibn Migash, in which the following observation is made:

> Nowadays, many people have appointed themselves as legal authorities, but the majority lack both a profound understanding of the *halakhah*, and any expertise in the legal opinions of the Geonim ... certainly, there are none who are on the level of being able to rule on halakhic matters directly from the *Talmud*. (*Responsa Ri Migash* no.114)

It is difficult to ascertain the extent to which this responsum reflects the general standard of the Spanish Jewish judges, and whether or not the picture it portrays is true of the entire period covered in the present chapter. The responsum does, however, support the claim that the class of competent halakhists in Spain at this time was a small one, and that expertise in the law was not a widespread phenomenon.

The existence of towns in which there were no qualified scholars constitutes the background to a responsum of Rabbi Solomon ben Adret (acronym *Rashba*) concerning the appointment as judges of unqualified individuals. According to the *Talmud* (*B. Sanh.* 7b) it is forbidden to make such an appointment, and *Rashba* was asked whether or not the practice of appointing ignorant judges in order to prevent Jews taking their cases to non-Jewish courts constituted a contravention of this prohibition. The question was a particularly important one for the preservation of Jewish judicial autonomy, since, if answered in the negative, it would mean that only in those few towns in which genuine experts were to be found could autonomy be preserved. *Rashba* replied that whilst the 'strict letter of the law' condemned this practice, the fact that without unqualified judges Jewish judicial autonomy would collapse justified the mandatory jurisdiction of such courts. It was 'an emergency hour' and a communal enactment granting authority to this type of judge bound all members of the community (*Resp.*

Rashba 2, no.190). *Rashba* cited the talmudic precedent of 'a court of common people' (*bet din shel hedyotot*) in support of his ruling and emphasized the need to rely on this institution in order to maintain the cardinal value of Jewish judicial autonomy in Spain.

In many communities, the jurisdiction of the local courts, which extended to both judicial and legislative activities, was supplemented by other bodies drawn from the lay leadership of the community. The development of such bodies was encouraged by the halakhic authorities, and, as a result, there arose in Spain a vibrant and active Jewish legal system, notwithstanding the relatively small number of expert halakhists living there.

The maintenance of judicial autonomy was also due to the steadfast opposition of Spanish rabbis to the practice of taking legal matters to non-Jewish courts. Although the *Talmud* mentions the prohibition on appearing before a gentile court (*B. Gitt.* 85b), it does not address practical questions such as the sanction, if any, for breaking this prohibition; the possibility of its subversion on the basis of a prior condition; or the case of a recalcitrant litigant who can only be compelled to appear before a gentile court.

The Spanish authorities supplied the answers to these questions and developed a rich body of law in this area. In relation to the sanction for attending non-Jewish courts, the authorities suggested excommunication (*Resp. Rif* nos.14, 221; *Resp. Rambam* (ed. Blau) nos. 26, 260; *Resp. Rashba* Vol.3 no.431). Conditions to the effect that a dispute arising out of an agreement be taken before a non-Jewish tribunal were declared void by *Rif*, on the grounds that they offended against the biblical prohibition mentioned above (see *Sefer Haterumot, Sha'ar* 62:1 no.4).

Rif's ruling was followed by R. Moses b. Naḥman (acronym *Ramban*, Naḥmanides) in his commentary on the *Torah* (*Exodus* 21:1), and attention was drawn by the latter to the contrast between gentile courts which are forbidden, and non-expert Jewish courts which are permitted under Jewish Law. *Rashba* is highly critical of any attempt to use conditions in order to circumvent this prohibition (*Resp. Rashba* Vol.6 no.254).

The prohibition on appearing before non-Jewish tribunals, and the strong stand taken by Spanish rabbis against any attempt to subvert it, produced a situation in which the appearance of Jewish litigants before a non-Jewish tribunal was an extremely rare phenomenon. There were, however, cases in which a Jewish litigant was swayed neither by the prohibition on recourse to gentile tribunals, nor by the means used by the rabbis to prevent Jews having recourse to them. In such a case, it was agreed that the ban on non-Jewish courts was suspended (*Resp. Rashba* Vol.1 no.57) on the grounds that a person is permitted to save his property from violent seizure, even if, in the course of so doing, the perpetrator of the violence suffers a loss (*Resp. Rambam* no.63). Similarly, it is permitted to sue a non-Jew in a non-Jewish court, because a loss would be suffered if this was not done (*Resp. Rashba* Vol.1 no.524). The general approach of the Spanish authorities to the problem of recalcitrant Jewish litigants is stated by Maimonides as follows:

> Where the Jews are subject to a gentile Government, and one of the litigants is a violent person who will not accept the authority of the Jewish courts, then recourse should first be made to the judges of Israel in order to resolve the matter. If the litigant refuses to obey the summons, then the plaintiff — with the permission of the Jewish court — may save his property by suing the defendant in a non-Jewish tribunal. (*Hilkhot Sanhedrin* 26:7)

This balance between prohibition and exceptions constituted the means by which Spanish halakhic authorities preserved the judicial autonomy of their communities throughout the period discussed in the present chapter.

3. *The Halakhic Literature of the Period*

The earliest extant halakhic material from Spain dates from the middle of the tenth century. This material consists of scores of responsa written by R. Moses b. Ḥanokh, and his son, R. Hanokh, who emigrated from Italy and whose arrival in Spain is celebrated in the famous legend of the four captives. (According to this tradition, four of the leading scholars in Babylonia were captured and sold into slavery in different countries, where they spread the Jewish faith. R. Moses b. Ḥanokh, according to this tradition, was sold into slavery in Cordova, Spain; was redeemed by his Jewish brethren; and came to be recognized as the leader of his community: see Abraham ibn Daud in *Ṣefer Haḳabbalah* — The Book of Tradition, ed. G.D. Cohen, 1967, pp. 63-69). There is, however, very little original halakhic development in this material. Fragments of the halakhic writings of R. Samuel Hanagid, a disciple of R. Hanokh and other early eleventh century sages such as R. Isaac b. Judah ibn Giyyat, are also extant. It was only with the arrival of *Rif* from North Africa at the end of the eleventh century that halakhic creativity began in earnest in Spain, and continued there for several hundred years.

Halakhic literature is commonly classified under the rubrics of commentaries and novellae, codes and responsa. Spanish authorities made important contributions to each of these areas in the period under discussion.

A. Commentaries and Novellae

Spain produced many important Bible commentators, amongst the earliest of which are R. Judah b. Balaam of eleventh century Toledo, and R. Moses b. Ezra, who emigrated from Toledo to Italy in the twelfth century. R. Jonah Gerondi, the teacher of Naḥmanides (d. 1263, Toledo), was also a notable Bible commentator. The most outstanding Spanish Bible commentator was undoubtedly Naḥmanides himself. His work (on the five books of the *Torah* and on *Job*) extends beyond the elucidation of the literary meaning of the text and enters into the conceptual analysis of the legal material in both individual verses and whole chapters. The importance of Naḥmanides' commentary stems from his halakhic eminence; in this respect, his commentary is unique amongst the Spanish scholars in both previous and succeeding generations.

The outstanding commentary in the area of rabbinic literature is Maimonides' *Commentary on the Mishnah*, which was the first complete commentary ever written on that work. *Rashi*'s earlier commentary (see p.313, below) was on the whole *Talmud*, but it did not include tractates in which there was *mishnah* but no *gemara*. Maimonides' aims in this commentary were the elucidation of the *Mishnah* in the light of the *gemara*, and the establishment of the *halakhah* in each case in which it was subject to a dispute in the *Mishnah*. Maimonides' work achieved great popularity and became a standard source of talmudic commentary.

The novellae literature is a form of interpretation in which the writer does not merely clarify the text, but aims to explain the motives or reasons behind the text, to settle potential contradictions between the text and other sources, and to discuss the legal (halakhic) issues that arise from it in a general manner. The earliest author in the genre field of talmudic *novellae* is R. Joseph ibn Migash, a disciple of *Rif*, and a prominent Spanish talmudist. Only a fraction of his *novellae* have survived. A similar fate befell the *novellae* of R. Meir Abulafia, another famous early Spanish talmudist. The *novellae* of Naḥmanides, *Rashba* and *Ritba* (R. Yom Tov Ashbili) are, however, readily available on almost the entire *Talmud*, and they provide a rich source of practical halakhic rulings, as well as conceptual analyses of the talmudic text.

B. Codes

This literary genre exists in two forms: *Ṣifre halakhot* and *Ṣifre peṣakim*. The former consist of analyses of the sources of the laws and their development in halakhic literature. The second presents only the final *halakhah*, without any additional information. This division is found in geonic literature and was followed by the Spanish halakhists. Some of the most important works in this field of Jewish Law are of Spanish origin, and two of them, i.e. the *Sefer halakhot* of *Rif* and Maimonides' *Mishneh Torah*, were used by R. Joseph Karo in the sixteenth century as two of the three major sources for the establishment of the definitive *halakhah* in his *Bet Yosef* and *Shulḥan Arukh*. The major codificatory works of this period are as follows:

i.   *Sefer halakhot* of R. Isaac b. Jacob Alfasi (*Rif*)

The *Sefer halakhot* is a condensed version of the *Talmud*, and was a popular form in geonic halakhic writings. In the course of time, however, these early condensations needed to be updated, and *Rif's* work combined the talmudic material with the legislation, responsa and customs which had accrued since the closing of the *Talmud*.

Rif's work is arranged according to the tractates of the *Talmud*; in each one, he extracts the halakhic conclusions together with the arguments upon which they are based. On occasion, he also cites rulings from the Jerusalem *Talmud* and the writings of the Geonim. In the light of the principles of contemporary relevance which guided his codificatory enterprise, *Rif* excluded all talmudic material on issues which possessed no contemporary application, e.g. laws relating to sacrifices and ritual purity, and those dealing with the Land of Israel.

The stature of the author and the wide scope of the *Sefer halakhot* gave it unprecedented halakhic status, both in its time, and in succeeding generations. A whole body of commentary grew up around *Rif's* work, consisting of both critiques of it and defences to those critiques.

ii. The *Mishneh Torah* of R. Moses b. Maimon (*Maimonides*)

Maimonides' *Mishneh Torah* is the most comprehensive and significant code of Jewish Law ever compiled. The fact that the *Shulḥan Arukh* of R. Joseph Karo is now the authoritative code of Jewish Law does not detract from the status of the *Mishneh Torah*, especially since it provides the basis for the vast majority of the decisions in the *Shulḥan Arukh* (see further Ch.12, pp.339ff., below).

Amongst Maimonides' aims in writing the *Mishneh Torah* was the halakhic education of the laity, which had suffered as a result of the gradual deterioration of *Torah* study in general, and of the *Talmud* in particular. Maimonides also fought against the teachings of the Karaites: one of the pervasive themes in the *Mishneh Torah* is, therefore, the uniqueness and unity of the halakhic system and the primary place occupied in it by the Oral Law. From a purely internal perspective, the *Mishneh Torah* was written in order to constitute a comprehensive and authoritative legal code. It is from this internal perspective that Maimonides himself justifies his great work in the introductory section:

> ... this compendium would embrace all the laws of the *Torah* ... outside of this work there was to be no need for another book to learn anything whatsoever that is required in the whole *Torah*, whether it be a law of the Scriptures or of the Rabbis.

The principal source for the *Mishneh Torah* is the Babylonian *Talmud*. Maimonides also used geonic writings in arriving at definitive rulings in the *Mishneh Torah*.

The halakhic material in the *Mishneh Torah* is classified according to subject matter, and is presented in a definitive form without any of the supporting arguments upon which the final ruling is based or a record of the differing opinions in talmudic literature.

In substantive terms, the influence of *Rif's Sefer halakhot* on the *Mishneh Torah* is clearly evident, since many of Maimonides' decisions are obviously based upon those of R. Alfasi. In terms of the structure of the two works, however, that of Maimonides is entirely original and owes nothing to his illustrious predecessor: Maimonides did not follow the classic format of the order of the talmudic tractates, as R. Alfasi had done. Rather, Maimonides' system of classifying the *halakhah* is highly sophisticated and unique. Although some of the Geonim had applied subject classification to specific areas of Jewish Law, none had applied it to the entire halakhic system. It is, indeed, the comprehensive scope of Maimonides' code which makes it unique both in relation to the Geonim and to the codifiers of subsequent generations.

The *Mishneh Torah* comprises fourteen books and is, therefore, also known as *Yad hahazakah* (lit: the strong hand; the numerical values of the Hebrew letters in the word '*yad*' is fourteen). The strictly legal areas of the *halakhah* are concentrated in the books on women, torts, property, civil law, criminal law and procedure. In general, Maimonides uses the casuistic method of the *Talmud* in his presentation of the law: the *halakhah* is expressed using a concrete example, such as: 'an ox that gored the cow' (Maimonides, *Hilkhot Nezikin* 9:3, following *B. B.K.* 46a), rather than through an abstract principle. In many instances, however, he combines it with an elucidation of the abstract principles governing the area of the law with which the case is concerned.

The truly revolutionary aspect of the *Mishneh Torah* is its anonymous style. The omission of the talmudic sources of its rulings made the *Mishneh Torah* a unique code of law in its time. According to Maimonides, this style was adopted in order to make the work more accessible, and, hence, much more efficient than other codes of Jewish Law. It was, however, this very anonymous style which aroused strong opposition amongst scholars, and stimulated Maimonides' successors to produce codes which were accessible but did not omit links to the talmudic sources. Notable examples of such codes are the *Tur* and the works of R. Joseph Karo (pp.338ff., below).

Notwithstanding the opposition to the *Mishneh Torah* during Maimonides' lifetime, and in the period following his death, it was universally acknowledged as the most important code of Jewish Law ever written, and its rulings were adopted by some communities [e.g. that of Yemen] as binding *halakhah* for all time. The *Mishneh Torah* gave rise to a vast body of commentary and 'super-commentary' (commentary upon commentary), the sole aim of which is to elucidate the sources of Maimonides' rulings and the analytical process involved in their formulation.

iii. The Halakhic Works of R. Moses b. Naḥman (Naḥmanides, *Ramban*)

Naḥmanides' *Torat Ha'adam* is undoubtedly his most significant contribution to the codification of Jewish Law. In this work, Naḥmanides deals with the laws governing diseases and their cures, the legal status and responsibility of the physician, the scope of the obligation to break the law in order to save human life, burial of the dead, the laws of mourning and the theological doctrine of reward and punishment. In each area, Naḥmanides cites the relevant talmudic material together with a wide range of views drawn from geonic and rabbinic works. In general, Naḥmanides reaches his conclusion on the basis of the Babylonian *Talmud* alone, and does not rely on the opinions of other commentators and codifiers. In this respect, his work resembles a geonic *Sefer halakhot*. The *Torat Ha'adam* is a major source for the *Tur* and the *Shulḥan* Arukh in the above-mentioned areas of Jewish Law.

Naḥmanides also compiled *Sifre halakhot* on specific topics in the area of ritual law which were modelled on *Rif's Sefer halakhot* and which followed the latter's halakhic rulings. In these works, Naḥmanides also adopted *Rif's* practice of using the Jerusalem *Talmud*, in the absence of any definitive

ruling in the Babylonian *Talmud*. Naḥmanides' *Hilkhot Niddah* is a
deviation from this pattern in that it is written in a clear and terse style, and
does not include any discursive material.

iv. R. Samuel Hasardi's *Ṣefer Haterumot*

This work deals with the law of obligations, and its significance lies in
the fact that it is the first halakhic code devoted entirely to the field of civil
law. It is arranged according to subject matter, and in each subject entry,
R. Samuel cites the talmudic material together with the opinions of the
Rishonim. Each entry concludes with an analysis of all the relevant
opinions, and a definitive ruling on the matter under discussion.

In contrast to the corresponding sections in the *Mishneh Torah*, the
present work discusses aspects of the laws of obligations which are only of
peripheral concern to the law of obligations *stricto sensu*. Matters which are
only hinted at by Maimonides are treated in great detail in the *Ṣefer
Haterumot*. There is no evidence of any system of decision-making. In each
subject, R. Samuel reaches a conclusion on the basis of his analysis of the
particular halakhic material relevant to the subject under discussion. In some
instances, however, the law is left undecided, e.g. if the matter is disputed by
early authorities and the dispute was never resolved. R. Samuel never rules
against the opinion of his teacher, Naḥmanides, whose views are often cited
verbatim in the *Ṣefer Haterumot*. The *Ṣefer Haterumot* is, therefore, also an
important source for the opinions and decisions of Naḥmanides.

R. Samuel's magnum opus incorporates opinions of many Spanish and
Provençal authorities, and is widely cited in the *Ḥoshen Mishpaṭ* section of
Ṭur.

v. The Halakhic Codes of R. Solomon b. Abraham Adret (*Rashba*)

Rashba's most important codificatory work is the *Torat habayit*, a book
devoted to matters of ritual law. The *Torat habayit* consists of two compilations entitled *Torat habayit ha'arokh* and *Torat habayit hakatsar*. In the
former compilation, *Rashba* discusses the talmudic material, cites the
opinions of the commentators from talmudic times until his own period, and
decides the *halakhah* on the subject under discussion. It is noteworthy that
Rashba relies heavily upon *Rashi*'s commentary on the *Talmud* (see Ch.11,
p.309, below); in the *Torat habayit*, at any rate, *Rashi*'s role becomes that of
a codifier and not only that of a commentator.

In the latter compilation, *Rashba* condenses all the material dealt with in the former one, and formulates the definitive *halakhah* without including any analysis of the material. The *Torat habayit* is divided into seven 'houses' (*batim*), each of which is sub-divided into 'gates' (*she'arim*). The contents of each gate are outlined in detail in a contents section at the beginning of the whole work (*mevo hashe'arim*).

Rashba selected this method of codifying the law in order to satisfy the needs of both scholars and lay people. For the former group, he wrote the lengthy *Torat habayit ha'arokh*. The latter group was served by the *Torat habayit hakatsar* with its brief summary of the halakhic material and definitive legal rulings. Scholars who required a brief summary of a halakhic topic or a statement of the final ruling would also use the *Torat habayit hakatsar*. The *Torat habayit* introduced a new concept into the codification of Jewish Law, i.e. the combination of a *Sefer halakhot* with a *Sefer pesakim*. The combined presentation fulfilled the previously incompatible goals of profound halakhic analysis and easy access to definitive halakhic rulings.

Explanatory notes and critical scholia on the *Torat habayit* were compiled by R. Aaron Halevi of Barcelona, a contemporary of *Rashba*, in a work entitled *Bedek habayit*. *Rashba* replied to the criticisms levelled at his work by R. Aaron Halevi in a work called *Mishmeret habayit*.

Rashba compiled additional works on specific areas of Jewish Law in the same style as the *Torat habayit*. In his *Sha'ar Hamayim*, *Rashba* deals with the laws of family purity, and provides a concise version of the *halakhah* in a companion volume entitled *Bet Hamayim*. Another work, *Avodat Hakodesh*, is devoted to the laws of the Festivals, and whilst only the short version is extant, it is evident that a long version did exist in the past. *Piske hallah* deals with the laws of taking the *hallah* portion from bread dough. The importance of these works lies not so much in the halakhic material contained in them but in the two-tier approach to the codification of Jewish Law which they exemplify.

C. The Responsa Literature

The judicial autonomy possessed by medieval Jewish communities, together with the developments in trade and industry which took place during this period, created a pressing need for halakhic solutions to everyday problems in the areas of civil, criminal, administrative and public law. Local courts were not always capable of providing such solutions, and the problems were often sent to the great halakhic authorities of the time for a definitive ruling. The Middle Ages was, therefore, a period during which the responsa literature grew and flourished.

As indicated in Ch.8, the responsa began as an independent branch of halakhic literature in the geonic period. During that period, questions were sent from various Jewish centres to the Babylonian Academies, which served as a supreme judicial body, the authority of which extended throughout the Jewish world. The Spanish authorities also replied to questions addressed to them from other centres such as France and Germany. The main bulk of their responsa, however, were sent to questioners within Spain, since the universal authority enjoyed by the Babylonian academies no longer existed.

The responsa of the early part of the Middle Ages played a vital role in the development of Jewish Law as a whole, and of public and administrative law in particular. Many of these responsa were later cited and discussed by R. Joseph Ḳaro in his *Bet Yoṣef* on the *Ṭur*. The responsa of Spanish authorities constituted an important contribution to this branch of the halakhic enterprise, and the remainder of this section is devoted to a summary of the major responsa collections of this period.

i.   Responsa of R. Isaac b. Jacob Alfasi (*Rif*)

Several hundred responsa of *Rif* are extant, and the majority were written during the latter part of his life, when he was a resident of Spain. As the greatest halakhic authority of his time, he received questions from Spanish and North African communities alike. The majority of the responsa are written in Arabic, and in their structure they resemble those of the Babylonian Geonim. Most of them deal with commercial and economic matters, family law, communal life, relations with gentiles and legal procedure. Some are concerned with marriage, ritual matters and liturgy. In general, *Rif's* responsa paint a picture of Jewish life in Spain during his times.

ii.   Responsa of R. Joseph ibn Migash

Some two hundred and fifty responsa attributed to R. Joseph ibn Migash have survived, and as early as 1150, nine years after his death, it was known that there was in existence a bound collection of his responsa. This entire collection was translated from the Arabic, with the exception of details such as the names of the questioners, the dates of the responsa and the halakhic sources upon which he relied in providing the answers, since none of these were necessary for knowing the definitive *halakhah*.

iii. Responsa of Maimonides

Maimonides' responsa were written in Egypt, in the period in which he became a central figure in the Jewish world. He was in touch with the major Jewish centres of both the East and the West, and his responsa cover all areas of Jewish Law. Included in his responsa are difficulties in the interpretation of talmudic discussions and enactments he was instrumental in passing in Egypt for the purposes of improving religious standards in the community, and the strengthening of communal life. The hundreds of Maimonides' responsa which have come down to us appear in various collections, in both Arabic and Hebrew translation. The most comprehensive edition is that of J. Blau, which was published in Jerusalem in 1958, and reprinted in 1986.

iv. Responsa of R. Meir Halevi Abulafia

The sole extant collection of R. Abulafia's responsa was published in a work entitled *Or Tsadikim* and published in 1808 in Salonica. This work contains seventy responsa, numbered from section 240 until 309, thus indicating that at least 239 responsa were lost. Some of these have been located in other rabbinic works, but the majority remain missing.

v. Responsa of Nahmanides

The majority of Nahmanides' published responsa are those sent to his disciple and colleague, R. Samuel Hasardi, and included in his *Sefer Haterumot* on the laws of loan. Other responsa, which do not appear in *Sefer Haterumot*, deal with a wide range of halakhic issues.

vi. Responsa of R. Solomon b. Abraham Adret (*Rashba*)

In terms of the quantity of responsa and their range, *Rashba* is one of the most prolific of Spanish responders, and possibly of all time. His responsa were sent to every part of the Diaspora, and his correspondents included R. Meir of Rothenburg, R. Menahem Hameiri, R. Aharon Halevi, and other luminaries of the period. There is hardly a single area of *halakhah* which does not figure in Rashba's responsa. The wide judicial and administrative autonomy enjoyed by the Jewish communities of medieval Spain is reflected in the fact that communal enactments and taxation constitute two major themes in the responsa of *Rashba*. There are more than three thousand responsa, published in eight volumes.

4. *Legal Practice: Communal Enactments* (*Takkanot Hakahal*)

The vitality of Jewish Law in Spain during this period is manifested most strongly in the area of communal enactments. The wide jurisdiction enjoyed by the community and its representatives is indicated in the following extract from a responsum of *Rashba*:

> The community is empowered to make all manner of enactments in the area of monetary matters ... and they are certainly binding when passed by a majority of the community. Every local community is considered as if it possessed the authority of the Geonim, whose enactments bound the whole of Israel. (*Resp. Rashba* 1, no 729).

Two important principles may be derived from this responsum with regard to the jurisdiction of the community in relation to communal enactments: the distinction between monetary and religious matters, and the legal status of the community.

The power of the community to enact legislation is limited to monetary matters, and does not extend to matters of a purely religious nature, which remained solely within the authority of the rabbinic authorities (see *Resp. Rashba* 3, no.411). There are, nevertheless, areas of religious life in relation to which communal enactments were of significance. Clearly, the community could make an enactment in order to *strengthen* religious observance, and a noteworthy Spanish contribution to this field was the enactment that no marriage ceremony was to be performed in the absence of a rabbi and ten adult males. This was not a requirement under talmudic law, and is a particularly dramatic illustration of communal power, since many enactments specified that the penalty for non-observance would be annulment of the otherwise perfectly valid marriage (*Resp. Rashba* 1, no.551). Notwithstanding the obvious ramifications of such an enactment for purely religious matters, there were many such enactments in force in Spain during this period.

Rashba compares the status of the community to that of the Babylonian Geonim, who enjoyed absolute authority in Babylonia. It is noteworthy that the Geonim were all outstanding halakhic authorities — which was clearly not the case with regard to the communal leadership of medieval Spain. In other responsa, *Rashba* goes further, and draws an analogy between the authority of the community and that of the *Sanhedrin*, or Great Court, which had its seat in Jerusalem and exercised jurisdiction over all of Israel (*Resp. Rashba* 3, no.417; 5, no.126).

The scope of communal authority was responsible for the development of a wide-ranging system of enactments, which in many areas, replaced the provisions of the *Talmud*. In a responsum on a question of tax law, for example, *Rashba* wrote that:

> ... the matters under discussion are not regulated by the laws of the *Talmud* but by local custom and enactment, and the operative principle in this area is that everything is in accordance with local practice. (*Resp. Rashba* 3, no.398)

Indeed, according to *Rashba*, the status of communal enactments is equivalent to that of the *Torah*'s commandments:

> It is clear that the community may pass enactments and make agreements in relation to any matter it deems fit, and its decisions possess the force of *Torah* law. Those who disregard these decisions may be fined or punished in various ways. (*Resp. Rashba* 4, no.185)

The area in which Jewish judicial autonomy assumed greatest significance was that of the criminal law. During most of the period of exile and dispersion, Jewish communities did not possess criminal jurisdiction, and as a result halakhic literature did not in general, address this issue. In Spain, however, criminal jurisdiction was possessed by Jewish communities, and halakhic authorities were required to deal with the practical aspects of criminal jurisdiction, including the power to administer capital punishment.

The means used for dealing with the practical ramifications of the capital jurisdiction of Spanish Jewry was the communal enactment, which, in effect, replaced the *Talmud* in this area of the law. *Rashba* relied upon the talmudic principle that the court may administer corporal and capital penalties 'even if they are not sanctioned by the *Torah*' (*B. Yeb.* 90b) in order to justify the punishments meted out by communal authorities for breaches of their enactments. This power was used on a temporary basis in order to safeguard public religion and morality, and was bestowed upon the community by virtue of its role as a Great Court. A precedent was provided by *Rif*, who ruled that although the restrictive *Torah* law concerning the fining of rapists and seducers could not be followed in Spain, the 'elders of the community may levy fines at their discretion in order to preserve public morality' (*Resp. Rif* no.36). *Rashba* used this principle in the context of both fines, corporal and capital punishment, mainly in order to provide a justification for meting out both types of punishments, notwithstanding the fact that the *Talmud* implied that there was no jurisdiction to do so in the post-biblical period (*Resp. Rashba* 4, no.310).

It is important to note that the criminal jurisdiction of Jewish communities in Spain was granted to them by the Muslims and was, therefore, halakhically legitimate in terms of the principle of 'royal approval' in Jewish Law. In his reply to a scholar in Toledo concerning criminal jurisdiction, *Rashba* mentioned both the authority of the community and royal authority as bases for meting out this type of punishment:

> It is necessary in criminal cases to consult with the elders of the city, and to mete it out only after careful consideration and for the sake of a vital public interest ... In my opinion, there is also royal authority for criminal jurisdiction, and since it carries royal approval, it is also halakhically valid. (*Resp. Rashba* 2, no.290)

It is noteworthy that the grant of criminal jurisdiction to Jews was highly irregular under Islamic Law, and was unique to Spain. The uniqueness of this jurisdiction is indicated in Maimonides' formulation of the law, which confines it to Spain or 'the West' (as Spain is referred to in rabbinic literature):

> And it is common practice in the cities of the West to kill proven informers who place the property of Israel in jeopardy. (*Laws of Damages* 8:11)

This jurisdiction was maintained in Christian Spain, and from the thirteenth century onwards the charters of Spanish Jewish communities contain details of procedures for the administration of the death penalty.

A special communal office was created for those dealing with criminal jurisdiction. In a responsum sent to the community of Jacca, *Rashba* refers to 'a local enactment empowering elected officials of the community to punish any transgressor and to levy fines' (*Resp. Rashba* Vol.3, no.318).

The halakhic literature of the period contains a wide range of principles governing communal enactments. The more important ones may be briefly summarized.

1. The authority to pass an enactment is vested in the majority of the community and the minority is bound by it, notwithstanding any objections to that enactment (*Resp. Rif* no.13; *Resp. Rashba* Vol.2, no.279; Vol.5, no.242). The view of *Rabbenu Tam*, a prominent twelfth century Tosafist (see p.311, below), that majority decisions were not binding upon a minority, was not accepted in Spain (see *Mordekhai, B.K.*, no.179).

2. The legal basis for the authority of the community is its status as a court; as a result, it is bound to follow the rule that all its proceedings must be open. Majority decisions will, therefore, only be binding if the whole community, or its representative body, is present at the time of the making of the enactment (*Resp. Rashba* 3, no.304).

3. The appointed representatives of the community are empowered to pass enactments; it is not necessary for the whole community to do so

(*Resp. Rashba* Vol.1, nos.40, 617; Vol.3, no.443).

4. Communal enactments bind all members of the community, including those who became members only after the time of its passage. The unborn are also bound by enactments of the community (*Resp. Rashba* 3, no.411).

5. It is a precondition of communal enactments that they gain the approval of any recognized halakhic authority (*adam ḥashuv*) residing in the community (*Resp. Rashba* 4, no.185).

6. An enactment must improve the situation and not make it worse: its social consequences must therefore be taken into account (*Resp. Rashba* Vol.2, nos.40, 279). It must also fulfil the requirement that 'the majority of the community find it possible to abide by enactment' (*Resp. Rashba* Vol.7, no.108). Enactments may not deprive the minority of its rights in an arbitrary fashion, and must apply equally to all members of the community (*Resp. Rashba* Vol.5, no.178). Retroactive enactments are invalid, since they offend against the principles of righteousness and justice (*Resp. Rashba* Vol.5, no.179).

5. The Leading Authorities

A. Rabbi Isaac ben Jacob Alfasi (*Rif*)

Rif was born in Qal'at Hammad, Algeria, in the year 1013, at the end of the geonic period, and was called by the *Rishonim* (the early commentators) 'The Gaon Rabbi Isaac'. According to the *Sefer hakabbalah harishon*, *Rif* attended the Kairouan *yeshivot* (academies) and studied with the Rabbi Nissim Gaon and Rabbi Ḥananel ben Hushiel. Though he did not refer to them as his rabbis (teachers), he did cite many of their teachings in his *Sefer Hahalakhot*. Following his studies at Kairouan he settled in Fez (Morocco) and stayed there until 1088. Then, in his 75th year, he was denounced to the authorities and fled to Spain. In Spain he stayed in Cordova a short while, and then moved to Lucena where he assumed the post of Head of the *Yeshivah* following the death of Rabbi Isaac ibn Ghayyat. Among his many students were, notably, Rabbi Yehuda haLevy and Rabbi Joseph haLevy ibn Migash who studied with *Rif* from the age of 12. *Rif* ordained Rabbi Joseph and entrusted him with his knowledge and teachings. He nominated Rabbi Joseph Head of the *Yeshivah* to succeed him a short time before he died though he had a son who was considered a wise scholar — Rabbi Jacob. *Rif* died at the age of 90 in Lucena in the year 1103.

B. R. Joseph HaLevy ibn Migash (*RY*)

RY was born in the year 1077, the son of Rabbi Meir. His grandfather was Rabbi Joseph — among the leading Rabbis of Spain in general and of Granada in particular. Rabbi Joseph was named after his grandfather. *RY* (Rabbi Joseph) studied with Rabbi Isaac ben Baruch from an early age in Seville, and moved to Lucena at the age of twelve when *Rif* settled there. In Lucena he studied with and served *Rif* for fourteen years. He was ordained by *Rif* while still in his youth. Following the death of *RY*'s father, *Rif* took him into his home and raised him as a son. Among his students are, notably, Rabbi Meir, his son, Rabbi Meir, his brother's son, and Rabbi Maimon, Maimonides' father. Maimonides, who learned the teachings of Rabbi Joseph ibn Migash through his father, is also considered one of *RY*'s students. According to *Meiri* (R. Menaḥem b. Shlomo Meiri, thirteenth century), *RY Migash* composed a commentary to the whole of the *Talmud*, but only his *novellae* (*ḥiddushim*) on *Bava Batra* and *Shavuot* are extant. From information found in several books of the *Rishonim* we learn that *RY* also wrote a book by the name of *Megillat Ṣetarim* and an article that interprets the shape of the Hebrew letters. Unfortunately those, like most of his literary work, have not survived. Following the death of *Rif*, Rabbi Joseph succeeded him and presided over the *Yeshivah* for 38 years, until his death (variously dated 1141 or 1145).

C. R. Moses ben Maimon (Maimonides = *Rambam*)

Rambam was born in the year 1135 in Cordova, Spain. His father, Rabbi Maimon, was the *dayyan* (judge of a Rabbinical court) of the city and a member of a family which had produced *dayyanim* for a number of generations. The Almohads conquered Cordova in the year 1148 and forced the Jews to convert to Islam. Many of the Jews apparently embraced Islam, but the family of Rabbi Maimon chose to leave Cordova and travel through the Christian part of Spain for a few years. During these years of wandering, *Rambam* composed his essay *Ḥibbur Millot Hahigayyon* (on logic) and an article *Ma'amar ha'ibbur* (on the Jewish calendar). At the same time he started writing his commentary to the Babylonian *Talmud* and book on the Jerusalem *Talmud*. In the year 1158 he started writing his commentary to the *Mishnah*. In 1159 the family moved to the city of Fez in North Africa where Maimonides studied with Rabbi Judah haKohen. In Fez he wrote his *Iggeret Hashemad* (a letter on forced conversion) also called *Ma'amar ḳiddush hashem* to strengthen and reassure the faith of converts to Islam who remained secretly loyal to Judaism, and urged them to move to places in which they would be able to worship God freely. There in Fez, *Rambam* also continued to write his commentary to the *Mishnah*, and pursued general studies, medicine in particular. Having lived about five years in Fez, the family was forced to leave again, and turned to the Land of Israel; they did not stay long, and were finally forced to emigrate to Egypt. Following a short stay in Alexandria, the family moved to Fostat, near Cairo. After the death of his brother David, who was a merchant and supported the whole family, Maimonides took it upon himself to provide for his family and started working as a physician. In spite of the fact that work occupied most of his time, especially following his nomination as the Sultan's physician, Maimonides still found time to write his articles and deal with public matters. He was nominated Head of the Community, *Nagid*, and struggled successfully against the Karaites who, in those days, commanded a majority among the Jews of Egypt. Maimonides completed his commentary to the *Mishnah* in Egypt, and in the year 1177 started writing his great work *Mishneh Torah*, which took him about 10 years. While in Egypt, he also wrote his famous letters *Iggeret Teiman* (his letter to the communities of Yemen) and *Ma'amar Tehiyat hametim* (*On Resurrection*). Maimonides' public esteem reached its peak with the publication of his *Moreh Nevukhim* (*The Guide to the Perplexed*). It is this book which may best reflect Maimonides' religious and philosophical beliefs. Maimonides' philosophy was greatly influenced by Aristotle. In his later years Maimonides published medical writings which afforded him great publicity and respect throughout the world. Most of his writings on medicine have survived and are available to us. Maimonides passed away at the age of 70 in Egypt in the year 1204, and, according to tradition, his bones were brought to the Land of Israel and buried in Tiberias.

D. R. Meir HaLevy Abulafia (*Ramah*)

Ramah (Rabbi Meir Halevy Abulafia) was born in the city of Burgos, Spain, around 1170. In his youth he moved from Burgos to Toledo and was nominated a *dayyan* there. His family was related by marriage to the social élite of the community of Toledo. *Ramah* played an active role in the leadership of that community and was recognized as the most important leader of the Jews of Spain in his day. Already at the start of his public career, around the year 1200, he initiated the first debate challenging

Maimonides' views with regard to resurrection and the coming of the Messiah — sending letters to the rabbis of Provence, led by Rabbi Jonathan haKohen of Lunel, and insisting that they express an opinion in the debate. He collected the correspondence on this issue and composed his *Kitab al-Rasa'il*. He wrote his commentaries to the *Talmud* which he called *Pirṭe Peraṭim*. According to *Tseidah Laderekh* (by R. Menaḥem b. Zeraḥ, Spain, fourteenth century), *Ramah* composed both a short and a long version of this book. Its scope is not generally agreed upon but, in any event, the entire volume of *Ramah*'s commentaries on certain sections of the *Talmud* were lost. The only commentaries to have survived are the ones on *Bava Batra* and *Sanhedrin*. In his commentaries *Ramah* represented the academic tradition of Spain in his time. In addition to his new commentary on the *Talmud* and his responsa, the majority of which were also lost, *Ramah* wrote the *Maṣoret seyag latorah* which deals with establishing exact spelling in the five books of the *Torah*. The *Torah* scroll which he wrote for himself served as an example for the purposes of accurate copying and supervision of *Torah* books in Spain, France, northern and central Europe, and North Africa. *Ramah* also wrote an explanation of the *baraita* of the thirteen *middot*, poetry, and was occupied with mysticism. He died in Toledo in the year 1244.

E.   R. Moses ben Naḥman (*Ramban*)

Ramban (Naḥmanides) was born in Gerona, Catalonia. His rabbis were Rabbi Nathan ben Rabbi Meir, Rabbi Judah ben Yaḳar, from whom he learned the teachings of the authors of the *Toṣafot* commentaries from the north of France, and Rabbi Jonah Gerondi. He was in contact with *Ramah* and with Rabbi Samuel haSardi to whom he sent most of the responsa which have come down to us. Among his most important students were *Rashba* and *Roeh* (R. Aharon b. Joseph Halevi). According to the testimony of his student *Rashba*, found in his responsa, *Ramban* made his living as a physician. When, in 1238, there developed a debate with regard to the writings of Maimonides he was addressed and adopted a moderate position, attempting without success to diffuse the disagreement. He started writing his commentary to the *Talmud* tractates of *Moed*, *Nashim*, and *Nezikin* at an early age, and most of them were published. His method combined the tradition of the rabbis of Spain with the teachings of the French authors of the *Toṣafot* as well as those of the Rabbis of Provence. In the area of *halakhah*, *Ramban* wrote such monographs as: *Dina degarme*, *Mishpaṭ haherem*, *Torat ha'adam*, *Hilkhot niddah* and writings complementing *Sefer haRif* in matters relating to the laws of *Nedarim*, *Bekhorot*, and *Hallah*. He also wrote *haṣaggot* — comments challenging *Ṣefer hamitsvot* by Maimonides and defended the writings of *Rif* against the *haṣaggot* of Rabbi Zerahia Halevy and the *Ravad* (R. Abraham b. David of Posquières) in his books *Milḥamot Adonai* and *Ṣefer Hazekhut*. *Ramban* also wrote essays on matters of faith and opinion, among them letters and sermons. In his last years he wrote a commentary to the Bible. He composed most of it in Spain, and made additions to it in the Land of Israel. In the year 1263 *Ramban* demanded a public debate with the convert Pablo Christiani on matters of faith and won great respect. The debate was recorded by *Ramban* in *Ṣefer havikuaḥ* (the *Book of the Debate*). Following the book's distribution there were calls among Dominican monks to punish *Ramban* for offending the Christian faith. In the year 1267, when he saw that he was in danger, *Ramban* decided to leave Spain and emigrate to the Land of Israel. In Israel, he organized the remnants of the community and built a synagogue in Jerusalem. He died 3 years after his arrival in Israel, in the year 1270.

F.   R. Samuel haSardi

R. Samuel was born in Barcelona around 1190 and lived there. From published documents it transpires that he owned a great deal of land. R. Samuel wrote a book on the laws relating to loans which is called *Sefer haterumot*. He does not cite his rabbis in the book, but its contents reveal that he was in close contact with *Ramban*, his friend, and incorporated his responsa (to questions by Rabbi Samuel) in his book. He was also in contact with Rabbi Nathan ben Rabbi Meir, *Ramban*'s rabbi, and with other rabbis. He died around 1255.

G.   R. Solomon ben Abraham Adret (*Rashba*)

Rashba was born in 1235 to a highly respected and wealthy family in Barcelona, where he lived and worked throughout his life. He is considered the greatest Rabbi of Spain in the generation following *Ramban*. He studied with *Ramban* and with Rabbi Isaac ben Abraham Narboni. He was appointed to the position of Rabbi of his city while he was still quite young, and within a few years came to be recognized as the leading rabbi of Spain and as one of the leaders of his entire generation; his opinions were also listened to beyond Spain. He wrote new commentaries on most sections of the *Talmud*. In his commentaries he was very much influenced by *Ramban*'s method. He also wrote a book on the legends of the *Talmud*. In the area of law (*pṣiḳa*) *Rashba* wrote the book *Torat habayit*, which was later challenged and commented on by his friend, Rabbi Aharon haLevy, in the book *Bedeḳ habayit*. He also wrote the books *Avodat haḳodesh*, *Sha'ar hamayyim* and *Piṣḳe ḥallah*. His greatest contribution to Jewish Law was in the thousands of responsa he wrote to those who turned to him throughout the Diaspora. His responsa gained him great fame and respect in his own lifetime, and were collected in special compilations. His responsa became a foundation stone in Jewish Law and were incorporated in the *Ṭur*, the *Shulḥan Arukh*, and throughout the literature of the *poṣkim* and responsa in later generations. His responsa still provide an extraordinary and unique source for the history of the people of Israel during his period as well as for general history. *Rashba* had also acquired a philosophical education, and was acquainted with the scientific literature of his age. In spite of that, he took a leading and crucial part in the partial *ḥerem* (ban) against the teaching of philosophy in 1305. Among his greatest students were Rabbi Yom Tov Ashbili (*Ritba*), Rabbi Shem Tov Gaon and Rabbi Baḥya ben Asher. He died in Barcelona in the year 1310.

6. *Important Contributions of the Spanish Sages to Specific Areas of Jewish Law*

A. The Status of the Woman in the Family

The issue of the woman's status in the family has been subject to many changes in the course of history. Under Biblical Law, for example, a man was permitted to marry more than one woman, and did not need her consent to a divorce. Under contemporary Jewish Law, however, the husband is not allowed to marry another woman as long as he is still married to his first wife, nor may he divorce his wife against her will.

The revolution in this area was brought about by the famous *takkanot* of the tenth century Ashkenazi scholar, R. Gershom Maor Hagolah. *Inter alia*, they forbade the practice of polygamy, and divorce of the wife against her will (*Shulḥan Arukh, Even Ha'ezer* 1:10; 119:6; see Ch.11, pp.315ff., below). These *takkanot* were only accepted by the Ashkenazi communities. They were not adopted by the majority of Spanish and Eastern communities. This does not mean, however, that polygamy was actually practised in Spain. From the talmudic commentaries of the Spanish halakhists, it is evident that local customs against the practice of polygamy were read into marriage agreements even if they were not stated there explicitly. The force of custom made the ban on polygamy into an implied condition of the marriage (*Ritva, Kiddushin* 7a).

This custom was also strengthened by an oath taken by the groom not to marry another woman during his bride's lifetime (see *Resp. Rashba* Vol.1 no.412; B. Shereshevsky, *Dine Mishpaḥah*, Jerusalem, Rubin Mass, 1971, 79-80). This condition against polygamy was imposed even in Egypt and other countries in which the dominant practice was, in fact, to take more than one wife (*Resp. Rambam*, ed. Blau, nos.234, 383).

The rulings of the Spanish Sages are of particular importance in relation to the grounds for divorce under Jewish Law. According to the *halakhah*, divorce is only possible if there is free consent on the husband's part. In the absence of such consent, he cannot be coerced into giving one against his will. The *Talmud* provides a limited list of instances in which coercion is expressly authorized (*B. Ket.* 77a) and there are additional lists, cited in different places, of grounds under which the husband is obliged to grant his wife a divorce. There is, however, no provision for any remedy in favour of the wife if her claim is one of emotional incompatibility per se. The closest talmudic precedent is the wife's claim of *ma'is alai* (*B. Ket.* 63b), 'he is repulsive to me', which is discussed in the context of a wife refusing to have intercourse with her husband. The *Talmud* maintains that in such circumstances, the wife is not to be treated as a rebellious wife (*moredet*) and penalised as such, but does not indicate whether or not she is entitled to ask for pressure to be put on her husband in order to make him give her a divorce.

Maimonides follows *Rif* (*B. Ket.* 63b) and rules that pressure may be applied to the husband in such a case, in order to secure a *geṭ* for the wife. In Maimonides' own words: 'she is not a prisoner so that she may be forced to have intercourse with a man she cannot abide' (*Laws of Marriage* 14:11). It ought to be noted that Maimonides' view was not by any means the universal one, and many authorities maintained that, in the absence of specific talmudic authorization, pressure might not be brought to bear on a husband in order to make him divorce his wife. Indeed, *Rosh* (R. Asher b. Yeḥiel; see Ch.12, p.342, below) in a responsum held this view and disagreed with Maimonides' position (*Resp. Rosh* no.43:6; 43:8). Maimonides' view is utilized by contemporary halakhists as an additional point in favour of coercing a *geṭ* in a case of a claim by the wife that the husband is repugnant to her (*ma'is alai*), and in cases where there is a doubt with regard to the validity of the marriage (*Resp. Tsits Eliezer* Vol.1

no.42:32; Shereshevsky, *Dine Mishpaḥah*, 255 n.72).

Maimonides' view is also operative in the context of conjugal relations: a husband may not force conjugal relations upon his wife when she claims that she finds him repulsive. But what is the position where the wife simply refuses to have relations with her husband, without any objective claim such as *ma'is alai*. The sixteenth century Spanish scholar *Mabit* (R. Moses ben Yoṣef di Trani) was of the opinion that even if the wife does not find the husband repulsive, but is merely rebelling against him with the intent of hurting him, she may not be forced to have intercourse with him. A woman is at liberty to refuse to have intercourse with any man, including her husband (*Kiryat Ṣefer, Laws of Marriage*, ch.14). *Mabit* observes that Maimonides rules specifically that having intercourse with a woman against her will constitutes an offence (*Laws of Forbidden Intercourse* 21:12); elsewhere he states that a husband may not 'rape his wife and have relations with her against her will, but only with her consent, and in an atmosphere of communication and happiness' (*Laws of Marriage* 15:17). This view of Maimonides was later to provide the basis for a decision of the Israel Supreme Court that the rape of a woman by her husband constitutes a criminal offence (*Cohen* v. *State of Israel* Cr.A. 91/80, 35 (3) P.D. 281).

It is noteworthy that Maimonides includes mutual respect between husband and wife in his codification of the *halakhah* in this area:

> The Sages instructed that a man should honour his wife more than himself, and should love her as himself. If he has money, he must promote her welfare in accordance with his financial capacity. He may not intimidate her, but should always speak to her calmly. He should neither be sad or angry with her. The Sages also ruled that a wife should greatly honour her husband; she should fear him and all her actions should be according to his word. He should be as a prince or a king in her eyes; she should behave according to his heart's desire, and should distance all things that he hates. And this is the custom of the daughters and sons of Israel who are holy and pure in their partnership. (*Laws of Marriage* 14:19-20)

Maimonides also made an important contribution to the law of maintenance. According to Jewish Law, the husband is obliged to provide his wife with all of her needs, e.g. medical expenses and jewellery (*Laws of Marriage* 13:6). Does the failure to provide maintenance constitute grounds for divorce? In discussing this point, the *Talmud* presumes that the failure to provide is motivated by malice on the husband's part. According to Rab, the woman is entitled to an immediate divorce since she 'is not required to continue living with a snake' (*B. Ket.* 77a). Samuel, however, maintains that an attempt ought to be made to persuade the husband to pay before resorting to the drastic step of forcing him to give her a *get*. Maimonides rules in accordance with Samuel's view, apparently in an attempt to limit the phenomenon of divorce as far as possible.

Maimonides also considers the husband's failure to pay maintenance as a result of lack of financial resources. This possibility is not discussed in the *Talmud*, but Maimonides rules that a wife is entitled to a divorce in such circumstances, since maintenance is a legal obligation upon the husband, and if he fails to fulfil it, then the marriage has lost one of its primary legal bases. In such circumstances, the husband is obliged to divorce his wife (*Laws of Marriage* 12:11; *Kesef Mishneh* and *Maggid Mishneh, ad loc.*).

B. Laws of Inheritance

In the middle of the thirteenth century the communities of Toledo, Molena, and some other Spanish towns promulgated *takkanot* which introduced significant changes in the area of succession law (See *Tur, Even Ha'ezer* 118). Three most important changes introduced by these enactments deserve mention.

1. According to classical Jewish Law, the husband succeeds to the estate of his wife. Under these *takkanot*, if a wife dies leaving children behind, her estate is divided between her children and her husband. If the wife dies childless, then the estate is shared by the husband and her legal heirs.

2. Under classical Jewish Law, a mother does not succeed to her children. The *takkanot* provided that if a mother had provided her daughter with a dowry, then in the event of the married daughter's death, the estate would be divided between the mother and the husband.

3. The classical halakhic position is that a widow is entitled to receive the entire *ketubah* money from the husband's estate. In order to ensure that some property would be left for distribution amongst the heirs, it was enacted that not more than half of the estate would go to the widow, and the rest would be left for the heirs.

C. Penal Law

The extensive juridical autonomy granted to the Jews of Spain included the power to administer capital punishment. As already observed, this power was not easily squared with the halakhic position regarding the death penalty in post-Temple times, and the halakhic justification for this aspect of judicial autonomy exercised the Spanish scholars to a significant degree. The major source for such a justification was the authority of the Sanhedrin, and courts in general, to mete out extra-judicial penalties — including death — where there was a need to protect public order and safety. Maimonides provides the following detailed description of this extra-legal jurisdiction:

> The court is empowered to flog him who is not liable for flagellation and to mete out the death penalty to him who is not liable to death. This extensive power is granted to the court not with the intention of disregarding the law but in order to build a fence around it. Whenever the court sees that a commandment has fallen into general disuse, the duty devolves upon it to safeguard and strengthen the commandment in any way which in its judgment will achieve the desired result. But whatever measure it adopts is only a temporary one and does not acquire the force of a law, binding for all time to come ... and similarly, the court at all times and in all places may flog a person concerning whom there are evil rumours and who is suspected of engaging in forbidden sexual relationships ... and so too the court is required to judge and to excommunicate even those not liable to excommunication in order to close the breach in public order and as deemed necessary in accordance with the exigencies of the hour ... also, a judge must ... whip evil-doers and tear out their hair and to abjure them in the name of God against their will that they will not commit offences, or have not done so in the past ... he may also tie up their hands and feet and imprison them ... all of these matters being in accordance with his understanding of the law in the specific situation and the requirements of the time. (*Laws of the Sanhedrin* 24:4-10)

The same principle is enunciated by *Rashba*, as follows:

> ... the *berurim* (communal leaders who carried out judicial tasks) are empowered to impose fines ... and administer corporal punishment in accordance with their discretion; this is for the general welfare of society for if one adheres in all matters to the laws specified in the *Torah*, and refrains from discretionary punishments ... then the world would be destroyed, since witnesses and warnings would be required before any punishment could be meted out, and as the *Talmud* observes: 'Jerusalem was destroyed only because they based their words on the laws of the *Torah*' (*B. B.M.* 30b). This is certainly the case in the Diaspora, where there is no talmudic authority for the levying of fines, and adherence to the *halakhah* would result in the breakdown of civilization and the desolation of the world ... and even though we do not have the authority to impose fines since there is no authority to impose them in Babylonia ... nevertheless, we levy them in all places ... in order to discipline the generation ... when we see that the time demands it in order to afflict those fools and youths who sink into wrong-doing ... the *berurim* may, therefore, inflict corporal and capital punishment and levy fines for the sake of the welfare of society ... and their actions are especially appropriate since they have obtained royal approval ... and at all times, their actions should be for the sake of heaven. (*Resp. Rashba* Vol.3, no.393)

It would appear that the most frequent form of punishment used in Spain was excommunication, which was particularly effective given the socio-religious context of the Middle Ages, in which it was virtually impossible to survive in any community in an excommunicated state.

Excommunication was normally imposed by either the *Bet Din* or the City Elders sitting in their quorum of ten. The actual ceremony of excommunication included various rituals such as the sounding of the *shofar* and the use of *Torah* scrolls. Excommunicated individuals were forbidden to cut their hair or to bathe; they were not included in religious ceremonies for which a *minyan* (religious quorum, of ten adult males) was required; other Jews were not permitted to associate with them, eat with them, study *Torah* with them or do any business with them. One major difference between the Spanish and the Ashkenazi authorities in this area was that the former permitted brief conversations with excommunicatees, whereas the latter forbade even this very limited contact (*Resp. Rambam* no.311; *Resp. Rashba* Vol.4 no.86).

Excommunication was used mainly in order to protect the autonomy of the community and the maintenance of its religious framework. Specific offences include attacking rabbinical authority (*Resp. Rambam* no.268; *Resp. Rashba* Vol.1 no.763; Vol.4 no.315; Vol.5 no.236); breach of a custom (*Resp. Rashba* Vol.4 no.186); dishonouring judges or scholars (*Resp. Rif* no.146; *Resp. Rambam* nos.111, 268, 290; *Resp. Rashba* Vol.1 nos.279, 417, 460, 475, 608; Vol.4 no.264) and communal officers (*Resp. Rambam* no.110; *Resp. Rashba* Vol.1 no.824) and having recourse to non-Jewish courts (*Resp. Rif* no.14; *Resp. Rambam* nos.26, 27, 221, 260; *Resp. Rashba* Vol.3 no.431). It was also applied against those transgressing communal regulations and conventions (*Resp. Rambam* nos.27, 183, 242, 270; *Resp. Rashba* Vol.1 nos.549; Vol.3 no.430; Vol.4 nos.186, 296; Vol.5 nos.279, 281); for breaches of excommunication (*Resp. Rif* no.146; *Resp. Rambam* no.349; *Resp. Rashba* Vol.1 nos.696, 697; Vol.4 no.264) and for forbidden betrothals and marriages (*Resp. Rif* no.180; *Resp. Rambam* nos.157, 346, 349; *Resp. Rashba* Vol.1 no.649; Vol.3 no.446; Vol.4 no.314).

The Spanish authorities also imposed fines, notwithstanding the talmudic ban on levying them outside the Land of Israel (*Resp. Rif* no.36). These fines were either collected by the local *Bet Din* (*Resp. Rashba* Vol.3 no.318) or the non-Jewish authorities (*Resp. Rashba* Vol.3 no.385).

A similar situation existed with regard to flogging. The punishment of lashes specified in the *Torah* was not put into practice in the Middle Ages, but halakhic authorities resorted to flogging in various cases, arguing that the concept was found in the sources of Jewish Law. Indeed, in one of his responsa, *Rashba* mentions the amputation of limbs as a legitimate penalty for 'breaching the fences of the traditions of Israel' (*Resp. Rashba* 4 no.264). There is, however, no record in halakhic literature of amputation being practised as a penalty, and *Rashba* himself restricts it to the most severe type of offence.

The Spanish responsa also yield principles of criminal procedure, such as the need to examine the criminal record of the accused in order to establish whether he had been a habitual offender or not (*Resp. Rashba* Vol.5 no.238). Sentencing criteria, such as the character of the accused, and the need to pass tough sentences in order to deter potential criminals, are also to be found in the responsa literature of this period (*Resp. Rashba* Vol.1 nos.475, 855; *Resp. Ri Migash*, no.161).

7. *Bibliography*

AA. VV., 'Spain', *Encylopedia Judaica*, Vol. 15, cols. 220-46.

Ashtor, E., *The Jews of Moslem Spain* (Philadelphia: Jewish Publication Society, 1973-84, 3 vols.).

Baer, Y., *A History of the Jews in Christian Spain* (Philadelphia: Jewish Publication Society of America, 1983, 2 vols., 2nd ed.).

Beinart, H., ed., *Moreshet Sepharad: The Sephardi Legacy* (Jerusalem: Magnes Press, 1992, 2 vols).

Elon, M., *Jewish Law: History, Sources, Principles*, trld. B. Auerbach and M.J. Sykes (Philadelphia and Jerusalem: Jewish Publication Society, 1994), ch.20 *passim* and s.v. 'Spain' (index).

Epstein, I., *Studies in the Communal Life of the Jews of Spain, as Reflected in the Responsa of Rabbi Solomon ben Adereth and Rabbi Simon Ben Zemach Duran* (N.Y.: Hermon Press, 1968, 2nd ed.).

Tchernowitz, Ch., (Rav Tzair), *Toledot Haposkim* (N.Y.: Jubilee Committee, 1946), vol.-1, pp. 131-306.

11

ASHKENAZIM TO 1300

by

AVRAHAM GROSSMAN

Hebrew University of Jerusalem

1. *Political and Juridical Background*

Although the term 'Ashkenaz' became the Hebrew designation for the land of Germany, its wider sense of a discrete cultural entity also embraces the Jewish communities of Northern France, the Slavic lands and England. The Jewish centre in Germany, at this period, was relatively small in terms of population, but it was of the greatest importance in the evolution of Jewish Law. While several Jewish communities are known to have existed in Germany as far back as the Roman period, these seem to have all but disappeared during the endless warfare engulfing Roman Gaul prior to the collapse of the Empire in 476 C.E. When Jewish settlement in Ashkenaz re-emerges at the beginning of the ninth century, it is intimately bound up with the efforts of the Carolingian rulers to stimulate trade and commercial activities across the far-flung lands of their kingdom.

The Jewish traders were considered an important element in the development of economic life. That the Carolingian rulers indeed welcomed their presence can be seen from the various *privilegia* which they were granted. These charters conferred a wide range of prerogatives on the Jewish traders, including exemption from certain tariffs, judicial autonomy, trade concessions, the engagement of Christian servants and the protection of life, limb and property from the 'insolence of the populace' (See Blumenkranz, *The Roman Church and the Jews*, 162). Granting special privileges to this group or that was an accepted phenomenon in medieval Europe, a familiar part of the feudal order.

The burgeoning economic activity drew additional Jews to Ashkenaz. The majority of newcomers originated from Italy, the minority from France.

Wealthy traders of distinguished family stood at the head of these immigrant groups, and it was they who received the charters from the ruler. Forming a community around a nucleus of prominent families was unique to the Jewish communities of Germany. It vitally affected the structure of society, its internal organization, some of its economic institutions and also the development of the spiritual life. Several of the ordinances enacted by the Jewish communities of those years were inextricably bound to this social structure, whether in relation to family law and practice or to litigation and commerce. The fact that many of these communities were so sparsely populated clearly affected the character of the communities and their legal system. While natural increase and continuing immigration did contribute to their growth, the Franco-German communities remained smaller than their counterparts elsewhere in the world.

Of the manifold factors shaping the social, spiritual and judicial life of Ashkenazi Jewry, seven basic facts deserve emphasis:

1. The immigrants originated from different places and brought with them a host of varying religious and social customs. These customs were faithfully, indeed zealously, handed down from father to son up until the devastations of the First Crusade in 1096, and to some extent even after. Custom played a vital role in community life; indeed nowhere else in the Jewish world did custom so nearly obtain the force of law. Since many of the immigrants originated from Italy, where affinity with the traditions of *Erets Israel* ran deep, the religious rites of tenth-eleventh century Ashkenaz were greatly influenced by those of ancient *Erets Israel*, and to a certain degree thereafter.

2. Family lineage was paramount in ancient Ashkenaz. Distinguished families and scholars were conceded pre-eminence not only in the spiritual life of the community but also in its political manoeuvrings. As late as the eleventh century, it was in fact the great scholars who received the Charters of Privileges from the rulers of Worms and Mayence. In no other Jewish centre of that period did scholars assume so vital a role in the leadership of society, and it was through their agency that several of the most important community ordinances were enacted.

3. The local community was vested with almost complete sovereignty, regulating its own affairs in nearly all facets of life. The authority wielded by the local community, which included powers of legislation, was as great as that of any other Jewish centre of the period.

4. The first settlers promulgated special ordinances aimed at protecting their economic interests against rivalry. Such was the *herem hayishuv*, the

right of a community to prevent new Jewish settlers from establishing domicile without common consent. As the communities prospered and grew, this ordinance loomed in the background of many a bitter dispute.

5. The nascent communities were small, often numbering little more than a few dozen souls. Shaping a legal system for so small a community could present a formidable task. True, the ruler had invested the community with legislative powers of a very broad nature, but not every community possessed suitably qualified judges. This had an impact on the community's judicial system, as we shall presently see.

6. The role of the individual in these communities was more important than anywhere else in the Jewish world, and this fact is clearly reflected in the legislation of the communities and in their social and spiritual make-up. Not for the talmudic academies of Ashkenaz, for example, the formality adopted by the academies of Babylonia and Spain. In Ashkenaz, the masters and disciples conducted the dialectics of learning in a lively give-and-take that allowed disciples a wider scope for exercising their individual powers, whether in openly challenging their masters' opinion or in carving out their own path while yet under their tutelage. Disciples were even permitted to launch their own local academies. Such conditions greatly spurred the development of spiritual creativity, as the toṣafist movement strikingly attests. Emerging in France towards the close of the eleventh century, the Toṣafists wrought a powerful impact on Jewish Law in France and Ashkenaz of the twelfth and thirteenth centuries, and it was indeed from the unique character of the Ashkenazi talmudic academy that the entire movement imbibed.

7. The Jews were in close social and economic contact with the world around them. To be sure, the persecutions of the First and Second Crusades (1096, 1147) adversely affected the development of these relations, and the sobering events of late thirteenth century Germany (particularly, the persecutions of Rindfleisch, 1298-1299) only heightened the antipathy between the Jews and their surroundings. But for the most part, close socio-economic ties persisted throughout the entire period. The dependence of the Jews on the economic activities of their neighbours proved decisive. If at first this was due to their commercial ventures along the routes of internat-ional trade, by the twelfth and thirteenth centuries it was due to their role in money-lending. This fact clearly left its imprint on communal legislation. Parallel with the increasing exclusion of Jews from medieval society, we find the Sages submitting their decisions with a view to mitigating the hardships of obtaining a livelihood, even at the cost of compromising with Jewish

Law. The force of this economic reality is well evident in the evolution of
Jewish Law in Ashkenaz.

Beginning with the twelfth century the emperors came to regard the Jews
as their own royal property, deeming them *servi camerae*: 'servants of the
Treasury'. While this did not have any real effect on their legal status,
inasmuch as they retained their freedom of movement and the right of any
free subject to bear arms, psychologically it was something of a millstone.
No less detrimental to their status was the gradual shift into money-lending.
The Jews had accumulated a great deal of capital during their years along the
high roads of international trade. Medieval Europe, for its part, was suffering
from a chronic shortage of ready funds, so that as the Jews progressively
penetrated the market they evolved into an increasingly dominant force.
Interest rates were high, loans were generally secured through the deposit of
collateral. Should owners be unable to redeem their pledged valuables, as
indeed often happened, they then reverted by default to the Jewish money-
lenders. Amongst those who regarded themselves as having been swindled
and cheated were knights and high noblemen, who resented this affront to
their honour.

The ability of Jews to take their place in the feudal order and engage in
cultivation of the soil was severely hampered by a number of factors. Not
the least of these deterrents was the administration of the feudal oath,
grounded on the basic tenets of the Christian faith.

The Jewish centre in Northern France waxed steadily and progressively
stronger, reaching its apex by the thirteenth century due to the expansion of
trade and commerce throughout the region. Spiritual and intellectual life also
experienced a great flowering in Northern France. Following the ravages of
the Crusading hordes in 1096, the renowned academies of Mayence and
Worms were no longer in ascendance. This fact, together with the establishment of the talmudic academy of Troyes by *Rashi* (p.311, below), greatly
spurred the establishment of new centres of Jewish learning throughout the
cities of Champagne. And indeed, one of the most important movements of
high medieval Jewry, the *Tosafot*, gathered its rapid momentum in these
flourishing cities of trade.

The intellectual ferment displayed by the Sages of Ashkenaz is most
impressive and diversified. Despite the smallness of the Franco-German
centre in the eleventh century, the range and scope of its literary creativity far
surpassed that of the redoubtable Babylonian centre, with its hundreds of
thousands of Jews. There was no realm of rabbinic creativity in which the
scholars of Ashkenaz did not try their hand. They wrote commentaries on the

Bible, *Talmud*, rabbinic expositions and liturgical poetry. Nor did scholars confine their activity to exegesis: their writings embrace a wide range of interests — religious law and custom, rabbinic ordinances and legal responsa. The rabbinic activity in several of these areas was not only vigorous but indeed innovative. Never before had such commentaries to the *Talmud* and the liturgical poems been written, nor had the customs of the masters been so assiduously compiled and redacted.

2. The Literary Sources

The following represents a brief survey of the literary activity of the Sages of Ashkenaz, with special emphasis on their role in the evolution of Jewish Law.

Somewhere around the year 1000, R. Gershom ben Judah (known as the 'Light of the Exile', *Me'or hagolah*) wrote the first systematic commentary to the Babylonian *Talmud*. There can be no comparing this comprehensive work with the fragmentary commentaries written by Rav Sherira and Rav Hai Gaon, who flourished close to R. Gershom's own time. R. Gershom's disciples and followers perpetuated his exegetical work in the talmudic academies of Mayence and Worms. Ultimately spreading into France, this exegesis culminated in *Rashi*'s classic commentary to the *Talmud*, which drew directly from the commentaries of the German Sages.

Between the years 1100-1300 a new branch of talmudic exegesis and study took root: the *Tosafot*. The Tosafists wrote collections of comments on the *Talmud* arranged according to the order of the talmudic tractates, taking *Rashi*'s commentary on the *Talmud* as their starting point, and using it to compare and analyse different talmudic passages, thus seeking to harmonise apparent discrepancies and distinctions (see further *Enc.Jud.* xv.1278-1283). Several elements of this new intellectual current are discernible amongst the scholars of Worms at the close of the eleventh century, but it was only in twelfth-thirteenth century France that they reached their finest flowering. Combining great erudition with a dialectical analysis of the talmudic text, the crystallisation of the *Tosafot* bears a significant resemblance to the manner in which the *Talmud* itself was composed. Both reflect the drawn-out debates of rabbinic academies. Like the *Talmud*, the various collections of *Tosafot* intersperse answers to questions with legal decisions. In the words of one eminent scholar:

> The Tosafists began where the *Talmud* left off and their writings became the new '*Talmudim*'. Just like [the *Talmud*] they too absorbed everything that

> happened within the academy: the give-and-take of study; the deeds and doings of the masters that were transmitted orally; the epistles, rulings and laws that were written down. (Urbach, *The Tosafists*, 525)

Every academy had its own collection of *Toṣafot*. But while the great majority are no longer extant, others have been preserved for all time in the *Talmud* itself, printed alongside the commentary of *Rashi*. And as on the printed page, so in the world of Jewish Law do the *Gemara*, *Rashi* and *Toṣafot* reign supreme. In the evolution of Jewish Law this combination was to prove a law-producing source of the first magnitude. Scholars often referred to these commentaries and novellae when deciding questions of law, and the very manner of studying the *Toṣafot* profoundly influenced jurists throughout Germany, France, England and the Balkans. Towards the close of the twelfth century and in the following generation more particularly, the *Toṣafot* even made their way into Spain, where they greatly influenced the study of *Talmud* and the writing of novellae and law codes over the next two centuries.

The scholars of Ashkenaz were primarily engaged in exegesis and the composition of legal responsa. Law codes as comprehensive as those written by Spanish Jewry were not undertaken in Ashkenaz. Yet the Ashkenazi centre did produce several important digests of Jewish Law. Particularly noteworthy are the works compiled by R. Eliezer ben Nathan (*Raban*) and R. Eliezer ben Joel Halevi (*Rabiah*) in twelfth century Germany, by R. Isaac ben Moses of Vienna (*Or Zaru'ah*) and R. Mordecai ben Hillel in the following century. In some respects, we may assign to the same group the *Piṣke haRosh* of R. Asher ben Yeḥiel, a German Sage who compiled his book in Spain after settling there in the early fourteenth century. There is also the *Ets Ḥayyim*, composed in late thirteenth century England by R. Jacob Hazan, who included matters of civil and criminal law.

Neither in France nor in Germany was an all-embracing law code ever composed according to the classic model of thematic division. Apart from R. Jacob Hazan's *Ets Ḥayyim*, which betrays the influence of Maimonides, all the legal codes mentioned above are arranged according to the order of the talmudic treatises rather than by subject matter. Even legal responsa are found interspersed in them. Yet their importance in the evolution of Jewish Law cannot be gainsaid. Notable differences often distinguish the legal rulings of Ashkenazi Jewry from those of their Spanish brethren, most particularly in ritual law. All such differences find faithful expression in these books.

Another kind of legal code consists of the short treatise on a specific theme. The great majority of them deal with Jewish holidays and liturgy; very little pertains to either civil or criminal law. The French Sages displayed a partiality for the genre and already in *Rashi*'s academy such works were being written. In general, however, the codifying efforts of the French school were eclipsed by their activities in exegesis and novellae. Such efforts as they did expend in the realm of legal decision-making went into the writing of responsa.

The responsa of the medieval rabbis are of the utmost importance, both as a source of history and as a mirror of Jewish Law and its evolution. Many of these responsa deal with questions arising out of the concrete problems of daily life and have direct bearing on both civil and criminal law. As local judges were not always equipped to resolve cases involving legal uncertainty, they often submitted the questions to a famous scholar for his authoritative decision. These responsa acquired the power of 'case-law' (though not individually setting precedents), and were eventually incorporated into the classic law codes. For example, the responsa literature greatly influenced the *Arba'ah Ṭurim* of R. Jacob ben Asher, which in turn, some two centuries later, exerted so profound an impact on the rulings of the *Shulḥan Arukh* (see further pp.338f., below).

The *responsa prudentium* of the rabbis occupied a vital role from the very beginning of Jewish settlement in Ashkenaz. As far back as the tenth century, questions were directed to Rabbi Kalonymos and his son, Meshullam. During the eleventh century the greatest Sages of Ashkenaz sent responsa well beyond their own communities, laying the foundations for the organized Jewish community and for such issues as family law and synagogue rites. Many hundreds of responsa have come down to us, but that many others have been lost is beyond doubt. Some of these responsa are still in manuscript form and have yet to be published.

From the twelfth century on, the drafting of responsa bears the imprint of the *Toṣafot*. The dialectics are generally more protracted and a wider range of deliberations comes into view.

Any list of the period's greatest respondents must include R. Jacob b. Meir (*Rabbenu Tam*) in France (p.311, below) and R. Meir of Rothenburg in Germany (pp.312f., below). R. Meir was the greatest respondent to flourish in the sphere of Ashkenazi Jewry. Throughout the entire fourteenth century, the disciples of R. Meir — or the disciples of his disciples — provided the leadership for the communities of Germany and Austria.

We have already seen that for dynamic interaction and unimpeded individuality, the academies of Ashkenaz were unique. The literary style of

the responsa may itself reflect this uniqueness. Beginning with the eleventh
century, the responsa of Ashkenaz refer *ex hypothesi* to the possibility of
diverging opinions and multiple views. Not so the responsa of the Babylonian Geonim or those of the early Spanish Sages. The rabbinic masters,
much like the Christian scholastics, encouraged their disciples to pursue their
own literary paths. One of the most interesting testimonies to this effect is
found in a ruling issued by several of the greatest Toṣafists of twelfth century
France. They ruled that a disciple is permitted to challenge his master's
opinion in public, to expound the Law in his living quarters and even to
launch an academy in the same city as his master. Both in letter and in spirit
this represents a sharp divergence from early rabbinic rulings, but the
Toṣafists deemed the old ways better suited to the talmudic period than to
their own. For whereas a disciple had formerly been dependent on his master,
this dependence had been obviated now and forever by the emergence of law
codes. Needless to say, neither the Geonim of Babylonia nor the Sages of
Spain accepted this ruling.

The religious customs of the great Sages nurtured a new and innovative
literary genre: books of customs (*ṣefer minhagim*). As early as the eleventh
century, numerous customs of contemporary Sages from Mayence and
Worms found their way into the locally composed *Ma'aseh haMakhiri*. Nor
had the thirteenth century elapsed before the disciples of R. Meir of
Rothenburg (1215-1293) reduced his customs to writing. Apart from France,
however, where the genre was somewhat less cultivated, these customs
attained the force of legal precedent, binding on communities far and wide.
At a later stage the Austrian communities also accepted the genre.

Books of customs had a certain impact on the evolution of Jewish jurisprudence, though primarily in the field of ceremonial law. Some of these
customs were later to resurface in the domain of Polish Jewry. Many of the
customs and beliefs adopted by the pietist circle of twelfth-thirteenth century
Ashkenaz are found concentrated in the *Ṣefer Ḥaṣidim* (*'Book of the Pious'*).
Composed in Germany during the early thirteenth century, the impact of this
book is well evidenced in non-pietist circles as well. The pietist movement
which emerged in eighteenth century Europe greatly revered *Ṣefer Ḥaṣidim*
and the book's influence permeated many of its customs. These customs had
somewhat less, though not an insignificant, impact in the centres strongly
influenced by the Spanish heritage. Following the move of several German
Sages to Spain in the late thirteenth and fourteenth century, some of these
customs penetrated the sphere of Spanish Jewry. Asher ben Yeḥiel, author of
the *Piṣke haRosh*, was one of the foremost figures in this respect.

3. *Legal Practice*

A. Communal Enactments *(Takkanot hakahal)*

Due to the special nature of German Jewry, community Sages and members enacted numerous ordinances for the public welfare, especially in matters of economics, family law and judicial procedure. This was never more true than in the eleventh and twelfth centuries, when the sovereignty of the local communities reached its zenith. Once the ordinances were reduced to writing they became the *jus cogens* of community life. The community was envisaged as a kind of self-governing body, the ordinances as its binding code of law. Some of these ordinances were enacted in rabbinic synods attended by leading Sages from far and wide, and their consequent prestige rendered them binding for many generations thereafter. Amongst the most important ordinances are those promulgated by R. Gershom ben Judah in early eleventh century Germany, and by R. Jacob ben Meir *(Rabbenu Tam)* in mid-twelfth century France. There are also the ordinances enacted during the twelfth-thirteenth centuries by the three Rhineland communities of Speyer, Worms and Mayence. Despite the fact that these ordinances were promulgated against a specific set of socio-economic circumstances, Ashkenazi Sages of a later period regarded them as binding precedents.

These ordinances exercised a vast influence over the evolution of civil and criminal law of Ashkenazi Jewry. Some of them — particularly in the domain of family law — continue to mould the life of Ashkenazi Jewry to this very day.

B. Courts and Procedures

Supervision of judicial procedures was invested in the community itself. While the Franco-German communities did not have a central institution governing their common interests, we do hear of meetings between community leaders in the great centres of eleventh century trade. During the twelfth century we find rabbinic synods convened by the leading Sages of France and Germany, in which decisions and ordinances were enacted on behalf of Franco-German Jewry as a whole.

Having been granted wide legal autonomy, the communities adjudicated most of the disputes between fellow townsmen. Communities were even empowered to choose their own leaders, and these were generally rich traders close to the ruling circles, or prominent rabbinic scholars.

During the eleventh and twelfth centuries, the communities enjoyed

almost complete internal jurisdiction. But beginning with the thirteenth
century we find localities being deprived of the right to have cases of civil
and criminal law tried before Jewish courts. One striking example of this is
found in the privileges issued to the community of Cologne in the year
1252. This charter orders Jews to submit all cases of theft, forgery, assault
and adultery to the Christian courts. Behind this development looms the rise
of the cities, and the struggle of the city burghers to widen their sphere of
jurisdiction. Yet another factor comes from the field of economics. These
gentile authorities were desirous of enriching their coffers with the fines
imposed on transgressors. Hence we occasionally find agreements between
city authorities and the Jewish leaders, whereby fines paid by Jews were
turned over in part to the city treasury. But this was only one expression of
the general trend, and from the thirteenth century on, various Christian
lawbooks refer to the legal status of the Jews in the most painstaking detail.
For sheer comprehensiveness, none surpasses the *Sachsenspiegel* of Germany. These laws have been discussed at length by G. Kisch in his classic
study, *The Jews in Medieval Germany*.

Not every community could boast of qualified judges and this was
especially true of the smaller communities. Community leaders frequently
served as a court of law. In this context, we may take a closer look at a most
curious ruling handed down by Meshullam ben Kalonymos around the year
1000. A Jewish Law of hoary antiquity rules that judgment must follow the
majority opinion and, indeed, such is the principle in the Bible itself
(*Ex.* 23:2). Nonetheless, we find Rabbi Meshullam ruling that:

> Of the three [judges] constituting a court of law, [it may happen] that two say
> this and one says that. If [they are] equal in wisdom then ignore the words of
> the one and abide by the words of the two; but if the one is to be preferred
> over the two, go with him who makes his words cogent. (*Responsa of the
> Early Geonim*, no. 144)

The decision of this responsum clearly runs counter to both biblical and
talmudic principles. One later Sage tries to explain this ruling as referring to
a court composed of an Academy Head and his two disciples, but there is no
hint of this in the text itself. Moreover, only when a court was composed of
untutored laymen might the majority opinion be overruled. Meshullam's
decision, we thus find, springs from the historical exigencies of his day and
age. Learned Sages were not always to be found in those early years of the
incipient European communities, and the ruling should be regarded as a
makeshift, an attempt to meet the needs of the hour. As such, it provides us
with valuable insight into Jewish society towards the latter half of the tenth

century, when in some emerging communities of Europe, lay courts were empanelled, by force of necessity.

C. Communal Autonomy

The early Sages of Ashkenaz strove to consolidate the rule of the individual community and to strengthen its authority. They ruled that no community had the right to interfere with another community, no matter how small or bereft of Sages the latter might be. One important ordinance in this spirit obliged every person to stand trial wheresoever accused, without being allowed to request trial in his own community (as permitted by talmudic law).

Generally speaking, a defendant could be compelled to stand trial in a Jewish court. In certain cases the Jewish courts even applied to the Christian authorities in order to ensure compliance. Sources often mention the talmudic 'seven good men of the city' vis-à-vis court procedure and local leadership, but this number was not always heeded in practice.

D. Penalties

Jewish courts made use of different penalties in order to enforce their decisions. Most frequent of these were fines, the ban of excommunication (*herem*), confiscation of property and, in certain cases, corporal punishment. The community was most severe with any Jew who had recourse to a non-Jewish court. At times a person who did so would meet with the same penalties imposed on informers: excommunication or the infliction of stripes and a monetary fine. Even a person who only threatened to make such an appeal was severely punished.

E. Appeals

The right of litigants to request an appellate review of court decisions was never uniformly resolved. R. Joseph Tov-Elem (Bonfils) and R. Jacob b. Meir (*Rabbenu Tam*), two of the most outstanding Sages of eleventh-twelfth century France, limited the right of appeal. In the opinion of the former authority, the right of a higher court to abrogate the decision of a lower court applied only to ritual matters and not to civil law. Talmudic law gives the litigant the right to request a written opinion from the judges. *Rabbenu Tam*, however, limited this to cases where the defendant had been summoned against his will to a certain court.

Nonetheless, court decisions were often appealed in Ashkenaz, and R. Meir of Rothenburg mentions that such appeals were a daily routine (*Responsa* of *Maharam of Rothenberg*, Prague ed., no.715). Appeals of another kind were made by the judges themselves, directed to the 'Great Ones of the Generation'. Confronted with cases of particularly complex or delicate nature, or problems of inter-communal dispute, the judges often appealed to a leading scholar for a definitive ruling. This procedure did not emanate from a formal and duly authorized institution, but rather from a general consensus over the ability of great scholars to dispense justice by force of their personality and their greatness in *Torah*.

Speyer, Worms and Mayence, three of the most important Rhineland communities of the period, established a superior court in the twelfth century in order to regulate their common affairs. From time to time they convened rabbinic synods, and since other communities willingly submitted to their authority, these synods became something of a supreme judicial authority for all Ashkenaz. The outstanding rabbinic figures of the day took part in these synods, acting once again by virtue of their prodigious learning and by the aura of their authority. But as these synods were only irregularly convened, Franco-German Jewry cannot be said to have instituted a High Court with plenipotentiary powers.

4. *The Principal Authorities*

Many of the Sages of Ashkenaz left their imprint on Jewish Law. Indeed, dozens come from the ranks of the Tosafists alone. As we cannot do full justice to these figures in the space at our disposal, we shall sketch the lives of just twelve, and even then with great brevity.

A. R. Gershom ben Judah ('The Light of the Exile') (950-1028)

Foremost Sage of eleventh century Germany, he was one of the most instrumental figures in shaping the communities of Ashkenaz and in fostering the study of *Torah*. He enacted numerous ordinances in relation to family law and the socio-organizational aspects of community life. He was the first to write a comprehensive and systematic commentary to the *Talmud*. He accustomed his disciples in the academy of Mayence to a free and open discussion devoid of all formality and distance. His responsa and ordinances influenced Jewish Law for all generations.

B. R. Joseph ben Samuel Tov-Elem (Bonfils) (980-1050)

The greatest of the French Sages during the first half of the eleventh century, he compiled an important anthology of the teachings and responsa of the Babylonian Geonim, thereby helping to disseminate their doctrine throughout Germany and France. He wrote many influential responsa about community organization, which were widely studied and quoted by later authorities as well. He deserves recognition as one of the principal architects of the several communities.

C. R. Solomon ben Isaac (*Rashi*) (1041-1105)

The most eminent of the French Sages, his commentaries to the *Talmud* and Bible represent literary creativity at its finest; his impact on the study of the Pentateuch is without peer. *Rashi*'s commentary to the Babylonian *Talmud* has become an inseparable part of the *Talmud* itself, uniformly printed in all editions since the very dawn of Hebrew printing. His disciples compiled various legal treatises under his direction and hundreds of his legal responsa are extant. Together, these sources greatly influenced later generations of jurists active in Ashkenaz. Despite great personal modesty his rulings reveal unfaltering confidence, and he played an important role in community leadership.

D. R. Jacob ben Meir (*Rabbenu Tam*) (1100-1171)

Rabbenu Tam was *Rashi*'s grandson was the greatest of the Toṣafists and one of the most renowned French Sages of all times. Students flocked to his academy from as far away as Italy and Russia. Most of the first Toṣafists in Germany and France were his disciples and his own *Toṣafot* are at the basis of many of the other collections. He took an active role in public life. The *Toṣafot*, rulings and commentaries of *Rabbenu Tam* provide a rich source for the evolution of Jewish Law.

E. R. Eliezer ben Nathan of Mayence (1090-1170)

The first Sage of Ashkenaz to compile a comprehensive legal code, his *Even ha'ezer* contains rulings, responsa, commentaries and *Toṣafot*; the laws are arranged according to the order of the talmudic tractates. Much of the book is devoted to problems arising from Jewish participation in trade and commerce, rendering it important not only for the history of Jewish Law but also for the socio-economic study of medieval Jewry.

F. R. Judah ben Samuel the Pious (1150-1217)

The dominant personality of German pietism (*Ḥaṣidut Ashkenaz*), a movement which elevated ethics and mysticism to the spiritual forefront of Ashkenazi Jewry. The fragments of writings that have come down to us are not from his own hand. Many of his teachings are interspersed in *Sefer Ḥaṣidim* (the '*Book of the Pious*'). Even jurists with little inclination towards pietism were influenced by his teachings. He strove to preserve the tradition of ancient Ashkenaz, and to this end rejected customs originating with the French Sages. *Sefer Ḥaṣidim* exerted a profound influence on many of the ethical works composed in later generations.

G. R. Eleazar ben Judah of Worms (1165-1238)

An outstanding disciple of Judah the Pious, he played a vital role in the development and dissemination of Ashkenazi mysticism. The author of numerous works of law, *ḳabbalah*, ethics, biblical commentaries, *Toṣafot*, liturgical poetry and esoteric commentaries to the prayers, his most important legal work is *Sefer haRoḳeah*, which deals mostly with ritual law and worship. It too betrays the clear imprint of German pietism.

H. R. Eliezer ben Joel Halevi (1140-1225)

One of the most important Sages of medieval Germany, he wrote the *Sefer Rabiah,* in which laws and legal decisions are arranged according to the order of the talmudic tractates. Responsa are also included. The book profoundly influenced Jewish Law even beyond Ashkenaz. Much of it was published in a very fine edition by V. Aptowitzer (2nd ed., Jerusalem, 1964), and additional sections have seen publication in recent years.

I. R. Isaac ben Moses of Vienna (1180-1250)

He flourished amongst various communities of Ashkenaz and towards the end of his days served as a rabbi in Vienna. His *Or Zarua*, which he spent some 30 years writing, is one of the most important law codes ever written in Ashkenaz. In it he sums up the more elaborate sophistries and discussions of earlier codifiers and also draws upon the ancient literature of Franco-German Jewry. The book is arranged in part by subject matter, and in part by the talmudic tractates. It contains both ritual and commercial law.

J. R. Meir of Rothenburg (1215-1293)

R. Meir (the *Maharam* of Rothenburg) was one of the most important

Toṣafists and spiritual leaders of Ashkenaz during the latter half of the thirteenth century; from the ranks of his disciples rose the leaders of an entire generation. His surviving responsa, approximately one thousand in all, constitute his principal contribution to the evolution of Jewish Law. They cover the entire spectrum of Jewish Law and were circulated through the communities of Ashkenaz, Austria, Bohemia, Italy, France and Spain. Questions of community jurisdiction and procedure were allotted considerable space. Numerous religious customs of the *Maharam* have been incorporated into the rites of Ashkenazi Jewry.

K. R. Mordecai ben Hillel (1240-1298)

Amongst the greatest of rabbinic authorities in late thirteenth century Ashkenaz, his law code, the *Mordecai*, follows the order of the *Ṣefer hahalakhot* of Isaac Alfasi. Over three hundred Sages and books are mentioned in this encyclopaedic work, which was rapidly disseminated in various editions. Its impact was felt beyond Ashkenaz into Spain.

5. *Characteristics of the Law of the Period*

The historical reality of medieval Ashkenaz profoundly influenced the formal judicial aspects of community life. Obviously, Jewish Law in Ashkenaz was founded on the *halakhah* of the *Talmud*. But historical reality affected the application of that *halakhah*. Changing circumstances required adjustment, and special ordinances were promulgated in many areas of life. That the reality was potent and its consequences most tangible, the following examples will show. They pertain to the fields of judicial procedure and law, community organization and family life. These examples will serve to demonstrate, moreover, just how dynamic and alive Jewish Law was in this period.

A. Fines and Excommunications

The *Talmud* lays down that fines cannot be imposed outside of *Erets Israel*. This decision was upheld by the Geonim of Babylonia and it crops up time and again in various sources, including those written by the early Sages of Ashkenaz. Nonetheless, the Jewish courts of Ashkenaz made wide use of this penalty and did so with great frequency. Through the responsa of Rabbi Meshullam and R. Gershom ben Judah we learn that fines were imposed from the very outset of Jewish settlement in medieval Ashkenaz. One Sage of thirteenth century Ashkenaz reconciled the contradiction by drawing a distinction between the biblically-ordained fines and those imposed by rabbinic enactments. It may very well be that the earlier Sages also adopted this line of reasoning, but there is no hint of it in any of their writings, despite the relative frequency with which they discussed the question. Apparently, then, this rationale is somewhat retroactive, an attempt to comprehend a rabbinic practice that ostensibly negates both the law of the *Talmud* and the rulings of the Geonim.

No more effective was a limitation on fines proposed by Isaac of Worms in eleventh century Ashkenaz. According to a ruling 'handed down from his Masters', monetary penalties were only to be levied by the 'seven good men' of the city. Such delimitation, however, is not to be found in any of the Franco-German sources. Quite the contrary is true, and there seems good reason to believe that both individual Sages and regular courts did impose fines.

We may reasonably assume that recurring defiance of community authority provided the major impulse behind the proliferation of fines and excommunications. Whatever socio-economic sanctions excommunication involved — and these could be heavy indeed — its element of sacrality resounded powerfully in both Jewish and Christian society, and thus rendered it a particularly effective means of coercion.

That both of these measures were needed, we learn from the testimony of Joseph Tov-Elem. Only by imposing excommunications and levying fines, he laments, was it possible to coerce the 'wicked men' of the age into compliance. Thus does an outstanding scholar paint the portrait of his generation, and there were others who even sought to alter court procedure by administering a warning of excommunication along with the courtroom oath. The dread of excommunication, they claimed, would make one and all more fearful of taking a false oath. R. Gershom ben Judah, however, rejected this idea. Nonetheless, this is valuable testimony to the power of excommunication, at least in the eyes of some, for throughout the Bible and various talmudic sources, the oath is imbued with a stern solemnity that is second to none.

B. Public Grievance

One of the more intriguing practices to emerge from the Ashkenazi communities was that known as 'Stopping the Services'. (Some scholars have traced the roots of this practice to *Erets Israel* during the talmudic period, but the evidence for this is obscure.) From the very outset of community life, any Jew who felt aggrieved or wronged had the inalienable right of rising to his or her feet in the synagogue and interrupting the divine service. When this occurred all prayers came to an abrupt stop, the reading from the Holy Scrolls halted mid-line, and the congregants heard out the grievance. Nor might they resume the service prior to finding some way of dealing with the problem, such as appointing a special committee to examine the complaint. The earliest evidence of the practice dates from the first half of the eleventh century, but it most probably existed even before. Be that as it may, the practice continued unabated over the centuries, even though it earned the opprobrium of the Christians, who ridiculed the Jews for such 'scandal-mongering' during the hour of sacred worship.

The Geonim of Babylonia objected to the practice in the most forthright of terms. Presumably, it was the very weakness of the early Franco-German communities which caused the practice to flourish amongst the Jews of Ashkenaz. As we have already noted, many of the communities were extremely small, and less-than-expert jurists often sat in their law courts. Equitable treatment of a wronged member had to come from the community itself if it was to come at all. But once the communities and their courts stood on a firmer footing, it was only natural that efforts were launched to put a check on the practice. Such is the trend of an ordinance ascribed to R. Gershom ben Judah, the Light of the Exile:

> If a man summons his neighbor to Court, and the latter refuses to appear, the plaintiff may not stop the morning or afternoon prayers or the reading of the *Torah* unless he has thrice interfered with the evening service or the completion of the morning service. After that he may stop all services until his case is tried. If there are two synagogues in the city he may only interrupt the prayers in the synagogue which the defendant attends. But if he has interrupted the prayers there thrice (without avail) he may stop the services in both synagogues. (Finkelstein, *Jewish Self-Government*, 128-29)

Even so, this practice continued to disturb the equanimity of the Jewish communities for years to come. As late as the thirteenth century, one synagogue had to forego the Sabbath prayer for two weeks running due to the refusal of one aggrieved individual to renounce his complaint.

Needless to say, the ability to stop the services gave each and every member of the community considerable power and emphasized his individual dignity and rights. This legal practice is found also in the documents of the Cairo Genizah from the eleventh century and subsequently amongst Spanish Jewry as well, though with less frequency than in the communities of Ashkenaz.

C. Place of Trial

Talmudic law gave the defendant the right to be tried in his own community, and this law prevailed throughout the geonic Period. Yet in one of the ordinances attributed to R. Gershom ben Judah a new practice required the defendant to stand trial wherever he was accused, even if at some distance from his own locality, so long as that court had competence to impose the ban.

> If a man passes through a community where there is a *herem bet din* and he is summoned to a Court under the *herem*, in the presence of the proper witnesses, even if he be summoned in the market-place, the *herem* is upon him until he repairs to the Court to plead his case. Even if no witnesses are present, the *herem* applies ... but a writ of insubordination can be issued only on the testimony of witnesses. After having made his plea, the defendant may proceed on his way. The plaintiff is responsible to see that the decree of the Court reaches him. (Finkelstein, *Jewish Self-Government*, 126)

An examination of the responsa from the first half of eleventh century Ashkenaz reveals that this ordinance was in fact practised. So, for example, we read of one German Jew who travelled to Hungary for his commercial affairs, only to be hauled before the local court by a Jew who was likewise from Germany (Responsum of Judah ha-Cohen, in *Responsa of Meir of Rothenburg*, Prague ed., no. 904.)

The change in judicial procedure was highly significant. At this time many Jews of Ashkenaz were sailing the high seas of international trade and, as a result, were often absent from home. Such journeys could last for extended periods of time — as a variety of documents attest — and tracking the wayfarers down was no easy task. Under these circumstances it was only too easy to dodge legal suits by tarrying in foreign parts. This is the historical background behind our ordinance. Later Sages also mention a similar practice. Concerning the *herem bet din* of his own city, Rabbi Samson of Sens (second half of the twelfth century) wrote that:

> Any townsman of ours who brings a case against a recalcitrant townsman must plead his case here. And [the defendant] cannot fob him off by saying 'Let us go to the *Bet Va'ad*' [lit. House of Assembly] or 'I'm going to take this to the Great Court'. (*Mordekhai, Sanhedrin*, no. 709)

And towards the end of the thirteenth century R. Meir of Rothenburg made a similar ruling:

> [If] Reuben says 'Let us plead the case here in Rothenburg' and Simeon says 'Let us go to the *Bet Va'ad* in Marienburg' ... we have a community

ordinance nowadays that in any locality with a proper law court, he may not put him off by saying 'Let us go to the *Bet Va'ad.*' (*Responsa of Meir of Rothenburg*, Berlin ed., p. 42, no. 290)

Having seen three examples of legislation concerning court procedure, let us now turn our attention to two famous ordinances from the realm of family law.

D. Polygamy

The fame surrounding the ban against polygamy derives largely from the name of R. Gershom ben Judah, the 'Light of the Exile'. Nonetheless, the ordinance has bred a host of lingering doubts. Was it really enacted by R. Gershom? What was the historical background behind its enactment? Some scholars have assumed that the ordinance is a late one, dating to the twelfth century. But the traditions ascribing it to Rabbi R. Gershom are ancient, and their value considerable. In discussing the date, scholars have overlooked the historical picture emerging from the documents of eleventh century German Sages. Although the sources are relatively abundant and exceedingly varied, not one of them offers even a single testimonium about a second marriage contracted during the lifetime of the first wife. We may dismiss from our discussion, of course, those second marriages required by religious law, i.e. when ten years of marriage failed to produce any issue. Thus we learn that already by the eleventh century, bigamous households were nowhere to be found in Germany. Special weight should be given to the fact that the Hebrew chronicles of 1096 make not the slightest mention of bigamy. Even more significantly, neither do the memorial book-lists of those who perished during the persecutions. These lists do not cite even a single family with more than one wife!

The question of the historical background has generated six principal solutions. Only three will be mentioned. According to Z.W. Falk, the strictly monogamous Christian surroundings were the prevailing force behind this ordinance. M.A. Friedman has suggested that the ordinance preserves an ancient tradition of *Erets Israel* from the mishnaic and talmudic period. In our own opinion, however, the ordinance was enacted in response to a real and pressing need. We have already seen that many members of the Ashkenazi communities were long absent from home during this period, plying the routes of international trade. Their travels washed them ashore such southern lands as Provence, Spain and North Africa, and their stay in these remote places often stretched out for years. On this point the responsa literature has preserved various testimonia. That Jewish merchants should contract a second marriage when so long away from hearth and home is scarcely surprising. Yet it was not only the contingencies of everyday life that conspired to bring about this development, but even the hallowed sources of Judaism itself. The Babylonian *Talmud* mentions two venerated Sages who were wont to take other wives when finding themselves away from home. Needless to say, the polygamous practices of the Muslim population in the lands of Islam, and even of some of the Jews, only exacerbated the problem. And, in fact, rabbinic literature of the time does mention 'strangers' from afar who married local women, dwelled together in wedlock, and then, when returning whence they came, either divorced their new wives or left them alone and disconsolate between one trading expedition and the next. Just how grave a problem this was we learn from Maimonides himself:

> Maimonides, of blessed memory, enacted an ordinance to regulate the position of the daughters of Israel, that we should not give a woman in marriage to a stranger [*nokhri*, here a Jew from abroad who was not a member of the community] anywhere in Egypt until he brings proof that he is unmarried, or swears an oath on the Pentateuch to that effect. And if he has a wife, let him write her a bill of divorce, and then we may permit him to marry in this country. And as for any stranger who marries a woman here and wishes to leave for another country, we will not allow him to go even if his wife has given her consent, until he writes and delivers to her a conditional bill of divorce, to come into effect at such time as may be agreed between them, being a year or two years or three years, but not longer. (*Responsa of Maimonides*, ed. Blau, vol. 2, p.624)

Of particular interest is that part of the ordinance which prevents 'foreign' Jews from leaving Egypt without depositing a conditional bill of divorce. Only a harsh reality in which wives were abandoned over protracted periods of time could explain so drastic a measure. Non-compliance would effectively curtail the activities of a Jewish merchant: we may recall that in this period Egyptian Jews were still accustomed to travelling abroad on business. Inasmuch as the socio-economic conditions of neighbouring countries resembled those of Egypt even prior to Maimonides' day, it is hard to imagine that the phenomenon was localized to twelfth century Egypt.

The ban against polygamy enacted by the Sages of eleventh century Germany cannot be considered in isolation from the socio-economic structure of the local Jewish communities. Two factors were of special importance: the large number of rich and well-connected merchants comprising the original nucleus of settlement; and the relatively high status enjoyed by women in these communities.

Under such conditions, well-to-do parents naturally keep an anxious eye out for the honour of their daughters and the rich dowries attending their marriage. While a second marriage during the first wife's lifetime was a rare and unlikely occurrence, a community ordinance would effectively guarantee the monogamous structure of the daughter's family life. Moreover, society as a whole was all the more ready to accept such ordinances in view of the prevailing attitude towards women.

E. Divorce

The force of these two factors — furtive marriages in far-away lands and the relatively high status of women — form the crux of another ban attributed to R. Gershom: the ordinance forbidding the divorce of a woman against her will. A straying husband who took a second wife entailed the risk of excommunication upon returning to his original community, or upon discovery of his secret by fellow-merchants likewise roaming the inter-national trade routes. Such a predicament could be circumvented by sending his first wife a bill of divorce; this may have been more frequent amongst childless couples. But once the first ordinance forbidding plural marriage was in effect, it was only natural to bolster it with another ordinance forbidding divorce *nolens volens*, whether or not the husband was away from home. Once again, the auspicious socio-economic conditions and high status of Jewish women within the German community are inextricably linked together.

F. Domestic Violence

The Sages of Ashkenaz adopted a severe attitude towards a husband who beat his wife, more so than in any other Jewish centre of the Middle Ages. While the Geonim of Babylonia penalized the offending husband with a fine, most of them felt that he need not be forced to grant his wife a divorce. The Sages of Spain concluded that the wife-beater should be so forced, but only after tedious and drawn-out hearings. Moreover, when the circumstances seemed ripe, they did permit a husband to beat his wife 'in the name of education'. So, for example, Maimonides ruled that:

> Any woman who refrains from doing work of the kind that she is obliged to do is forced to do it, even by means of whipping. (*Mishneh Torah*, Matrimonial Laws, 21:10)

That a husband might beat his wife into performing chores is an opinion without parallel in the writings of any Jewish Sage active in Christian Europe. It is no coincidence that Rabbi Abraham ben David of Posquières (*Rabad*) told Maimonides *à propos* this decision, 'I have never heard of chastising women with rods.'

The Sages of Northern France, the Toṣafists, ruled that the husband should be fined and compelled to grant his wife a divorce, should she be so inclined. From a legalistic point of view, a wife-beating husband and a man who hit a stranger incurred one and the same judgment, as we find in this ordinance of R. Perets ben Elijah:

> The cry of the daughters of our people has been heard concerning the sons of Israel who raise their hands to strike their wives. Yet who has given a husband the authority to beat his wife? Is he not rather forbidden to strike any person in Israel? Moreover R. I(saac) has written in a responsum that he has it on the authority of three great Sages, namely R. Samuel, R. Jacob Tam and R. I(saac), the sons of R. Meir, that one who beats his wife is in the same category as one who beats a stranger. Nevertheless, we have heard of cases where Jewish women complained regarding their treatment before the Communities and no action was taken on their behalf.
>
> We have therefore decreed that any Jew may be compelled on application of his wife or one of her near relatives to undertake by a *ḥerem* not to beat his wife in anger or cruelty or so as to disgrace her, for that is against Jewish practice.
>
> If anyone will stubbornly refuse to obey our words, the Court of the place to which the wife or her relatives will bring complaint shall assign her maintenance according to her station and according to the custom of the place where she dwells. They shall fix her alimony as though her husband were away on a distant journey.
>
> If they, our Masters, the great Sages of the land agree to this ordinance, it shall be established. (Finkelstein, *Jewish Self-Government,* 216-18)

The stringently-minded rabbis of this ordinance constitute the greatest Toṣafists of twelfth century France. At the same time, this source apprises us of the difficulty in combating a phenomenon which was well-known in the neighbouring Christian milieu.

The stand adopted by the German Sages on this issue is of great interest. Utmost severity was the note sounded by the greatest of Sages who referred to the matter throughout the twelfth-thirteenth centuries. They were not content like the French Sages merely to fine the husband and force him to grant a divorce. Instead, they ruled that he must also receive corporal punishment. Thus, for example, writes Rabbi Simcha of Speyer:

> Therefore penalize him severely, whether physically or financially, for what has happened. Great repentance is necessary, and deal severely with him in

the future as you see fit.

R. Meir of Rothenburg was even more uncompromising:

> The beater must be ostracized and excommunicated, flogged and punished with all kinds of beatings, and even have his hand cut off if he is accustomed to beating her.

We have already noted that the pietists of Ashkenaz greatly influenced the Sages of Germany: severity against wife-beaters seems to provide yet other example. Pietist circles accorded women great respect, and considered it a sin to subject any person to insult or shame. In the case of wife-beating, financial compensation was insufficient. Atonement was necessary as well and for this the husband required punishment: in the eyes of the pietists, repentance could only be achieved in a manner commensurate with the sin. Sentencing the husband to corporal punishment, so it appears, was designed to expiate the sin *quid pro quo*.

6. Bibliography

Agus, I.A., *The Heroic Age of Franco-German Jewry* (New York: Yeshiva University Press, 1969).

Agus, I.A., *Urban Civilization in Pre-Crusade Europe* (Leiden: E.J. Brill, 1965, 2 vols.).

Blumenkranz, B., *The Roman Church and the Jews* (Tel-Aviv, Massadah Publications, 1966).

Elon, M., *Jewish Law* (Jerusalem: Magnes Press, 1973, Hebrew); Engl. ed., *Jewish Law: History, Sources, Principles*, trld. B. Auerbach and M.J. Sykes, Philadelphia and Jerusalem, Jewish Publication Society, 1994, 4 vols., esp. chs. 19, 31.

Finkelstein, L., *Jewish Self-Government in the Middle Ages* (New York: Feldheim, 1964).

Frank, M., *The Communities of Ashkenaz and their Courts* (Tel Aviv: Dvir, 1937, Hebrew).

Grossman, A., *The Early Sages of Ashkenaz* (Jerusalem: Magnes Press, 1981, Hebrew).

Grossman, A., 'Medieval Rabbinic Views on Wife-Beating, 800-1300', *Jewish History* 5 (1991), 53-62.

Katz, J., *Exclusiveness and Tolerance: Studies in Jewish-Gentile Relations in Medieval and Modern Times* (New York: Schocken Books, 1962).

Kisch, G., *The Jews in Medieval Germany* (New York: Ktav Publishing

Co., 1970).

Rakover, N., *Multi-Language Bibliography*, s.v. 'Regulations. Legislation' (pp. 75-77); Responsa (pp. 294-298); Communities — Organization and Administration (pp. 390-394); Germany (pp. 413-418); France (pp. 446-451); personal bibliographies (pp.740-742, 747, 750-752, 756-758).

Schwarzfuchs, S., *Kahal: La communauté Juive de L'Europe Mediévale* (Paris, Maisonneuve et Larose, 1986).

Soloveitchik, H., 'Can Halakhic Texts Talk History?', *AJSReview* III (1976), 311-357.

Stow, K.R., *Alienated Minority* (Cambridge MA: Harvard University Press, 1992).

Urbach, E.E., *The Tosafists* (Jerusalem: Mosad Bialik, 1980, 4th enlarged ed., Hebrew).

Weisbard, P. and Schonberg, D., *Jewish Law: Bibliography of Sources and Scholarship in English* (Littleton: Fred B. Rothman & Co., 1989), s.v. Takanot (pp. 21-22).

12

TOWARD SUNRISE
IN THE EAST 1300-1565

by

STEPHEN M. PASSAMANECK

Hebrew Union College-Jewish Institute of Religion

Los Angeles

1. *Historical Introduction*

When Rabbi Meir b. Barukh of Rothenburg died a prisoner held for ransom in the fortress of Ensisheim in 1293, his mantle of authority as the ultimate legal expert of his generation among German (Ashkenazi) Jews devolved upon his younger contemporary and pupil, R. Asher b. Yeḥiel — variously known as *Rabbenu Asher*, *Rosh* (the acronym for *Rabbenu Asher*), and *Asheri*. When R. Asher assumed by consensus the dignity of ultimate authority among German Jews, R. Solomon b. Adret, the businessman turned legal scholar and jurist, held the same consensus position amongst Iberian Jews. Between the time that these two towering figures flourished and the publication of Joseph Ḳaro's *Shulḥan Arukh* in 1565 (with glosses by the Polish authority, Moses Isserles, following a few years later) both German Jewry and Iberian Jewry experienced changes, upheavals, and dislocations which profoundly altered these communities and consequently presented occasion for further challenge to and development in Jewish Law. No account of Jewish Law during this period between 1300 and 1565 can proceed without reference to the momentous occurrences in Jewish history during that time or without some, albeit brief, reference to those major events of European history which affected the status and condition of the Jews.

To begin with, this general period includes numerous European dynastic wars on both smaller and larger scales: the Hundred Years' War which devastated Northern France and the continuing reconquest of Spain in which Christian monarchs steadily pushed the Muslims from the land, eventually expelling them altogether in 1492. Further, the black death ravaged Europe in the fourteenth century, and its effects lingered for two generations in terms of social and economic dislocation. This was also the period of the Renaissance for art and letters, which of course affected different parts of Europe at different times and to different degrees. There was also the Reformation and the Counter Reformation. And for the last 100 years of the period, the introduction of moveable type printing in the fifteenth century occasioned change in western society at many levels. Even though the particular institutions and phenomena of Jewish Law to be discussed do not appear to refer or relate directly to these major historical events, the fates of communities and of individual Jews, all of which affected the practice and development of Jewish Law, were always swept along by the larger historical tide.

Parenthetically, we should also note that the great centres of Jewish cultural, political, social, and legal activity at the time under notice — Barcelona, Toledo, Cracow, Salonika, Venice, Vienna, Wiener Neustadt, and all the others — were by modern standards small towns, crowded and squalid, and not the modern urban centres which, though often equally crowded and squalid, are many degrees removed from their medieval ancestors.

In the year 1300, *Rosh*, then about age 50, was the most prominent rabbinic jurist among German Jews, who were generally concentrated in the areas of southwestern and southern Germany, parts of Bohemia, Moravia, Slovakia and Austria. At the same time, R. Solomon b. Adret was the most prominent rabbinic jurist in Spain, and Spanish-Jewish communities flourished in Catalonia, Aragon, Castile, Murcia, Valencia, and Andalusia. By the end of the period, 1565, a significant population of German Jews had emigrated to Poland, at the invitation of the Polish Crown, and the foundations of the great communities of Eastern Europe had been laid. By that same time, the Spanish Jewish world — which had produced statesmen and jurists of the first rank for centuries — had disappeared, banished from Spanish territory in 1492, just months after the last enclave of Moslems had been defeated and exiled. Ferdinand and Isabella of Spain had completed the Christian reconquest. The Spanish Jewish refugees who survived the brutal rigors of seeking new homes (and many thousands did not survive) found themselves in Algeria, Morocco, Venice, and especially Greece, Turkey, Palestine, and Egypt, then parts of the Ottoman Empire, the most powerful and splendid Empire of its time. Thus, during this period of Jewish legal development, new population centres were created, some out of choice and some from dire necessity, with all the attendant problems that uprooting and resettlement cause.

Given the enormous historical tapestry which has been described only in the briefest outline, the task of following the single thread of Jewish Law, albeit a bright and significant thread, obviously would lead us into a welter of detail, not to mention drama, that would at length tend as much to obscure as to illuminate. Therefore the discussion of general background of the period, in terms of both German and Spanish Jewish legal life, will concentrate on a characteristic time and place for each, within the total historical and geographical possibilities of the era. The specific time and place chosen does of course reflect what has gone before and presages what would come later.

The period between *Rosh* and Joseph Ḳaro, the last era of the *Rishonim* (the so-called 'earlier' authorities), is marked by an eastward movement in European Jewish life in general. This age also presents us with a series of distinguished rabbinic jurists who are among the most frequently quoted authorities in Jewish Law and an equally distinguished catalog of rabbinic legal works which are among the most frequently cited Jewish legal writings.

2. *Juridical Background and Legal Practise of the Period*

A. Germany

First, the Germans. Professor Shlomo Eidelberg has written extensively on Jewish life in Austria in the fifteenth Century. That place, and that time, provide us with a good look at the state of Jewish Law and legal practice for German Jewry.[1]

The Jews of Austria (or of the various German principalities) were of course not citizens and were viewed as an alien, if ancient, part of the population. The Jews formed a particular community unto themselves, had developed their own organizational structure, were responsible for their own poor, indigent and sick, taxed themselves for their particular community requirements, and raised taxes for the non-Jewish political authority, to which of course they were answerable for maintaining their own communal order and discipline. To these ends, Jewish communities had maintained their own courts and judges for centuries.

In the fifteenth century, Jewish communities had an important degree of autonomy for handling offences of various types (Eidelberg, 86). The Jewish court was headed, wherever practicable, by a rabbi, selected by community leaders; the rabbi had become a salaried official by this time (Eidelberg, 66). Larger communities also employed salaried magistrates, who, together with the rabbi, formed the competent court for the adjudication of all religious matters — which included the superintendence of the dietary laws, problems in the legality of marriages and divorces, the standards for the ritual bath, for donating charity, and the like.[2]

The synagogue itself, or an adjoining room, served as the actual court-room (Eidelberg, 71). The *Torah* scroll was conveniently available to the court for use in the administration of oaths, and the synagogue and its precincts were neutral ground, where all members of the community gathered as more or less equals (social distinctions of learning or wealth being what they were) for prayer and other public purposes.

Where a community for one reason or another did not employ a rabbi — who would both enjoy and exercise considerable judicial authority on the basis of traditional law and practice — a lay court adjudicated all cases except those involving questions of religious validity or religious propriety (which of course had to be referred to a competent rabbi — Eidelberg, 66). These lay courts did handle a good many pecuniary cases, but even here their discussions were subject to review by a rabbi if one of the parties to the suit chose to carry the case before such authority (*ibid.*). Indeed some rabbis wanted the lay courts' authority restricted to the taking of testimony alone (Eidelberg, 67).

Cases that involved pecuniary matters only were generally resolved through compromise negotiated between the parties under the supervision of the court rather than by the strict application of talmudic provisions bearing on the dispute (*ibid.*, and notes thereto). This occurred for two main reasons. Talmudic Law itself permitted parties in a pecuniary matter to adjust their differences through negotiation and compromise. Secondly, the expertise of a rabbinic talmudic authority did not have to be secured for every minor monetary dispute, so the business of the law moved more swiftly. Indeed some rabbis chose not to involve themselves very often in deciding pecuniary cases unless the parties had previously bound themselves in a written agreement to accept the rabbinical decision, which obviously could be substantially different from their own negotiated settlement. Rabbinical judges did not often, at this time and place, constrain a party in a pecuniary case to accept a monetary judgment against his will (*ibid.*). This practice became more common in Poland in the sixteenth century.

Cases that involved strictly religious questions required the rabbinic court, as has been mentioned. Other causes as well demanded the knowledge and the authority of the rabbinate for proper adjudication. These cases cover a broad spectrum that would generally tend to be considered criminal matters today. They include quarrelling in the synagogue, gambling, adultery, licentious behaviour, and informing (Eidelberg, 83).

The matter of informing demands some special notice. Of all the misbe-haviour that might come to the attention of a rabbinic court, informing was far and away the most dreaded and feared.[3] If a Jew gave information to the gentile authorities, which information exposed Jewish lives or property to danger, the informant was subject to a charge of informing. The heaviest penalties were applied to such a person, since what he (or she) did amounted to treason against the community and threatened whatever internal cohesion and discipline the community struggled to exercise for its survival. Obvi-ously combinations of fear and greed in various proportions prompted people to inform to the gentiles and the consequences of such treachery could be disastrous.

Cases of battery and forgery involving only Jews usually went to a gen-tile court, where corporal punishments were brutal, but a small number of Jewish communities had been granted the authority to inflict corporal punish-ments — mutilation or amputation — for various offences, although in such instances the sentences of the Jewish court were actually carried out by gentile officers (Eidelberg, pp.88f.).[4]

Theft among Jews was another cause that usually came before a gentile tribunal (Eidelberg, 88f.). Here, too, a few Jewish communities had autho-rity to hear and decide the matter. Theft was, however, a capital offence under gentile law at the time, so Jewish communities customarily used every means possible to ransom a Jew charged with theft. Capital jurisdiction was no part of Jewish jurisdiction in Germany and Austria (*ibid.*).

Despite the absence of capital jurisdiction, homicide received the severest possible treatment that the rabbinic court could invoke. Indeed there is one instance in which a Jew who had murdered another Jew had upon conviction been blinded by the Jewish court, although this case was apparently kept secret from gentile authorities (Eidelberg, 89) — a rather monumental job of security when one considers the possibility for informing that existed: the relatively small (by our own standards) size of cities, and the crowded, gossipy nature of those medieval towns.

Probably the more common method of dealing with a case of homicide in the Jewish community when it came before a Jewish court — and side-stepping gentile law if at all possible — was through the imposition of indemnities for the surviving family and an extremely long regimen of repen-tance and public humiliation (see below pp.347-350). How the indemnities could be paid by a poor defendant was doubtless a problem, but the defendant in at least one case became in effect the breadwinner for the widow and orphans.

The most feared punishment available to the Jewish court was excommunication.[5] This penalty literally rendered a person an out-law and in its severest form isolated a person from every contact and comfort that life had formerly included and even continued after death with the denial of funeral rites (see also pp. 330, 335 below). Excommunication was invoked for the continued non-observance of Jewish Law, which allowed the court an enormous latitude to employ this punishment for all manner of offences. The court could declare such a ban for the offence against Jewish legal practice (and moral rectitude) of summoning another Jew before a gentile tribunal, and for offering insult to Rabbis and other learned persons. Contempt for community leadership doubtless represented almost as much of a threat to community solidarity and safety as informing.

In the fifteenth century at Wiener-Neustadt, gentile law supported the rigor of the ban. A statute provided for confiscation of an excommunicated Jew's property, if that Jew did not accede to the community's demands upon him within 30 days (Eidelberg, 87). This sort of procedure certainly focused the attention of all excommunicants — except perhaps the poorest and most isolated to begin with — upon a program of prompt compliance with community standards and requirements.

The Jewish courts also imposed various indemnities and payments on convicted persons, even though under the strict interpretation of talmudic Law, no court could impose a fine as such.[6] That authority had resided only in ordained Judges of the Land of Israel and they had not been present for a thousand years.

Parties to a suit could and did call upon advocates to present their arguments before the court, but these advocates were not permitted to have any financial interest in the matter they presented; a contingency fee or a portion of the settlement if any was wholly out of the question.[7] Such advocates probably received a fixed rate for service as provided under a contract.

Although summoning a Jew before a gentile court was an offence punishable by excommunication, there was a procedure by which a case involving two Jews could be heard by a gentile magistrate (Eidelberg, 87f.). The matter would first come to the Jewish court. If one of the sides requested a change of venue to the gentile court, the change had to be granted and of course no excommunication was in order.

When legal problems arose between Jews and gentiles, which happened frequently enough owing to the close proximity in which Jews and gentiles lived, they came before a magistrate with the title of *judex judaeorum*

(Eidelberg, 33ff.). This judge was appointed by a local city council. He was a non-Jew of good background who was charged with hearing and deciding cases between Jews and gentiles and cases between two Jews when one party had requested a change of jurisdiction to a gentile court. In these instances, presumably the Jewish community was not necessarily pleased with the change of venue, but the laws governing the status and privileges of the Jews allowed for it and that was that. The *judex* certified notes and mortgages between Jews and gentiles and registered them. In the fifteenth century there was also, for a while, a mixed court, composed of equal numbers of Jews and gentiles under the chairmanship of the *judex*. This tribunal heard cases between Jews and gentiles and used the services of Jewish scribes and translators. The local rabbi was kept informed of testimony presented by Jews in this court. The regular municipal courts later assumed jurisdiction in Jewish-gentile cases when gentile merchants in various communities accused these courts of bribery and corruption. While Jewish Law was certainly not the law which governed this tribunal — or the *judex* for that matter — the *judex* and the court did from time require consultation on Jewish legal rules and procedures.

The traditional Jewish Law, based on the Babylonian *Talmud* as amplified through commentary and responsa and recast in the restatements, formed the legal infrastructure which obtained within the Jewish communities of Germany during the period in question. This infrastructure was supplemented by local community ordinances; and of course its scope was affected by various gentile statutes and ordinances. Local ordinances often provided means of dealing with purely local situations, and these ordinances were carefully crafted to amplify the traditional law or to supply this or that procedure which had not heretofore been specified. In any event, local legislation always remained very much aware of talmudic law as a living and functioning system which governed all aspects of a Jew's life to the fullest extent permitted by external circumstance.[8]

The legal forms and procedures of German Jews which they carried with them to Poland in the sixteenth century became the basis for Polish Jewish legal practice, which is examined in the next chapter.

B. Spain

We turn now to the Spanish domains and Spanish Jewry.[9] If Jewish Law was a complex phenomenon in German territory, it was all that and more in Spain. The Jews of Spain were by and large treated as virtually an alien state within a state, notwithstanding Jewish presence in Spain since late Roman times. Each community possessed its own particular charter of rights and privileges. Among these charters (promulgated by monarchs of Castile or Aragon and so forth), which were reconfirmed and revised periodically, no two were exactly alike; each community charter was a special act of enablement in its own right.

The research into fourteenth century Spanish-Jewish life affords us a sort of cross-section, or sample, reflecting what went before and suggesting what occurred later, in the area of Jewish Law. From it, we can gather a rather accurate picture of the general shape of the Jewish community and the Jewish Law out of an enormous mass of specific detail. Abraham Hershman's study of the life and works of R. Isaac b. Sheshet Perfet, 1326-1408, provides an admirable starting point for the development of this cross-section of Jewish communal and legal activity between 1300 and the tragic expulsion of 1492 (see bibliography, pp.353ff. below). This particular cross-section covers the era of the black death in Spain and its baleful consequences; and the sustained and grisly anti-Jewish outbreaks of 1391 that marked the beginning of the end for Spanish Jewry, as well as the constant process of Christian reconquest of the entire Iberian peninsula.

To begin with, the Jewish communities of this era enjoyed a large degree of independence, granted by the Crown, to conduct their internal affairs, including communal taxation and adjudication of various religious, pecuniary and criminal matters.[10] These communities, or *aljamas*, developed a complicated set of institutions to carry out the powers accorded them by the civil, that is the royal, authority. The Jews were thus foremost king's men, although the sovereign could and did at times grant the revenues of this or that *aljama* to this or that favourite, or politically helpful, nobleman.

The degree of jurisdiction among the communities varied significantly: some charters granted jurisdiction in matters involving corporal or capital punishment, although such punishments, when imposed, were customarily carried out by officers of the civil government (Hershman, 103; see also Epstein, *The Responsa of Solomon b. Adreth*, pp.46ff.). This was the situation in Lerida and Murviedro (Hershman, *ibid.*). Valencia's charter did not grant capital jurisdiction, while Barcelona, by its charter of 1241, could inflict exile and excommunication but capital jurisdiction was not granted until 1377 (Hershman, 101f.). The most potent punishment within the community was the excommunicatory ban. Lesser punishments included flogging, banishment and fines, notwithstanding the provision that judges who had not been properly ordained in the Land of Israel could not impose fines (see note 6). When the occasion called for a fine, the judges found some means of imposing it. The Crown or perhaps a baron would appoint a bailiff to collect fines and administer such other punishments as the Jewish court ordered. Doubtless the bailiff was an excellent source of information for the Crown on the state of his Jewish subjects.

Privileges granted can also become privileges revoked. The community of Majorca enjoyed the power to adjudicate civil claims. In 1315 all its privileges were revoked because the community, most unwisely for that time and place, accepted two Roman Catholics as converts to Judaism (Hershman, 102.). Two generations later Majorca was allowed to exercise capital juris-diction in cases involving informers and other types of criminal jurisdiction, but it never again regained any civil law powers (*ibid.*).

The internal Jewish legal system was authorized to use both traditional Jewish Law and the local communal ordinances, both Jewish and gentile, in the matters that came before it. Jewish magistrates did not hold that civil law as such was binding on them and even presumed to interpret and define royal, baronial and curial decrees in the context of Jewish Law, and thereby determine their scope and application for Jews (Epstein, *Ben Adreth*, 53). The Crown appears to have had a rather high regard for Jewish Law and thus when a civil court occasionally heard a case in which Jews were the parties to the suit, that court was under instruction to decide the matter according to Jewish Law (Epstein, *Ben Adreth*, 48; Hershman, 99). Special Crown tribunals appointed to hear cases between Jews received the same instruction. Jewish litigants were able to sue in either a Jewish or non-Jewish court, a freedom of action disallowed in German Jewish legal practice; but even so, it was often deemed embarrassing and dangerous by Spanish Jewish authorities to do so. The Jewish authorities could and did condemn this sort of airing of Jewish quarrels in gentile courts; but they could not prevent it. The civil court might even refer Jewish litigants to Jewish courts for hearing and at times even after the civil court had decided a case, the civil court could permit the case to be reheard before a Jewish court (Epstein, *ibid.*).

The obvious risk that a party ran by seeking hearing before a civil court was the accusation of informing, which was no less feared, dreaded, and condemned among Spanish Jews than among German Jews. Indeed some Jewish communities would pay for the privilege of trying informers and some *aljamas* enjoyed the privilege of trying and condemning informers to corporal or even capital punishment, which punishment was actually carried out by civil officers, appointed by civil authority (Epstein, *Ben Adreth*, 49f.).

The individual charters of course provided various prescriptions for dealing with suits between Jews and gentiles. The charter of Saragossa offers an example: the Jewish court could hear pecuniary cases between Jews and gentiles, but the gentile was not obliged to accept the court's decision unless he had contracted formally to do so in the presence of the town clerk (Epstein, *Ben Adreth*, 47). Execution of any judgment was reserved to the Crown. Other communities could execute judgment themselves, presumably using a Crown or baronial bailiff to do so.

Parties could use the services of advocates before both Jewish and civil courts (Epstein, *Ben Adreth*, 52f.; see above p.328). These advocates were under contracts which generally ran for specific terms: weekly or monthly. It was the usual practice for female litigants to be represented by an advocate rather than appear in person. Male litigants did have to appear in person, with or without an advocate.

Jewish Law forbids judges and litigants to be related by family ties. When a case arose in which the judge and a litigant were related, as must have happened more frequently in the smaller communities, some *aljamas* allowed the case to be heard by the unrelated judges of the *Bet Din*, that is, by a smaller judicial panel; other communities allowed the judges to select another unrelated judge to sit with them for the case (Hershman, 115).

Litigants customarily presented their argument orally. Although the reported cases of the period do reflect instances of written statements and depositions, R. Isaac b. Sheshet did not allow arguments to be submitted in writing: first, he thought it unnecessarily expensive, and therefore improper, to require a defendant to secure a copy of the plaintiff's statements; secondly, the oral statements, unlike skillfully crafted words on a page, would possess a ring of truth or untruth which the judges could detect (*ibid.*). The court, however, provided a clerk to maintain a record of all arguments. The litigants paid the fees of the clerk.

The usual composition of the Jewish courts must also be discerned from a mass evidence present in the individual community charters. We encounter differing nomenclature for officials, all of whom made up the Jewish judiciary in medieval Spain.

First, the rabbi was the head of the rabbinical court, the *Bet Din*, which heard questions involving ritual law and the validity of marriages and divorces. The greatest rabbinic personages of the era staffed these courts. A rabbinical court usually consisted of three men, one of whom was generally a distinguished legal scholar (Epstein, *Ben Adreth*, 46ff.; Hershman, 114f.). The members of a *Bet Din* generally had the title of *dayyanim* 'judges' or ḥakhamim, 'Sages'. This court could be either a standing communal institution, whose members were elected or selected for a term, or simply appointed ad hoc. The *Bet Din* might be called upon to hear various sorts of cases, but it appears generally to have had the option of referring litigants to courts of arbitration composed of community selectmen or other members of the laity who were expert in the matter at hand. Cases of ritual or religious significance or cases which involved personal status were not of course referred.

Second, the communities were governed by elected officials variously known as *ne'emanim*, 'trustees,' *mukdamim*, foremen, or *berurim*, selectmen (Hershman, 104). The titles vary with the charters. These officials or some of them also formed a judiciary in addition to the rabbinate. In Barcelona, trustees were active in the prosecution of informers and worked with the *berure averot*, the 'selectmen for transgressions,' who formed a special court for criminal matters including affronts to morality and pious behaviour.[11] In Valencia, 'foremen' were permitted to try all suits between Jews of that community (Hershman, 108). The 'foremen' or 'selectmen' of Saragossa apparently acted as fact finders, investigating cases that had been brought before the *dayyanim*. They submitted the results of their investigation to the magistrates who rendered a decision, whereupon the foremen (or selectmen) executed the decision (Hershman, 110).

These officials cooperated with the rabbinical courts, but had important judicial authority in their own right. The charter could grant them jurisdiction in pecuniary matters, informing, theft, and violation of sacred oaths. They had authority to fine, to excommunicate, and — if the charter so specified — to impose corporal or capital punishment.

In some communities there were also courts of *berure teviot*, 'selectmen for money claims', hearing what amounts roughly to 'civil' suits (Hershman, 115).

These elected officials were not always drawn from the ranks of the most learned, but they apparently enjoyed the backing of the community in general or at least its most powerful elements, and they could of course call upon rabbinic authority for guidance in the law or rabbis could review their decisions. The rabbinic court in effect acted occasionally as an appeals court, or a court of review, in respect to the *berure averot*.

In some *aljamas* of Aragon there was a judge of appeals (Hershman, 120, the *dayyan hasilluqin*). Either or both litigants could ask this official to review the decision of a lower court, set it aside, and hear the case himself. Such petitions for review were submitted in writing. The judge had the option of hearing the case himself or of studying the record of the litigants' arguments and rendering his decision on that basis. On the whole it would seem that he would pronounce upon the law in the matter, after the fashion of an appellate judge.

The Spanish-Jewish community maintained a highly structured and effective legal apparatus virtually to the time of exile in 1492. Depending on the provisions of a particular charter, Jewish jurisdiction applied more or less broadly to all internal Jewish cases, and in some instances even to capital matters.

C. The Ottoman Empire

When so many refugees from Spain settled in the Ottoman Empire at the invitation of the Sultan in the late fifteenth and early sixteenth centuries, the indigenous Jewish communities of the Empire were bound to be seriously affected. But not only Spaniards came to Turkey in the early sixteenth century. Groups of Ashkenazi Jews, from Italy, Germany, and Hungary also relocated in the more hospitable atmosphere of the Turkish Empire. The Spaniards of course fled because of a particularly cruel edict that struck them rather suddenly, but all the European Jews who made their way to the Ottoman Empire were victims of vicious and often bloody oppression.

Before the Spanish exiles, and the various other European Jews, came to Turkey, the rather small Jewish communities had been under the authority of the *ḥakham* appointed by the Sultan.[12] All the Jews of a given town belonged to the same 'community,' and all communities looked to the central leader, who was their representative at court.

When the newcomers arrived from their various countries of origin, each ethnic or national group constituted a separate 'community' (Goodblatt, *Jewish Life in Turkey in the XVI Century*, 61). There were the Castilians, the Aragonese, the Germans, the Italians, and so forth. Each of these national communities was autonomous, each had its own structure. The days of central authority were forever gone. Each individual Iberian community evolved structures that were roughly similar to the communal structures that had obtained in pre-exile Spain.

Each community — and there were several in each major city — had its own court, which administered Jewish Law and the local ordinances which the community framed as part of its autonomous and self-governing character (*ibid.*). The legal system was administered by either a Rabbi and his *Bet Din* or by a three-man lay court of arbitration (Goodblatt, 86).

In Salonika, each community had its own court, and if the litigants belonged to two different communities, the defendant's court took jurisdiction. When a town had a competent court of qualified judges, no resident of that town could repair to another city for a legal ruling (*ibid.*).

All courts enjoyed the same range of powers, but the learning and scholarship of the judges serving on a particular court would confer upon it a cachet of prestige and importance not accorded to courts of lesser learning (*ibid.*).

The Jewish courts of the Ottoman Empire did not exercise criminal or capital jurisdiction. They superintended the community as a quasi-administrative body, framed ordinances for the internal regulation of the community, and heard all cases relating to pecuniary matters, religious questions (including marriage and divorce), and all cases involving its own ordinances (*ibid.*).

Within the limits imposed on its jurisdiction, the Jewish court was extremely active. No Jew was permitted to bring another Jew before a gentile court, and anyone who attempted to do so risked excommunication (*ibid.*). One authority considered it totally wrong to go to a gentile court even if the gentile law in the matter to be decided were precisely the same as Jewish Law in that case, and it was wrong even when the Jewish court did not even have jurisdiction in the matter (*ibid.*). Clearly the concern over informing was as real as ever and informing remained the most monstrous crime of all in the eyes of the Jewish court.

There was, however, apparently one exception to the rule against going to a gentile court (Goodblatt, 88f.). If a Jew refused to appear as a defendant when summoned to do so by the competent Jewish court, or if a Jew refused to swear an oath required by a Jewish court, the plaintiff could then petition the court to have the matter heard by the competent gentile jurisdiction.

The most powerful enforcement tool the Jewish court in the Ottoman Empire could invoke was the excommunicatory ban, which we have already encountered both in German Jewish jurisprudence and in Spanish Jewish jurisprudence. There were three forms of the ban, a mild one which was temporary; a more severe one, which denied the banned person certain civil dignities and religious status for a period of time; and the most severe ban which was indefinite in duration and which, as has been indicated, rendered the person a pariah, unfit in every respect for intercourse with Jews.[13] Bans of lesser severity had also been part of the enforcement arsenal in both German and Spanish Jewish communities.

The severest form of excommunication was imposed for any of these offences: insubordination to a rabbi or community official; violation of community ordinances; defaming a Jewish woman; persistent immoral conduct; refusal to testify in a Jewish court when duly summoned three different times; and informing (Goodblatt, 89). Counterfeiting might also be punishable by excommunication; this offence could obviously expose the Jewish community to rather severe government reaction (*ibid.*).

Excommunication was so severe that it was imposed only after three warnings had been given and after a lapse of 30 days (*ibid.*). Rabbinic concurrence was necessary if lay officials wished to have the ban declared; of course, the rabbi could pronounce the ban himself against a member of the laity who had insulted and defamed him — no lay approval was needed. The actual ceremony of excommunication was surrounded with the most stark and solemn pageantry.

Upon evidence of sincere repentance, remorse, a new life of unimpeachable rectitude, and the making good of any matters outstanding, the ban could be revoked (*ibid.*).

Community ordinances, and occasionally private contracts, included a provision that whoever violated the ordinance (or private contract) would be subject to the ban in all its rigors. The explicit threat of excommunication tended to secure compliance with the law (Goodblatt, 90). Jewish Law allows a group, or an individual, to undertake to do something, or to refrain from doing something, under the threat of express penalty for violation of the undertaking. Excommunication was thus a standard penalty that each community member accepted as a contingency, merely by virtue of his membership in the community. Appending an excommunication clause to a private contract had to be a voluntary act.

The use of the solemn oath was another procedure by which compliance with community regulations and legal decisions was sought (Goodblatt, 91). Community regulations were confirmed by members of the community through their solemn oath to observe the enactment in all its particulars; and litigants in the Jewish courts were placed under oath to abide by the court's judgment.

Since the solemnity and sacredness of the oath were exceptionally serious matters in Jewish Law, the breaking of an oath constituting a grievous religious offence, an oath was a reasonably effective means of achieving compliance with the law (*ibid.*). If a person dared to break the oath the graver penalties of the ban awaited him in due course.

We have looked at examples of Jewish procedure and jurisdiction in the Ottoman Turkish Empire, in which the Jewish community in many respects reached its zenith in the sixteenth century. Although the Polish Jewish community also dates from this period (and we shall encounter a famous rabbinic jurist or two from that community) , on the whole the ascendancy of the Polish community falls in the sixteenth-seventeenth centuries (see further ch.13, below).

3. *General Character of the Sources*

It must always be borne in mind when considering the written sources of Jewish Law that no post-talmudic legal source, not even the comprehensive restatement of Maimonides, ever in fact superseded earlier works entirely or substantially.[14] No authority was bound by precedent and every authority was free to examine all the previous legal opinion, from the *Talmud* to the latest novellae, in order to frame an opinion for inclusion in a responsum or a paragraph in a restatement. The importance and authority of a given source depended upon its author's or compiler's reputation for learning and scholarship and also upon the source's clarity, thoroughness, and incisiveness in treating the subject matter. In effect, each work was exposed to rigorous examination by both its author's contemporaries and later authorities. Those collections which received the greatest approbation from rabbis have been cited down through the centuries, each possessing a degree of persuasiveness or authority.

First, the major legal works. The legal works of this period fall into the three standard categories of post-talmudic halakhic literature: codes or restatements, commentaries, and responsa.[15]

Three major restatements require some attention. First, in historical order came the compendious work *Rabbenu Asher* or *Hilkhot Asheri* (*Piṣke haRosh*), compiled by *Rosh*, a restatement or abstract of talmudic law, which has the format of a commentary but which is really a restatement of those portions of the law which he deemed practical in the sense that they applied outside the Land of Israel. His general plan was therefore akin to and followed the major work of R. Isaac Alfasi, but *Rosh*'s work, while composed during the latter part of his career when he lived in Spain, reflects also his Ashkenazi methodology that affected all subsequent major halakhic restatements.

Rosh begins with the talmudic material itself but then cites both German and Spanish authorities in his discussion of the law. The Toṣafists and important jurists of the German school of talmudic commentary are cited along with the Sephardi masters, particularly Alfasi and Maimonides. The combination of the two streams of legal style and interpretation reveal *Rosh* as a master of both, and no major subsequent work in talmudic law could really achieve greatness unless it also presented both schools and styles. The *Rabbenu Asher* became so enormously popular as a legal text and a legal commentary that it was published as an appendix to the first edition of the Babylonian *Talmud* in the sixteenth century and with most editions ever since. Citation of *Rabbenu Asher* is also encountered in later restatements, commentary and responsa down to the present; and it attracted its own mass of commentary by eminent authorities of later generations, which in the course of time were also printed along with the *Rabbenu Asher* appendix to the *Talmud*.

R. Asher b. Yehiel's son, R. Jacob b. Asher, had preceded his illustrious father to Spain. Like his father, the son was learned in both German and Spanish legal traditions. Principally through his own restatement, the *Arba'ah Turim*, 'The Four Rows', R. Jacob b. Asher achieved recognition as a major figure in Jewish legal scholarship and his work, known simply as the *Tur*, which appeared first in Spain before 1340, rose to be the primary restatement of the law for more than 200 years.

R. Jacob b. Asher eschewed the talmudic commentary format, which follows the classic order of the tractates, as Maimonides had done a century and a half before. He chose a four volume format that included only those laws and practices which were current, of immediate interest and value in the Diaspora. Thus the *Tur* was not a comprehensive restatement after the fashion of Maimonides.

The titles he gave to each book of his four volume work became the standard for division and categorization of practical *halakhah* which was adopted by later authorities for their own works and for divisions and indices for later collections of responsa. The four books are *Orah Hayyim* (the 'path of life'), which covers the liturgical calendar: daily, Sabbath, festival, and holyday regulations; *Yoreh De'ah* ('the one who will teach knowledge'), which covers ritual matters unrelated to calendar, e.g. dietary laws, circumcision, charity, death, burial and mourning regulations; *Even Ha'ezer* ('the rock of help'), which covers marriage, divorce and related matters; and *Hoshen Hamishpat* ('the breastplate of justice'), which includes rules on the judiciary, courts, pecuniary matters of all kinds, loans, sales, bailments, and also rules concerning damage to property, battery, homicide, etc.

The work proved so useful and so popular as a standard authority that it was one of the first books ever printed in Hebrew, appearing in a complete edition in 1475.

The work itself does not cite talmudic sources as such, but it cites a rule drawn from the *Talmud* and proceeds to demonstrate the amplification or modification the rule received through the principal commentators, particularly *Rashi* and *Tosafot*, the opinions of Alfasi and Maimonides, and the opinions of other major authorities including his own father, whose responsa are occasionally cited extensively. The material is masterfully arranged so that the reader can perceive the development of the talmudic rule as it came to be applied in practice and as it was affected by various permutations of fact.

The *Tur* itself attracted numerous commentators, among them R. Yosef Karo and R. Moses Isserles, sixteenth century authorities whose work is the third major restatement of the period between 1300 and 1565.

R. Yosef b. Ephraim Karo compiled the *Shulhan Arukh*, which, with the glosses of R. Moses Isserles, interspersed in the original paragraphs of Karo, remains to this day the standard restatement of those portions of Jewish Law which, in theory or in practice, apply to Jews everywhere.

Karo had written an extensive commentary to the *Tur*, entitled *Bet Yosef*, which is in fact his most erudite and intricate contribution to the field of Jewish Law. He examined many sources and opinions which did not figure at all in *Tur*. The upheaval in Jewish life owing to the Spanish exile (Karo himself was a first generation refugee), the development of new communities in the Ottoman Empire, and the fact that in order to use the *Tur* competently one needed a good deal of prior study, prompted Karo to design a new restatement, more briefly put and directed towards the requirements of beginning students. It was his hope to spread a feast of information on practical law, thus the title *Shulhan Arukh* ('The Prepared Table'). He also suggested that the book, which gave the law in crisp and unadorned style, would also be useful as a review for more advanced scholars.

Karo chose the highly esteemed *Tur* as his model and format; thus the *Shulhan Arukh* has generally the same titles and divisions for books, sections and chapters as the *Tur*. The *Shulhan Arukh* does not, however, present a logical and detailed array of sources like the *Tur*.

Karo chose three major authorities as the primary referents for any given rule: Alfasi, Maimonides and *Rosh*. If all three authorities, or two out of three, agreed on a rule, Karo stated the rule according to that consensus, but without citing sources. If however a majority of earlier authorities disagreed with the three primary authorities or followed the minority opinion among the three, the earlier authorities' opinion or the relevant minority opinion was upheld, again without citation of sources. Obviously his earlier experience in the development of the *Bet Yosef*, had immersed Karo in all the relevant opinions and had made him a master of them.

The *Shulhan Arukh* appeared in print in Venice in 1564-65. It is the first major work of its genre that does not have a tradition of manuscripts behind it.

R. Moses Isserles, Rabbi of Cracow, and Karo's somewhat younger contemporary, also wrote a commentary to the *Tur*, the *Darkhe Moshe*, which was also a sort of critical supplement to the *Bet Yosef*. Isserles saw one or more of the early editions of *Shulḥan Arukh* — the work was reprinted several times between 1565 and 1580 — and believed that the work was too terse and brief, excluding valuable opinions that were in his view extremely useful. Isserles undertook to supplement the paragraphs of *Shulḥan Arukh* with interspersed glosses — not a commentary designed for the margin of the page, but glosses that fit into, and often split into segments, the original Karo text. He called his glosses the *Mappah*, the 'tablecloth' for the prepared table.

The usual assessment of Isserles's purpose was that he wished to give greater emphasis to Ashkenazi views upon the *halakhah*. This opinion is correct up to a point. In ritual matters, the German (and later the Polish) style of ritual did differ substantially from the Spanish. Isserles does give the alternate German view or views in ritual matters. In many other areas of the law, however, Isserles is as apt to quote a leading Spanish authority as a leading German one. Isserles will cite R. Solomon b. Adret or R. Isaac b. Sheshet or some other Spanish jurist without any hesitation. On the whole, therefore, it would seem that Isserles was as much concerned with providing a more thorough and rounded statement of a given law, with optional procedures clearly stated, as he was with giving due weight and consideration to the wealth of ritual practice which had developed among German Jews.

The first complete edition of *Shulḥan Arukh*, with Karo's text set in one typeface and Isserles's interspersed glosses set in another, appeared in Cracow in 1580. Since that time the *Shulḥan Arukh* text has always been printed in its glossed form. The work may justly be termed the Karo-Isserles *Shulḥan Arukh*, though of course the two men never collaborated in the usual sense of the word.

The *Shulḥan Arukh* enjoyed a tremendous popularity. Numerous editions, first of Karo's text alone and then those with the glosses, were printed in Venice and in Cracow between 1565 and 1600. The work was not, however, without its powerful detractors — who deemed it too elementary, too brief, too much of a schoolboy's primer, to be of any real value. There was also criticism of it in terms of its substantive rules. Despite the cachet that the work enjoyed because of the fame of its 'authors' and its obvious popularity, the *Shulḥan Arukh* did not emerge as the preeminent restatement of the law, outdistancing its rivals and silencing its rather harsh critics, until a century had passed. In the seventeenth century a brilliant array of rabbinic jurists chose *Shulḥan Arukh* as the focus for their own extensive legal commentary, which now appears in the printed text along with the Karo-Isserles rulings. The critical commentary of those savants revealed the work as an excellent statement of the law and raised it to a prominence among post-talmudic restatements of the law that has not yet diminished.

In addition to *Rabbenu Asher*, *Ṭur* and *Shulḥan Arukh*, there were several restatements of smaller scope that are worthy of mention. R. Solomon b. Adret composed an excellent compendium on dietary law and ritual purification, *Torat habayit*, and another on Sabbath and festival law, *Avodat hakodesh*. Another Spaniard, R. Samuel b. Isaac Hasardi, wrote a compendium on civil suits, the *Ṣefer haterumot*, as did R. Asher's pupil Jeroham, the *Ṣefer Mesharim*. R. Asher's contemporary and fellow pupil of R. Meir of Rothenburg, R. Mordecai b. Hillel, compiled a tractate by tractate compendium, known simply as the *Mordecai*, which preserves an enormous amount of German rabbinic legal literature including many responsa of his teacher. The *Mordecai* is appended to the *Hilkhot Alfasi* in the Vilna edition of the Babylonian *Talmud*.

The field of talmudic commentary, itself a written source of Jewish Law, was also pursued during this period.[16] The principal commentators to portions of the *Talmud* were R. Solomon b. Adret, R. Yom Tov b. Abraham, and R. Nissim b. Reuben Gerondi among the Spaniards; R. Obadiah di Bertinoro, and R. Bezalel Ashkenazi among the Ottomans; and R. Solomon Luria, the great Polish commentator of the sixteenth century.

The list of jurists who produced volumes of responsa is enormous (see n.15 below). Among them are, in addition to R. Solomon b. Adret and *Rosh*, R. Judah b. Asher (another of *Rosh's* sons who settled in Spain), R. Yom Tov b. Abraham (the talmudic commentator), R. Nissim b. Reuben Gerondi, R. Isaac b. Sheshet Perfet, R. Shimon b. Zemaḥ Duran and his son R. Solomon b. Simon Duran, among the earlier Spanish and North African jurists. The Ottoman Turkish Rabbinate produced a glittering circle of legal authorities whose responsa are still cited: in addition to Karo, there were R. Samuel di Medina, R. Joseph ibn Lev, R. Moses Capsali, R. Elijah Mizraḥi, R. David ibn Zimra, R. Moses Alshech, R. Joseph Berab, R. Levi ibn Habib, R. Moses di Trani, and R. Joseph Trani. German respondents of the period include R. Israel Isserlein, R. Jacob Weil, R. Israel b. Ḥayyim of Brunn, and R. Moses b. Isaac Minz. The Italian rabbinate, which was under the intellectual influence of the German rabbinate, included the highly respected fifteenth century scholar Joseph Colon and the German-born Meir b. Isaac Katzenellenbogen, who was active in Padua. Both R. Moses Isserles and R. Solomon Luria composed important collections of responsa reflecting life in sixteenth century Poland.

One other work of halakhic importance, which is not really a restatement, a commentary or a collection of responsa is the *Sefer Maharil* of R. Jacob Halevi Moellin.[17] He collected and collated a large number of the classic customary procedures of German Jewry. This book on customs figured importantly in R. Moses Isserles's amplification of ritual law in his glosses to the *Shulḥan Arukh*, and also in various responsa and commentaries.

The foregoing lists of commentators and respondents gives some idea of the vigorous and lively condition of Jewish Law in the period under notice. The writings of any one of the personalities listed, not to mention *Rosh*, Jacob b. Asher, and Ḳaro, can and do contain opinions and rulings which may bear upon questions heard by rabbinical courts today.

4. *Principal Authorities of the Period*

From all the personages named, seven of the greatest have been selected here for brief biographical treatment. Any short list of the outstanding figures of the period would include most if not all of the personalities here chosen.[18]

A. Spain and the Ottoman Empire

1. R. Isaac b. Sheshet Perfet, Spain and North Africa, 1326-1408. *Ribash*, as he is known by acronym, was born in Valencia but was raised in Barcelona.[19] He studied with R. Ḥasdai Crescas and R. Nissim Gerondi. He achieved a widespread reputation as a talmudic authority but he made his living in a family business. After he had been falsely accused and imprisoned, he fled Barcelona a poor man and took a position as Rabbi in Saragossa. In 1391 when the anti-Jewish fervour of the mob racked all of Spain, he fled again. At age 65, *Ribash* crossed the Mediterranean to Algiers, where despite the opposition of the incumbent rabbi, the great and learned R. Simon Duran, he became a Chief Rabbi as well. The Algerian Jewish community was split rather seriously because of this rabbinical quarrel. *Ribash*, with help from lay leaders of the community, who interceded on his behalf with the King of Algiers, secured the appointment of

Rabbi of the Spanish émigrés in Algiers. Eventually, even Duran recognized *Ribash* as a superb choice to be a Chief Rabbi, even though Duran was firmly against non-Jewish interference in Jewish internal matters.

Ribash's collection of responsa is among the most authoritative works in all responsa literature, and his decisions figure in both the *Shulḥan Arukh* and numerous later commentaries and responsa.

2. R. David ibn Zimra, 1479-1589, Spain, Israel, Egypt. *Radbaz*, as he is known by acronym, was about 13 when all Spanish Jews were forced into exile. He settled as a youth in Safed, where he studied rabbinic law and lore and eventually moved to Cairo.[20] He became a member of the Cairo rabbinical court and in 1517 the Chief Rabbi of Egypt, a post he held for 40 years. He was independently wealthy and participated in the community life of Cairo as well as in legal scholarship through correspondence with authorities from all parts of the Ottoman Empire and beyond. When he was 90, he resigned the Chief Rabbinate, distributed his wealth to the poor, and resettled in Jerusalem. Although no longer wealthy, he became the target of extortion by Turkish officials. He left Jerusalem for Safed where in extreme old age he served on the rabbinical court, which was headed by another Spanish refugee, R. Joseph Ḳaro.

Radbaz left about 3,000 responsa, which are considered models of lucidity and are still cited today.

3. R. Joseph b. Ephraim Ḳaro, 1488-1575, Spain, Greece, Israel.[21] At the age of four Ḳaro was a victim of the Spanish expulsion. His family settled first in Nicopolis in Macedonia where Joseph studied with his father. He also studied in Adrianople and there was attracted to religious mysticism. He became a mystic and coupled legal erudition in the highest degree with a life-long devotion to mystic religious practice and belief. He also studied at Salonika and from there made his way to Safed where he settled in 1535. He was active in the attempt to revive the ancient forms of rabbinical ordination, but these attempts were powerfully opposed by numerous rabbis of the period and came to nothing.

As a legal authority, he was known throughout the Jewish world. His *Bet Yoṣef*, which he had begun in Adrianople, was completed in 1542 in Safed; and from that monumental work came the seed of the *Shulḥan Arukh* which Ḳaro produced in his later years. He lived and worked among the great jurists and mystics of Safed, and his reputation as a respondent and as an authority in all areas of Jewish Law is undimmed after more than 400 years.

B. Germany and Poland

1. Rabbenu Asher b. Yeḥiel, *Rosh*, was born in Cologne in 1250 and died in Toledo in 1328. After early studies at home he became R. Meir of Rothenburg's most famous pupil and R. Meir appointed him to the rabbinical court at Worms. When R. Meir died while in prison, *Rosh* became the consensus premier rabbi of German Jewry.[22]

The lesson of his teacher's fate was not lost on *Rosh* who, when past 50, managed to leave Germany for Spain. He was welcomed most cordially by the aged R. Solomon b. Adret in Barcelona. *Rosh* took residence at Toledo, where his reputation as a jurist of international repute had moved the leaders of that community to appoint him both chief judge and rector of the rabbinical college in the city. Although a foreigner, the Spanish community warmed to him and he rose rapidly in their esteem. He became as thoroughly expert in the Spanish-Jewish interpretation of the law as he was in the German-Jewish interpretation. His mastery of both major streams of talmudic learning and law allowed him to integrate them both into his principal work, the *Rabbenu Asher* or *Hilkhot haRosh*, which has already been discussed. From the death of Solomon b. Adret in 1310 until the Spanish expulsion 182 years later, no rabbi in Spain surpassed the reputation of *Rosh*. Indeed, after his death in 1327, the community of Toledo adopted a rule of precedence of authority in its local court which provided that the restatement of Maimonides was to be taken as authoritative except where *Rosh*'s opinion on the law differed — a high accolade for the refugee rabbi from Germany.

In addition to *Rabbenu Asher*, *Rosh* wrote a talmudic commentary and a collection of approximately 1000 responsa, which set a high standard both for style and mastery of the law.

2. R. Israel b. Petaḥiah Isserlein, 1390-1460, Germany, the premier rabbi of Germany in the fifteenth century.[23] A native of Regensburg, he served the communities of Marburg and of Wiener-Neustadt, with which latter city he is usually associated. He studied with his uncle in Wiener-Neustadt, but in 1421 he fled that area owing to anti-Jewish riots in which his mother and his uncle were murdered. He took refuge in Italy for many years, but was called back to Wiener-Neustadt in 1445 to be the Rabbi of the community and the head of its rabbinical college.

Isserlein left two collections of responsa, the *Terumat Hadeshen* of 354 decisions and the *Peṣaḳim Uketabim* of 267. Both works were published in one volume by his students, the smaller collection an appendix to the larger one. Ḳaro cited Isserlein extensively in *Bet Yoṣef*, as did Isserles in *Darkhe Moshe*, and Isserlein's legal opinions still enjoy significant authority.

3. R. Joseph b. Solomon Colon, 1420-1480, Italy, acronym *Maharik*. Born in Savoy, he lived in various communities, eventually founding a rabbinical college in Mantua, and later moving to Pavia where he was both Rabbi and head of the rabbinical college.[24] His school attracted students from Germany, Poland and the Balkans as well as Italy. Colon's training had been under the influence of the German masters — he may have been a pupil of Moellin, who described so much of German customary practice, and he studied with pupils of Isserlein whose methodology also profoundly impressed him. He was a master of the German school of interpretation, but he framed his decisions with an Italianate clarity and grace of style. His decisions occasionally tended to lenience in some ritual cases. He did not however compromise his personal code of strict piety. He resolutely argued his interpretation of the law and was not averse to extended debates and quarrels with learned colleagues. He was nonetheless a man of great piety who also asked forgiveness from a rabbinical adversary, when he realized that because he had been misled as to certain facts, his opinions and arguments had caused the other man undue and unfair embarrassment and hardship.

Colon's responsa, collected by his son-in-law and his pupils after his death, have become an authoritative classic in Jewish legal literature. Ḳaro of course made use of Colon's decisions in *Bet Yoṣef*.

4. R. Moses b. Israel Isserles, 1520-1572, Cracow, acronym *Rema*. The *Rema* came from a wealthy and prominent family.[25] He was a kinsman to his redoubtable contemporary R. Solomon Luria and the two of them were rabbinical students together. They maintained a close friendship despite differences over various interpretations of the law. Both men strove to achieve precision and accuracy in their decisions and both emphasized the role of custom in religious practice. They parted company, however, over the permissibility of studying philosophy. Isserles took a lively interest in philosophical studies and also enjoyed the study of history, astronomy, and mysticism. He did not believe that these pursuits detracted from his piety or devotion to Jewish Law.

Isserles founded a rabbinical college in Cracow and used his personal funds to support his pupils. He became a Rabbi and a member of the rabbinical court in Cracow in 1553. He was an active participant in Jewish communal affairs as well, and took a leading role in the work of the Council of the Four Lands, the Jewish administrative organ for the growing communities of Eastern Europe.

His major contributions to Jewish Law, the *Mappah* and the *Darkhe Moshe*, have already been mentioned. He also wrote authoritative responsa and even some works on philosophy and mysticism.

Isserles had already gained an international reputation as a jurist when he was still quite young. His fame as a scholar and legal writer, and especially as a champion of customary practice as a crucial element in ritual law, continues to the present day.

5. *Some Examples of Substantive Law in the Period*

Because medieval society generally considered the Jews as a separate and foreign, not to say alien, people — despite the fact that Jewish habitation in this or that region might have dated from Roman times — Jewish Law perforce became part of the infrastructure and social fabric of the Jewish community, whether Spanish, German, Turkish, or Polish. Whatever standing Jews may have had in gentile law and before gentile courts was tenuous at best, and the Jew could easily find himself or herself at a disadvantage in respect to oaths and credibility owing to the particular social esteem and political position of the Jews at specific times and places. Thus Jewish Law obtained within the Jewish community as a living law, and the range and scope of its concerns were enormous. It is therefore extremely difficult to select just a few institutions or trends as a demonstration of the characteristics of this entire period. With this in mind, let us take a brief look at two examples of substantive law.

A. Criminal Law

On occasion Jewish courts of this period heard and decided what we today would deem serious criminal cases, including homicide. Perhaps the matter of homicide, an area of the criminal law which arouses strong fears and passions, affords a glimpse into Jewish communal life and the processes of Jewish Law at this period as no other area of the law can do. As we have noted, some communities in Spain exercised capital jurisdiction under royal patent in cases of, e.g., homicide, and the responsa literature of the period presents the rather positive attitude toward capital punishment, and severe corporal punishment, espoused by rabbinic jurists.[26] These responsa disclose a vibrant and complex period in Jewish criminal law.

No less vibrant and complex was the world of Ashkenazi Jewry at this time. But the Ashkenazi communities did not have a grant of capital jurisdiction from anyone. Thus a fifteenth century German responsum, concerning a drunken brawl and a homicide, preserved in the responsa of R. Israel b. Hayyim of Brunn, reveals an enormous resourcefulness in dealing with a case of homicide when capital punishment was not an option. For a case of homicide to come before an Ashkenazi rabbinical court at all bespeaks the unusual, which surely obliged the court to operate with the greatest care and circumspection lest gentile authority which ordinarily exercised capital jurisdiction assert its power and remove the case from Jewish hands.

R. Israel's responsum appears as nos. 265 and 266 in his collected responsa, ed. Salonika, 1798.[27] The case is especially interesting because of the form of punishment which R. Israel defined and described in the matter of homicide. Further, under classical talmudic procedure, a capital conviction required a minimum of two competent eye witnesses to the act itself, and the satisfaction of some other procedural standards as well, e.g., a warning to the accused before the act was committed (although these safeguards were often waived in the procedure of the Spanish rabbinic courts that imposed capital sentence). A confession by the accused was always inadmissible in Jewish Law with respect to a capital crime. The ancient rule against self-incrimination is well known and has been examined in detail.[28] In the case under notice, there is a vague mention of eyewitnesses, one is apparently named, and there is a confession by the accused. The confession was, however, *not* inadmissible in the case since capital punishment could not apply! The decision of the judge rests entirely on the confession of the accused as an indication of his sincerest remorse, regret, and repentance. The text:

> *Question*: Greetings to the community of Lemberg (Posen) ... On the matter of the murder which occurred in your city: a certain wicked fellow, Nahman, struck the first murderous blow, and a certain Simhah finished the murderous deed. It has been deposed that Nahman stabbed Nissan in the head with a knife, wounding him in the head. According to testimony given in the community of Frieslow (?), whose members had had a report from the eyewitnesses to the murder, he (Nahman) also wounded him so that he could not rise to his feet any more. Nahman moved the wounded man about by his head; then he called to Simhah, 'Get him.' Simhah ran and struck Nissan with a cudgel until he fell to the floor. (Apparently Nissan had been seated. The first blow left him unable to rise. Simhah's *coup de grace* left Nissan dying on the floor.) While Nissan was on the floor Simhah struck him three more times.
>
> Moses b. Asher testified that Simhah was drunk at the time. He testified concerning Nissan that he was ignorant and illiterate, had never even put on

tefillin, and there was not even a veneer of piety about the man. He (Nissan) had begun the fracas by hurling two chunks of wood at Simḥah. It is also inscribed how Simḥah is filled with remorse and seeks to repent; Naḥman has shown no remorse or inclination to repent. Nissan died that night ...

Answer: You have called Naḥman by his name Naḥman; you have called Simḥah a murderer. *I name them both murderers*, utterly guilty before the divine tribunal, but (alas) beyond the jurisdiction of the human court! In *B. Sanh.* 78a, we have the provision that if the assailants strike a man mortally, whether they do so simultaneously or consecutively, they cannot be tried for murder under Jewish Law because the Bible clearly states, 'if *one* kills a man' (*Lev.* 24:18), which is interpreted as meaning that one murderer must perform the entire act of killing. This is also brought out in *B. B.K.* 26b. Even though R. Judah (in the *Sanhedrin* 78a citation) takes issue and opines that the last one to wound the deceased is guilty of an indictable crime (since his blow presumably finished off the victim), the majority view of non-culpability for all of them prevailed. The rule holds even if each of the blows could have been fatal; for if the first blows could not possibly have been fatal, even the majority of talmudic authorities would hold the last one to strike (i.e., the final fatal blow) guilty of murder (which could be tried in the rabbinic courts). This is indicated explicitly, *B. Sanh.* 78a, and the *Toṣafot* also demonstrate this in the commentary to *B. B.K.* 10b ...

The iniquity of causing death is shared equally. The reservations, applicable in the case of one who committed manslaughter, that the victim may have in some way aggravated his injury or some natural process may have aggravated his injury (cf. *Toṣafot* to *B. Gitt.* 70b) *do not apply* to willful murder.

I say of both of them: 'Their hands are full of blood' *(Is.* 1:15); of Naḥman I say (cf. *I Sam.* 24:13): 'From the wicked, a wicked man comes forth' — for he sinned and caused Simḥah to sin, as shown in the evidence, because he called to Simḥah, 'Kill him!' Thus he is a 'pursuer' (i.e., one who pursues his fellow to kill him, cf. Maimonides, *Hilkhot Rotseaḥ* 1:6).

As for Simḥah, the testimony of the witness that Simḥah was drunk is irrelevant, as long as he had not become as drunk as Lot who was so drunk he did not know when his daughter lay down and when she got up (i.e., the episode of incest, *Gen.* 19), as we have it in *B. Eruv.* 65a. There in the *Talmud* it is laid down that if an intoxicated person committed a transgression punishable by death (assuming Jewish jurisdiction in such matters), he is put to death. The *Talmud* qualifies this by providing that the degree of intoxication in the situation has not reached the point of Lot's drunkenness ... Simḥah confessed his part in the whole matter the next morning, he was completely rational (i.e., he had full recollection of the previous night's events) ...

Concerning that scoundrel Naḥman, I shall prescribe no procedure for atonement because he spurns repentance; he is not shaken and remorseful over his iniquity ... (No. 266) Now I shall prescribe the procedure for repentance required of Simḥah, according to what appears to be correct on the basis of the documents (which describe such matters). However, I do not know the man (Simḥah), his manner, or his nature. Thus, if it seems (correct) to the scholars of Posen to add or detract (from the program I shall propose) they are free to do so. This is the program of his repentance:

He shall journey about as an exile for a full year. Every day he shall appear at a synagogue — or at least on every Monday and Thursday. He shall make for himself three iron bands, one to be worn on each of his two hands, which were the instruments of his transgressions, and one to be worn about his body. When he enters the synagogue, he shall put them on and pray with them on. In the evening he shall go barefoot to the synagogue. The *hazan* shall seat him (publicly) prior to the *Vehu Raḥum* prayer.[29] He shall then receive a (symbolic [?] public) flogging and make the following declaration: 'Know ye, my masters, that I am a murderer. I wantonly killed Nissan. This is my atonement. Pray for me.'[30] When he leaves the synagogue he is to prostrate himself across the doorsill; the worshipers are to step over him, not on him. Afterwards he is to remove the iron bands.

He is to fast every day for a full year, except for those days on which penitential prayers are not said (e.g., Sabbaths, holidays). He is neither to partake of meat or wine nor to become drunk on strong liquors, and it is particularly appropriate for him to refrain from the type of drink he had on the night of the murder, because drunkenness from it caused the tragedy. He is not to sleep on a soft bed except on Sabbaths and holidays, including *Ḥannukah* and *Purim*. During his exile he is not to trim his hair or his beard, for this is a mode of repentance noted in *B. Sanh.* 25a. He is not to wash with hot water except on the eves of Sabbaths and holidays. He is to cleanse his hair once a month. He is to wash his clothes once a season. He is not to frequent taverns, for in such a place did the mischief first occur. He is not to engage in any game of chance: the killing occurred because of an argument over a game of chance. If people insult him with the epithet 'Murderer!', he is to hold his peace and accept in love whatever insults are hurled at him; he is to say: 'This is my atonement.' He is to be very careful in reciting the *Shema* and *Tefillah* portions of the public liturgy. He is to make the well-known formal confession of sins three times each day and to declare after each recitation: 'Please Lord, accept my repentance, for I have transgressed and shed innocent blood; may my humiliation and shame be my atonement.'

After one year he shall continue his fasts on Mondays and Thursdays. He shall, for the rest of his days, carefully observe the anniversary month and the anniversary date of the killing. He shall fast at that time (the date) three consecutive days if he is healthy or only two days, the day of the wounding and the next day, the day of Nissan's death, if he is infirm. He shall, for the rest of his days, be active in all enterprises to free imprisoned Jews (i.e., hostages held by gentiles), charity, and the saving of lives. He shall work out an arrangement with his (Nissan's) heirs (i.e., his orphans) to support them properly. He shall ask their pardon and the widow's pardon. He shall return to God, and He shall have mercy on him.

And since Simḥah has expressed remorse and seeks repentance and atonement, immediately upon his submission to the program of public degradations, he becomes our brother once again for every religious purpose (i.e., the quorum for worship, cf. *B. Makk.* 23a). *Rabbenu Tam*, the Tosafist, demonstrated that acceptance of the program of repentance is sufficient (indication of atonement for reaccepting the person as a brother); I find difficulty with this view, but this is not the place to go into that (cf. *Tosafot* to *B. Bekh.* 31a) ... Israel of Brunn.

B. Family Law

Two more cases from the responsa literature,[31] one from Spain and one from Germany, demonstrate both the general view of prominent legal authorities on a matter of family law. Both texts discuss the matter of a wife's application to the rabbinical court for a divorce. The two petitions both refer to gambling husbands and reveal some specific detail of the social conditions in the respective Jewish communities.

The Spanish case comes from R. Yom Tov b. Ashbili, responsum no. 122 from the Jerusalem, 1958 edition; the author was a younger contemporary of *Rosh*. The German case comes from R. Jacob b. Judah Weil, a student of Moellin and perhaps of Isserlein; the text is responsum no. 135 from the Venice, 1549 edition.

First the Spanish case:

You further asked: What is to be done about women whose husbands gamble away their money and who insist on being divorced from these husbands on the grounds that 'they are repulsive.' Should I give you leave in this case to force the men to divorce their wives on the basis of Maimonides' opinion, which admits a plea of 'repulsiveness' as sufficient ground for divorce because Jewish women are not deemed to be prisoners who are compelled to live with masters hateful to them ...?

Answer: You have already learned a long time ago that my teacher of blessed memory, R. Moses b. Nahman, and many other great authorities, and my masters of blessed memory, did not agree with that great teacher, Maimonides, of blessed memory, in this case — nor do I, who am but a tail to those lions! Although there are indeed some in these districts who do render judgment according to Maimonides, who do not listen to us who oppose that great lion (Maimonides). It seems to them that through their acts there is an amelioration of the condition of Jewish women. Nevertheless, Heaven forbid that I follow his (Maimonides') ruling, in opposition to the opinion of my masters of blessed memory, and the other lions who oppose him, in a matter as serious as this: i.e., bringing doubt and unclarity into questions of a married woman's status (whether she is married in the eyes of the law or lawfully divorced).

Even in the case of these gamblers, we can give no leave, according to our principles and opinion, to compel divorce, except as we see that they are not satisfying their marital obligations in the matter of food, clothing, and conjugal society. (Men who do not fulfill these duties) are among those who can be forced to divorce, when no other solution (to those domestic problems) is possible. Marriage is, of course, a duty incumbent upon every man. (Yet,) as has been said in the Palestinian *Talmud* (*Y. Gittin* 9:9, 50d): If we can compel a man to divorce his wife on her complaint that he chronically has impossibly foul breath, how much the more can the marriage bond be legally severed for a cause which affects life itself! So if the evil act men commit causes them to make their wives sin and transgress, and it is impossible to remove the men from their sinful ways by any other compulsion, then it is possible to compel a divorce, for no one lives 'with a poisonous serpent in a basket' (*B. Yeb.* 112b). (The woman cannot be forced to live with such a wicked influence.) However, without such a dire danger, we do not compel divorce — on the strength of a claim of mere 'repulsiveness'.

However, I have seen an opinion of my teacher (R. Moses b. Naḥman) of blessed memory, in a similar case. He penalized the men by permitting their wives to refrain from taking care of them, not holding these wives to be 'rebellious women'. (Such behaviour by wives would normally be grounds for divorce!) This was in order that they (the men) be punished. Or the rabbinical court could deal with the men, in similar fashion, as they saw fit: according to the sort of men they were, so that they might turn from their evil path. But divorce? — We may urgently request it, but we cannot compel it. Know this!

Now the German Case:

Reuben and his daughter's attorney have told how her husband, Simon, throws his money away by gambling and by frequenting gentile taverns where he becomes drunk and ill. The wife pleads that she abhors this husband of hers and wants (a divorce and) the money from her wedding contract. Simon, the husband, responds that he had done nothing improper. (He has indulged a bit in wagers and drink) at *Ḥannukah* season — as is usually done![32] And also occasionally he went to toast the health of friends and dine with them, as was customary in the district. If it is proper, as Reuben and his daughter's attorney claim, that on these grounds a woman may plead the husband's 'repulsiveness' and force him (to divorce) and pay off the wedding contract — if this is so, you have not left a single daughter of our father Abraham who would live peacefully with her husband! (What wife could not call attention to occasional excesses of food and drink and get a divorce!) This does not seem right to me! This is a mere pretext (to get a divorce and a financial settlement); I need not expand up the (weakness of) these shabby arguments. ...

Moreover, Simon has written: 'Again today Simon, her husband, declares before the Chief Judge and the Selectmen of the city, 'My father-in-law will suffer not loss on my account. Upstanding and decent men will guide me and I shall undertake to accomplish what they advise. There will be no loss on my account.'' And in a second plea he wrote: 'Indeed Simon stands ready to correct the faults his father-in-law alleges.' Since this is so, that Simon wants to correct himself and improve himself according to the advice of upstanding and decent men, by what right do his wife and her father complain and doubt him? Even if it were so that Simon had acted improperly, and had strayed from the straight and narrow path in some respect, indeed he now wants to correct himself and to undertake not to return to this wrong path! As for what Reuben's daughter's attorney wrote, that her husband should establish some guarantee that he will mend his ways — it seems that here as well she is going too far. There is apparently no fault or flaw in Simon that prevents one from believing that he will perform what he undertakes to do. (Whatever his faults, he is not a liar!)

Since this is so, that Simon wants to mend his ways according to the advice of upstanding and decent men, he has thereby fulfilled his obligations (or at least he has made a laudable beginning). As clarified in the stipulations (between the parties) that each side would take a negotiator, etc., so should they do! The negotiator would work matters out. If the negotiators were unable to come to an agreement, then they would refer the matter to the arbitrator.

He has claimed (presumably the attorney) that Reuben's daughter was at a distinct disadvantage in her mother-in-law's house — because her mother-in-law heaped insult on her. Simon has responded that the couple have taken their own quarters and the wife has no contact with the mother-in-law except at meals. Furthermore, today, if she does not wish to live in her mother-in-law's household, then she may stay in her own house and her old mother-in-law will not go near her or have any dealings with her — in this matter it also appears that Reuben's daughter is seeking some sort of pretext (for a divorce). What more can the old woman do? Is this not enough and more than enough (i.e., to be *non grata* in her own son's house)?

As long as Reuben's daughter conducts herself with persistent rebellion against her husband, her husband is under no obligation to provide for her keep. And this requires no involved talmudic discussion and analysis ... Jacob Weil.

In neither case did the woman's plea convince the Rabbi to compel the husband to issue the divorce. Although the law provided that indeed the wife could petition the court to compel a divorce in some specific situations, the judges were not inclined in these cases to broaden such grounds. Some rabbinic judges in Spain did view gambling as a corrosive and destructive element in a marriage, but clearly R. Yom Tov, a leading authority did not. For him, the gambler had necessarily to reach the point where he had degraded the marriage completely in respect of food, clothing, and so forth. Gambling in itself was not sufficient ground, one gathers, as long as the minima for a marriage still exited. The German authority appears inclined to enlist every means of negotiation and arbitration between the parties to restore marital harmony. He would not allow the woman to use the power of the court to compel a divorce; public drunkenness and gambling were for him insufficient grounds for divorce. He hints that these indulgences would jam the floodgates of divorce wide open to inundate unknown numbers of marriages. For both authorities, the fact of marriage seems to rise superior to the quality of the relationship between husband and wife. What effect all this might have on the children of such a marriage receives not a word.

6. Conclusion

By the year 1580, when the first complete Ķaro-Isserles *Shulḥan Arukh* appeared in print, the German community, while still numerous, had already looked on while many of its members had moved eastward to found the great Eastern European communities that achieved dominant positions in later centuries. The ancient Spanish community was no more, its glory dispersed along tragic highways to North Africa, Italy, and especially to all the Ottoman Turkish domains. New communities arose in the East, where the sun rose again on the vigour of Jewish Law.

7. Bibliography

The Bibliography for this period of Jewish Law in languages other than Hebrew is quite large. The booklist given here offers a general idea of its extent. Some of the works, of course, are relevant to other periods of legal history as well as this one, but each book, after its fashion, is useful in reconstructing both the law and its development and the lawyers and events that were prominent in that development.

The books listed are all standard works. Some of the secondary material on Jewish Law of this period is framed as history or biography, insofar as biography can be reconstructed from the available sources. Such works rely heavily on the responsa literature of the period.

Abrahams, I., *Jewish Life in the Middle Ages* (Philadelphia: Jewish Publication Society, 1911).

Baer, B., *The Jews in Christian Spain* (Philadelphia: Jewish Publication Seminary of America, 1961-66, 2 vols).

Bazak, J. and Passamaneck, S.M., *Jewish Law and Jewish Life* (New York: Union of American Hebrew Congregations, 1977).

Eidelberg, S., *Jewish Life in Austria in the XV Century* (Philadelphia: Dropsie College, 1962).

Elon, M., *Jewish Law* (Jerusalem: Magnes Press, 1973, Hebrew); Engl. ed., *Jewish Law: History, Sources, Principles*, trld. B. Auerbach and M.J. Sykes (Philadelphia and Jerusalem: Jewish Publication Society, 1994), esp. Vol.III, ch.39.

Epstein, I., *The Responsa of R. Solomon Ben Adreth* (New York: KTAV Publishing House, 1968).

Epstein, I., *The Responsa of R. Simon B. Zemah Duran* (New York: KTAV Publishing House, 1968).

Falk, Z.W., *Jewish Matrimonial Law in the Middle Ages* (London, Oxford University Press, 1966).

Finkelstein, L., *Jewish Self-Government in the Middle Ages* (New York: Feldheim Publishing Co. 1964).

Freehof, S.B., *The Responsa Literature* (Philadelphia: Jewish Publication Society of America, 1955).

Goldman, I.M., *The Life and Times of R. David ibn Abi Zimra* (New York: Jewish Theological Seminary of America, 1970).

Goodblatt, M., *Jewish Life in Turkey in the XVI Century* (New York: Jewish Theological Seminary of America, 1952).

Hershman, A., *Rabbi Isaac B. Sheshet Perfet and His Times* (New York: Jewish Theological Seminary of America, 1943).

Kirschenbaum, A., *Self Incrimination in Jewish Law* (New York: Burning Bush Press, 1970).

Neuman, A., *The Jews in Spain* (Philadelphia: Jewish Publication Society of America, 1942, 2 vols).

Passamaneck, S.M., *The Traditional Jewish Law of Sale* (Cincinnati: Hebrew Union College Press, 1983).

Quint, E., *A Restatement of Rabbinic Civil Law*, vol. I, *Laws of Judges, Laws of Evidence* (Northvale, New Jersey, London: Jason Aronson Inc., 1990).

Quint, E. and Hecht, N.S., *Jewish Jurisprudence* (CHUR, London, Paris, New York: Harwood Academic Publishers, 1980-86), 2 vols.

Rabinowicz, H., *Life and Times of Rabbi Joseph Colon* (London: University of London, 1947).

Steiman, S., *Custom and Survival* (New York: Bloch Publishing Co., 1963).

Werblowsky, R.J.Z., *Joseph Karo: Lawyer and Mystic* (Oxford: Clarendon Press, 1962).

Of particular interest for the present period are the bibliographies in Nahum Rakover, *The Multi-Language Bibliography of Jewish Law* (Jerusalem: Library of Jewish Law, 1990), noting articles on communal organization and administration in Spain and Portugal (p.436), Germany (p.413), Poland, Lithuania and Russia (p.438) and Turkey (p.432)

Rakover's sections on legal procedure and the attorney (pp. 489-92) are useful. He has a lengthy section on penal law, with a special subsection on homicide (pp. 517-47), as well as a section on tort law (pp. 677-714). There is also a detailed section on family and inheritance (pp. 623-73).

Phyllis H. Weisbard and David Schonberg, *Jewish Law: Bibliography of Sources and Scholarship in English* (Littleton: Fred B. Rothman & Co., 1989), presents a less detailed format, but is rather easier to use for that reason. It contains sections, among many others, on criminal law, evidence, family law, property and torts, with explanations of the contents of each category — useful because Jewish legal classification differs from English legal classification enough to cause some unnecessary confusion for persons unfamiliar with the categories of Jewish Law.

Notes

1   See the bibliography at the end of this chapter. Eidelberg's work is used extensively in the development of a 'cross section' of German Jewish legal institutions and practice of the period.

2   The areas of ritual law and marriage and divorce law were treated with the utmost seriousness in this period as in other periods. Jewish Law was self-consciously an ecclesiastical law, and one's proper relationship to the deity — maintained through law, ritual and so forth — was a major concern of the law.

3   *Ibid.* see also J. Bazak and S.M. Passamaneck, *Jewish Law and Jewish Life* (New York: Union of American Hebrew Congregations, 1977), Book 7, pp. 31-36.

4   Articles on capital punishment, and informers are also most useful. See bibliography at the end of this chapter.

5   Eidelberg, 86; see *supra*, pp.330 and 335f. The excommunicatory ban, the ḥerem, is discussed in numerous articles; see the bibliography at the end of the chapter.

6   Quint and Hecht, *Jewish Jurisprudence*, vol. 1, pp. 75-121. See also Bazak and Passamaneck, *supra* n.3, at Book 6, p. 33; Book 1, pp.17f., 45f., and *supra*, p.326.

7   See note 6, *supra*. The article 'Attorney' in the *Encyclopaedia Judaica* is most useful.

8   See for instance Louis Finkelstein's classic study, *Jewish Self-Government in the Middle Ages* noted in the bibliography at the end of this chapter.

9   The terms 'Spanish' as used here refer to all of Iberia, including Majorca, and to the Spanish-Jewish communities that developed in North Africa in the 14th century.

10   Hershman, 99; and Isidore Epstein, *Studies in the Communal Life of Spain,* 46ff. See bibliography at the end of this chapter.

11   Hershman, 108, 115; See also S.M. Passamaneck, 'The *Berure Averot* and the Administration of Justice in XIII and XIV Century Spain', *Jewish Law Association Studies IV. The Boston Conference Volume*, ed. B.S. Jackson (Atlanta: Scholars Press, 1990), 135-46.

12   See the bibliography at the end of this chapter. The cross-section of Jewish legal institutions and practice in the Ottoman Empire relies extensively on Morris Goodblatt's study, *Jewish Life in Turkey in the XVI Century.* Israel Goldman's book on David ibn Abu Zimra is also most useful.

13   Goodblatt provides a detailed discussion of excommunication in all its forms practised in Ottoman Turkish Jewish courts: 88-90.

14   See M. Elon, *Jewish Law: History, Sources, Principles*, trld. B. Auerbach and M.J. Sykes (Philadelphia and Jerusalem: Jewish Publication Society, 1994, 4 vols.).   This massive study provides a more complete statement on the sources of law, their character, inter-relationships, and development, for this (and every other) period.

15   Elon's *Jewish Law* is the best general non-Hebrew source for specific discussions of codes, responsa, and commentaries; S. Freehof's *Responsa Literature* is the most comprehensive work in English on that subject; and Louis Ginzberg's essay on the 'Codification of Jewish Law' in *Jewish Law and Lore,* New York, Jewish Publication Society of America, 1955, is still quite useful.

16   There is some discussion of commentaries in the encyclopaedia articles about the work to which commentary is annexed. For instance, in the articles on 'Talmud', there is some discussion of talmudic commentary.   More information comes from articles on the men who wrote the various commentaries.   There is no general work on legal commentary *per se* in medieval rabbinic legal literature available in English.

17   See the bibliography at the end of this chapter. Sidney Steiman's *Custom and Survival* draws heavily upon the work of Moellin.

18   See the bibliography at the end of this chapter. Several works give brief biographical sketches of the lives and careers of major authorities: Bazak and Passamaneck, Freehof, Werblowsky; and of course there are the book length studies of some of the major personalities: Eidelberg on Isserlein, Epstein on *Rashba* and so forth. There are of course encyclopaedia articles on each of

them.

19 See Hershman, *op. cit.,* passim; Bazak and Passamaneck, *supra* n.3, at Books 7 and 8 combined, xxxv-xxxvi; and Freehof, *op. cit.,* 68-71.

20 See Israel M. Goldman, *The Life and Times of R. David ibn Abu Zima* (New York, Jewish Theological Seminary of America, 1970), *passim*; and Freehof, 80-82.

21 See R. J. Z. Werblowsky, *Joseph Karo: Lawyers and Mystic* (Oxford: Clarendon Press, 1962), *passim.*

22 See Bazak and Passamaneck, *supra* n.3, at Books 7 and 8 combined, xxxiii-xxxiv.

23 See *ibid,* p. xxxviii; and Freehof, 74-76.

24 See Bazak and Passamaneck, *supra* n.3, at Books 7 and 8 combined, p. xl; and Freehof, 76-80.

25 Max Seligsohn, 'Isserles, Moses b. Israel', in *The Jewish Encyclopedia* (New ·York and London: Funk and Wagnalls, 1904), vi.678a.

26 See Bazak and Passamaneck, *supra* n.3, at Books 7 and 8; S.M. Passamaneck, 'R. Judah b. Asher on Capital Penalties', in *Jewish Law Association Studies VII. The Paris Conference Volume,* ed. S.M. Passamaneck and M. Finley (Atlanta: Scholars Press, 1994), 153-72.

27 The translation of the responsum is reproduced here with the kind permission of the Union of Hebrew Congregations, publishers of Bazak and Passamaneck, *Jewish Law and Jewish Life, supra* n.3, at Book 7.

28 See Aaron Kirschenbaum, *Self Incrimination in Jewish Law* (New York: Burning Bush Press, 1970). The work explores the question of self-incrimination in great depth and detail. It was clearly inadmissible in capital cases.

29 I.e. the meditation which describes God as merciful — *raḥum* — and a pardoner of sins; this occurs immediately before the commencement of the formal liturgy, the call to worship.

30 Lit.: seek mercy — Hebrew, *raḥamim,* a word from the same verbal root as *raḥum* in the next-following element of the liturgy.

31 The translations of both the Spanish case and the German case come from Bazak and Passamaneck, *supra* n.3, at Book 8, and are reproduced here in abbreviated form with the kind permission of the publisher, the Union of American Hebrew Congregations.

32 Some drinking and gambling traditionally punctuated the winter *Ḥannukah* observance, but this was supposed to be kept within the bounds of moderation.

13

JEWISH LAW FROM THE
SHULḤAN ARUKH
TO THE ENLIGHTENMENT

by

EDWARD FRAM
Ben Gurion University

1. *Political and Juridical Background*

The dawn of the seventeenth century brought few immediate changes to most Jewish communities. During the course of approximately the next 150 years, however, Jewish communities in Europe, North Africa, and the Ottoman Empire would experience dramatic events that would help reshape the character of Jewish life.

In 1600 Polish Jewry was in the midst of a Golden Age that would be jarred by the Cossack revolts and Swedish invasions from 1648 to 1658. These wars decimated many Jewish communities, particularly in eastern sections of the country, and contributed to an ever growing westward trend in Jewish migration. In the mid-eighteenth century, Hasidism would begin to develop in eastern Europe although it would only be forged into a movement by the successors of Rabbi Israel Baal Shem Tov (d. 1760). In the wake of the religious battles in the West, so-called 'court Jews' emerged in the German absolutist States. Their wealth and political influence often put them beyond the reach of the traditional Jewish community and rabbinic control and eased their acculturation into general society.

The Sephardi Diaspora that had begun in the late fourteenth century continued and even found new centres such as Amsterdam where *conversos* de facto enjoyed freedom of religion as well as economic opportunities. The major upheaval of the seventeenth century was the proclamation of Shabbetai Zevi as Messiah in 1665. Jewish communities throughout the Ottoman Empire as well as in Europe and North Africa became caught up in the excitement only to learn that when faced with the choice of apostasy or death, the supposed Messiah abandoned his people for Islam (1666). The disappointment left an indelible mark on future developments in Jewish communities, although it was of almost no discernible consequence in the realm of Jewish Law.

Despite the obligations imposed by Jewish Law in all walks of life, Jews in the seventeenth and eighteenth centuries tended, as they had in the Middle Ages, to observe the ritual law but at times neglected a strict observance of commercial law. While lapses in ritual observance occurred — there was always an unscrupulous butcher or someone tempted by a worldly, but forbidden pleasure — such cases were exceptions in a society where observance of ritual helped define Jewish self-identity in a Christian or Muslim context. Few, however, could afford to defy the practices of the market in an age when most people lived on the cusp of survival.

As it had for centuries, Islamic Law guaranteed the rights of Jews to practise their religion and enjoy some degree of judicial autonomy. Such was not the case for Jews living in Christian lands where Jewish settlement and the level of Jewish judicial autonomy continued to depend on Jewish communities securing rights or privileges from the host authorities. Rights were commonly negotiated when Jews came to dwell in an area and were often articulated in charters that Jewish communities were careful to renew with each subsequent leader. Frequently included were rights to judge fellow Jews, make enactments fostering religious observance, and tax members of the community.

Generally, any community wealthy enough to employ a Rabbi had some form of Jewish court or arbitration. A notable exception was Amsterdam which, although it had a significant Jewish community, apparently did not have a Jewish court before 1632. Prior to that, the Jewish refugees from the Iberian peninsula who lived in this commercial centre went to municipal courts to settle their disputes.

The extent of Jewish judicial autonomy varied from place to place and often reflected developments in the non-Jewish environment. For example, Jews enjoyed traditional forms of self-government in much of Southern, Central, and Western Germany during the early to mid-seventeenth century. As that century progressed, however, the political doctrine of absolutism took hold in the German States and called for the elimination of independent entities within the State. In seventeenth century Venice, too, Jews faced opposition from a Government that was trying to exert its jurisdiction over all its citizens — including members of the Catholic clergy — in civil and criminal matters. Theorists argued that the prince must be recognized as the final authority in all temporal matters. Nevertheless, despite the interdictions of the Venetian Government, Jewish courts continued to try both civil and criminal cases there and even fined Jews who took their disputes to non-Jewish courts.

Opposition to Jewish self-adjudication in civil and criminal matters was motivated not only by political considerations but by religious concerns as well. Many Christian thinkers, both Protestant and Catholic, believed that Jews were to be a subjugated people and that granting Jews judicial dominion over civil and criminal matters was incompatible with their lowly status. Muslim theologians, whose influence was steadily growing in the Ottoman Empire of the seventeenth century and who were obliged to humble the *dhimmi* (non-Muslim subjects of the Muslim State), also kept a wary eye on Jewish legal independence.

Even in states that demonstrated a benevolent attitude towards Jewish judicial control in civil and criminal matters, such as in Mantua and Tuscany, communities continually had to urge the authorities to enforce and augment their powers. Early in the seventeenth century, the Mantuan Jewish community strove to obtain official recognition of its decisions in civil matters as well as in all matters of personal status. Although the Government eventually recognized the authority of Jewish courts, it still allowed Jews to take matters to non-Jewish courts, which they did. The demands of Jewish Law that Jewish litigants come before a rabbinic court that judged matters on the basis of Jewish Law were not always enough to outweigh the temptation of exploiting a discrepancy between Jewish Law and the law of the land or the ease of going to a non-Jewish court. Only in 1626 did the Mantua community receive a privilege granting it exclusive authority over cases between Jews. Nevertheless, Jews continued to go to non-Jewish courts leaving the community (from 1647 with the blessing of the Duke) to threaten such people with fines and punishments. As in Poland, cases between Jews and non-Jews were judged in a special court presided over by a Government-appointed non-Jewish judge. A Jew who violated the law of the state generally fell into the hands of the state.

Ottoman authorities generally did not interfere in religious life and, although Jewish courts were not recognized by the Government and therefore could only resort to limited social pressures to enforce their decisions, cases between Jews seem to have continued to be judged in Jewish courts. However, when large sums were at stake or when litigants thought it in their best interest, Jews tended to turn to non-Jewish courts. Jewish courts had no jurisdiction over criminal matters.

Similarly, in England — which, under Oliver Cromwell, readmitted Jews to its shores in 1656, after an hiatus of 362 years — Jewish communities were completely devoid of political power, and compliance with Jewish judicial rulings, as well as membership in the Jewish community itself, was strictly voluntary. With Jews enjoying full access to state courts and the, at best, tenuous connection of many English Jews to the traditional community, rabbinic courts were generally left to deal with matters of personal status. By contrast, Polish Jewry boasted local, regional, and national councils each of which enacted ordinances ranging from rules governing the marketplace to sumptuary laws. Residents were obliged to observe such laws and each organ of Government had courts to ensure that they did.

While Jews continued to enjoy judicial autonomy in eighteenth century Poland prior to the country's partition and demise as an independent nation in 1795, Jewish courts in regions owned by Polish noblemen were not independent but were part of the landowner's own court system. Jews in these areas could appeal against decisions of Jewish courts to the landowner or his representatives, although rabbis were often invited to hear the appeals together with the landowner. Landowners were also known to interfere with Jewish courts if they believed it in their best interest. While rabbis opposed this loss of sovereignty, there was little that they could do to prevent it.

In Western Europe, the mid-eighteenth century brought with it discussion of emancipation for the Jews and the notion that they would take their place as full citizens of the state and bring their legal disputes to state courts. Yet when French Jews attained full emancipation (September 1791) they tended to guard their ritual traditions and were not immediately drawn into French society. In Austria, however, Jewish legal autonomy was abolished in 1785 as part of the emancipation of Jews. Elsewhere the failure of Jews to attain full emancipation until the nineteenth and even twentieth centuries helped perpetuate independent Jewish legal systems, particularly in Russia where the Czar encouraged a rigid legal separation of the Jews from Russian society.

2. *Legal Sources*

The literary genres of Jewish Law have remained relatively constant over the ages and the early modern period was no exception. Codes, commentaries, and responsa formed the basis of Jewish legal literary creativity during this period while ordinances of Jewish self-governing bodies guided communal activities.

As they had in previous centuries, Rabbis used responsa to answer legal questions from laymen and colleagues that appeared to be without clear precedent or which seemed to be mired in controversy. The nature and limits of Jewish self-government, questions of ritual, as well as civil and criminal law, were all treated in the responsa literature. The question and answer format of responsa was also used by a number of rabbis, such as R. Aryeh Leb Gunzberg (1695-1785) who served in Lithuania and later in Metz, to deal with topics of interest to themselves rather than respond to actual conundrums.

No one appointed Rabbis to write responsa. Questioners turned to men that they believed to be outstanding and God-fearing scholars. However, a Rabbi whose answers were too often at variance with the values of his questioners would soon find people sending their queries elsewhere. The authority of a responsum generally depended on the personal prestige of its author.

While responsa remained a mainstay of halakhic development throughout the period, the first half of the seventeenth century produced a shift in the focus of Jewish legal thought, one that pushed commentaries to the forefront and almost eliminated codes as a creative genre in the Ashkenazi world for the remainder of this period. The last half of the sixteenth century had witnessed the publication of Joseph Karo's *Shulhan Arukh* and the accompanying glosses of Moses Isserles, although this was not the only code written in the late sixteenth century.

Rabbi Solomon Luria (d. 1574), who served as Rabbi of Ostrog, Brest-Litovsk and later Lublin, rejected the notion of a definitive code stating only normative conclusions and, heeding what he believed to be a heavenly charge, wrote a lengthy code in which he considered previous scholarship on each issue before arriving at a decision. Unlike Karo's code, Luria followed the rather haphazard organization of the *Talmud*. Cumbersome albeit brilliant, incomplete, and not fully printed until the mid-eighteenth century, the work was not a viable alternative to Karo's masterpiece of legal brevity.

A student of both Isserles and Luria, Rabbi Mordekhai Jaffe (d. 1612), a native of Bohemia who served as Rabbi in Prague and Poznan, Poland, was also dissatisfied with the terseness of the *Shulhan Arukh* and criticized its failure, on both pedagogic and methodological grounds, to give rationales for laws. Jaffe composed a code of his own entitled *Levush Malkut*, a code that he believed would be useful to students as well as accomplished scholars.

Jaffe's work seems to have quickly garnered popularity among students who used his conclusions in arguments before many a teacher. Some argued that Jaffe should be followed because his conclusions took Ḳaro's and Isserles's views into account. Legal scholars of the first rank, however, did not concur. Rabbi Benjamin Slonik (around 1550-1619, Poland) wrote to one questioner regarding Jaffe's code:

> And do not pay attention to the words of Rabbi Mordekhai Jaffe in his book, the *Levush*, because he is nothing but a scribe who copies from books and does not investigate (the opinions of) the authors ...

Nevertheless, Jaffe's work proved popular, at least among Polish Jews, in the first decades of the seventeenth century.

In the early seventeenth century neither Jaffe's or Ḳaro's code had achieved dominance. An outstanding authority and influential teacher of the period, Rabbi Me'ir ben Gedaliah of Lublin (1558-1616), wrote: '... it is not my way to deal with the *Shulḥan Arukh*...' — although he certainly made reference to the book from time to time. Jacob ben Asher's venerable *Ṭur* remained the focus of most legal commentaries of the period. In the 1640s in Poland, however, a number of legal commentators working independently chose to consider new halakhic ideas that had been raised since Ḳaro, plus their own insights, in glosses to Ḳaro's *Shulḥan Arukh* rather than the *Ṭur*. David ben Samuel ha-Levi's *Ṭure Zahab* and Shabbetai ben Me'ir ha-Kohen's *Sifte Kohen* not only comprehensively weighed the relative merits of Ḳaro's and Isserles's positions but used Ḳaro's code as a point of departure for broad legal discussions, including consideration of other legal texts. Ultimately they engendered a lively give and take not only among themselves but, as their commentaries became authoritative texts in their own right, the criticisms of succeeding generations as well. Other commentaries that became standard in subsequent editions of *Shulḥan Arukh* include Rabbi Abraham Gombiner's (around 1637-1683) *Magen Abraham* on ritual law and Rabbi Joshua Falk's (1555-1617) *Ṣefer Me'irat Eynayim* on civil, commercial, and criminal law. Both of them also lived and worked in Poland.

The decision of authors to base themselves on portions of Ḳaro's code and the printing of these works in the margins of Ḳaro's text was crucial in establishing the place of the *Shulḥan Arukh*. While Jaffe's work attracted the glosses of at least one notable scholar, the stature of those who wrote on Ḳaro's code not only made the *Shulḥan Arukh* the basic legal code of Jewish Law but created a literary genre of commentaries and super-commentaries on the *Shulḥan Arukh*. Jaffe's work was still referred to, but often the reference was derisive and it usually appeared in the margins of the *Shulḥan Arukh*.

There was intermittent opposition to Ḳaro's code — most notably when, in 1692, the Palestinian scholar Rabbi Hezekiah Da Silva (1659-1695) published the first volume of his *Pri Hadash*, a biting critique not only of Karo but of all earlier codifiers save Maimonides. When the work reached Egypt a controversy ensued and attempts were made to ban the book. Ultimately though, the position of the *Shulhan Arukh* could not be challenged and in the eighteenth century Da Silva's work, somewhat muted by the publishers, appeared within the covers of an ever expanding *Shulhan Arukh*.

By the mid-eighteenth century the *Shulhan Arukh* took on another role, becoming a point of departure for *pilpul* — a legal and pedagogic methodology based on sometimes wildly abstruse casuistry. Most notable examples of this genre were the *Kereti uPeleti* of Rabbi Jonathan Eybeschütz (1690/95-1764) and the *Kitsot haHoshen* and *Avne Milu'im* of Rabbi Aryeh Leib Heller (around 1745-1813).

The publication of the *Shulhan Arukh* and its broad acceptance unwittingly created an intellectual line of demarcation in Jewish legal history. During the second half of the seventeenth century, Rabbis who had lived before the end of the fifteenth century were accorded a higher level of authority than their successors. Later jurists (*Aharonim*) could discuss the views of their predecessors (*Rishonim*; lit., 'first ones') but they could not overrule them. This was not a new notion. From talmudic times, legal scholars had believed that earlier generations were closer to the Sinaitic revelation and that the knowledge of subsequent generations had somehow been whittled away. One notable exception to this line of thought was Rabbi Elijah ben Solomon (1720-1797) of Vilnius who regularly disagreed with earlier post-talmudic authorities.

Karo's work had met the need for codification but the ever-mounting maze of controversies and opinions that occupied the margins of the *Shulhan Arukh* made the work far too complicated for even the educated layman to use. The four slim volumes that had been published in Venice in 1564-1565 were well on their way to their modern form of ten, heavy, folio tomes laden with commentaries and super-commentaries in the tiniest of prints — rather an ironic fate for a work intended to be a review tool for scholars and a legal primer for young students.

From time to time the provisions of the *Shulhan Arukh* proved insufficient to maintain Jewish life and it was necessary for rabbis to enact ordinances to protect communal observance. Such *takkanot* (or *haskamot* in the Sephardi world) were generally regional and not binding on non-residents. In 1607, with the agreement of the lay leadership of Polish Jewry, Falk introduced a number of such ordinances aimed at ensuring the suitability of ritual slaughters and developing a legally acceptable method of charging interest on loans between two Jewish parties. In Constantinople, Rabbi Joseph di Trani (1568-1639) instituted overseers to ensure that local Jews did not continue to flaunt the law. Even if they did not enact the ordinances themselves, Rabbis were often asked to interpret the scope of community rules. Rabbi Judah Ayash (around 1700-1760, Algiers) was asked whether a Jew could send a non-Jew to buy fish for him after the community had prohibited Jews from buying fish because of price gouging by non-Jewish fish mongers (he ruled that he could not).

Ordinances were not only made by Rabbis. Communities, associations, and other social organizations within the Jewish community enacted rules of behaviour, at times with the approbation of the local Rabbi. These *takkanot* were recognized as part of the community's traditional rights and were binding on community members 'forever' — unless a time limit was specified. Ordinances were enacted by communal leaders without the explicit approval of local residents (there were no provisions for referenda) and were recorded in the community, association or society record book.

3. *Legal Practice*

A prominent Rabbi of a town was likely to receive many letters seeking his legal advice, some from people far from his community. Not responsible to those who did not employ him, such a Rabbi could choose the questions to which he wished to respond and those which he wished to ignore. Judges sitting on tribunals did not enjoy this luxury.

Judges were not always Rabbis or even trained in Jewish Law. While communities of Jews who had fled the Iberian peninsula for the Ottoman Empire generally set up rabbinic courts, similar communities in Western Europe established courts in which lay leaders served as judges. In much of the Ashkenazi world there were simultaneously two types of Jewish courts: a rabbinic court and a lay court. Rabbinic courts dealt with matters of personal status (e.g., a bill of divorce), occasionally criminal matters (which for political reasons were often decided by the lay leadership), and monetary matters. However, Rabbis such as Ezekiel Landau of Prague (1713-1793) complained that Rabbis were all too often handling petty monetary cases while important matters were being taken to lay courts.

Lay courts were presided over by businessmen or other men (usually three) with some life experience (women did not serve on rabbinic or lay courts). Judges were generally appointed — sometimes against their will — by Jewish political leaders. In Poznan, for example, the electoral college chose the various levels of judges who decided monetary and religious matters. In Fez judges were appointed from among the members of the ruling council and generally held their positions for life. But as the demands of business often had to be settled quickly in a place without a sitting court, cases were not always brought before an established court. In such instances, each litigant could choose one judge and the two judges would choose a third, all on an *ad hoc* basis.

In early seventeenth century Cracow, established lay courts met on a regular basis and were divided into courts dealing with small sums (up to 10 gold pieces), medium sums (between 10 and 100 gold pieces), and large sums (over 100 gold pieces). The latter met on Sundays and Mondays (and Thursdays if necessary) while the other courts met daily from Sunday to Thursday. Courts could summon parties, although they could only resort to religious threats to force testimony from possible witnesses. For faster justice, arbitration could be used. The Cracow ordinance declared that arbitrators had to hear a case within 24 hours of being chosen and render a decision within 3 days. Lay courts were also set up at fairs to handle matters between merchants.

Unlike rabbinic courts that decided matters on the basis of *halakhah*, lay courts used a 'common sense' approach that was probably based on local commercial custom. In some circumstances, judges could be held liable for gross errors in judgment. From time to time lay judges in Sephardi centres consulted rabbinic scholars for advice or simply referred matters directly to them. Decisions of rabbinic courts could be, and often were, appealed to a rabbinic authority, usually one living in a different city and who enjoyed great prestige. To the chagrin of many Jewish communities, decisions were frequently appealed to non-Jewish courts.

In Poland during the seventeenth and eighteenth centuries, legal questions that crossed geographic jurisdictions could be referred to a regional court presided over by the Chief Rabbi of the region (usually the Rabbi of the regional centre). Such courts appear to have met irregularly.

Litigants in both rabbinic and lay courts paid a fee for justice according to the value of the case. Fines assessed by the courts often went for charitable purposes. Communities could do a number of things to see that a ruling was enforced, from denying a recalcitrant individual certain religious privileges to excommunicating him from the community. Enforcement also depended on the extent of State support for Jewish judicial and communal autonomy.

Oaths were commonly taken before testimony was accepted. If the case was in a Jewish court then the witness was warned about the grievous nature of false testimony in religious terms. In Government courts in Poland, Jews were permitted to take a special oath, since the oaths used by Christians invoked the name of Jesus and were therefore religiously objectionable to Jews. In 1604, a Jew in Cracow took an oath in a Polish court beginning, 'I, Zacharias, swear to omnipotent God who created heaven and earth, who gave the Ten Commandments on Mount Zion (sic!) by his faithful servant Moses ...' and concluded by reaffirming that the statement was true, based on God as the giver of the Ten Commandments. If it was not true the witness asked that his flesh and blood be punished. Muslim courts did not accept the testimony of a Jew against a Muslim.

Testimony in Jewish courts was generally given in the vernacular rather than Hebrew. Legal representation was prohibited in the Jewish courts of Mantua until 1676-1677, when the local judicial system was reformed. Court decisions were recorded by court scribes in a special book for this purpose.

Certain cases, such as those dealing with the ever-vexing problem of abandoned wives, *agunot*, often required sending legal documents from one community to another. Testimony was often heard in the locale of one of the witnesses, notarized by the local scribe or Rabbi, and sent on to a prominent Rabbi for his consideration (see the section on family law below). Polish Rabbis also met at the major fairs to consult regarding difficult legal matters.

In an age when plagues still ravaged cities and highwaymen thought little of killing their victims, orphans were all too common a phenomenon. Communities took it upon themselves to appoint guardians to care for the interests of orphans. Guardians appear to have been responsible to the community and not to the courts.

4. *Leading Rabbis of the Age*

Major centres of Jewish life in the seventeenth and eighteenth centuries such as Lwów, Cracow, Prague, Hamburg, Venice, Algiers, Constantinople, and Salonika, generally engaged the leading rabbinic scholars of the generation as their spiritual leaders. Some were prolific, others were not; among the prolific, the scholarship of some caught the imagination not only of their contemporaries but of subsequent generations as well. The following list, while not exhaustive, focuses on Rabbis whose influence far outlasted their own times.

A. A critic of the *Shulhan Arukh*, Rabbi Joel Sirkes (around 1541-1640) served as Rabbi of numerous Lithuanian and Polish communities before coming to Cracow in 1620. Sirkes authored a lengthy commentary on Jacob ben Asher's *Tur* in a vain attempt to restore the *Tur* to the centre of Jewish legal study. Although his views were often rejected when in conflict with Karo's, he was regularly cited by the commentators on the *Shulhan Arukh*. Sirkes's rulings allowing the sale of leaven on Passover without its physical removal from the Jew's property and his allowance of *hadash* in the Diaspora (lit., 'new'; see *Lev.* 23:9-14) remain the basis for contemporary practice. Sirkes's responsa and textual emendations to the Babylonian *Talmud* are standard works.

B. Although Shabbetai ben Me'ir ha-Kohen (1621-1662) served as a Rabbi and judge in his native Lithuania and later in Moravia, he was best known for his commentaries on the *Shulhan Arukh*, particularly his work on ritual law. With a clause by clause analysis that used logic, a wide range of sources, and casuistry, Shabbetai championed Karo and Isserles's code and firmly rejected many of the views of jurists who lived between the publishing of the *Shulhan Arukh* and his own time. Shabbetai also introduced numerous legal works from Ottoman authorities into Ashkenazi legal discourse.

C. Born in Safed, Rabbi Joseph di Trani arrived in Constantinople in 1604 to head the talmudic academy and five years later became the Rabbi of the city. Rarely citing earlier authorities in his responsa unless to buttress his point, di Trani based his opinions on talmudic sources. Like so many of his contemporaries in the Sephardi world, he was forced to consider the status of Marranos in Jewish Law.

D. Rabbi Zvi Hirsch Ashkenazi (1658-1718) and his son, Rabbi Jacob Emden (no.5, below), both engendered much controversy during their careers but both remained influential jurists. Ashkenazi, who, although Polish by birth, studied with Sephardi teachers, served in Sarajevo, Altona, Amsterdam, and Lwów. His responsa entitled *She'elot uteshubot hakham Zebi* (Amsterdam, 1712), answered questions from across Europe and helped define how Ashkenazi and Sephardi Jews should interact in the world of ritual where their customs often conflicted.

E. Unlike his father, Rabbi Jacob Emden (1697-1776), with one brief
exception, did not hold communal office. A prolific author and virulent
opponent of those who harboured lingering beliefs in the pseudo-messiah of
the 1660s, Shabbetai Zevi, Emden believed that one may not simply rely on
legal precedent but must recheck the talmudic sources on each issue. His
legal independence led him not only to question the views of many
commentators on the *Shulhan Arukh* but the legal authority of the *Shulhan
Arukh* itself. Emden also rejected unfounded stringencies believing that
'someone who prohibits what is permitted will ultimately allow what is
prohibited.'

F. Rabbi Ezekiel Landau, a native of Poland, assumed a judicial post at
the age of 21 and, in 1754, was invited to become Chief Rabbi of Bohemia.
Landau produced over 850 published responsa notable for their wide use of
earlier sources, talmudic commentaries, sermons, and other rabbinic writings.
Like Emden before him, Landau spearheaded the efforts of the Jewish
community against laws demanding the delay of burial of the dead until three
days after the cessation of bodily functions, in accordance with then current
scientific beliefs, Government orders in Brunswick, Germany (1783),
Bohemia (1786), and Austria (1787), and the views of Jewish modernists. A
strong supporter of the authority of tradition, Landau believed that the
principles of Jewish Law could not be outweighed by scientific postulates.

G. One of the most revered figures of the period was Rabbi Elijah ben
Solomon Zalman of Vilnius (1720-1797), who was known and, indeed, is
still referred to, simply as 'the Gaon' by Ashkenazi Jewry (but not to be
confused with the Geonim of some 800 years earlier). Although Elijah did
not occupy a rabbinic position, he was able to mount a virulent campaign
against the emerging Hasidic movement in Eastern Europe on the basis of
the respect that he had earned for his scholarship. Elijah lectured to a small
group of disciples, a number of whom became rabbinic leaders in the nineteenth century. His works, including commentaries to both the Palestinian
and Babylonian *Talmudim* and the *Shulhan Arukh*, were published
posthumously and are characterized by textual comparisons and emendations.

H. In the Sephardi world Rabbi Judah Ayash was renowned. The son of
an outstanding jurist, Rabbi Isaac Ayash (d. 1727), Judah became the head of

the rabbinic court in Algiers in 1728 and corresponded with communities around the Mediterranean. His responsa considered matters of communal authority and commercial practice but the majority of questions asked of him dealt with ritual practices. Like many outstanding rabbinic leaders, Ayash also maintained a talmudic academy where he taught *Talmud* and Jewish Law.

I. Another Sephardi leader from a prominent rabbinic family was Rabbi Yom Tob Algazi (1727-1802). Algazi, whose scholarship was warmly praised by the Hungarian Rabbi of the next generation, Moses Sofer, became a member of the rabbinic court in Jerusalem and was signing local enactments by the year 1762. In 1780 he assumed the Chief Rabbinate of Jerusalem. His work included responsa and a commentary on Maimonides' *Mishneh Torah*.

5. *Developments in Halakhah*

A. Voting Rights

Control of the Jewish community has been an enduring issue in Jewish life. While Jewish communities held elections on a regular basis, in many communities only taxpayers were allowed to vote and the wealthy who contributed the most to the community chest often enjoyed an unequal say in running the community. Rabbi Menahem Krochmal (around 1600-1671), a native of Poland who eventually became Chief Rabbi of Moravia, was asked to interpret a number of communal ordinances concerning the claims of poorer taxpayers who felt that their rights were being usurped by the wealthy. Krochmal wrote

> When I came to the holy community of Kromeriz (1636) which accepted me as teacher [of the law, i.e., Rabbi], a disagreement took place in the community regarding the hiring of the beadle. In the community there were fifty taxpayers and among them there was one individual with his two sons and two sons-in-law who were rich and paid three-fifths of the communal expenses and the rest [of the community] together paid only two-fifths ... And the community had an ordinance regarding hiring a Rabbi, cantor, and beadle and this is its language: 'The ordinance for hiring a Rabbi, cantor, and beadle: all the taxpayers will gather together [and vote and a] numeric majority and a majority of the money [i.e., those who contribute at least fifty percent of the taxes] must be in agreement' ... And now this individual with his sons and sons-in-law did not agree on the beadle that the rest of the community wanted to hire. And because of this they had to cancel their plan [to hire the beadle] ... (Krochmal, *Responsa*, no. 1)

According to the Jewish community of Kromeriz's own ordinance that had been agreed to by previous generations, there had to be a concurrence of both the majority of taxpayers and those who provided the majority of funds to the community to hire communal functionaries. Since the five family members contributed more than half of the community's total tax receipts, they could effectively block the hiring decision of the majority of the community. The forty-five other taxpaying members of the community came to Krochmal fearing that these five family members would continue to control communal appointments. They maintained that the ordinance was a 'decree that the community could not endure' and, in accordance with talmudic precedent, should be cancelled. Krochmal, who during his career had to decide a number of questions of minority rights, did not attempt to overturn the ordinance of early generations but carefully reinterpreted its implications. He responded:

> ... According to custom, half the salaries of the Rabbi, cantor, and beadle are collected based on tax contributions and half based on the number [of taxpayers]. Therefore, since forty-five taxpayers agreed on the appointment of this beadle, even though the five rich ones did not, nevertheless, there is agreement of the numeric majority and the majority of contributions in these forty-five taxpayers. Although it is true that if the custom of the community was to pay the salaries ... based on contributions then the law would be with these rich taxpayers ... since they give most of the contributions but based on the custom of the community ... the forty-five ... are the majority.
>
> And I will explain how. For example, if they pay the beadle fifty golds annually, the first twenty-five golds are collected per capita, half a gold per taxpayer. This means that the forty-five taxpayers contribute twenty-two and one-half golds to the first twenty-five golds of salary ... And of the half collected based on contributions these five rich men pay (three-fifths or fifteen golds) and the remaining forty-five taxpayers give two-fifths or ten golds. We find when we add the amounts that the rich only give seventeen and one-half golds and ... the rest of the community together gives thirty-two and one half golds. Thus the community of forty-five taxpayers has the numeric majority and the majority of contributions ...

The rich man appealed Krochmal's decision to the regional political leaders, arguing that the framers of the ordinance never intended to allow those who contributed the majority of communal funds to lose their (unequal) share of control over communal affairs. His appeal was of no avail.

B.   Family Law and Personal Status

A clever insight may help solve the most perplexing of quandaries, and in no area was this needed more than in cases of deserted wives. Jurists in every generation had to deal with this issue but the problem became acute after the 1648 Cossack uprising in Poland in which Jews were not only slaughtered and scattered but also taken captive and sold to the Ottomans. The break-up of families left many women unaware of the fate of their husbands and, often desperate to avoid a life of loneliness and all too often of poverty, they sought rabbinic advice as to whether they could remarry.

Although Rabbis were under great pressure to find a way of being lenient in such cases there was no methodological breakthrough that allowed women to remarry more easily. Each case continued to be weighed carefully by jurists who often had to sift through a maze of material to find an allowance. Even with witnesses at hand, the process of gaining permission to remarry for a woman could take well over a year and sometimes longer. Decisions in this field generally required great legal creativity and many Rabbis were not willing to rely on their own ruminations to allow a woman to remarry without the agreement of at least two colleagues. Sometimes, albeit rarely, no allowance could be found and the woman was forced to look for more evidence or remain alone. The Council of Four Lands, the governing body of Polish Jewry until 1764 when it was abolished, realized the difficulty of finding additional evidence, especially from distant places, and hired people to search for information, a search that sometimes dragged on for years.

Once permission to remarry was granted, a copy of the release was given to the woman. Courts gave similar letters to women whose husbands were killed. An example from Lublin, Poland in 1656 read:

> It is true that Mr. Samuel son of Jacob, husband of Mrs. Gittel daughter of the martyred Rabbi Jacob, was murdered in the holy community of Lublin and I, the undersigned, buried him with my own hands. At the same time the aforementioned Mrs. Gittel was pregnant. All this I have written and signed as testimony and a proof.
>
> 1 Heshvan 5416
> Eliyah Harodner, teacher
> Mattiyah son of my father and teacher, Rabbi Ḥayyim of blessed memory, beadle.

In the area of divorce too there was no major change in halakhic thought. The seventeenth and eighteenth centuries each witnessed major controversies over specific bills of divorce, one in Vienna in 1611 and a second, broader dispute, in Cleves in 1766-1767. Each controversy centred on perceived deceptions in marriage and divorce but neither gave immediate rise to broad legal change.

Personal status remained an issue in Sephardi centres and Rabbis such as Samuel Aboab (1616-1694), Rabbi of Venice in 1650, had to determine whether the children of Marranos were to be considered Jews or apostates. Aboab responded to one such question from Jews in Hamburg.

> ... the matter is an ancient one and we should not budge from the opinions of Rabbi Isaac ben Sheshet (d. 1408, Spain, Algiers) and Rabbi [Jacob] ben Habib (d. 1516, Spain, Salonika) quoted by Rabbi Elijah Mizraḥi (d. 1526, Constantinople) in his responsa and others and Rabbi David [ben Hayyim] ha-Kohen [of Corfu] (d. 1530) agrees with them in part in his responsa. However, in section 28 [of his responsa, David ha-Kohen] appears to recant his opinion and decide that Marranos have the law of apostates. And, at first, I had doubts and wanted to say that [David ha-Kohen thought] that only those who were Jews, who knew the nature of the religion of Moses and Israel, and who were forcefully converted and could not possibly be mistaken in thinking of some permission to worship idols for whatever reason but [continued in their ways] simply because their desires have sway over them, should be judged as apostates. But their children and their offspring who never knew or saw the light of *Torah*, what difference is there between them and a child captured by the nations [i.e., non-Jews; who is not responsible for his unlawful ways and is still considered a Jew] or the Karaites whom Maimonides had mercy on for this reason.
>
> However, I saw afterwards that this was not the road taken by Rabbi David ha-Kohen in section 8 where he 'remembers the sin of the fathers on the children' (*Ex.* 34:7) and inferred *a minori ad maius* an analogy that the children are like the father, assuming that the fathers teach the children what they know. And it is a well known fact that this claim is incorrect with regard to many of them and even those who reveal a small number of the commandments to their children do so in fear, with trembling voices, telling them that one only violates the prohibition of idol worship when one's heart concurs with one's actions. However, when one is not sincere and all one's actions are because of fear of the non-Jews, one is absolved from punishment according to the laws of heaven ... and how can these children whom the sun of tradition has not shone upon be considered apostates? ... (Aboab, *Responsa*, no. 45)

Aboab staunchly defended the tradition of recognizing the children of Marranos as Jews even though he was willing to entertain the possibility of writing off the parents.

C. Commercial Law

With the expansion of commerce in the seventeenth century and the beginning of industrialization in the eighteenth century, no segment of Jewish Law came under greater pressure than commercial law. However, businessmen could hardly wait for Rabbis to solve their problems; by the time that happened a potential deal could be lost. As a result, businessmen seemed to have done what they needed to do and either did not ask questions or did so after the fact. In the realm of interest-bearing loans, Jews took interest from one another well before a sound legal argument was advanced in 1607 by Joshua Falk that turned loans between Jews into business partnerships in which the creditor shared in the debtor's profits (the *heter iṣka*). In seventeenth century Poland bearer notes passed from hand to hand without a legally recognized form of transfer. Their use was taken for granted by everyone, including the Rabbis themselves. In mid-seventeenth century Amsterdam, the Jewish community did not even attempt to judge disputes between Jews over bills of exchange but simply referred them to municipal courts. While voluminous glosses were being written on the sections of the *Shulḥan Arukh* dealing with commercial and criminal law, these sections of law were largely being ignored in the marketplace, where Jews could rarely set the rules.

However, Jews were less likely to violate ritual laws openly. As Professor Jacob Katz has shown (see bibliography), industrialization placed great pressures on Sabbath observance. Jews involved in estate leasing, cloth manufacturing, and sales could hardly expect to close their business on the Sabbath and remain competitive with non-Jewish businessmen operating six days a week. Sabbath closings would not only financially harm owners but also the many Jews who benefited either directly or indirectly from successful Jewish enterprises. Rabbis could not be insensitive to such matters and so they sought legal means to allow factories, mills, and estates to operate on the Sabbath, often by using non-Jews. A non-Jewish manager might, for example, be made a partner who would control the business on the Sabbath and whose share of profits would, at least legally, come from Sabbath operations. There were, however, limits to such allowances. In a responsum quoted by Katz, Rabbi Ezekiel Landau was asked whether a Jew could have a stamp with his signature made so that when he sat in the office on the Sabbath with important individuals he could tell a non-Jew to 'sign' (i.e., stamp) his signature when necessary. Allowances could be made in a case of severe financial loss if a non-Jew was told what to do before the Sabbath began but to tell a non-Jew directly on the Sabbath to violate a biblical prohibition was more than Landau would allow.

The seventeenth and eighteenth centuries were a period of great creativity in Jewish Law, particularly on the margins of the *Shulḥan Arukh* and in a blossoming responsa literature. However, the Enlightenment placed tremendous pressures on the traditional Jewish community in Europe. While Rabbis in Eastern Europe and the Islamic world were not immediately affected, leaders in Western Europe had to spend much of the early nineteenth century confronting the challenges of modernity.

6. *Bibliography*

Nahum Rakover's *The Multi-Language Bibliography of Jewish Law* (Jerusalem: The Library of Jewish Law, 1990) is the most useful bibliography of articles written in western languages about Jewish Law. Its list of bibliographies and encyclopedias relevant to Jewish Law (pp. 725-26) is particularly useful. The numerous entries are organized topically and include works on arbitration (p. 488), bills of divorce (pp. 651-57), abandoned wives (pp. 657-58), and usury (pp. 694-696). Topics are not delineated by century and discussion relevant to the seventeenth and eighteenth centuries must be searched out. The section on organization and administration of the Jewish community (pp. 391-425) is arranged in a helpful format, country by country and city by city.

Phyllis Weisbard and David Schonberg's *Jewish Law: Bibliography of Sources and Scholarship in English*, with a Foreword by Menachem Elon (Littleton: Fred Rothman and Company, 1989), is also arranged topically. It has a useful appendix on community studies (pp. 473-504).

The following works, in whole or in part, discuss various aspects of topics covered above.

Baron, S.W., *The Jewish Community* (Philadelphia: Jewish Publication Society of America, 1942), 3 vols.

Freehof, S.B., *The Responsa Literature* (Philadelphia: Jewish Publication Society of America, 1955).

Fuss, A., 'Assignability of Debt and Negotiable Instruments in Jewish Law,' *Diné Israel* 12 (1984-1985), 19-37.

Gerber, J., *Jewish Society in Fez 1450-1700* (Leiden: E.J. Brill, 1980).

Katz, J., *Out of the Ghetto* (Cambridge, Mass.: Harvard University Press, 1973).

Katz, J., *The Shabbos Goy* (Philadelphia: Jewish Publication Society of America, 1989).

Katz, J., *Tradition and Crisis* (New York: Free Press of Glencoe, 1961).

Lewis, B., *The Jews of Islam* (Princeton: Princeton University Press, 1984).

Rosman, M.J., *The Lords' Jews* (Cambridge, Mass.: Harvard University Press, 1990).

Rothkoff, A., 'The Divorce in Cleves, 1766,' *Gesher* 4 (1969), 147-69.

Shochet, E., *Rabbi Joel Sirkes: His Life, Works, and Times* (Jerusalem and New York: Feldheim Publishing Co., 1971).

Simonsohn, S., *History of the Jews in the Duchy of Mantua* (Jerusalem: Kiryath Sepher, 1977).

Twersky, I., 'The *Shulhan Arukh*: Enduring Code of Law,' reprinted in *The Jewish Expression*, ed. Judah Goldin (New Haven: Yale University Press, 1976), 322-34.

14

MODERN RESPONSA:
1800 TO THE PRESENT

by

DAVID NOVAK
University of Virginia

1. *Juridical Background*

The period begins, in effect, with the French Revolution and reflects the growth in importance of the modern nation state. For Jews, this political revolution radically changed their social reality, especially during the reign of Napoleon with its ramifications throughout Europe. The transformation in Jewish history which occurred from 1800 to the present has proved every bit as radical as the period from the destruction of the Second Temple in 70 C.E. to the canonization of the *Mishnah* around 200 C.E. In both periods the primary institution that determined the social and religious character of the Jewish community had disappeared and been replaced by other determining institutions. In the former period it was the destruction of the Jerusalem Temple (*bet hamikdash*); in the latter period it was the demise of the social and religious autonomy of the traditional Jewish communities (*kehilot*). In both periods, historical transformations produced deep and wide-ranging legal consequences.

The demise of the social and religious autonomy of the *kehilot* was the result of the process of political emancipation of West European Jewry that began at the end of the eighteenth century. Whereas the traditional Jewish communities had a contracted status as a tolerated foreign enclave in pre-modern European nations, political emancipation gradually gave Jews rights as *individual* citizens in the new modern states while simultaneously eliminating the *collective* privileges of the traditional communities. Individual rights and collective privileges were seen as being incompatible in modern states, where the basic political bond was to be one between the individual and the State rather than one between various communities and the sovereign. In this sense, the demise of the social and religious authority of the *kehilot* was a result of the demise of the *ancien régime* in general, a historical process having revolutionary impact on the whole populace as well as on the Jews.

The social and religious results of political emancipation even as early as 1800 can be seen in four areas of Jewish Law: (1) ritual practice; (2) family status; (3) relations between Jews and non-Jews (including the whole institution of *gerut*, conversion of gentiles to Judaism); (4) civil and criminal procedures. In the first three areas the responsa of this period reflect the considerable ingenuity required of halakhic authorities to bring the classical sources to bear on many frequently unprecedented new questions arising from the radically transformed social and religious realities of modern Jewish life. As for the fourth area, however, that pertaining to civil and criminal procedures, one sees a marked decrease in the number of responsa, precisely because questions in this area much more than in the others presuppose the collective autonomy of the traditional Jewish community, an autonomy that was fast disappearing in this period of history. With the growing assimilation of Jewish political and economic activity into the larger secular society (even by otherwise halakhically observant Jews), fewer and fewer questions of civil and criminal law were or even could be referred to traditional rabbinical courts (*Bate Din*) for adjudication.

2. *Legal Practice*

A. Ritual Practice

The rise of Reform Judaism early in the nineteenth century raised important new questions in the area of ritual practice especially. These questions began to be the subject of intense debate with the opening of the first explicitly Reform temple in Hamburg in 1819. In order to understand the intensity of this debate, one has to be aware of the conflicting explanations and justifications offered for the desire to change the synagogue service at this particular time and the intense opposition to it. These changes involved such things as shortening the liturgy, reciting some of it in the vernacular, and the introduction of instrumental music in worship.

For the pro-reform party, the traditional synagogue service had become an impediment to religious devotion (*kavanah*) because its language, its tone, its very ethos were so estranged from the spiritual life of the newly emancipated German Jews. The reformers thus argued that the general purpose of retaining the religious loyalty of modern Jews (especially since Germanic culture was so intimately connected to Protestant forms of worship) required that specific changes be instituted in the prevalent mode of Jewish worship. For their essential justification they frequently cited the biblical verse, 'it is time to act for the Lord; they have negated Your *Torah*' (*Ps.* 119:126), which in rabbinic interpretation came to be read as 'at times, specifics of the *Torah* must be voided for it is time to act for the Lord in general' (*M. Ber.*, end and *Rashi* thereon).

But for the anti-reform party, the desire to change the synagogue service was seen as being the result of a more basic desire to assimilate into the general society and culture by copying the ways of the gentiles, even in communal worship, an institution previously regarded as a uniquely Jewish preserve. For this reason, the anti-reform party justified its growing emphasis on the strictest possible interpretations of ritual law. This essentially theological debate was most evidently conducted over ostensibly halakhic issues.

The major innovations of the Hamburg Temple had already been argued for halakhically by R. Aaron Chorin (1766-1844), primarily in his widely read responsum, *Kin'at Ha'emet* ('the zeal for truth'), published in 1818. There he countered the major objections that could be raised by traditionalists against the proposed innovations of the reformers in Hamburg, reforms that had been already instituted by Israel Jacobson (1768-1828) in his private synagogues, first in Seesen and then in Berlin. For example, basing himself on the *Mishnah* (*Sot.* 7:1), Chorin argued that all the prayers, even the most important ones like the *Shema'* and the *Shemoneh Esreh*, could be recited in any language. He, nevertheless, moderated that argument by suggesting that the main portions of the liturgy should still be recited in Hebrew. The reason for the innovation was to allow greater participation in religious services, but these services were still to be recognizably Jewish, having basic continuity with Jewish tradition.

As for the use of an organ in the synagogue services, Chorin found a precedent in the permission by the sixteenth century authority, R. Moses Isserles (*Rema*), of musical instruments when they are needed for a *mitsvah* requiring joyous celebration, even though the general use of these instruments was discouraged because of the perpetual mourning mandated for the destruction of the Second Temple (note on *Shulḥan Arukh: Oraḥ Ḥayyim*, 560.3; cf. *B. B.B.* 60b). The Ashkenazi Hamburg reformers also proposed adopting the Sephardi pronunciation of Hebrew in the services of the new temple. Against those who objected to this reversal of custom (*minhag*), Chorin argued that this pronunciation was more authentic Hebraically.

Finally, in answer to the objection that synagogue reform violated the prohibition of 'walking in the statutes of the gentiles' (*ḥukot hagoi* — see *Lev*. 18:3 and *Ṣifra* thereon), Chorin argued that this only applies to practices that are overtly idolatrous or which cannot be justified by any Jewish religious reason. But if such practices can be so justified (*leshem shamayim*, i.e. for the sake of God), then they do not violate the prohibition.

The main thrust of virtually all of Chorin's arguments was aesthetic. It was consistent with the growing emphasis on *Kultur* in Germanic countries. Many newly acculturated Jews came to find the traditional synagogue services unaesthetic and thus uninspiring. For this reason, the introduction of prayers in German was seen as enabling Judaism to become a modern European religion and not remain an ancient oriental one. So, also, the use of the organ was seen as the means for enabling Jewish liturgy to be conducted with Western-style music. And, the use of the Sephardi pronunciation (which, unlike the former two innovations, did not become prevalent in Reform worship after 1819) seems to have been the result of admiration for the aristocratic Sephardim of the Portuguese congregation in Hamburg, in whose synagogue more decorous ritual was conducted and in which a more acculturated laity participated.

The traditional rabbinical court (*Bet Din*) of Hamburg responded to the establishment of the new temple with predictable alarm. The judges (*dayanim*) quickly solicited the opinions of the leading rabbis of Europe and published them in 1819 in a collection called *Eleh Divre Haberit* ('these are the words of the covenant' — taken from *Deut*. 28:69, the conclusion of the curse pronounced on Israel if she abandons God's *Torah*). To a man these Rabbis condemned all the innovations of the new temple. The debate over the opening of the Hamburg Temple set the content and tone of the halakhic disputes between those in favour of innovation and those opposed to innovation, a debate that has very much continued into the present.

The main thrust of traditionalist arguments was that the reformers had distorted the rabbinic sources, essentially taking sources that permit certain individual and exceptional practices and making them function as the basis of regular communal religious proceedings. Reform was attacked as an attempt fundamentally to reconstitute Jewish life itself by an elevation of the role of individual prerogative (itself a result of the Enlightenment), an elevation that necessarily undermined the very reality of traditional Jewish communal existence. In other words, traditionalists were quite aware that the reformers were intent on a thorough reconstitution of Judaism, not just a few halakhic adjustments here and there. For not only were the reformers interested in changing the language and tone of Jewish worship, they were even more interested in changing its content. It was thus recognized that the full intent of religious reform was ideological not just aesthetic. Much of the responsa literature of this whole period in the area of ritual observance reflects the attempt to reassert the authority of the tradition per se in the face of what were seen as Reform or crypto-Reform efforts to undermine that authority piecemeal. Thus the leading opponent of Reform, R. Moses Schreiber (1762-1839) wrote:

> If we had the political authority, my opinion would be totally to separate them from ourselves (*lehafrisham me'al gevuleinu*), not to marry their sons or their daughters so that our sons and our daughters not be drawn after them [and their ways]. They should be regarded as Sadducees [and other heretical sects] ... Of course, all of this it seems to me can only be theoretical and not actual practice (*lehalakhah velo lema'aseh*) without the permission of the Government. (*Responsa Ḥatam Ṣofer*, 6, no. 89)

Clearly, the attempt was totally to isolate the reformers by separating them from the very corporate body of the people of Israel. Schreiber sees the only impediment to this attempt as being the non-Jewish Government. The implication of this admission, however, is itself indicative of the radically changed state of affairs for European Jewry. For when the Jews were recognized by their non-Jewish host societies as a tolerated foreign enclave within the body politic, the Jewish authorities did have the power to excommunicate those members of the community regarded as heretics. One sees this as late as 1656 in the relatively liberal atmosphere of Holland in the excommunication of the philosopher Baruch Spinoza by the Amsterdam rabbinate. But one of the prices Jews had to pay for their political emancipation was the relinquishment of the communal power of excommunication (best argued by Moses Mendelssohn in *Jerusalem*). The loss of this power made ideological dissent a real social option.

Because of considerable Reform inroads, traditionalist Jews in Central and Western Europe began a process of self-segregation in those communities in which Reform had made any type of real headway and where its proponents controlled the institutions of the Jewish community. This separation, in some places more partial and in others more complete (like Frankfurt-am-Main, under the leadership of R. Samson Raphael Hirsch, beginning in the 1850s), led these traditionalists to designate themselves as 'orthodox' or '*Torah*-true', as opposed to those Jews who either advocated reforms (the 'liberals'), or who were willing to coexist with them (the 'conservatives').

Increasingly, the responsa from this period, especially to ritual questions, reflect a notion that *halakhah* is exclusively the domain of those deemed unswerving in their religious loyalty, even if they now constituted only a minority in Jewry.

B. Marriage and Divorce: the *Agunah*

Considering the vast social, political and economic changes in the world at large during this period, changes that had profound effects on the Jewish community, it is obvious that these changes would have effects on the most elementary unit of the community, the family. Whereas in the past Jewish marriage and divorce were under the exclusive domain of the rabbinical authorities, beginning with the Sanhedrin of Jewish notables assembled by Napoleon in 1806 in Paris, neither marriage nor divorce could be conducted without the prior approval of the State. In other words, marriage and divorce were now considered to be primarily contracts between individual citizens, which the State regulated in the public interest. Religious considerations were considered to be private options that these individual citizens could exercise or not, however they chose.

The essentially communal character of Jewish marriage (and divorce), expressed by the talmudic principle, 'anyone who marries only does so with rabbinic consent' (*B. Gittin* 33a), was now effectively reduced to a private option, one which civil society was no longer interested in regulating. Accordingly, most of the communal controls of the institution of marriage that had evolved over the centuries in Jewish Law were no longer operative *de facto*, but only *de jure*, since the power of the traditional Jewish community to enforce these controls had been eliminated by the political emancipation of the Jews. Because of these radical changes, the problem of a woman whose husband refused to give her a Jewish divorce (*get*), although certainly not unprecedented in earlier times, became particularly acute in modern times.

In biblical law it seems that a man could divorce his wife for no objective reason (see *Deut.* 24:1), but that a woman could not even sue for a divorce from her husband for any objective reason. However, in the development of the law in the rabbinic period, it became necessary for a man to have an objective reason to divorce his wife (see *M. Gitt.* 9:10), and it became possible for a woman to sue for a divorce from her husband for certain objective reasons (see *M. Ket.* ch.7; also *B. Ket.* 63b). To sue for divorce in Jewish Law means that even though the woman herself cannot initiate the divorce proceedings, a rabbinical court acting on her behalf can force her husband to do so if they judge her reasons to be valid (see *M. Gitt.* 9:8). Nevertheless, all of this is virtually inoperative when the Jewish communal authorities have no political control over husbands who refuse to divorce their wives when, according to the law, they ought to do so. In the modern period membership in the Jewish community became voluntary as the religious community became in effect a corporation, having no more power than that which the individual was willing to grant to it. The individual having this power could always secede from the religious community and its control at will.

Because a Jewish woman cannot remarry without a Jewish divorce, pious women who had been divorced by their husbands in civil courts were still unable to remarry under Jewish religious auspices. In the premodern period, when there was no institution of civil divorce, men who had abandoned their wives could not do so with impunity. There were even times when the Jewish religious authorities successfully utilized the non-Jewish authorities to bring such lawbreakers back under the control of Jewish justice. However, in modern societies where civil divorce is a real legal institution, a man who refuses to grant his wife a Jewish divorce, even when she is entitled to one according to Jewish Law, is not a lawbreaker in the eyes of the state authorities. In their eyes he has not unlawfully abandoned his wife. For the most part, they have decided that this particularly religious problem is none of their business.

This problem became more and more acute with the mass migrations of Jews from Eastern Europe that began in the nineteenth century. Literally thousands of Jewish women were abandoned by morally unscrupulous husbands, and unlike in the past, the Jewish community seemed to be virtually as helpless as were the unfortunate women themselves. Because of this affront to morality, by the early twentieth century halakhists were beginning to propose various legal remedies to help alleviate this growing social scandal. This concern is reflected in some of the most interesting responsa, especially beginning early in the twentieth century.

In 1907, almost exactly 100 years after West European Jewry living under French rule had been required by Napoleon to accept civil marriage and divorce as part of the price of their political emancipation, the French rabbinate proposed that all Jewish marriages should be initiated conditionally. They formulated the following condition to be uttered by the bridegroom to the bride at the moment of the inauguration of the marriage:

> Behold you are consecrated unto me in a manner that precludes your becoming an *agunah* on my account. If the civil judges decree a divorce, then

the marriage will be annulled (*lo yaḥulu hakiddushin*) and the woman shall be released and be free to remarry with regular Jewish marriage rites. (Quoted in A. Freimann, *Ṣeder Kiddushin Venisu'in* (Jerusalem: Mosad Harav Kook, 1945), p.390)

It was soon charged, however, that this proposal was in effect: (1) a condition designed to evade the traditional Jewish laws of marriage and divorce; (2) that it took a matter subject to Jewish jurisdiction and made it subject to civil jurisdiction; (3) that in contradiction to the *Torah*'s prescription, it enabled the woman to initiate her own divorce. But, in a second, more conservative version of this conditional formula of betrothal, it was stipulated that the marriage became null and void *only* if the husband refused to give his wife the *get* to which she was entitled. In other words, the second version escapes all of the previous objections, since: (1) it is no longer a proposal to evade Jewish divorce law, for it only applies to exceptional cases; (2) it no longer gives the civil courts jurisdiction in Jewish matrimonial matters, since it is the Jewish court that now determines the grounds for the dissolution of the marriage; (3) it is now the Jewish court, not the woman herself, who initiates the dissolution of the marriage. Nevertheless, this proposal was almost universally rejected as being too radical a departure from precedent, even though the Turkish rabbinate actually instituted it in 1924.

In the United States, immediately after the huge population disruptions of the First World War, the *agunah* problem became especially acute. Here there were literally thousands of Jewish men who had left their wives in Europe without freeing them through a *get*. An American Rabbi, Louis M. Epstein (1887-1949), offered a novel solution to the *agunah* problem, which although not of help to those women who were already *agunot*, would at least prevent many others from becoming *agunot* in the future. In 1930 Epstein proposed that at the time of the marriage the husband authorize a rabbinical court to grant his wife a divorce in his absence and appoint the necessary witnesses and agents for this purpose. He suggested that this authorization for divorce by proxy (*minui shelihut*) be included as part of the *ketubah*, the marriage contract, an institution about which he wrote a major study (*The Jewish Marriage Contract*, New York: Jewish Theological Seminary of America, 1927).

The chief legal difficulty with this solution is that the husband must personally appoint the scribe and the witnesses for the divorce. This is, of course, quite unfeasible, because if a man would make these appointments, he would also be giving his wife the *get*. So Epstein suggested that the husband appoint his own wife as his agent to write for herself her own *get* with rabbinical approval and under rabbinical supervision. This is a *fictio juris* to be sure, but there are ample precedents for *fictio juris* in the halakhic literature from the earliest rabbinic sources. Thus Epstein came up with the following betrothal formula:

> I do hereby appoint my wife ___ in her presence and ___ in their presence ... that any one of them shall write a divorce for my wife ... I further declare that I grant this authorization for the writing of the divorce only if at any time I disappear or fail to support her or fulfill my conjugal duty for a period of three years, or if we are divorced from each other by the action of the civil court. (*Proceedings of the Rabbinical Assembly* IV [1930-32], p.235)

Aware of the universal rejection of the conditional marriage proposal of the French rabbinate in 1907, but believing his proposal more cogent halakhically, Epstein solicited the opinions of halakhists throughout the world. The response here was just as negative, however, causing Epstein to withdraw his proposal in 1936 because he feared that it would only aggravate an already grave problem. And just as the French proposal led to a series of condemnations published in the 1930 pamphlet *Eyn Tenai Benisu'in* ('there is no conditional marriage'), so the Epstein proposal led to a series of condemnations published in the 1937 pamphlet by the American Orthodox *Agudat Harabbanim* called *Ledor Aharon* ('a warning to future generations').

Any solution to this grave modern problem, involving as it does the very moral integrity of Jewish Law, seems to require a unanimity of rabbinical opinion and action that is much too improbable even to hope for in the post-emancipation Jewish world. Because of this political impasse, made even more problematic by the abandonment of Jewish divorce by the Reform movement in America (and elsewhere) as early as 1869 (following the opinion of the German reformer Samuel Holdheim [1806-1860] as early as 1843), the *agunah* problem is one that has continued to fester up to the present.

In order to deal with this problem, albeit in a partial way, many contemporary halakhists have been following the lead taken by R. Moses Feinstein (1895-1986), who sought to make the process of retroactive annulment easier in cases where a divorce cannot be obtained. Feinstein ruled that the presence of any major non-traditional factors in the initial marriage ceremony (such as being conducted under civil or Reform auspices) is sufficient grounds for annulment, even if the couple have been living together as a marital unit for a long period of time (*Iggrot Mosheh: Even Ha'ezer*, nos.75-76).

C. Conversion

The demise of the autonomous pre-modern Jewish communities did much to lessen the political and economic isolation of the Jews from the rest of the population of the new nation states in which they now lived. This growing integration into the general society also had the effect of creating greater social and personal interaction between Jews and gentiles. One area where this began to be especially manifest was marriage, i.e. intermarriage between Jews and non-Jews. The greater number of mixed marriages between Jews and non-Jews reflects the lessening of social barriers between the two groups.

Although some of the radical reformers, following the example of Samuel Holdheim, were willing to tolerate intermarriages, and actually celebrate them with Jewish religious rites, even most of the more liberal rabbis refused to make such a fundamental departure from tradition. But the responsa of this period do deal with the growing phenomenon of non-Jews willing to convert to Judaism as part of the process of marrying a Jew. The question faced here was how to deal with the halakhic rule that even though such conversions are valid *ex post facto*, nevertheless they are not to be conducted *ab initio* (see Maimonides, *Mishneh Torah, Iṣure Bi'ah*, 13:17). Some traditional Jewish authorities, convinced that virtually all conversions in the modern period are only ruses for the sake of marriage (even when professed to be for the sake of Judaism per se), actually refused to perform any conversions at all. Such was the case in Argentina and in the Syrian Jewish communities in North America earlier in the twentieth century.

Other halakhists, however, took a different stand. Two important halakhists earlier in this century, R. David Zvi Hoffmann (1843-1921), the rector of the Orthodox Rabbinical Seminary in Berlin and the leading halakhic authority of German Jewry, and R. Ben Zion Uziel (1880-1954), the Sephardi Chief Rabbi of the then Palestine, dealt with this question, both recognizing that a lack of rabbinical leniency here would most likely lead to civil marriage and the inevitable loss to Judaism of both the Jewish partner in such a marriage and the children born from it.

On the one hand, Hoffmann approaches the question in the spirit of making the best of an inevitably bad situation by bending the law somewhat, lest a far worse transgression result. He furthermore suggests that the convert make a formal declaration or promise (*Eidesstattliche Versicherung*), something a little less grave than an actual Jewish oath (*shevu'ah*), to observe such basic Jewish laws as the Sabbath and the dietary restrictions

(*Responsa Melamed Leho'il*, 2, no. 83).

Uziel also emphasizes that one must make the best of a bad situation, insightfully bringing the talmudic justification (*B. Kidd.* 21b) for the biblical permission to convert and marry a gentile war bride (*eshet yefat to'ar*) because 'Scripture takes into account human inclination (*yetser hara*)' (*Responsa Mishpaṭe Uziel: Even Ha'ezer*, no.18). Moreover, in his conclusion to this important responsum, written in 1944 in reply to a query from the Chief Rabbi of Istanbul, Uziel makes a striking point. He argues that the reason for the conversion of the non-Jewish partner 'is because this Jewess or this Jew does not want to transgress, but rather (*aderaba*) wants to save herself or himself from transgression.' Here we see an extraordinary sociological insight in the very heart of a halakhic judgment. What Uziel recognized is that the sociology of intermarriage has changed in modern times. Whereas in earlier times intermarriage was most often an expression of apostasy, in modern times it has become a consequence of greater social interaction between Jews and non-Jews. Thus the modern Jew who is drawn into a love relationship with a non-Jew, and who urges the non-Jew to seek conversion to Judaism, is attempting to reconcile his or her personal involvement with his or her own authentic commitment to Judaism. The motivation, then, is the exact opposite of that which seeks apostasy.

D. The Holocaust

The horrendous experience of the Holocaust has certainly had an enormous impact on all aspects of Jewish life from the middle of the twentieth century until the present. That impact is seen in the responsa written during this period. The systematic murder of one third of the Jewish people during the years 1939-1945, along with the destruction of the civilization of Central and Eastern European Jewry by the Nazis and their cohorts, has raised numerous questions of Jewish Law. Proper response to these questions has required great spiritual sensitivity to the frequently unprecedented situations of Holocaust victims and survivors, coupled with thorough research and imaginative application of the classical legal sources.

One of the most important respondents to questions arising out of the Holocaust was R. Ephraim Oshry, formerly the rabbinical judge (*dayan*) of the Kovno Ghetto during the German occupation of the early 1940s, and who later settled in New York after surviving the war, where he published his wartime responsa in the 1960s. His collection of responsa, *Mima'amakim* ('From the Depths', cf. *Ps.* 130:1), published in New York in 1963, is the work of an authority who had direct responsibility for giving legal direction to victims and survivors in the most trying circumstances imaginable.

In one responsum (pt.3, no.7), R. Oshry himself was asked by a group of Lithuanian Jewish survivors in the fall of 1943 whether a man who had complied with the request of a fellow prisoner in a work detail to kill him, because he could no longer stand his suffering at the hands of the Nazis, could be appointed their leader of public worship (*shaliah tsibur*) for the high holy days of Rosh Hashanah and Yom Kippur. R. Oshry's judicial dilemma was that, on the one hand, causing the death of another person is considered murder even if done at their request out of compassionate motives (*B. B.K.* 91b; cf. *B. A.Zar.* 18a); but, on other hand, the man who committed this act was contrite about it and evidenced sincere repentance for what he thought at the time, under terribly extreme circumstances, was the right and good thing to do. Moreover, there is the sense in reading this responsum that R. Oshry knew that this ruling would become a precedent for other survivors themselves deeply troubled by similar acts they committed *in extremis*.

R. Oshry ruled that the man in question could be appointed the leader of public worship, even for the high holy days. He argued that this man was in fact only the indirect cause (*gorem*) of the death of his fellow prisoner, only having pushed him down to the ground several times, an act from which death did not immediately follow. As such, his act was really manslaughter (*bishegagah*) rather than literal murder (*bemezid*). For this type of act, he found an earlier ruling of R. Moses Isserles (*Rema on Shulhan Arukh: Orah Hayyim*, 53.5) that concluded that in a similar case proper repentance (*teshuvah*) was sufficient to enable the repentant sinner to be a leader of public worship. What R. Oshry (along with other Holocaust respondents) accomplished in this moving and insightful responsum was to avoid condoning clearly prohibited acts even when done *in extremis*, and at the same time to aid Holocaust survivors in the painful process of their spiritual and emotional healing.

E.   The State of Israel

The re-establishment of Jewish sovereignty in the Land of Israel in 1948 has had an enormous effect on the life of the Jewish people, both in Israel itself and throughout the Diaspora. It has raised numerous new questions of Jewish Law, especially questions pertaining to political and military matters. These questions, which even in the recent past would have been purely academic, are now very much matters of practical import and the subject of active discussion among those who have the responsibility to respond to them. What we are now seeing in this area of Jewish Law is the rehabilitation of the whole Jewish political tradition, most of which had been practically dormant heretofore.

Probably the most prominent legal authority in the State of Israel today is the former Sephardi Chief Rabbi, R. Ovadia Yoṣef. Possessing an encyclopedic knowledge of the classical legal sources along with more recent discussions and applications of them, and having a large following among both Israeli and Diaspora Jews, R. Yoṣef's numerous decisions have made a great impact on contemporary Jewish life.

One of the most important questions to emerge from renewed Jewish political sovereignty is the status according tradition of those who have political authority in the new Jewish state. For example, what is the Jewish status of the head of state: the President (*Nasi*)? Is his office comparable to that of a king in the classical sources or not? A specific question asked of R. Yoṣef along these general lines (*Yehaveh Da'at*, Jerusalem, 1978, pt.2, no.28) is whether one, when seeing the President of the State of Israel in person, must say the traditional blessing mandated when one sees a king: 'Blessed are You O Lord our God, king of the universe, who has given some of his glory (*mekevodo*) to flesh and blood' (*B. Ber.* 58a). (Interestingly enough, this formula of the blessing is mandated when seeing the king of a non-Jewish state, inasmuch as there cannot be a king in a Jewish state in the Land of Israel without the institution of both *Sanhedrin* and prophet to approve his appointment. See Maimonides, *Hilkhot Melakhim*, 1.2.)

The answer to this question turns out to be contingent on whether one interprets kingship literally or functionally. If one interprets it literally, then R. Yoṣef points out earlier sources that rule that the 'glory' of the king for which God is being praised in the blessing is present only when the king appears in uniquely royal garb, which symbolizes his superiority to the people beneath him. Since, however, modern presidents head democracies, the very egalitarian nature of democracies requires that even the president dress like an ordinary citizen. But, on the other hand, if one interprets kingship functionally, then R. Yoṣef points out, basing himself on other earlier sources, kings have the power of life and death over their subjects. And, even though presidents of democratic states may not execute anyone on their own authority, they do have the power to grant clemency to criminals sentenced to death by the courts. This is a sufficient functional analogy to classical kingship to cause R. Yoṣef to be inclined to require the recitation of the prescribed blessing for kings when one actually sees the President of the State of Israel.

Nevertheless, R. Yosef does not come to any definite conclusion in the question before him. In fact, he twice mentions the talmudic rule that when there is a doubt (*safek*), a blessing should either not be said at all (*B. Shab.* 23a), or according to later practice, it should be said in a truncated form without formal mention of God's name (*shem*) or kingship (*malkhut*). By leaving the matter at that level, R. Yosef reveals much of the ambivalence of even those Israeli religious authorities who support the State, yet who cannot fully endorse the religious legitimacy of a secular state. For in the classical sources there seems to be no recognition of a *Jewish* secular state. A Jewish state is seen as being religious *ipso facto*; only non-Jewish states have the option of being secularly constituted (see *B. B.B.* 54b and *Rashbam* thereon). Thus Jewish political and legal thinking about the meaning of Jewish statehood in the contemporary world is only in its infancy.

3. *Principal Authorities*

The radical changes brought to the life of the Jewish community and to the lives of individual Jews by the sudden and rapid prevalence of modernity called for great ingenuity on the part of halakhic authorities. Whether these authorities tended to be opponents of modernity altogether, or were willing to come to some sort of accommodation with it, it soon became quite clear that no responsible halakhic rulings could possibly be made without clear recognition of this radically changed Jewish environment.

Some of the leading and most influential halakhic authorities since 1800 have been the following:

A. Moses Schreiber (1762-1839) known as *Ḥatam Ṣofer*. Leading the important traditionalist community in Pressburg, Hungary, Schreiber became the originator of what might be termed the Jewish 'Counter Reformation', coining the important slogan 'What is new is prohibited by the *Torah*.' However, although he was an opponent of innovations coming from outside what he saw as the parameters of the *halakhah*, he himself was at times quite innovative in his own rulings, which he saw as being within the parameters of the *halakhah* and necessary for its survival. His principal halakhic work is the collection of responsa known as *She'elot uteshuvot Ḥatam Ṣofer* (Pressburg, 1851-1864).

B. David Hoffmann (1843-1921). Directing the Orthodox Rabbinical Seminary in Berlin, Hoffmann became the acknowledged authority for

German-speaking Jewry. Although zealous to fight the inroads of Reform, he was nevertheless quite willing to come to terms with modernity and to make the *halakhah* responsive to the radically changed situation of observant Jews living as a minority among largely non-observant Jews, as has been the case in Western Europe and the United States. His responsa are published in the volume *Melamed leho'il* (Frankfurt-am-Main, 1926).

C. Chaim Grodzinski (1863-1940). As the leading halakhic authority for Lithuanian Jewry, Grodzinski had to confront the growing inroads of secularism and especially secular Zionism in what had formerly been the bastion of East European traditionalism and talmudic scholarship. Although he was vehement in his opposition to all changes in Jewish communal life, he was at times lenient in recognizing changes in the personal lives and circumstances of even fully observant Jews. His responsa are published in the collection *She'elot uteshuvot Aḥiezer* (Vilna, 1922).

D. Ben Zion Uziel (1880-1954). As the Sephardi Chief Rabbi of the State of Israel, Uziel had to confront the changes that modernity had brought to Jewish life, especially once the Jewish state had been re-established. His responsa reflect a decidedly lenient attitude on many issues, following the traditional Sephardi tendency not to prohibit what earlier sources had not explicitly prohibited. His major responsa are published in the volumes *Mishpeṭe Uziel* (Tel-Aviv, 1935-1964).

E. Solomon Freehof (1893-1990). Although the Reform Movement does not recognize the absolute governance per se of the *halakhah*, it has taken a great interest in traditional sources as guides for its own practices. Freehof was the most important Reform halakhist of the twentieth century, drawing upon the *halakhah* to justify many Reform innovations, and also using it to argue for what Reform practice should and should not be. His responsa appear in the volumes *Reform Responsa* (Cincinnati: Hebrew Union College Press, 1960-90).

F. Isaac Klein (1905-1979). As the leader of the traditionalist wing of the Conservative Movement, Klein attempted to justify Conservative practices he saw as halakhically justifiable, and to argue against Conservative practices he saw as halakhically unjustifiable, especially in areas of ritual observance. His major work is *A Guide to Jewish Religious Practice* (New York: Jewish Theological Seminary of America, 1979).

G. Moses Feinstein (1895-1986). Feinstein became the leading Orthodox halakhic authority in the United States (but with an international influence) because of his willingness to deal with the problems facing observant Jews living in the radically changed world of modernity. Although strongly opposed to any non-orthodox forms of Judaism, he was often quite lenient in decisions that alleviated serious problems of Orthodox Jews, especially in areas of family status. His responsa are the most widely cited of any modern authority. They appear in the volumes *Iggrot Mosheh*, published privately in New York, which began to appear in 1959.

4. *Summary*

The radical changes in the political, economic and social life of the Jews after 1800, and the religious ramifications of these changes, could not go unnoticed by any halakhic respondent during this period. They generated many unprecedented questions. What we see during this period are two contrary trends among respondents. On the one hand, there was an attempt to stretch the law in order to make it applicable to the new situation at hand. This was especially the case when human suffering was involved, and when leniencies were not being sought for ideological reasons. But, on the other hand, there was also an attempt to make the law as strict as possible, seeing such strictness as the only means to save those Jews still faithful to Jewish tradition from gradually having their faithfulness diminished by a cumulative process of accommodation to a non-traditional environment. Indeed, it was this attitude primarily that gave rise to the phenomenon of many traditional Jews calling themselves 'orthodox'. Some respondents emphasized the first approach, others the second, and some tried to employ both, depending on how they viewed the overall implications of any particular question. Clearly, this period saw a radical new contextualization of *halakhah* irrespective of who was applying it. That radical recontextualization continues to this very day. In that sense, even *halakhah* and its decisors have in effect recognized that modernity, for good or for ill, is irreversible.

5. *Selected Bibliography*

Ellenson, D., 'Representative Orthodox Responsa on Conversion', *Jewish Social Studies* 47 (1985), 209-220.

Katz, J., *The 'Shabbes Goy': A Study in Halakhic Flexibility*, trans. Y. Lerner (Philadelphia: Jewish Publication Society of America, 1989).

Klein, I., *A Guide to Jewish Religious Observance* (New York: Jewish Theological Seminary of America, 1979).

Novak, D., *Halakhah in a Theological Dimension* (Chico, CA: Scholars Press, 1985).

Novak, D., *Law and Theology in Judaism* I (New York: KTAV, 1974).

Petuchowski, J.J., *Prayerbook Reform in Europe* (New York: World Union for Progressive Judaism, 1968).

Rosenbaum, I.J., *The Holocaust and Halakhah* (New York: KTAV Publishing House, 1976).

Schweid, E., 'The Attitude Toward the State in Modern Jewish Thought Before Zionism', in D.J. Elazar, ed., *Kinship and Consent* (Ramat Gan and Philadelphia: Turtledove Publishing, 1981), 127-147.

Zimmels, H.J., *The Echo of the Nazi Holocaust in Rabbinic Literature* (New York: KTAV Publishing House, 1977).

15

JEWISH LAW IN THE
STATE OF ISRAEL

by

DANIEL SINCLAIR

Jews' College, London

1. *Introduction*

This chapter is divided into two main sections. The first deals with matters of personal status, and the second relates to all other areas of law. Matters of personal status have been within the sole jurisdiction of the Rabbinical Courts — which are staffed by religious judges applying traditional *halakhah* — since the very establishment of the State of Israel. Other areas of Israeli Law are influenced by Jewish Law, but the extent to which this influence is a binding one is a matter of debate. The generally accepted view amongst the members of the Israeli judiciary is that Jewish Law is a valuable source of legal enrichment, but its provisions are not binding upon them. The debate regarding this question took place in the wake of the enactment of the Foundations of Law Act 1980, which is discussed in detail below.

The application of Jewish Law in non-status matters is commonly referred to as *Mishpaṭ Ivri* (Hebrew Law), and has been the subject of much theoretical discussion in Israeli jurisprudence.[1] The selective application of Jewish Law in accordance with the needs of the modern, secular, pluralist society of Israel does not please the purists, either jurisprudentially or politically. The pragmatists oppose the enterprise on the grounds that secular judges are unable to establish the position of Jewish Law on any particular issue because of the difficulties involved in understanding halakhic sources, and they also express doubts with regard to the ability of Jewish Law to deal with issues which are of significance to the modern State. In the final analysis, the *Mishpaṭ Ivri* enterprise is an aspect of the general tension in Israeli culture between tradition and modernity, and its fate will be decided in the context of the developments in Israeli society in general. The wide range of cases involving Jewish Law discussed in the present chapter indicates that it has never ceased to play a part in the development of Israeli Law, and this is significant for its future as an integral part of Israeli jurisprudence.

2. *Jewish Law During the Period of the British Mandate*

In practical terms, the bulk of the legal business of the Jewish settlement in Mandatory Palestine was conducted in the Mandatory courts, which applied Ottoman law as it was on 1st November 1914 together with the Ordinances and Regulations enacted by the Mandatory Government. According to article 46 of the Palestine Order in Council 1922, legal problems to which there was no solution in existing law were to be solved by reference to the principles of common law and equity as they were applied in England. A proviso was attached to this Article to the effect that the principles of common law and equity were to apply 'only in so far as the circumstances of Palestine and its inhabitants and the limits of His Majesty's jurisdiction permit, and subject to such qualification as local circumstances render necessary'. The Mandatory legal system, therefore, incorporated the jurisdiction of religious courts in most areas of personal status, and elements of Islamic Law (Mejelle), Ottoman Civil Law based upon the Code Napoléon (Ottoman Civil Procedure Law, 1879), Mandatory Ordinances, and principles of common law and equity as applied in English courts.

It is interesting to note that some litigation was handled by a loose system of arbitral bodies applying a procedure known as *Mishpaṭ Hashalom Ha'ivri*. This system was founded in the pre-Mandatory period, and served both as an expression of Jewish nationalism, and as a reaction to the gross corruption and inefficiency of the Ottoman courts. The *Mishpaṭ Hashalom Ha'ivri* system was, however, extremely informal, and possessed none of the intellectual rigour of the projected system of Jewish Law championed by the members of the *Mishpaṭ Ivri Society*, which consisted mainly of academic jurists interested in developing an integrated legal system based upon the rules and principles of Jewish Law. The majority of its officers lacked both legal and rabbinic expertise, and the decisions of the courts were of a purely ad hoc nature. During the Mandatory Period, the *Mishpaṭ Hashalom Ha'ivri* courts were recognized arbitral bodies (Arbitration Order 1926, s.2) but they fell into disuse: the Mandatory courts did not suffer from the same defects as their Ottoman predecessors, and there was, therefore, no strong practical reason for using them in preference to the regular courts. The *Mishpaṭ Hashalom Ha'ivri* system was abolished in 1949, in the wake of the establishment of the State of Israel.

As already observed, the jurisdiction of the Rabbinical Courts in many areas of personal status was part of the Ottoman Law and was incorporated by the British mandate into the legal system of Palestine (Articles 51-53 of the Palestine Order in Council 1922). Not all matters of personal status, however, were settled exclusively by Jewish Law. According to the Succession Ordinance 1923 s.21, women heirs were not to be deprived of certain types of property even if Jewish Law excluded them from inheriting it. The Mandatory legislator also established a Special Court consisting of two Supreme Court judges and one senior religious judge for dealing with disputes regarding jurisdiction in personal status issues (Article 55 of the Palestine Order in Council 1922). The trend to ensure the equality of women in matters of personal status (other than marriage and divorce) was continued in the legal system of the State of Israel, as was the institution of the Special Court in this area. As far as other areas of the law were concerned, the Rabbinical Courts served as recognized arbitral bodies, and they continue to do so to the present day.

The creation of the Chief Rabbinate in 1921 provided an opportunity to centralize the Rabbinical Courts, and a major step in this direction was the establishment of the Rabbinical Supreme Court of Appeals in that year. The concept of a regular appellate tribunal was a novel one in the *halakhah*, and its creation was achieved by means of a *takkanah* (rabbinical enactment). The institution of the *takkanah* was suggested by R. Abraham Kook, the first Ashkenazi Chief Rabbi, as the means by which the Chief Rabbinate would be able to deal with problems created by the tension between traditional *halakhah* and the renewal of Jewish national life in the Land of Israel. In the period prior to, and just after the establishment of the State, the Chief Rabbinate did indeed pass several *takkanot* in the area of family law. These included the fixing of a minimum sum in a *ketubah*, the obligation to maintain children over the age of 6 years, the legal age for marriage, and rules of procedure for the Rabbinical Courts. After this period, however, the Chief Rabbinate virtually ceased to enact *takkanot*, and the approach of the Rabbinical Courts to the pressing problems of this area of the law (e.g. *agunot*, deserted wives) has been a highly conservative one.

A noteworthy exception to this approach was Rabbi Dr. Isaac Halevi Herzog, the first Ashkenazi Chief Rabbi of the State of Israel. In the 1940s, R. Herzog prepared detailed *takkanot* for matters of inheritance, which struck

a compromise between the purely secular law and the principles of Jewish
Law. In R. Herzog's own words:

> ... the majority of my colleagues were not inclined to enact any *takkanot*
> whatsoever ... In the end the matter was shelved; the Government acted as it
> saw fit ... and a law ... was enacted, entirely contrary to the Law of Moses
> and Israel. Perhaps some of our colleagues now regret this. At that time, not
> one of them raised any halakhic arguments to refute my recommendations,
> with the exception of one well-known scholarly rabbi, to whom I replied in a
> responsum.[2]

3. *The Establishment of the State of Israel*

A. Personal Status

i. Marriage and divorce

The legal system which came into existence at the time of the Establishment of the State was that of the Mandatory period (Law and Administration
Ordinance 1948, s.11), with the result that, in principle, matters of personal
status remained in the hands of the religious courts. The jurisdiction of the
Rabbinical Courts in matters of marriage and divorce was codified in the
Rabbinical Courts Jurisdiction (Marriage and Divorce) Law, 5713-1953, the
first section of which provides that 'matters relating to the marriage and
divorce of Jewish citizens or residents of the State of Israel shall be within
the sole jurisdiction of the Rabbinical Courts.' This statute also provides
that the law to be applied in these matters is the 'law of the *Torah*' (s.2). It
is noteworthy that s.6 of the Law provides that a recalcitrant husband who
refuses to give his wife a *get* (bill of divorce) when a Rabbinical Court has
ordered that he be compelled to do so, may be imprisoned. The Rabbinical
Courts, however, have tended to avoid ordering a husband to divorce his wife,
due to their fear that this will result in a 'forced *get*'. In order for a *get* to be
valid, it must be given voluntarily, and although physical force may be
applied by a Rabbinical Court to a recalcitrant husband, he must, at the end
of the day, declare his sincere intention to divorce his wife. In the absence of
such a declaration, the *get* is a 'forced *get*', and is invalid. Moreover, the
question whether or not such coercion is appropriate in the context of a
wife's petition for divorce is the subject of a debate between Maimonides
(*Laws of Marriage* 14:8) and *Rabbenu Tam* (*Toṣafot, Ket.* 63b s.v. *aval
amrah*). The Rabbinical Courts, however, have evaded the issue by consistently avoiding the use of any language that could be interpreted as 'forcing' a

get,[3] with the result that imprisonment is rarely, in fact, a real option.

It is worthwhile mentioning that the jurisdiction of the Moslem courts includes the entire sphere of personal status, and extends to certain areas of property law. Indeed, although the Land Law, 5729-1969, abolished the Ottoman land law in the legal system of Israel, the special status of the Moslem *waqf*, i.e. property dedicated to religious purposes, remains in force.

The sole jurisdiction of the Rabbinical Courts in matters of marriage and divorce is strongly entrenched in Israeli Law; for example, the Declaration of Deaths Law, 5738-1978 provides that an official declaration of death is not evidence for purposes of the laws of marriage and divorce (s.8). Hence, a woman whose husband's death is made official under this law will still need to await the decision of a Rabbinical Court before she may remarry. Proof of death in this context is a complex halakhic issue, and although the rabbinic tradition tends to favour the goal of permitting remarriage over that of fulfilling the halakhic rules of evidence, the evidentiary requirements are more difficult to fulfil than they are under secular law.

ii.   Other Areas of Personal Status

In areas of personal status other than marriage and divorce, the Rabbinical Courts do not possess sole jurisdiction, and they are subject to certain laws specifically directed at tribunals trying personal status matters. The foremost example of such a law is the Women's Equal Rights Law, 5711-1951, the provisions of which bind all courts empowered to deal with personal status matters, unless the parties are over the age of 18 years, and they specifically agree to abide by Jewish Law alone (s.7). A Rabbinical Court which ignores the provisions of this law is subject to judicial review under s.7 of the Courts Law, 5717-1957.[4] In the *Nagar* case,[5] the Special Court criticized the decision of the District Rabbinical Court in a decision concerning the education of the children of divorced parents. The Rabbinical Court authorized the father to decide the type of school his children would attend, on the grounds that he alone was subject to the halakhic obligation to educate his children, and, therefore, control of their education ought to be in his hands. The court pointed out that according to *halakhah* a strong argument could be made in favour of extending this obligation to mothers in contemporary times, since fathers no longer teach their children directly and simply pay teacher's fees. It was also observed that the gap between women and men in terms of commitment to Jewish education is much smaller today than it was in the past. Elon J. suggested that the narrow view of the best interests of the children adopted by the District Rabbinical Court would not have been taken by the Rabbinical Appeals Court, especially in the light of the Women's Equal Rights Law, 5711-1957, which binds all courts dealing with matters of personal status.

Judicial review of a Rabbinical Court in the context of personal law is also possible if the court has ignored the requirements of natural justice. In *Vicki Levi* v. *Regional Rabbinical Court of Tel-Aviv and Yaffo*, H.C.10/59, P.D.13, 1182, the Rabbinical Court changed a maintenance order on the basis of the husband's complaint that his estranged wife had moved out of the matrimonial home. The wife was not present at the proceedings, but her counsel argued that the move was due to beatings inflicted upon her in the home by her husband and requested a further hearing in which the wife could present her account of the move to the court. This request was denied, and the wife's maintenance was reduced in accordance with the husband's version of the situation. The wife petitioned the High Court of Justice for relief on the grounds that she had been denied the natural right of being heard by the tribunal passing judgment upon her, whilst her adversary had enjoyed such a hearing. The High Court found in her favour and nullified the new maintenance order. Silberg J. also criticized the Rabbinical Court on the basis of Jewish Law, according to which absolute impartiality is the hallmark of all judicial proceedings.[6]

The secular justification for the imposition of the principles of natural justice, and the provisions of the Women's Equal Rights Law, 5711-1951, on the Rabbinical Courts in matters not strictly defined as personal status issues under Israeli Law (and thus not within their exclusive jurisdiction), is that their jurisdiction in these areas is derived from secular Israeli Law.[7] Halakhic justification was provided by R. Kapah, the rabbinical judge in the *Nagar* case, who based it upon the general principle in Jewish Law according to which there is freedom of adaptation in matters not strictly falling into the category of religious law.

As already suggested, the trend in the State of Israel has been to restrict the sole jurisdiction of the Rabbinical Courts to marriage and divorce, and to place the rest of personal status law in the hands of the secular courts. The list of secular personal law is a fairly long one, and includes maintenance — albeit with different levels of application according to whoever is liable to maintenance,[8] financial relations between spouses,[9] paternity,[10] adoption,[11] guardianship[12] and rights of succession.[13] Although the jurisdiction in these areas is in the hands of the secular courts, the laws which they apply are those of Jewish Law, or they are influenced by concepts and principles drawn from that system. The Family Law Amendment (Maintenance) Law, 5719-1959, states explicitly that the law to be applied is the personal law of the parties to the case (ss.2-3). The Succession Law, 5725-1965, contains a clause specifically excluding the application of Article 46 of the Palestine Orders in Council 1922-1947, thereby paving the way for the adoption of rules and principles of Jewish inheritance law in this statute. A striking example of the adoption of a halakhic principle in this law is the provision that 'the fact that a child is born out of wedlock shall have no effect upon succession rights' (s.93). This principle, which was certainly unique to Israeli Law in 1965, is based upon Jewish Law, according to which illegitimate offspring do not suffer any disadvantage with respect to rights of succession.[14]

Another example of the influence of Jewish Law on a personal status issue controlled by secular law is the application of the halakhic principle of avoiding bastardy (*mamzerut*) to the question of whether or not to order a tissue-typing test for determining paternity in the case of a child of a married woman.[15]

Secular personal status law is, nevertheless, basically secular in nature. Court procedure takes no account of the requirements of Jewish Law with regard to the laws of evidence or the qualifications of the judiciary.[16] More significantly yet, a civil marriage performed outside the State of Israel will be recognized for the purposes of Israeli personal status law in areas other than marriage and divorce, e.g. maintenance and custody. The only relevant factor is the validity of the civil marriage under the rules of private international law.[17] The courts have also recognized a private marriage performed in Israel between two Jewish residents of the State, for purposes of registration under the Population Registry Law, 5725-1965, which specifically excludes any application to matters of marriage and divorce. In *Gorfinkel-Haklai* v. *Minister of the Interior* H.C.80/63, P.D.17, 2048, the court recognized a marriage between a *kohen* (male member of a priestly family) and a divorcee, notwithstanding the prohibition on such a marriage in Jewish Law. The court cited the halakhic position: such a marriage, though forbidden, is nevertheless valid once performed, but the couple are required to divorce and their relationship is regarded as a sinful one. The court distinguished between the legal position in Jewish Law, according to which the marriage was a valid one, and the purely religious one, which regarded the union as sinful. It went on to argue that as a secular court, it ought not to be subject to purely religious aspects of personal status matters, and was, therefore, prepared to recognize the marriage. The majority decision, given by Landau J., emphasized the policy of not forcing religious prohibitions upon the secular citizens of the State of Israel.[18] In his minority judgment, Silberg J. objected to the wrenching apart of the religious from the legal in the context of Jewish Law, in which these two elements are so closely intertwined.

It is noteworthy that in another private marriage ceremony case, where the couple simply objected to a Jewish marriage ceremony, but were not halakhically barred from marrying each other, the court refused to recognize the marriage. The reasoning in that case was pure policy: recognition of private marriages is solely for the purpose of avoiding what are regarded by the court as the harsh consequences of applying the *halakhah* in matrimonial law. In the absence of such harshness, there is no reason to undermine the spirit of the Rabbinical Courts Jurisdiction (Marriage and Divorce) Law, 5713-1953, according to which the marriage and divorce of Jewish residents of the State of Israel should be governed by Jewish Law. The court also pointed out that it would be bad policy to encourage clandestine nuptials.[19]

It is in the context of citizenship and registration under the Population Registry Law, 5725-1965, that the most striking illustrations of the secular nature of Israeli personal status law are to be found. According to the Law of Return, 5710-1950, 'every Jew has the right to come into this country as an *oleh* (immigrant).' In the celebrated case of *Oswald Rufeisen* v. *Minister of the Interior*, H.C. 72/62, P.D. 16, 2424, the High Court of Justice ruled that the petitioner, although born to a Jewish mother, and hence halakhically Jewish, would not be recognized as a Jew for purposes of automatic citizenship under the Law of Return, since he had converted to Catholicism during the Second World War, and now stood before the court as Brother Daniel, a Carmelite monk. The court drew a distinction between the term 'Jewish' used in the Rabbinical Courts Jurisdiction (Marriage and Divorce) Law, 5713-1953, in which the word had to be interpreted in accordance with *halakhah*, and the present law, which was a secular one and did not, therefore, need to be understood in purely halakhic terms. The definition adopted by the majority of the justices was based upon the concept of historical and religious affinity with the Jewish people, and on this definition, Brother Daniel could not be recognized as a Jew. In his dissenting judgment, Cohn J. argued that this affinity ought to be interpreted in a dynamic fashion, and that in the light of the principles of comity with other nations, and the prophetic vision of 'freedom, justice and peace' enshrined in Israel's Declaration of Independence, Brother Daniel should be granted citizenship under the Law of Return.

The secular approach to Jewish identity adopted in the Brother Daniel decision was followed in two highly controversial cases (*Funk-Shlesinger* v. *Minister of the Interior*, H.C. 143/62, P.D. 17, 225; *Benjamin Shalit* v. *Minister of the Interior*, H.C.5 8/68, P.D. 23, 477) and in the wake of the public furore sparked off by these decisions, an amendment was made to the Law of Return in an attempt to satisfy both religious and secular sensibilities on this emotive issue. The 1970 amendment defined a Jew as someone 'born to a Jewish mother or converted to Judaism and who is not a member of another faith' (s.4b). The traditional *halakhah* and the Brother Daniel decision were officially incorporated into Israeli Law in a move to satisfy religious and secular alike. The purely secular approach, however, was consolidated in s.4a, which provided that the 'rights of a Jew under this Law ... are also vested in a child and a grandchild of a Jew, the spouse of a Jew, the spouse of the child of a Jew and the spouse of a grandchild of a Jew, except for a person who has been a Jew and has voluntarily changed his religion.' The concept of vested rights under the Law of Return reflected previous administrative policy in this area of the law.

The amended version of the Law of Return has given rise to a number of problems. The definition of 'member of another faith' has not proved an easy one to formulate, and in 1987 the High Court was faced with the question of defining that phrase in relation to two Messianic Jews, both of whom were born to Jewish mothers. The court decided that the fact that there was no clear evidence of baptism was irrelevant, since membership of another faith was decided in accordance with Israeli Law and not the entrance requirements of the other faith. Since belief in Jesus was not compatible with the definition of Judaism formulated by the court in the *Rufeisen* and *Shalit* decisions, the petitioners failed in their bid to become citizens under the Law of Return.[20] It has also been necessary to confront the issue of conversion to Judaism, and the courts have persistently refused to limit the scope of valid conversions to those performed in accordance with strict *halakhah*. In *Association of Torah Observant Sefardim-Tenuat Shas* v. *Director of the Population Registry*, H.C. 264/87 etc., P.D. 33(2) 723, the court held that the requirements of the Population Registry Law, 5725-1965, were fulfilled 'for the purposes of establishing conversion to Judaism under this Law, when the convert made a statement to the effect that he or she had been converted to Judaism in a Jewish community in the Diaspora, and a document attesting to the conversion was produced'. It is noteworthy that in the case of *Shoshana Miller* v. *Minister of the Interior*, H.C. 230/86, P.D. 40(4) 436, the court struck down an attempt by the Minister of the Interior to have the word 'convert' added to the registration document of a Reform convert, both on the grounds that such a change in registration procedure could only be achieved by passing a law to that effect, and that Jewish Law itself prohibited the slightest insult to a convert by reminding him or her of their previous gentile status.

In concluding this section, it ought to be emphasized that the line dividing Jewish and secular law in personal status matters other than marriage and divorce is not a hard and fast one. The secular courts have followed the decisions of the Rabbinical Courts in determining the amount of maintenance to be paid to a wife working outside the matrimonial home,[21] and the Rabbinical Courts have been instructed with regard to the correct halakhic principle underlying the concept of the child's welfare in custody matters in the above-mentioned case of *Nagar*.[22] It is also significant to note the analysis of the halakhic status of secular Israeli Law in Rabbinical Court decisions. In the *Vilozhni* case,[23] the court dealt with this issue and cited the current theories according to which secular Israeli Law falls into the category of 'the law of the land' or the canons of general usage.

B.   Areas Other than Personal Status

The legal system which came into existence with the establishment of the State of Israel was that of the British Mandate, including the provision that gaps in the law were to be filled in on the basis of English common law and equity. In fact, this provision was restricted in the early years of the State to laws applied in Palestine prior to 1948, and there was, therefore, no obligation to turn to England for guidance in any issue which was not already part of Mandatory Law.[24] Nevertheless, the very existence of this link aroused the ire of the supporters of *Mishpat Ivri*. Realizing that Jewish Law would not be adopted as the legal system of the State, they argued that at the very least, it should function as the official source for filling in gaps in the existing law. Their efforts during the early years of the State's existence were, however, in vain, and it was not until 1980 that the link with English Law was severed, and replaced with a section requiring a judge to resolve a problem to which there was no solution in the existing law on the basis of 'the principles of freedom, justice, equity and peace of the heritage of Israel' (Foundations of Law Act, 5740-1980 — see pp.411-15 below for a detailed discussion). Opposition to granting an official role to Jewish Law in matters other than personal status was justified in the Knesset in terms of both the practical problem of non-specialists attempting to establish the legal position in Jewish Law on any particular matter, and the ideological issue of the suitability of Jewish Law for a modern, pluralist society. Israeli Law developed independently of the Jewish legal tradition. It borrowed from other systems — both Common law and Civil law forms, and created a uniquely Israeli system. Notwithstanding its lack of any official role, Jewish Law did, nevertheless, play a part in the development of Israeli civil, criminal and public law, and it is to a description of this role that the following section is devoted.

i. Legislation

Rules and principles of Jewish Law are often referred to in the course of parliamentary debates on proposed legislation, and it is routine practice for all draft bills to be sent to the Deputy Attorney General and Advisor on Jewish Law for comment. On occasion, the Jewish Law material discussed in the Knesset is incorporated into the preamble to the final law.

One example of such a law is the Wages Protection Law, 5718-1958, which requires employers to pay their workers on time. The principle of prompt payment is found in the Bible (*Lev.* 19:13; *Deut.* 24:15) and is discussed in the *Talmud* and codes.[25] These sources were referred to in the Knesset deliberations, and the preamble to the law mentions its Jewish Law background. Nevertheless, none of the sections of the actual law are based upon halakhic principles, and the detailed provisions which they incorporate are to be found in many modern legal systems. Moreover, in the course of the Knesset discussions, the 'interesting' suggestion that 'any problem arising in relation to the implementation of this law be resolved by reference to Jewish Law', was summarily dismissed by the Minister of Justice on the grounds that it was neither practical nor wise.[26]

Jewish Law played a similar role in relation to the Co-operative Housing Law, 5713-1952. According to Jewish Law 'the house and the top storey' may be owned by separate individuals (*B. B.M.* 116b). The concept of separate ownership in a multi-storey building also exists in English and American Law. It was not, however, part of Mandatory Law which accepted the Roman Law doctrine of ownership extending above the land and below it. The Israeli legislature adopted the model of separate ownership and incorporated references to Jewish Law into the preamble to the 1952 law. Nevertheless, the Minister of Justice took the trouble to observe that it was not 'Jewish Law doctrine' but 'economic reality' which had tipped the scales in favour of separate ownership. The housing shortage in Israel together with the high price of property militated against the Roman Law doctrine, and it was this practical consideration which lay at the base of the Knesset's decision to opt for separate ownership.[27]

Other laws in relation to which Jewish Law played a similar role include the Severance Pay Law, 5723-1963, and the Bailees Law, 5727-1967.[28]

It is necessary to observe that there are many instances in which Israeli legislation deviates from Jewish Law. One such instance is the Limitation of Actions Law, 5728-1968, which codifies a legal doctrine which, strictly speaking, does not exist in Jewish Law. According to the *Talmud* 'the creditor's claim is never extinguished by the passage of time' (*B. Ket.* 104a-b) and this is the accepted principle in the *halakhah*. Although custom and communal enactments played a role in limiting legal actions in various communities during various periods, the principle of unlimited actions was always the regnant one. Another oft-quoted example of deviation is the Guarantee Law, 5727-1967, which gave the creditor the right to proceed against the guarantor after having merely notified the debtor, and without having taken any legal action against him. Under Jewish Law, the debtor must be sued before any action can be taken against the guarantor, and much was made of this deviation by opponents of the law during the preliminary debates. In fact, the law has been changed and it is now necessary to exhaust all legal remedies against the debtor before suing the guarantor. It is, nevertheless, noteworthy that there is a fundamental difference between the halakhic concept of guarantee and the principle underlying the Guarantee Law. According to many authorities, Jewish Law places the guarantor's property at the disposal of the creditor as if it were part of the debtor's assets. It is, therefore, necessary to sue the debtor first. Under Israeli Law, however, the guarantor is liable to the creditor, and, therefore, suing the guarantor makes legal — if not moral — sense.[29] It should also be observed that economic and social factors, such as the shortage of housing for rent and banking practices, influenced both the 1967 law and the recent changes in it.

Jewish Law is clearly a pervasive presence in the Israeli legislative process. It does not, however, constitute part of non-personal status legislation, and usually figures in preliminary debates and preambles to laws. The one law in this area which specifically deals with the role to be played by Jewish Law is the Foundations of Law Act, 5740-1980 (see p.411, below), and its concern is with judicial decisions, which is by far the most fertile ground for the direct application of Jewish Law in the Israeli legal system.

ii. Case law prior to the Foundations of Law Act, 5740-1980

In the early days of the Israeli legal system, the question of interpreting legal terms in the light of Jewish Law was discussed by the judiciary. This type of interpretation is a natural result of the fact that Hebrew is the language of Israeli Law, and the rich legal heritage of the *halakhah* provides much of its vocabulary. Although the justices differed on this question, the majority view was expressed by Heshin J. in *Mitoba* v. *Kazan*, P.M. 89\51, P.D. 6,4 as follows:

> Even if it is abundantly clear that the (semantic — D.B.S.) origin of a particular term or expression lies in the *Talmud* ... a distinction must be drawn between the terms and their substantive content. The terms are borrowed from one place, but the content with which they are filled is original and is drawn from a different source.

There is, therefore, no necessary link between a legal term borrowed from Jewish Law and its significance in Israeli Law. In certain cases, however, the courts have cited the halakhic background of ambiguous terms in the course of arguing for a particular interpretation of it. The term *gemirat da'at* is widely used in Jewish Law to indicate that the parties to an agreement have manifested their intentions in an objective manner. The same term is used in the Law of Contracts (General Part), 5733-1973, and in *Zandbank* v. *Danziger*, C.A. 440\75, P.D.30(2), 260, the court held that the objective approach was also the one to be adopted in relation to this law. In *Russian Ecclesiastical Mission* v. *Attorney General*, C.A. 831\75, P.D. 31(3), 317, the problem facing the court was whether or not the word 'hearing' in an ordinance dealing with the Attorney General's right 'to be heard' (*hashmi'a*) extended to the presentation of evidence to the court. The ruling was in the affirmative, and Cohn J. adduced proof from the Biblical verse: 'Hear (*shamo'a*) the causes between your brethren and judge righteously' (*Deut.* 1:16), which is interpreted by the Rabbis to teach that evidence must be brought in order for a 'hearing' to take place (*Sifre, Deut.* 1:16).

In addition to the interpretation of terms, Jewish Law has been cited with a view to elucidating a legal concept, or aiding the court in choosing between different approaches to a legal principle. This is especially the case when issues of morality and justice are at stake, although Jewish Law has also been referred to in the context of purely legal issues. A selection of matters dealt with by the court in recent years includes illegal contracts,[30] defining 'public policy' and 'good faith',[31] illegal custody,[32] the necessity plea in criminal law,[33] liability for negligent misstatements,[34] and the definition of prescription.[35]

One of the most dramatic cases in which Jewish Law played a role was *Moshe Cohen* v. *State of Israel*, Cr.A. 91\80, P.D. 35(3), 281, in which the petitioner was charged with the rape of his wife. The relevant section of the 1977 Penal Law defines rape as 'illegal' intercourse, and the Common law position was then that a husband could not have 'illegal' intercourse with his wife, since such intercourse constituted one of the basic conditions of the marriage agreement entered into by both parties. The origin of this position lies in the Christian concept of the conjugal debt owed by a wife to her husband. The prosecution argued that the term 'unlawfully' should be interpreted in the light of the petitioner's personal law, which in Cohen's case was Jewish Law. Upon examination of the relevant sources it became evident that the *halakhah* forbids the use of force in the context of marital intercourse,[36] although there is no criminal sanction against a husband who disregards this prohibition. The court held that it was permissible to extrapolate from the realm of pure halakhic prohibitions to the criminal law, and Moshe Cohen was found guilty of raping his wife. Bekhor J. commented on the progressive approach of Jewish Law in this area, and contrasted the positive attitude towards female sexual fulfilment in Jewish sources with the generally negative one found in many Christian writings. It is noteworthy that the law has since been changed in both the United Kingdom and the United States in favour of the wife.[37] In this case, Jewish Law was applied in order to achieve a result which was a morally progressive one, and it is in this type of enterprise that the courts have excelled at drawing inspiration from the *halakhah*.

Another case of this nature is *Becker* v. *Eilat*, H.C. 172\78, P.D. 32(3), 372, in which the petitioner was a road-safety expert who had been summoned to testify in a homicide case. He declined to take the witnesses' oath — which was taken on the Bible — because he was an agnostic. Under the existing law, a witness could be excused from taking an oath on the grounds of 'religion' or 'conscience', and would then merely have to affirm that the testimony was true. The judge rejected the petitioner's claim to be excused from taking the oath. He decided that agnosticism did not qualify as a basis for exemption from the witnesses' oath since it constituted neither 'religion' nor 'conscience'. Moreover, the petitioner's request to be excused from taking the oath was not made in 'good faith' as required by the law. The High Court reversed the lower court's decision both in terms of the interpretation of the exemption qualifications, and the issue of 'good faith'. Elon J. pointed out that under Jewish Law there is no witnesses' oath, since all witnesses are subject to the Biblical prohibition against 'bearing false witness against your neighbour' (*Ex.* 20:13; *Deut.* 5:17). According to talmudic law, witnesses are warned about the terrible consequences of lying to the court, but there is no formal oath to tell the truth. A change occurred in the Middle Ages — possibly under non-Jewish influence — and the court was given discretion to impose an oath should it feel that this step was necessary for the establishment of the truth.[38] This approach was recommended to the Israeli legislator by Elon J. as being commensurate with the demands of both justice and the Jewish tradition in a modern context. Shortly after this decision the law was indeed changed, and under the Evidence Law Amendment (Warning of Witnesses and Removal of Oath) Law, 5740-1980, there is no mandatory witnesses' oath in Israeli courts. Instead, the witness is warned to tell the truth and the judge has the discretion to impose an oath if this step would facilitate truthful evidence. The witness preserves the right to request exemption from such an oath on grounds of 'conscience' and 'religion', provided that the request is made in 'good faith'.

In both of these cases, the results obtained under the inspiration of Jewish Law were acceptable under general jurisprudence and morality. It is noteworthy that where this is not the case, then the court is very firm in its rejection of Jewish Law as a source for considering the solution of the problem with which it is dealing.[39] Israeli courts have turned to Jewish Law — notwithstanding its lack of official status — for guidance with respect to general issues of morality and justice from the early days of the establishment of the State. This pattern continues to be followed in the period after the Foundations of Law Act, 5740-1980, the main features of which are discussed in the following section.

iii.   The Foundations of Law Act, 5740-1980 and subsequent case law

This Act replaces the section linking Israeli Law with that of England and provides as follows:

> Where a court finds that a question requiring a decision cannot be answered by reference to an enactment or a judicial precedent or by way of analogy, it shall decide the same in the light of the principles of freedom, justice, equity and peace of the heritage of Israel.

It is noteworthy, that according to the Declaration of Independence, the State of Israel is 'based upon freedom, justice and peace as envisaged by the prophets of Israel'. Equity was included in article 46 of the Palestine Order in Council 1922, and became part of the law of the State of Israel under the

Law and Administration Ordinance of 1948.

In order for a court to be required to turn to the 'heritage of Israel' — and there is no doubt in the mind of the Israeli judiciary that this term applies to Jewish Law — there must be a legal issue to which there is no answer in the existing law, even by way of analogy. It is interesting to note that some learned authors felt that prior to this Law, the option of using analogy was not available to the Israeli judge, and that he or she was bound, in such a case, to follow English Law.[40] Now, gaps in the law are very unlikely. Such a situation is not likely to arise often, and in the words of one of the supporters of the bill, 'it is doubtful whether even half a per cent of the cases before the court would fall into the category of a lacuna.'[41] It was also emphasized by the same Knesset member that the law 'was not intended to possess any far-reaching practical consequences; its significance was primarily symbolic.'

The majority of Israeli jurists would appear to subscribe to the belief that the large body of law which has grown up in Israel over the last two decades is comprehensive enough to ensure that no lacuna will ever be discovered. Indeed, the 1980 Act is itself responsible for this situation, since it makes legal analogy an official source of Israeli Law — something which had not been clear prior to the Act — and there is no reason why analogy should not produce the answer to every legal problem, as it does in other legal systems.[42] This approach is also supported by the case-law both prior to and after the Foundations of Law Act, 5740-1980.

According to Elon J., however, the scope of the Foundations of Law Act, 5740-1980, is not restricted to the filling in of lacunae in the law. In his view, it extends to the interpretation of general terms such as 'good faith' and 'public policy', which should be interpreted in accordance with the principles of the 'heritage of Israel', before turning to any other system for inspiration. He also argued that this type of amplification of general concepts was closer in nature to the filling of lacunae than it was to regular legal interpretation. Elon J.'s approach was rejected by the majority in the leading case of *Kupat Am Bank* v. *Hendeles*, F.H. 13/80, P.D. 35(2), 785, in which both Landau J. and Barak J. argued that the jural postulates of Israeli Law were quite different from those of Jewish Law, and that it would, therefore, be ill-advised to mix the two systems at any level of interpretation. Moreover, the fact that the Act was couched in such wide terms served as an indication that the legislature did not intend to impose Jewish Law upon the judiciary, even in relation to lacunae. Clearly, it was not the legislator's intent to make Jewish Law binding upon Israeli courts in matters of interpretation at any level of generality.

The issue before the court in *Kupat Am Bank* v. *Hendeles* was the ownership of promissory notes found on the floor of the safety-deposit box room of the bank. The notes remained unclaimed, and their ownership was contested. The Restoration of Lost Property Law 1973, provides that 'a person who finds lost property in another person's domain ... shall deliver up the property to him' (s.3). The majority decision was in favour of the bank in whose 'domain' the notes were found. In his minority opinion, Elon J. came to the opposite conclusion on the basis of Jewish Law, which requires that the owner of the domain be in actual physical control of it before it can be used as a basis for acquiring the ownership of lost articles. In the present case, the bank had no such control over the safety-deposit box room, and the finder was, therefore, the owner. In the Further Hearing, which was devoted specifically to the Foundations of Law Act 1980, the majority view was that the term 'domain' was not an unclear one in Israeli Law, and its interpretation did not, therefore, fall under the terms of the Act. The majority also held that the amplification of general concepts did not fall within the scope of the Act. It was also emphasized that Israeli courts should not use rabbinical authorities as expert witnesses in determining the Jewish Law position on a particular issue. Rather, they were to go directly to the sources of Jewish Law and derive the legal position on the basis of first-hand research. On the basis of this decision, and in the light of the cases decided after the Act, it is evident that the mandatory imposition of Jewish Law upon Israeli judges was not the aim of the legislature in passing it. The Act simply made official the existing practice of judges and lawyers learned in Jewish Law of making use of it in cases in which it would help the court to arrive at a decision based upon 'freedom, justice, equity and peace'.

The major influence of Jewish Law in the Supreme Court, since the passage of the Act in 1980, has been in areas of ethical significance. These areas include a convict's right to vote in the Knesset elections,[43] free speech,[44] immoral contracts,[45] and the extent to which a testator's freedom to dispose of his property should be bound by formal legal requirements.[46] In this respect, the pattern set for the application of Jewish Law before the passing of the Foundations of Law Act 1980 persists after its passing.

In its non-mandatory capacity, Jewish Law continues to make its mark in Israeli jurisprudence. A case in point is *Belker* v. *State of Israel*, Cr.A. 341/82 P.D. 41(1) 1, in which the Supreme Court addressed the issue of whether or not causing brain death constituted the *actus reus* of murder under s.300 of the Penal Code 1977. The appellant's wife was brought to hospital in a critical condition after having fallen out of a fourth floor window. Upon arrival at the hospital, the physicians concluded that she was brainstem dead, i.e. whole brain death. She was connected to life-supporting devices for the purpose of establishing the possibility of transplanting her organs, but when no donee was found, the devices were disconnected and she was declared dead. The trial judge found that the appellant had pushed his wife out of the window, and the issue before the court was whether or not this act constituted murder. In his decision, Beiski J. reviewed the position in Jewish Law, and arrived at the conclusion that cessation of respiration was the definitive criterion for establishing death and that the appellant's act did, therefore, amount to murder. He also cited the decision of the Israeli Chief Rabbinate in 1987, which relied upon this criterion in order to permit heart transplants, which involve the transfer of a still-beating heart from the body of a brainstem dead donor to a donee. It is the brainstem which controls respiration, and once it has been irreversibly damaged, the person may be declared dead, and his or her still-beating heart may be used to save the life of the donee. The appellant was found guilty of murder and sentenced accordingly.

Another case in the biomedical area was *A.* v. *B.*, M.P. 103/92 in which Bazak J. of the Jerusalem District Court was summoned to a hospital in order to resolve a problem concerning a woman suffering from terminal lupus, who was also in the twenty-eighth week of her pregnancy. Her husband did not wish to consent to a Caesarian section on her behalf, since the doctors could not assure him that the baby would emerge healthy. In a previous case involving a similar situation, another District Court judge had ruled that the Caesarian section could not be authorized by a guardian ad litem, since there was no provision under the Capacity and Guardianship Law 1962 for appointing such a guardian for a foetus. The only option available to him, therefore, was to leave both mother and foetus to their fates. In the present case, Bazak J. applied the Foundations of Law Act 1980 and cited a talmudic ruling that 'if a woman who has been sitting on a birthstool died on the Sabbath, one may bring a knife and cut her womb open to take out the child' (*B. Arakh.* 7a). On the basis of this ruling, Bazak J. argued that Israeli Law ought to recognize a foetus, under such circumstances, for the purposes of legal guardianship, since halakhically the Sabbath could be profaned in order to save its life. Bazak J.'s decision was that once the woman had lost any independent capacity in her brainstem — in accordance with the Israeli Chief Rabbinate's decision — the foetus was to be removed by Caesarian section.

Amongst the other issues discussed and informed by Jewish Law in recent years are kidney transplants from mentally incompetent patients,[47] protection of privacy and the status of evidence obtained by non-consensual medical procedures,[48] conscientious objection,[49] prisoners' right to marital relations,[50] and judicial bias.[51] The courts continue to refer to Jewish Law, especially in relation to issues of ethical significance, and the existence of the Foundations of Law Act, 1980 is a spur to this type of creative judicial activity.

C. The Halakhic Status of Israeli Law in the Rabbinical Courts

There are two main models available for the halakhic justification of secular Israeli Law: the talmudic rule that 'the law of the land is the law' (*dina demalkhuta dina*), and the institution of the communal *takkanah*. The rule regarding the law of the land was propounded during the period of the Babylonian *Talmud* (*B. B.K.* 113a-b) and has served, from that time onwards, as the means for regulating the legal relations between Jewish communities and the non-Jewish ones in which they lived. The communal *takkanah* was the major instrument for the adaptation of *halakhah* to the needs of communal life during the Middle Ages, and Jewish public and administrative law is basically a commentary on these enactments. The majority of rabbinic authorities during the Mandatory period, and in the early years of the State of Israel, rejected the idea that secular law could fall into the category of a *takkanah*, on the grounds that the laws in question were propounded by secular people and the institution of the *takkanah* was only operative in the context of a religious society. Hence, the laws passed by the Knesset were, at best, to be regarded as 'the law of the land'. The result of this classification is that Israeli Law is not regarded as an integral part of the halakhic system, which would be the case if it did fall under the rubric of the communal *takkanah*, but as an external phenomenon, binding on the basis of the purely pragmatic principle of the preservation of the social order. It is noteworthy that even the most extreme view, which denies the status of 'the law of the land' to Israeli Law, does, nevertheless, accept as binding those laws passed by the Knesset for the purpose of maintaining civilized society. The basis for this very limited acceptance of secular law lies in the rabbinic tradition of accepting any governmental authority — Jewish or non-Jewish — in order to ensure that people do not 'swallow each other alive'.[52]

This negative approach to the halakhic status of Israeli Law is characteristic of the Rabbinical Courts, which, with one exception in the area of tenant protection legislation,[53] have never recognized any secular law as

constituting a communal *takkanah*, and hence as possessing normative force
in halakhic terms. The secular court system has criticized the attitude of the
Rabbinical Courts towards Israeli Law — which is undoubtedly responsible,
to a certain extent, for the generally negative approach of the former system
towards the latter. In *Yosef* v. *Yosef*, F.H. 23/69, P.D. 24(1) 792, the
Supreme Court dealt with the question of a secular court's obligation to
decide matters of Jewish Law in accordance with the decisions of the
Rabbinical Courts. Berenson J. observed that whilst the courts 'would place
the highest weight on such decisions, and would, in general, feel obliged to
follow them', it was unfortunate that the Rabbinical Courts 'did not adopt
the same respectful attitude' towards the law of the State, and legally require
obedience to 'the decisions of competent secular courts in matters arising
before them' (*ibid.*, 813).

D. The Debate Concerning the Theoretical Legitimacy of *Mishpat Ivri*

The *Mishpat Ivri* movement has been criticized on the grounds that it
constitutes a secularization of Jewish Law. One reason for this charge is the
fact that the areas of the *halakhah* chosen by the proponents of the
movement — for purposes of both academic research and practical application in the legal system of the State of Israel — are confined to civil and
criminal matters. The field of religious law is almost entirely neglected,
notwithstanding the fact that it includes procedural matters such as the laws
of evidence and judicial discretion, which apply to all areas of Jewish Law.
Another critique is that the unique feature of Jewish Law is its concept of
justice and righteousness rather than its substantive solutions to particular
legal problems. Only a judge steeped in the traditional ethos of the *halakhah*
is in a position to elucidate this feature of Jewish Law in the case before
him, and to apply it in practice. It is also argued by critics of *Mishpat Ivri*
that the research methodology used by its principal champions is historical
rather than normative, and yet they claim that the results of this research
should be applied in the legal system of the State of Israel, which is, after
all, a normative legal system.

The defenders of the *Mishpat Ivri* enterprise maintain that the distinction
between civil and religious law is an internal one, and the former is
traditionally much more flexible than the latter. The rule that 'the law of the
land is law', for example, applies to matters of civil law, but is inapplicable
in the context of religious law. It is also claimed that *Mishpat Ivri* presents
itself as the process of analysing *halakhah* (*lamdanut*) rather than deciding it

(*pesikah*). The division between these two areas is a traditional one, and those involved in the *Mishpat Ivri* enterprise are basically adopting the educational role of the *lamdan*, rather than the judicial one of the *posek*. In the light of both of these arguments, the charge that *Mishpat Ivri* is an attempt to secularize Jewish Law is unfounded, since the features which constitute the basis for the charge are, in fact, part of traditional *halakhah*. Both the selective nature of *Mishpat Ivri* and the secular context in which it operates, are, therefore, compatible with the division between civil and religious law and the distinction between *lamdanut* and *pesikah* in classical halakhic thinking. This argument is also a valid one in the context of research methodology, since it justifies the adoption of an analytical, as opposed to a strictly normative, approach to the law.

Finally, the champions of the *Mishpat Ivri* movement make the point that there is no empirical evidence of any secularization of Jewish Law as a result of its existence, and the net result has, in fact, been a very positive one — in educational terms — for both the legal profession and Israeli society at large.[54]

4. Bibliography

Elon, M., ed., *The Principles of Jewish Law* (Jerusalem, Keter, 1974).

Frimer, D., 'Israel Civil Courts and Rabbinical Courts Under One Roof', *Israel Law Review* 24 (1990), 553-559.

Jackson, B.S., ed., *Modern Research in Jewish Law* (Leiden: E.J. Brill, 1980).

Lifshitz, B., 'Israeli Law and Jewish Law — Interaction and Independence', *Israel Law Review* 24 (1990), 507-524.

Rakover, N., ed., *Jewish Law and Current Legal Problems* (Jerusalem: Library of Jewish Law, 1984).

Shifman, P., 'Family Law in Israel: The Struggle Between Religious and Secular Law', *Israel Law Review* 24 (1990), 537-552.

Shochetman, E., 'Israeli Law and Jewish Law — Interaction and Independence: A Commentary', *Israel Law Review* 24 (1990), 525-536.

Sinclair, D., 'Jewish Law in the State of Israel', regular column in *The Jewish Law Annual*, Vols.I-V published by E.J. Brill, Leiden, 1978-75; vols. VI-XI published by Harwood Academic Publishers for the Institute of Jewish Law, Boston University School of Law, 1987-94; in progress.

Notes

1   See B.S. Jackson, ed., *Modern Research in Jewish Law* (Leiden: E.J. Brill, 1980).

2   B. Greenberger, 'Rabbi Herzog's Proposals for *Takkanot* in Matters of Inheritance', in *The Halakhic Thought of R. Isaac Herzog,* ed. B.S. Jackson (Atlanta: Scholars Press, 1991), 57-58 (Jewish Law Association Studies 5).

3   *Gutman* v. *The Rabbinical Court,* H.C. 644/79, P.D. 34(1) 443.

4   *Sidis* v. *President and Members of the Supreme Rabbinical Court,* H.C. 202/57, P.D. 13, 1182; *Strait* v. *Strait,* H.C. 302/63, P.D. 18(1), 598; *Yosef* v. *Yosef,* F.H.23/69, P.D. 24(1), 792; *Vilozhni* v. *Supreme Rabbinical Court,* H.C. 823/81, P.D. 36(2), 733.

5   *Nagar* v. *Nagar,* F.H.1/81, P.D.38(1), 365.

6   Maimonides, *Laws of the Sanhedrin* 21:1-3; *Resp. Rema* no.108.

7   *Vilozhni* v. *Supreme Rabbinical Court,* H.C. 823/81, P.D. 36(2), 738-39.

8   Family Law Amendment (Maintenance) Law, 5719-1959.

9   Spouses (Property Relations) Law, 5733-1973.

10   *Boaron* v. *The District Rabbinical Court of Tel-Aviv-Yaffo,* P.D. 26(2) 727.

11   Adoption of Children Law, 5741-1981.

12   Capacity and Guardianship Law, 5722-1962.

13   Succession Law, 5725-1965.

14   Maimonides, *Laws of Inheritance* 1:7; *Shulhan Arukh, Hoshen Mishpaṭ* 76:6.

15   *Sharon* v. *Levi,* C.A. 548/78, P.D.35(1) 736.

16   *Kotik* v. *Wolfson,* C.A. 26/51, P.D. 5, 1341.

17   *Skornik* v. *Skornik,* C.A. 191/51, P.D. 8, 141.

18   See also *Rodnizki* v. *Supreme Rabbinical Appeals Court,* H.C.51/69, P.D. 24(1) 204.

19   *Segev* v. *District Rabbinical Court of Zfat,* H.C. 130/66, P.D. 21(2) 541; *Zonen* v. *Stahl,* C.A. 32/81, P.D. 37(2) 761.

20   *Beresford* v. *Minister of the Interior* H.C. 265/87, P.D. 43(4) 793.

21   *Yosef* v. *Yosef,* F.H. 23/69, P.D. 24(1) 792.

22   *Supra* n.5.

23   *Supra* n.4.

24   *Kohavi* v. *Becker,* C.A. 92/55, P.D. 11, 236.

25   *B.B.M.* 111a-112a; *Mordekhai, B.B.* no.468; *Or Zarua, B.M.* no.181.

26   *Divre Haknesset* 33, 5721-1961, 1303.

27   *Divre Haknesset* 8, 5711-1951, 775.

28   See H.H. Cohn, 'Jewish Law in Israel', in *Jewish Law in Legal History and the Modern World,* ed. B.S. Jackson (Leiden: E.J. Brill, 1980), 124-46.

29   See B. Lifshitz, 'Israeli Law and Jewish Law — Interaction and Independence', *Israel law Review* 24 (1990), 519.

30 *Jacobs* v. *Cartoz*, C.A. 110\53, P.D. 9(2), 1401; *Howard* v. *Miarah*, C.A. 311\81, P.D. 35(2), 505.

31 *Roth* v. *Yeshufeh*, C.A. 148\73, P.D. 33(1), 617; *Dicker* v. *Mokh*, C.A. 566\77, P.D. 32(2), 141.

32 *State of Israel* v. *Abukassis*, M.H. 71\78, P.D. 32(2), 240.

33 *Afangar* v. *State of Israel*, Cr.A. 89\78, P.D. 33(3), 141.

34 *Amidar* v. *Aaron*, C.A. 86\76, P.D. 32(2), 337.

35 *Gilberg* v. *Panus*, C.A. 213\76, P.D. 31(2), 272.

36 *B. Erub.* 100b; Maimonides, *Laws of Marriage* 15:17; *Shulḥan Arukh, Even Ha'ezer* no. 25:2.

37 J. Barton, 'The Story of Marital Rape', *Law Quarterly Review* 108 (1992), 260-71.

38 *Shulḥan Arukh, Ḥoshen Mishpaṭ* no. 28:2.

39 See e.g. *Kitan* v. *Weiss*, C.A. 350/77, P.D. 33(2), 785.

40 G. Tedeschi, 'The Problem of the *Lacuna* and s.46 of His Majesty's Order in Council', in *Meḥḳarim bamishpaṭ artsenu* (Jerusalem: Magnes Press for the Hebrew University of Jerusalem, 1959), 150-51 (in Hebrew).

41 *Divre Haknesset* 89 (1980) 4025.

42 See A. Levontin and C. Goldwater, *Choice of Laws and s.46 of the King's Order in Council* (Jerusalem: Magnes Press for the Hebrew University of Jerusalem, 1974); I. Zamir, *Israeli Administrative Law and s.46 of the King's Order in Council* (Jerusalem: Magnes Press for the Hebrew University of Jerusalem, 1974); G. Procaccia, 'Foundations of Law Act, 5740-1980', *Iyune Mishpaṭ* 15 (1984),145; A Barak, 'The Lacuna Problem in Modern Israeli Law', *Mishpaṭim* 5 (1973), 99.

43 *Hukmah* v. *Minister of the Interior*, H.C. 337/84, P.D. 38(1) 826.

44 *Neiman* v. *Elections Committee of the Eleventh Knesset*, C.A. 32/84, P.D. 39(2) 225.

45 *Agmian Shahah* v. *Yagisha Dardarim*, C.A. 466/83, P.D. 39(4), 734.

46 *Koenig* v. *Cohen*, F.H. 40/80, P.D. 36(3), 701.

47 *A.G.* v. *X*, M.L.A. 698/86, P.D. 42(2) 661.

48 *Military Appeals Court* v. *Vaknin*, F.H. 9/8, P.D. 42(3), 837; *Kortam* v. *State of Israel*, Cr.A. 480/85, P.D. 40(3), 637.

49 *Shein* v. *Minister of Defence*, H.C. 734/83, P.D. 38 (3), 393.

50 *Weil* v. *State of Israel*, H.C. 114/86, P.D. 41(3) 476.

51 *State of Israel* v. *Maman*, M.Cr.A. 341/89, P.D. 43(2) 441.

52 *M. Avot* 3:2.

53 *Vilozhni* v. *Supreme Rabbinical Court* H.C. 823/81, P.D. 36(2) 733.

54 See B.S. Jackson, ed., *Modern Research in Jewish Law* (Leiden: E.J. Brill, 1980).

16

POSTSCRIPT:
THE JUDICIAL PROCESS AND
THE NATURE OF JEWISH LAW

by

HANINA BEN-MENAHEM
Hebrew University of Jerusalem

1. *Introduction*

Modern scholarship in Jewish law is dominated by the modern, Western concept of law. The very term *Mishpaṭ Ivri* is a modern invention, a literal translation of 'Jewish law' (*jüdisches Recht*). It has quite different connotations from the traditional Jewish term, *halakhah.*

The modern, Western concept of law reflected in *Mishpaṭ Ivri* scholarship is dominated by three basic claims: (1) laws belong to a unified system; (2) within any such system, there are authoritative sources of law, and any valid application of the law must be justified by reliance upon those sources; (3) the system itself provides the means by which those rules may be recognised as authoritative. These claims combine into what is sometimes called the Rule of Law. In the West, this doctrine has a political history. It was a reaction against forms of absolutist monarchy, hence the expression 'governed by rules, not by men'. This political history, in modern Europe, in some ways recapitulates the history of law in Greece and Rome, where the origins of the Rule of Law doctrine may be found.

The Rule of Law, in this sense, certainly came to infiltrate halakhic thinking, and for long has formed the dominant strand. But it never represented an exclusive view within the *halakhah*. A very different conception — arguably the original conception — may be identified, one which adopts a pluralistic attitude towards the sources of Jewish law, and rejects the view that any valid application of the law must be justified by reliance upon those sources which are regarded, by the rules of the system, as the authoritative ones. It does so by reliance upon a religious ideology. Law is a matter of governance by men, not by rules. But not any men. It is the governance of men who were regarded originally as divinely inspired, later as at least divinely authorised, to depart from the rules of the system.

The purpose of this Postscript is to show a number of manifestations of the religious ideology of the *halakhah*, and to suggest that it continues, even to the present day, to exert an influence on halakhic thinking. This ideology is most prominently found in the *Talmud*. There is an essential difference between the *Talmud*'s conception of the legal process and that of classical Western thought. The maxim 'governed by rules, not by men' reflects the Western ideal, but conflicts with the talmudic conception. Implicit in the former is a litigant who is in court to claim his due rather than to plead for succour. The litigant claims that he is entitled to a favourable verdict. Such a claim requires the court's subordination to an established, integrated set of rules (no departure from which is brooked), one of which, the litigant contends, entitles him to the verdict he seeks. In a talmudic court a litigant cannot claim a right to a favourable verdict even if a legal rule exists which apparently entitles him to it. His position, rather, is that of one who pleads for succour; 'governed by men, not by rules' thus expresses the talmudic view of the judicial process.

The doctrine that emerges — that the law and the generally accepted norm do not necessarily represent the way in which the court decides a given case — is complemented by another talmudic principle, namely, that the legal norm does not necessarily represent the mode of behaviour desired of the individual. For example, the phrases, 'the Sages are pleased with him' and 'the Sages are displeased with him' constitute recommendation, even prescription, that individuals adopt a certain mode of behaviour in spite of the existence of an exempting legal norm, or avoid a given mode of behaviour in spite of a legal norm authorizing it.

This tension between legal norm and recommended behaviour is fascinating. The phenomenon of the existence of a legal norm alongside a parallel but different recommended norm is unknown in Western law. Western law contents itself with stating what is permitted and what forbidden and with defining procedures for the accomplishment of desired ends, such as writing a will, making a contract, etc. It does not suggest recommended modes of conduct and sets no values beyond what is required for the law to evaluate an individual's behaviour. The difference between the two levels in the context of the judicial process remains unarticulated, but its existence is manifest to any student of talmudic jurisprudence.

This distinctive conception of the judge's authority, which, as we saw, entails perception of the litigant as seeking succour from the court, can exist only in a society where the judge's standing derives not from his having been formally appointed, but from his being recognized as a spiritual leader. A judge is accepted because his virtues and personal qualities endow him with the status of guide and mentor; the community bows to his authority willingly. This voluntary surrender is termed *kabbalah*, and its place in the halakhic system merits further investigation.

2. *Biblical Origins*

The religious ideology of the judicial process is found in the Bible itself. The charge to the judges in *Deut.* 16:18-20 makes no mention of a duty to apply rules of law, but simply enjoins them (with the support of a proverb) to do justice and avoid corruption:

> You shall appoint for yourselves judges and officers tribe by tribe, in every settlement which the Lord your God is giving you, and they shall dispense true justice to the people. You shall not pervert the course of justice or show favour, nor shall you accept a bribe; for bribery makes the wise man blind and the just man give a crooked answer. Justice, and justice alone, you shall pursue, so that you may live and occupy the land which the Lord your God is giving you.

The same view is found in the account of the reform of Jehoshaphat (a not insignificant name, in this context), where the judges are assured that God will be 'with you' in rendering justice (*2 Chron.* 19:5-7):

> He appointed judges in the land in all the fortified cities of Judah, city by city, and said to the judges, 'Consider what you do, for you judge not for man but for the Lord; he is with you in giving judgment. Now then, let the fear of the Lord be upon you; take heed what you do, for there is no perversion of justice with the Lord our God, or partiality, or taking bribes.'

By contrast, it has been argued, the original function of the written law book, was primarily didactic.[1]

The *Talmud* itself recognises that the judge's function, according to the Bible, went beyond the application of a legal rule to a given case; that he participated, as it were, with God in the act of judging:

> And the judges should know whom it is they judge and before whom they judge and who will demand an account of them, as it is said, 'God standeth in the congregation of God [in the midst of judges doth He judge]' [*Ps.* 82:1] and thus it is said, concerning Jehoshaphat, 'he said to the judges, consider what ye know, for ye judge not for man but for the Lord.' (*B. Sanh.* 6b)

The *Talmud* thus recognises the divine mission of the judges as reflected in the charge given to them by Jehoshaphat. Yet its proof text is not, perhaps, the strongest which could have been chosen. The sentiment that the judges 'judge not for man but for the Lord' merely makes them divine representatives; the continuation of the biblical verse tells them that God 'is with you in giving judgment' (*ve'imakhem bidvar mishpaṭ*), i.e. that God will actually inspire their decisions. Yet even the weaker conception — divine authorisation rather than divine inspiration — was to prove capable of generating pluralistic conceptions of laws.

Certainly, within the biblical period itself, the role of the judge as applying the rules of the '*torah* of God' arose (see Westbrook, pp.3f. above, on Ezra). Indeed, we may contrast the Deuteronomic/Jehoshaphat type of charge to judges with that in *Ezra* 7:25:

> And you, Ezra, according to the wisdom of your God which is in your hand, appoint magistrates and judges who may judge all the people in the province beyond the River, all such as know the laws of your God; and those who do not know them, you shall teach.

Nevertheless, the original conception of the judge as an inspired (rather than learned) decision-maker was to leave significant traces on the later history of Jewish law.

It is in this context that we should understand the biblical tradition of the 'prophet like Moses', whose commands the people were required to obey in all matters other than idolatry (*Deut.* 18:18).[2] The precise scope of such powers was undefined in the Bible, and became a source of major controversy later. It belongs to a period when prophetic revelation was regarded as the primary source of law (Moses, of course, was himself regarded as the leading example: *Deut.* 34:10). There was no demand that every prophetic revelation of law be consistent, verbally or in terms of substance, with every other. Its authority resided in its source — direct divine revelation — rather than its belonging to an overall, rational system. That same feeling is reflected in the Talmud's later comment on the phenomenon of contradictory rulings (between Bet Hillel and Bet Shammai): the dispute, it tells us, was resolved by the intervention of a heavenly voice (*bat ḳol*) which proclaimed: 'both opinions are the words of the living God' (*elu ve'elu divre elohim ḥayyim, B. Erub.* 13b).[3] Divine law is thus conceived to be pluralistic, on the authority of a direct revelation (here, not even through a prophet) from God himself.

3. *The 'Legal System' and the Judicial Process in the Talmud*

Of the different legal orders that can be identified in the Diaspora communities over the generations, the talmudic period is that which most invites investigation.   Though the talmudic period can itself be sub-divided — there is a clear distinction between Palestine and Babylonia, and even within Babylonia different periods and locales must be distinguished — nevertheless the talmudic period can be seen, from the normative point of view, as a single era characterized by a coherent legal system, one which could be deviated from but which could not be ignored.

The judicial process as described in the *Talmud* seems to take place in a quasi-vacuum, with no interference by external constraints.   There are, of course, traces of the cultural, social, economic and political background of the time, but they are visible only dimly and cannot be uncovered without effort.   Certainly, the overall impression is that of an autonomous system. For example, when, after the destruction of the Temple, courts began to refrain from handling capital cases, the *Talmud* attributes this reluctance to internal factors and not to the prohibition which had been imposed by the conquering power.   This attitude made it easy for succeeding generations to use the *Talmud* as a self-contained model, albeit one which could be adapted to particular needs and conditions.

It was the role of the Gaonate, in particular, to impose the authority of the Babylonian *Talmud* on the entire Diaspora.   Indeed, the *Talmud* is the last cultural-legal work to be accepted by all Jewish communities, and therefore enjoys a special status with respect to the works that followed it.   In the *Sefer Kabbalah* (eleventh or twelfth century), R. Abraham b. David of Toledo states that 'it spread among all Jews and they accepted its authority and the Sages of each generation studied it in public and all Jews were in agreement on it; to it nothing should be added and from it nothing sub-tracted.'[4]   And in his introduction to the *Code*, Maimonides states: 'but all things written in the Babylonian *Talmud* are binding on all Israel, and every city and every country is to be compelled to adopt the conduct prescribed by the talmudic Sages, because all Israel agreed to all the things written in the *Talmud*.'

The talmudic sources contain a wealth of material relating to various aspects of the judicial process.   The issues discussed include: alternatives to the judicial process, such as arbitration and compromise, and how these processes are related; appointment of judges; qualifications for judging; payment for judging; composition of the bench; representation of litigants in court; conditions for ensuring fair process and equal treatment for both parties; prohibition of personal or financial involvement on the part of the judge in the process or its consequences; writing of the verdict; presentation and publication of the reasoning behind the verdict; the status of the verdict with regard to future cases; appeal; and enforcement. There is also extensive discussion of the nature of admissible evidence and of whether judges may take personal knowledge into consideration if it has not been introduced in court as evidence.

The *Talmud* thus presents a picture — one made normative for later generations — of a unified legal system. But is it an accurate picture of the legal practice of the time? From a sociological perspective, the most important question is which of these sources reflect lived reality and which are theoretical discussions that address an ideal model of the judicial process. One passage in the *Talmud* tells of a corrupt legal order in which the judges obviously did not proceed in accordance with talmudic precepts (*B. Shab.* 139a). Much research focuses on the problem of isolating the descriptive material from the theoretical. The talmudic scholar Y. Weiszburg noted some 90 years ago that the most reliable sources for description of judicial practice are accounts of court cases interspersed in the abstract legal discussions.[5] However, this principle, though basically correct, is not foolproof, since the identification of cases is in itself a difficult and complex task, due to the casuistic nature of the *Talmud*. Criteria for the identification and individuation of talmudic cases, distinguishing them from hypothetical and theoretical questions, must be established.[6]

Such an exercise yields, out of the entire *Talmud*, a meagre crop of several hundred cases. This is indeed a disappointing number in view of the scope of the legal concerns covered in the *Talmud* and the extensive period it documents. Nevertheless, it is highly significant because it indicates that most talmudic discussion is concerned with hypothetical questions, and that, for the most part, the development and perfection of the law is not based on the practices of the courts. Talmudic law developed mainly in the academy, where actual court activity did indeed take place, but only as an incidental adjunct to academic study. The precept 'study and you will be rewarded' (*B. Sot.* 44a) reflects the presumption that study of the law was undertaken for its own sake.

4. *Pluralistic Traditions in the Talmud and Judicial Discretion*

By studying the way in which these decided cases are presented in the

Talmud, light may be cast on the attitudes of both the judges of that period, and the editors of the *Talmud* toward judicial practice. For the most part, the judges do decide cases according to the law; their decisions are anchored in a definite and familiar set of norms made available to them by the legal system. That is not to say that the law was taken as decided on all points. There is recognition of cases where divergent views exist, without any authoritative resolution between them. For example, there was a dispute regarding the capacity of the heirs of a creditor to require payment of a debt from the heirs of the debtor. Rab and Samuel held they could not, since they were unable to take the oath (that the debt was still outstanding) that would have enabled the creditor himself to recover from the heirs of the debtor. Against this view there was another opinion, endorsed by R. Eleazar, permitting the heirs of the creditor to take a similar oath, that their father did not give them any instruction that the debt had been paid, and then they are entitled to exact the money from the heirs of the debtor (*B. Shebu.* 48a). After various unsuccessful attempts to decide which of the two opinions should prevail, the *Talmud* concludes:

> R. Hama said: Now since the law has not been stated either in accordance with the view of Rab and Samuel or in accordance with the view of R. Eleazar, if a judge decides as Rab and Samuel it is legal; if he decides as R. Eleazar it is legal.[7]

The inability to decide on the merits of the case is solved by adopting both opinions. Consequently, on the judicial level there is no doubt. Both opinions are correct and the judge is called upon to choose one of them. A very concrete manifestation of the pluralism which results from this solution is found in R. Papa's comment that the fate of the debt depends on the judge before whom the document is presented. No doubt, this sounds like an extremely realistic evaluation of the law. The heirs of the creditor come before the court to seek justice but they cannot claim that they have a right to a specific ruling. But, unlike the American realists, R. Papa does not deny the concept of normativity. He does not regard this as a case of a 'lacuna' in the law, which the judge must fill through the exercise of his discretion. Rather he calls attention to the consequence of having *two* conflicting, but equally binding, norms incorporated into the system. The judge may here choose between two contradictory, but equally authoritative, rules: either the one or the other — but not, by implication, something different from either (as would be the case in a genuine lacuna). We will call this the 'either-or' approach. It presupposes a pluralistic legal structure.

5. *Judicial Deviation in the Talmud*

What was the legal system's response to judges who deliberately and openly deviated from the law, basing their decisions on extra-legal considerations? Study of the Jerusalem *Talmud* and the Babylonian *Talmud* and examination of parallel passages reveal a systematic difference in their respective attitudes toward the judge's role. This difference is particularly pronounced in passages dealing with cases where judges openly deviate from the law. Such open deviation may be illustrated from *B. Ket.* 50b:[8]

> R. Eleazar intended to allow maintenance out of movable property. Said R. Simeon b. Eliakim to him: Master, I know that in your decision you are not acting on the line of the law but on the line of mercy (*midat rahmanut*), but [the possibility] ought to be considered that the students might observe this ruling and fix it as a *halakhah* for future generations.

The Jerusalem *Talmud* is usually opposed to judicial deviation from the law and strives to understand and account for early traditions reflecting such deviation. It also manifests a clear tendency to limit the scope of legal rules authorizing deviation from the law. Overall, the Jerusalem *Talmud* rejects the possibility of judicial deviation from the law.

In contrast, the Babylonian *Talmud* is unconcerned by early traditions reflecting deviation from the law and does not attempt to bring the practice of judicial deviation within the limits of rules expressly authorizing exceptions to the law (such as 'the needs of the hour' — *hora'at sha'ah*). Generally speaking, the Babylonian *Talmud* accepts the possibility of judicial deviation from the law and at times even views such deviation favourably.

The difference between the conception of the judicial process reflected in the Jerusalem *Talmud* and that reflected in the Babylonian may be related to the different social realities that existed in Palestine and Babylonia. In Palestine, sects such as Christianity had emerged which, despite their break with Judaism, claimed to be its successors, and retained certain core tenets of traditional Judaism. In their polemics with the Sages, these sects attempted to justify the permissive positions they adopted on various issues by citing the sources considered authoritative by the Sages, but interpreting them differently. In particular, they often quoted biblical and rabbinic sources evidencing deviation and departure from the law.[9] The Sages were thus forced to confront an attack from within. It is not surprising that the constant struggle with these sects gave rise to a tendency to insist upon the supremacy and exclusiveness of the law and fiercely to oppose any deviation from it.

The situation in Babylonia was entirely different. The distance between the Jewish community and the surrounding pagan society was so great that no comparable danger existed. In Babylonia, therefore, greater flexibility and tolerance of deviation from halakhic norms was possible. What is important for our purposes is not the actual frequency of such deviation but rather its possibility. In most cases, a court's verdict did indeed correspond to the decision reached in the Talmud's theoretical discussion, but the talmudic judge was not shackled to the legal norm and did not hesitate to deviate from it when, in his opinion, the circumstances of the case warranted such deviation. Obviously, we are not speaking of arbitrary, wanton deviation. When a judge deviates from the law he does so in order to enforce the true intent of the *Torah* — the law — as he understands it, though the intent of the *Torah* is a concept that defies definition in terms of norms.

Different types of consideration may motivate deviation, such as a litigant's inferior economic status or improper conduct, not necessarily related to the case at hand. For example, the *Torah* explicitly forbids courts to take into consideration a litigant's inferior economic status: 'Thou shalt not give a poor man preference in his litigation' (*Ex.* 23:3). This idea is developed and refined in many homiletic exegeses (*midrashim*) and is frequently cited in legal texts. The poverty or wickedness of a litigant must not be a relevant consideration in reaching a verdict. However, the fact that these *midrashim* are never mentioned in the classical passages of the Babylonian *Talmud* on the legal process is instructive. Moreover, in a number of cases, despite the normative prohibition, the inferior status of a litigant is indeed taken into account.[10]

The practice of judical deviation is well-anchored in the legal tradition and is documented in a series of precedents set by talmudic courts. The tradition is ascribed to the Tanna R. Eliezer b. Jacob in an adage that summarizes this aspect of the legal process succinctly: 'I have heard that the court may impose punishment and penalty not specified in the *Torah*' (*B. Sanh.* 46a). Commentators on the *Talmud* often invoke this adage, viewing it as the basis for the talmudic precedents where judges deviate from the legal norm.

It is noteworthy that during the period of censorship of the *Talmud*, the far-reaching implications of this adage did not escape the censor, who demanded that, in the text approved for print, its scope be restricted to the Great Court in Jerusalem, thereby giving it merely historical significance. Other scholars, such as R. Nissim (1315-1375) and Don Isaac Abrabanel (1437-1508), were also sensitive to the considerable authority accorded courts by this postulate, and attempted to harness theoretical considerations to limit its applicability to the Great Court in Jerusalem, but these minority views do not capture its original sense, and are incompatible with the evidence of the talmudic precedents.

6. *Manifestations of Pluralism Through the Ages*

In the context of Jewish law, a description of the judicial process can only be made within the framework of a specific time and place. With the possible exception of the Second Commonwealth period, Jewish law has never been centralised in a single State. Rabbinic authority has been geographically dispersed, right from the destruction of the second Temple. The judicial system in Palestine at the time of the *Mishnah* has a number of unique features, such as its distinction between expert judge and layman. In the post-talmudic period, the degree of divergence between the practices of different communities could only increase. Indeed, the differences between orders established at different times, or even in the same era but in distinct geographical areas, are so great as to suggest that we are looking at different systems altogether.

Whereas 'custom' (*minhag*) within the context of *national* legal systems often refers to 'local custom', for the *halakhah*, *minhag* often assumes a national dimension: *minhag ashkenaz*, etc. Legislation, too, has rarely even claimed to be binding upon all the subjects of Jewish law: think, for example, of the *takkanot* of Rabbenu Gershom (see pp.317ff., above).[11] Nor even do the so-called 'Codes' claim universal legislative authority. They too have had distinct geographical spheres of influence, and are generally not considered 'statutory' in the sense of modern legislation.[12] The Yemenite community accepted the legal authority of Maimonides; the Sephardi, that of R. Joseph Karo as expressed in the *Shulhan Arukh*; and the Jews of Central Europe usually followed the rulings of R. Moses Isserles.

The judicial process during the geonic period in Babylonia differs greatly from that of fifteenth century Central Europe; similarly, there are significant differences between the judicial system in Palestine under Roman rule and that which existed in Spain before the Expulsion. More generally, there is no strict system of precedent in Jewish law: if a *posek* decides to publish his decision in an actual case, the authority of his published judgment will derive from the authority it enjoys, or acquires, as a 'responsum', rather than from the judicial determination.[13]

All this indicates that the rule for identifying binding legal norms — the rule of recognition — varies from one community to the next, with no supreme authority to which all defer. Indeed, the whole range of what Hart called 'rules of recognition' is so broad in Jewish Law that we may wonder whether Hart's concept is truly applicable, if it is a criterion of a 'rule of recognition' (as Hart has it at one point[14]) that it provides a 'conclusive affirmative indication' whether a supposed primary rule belongs to the legal system or not.   Obviously, in terms of content, there are undeniable similarities between the legal systems in question. However, the integrated structure characteristic of a single legal system is lacking.

7.   *The ḳim li Argument*

In the fifteenth century (and not, as some scholars mistakenly argue, earlier), we encounter a plea known as *ḳim li* in the responsa literature.[15] The essence of the *ḳim li* argument is as follows: two incompatible halakhic opinions are brought before a court hearing a monetary case, one advanced by the plaintiff, the other by the defendant. The judge's assessment of the case leads him to decide that the law supports the plaintiff's position. In spite of this, the defendant can use the *ḳim li* plea to repel the suit — not by convincing the court of the correctness of his position, but by arguing that the court is estopped from giving a ruling against him since there exists a divergence of legal opinion, within which an opinion favouring his position may be found.

Note that there is a clear distinction between this plea and the legal rule 'the burden of proof rests on the plaintiff' (*M. B.K.* 3:11). That rule is cited in the *Talmud*, and though explicitly mentioned only in the context of factual doubt, it was undoubtedly applied in cases of legal doubt as well. In other words, if the judge is doubtful as to the law, the suit is dismissed.

The *ḳim li* argument differs markedly. It does not rest on the judge's own view of the law, but is raised by the defendant. Indeed, it overrides the judge's opinion: even if the judge thinks that the plaintiff has indeed shown that the balance of opinion is on his side, the defendant can still insist that judgment be given for him, on the basis of the contrary opinion he can cite. That *ḳim li* is essentially a defence plea is evident from the legal debates on whether it can be put forward by a woman, or by an uneducated person, or by the court on behalf of the defendant.

I give here one concrete example. Most rabbinic authorities hold that a legal obligation can be created for an unspecified undertaking, for example covering all expenses of curing a sick person.[16] Maimonides, however, is of the opinion that unless the obligation is fixed and known exactly at the time of its undertaking, no legal obligation can be created.[17] Now suppose A undertakes to pay all expenses of curing B's sick child and suppose that later A wants to withdraw from his undertaking. According to the doctrine of *ḳim li* A could avail himself of Maimonides' view and plead that this is the correct ruling — therefore he is not bound by his undertaking — thereby inhibiting the court from giving judgment against him, even though the court holds that such an undertaking is legally valid.

The *ḳim li* plea emerged in Central Europe in the fifteenth century, a period characterized by exceptional scholarly humility and by an almost total self-effacement on the part of contemporary scholars in favour of their predecessors. A number of responsa from this era stress that the plea is of recent origin and lacks explicit formulation in the *Talmud*.[18]

There are at least two ways to account for the inability of the court to give judgment against the defendant when the latter raises the *ḳim li* argument. The prevailing view is that the very existence of conflicting halakhic opinions creates an objective legal doubt. The individual conviction of the judge that the law actually follows one opinion rather than the other cannot suppress or overcome the objective doubt. Hence, the principle that no money can be recovered unless the plaintiff can show that the legal basis for his claim is correct, is applied. Even though the court thinks that the plaintiff has discharged the burden of proof (as to the applicable law), objectively, he has not, because of the authority cited by the defendant. The underlying assumption is that every legal question yields one (and only one) correct answer. The existing halakhic disputation casts doubt on the correctness of the proposed ruling of the court and hence the court lacks the power to exact money from the defendant. Under this account, the objections which have been voiced against the doctrines of *ḳim li*[19] are well understood. The court is deprived of the main function habitually assigned to courts, viz. to give an authoritative interpretation of the law.

There is, however, an alternative approach. I suggest that the *ḳim li* argument can be explained in terms of a pluralistic conception of the law, conceptually similar to that noted in §4 above (the 'either-or approach'). The very existence of halakhic controversy manifests the fact that the system contains more than one arrangement that might govern the case at issue. It is not a case of doubt as to which of the opinions is the correct ruling. The proposed ruling of the court does represent the law, but the law also provides that there is an equally valid parallel arrangement that governs the case at issue. Here, in monetary matters, the fact that the defendant has one such authoritative rule on his side is sufficient for him to resist the claim of the plaintiff.

The *kim li* plea met with strong opposition, however, in both earlier and later periods. The geonic period had been a time of vigorously-asserted authority and self-confidence on the part of the halakhic leaders. During this period there had been no place for such a doctrine. Indeed, the Geonim explicitly repudiate the possibility of such a plea,[20] though this repudiation is anticipatory, since the plea had yet to emerge in Jewish law; it may be that the reference is to a similar procedure in Islamic law known as *Taqulid*, which is mentioned by Jewish scholars of the late geonic period. Similarly, the scholars of Safed at the time of R. Jacob Berab, in the sixteenth century, enthusiastic over the plan to reintroduce ordination (*ṣemikhah*) and ultimately the *Sanhedrin* (thus giving rise to hopes that halakhic hegemony would be strengthened) make almost no use of the *kim li* plea. Amongst later Jewish authorities there were those who showed great reservation towards this institution and were reluctant to apply it.[21] Consequently many restrictions were imposed on the doctrine and its applicability was limited. Opposition to *kim li* may be taken to reflect an orientation towards the ideology of a unified legal system, one (in Hart's terms) with secondary rules of change as well as recognition and adjudication. However, the plea has survived and still occurs — though in a much more technical form — in the decisions of the Rabbinic Courts in Israel, where reference to it is made very frequently.

8. *Modern Reflections of the Religious Ideology of Jewish Law*

The pluralistic conception, which allows a judge to deviate from the law in particular cases, has not been lost from the halakhic tradition. Two modern expressions of it may be cited. The first is a quotation from R. Uziel, a contemporary halakhic authority and distinguished judge:

> Knowledge of jurisprudence, both theoretical and practical, does not suffice for one to qualify as a judge. A judge must also be a vigorous individual with the courage to deviate from the law, to acquit or convict, when the circumstances call for this.[22]

The second is found in a responsum issued by R. Kook, the first Chief Rabbi of Israel, who died in 1935. His decision permitting the use of specially-prepared legume oil on Passover evoked much agitation, and various arguments against it were put forward. One such argument was that the *Ḥatam Ṣofer* (Moses Schreiber, nineteenth century Hungary, an undisputed halakhic authority: see p.392 above) had taken a strict [prohibitive] stance on such matters. R. Kook responded to this argument as follows:

> Let me explain to you. The reason for the strict attitude evinced by the *Ḥatam*

Sofer in this regard was the need of the time. Since the Reform movement, which sought to reform the Jewish religion, was then in its heyday, any ruling against the prevailing custom would have provided the rebels with ammunition. The *Hatam Sofer* was not willing to introduce a new custom lest it encourage further reform. However, in our time this fear no longer exists, since those who wish to break off from religion do not seek any authority, but do as they please, reform no longer being an issue. There is thus no risk in sanctioning that which is halakhically permissible though contrary to prevailing custom. On the contrary, knowing full well the inclinations of our generation, I recognize that by permitting what may be permitted people will realize that what we do not allow cannot possibly be permitted.[23]

Custom prohibits, but R. Kook permits, explicitly taking account of the social considerations which distinguish his decision from that of the *Hatam Sofer* in an earlier generation.

9. *Conclusion*

From this brief historical overview, we are justified in doubting the sufficiency of the modern, Western concept of law for the purposes of describing the *halakhah*. Of the three elements of this ideology identified in §1 above, the first, the claim that laws belong to a unified system, is already cast into doubt by the general diversity of halakhic history: we have in fact a plurality of legal orders from a wide variety of societies, which, though having much in common in socio-cultural terms, are at the same time quite distinct. From the jurisprudential point of view, the legal orders in question can hardly be viewed as constituting a single legal system.

The second claim, that within any legal system, there are authoritative sources of law, and any valid application of the law must be justified by reliance upon those sources, is falsified by the practice of judicial deviation, a phenomenon most prominently endorsed in the Babylonian *Talmud*, but on occasion justified even in the modern era. The justification for such deviation, it is suggested, is a religious one: the divine authorisation of the judge.

Pluralism in Jewish law, however, goes beyond this. Stemming from the original prophetic concept of divine revelation, the concept persisted that rival, apparently (to humans) contradictory traditions could subsist simultaneously, each claiming the validity of divine law. No 'rule of recognition' (such as is asserted by the third claim of the Western Rule of Law) could deprive such revelation of its validity. From this stems the understanding here propounded of both the 'either-or' phenomenon of the *Talmud* and the *ḳim li* argument of post-medieval Ashkenaz.

It is not claimed in this article that this religious ideology excludes any halakhic endorsement of a Rule of Law ideology. The latter, as already indicated, represents the dominant view. It may be tempting to seek to resolve the tension between these two ideologies in historicist terms: to argue that the original religious conception was replaced, at a rather early period, by a 'secular' view: one which still required that the judges possess religious qualifications but at the same time subjected them to the Rule of (Jewish) Law. But there is strong evidence against such an historicist solution. We have noted that the Rule of Law idea already appears to inform the account of Ezra's legal structure. In the talmudic period, despite the evidence of judicial deviation and the proclamation of *elu ve'elu*, the Rule of Law (in the form of a recognition rule of majority opinion, to the exclusion of any 'heavenly voice') is graphically illustrated by the story of the 'oven of *Okhnai'* (*B. B.M.* 59b).

There is, in fact, neither need not warrant for us to choose between a religious ideology and that of the Rule of Law. Rather, it may be necessary to conclude that the very ideology of Jewish law is itself pluralistic.

The independence permitted to the judge, anchored in the conception that judges are carrying out a religious duty and fulfilling a divine mission, does not, however, guarantee greater flexibility in the law than might otherwise be expected. For this conception may give rise to two opposed tendencies on the part of the judge: on the one hand, awe at pronouncing judgment and a paralyzing fear of distorting the law; on the other, emancipation from the feeling of being shackled to a legal rule that is formulated on the strength of human understanding and to that extent limited. In the words of R. Uziel, quoted above, we still need 'a vigorous individual with the courage to deviate from the law.' When we have such individuals, the pluralism inherent in the judicial role may admit of the resolution of practical problems on an individual basis, even if the pluralism of true legislation has been lost, with the cessation of prophecy and the rejection of the *bat ḳol*.

Notes

1   B.S. Jackson, 'Ideas of Law and Legal Administration: a Semiotic Approach', in *The World of Ancient Israel: Sociological, Anthropological and Political Perspectives,* ed. R.E. Clements (Cambridge University Press: 1989), 185-202, esp. 186-188.

2   B.S. Jackson, 'The Prophet and the Law in Early Judaism and the New

Testament', *The Paris Conference Volume*, ed. S.M. Passamaneck and M. Finley (Atlanta: Scholars Press, 1994), 72f. (Jewish Law Association Studies, VII).

3   For further discussion, see B.S. Jackson, 'Jewish Law or Jewish Laws', *The Jewish Law Annual* 8 (1989), 28-30.

4   A.D. Neubauer, ed., *Mediaeval Jewish Chronicles* (Oxford: Clarendon Press, 1887), I.59.

5   Y. Weiszburg, '*Odot Bate Hadin Bizeman Hatalmud*', *Festschrift zu M.A. Bloch* (Budapest, 1905), 76.

6   Discussed in H. Ben-Menahem, *Judicial Deviation in Talmudic Law* (Chur: Harwood Academic Publishers, 1991; Vol. I of *Jewish Law in Context*, a series of the Institute of Jewish Law of Boston University), ch.2.

7   *Shebu.* 48b. See further, on this and other examples of the 'either-or' approach, H. Ben-Menahem, 'Is There Always One Uniquely Correct Answer to a Legal Question in the Talmud?', *The Jewish Law Annual* 6 (1987), 169-173.

8   Discussed in *Judicial Deviation, supra* n.6, at 70-74.

9   E.g., *Matt.* 12:1-4 and parallels, citing David's authorisation of eating the shewbread, to justify gleaning on the Sabbath: see further Jackson, *supra* n.2, at 77f.

10 Discussed in *Judicial Deviation, supra* n.6, at 118-124, esp. 121f.

11 See Z.W. Falk, *Jewish Matrimonial Law in the Middle Ages* (Oxford: Clarendon Press, 1966); *Encyclopedia Judaica*, IV.986-987.

12 Significantly, M. Elon, *Jewish Law: History, Sources, Principles*, trld. B. Auerbach and M.J. Sykes (Philadelphia and Jerusalem: Jewish Publication Society, 1994), deals with the Codes in Part III of his work, entitled 'The Literary Sources of Jewish Law', quite separately from his treatment of legislation, considered in Part II as one of the 'legal sources of Jewish law'.

13 M. Elon, *The Principles of Jewish Law* (Jerusalem: Keter, 1975), 110-117; *idem, Jewish Law, supra* n.12, at Vol. III, ch.39.

14 *Concept of Law* (Oxford: The Clarendon Press, 1961), 92.

15 See further H. Ben-Menahem, 'Towards a Jurisprudential Analysis of the *kim li* Argument', *Shenaton Hamishpat Ha-Ivri* 6-7 (1979-80), 45-59 (Heb.); *idem, supra* n.7, at 173-175. For an introduction, see Elon, *Jewish Law, supra* n.12, at III.1282f. and n.180, citing later halakhic authorities who attribute the origins of the doctrine to authorities of the thirteenth century.

16 See *Tur, Hoshen Mishpat,* 60 sec.9.

17 *Maimonides, Mekhirah* 11:16.

18 See *Pahad Yitshak* by Isaac Lampronti, s.v. *Kim Li.*

19 See *Arukh hashulhan* by Jehiel Epstein, *Hoshen Mishpat* 25:13.

20 A. Harkavy, *Teshuvot haGe'onim* (Berlin: Mekitse Nirdamim, 1887), #347 (Studien und Mittheillungen aus der Kaiserlichen Oeffentlichen Bibliothek zu

St. Petersburg).

21 See Yeḥiel Epstein, *Arukh hashulḥan*, *Ḥoshen Mishpaṭ* 25:13.

22 B.M. Uziel, *'Dayan umishpaṭ'*, *Sinai* 17 (1945), 107.

23 A.I. Kook, *Orakh Mishpaṭ* (Jerusalem 1937), 126.

The order of Books follows the conventional order for the Hebrew Bible,
tannaitic and talmudic literature. The order for the post-talmudic literature is
alphebetical. This index does not claim to be comprehensive;
responsibility for its shortcomings resides with B.S.J. and S.M.P.